PHONOLOGICAL DEVELOPMENT

PHONOLOGICAL DEVELOPMENT
Models, Research, Implications

edited by
Charles A. Ferguson
Lise Menn
Carol Stoel-Gammon

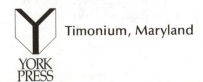 Timonium, Maryland

YORK
PRESS

This book was manufactured in the United States of America. Typography by Brushwood Graphics, Inc., Baltimore, Maryland. Printing and binding by Maple-Vail Book Manufacturing Group, York, Pennsylvania. Cover design by Joseph Dieter, Jr.

Library of Congress Cataloging-in-Publication Data
Phonological development : models, research, implications / [edited by] Charles A. Ferguson, Lise Menn, Carol Stoel-Gammon.
    p.   cm. — (Communicating by language)
    Includes bibliographical references and index.
    ISBN 0-912752-24-6
    1. Language acquisition. 2. Grammar, Comparative and general—Phonology. I. Ferguson, Charles Albert, 1921–   . II. Menn, Lise. III. Stoel-Gammon, Carol. IV. Series.
P118.P484 1992
401'.93—dc20
                                                        92-1152
                                                        CIP

Contents

PART I   **MODELS**

Second Language Acquisition

Views from Outside

Foreword

The National Institute of Child Health and Human Development (NICHD), one of the 13 component Institutes of the National Institutes of Health (NIH), was very pleased to be able to provide support for the conference on phonological development, which led to this book. The NICHD has, since its inception in 1963, supported conferences as part of its mission to stimulate, support, and develop research into the broad areas of human development, examining both normal and pathological processes in the whole individual as well as specific systems. In April of 1964, the Human Communication Program (one of the ten original programs in the NICHD) sponsored "The Speech Process," the first conference in the series *Communicating by Language,* and one of the first conferences sponsored by the new NIH.

The purpose of that conference and each subsequent conference in the series was to reveal existing and potential descriptions for study and to identify the roles various disciplines can and do play in expanding that knowledge. The conferences have reflected both the interdisciplinary and international interests of the NICHD. For each discussion topic experts in different disciplines from different countries were brought together to speak at the cutting edge of their knowledge and to speculate about tomorrow's research.

To date, fourteen *Communicating by Language* meetings have been held, generating subsequent publications. The series has included *Language by Ear and by Eye* (MIT Press, 1972), *Otitis Media and Child Development* (York Press, 1986) and *The Language Continuum* (York Press, 1991).

As James Jenkins wrote in the introduction to *Speech and Language in the Laboratory, School and Clinic* (MIT Press, 1978), "In retrospect each conference [in the Communicating by Language series] seems to contain the seeds of its successor." Indeed, that is, I suppose, the essence of a series, that there is some link between its several components. Moreover, each conference was designed to reveal existing and potential directions for fundamental research in the communicative processes, research that the NICHD could appropriately support. These conferences have helped the Institute accomplish its mission and have assisted the scientific community and, ultimately, all who wish to communicate with language.

The seventh conference and its two-volume proceedings, *Child Phonology* (Academic Press, 1980) were particularly successful in revealing existing information about a relatively new, multidisciplinary field and helped to stimulate much exciting research—so successful, in fact, that the NICHD agreed that, after only ten years, it was indeed time to hold another multidisciplinary conference on this topic.

This book, as have the other conference proceedings, provides new goals and new research directions in the field of child phonology.

James F. Kavanagh, Ph.D.
National Institute of
Child Health and Human Development

Preface

Every child, as part of his or her development, learns within a few years after birth to perceive and produce the speech sounds of the surrounding (ambient) language with a precision that sophisticated electronic speech recognition and synthesis devices are not yet able to match. Understanding the biological, social, and linguistic/cognitive aspects of the processes of phonological development can offer the key to a host of challenging scientific puzzles as well as provide a basis for assessment and intervention in this component of child development. Study of this normal phonological development is often called *Child Phonology*.

In 1978, the National Institute for Child Health and Human Development sponsored a national conference on child phonology in Bethesda, Maryland, that resulted in the book *Child Phonology*, edited by G. H. Yeni-Komshian, J. F. Kavanagh, and C. A. Ferguson (1980), which became a basic reference work for the field. At the time of that conference, investigation of the processes by which the normal child acquires the sound system of the ambient language was a relatively new area, but the preceding ten years had seen an "explosion" of child phonology research, and the organizers of the conference felt it was a good moment to "pause and take stock" (quotes from Yeni-Komshian et al. 1980).

Ten years later, in 1989, NICHD funded an international successor conference on phonological development at Stanford University, sponsored by Stanford's Department of Linguistics. The present volume is an outcome of that conference, and reflects the research activity of European and North American linguists, psychologists, and speech scientists who have been studying the processes of children's normal acquisition of the sound system of the ambient language. In addition to reporting on various lines of research, this volume differs from the earlier one in two important ways: it includes a substantial section on explicit theoretical models of phonological development, and it explores the implications of child phonology research for related fields such as phonological disorders, reading, second language acquisition, and animal communication.

The interest in theories and models is not simply the result of the greater amount and variety of research in the field, it also reflects the increasing concern for explicit theory building in the language sciences as well as the different theoretical perspectives of the various disciplines represented by child phonology researchers. The interest in implications for related fields is an indication of the fact that it is no longer possible to have general treatments of language development, phonological theory, speech perception, diachronic language change, or speech disorders without drawing on the findings of normal phonological development in children.

Although the participants in the Stanford conference, hence contributors to this volume, come from varied disciplinary backgrounds, they have all conducted empirical research with children's phonological development. Their attitudes toward research goals, theoretical foundations, and wider implications of the field may sometimes differ sharply, but they share a common interest in achieving better understanding of the processes of phonological development, and their discussions at the conference and in their papers are impressively free of the kind of polemics and turf-defending that sometimes characterize interdisciplinary efforts. The discussions at the conference and afterward were constructive and, in a number of instances, led to modifications of the original papers to take account of other perspectives or to clarify the authors' own positions so that others could better appreciate them.

Two "outsiders" who had done no child phonology research expressed an interest in the conference and were invited to give informal comments on their perceptions of the conference itself and of the field; K. P. Mohanan from the viewpoint of phonological theory, and Marc Hauser from that of animal communication. Both offered useful comments, and their papers are included in this volume. Hauser was joined as co-author by his colleague, Peter Marler, the well-known researcher and author on animal communication.

The field of child phonology research is very active, and it is earning a solid place in several disciplines, but it does not present a unified face. The papers collected here, however, give a vivid picture of the present state of research, and they open exciting pathways to consolidation of findings and to new discoveries. Each section of the book is preceded by an editor's assessment of the present state of things: theory-making; methods and directions of research; and implications for related fields. What the book may lack in the unity that a single author might give it is, we hope, more than compensated for by the richness of perspectives and the insights into some highly productive and promising lines of research.

In 1970, one of the editors of this volume produced an annotated bibliography of key references on child phonology that circulated in multilith form. At that time it was possible to keep such a list to twenty-five items, and one person could read and digest all of them. Now the major references run into the hundreds, and probably no one has read them all. A quick look at the references section to each chapter in this volume reveals that no items appear in *all* the lists and a surprising number appear only in a single *one* of the lists. This simple fact illustrates what was already noted by Jenkins in 1978: the number of specialized areas that investigators of phonological development need to know about puts a "staggering burden" on them (Yeni-Komshian et al. 1980, Vol 2:218). At the very least, the child phonology researcher must be familiar with principles of developmental psychology (especially of course, language development), speech and hearing science (including articulatory, auditory, and acoustic analysis), and linguistics (particularly phonological analysis). Furthermore, many researchers think of phonological development as a special aspect of cognitive development, and many see it as related to and drawing on clinical experience with phonological disorders.

All three editors are linguists by education and professional identity, but do not offer the book primarily as a contribution either to or from linguistics. We see it as a cooperative effort to help all those who, like ourselves, have a serious intellectual interest in understanding how children "learn to pronounce" the language spoken around them. Such understanding must draw on various sources and in turn may contribute to other larger or more specialized fields, but answering the question "How do they do it?" is a fascinating and important field of inquiry on its own.

Acknowledgments

A few people whose names do not appear in the table of contents to this volume played key roles in mounting the conference that led to this book and in the production of the book itself. First, we are grateful to our institutional backers, the National Institute of Child Health and Human Development, which provided most of the funds for the conference, and the School of Humanities of Stanford University, which, together with the Department of Linguistics, supplemented the NICHD grant. On the Stanford side, it was Dr. Ewart Thomas, then Dean of the School, Dr. Dorothy A. Huntington, then Chair of the Department, and Gina Wein, departmental Administrator, who pushed the supplemental grant through, and we thank them.

On the NICHD side, we owe more than institutional gratitude to Dr. James F. Kavanagh, Deputy Director of the Center for Research for Mothers and Children, NICHD. He not only helped the organizers of the conference with advice on their proposal writing, but was instrumental in having the conference become one of the series on "Communication by Language." That began in 1964—the early days of NICHD —and resultant volumes have included *Genesis of Language, Language by Ear and by Eye,* and our predecessor conference publication *Child Phonology.* We are grateful for his efforts. We missed his presence at the conference itself but appreciated the cordial written message he sent to the participants.

It was Grace Yeni-Komshian who steered us to NICHD as the source of funds, and we hope she will be gratified by the success of the conference and the contents of this volume.

Michelle Collette Murray of the office staff of the Department of Linguistics at Stanford served as Conference Coordinator. She cheerfully undertook responsibility for the innumerable tasks involved in the operation of a tightly scheduled, international meeting, for the participants who mostly did not know one another personally, and for many papers, some lengthy and last-minute. She also arranged social events in and around the conference to encourage interaction. We give her our heartfelt thanks. Michelle was assisted by other staff members, in particular Sonia Oliva, and their work is gratefully acknowledged.

Finally, Elinor Hartwig of York Press has been both enthusiastic and patient managing the whole process of dealing with delayed manuscripts, three editors in different locations, and a book larger and more demanding than she had expected. We have enjoyed working with her, and we appreciate more than she knows her professional and personal contribution to the volume.

Five contributors to the conference must be especially identified: Ferguson, Jusczyk, Lindblom, Menn, and Richard Schwartz. These five researchers in phonological development composed the Steering Committee that planned the conference, and three of them were doubtless relieved to be able to turn over the editorial responsibility to a somewhat different team. Ferguson expresses particular acknowledgment also to Marilyn Vihman for her willingness to listen and respond to his reflections during the period of proposal writing: she was often, in effect, a co-opted member of the Steering Committee.

Charles A. Ferguson
Lise Menn
Carol Stoel-Gammon

Contributors

David Barton
  Department of Linguistics
  Lancaster University
  Lancaster LA1 4YT
  United Kingdom
Bénédicte de Boysson-Bardies
  Laboratoire de Psychologie
    Experimentale
  Centre National de Recherche
    Scientifique
  54, Boulevard Raspail
  Paris 75270
  France
Lynette Bradley
  Department of Experimental
    Psychology
  University of Oxford
  South Parks Road
  Oxford OX1 3UD
  United Kingdom
Daniel A. Dinnsen
  Department of Linguistics
  University of Indiana
  Memorial Hall 322
  Bloomington IN 47405-2201
Loekie Elbers
  Rijksuniversiteit te Utrecht
  Vakgroep Psychonomie
  Postbus 80.140
  3508 TC Utrecht
  The Netherlands

Charles A. Ferguson
  Stanford University
  Stanford CA 94305
James Emil Flege
  Department of
    Biocommunication
  Box 503 UAB Station
  Birmingham AL 35294-0019
Pamela Grunwell
  School of Health and Life
    Sciences
  Department of Human
    Communication
  Leicester Polytechnic
  Scraptoft Campus
  Leicester LE7 9SU
  United Kingdom
Marc D. Hauser
  Animal Communication Lab
  University of California, Davis
  Davis CA 95616-8761
David Ingram
  Department of Linguistics
  University of British Columbia
  Faculty of Arts
  #369–1866 Main Mall
  Vancouver BC V6T 1Z1
  Canada
Peter W. Jusczyk
  Department of Psychology and
    Center for Cognitive Science

State University of New York
at Buffalo
Buffalo NY 14260

Ray D. Kent
Waisman Center
University of Wisconsin-
Madison
1500 Highland Avenue
Madison WI 53705-2280

Laurence B. Leonard
Audiology and Speech
Sciences
Purdue University
1353 Heavilon Hall
West Lafayette IN 47907-1353

Bjorn Lindblom
Department of Linguistics
University of Texas at Austin
Calhoun Hall 501
Austin TX 78712-1196

John L. Locke
Director and Senior Research
Scientist
Neurolinguistics Laboratory
Massachusetts General
Hospital
15 River Street
Boston MA 02108

Marlys A. Macken
Department of Linguistics
University of Wisconsin
Madison WI 53706

Lorraine McCune
Department of Educational
Psychology
Rutgers University
Graduate School of Education
New Brunswick NJ 08903

Lise Menn
Department of Linguistics
University of Colorado
Boulder CO 80309-0295

K. P. Mohanan
Department of English

Language and Literature
National University of
Singapore
Kent Ridge 0511
Singapore

D. Kimbrough Oller
Departments of Psychology,
Pediatrics, and
Otolaryngology
University of Miami
Mailman Center for Child
Development
PO Box 016820
Miami FL 33101

Joseph Paul Stemberger
Department of Linguistics
University of Minnesota
142 Klaeber Court
320 16th Avenue, SE
Minneapolis, MN 55455

Carol Stoel-Gammon
Department of Speech and
Hearing Sciences
University of Washington
1417 NE 42nd Street
Seattle WA 98195

Marilyn May Vihman
Educational Psychology
10 Seminary Place
Rutgers University
New Brunswick NJ 08903

Janet F. Werker
Department of Psychology
University of British Columbia
2136 West Mall
Vancouver BC V6T 1Z4
Canada

Henning Wode
English Department
Englisches Seminar der
Universität Kiel
Olshausenstraße
2300 Kiel
Germany

PART · I

Models

Overview

Building Our Own Models
Developmental Phonology Comes of Age

Lise Menn

RETROSPECTIVE

In a metatheoretical/historical contribution to the first conference on phonological development, organized by Yeni-Komshian, Kavanagh, and Ferguson (Menn 1980), I described our field as having passed through two phases in its recent history, and being about to start on the third. (Of course, like all "stage" accounts, this is an oversimplification.) The first phase, dominated and exemplified by Roman Jakobson, had extremely little data to go on, and so it could theorize about child phonology only by using frameworks that had been developed for the description of adult language—first structuralist, then generativist.

The second phase, which I called the "comparison" phase, was led by Charles Ferguson and students of his work at Stanford and elsewhere. Researchers began to amass longitudinal and cross-sectional data in order to test the ideas of Jakobson and of David Stampe, among others, and to trace the emergence of various basic theoretically defined elements (phonemes, features, contrasts). We saw, during these

I am grateful to Marc Hauser, Mike Mozer, Ed Matthei, K. P. Mohanan, Dan Dinnsen, Paul Smolensky, Bill Bright, and Charles A. Ferguson for discussions relevant to many of the points in this chapter.

years, that we were not going to be able to describe phonological development purely in adult-centered terms; new concepts, with a more psycholinguistic flavor, began to appear in the work of many of us. We also made progress using concepts from the prosodic phonology of J. R. Firth, as applied to child phonology by Natalie Waterson in England (see now Waterson 1987), and the newly developing autosegmental theory (see now Goldsmith 1990). However, I claimed that the metatheoretic bottom line was still that adult-based theory had no apparatus to handle the difference between the skilled and the unskilled speaker, because it had no need for such an apparatus. Therefore, it was going to be up to us developmentalists to come up with that apparatus; in our third phase we would have to modify and extend phonological theory ourselves, and furthermore, frame our questions and our problems in our unique terms. "Fergie," over the years, had called attention to many of these essential differences—for example, the problematic status of the notion of "contrast" in a tiny lexicon that may afford no near-minimal pairs (Ferguson 1963); the evidence for the word as a minimal phonological unit (Ferguson 1978); the child's immersion in a universe of words that he or she cannot yet say, and the consequent need to handle the child's choice of certain words to attempt from that universe (Ferguson, Peizer, and Weeks 1973; Ferguson and Farwell 1975); and the apparent autonomy of syllables as units in some, but not all, children (Ferguson, Peizer, and Weeks 1973).

The third phase, with this more mature angle on our topic, had begun by the end of the '70s; but in 1980 I felt there was little I could say about it because it was still so new. Now, a decade later, I have the welcome opportunity to take a good look at the third phase in this overview, focusing on the "models" aspects of current work in developmental phonology.

MODELS AND DISCONTINUITIES

First, a word about this notion of a theoretical apparatus to handle the behavior of the unskilled speaker/hearer (or the unskilled performer in general). An argument that has become quite popular in many areas of language development, and is associated most recently with the work of Steven Pinker, is called the "discontinuity argument" (Pinker 1984). It is often found in the following form: one should not postulate entities in developmental theory that differ from, or are in addition to those needed in adult theory, because then one will have to explain how to get rid of them or how to replace them with their adult counterparts. Discontinuity is, thus, a bad thing in developmental theories and models.

But this is true only if we posit such entities and then neglect to explain precisely how and why the entities change or disappear. What William of Occam said, after all, was that entities should not be multiplied *beyond necessity (praeter necessitatem)*. Sometimes, it is necessary to come up with what, from a description of normal adult behavior, is a new entity. Children crawl, adults walk. Caterpillars (in their last developmental stage) can make silk, butterflies cannot. Yet caterpillars do become butterflies; and crawling in humans remains as an adult form of locomotion in certain rare, generally overlooked, but quite statable conditions (e.g., avoidance of overhead hazards such as smoke or bullets; or giving children "horsie-back" rides). Our absolutely obligatory job as developmentalists is to account fully for the metamorphosis, withering-away, or disappearance of any child-specific apparatus that we posit. But if we do this, the discontinuity argument need not keep us from being faithful to what we see in our data. Only if we cannot find well-motivated arguments as to why the metamorphosis and other changes should happen are we necessarily better off sticking to continuity, to adult-based concepts. In fact, once a construct has been invoked for child data, it may turn out to have a place in a complete theory of adult behavior—as witness the example of crawling, above. To quote Ferguson and Farwell (1975): "Our approach is to try to understand children's phonological development in itself in order to improve our phonological theory, even if this requires new constructs for the latter" (p. 437).

As a brief example of these points, consider the two-lexicon model of child phonology, discussed and revised in the chapter by Menn and Matthei in this volume.[1] One part of its child-specific apparatus—the selection rules (see figure 2, Chapter 7) that choose which aspects of the adult word the child would attempt to represent in output—had to expand definitionally to take in the whole target as the child became able to deal with all of the details of the adult language. Thus, these rules were designed to metamorphose into the part of the adult apparatus that relates a stored phonological representation to the actually produced form. On the other hand, the input/output division of the lexicon itself, having been invoked for the child, appeals to some phonologists, like K. P. Mohanan (personal communication), as a way of handling such phenomena as the discrepancy between the large set of dialects we can comprehend versus the much smaller set of dialects we can produce.

---

[1]Hereafter, papers in this volume will be referred to simply as "the X paper" or "the paper by X."

MODELS AND THEORIES

What is the difference between these two terms? *Theory* seems to be more ambitious, but also more nebulous; it is easier to imagine a productive debate about the claim "X's model is no model" than about the claim "X's theory is no theory." I think this is because we expect a theory to give us a description of events plus a feeling of insight, and there is a heavy subjective component to the evaluation of insightfulness. Theories also claim implicitly to be "true"; yet at the same time we admit in advance that we cannot completely prove their truth, and so there is another subjective element in deciding whether we are going to accept their invitation to belief.

Models are conceived of as more prosaic descriptive objects: we ask whether they work and how well they work, and if they do not work, they are not models. We want them to be comprehensible and possibly insightful, but belief plays a much smaller role. If you call something a model, you imply that you will be quite willing to abandon it if a better approximation to the data comes along (although one does develop some emotional attachment to one's creations); and more importantly, you imply from the start that its concepts—input lexicon, connection weights, or whatever—are not "real things," but at best *correspond* to "real things." The stress in a theory is a little different: the best I can do is to say that the entities in a theory are treated as if they are indeed the names of real things, but one has a correspondingly lighter commitment to being able to say exactly how they work. What makes an account a model is a focus on "how" something happens, within the limits of what a discipline considers its responsibility. It seems to me that the division between linguistic and psycholinguistic approaches to the study of phonological development lies here, rather than in the subject matter. So, for example, the suggestions in Ingram's chapter, about changes from phonetic to phonological representation, exemplify what a psycholinguist's model must explain.

The Werker and Pegg chapter also is illuminating to consider from the point of view of the difference between a theory and a model. They discuss models/theories of perceptual reorganization—specifically, the developmental reduction of the ability to perceive phonetic distinctions that are subphonemic in the ambient language. The studies they cite differ not only in their explanations, but also in what is considered to count as an explanation. For example, Mattingly and Liberman (1989) account for this reorganization by saying that it is due to parameter resetting in a phonological module. From the psycholinguistic point of view, this is a theory and not a model, because no mechanism is provided. There is only the invocation of the primitives *parameter* and *module.* To make the Mattingly and Liberman account into a model, these primitives would have to be given a psychological interpretation.

Let us now consider the notion of *model* in more detail. What do we expect of a model, and how are models to be evaluated? A model works, i.e., tells you how it operates, but only up to a certain level of explicitness. A psycholinguist's model is considered to be acceptable if it treats constructs that are clearly in someone else's department as if they were available "off the shelf"—for example, *long-term memory* or *neural commands.* Of course, this may be a fiction: the psychologist may tell you that, in his or her opinion, no satisfactory model of long-term memory exists. But even the most interdisciplinary of us cannot take responsibility for every step; having ascertained that a construct we want to use is not considered a laughable absurdity by our neighbors, we are entitled to invoke it, assuming (provisionally, as always) that it will be available some fine day. However, some of the most fascinating advances in fact come when one of us develops a construct that lies within an interdisciplinary gap—for example, Kent's chapter applying the physics of tongue control. Many good research paths can be discovered by crossing discipline boundaries in search of mechanisms invoked by psycholinguistic models.

Our models also sometimes fail to be explicit about all of their mechanisms, even within what appears to be our own domain. That failure is a basis for criticism, but not necessarily for condemnation. A model that does not seem satisfactorily explicit may still be of great value in two ways. It may be very useful if taken as metaphor, i.e., as a vehicle for conceptual analysis of a problem. And it may usefully present an outline to be filled in; its value may be in making clear where the holes are and what the next tasks must be.

Ferguson uses the term *theoretical models* in the preface to this volume, which is an appropriate compromise between calling our work *models* or *theories.* On the one hand, of all the models here, only Lindblom's has been (largely) simulated on a computer; so we do not in fact know if they work. On the other hand, most of us model builders intend our constructs to be taken fairly seriously as theoretical entities. Speaking for myself, I stay away from the term *theory* because it seems too grandiose, and because I think that the terms of explanation that will provide insight will not be part of a deductive system. Instead, they will be closely controlled by empirical circumstances: by articulatory, acoustic, and auditory phonetics; by the nature of exposure to ambient language; by the nature of human neural development, memory, and processing; and by modes of category formation that will have general application, and will not require an elaborated and linguistically specialized theoretical apparatus.

However, this view is not shared by all the contributors to this volume; in particular Dinnsen, Macken, and Ingram hold far more rationalist positions. My reading of history tells me that this kind of tension within a field is not only inevitable but beneficial (at least as long as folks keep talking to each other): opponents provide constant challenges to the adequacy of each other's data and the accuracy of each other's reasoning. Without it, there would be complacency and stagnation.

MODELS, RESEARCH, IMPLICATIONS

Our description of this book as "models, research, implications" doesn't mean that the chapters in it can be divided into three groups with these as headings. My charge is to provide some orienting notes about the models that appear throughout the book, and to call attention to the remarks in all of the chapters that should be taken to heart by model builders.

The issues in these chapters also can be linked to some theoretical questions framed in past writings within our field, including those of Ferguson and his co-authors. After all, one of our problems is that we forget that some issues have been around for a long time, and that some insights were achieved years ago. For example, Ferguson and Farwell (1975) make a basic working assumption, which connectionist models also use:

> . . . we assume that a phonic core of remembered lexical items and articulations that produce them is the foundation of an individual's phonology and remains so throughout his linguistic lifetime. Lexical items of particular phonetic shapes are acquired together with notions of appropriateness of use in particular social frames, and changes in the phonic core are to be understood and accounted for in terms of at least lexical, phonetic, and social parameters. Thus we assume the primacy of lexical learning in phonological development, even though it may be heavily overlaid or even largely replaced by phonologically organized acquisition processes in later stages. Lexical primacy has many implications which cannot be developed here, such as the need for assuming a nonphonologically organized phonetic storage and the need for rethinking the notion of '*the* phonology of a language' [emphasis original] . . . [S]ince children have different inputs and utilize different strategies, the gradual development of phonological organization and phonological awareness may proceed by different routes and at different paces so that adult phonologies may differ from one another just as the lexical stocks of individuals may differ (p. 36).

Here it seems relevant to reiterate a point about the nature of many phonological (and other) universals: the general statements that we can make very often do have exceptions; yet, as probabilistic statements, they remain valid. Probabilistic universals may be philosophically inferior to absolute ones because they are hard to falsify: it may take hundreds of counter-examples rather than just one. However, that seems to be the way things are, and philosophical considerations are not the deciding ones in science. Once we accept that these are the kind of universals that we are stuck with, our task is the same as always: to find out why events (such as the onset of repetitive babbling), or orderings of events (mastering of initial stops, and sometimes final fricatives, before initial fricatives), happen the way they do. A probabilistic truth is no easier to explain than an absolute one. Our models, then, must take the form of providing a temporal *probability envelope* for the events of phonological development: they must account both for the shape of this envelope and the variability of the events within the envelope.

Let me return, now, to the issue of phonological units raised by Ferguson and Farwell, for two reasons: first, because a major goal for our models is to get them to simulate the phonological organization used by the child; and second, because this seems to be an area of continuing controversy and, in fact, outright confusion. What does it mean to say that the word is the first level of phonological organization, and what is the route that the child follows to get to the segmental/autosegmental organization of the adult? One set of answers to these questions has been offered by Macken (this volume). The following is a summary of her views:

(i)   There are two broad types of learners/grammars, harmony and melody types.

(ii) Both types are controlled by constraints across nonadjacent consonants in polysyllabic words that closely resemble adjacency restrictions in adult languages, like the typical content of linked structures and minimal distance constraints on tautosyllabic clusters.

(iii) There is little or no evidence, at this stage, of fixed CV syllabic units where V is other than a default vowel.

These facts and others show that these first grammars are built on templates with C-V planar segregation, and that the first constituent is the prosodic word, not the syllable.

As for the routes followed, the Lindblom chapter provides in some respects the most elaborated model, and the discussions in the chapters by Oller and Lynch and by Werker and Pegg are also highly relevant.

MODELS, BIOLOGY, AND INNATENESS

The chapters in this book that bear on the making of models interconnect with each other, although they have differing points of departure.

Some (Dinnsen; Ingram; Macken) are more traditionally phonological; some more biological—that is, anatomical or ethological (Kent; Jusczyk; Locke and Pearson; Werker and Pegg; Hauser and Marler). Some point to hoped-for computer simulations of the acquisition of articulatory targets and contrasts (Menn and Matthei; Stemberger), or even to partially implemented ones (Lindblom). In many, we see the tremendous impact that the idea of the self-organizing system now is having on the study of phonological development, after having been initially explored by Lindblom. Mohanan's chapter, the most "phonological" of all, is also the one that spends the most time explaining this notion in general, and connecting it with the sciences in which it is more fully developed than ours; readers less familiar with the notion might like to start with his exposition of it. On the other hand, several chapters (Elbers and Wijnen; Macken; Wode), offer important comments on what currently appear to be limitations of the self-organizing system approach, and these should be taken as reminders of the distance yet to be traveled.

Most of these chapters show the impact that the last decade's studies of prespeech vocalizations have had on models of phonological development; many of them are concerned with explicit accounts of how, during this period, the child might be beginning to learn the relations between articulatory gestures and the sounds they produce. This is the system that is organizing itself; a major consequence is that the interaction between phonological universals and individual differences can now be placed in a much more general context.

It is fascinating to see how some of the biological aspects of language development have been enriched by cross-species comparison; Hauser and Marler, and Locke and Pearson, suggest the possibility of intensely specialized periods of attending to particular types of stimuli. Their ideas indicate a new understanding of the interplay between, on the one hand, innate predispositions to undertake species-specific communication, and, on the other hand, the opportunities that exist for learning exactly how to do it. This is a way of thinking about innateness that may be more acceptable to developmental phonologists than are proposals of innate phonological universals.

The problem with claiming strong innate linguistic universals always has been that one thereby surrenders all hope of (nonphylogenetic) explanation. But explanation for phonological universals has looked much too tantalizingly possible, whatever the case may be for syntax. No surrender! say the phonological model-makers here. This does not mean "No innateness"; but it does mean that what are granted as innate are things such as processing abilities, learning abilities, developing abilities of fine motor control, auditory sensitivities, potential auditory categorizing abilities, and proclivities for attending to certain kinds of stimuli. Phonology emerges from this matrix; the challenge accepted by the model-makers, to one degree or another, is to show how it might do so. As Mohanan says, there may be some phenomena that will continue to defy extralinguistic explanations; but how will we know which they are if we do not at least try to explain everything?

However, we must pay attention to Dinnsen's caution (personal communication) that it is easy to talk ourselves into believing plausible explanations that are untested. After all, it is but a short time since speech disorders were blamed on a literal "tongue-tie" and treated by cutting the frenum, that bit of membranous skin under the tongue. Current, much more sophisticated hypotheses about the role and means of oral motor control are still just that—hypotheses—and they will remain so until we know much more about how neural impulses activate the vocal organs. Fortunately, there is research under way in this area, and we hope for more.

Because I have raised the issue of innateness, let me relate it more specifically to the types of models that the contributors to this volume consider. All students of language acquisition must agree that some role is played by genetically specified innate human properties, and that some role is played by learning from the environment; the intense disagreements in our field concern the nature and the amount of the contribution from these two sources and the nature of their interaction. In particular, I venture to suggest that many of the psycholinguistically oriented authors in this volume, like me, have some difficulty with the Chomskian concept of "innate knowledge" for two reasons. First, we are not at all clear about what it is supposed to apply to, other than aspects of language knowledge, and this makes it difficult to reason about its nature. Second, we are not clear how it could arise, and how it could interact with that which is learned. Without presuming to claim understanding of what Chomsky might mean, I suggest we bear the following in mind.

As Hauser and Marler remind us, most birds produce species-appropriate songs without exposure to adult songs as models. Their songs—or, if you prefer, their ability to produce their songs—are as innate as their feathers. For the many birds that do require exposure to models in order to learn to sing, however, there is still an innate component—in fact, Marler (1984) argues, there are at least two types of innate components. The data he presents show a very rudimentary level of species-specific song patterning, which we might call a "motor" level, even in deafened birds. A richer level of species-specific song patterning, which we might call the "motor + feedback" level, occurs in normal birds reared in isolation; normal song, in such species, occurs only in hearing birds exposed to appropriate adult model songs. It is the large incremental gain between the "motor" and the "motor + feedback" levels of abnormal song that is of interest here. The existence of this increment tells us that these birds, even though they are untutored, get something essential from hearing themselves sing. Presumably, they have an innate knowledge about what sounds "good" or "bad" in their attempts to sing, a knowledge that goes far beyond the content of the "motor" mechanism operating in the deafened birds. Marler (p. 291) describes this information as contained in "central auditory templates guiding vocal development by feedback control." We can take these birds to represent the category of innate auditory/vocal knowledge, and then ask ourselves what in human behavior, if anything, might be like theirs in some measure.

Until very recently, the long-known fact that neonates prefer to listen to human voices rather than to other environmental sounds has been presumed to show that a similar kind of innateness, although to a lesser degree, must be present in humans; see the Werker and Pegg chapter. I would like to point out, however, that recent findings on human prenatal auditory learning, mentioned by several of our contributors, call this conclusion into question. Before the standard claim can be sustained, we will have to look at hearing children of deaf parents who use sign language, to see if they orient preferentially to human voices in the same way that hearing children of hearing parents do. If they do not, then infant preference to human voices will have to be reclassified as learned behavior.

Hauser and Marler also bring up a number of points relevant to the problem of model making, and their ethological basis gives rise to some subtly different conceptualizations. They suggest that subsong in song-learning species, as well as babble in human babies, might both be regarded as the "substrate out of which a subset is subsequently selected" in order to build the adult system. This phrasing poses the questions, "On what is the substrate itself based?" and "What is the selection process?" It will be interesting to see whether the resemblances between song-learning birds and human infants hold up or break down as these questions are resolved for the two species.

With regard to the question of how innate knowledge can be instantiated in a psycholinguistically plausible way, there appear to be many options, since I imagine that the end result of "innate knowledge"—or an end state empirically indistinguishable from the state of having innate knowledge—can be derived from having properly preset processing mechanisms (as I suggested for the birds who need auditory feedback, mentioned above). The main reason I bring up this point is that some researchers who dislike self-organizing models seem to assume that they are necessarily blank-slate models (a case of guilt by associationism). However, this is very far from being the case. Connectionist models, for example, offer plenty of opportunities for "initial settings"—in fact, this is one of their weaknesses, according to some critics, because they are thus all too flexible. I certainly do not mean to claim that any desired kind of innate knowledge can be modeled by the right adjustments of a connectionist or other self-organizing model; I have no idea whether this is the case or not. However, out-of-hand rejections either of strong-innateness theories or of self-organizing systems models cannot be made on the grounds that they are prima facie incompatible with one another. It is rather their partisans who tend to be incompatible.

REORGANIZATION AND OTHER CHALLENGES
TO SELF-ORGANIZING SYSTEM MODELS

Other capacities that a model of developmental phonology must be able to represent are attention, effort, and awareness, as the Elbers and Wijnen chapter makes clear. Of course, these variables are needed elsewhere in psychology, and so disciplines other than ours will have to work on modeling them as well. On a more specific level, the developmental phenomena considered in the Leonard chapter provide the potential for a particularly stringent test of single-lexicon connectionist models, and his chapter provides an elegant example of the way in which data should be brought to bear on the evaluation of models in our field.

Connectionist models are likely to find it easy to incorporate Ingram's suggestion that functional load should play a major role in the order of output phoneme acquisition, and likewise the specific findings of the effect of the ambient language on perception, which are reported in the chapter by Werker and Pegg. Apparently, these phenomena can be tied to frequency and to co-occurrence patterns, which are the kinds of variables that connectionist models are already built to handle.

It would also seem that another goal of model making would be to account for the correlational developmental findings relating aspects of production and perception that are presented in the Stoel-Gammon chapter. Here, however, a caveat is in order. If it turns out that there are individual exceptions to the general correlational pattern, a model that ties them together strongly will be unsustainable unless it postulates modality-specific abnormalities in those exceptional individuals. That can always be done, but it will not be satisfactory unless such abnormalities actually can be demonstrated.

A final general point to be considered with regard to self-organizing models is the question of whether they can simulate developmental discontinuity/reorganization of the types currently believed to exist. This matter is very far from settled. Such power certainly is going to be required, for the general psychological phenomena of "chunking" and schema formation are quite well established. It appears that schemas of some sort must also be emergent to give a realistic account of language learning. In other words, self-organizing system models must have something equivalent to pattern extraction/recognition if they are going to do justice to our data (see also Peters and Menn 1990). Macken's chapter exemplifies the specific demands of our field, as it argues for the emergence of a phonological level of organization distinct from the phonetic level; the emergence of phonemes, as given by the model in Lindblom's chapter, may not be able to take us deep enough into phonology. Connectionist artificial intelligence modeling is still very bottom-up in its operation, and is relatively weak in representing hierarchies of organization (Paul Smolensky personal communication). Therefore, a major goal for the future must be to bring self-organizing system models for the acquisition of phonology up to the needed level of sophistication.

REFERENCES

Ferguson, C. A. 1963. Contrastive analysis and language development. *Georgetown University Monograph Series* 21:101–112.
Ferguson, C. A. 1978. Learning to pronounce: The earliest stages of phonological development in the child. In *Communicative and Cognitive Abilities: Early Behavioral Assessment*, ed. F. D. Minifie and L. L. Lloyd. Baltimore, MD: University Park Press.
Ferguson, C. A., and Farwell, C. B. 1975. Words and sounds in early language acquisition. *Language* 51:419–39.
Ferguson, C. A., Peizer, D. B., and Weeks, T. 1973. Model-and-replica phonological grammar of a child's first words. *Lingua* 31:35–65.
Goldsmith, J. A. 1990. *Autosegmental and Metrical Phonology.* Oxford: Basil Blackwell.
Macken, M. A. 1978. Permitted complexity in phonological development: One child's acquisition of Spanish consonants. *Lingua* 44:219–53.
Macken, M. A. 1979. Developmental reorganization of phonology: A hierarchy of basic units of acquisition. *Lingua* 49:11–49.
Macken, M. A. Personal communication.
Marler, P. 1984. Song learning: Innate species differences in the learning process. In *The Biology of Learning*, eds. P. Marler and H. S. Terrace. Dahlem Konferenzen 1984. Berlin: Springer-Verlag.
Mattingly, I. G., and Liberman, A. M. 1989. Speech and other auditory modules. In *Signal and Sense: Local and Global Order in Perceptual Maps*, ed. G. M. Edelman, W. E. Gall, and W. W. Cowan. New York: Wiley.
Menn, L. 1980. Child phonology and phonological theory. In *Child Phonology: Production, Vol. 1, Perception, Vol. II*, eds. G. Yeni-Komshian, J. Kavanagh, and C. A. Ferguson. New York: Academic Press.

Mohanan, K. P. In press. Universal attractors in phonology. In *Rules and Constraints*, ed. J. Goldsmith. Chicago: University of Chicago Press.

Mohanan, K. P. Personal communication.

Peters, A., and Menn, L. 1990. The microstructure of morphological development. Distributed by the Institute for Cognitive Science, University of Colorado. Technical Report 90-19.

Pinker, S. 1984. *Language Learnability and Language Development.* Cambridge, MA: Harvard University Press.

Smolensky, P. Personal communication.

Waterson, N. 1987. *Prosodic Phonology: The Theory and its Application to Language Acquisition and Speech Processing.* Newcastle upon Tyne: Grevatt and Grevatt.

Chapter • 1

Developing Phonological Categories from the Speech Signal

Peter W. Jusczyk

At first glance, acquiring the phonological categories for one's native language appears deceptively easy. It would seem to be a matter of identifying the basic set of elementary sound units that are used to form words in the language. However, this simplified account presupposes many things. Some of these concern basic abilities in the area of speech perception. Thus, one necessary ability is to segment the speech signal into units such as words, syllables, and, ultimately, phonetic segments. A second important ability is categorization of speech. A child must discriminate different speech sounds from one another and recognize when different sounds should be treated as belonging to the same category. As efforts to produce machine recognition of speech have shown, neither of these prerequisite tasks is trivial to achieve. The problems involved in extracting segments from the acoustic signal are well documented (e.g., Klatt 1979; Liberman et al. 1967). Because speech sounds are coarticulated, information about more than one segment often is encoded in the same portion of the acoustic signal. In addition, depending upon the context in which they

Preparation of this paper was supported by a grant from NICHD (#HD-15795). In addition, I want to thank Douglas Hintzman, Asher Cohen, Charles Ferguson, Lise Menn, David Pisoni, and Ann Marie Jusczyk for their comments on earlier versions of this manuscript.

occur, the same acoustic properties can give rise to the perception of more than one segment (Liberman, Delattre, and Cooper 1952; Repp et al. 1978). Moreover, once the learner arrives at the correct description of the phonetic categories that appear in the language and is able to represent speech in terms of these, he or she still is faced with an additional mapping problem—namely, how do these phonetic categories relate to the phonological categories of the language? Discovering the mapping here involves learning not only the allophonic variants for each category, but also something about the contexts in which they occur. For example, in English the phonological (or phonemic) category /p/ includes, among its allophones, unaspirated [p] and aspirated [pʰ]. However, which variant will occur in a word is constrained so that [pʰ] appears only in the initial position of a syllable. Thus, having a fully developed phonological representation requires learning the set of constraints (called phonotactic) concerning which phone can occur in which contexts.

To account for the way that phonological categories are derived from the speech signal, one must know something about when the infant possesses the prerequisite abilities. However, one must also keep in mind the situation in which the infant is acquiring knowledge about the sound structure of the native language. It is not simply a question of learning about the structure of the phonology of the language for its own sake, in the way that one might take apart some mechanical object to see how it works. Rather, the infant learns about the sound structure in the context of acquiring a communication system. Learning the correct set and permissible sequences of sounds in the language provides infants with the means to express their wants and desires and to gain information from those around them. Understanding the way in which infants progress toward phonological categories in the native language also requires some understanding of the communicative needs at the moment. Elsewhere, I have suggested that the development of speech perception capacities should be viewed in relation to the goal of building an input lexicon for recognizing words (Jusczyk 1985, 1986, in press b). Similarly, on the output side, the learner is engaged in the task of producing strings of sounds that will permit others to recognize his or her intentions. Consequently, it is likely that success in communication is an important impetus for change in the representations of sound structure that the infant employs. This is not to say that communicative effectiveness is the only factor pertinent to the development of phonological categories in the native language. Children also rapidly pick up patterns of allophonic variation associated with particular dialects. So, one can recognize whether a 4-year-old comes from Philadelphia or New York (Ferguson personal communication). Thus, some desire to imitate, or identify with, the speech patterns of one's cultural group helps to shape phonological categories.

Finally, one cannot neglect the role of genetic preprogramming in acquiring the phonological structure of the language. Thus, the aspects of the signal that capture the infant's attention may be the result of certain innate predispositions. Similarly, there may be strong constraints on the organization that infants are likely to impose on speech sounds in perception as well as in production. Certainly, in other organisms with well-developed oral communication systems, such as birds, there is evidence that acquisition of communicative repertoire is the result of an innately guided learning system (e.g., Gould and Marler 1987; Marler 1991).

In what follows, evidence about the infant's possession of the prerequisite capacities for deriving phonological categories from speech is examined. Wherever possible, attention is given to how these capacities develop. Areas in which critical information is lacking are noted and discussed. Consideration is given to the way in which changes in productive and perceptual capacities relate to one another and what implications this has for the development of phonological categories. Last, we put forth a tentative model of the way that phonological categories may evolve from basic speech perception capacities.

BASIC SPEECH PERCEPTION CAPACITIES IN INFANTS

Discrimination of Speech Contrasts

Soon after birth, infants can discriminate many fine distinctions between speech sounds. Rather than attempt an exhaustive listing of these, we focus on the few that are most relevant for our purposes (for more comprehensive reviews see Aslin 1987; Aslin, Pisoni, and Jusczyk 1983; Kuhl 1987).

Eimas et al. (1971) demonstrated that not only are infants as young as one month of age capable of perceiving the fine distinction in voicing between syllables such as [ba] and [pa], but they do so in a categorical manner. Using the high amplitude sucking (HAS) technique, Eimas et al. (1971) found that infants, habituated to tokens from one of these syllable types (e.g., [ba]), displayed significant increases in sucking for tokens from the other syllable type (e.g., [pa]). By comparison, infants presented with differences of an equal order of magnitude involving two different tokens from within the same syllable type showed no evidence of significant increases in sucking. These results parallel categorical perception results observed for adults (e.g., Liberman et al.

1967). They provide an indication that infants have the capacity to do some preliminary grouping of speech sounds into different perceptual categories.

The categorical discrimination capacities that Eimas et al. (1971) observed are not restricted to voicing contrasts. Such capacities have also been shown to exist for other types of speech contrasts such as place of articulation (Eimas 1974) and manner of articulation (Eimas 1975). Moreover, these capacities for discrimination are not dependent on a long period of experience with the contrasts. Thus, even newborn infants are sensitive to some speech contrasts (Bertoncini et al. 1987; Bertoncini et al. 1990). Furthermore, the distinctions to which they respond include ones not present in the immediate language learning environment. Streeter (1976) found that Kikuyu infants discriminate the [ba]/[pa] contrast even though it does not occur in their native language. Similarly, Trehub (1976), Werker and Tees (1984a), and Best, McRoberts, and Sithole (1988) have all reported findings demonstrating that American infants can distinguish contrasts not found in their native language. Hence, the variety of contrasts that infants can discriminate is quite wide ranging.

These studies provide evidence that infants are able to distinguish between utterances that differ by a single phonetic segment. Whether the infant perceives the distinctions as phonetic ones is another story. Parallels noted in infants' responses to speech and nonspeech contrasts (e.g., Jusczyk et al. 1980; Jusczyk et al. 1983; Jusczyk et al. 1989) have cast doubt on whether early speech discrimination skills are mediated by phonetic as opposed to general auditory processes. Even if there were conclusive evidence that phonetic processing occurs in the infants' discrimination of speech sounds, questions still would remain about how fine-grained these representations of speech are. For instance, it may be that infants compare the items as wholes without decomposing them into constituent phonetic segments.

Regardless of whether a holistic comparison process occurs in discriminating speech sounds, we can say that, within some utterances, the ordering of information appears to be preserved in the infant's perception of them. Bertoncini and Mehler (1981) found that infants distinguished [pæt] from [tæp]. Similarly, Miller and Eimas (1979) found that infants habituated to a fixed sequence like [ba]-[dæ] show significant increases in sucking to the sequence [bæ]-[da]. Whether strict ordering of features is retained in all cases is not yet known. It is possible that some ordering phenomena may be more salient than others.

The subject of the infant's representation of speech is discussed in greater detail later. For the moment, note that during the first few months of life infants have the capacity to detect contrasts as fine grained as those involving a single phonetic feature.

Coping with Variation in the Speech Signal

A problem in building a lexicon in the native language is coping with variability that is unrelated to changes in meaning among different utterances. One such source of variability is that no two vocal tracts are exactly alike. Therefore, because speech sounds are very much a product of the shapes of the vocal tracts that produced them (Fant 1960), different speakers' productions of the same word differ in their acoustic characteristics. In order to develop a perceptual representation of the sound structure of a word that accesses the appropriate meaning, the infant must ignore or "hear through" differences that arise whenever different talkers pronounce the same word. Adult listeners can adjust very rapidly to changes in speaking voice (Bladon, Henton, and Pickering 1984; Martin et al. 1989; Mullennix, Pisoni, and Martin 1989; Summerfield 1975; Summerfield and Haggard 1973; Verbrugge et al. 1976).

Kuhl (1979, 1983) has explored the ability of infants to ignore variability introduced by changes in the speaking voice. She trained six-month-olds to turn their heads toward a visual display box whenever they detected a phonetic change from a repeating background stimulus to a test stimulus, both produced by the same talker (e.g., from [a] to [i]). Once the infants mastered this response, new tokens of the background and test stimuli, produced by a number of different talkers, were introduced. The infants succeeded in detecting the phonetic change despite the increased acoustic variability from repeated changes in the speaking voice. Perhaps the most remarkable demonstration of infants' abilities to cope with such variation came in a study (Kuhl 1983) in which the vowels [a] and [ɔ] were used. There is considerable acoustic overlap among the tokens of these vowels. Nevertheless, the infants responded correctly to the phonetic change.

Recent research from our laboratory (Jusczyk, Pisoni, and Mullennix in press; see also Jusczyk in press a) suggests that even two-month-olds display some ability to cope with talker variability. Using the HAS procedure, we demonstrated that even when listening to tokens produced by 12 different talkers (6 males and 6 females), two-month-old infants detected a change between [bʌg] and [dʌg]. Moreover, the infants' success was not attributable to an insensitivity to talker differences. When presented with pairs of items that were phonetically identical (e.g., two utterances of [bʌg]) but produced by different talkers, the infants could discriminate the utterances. So, there is evidence that although two-month-olds perceive the similarities among tokens uttered by different speakers, they are also sensitive to differences among them.

Finally, there is some indication that the multiple-talker situation does present infants with more complexity than those of single talkers. The difference in the two situations was evident when we examined the consequences of imposing a two-minute delay period between familiarization to one syllable and testing with the other syllable. In particular, significant decrements in performance were observed for the multi-talker condition, but not for the single-talker condition. Hence, infants exposed to tokens produced by a single talker discriminated the utterances equally well whether testing was immediate or delayed for two minutes. In contrast, infants listening to tokens from multiple talkers only gave evidence of discrimination when testing occurred immediately. Interestingly enough, Martin et al. (1989) found that adult performance on an associated memory task was adversely affected for multi-talker as opposed to single-talker conditions.

Perception of Prosodic Information

In addition to its full complement of distinctive segmental elements or phonemes, the sound structure of a language is patterned with respect to its characteristic prosody, which includes intonation and rhythm among its elements. Increasing attention has been given to the role of prosody in speech recognition (e.g., Buxton 1983; Cutler and Carter 1987; Cutler and Norris 1988; Shillcock 1990). Indeed, there are suggestions that the prosodic organization of languages directly affects the kinds of speech recognition strategies that adult listeners are likely to pursue (Cutler et al. 1986).

Although not as extensively studied as segmental cues, the infant's perception of prosodic features has been examined also. One of the earliest studies (Kaplan and Kaplan 1971) demonstrated that by eight months of age, infants can detect differences in intonational contour of simple English sentences. Subsequent research showed that sensitivity to prosodic differences is present well before this time. For instance, Morse (1972) demonstrated that two-month-olds discriminate two phonetically identical syllables ([ba]), differing only in pitch contours (i.e., rising versus falling). Similarly, infants in this age range can discriminate bisyllabic utterances that differ only in whether stress occurs on the first or second syllable (Jusczyk and Thompson 1978; Spring and Dale 1977).

Infants' sensitivity to prosody seems to go well beyond merely being able to discriminate contrasting prosodic patterns. Indeed, there are indications that sensitivity to prosodic variables may help to direct infants to other important aspects of language. Thus, Fernald (1985; Fernald and Kuhl 1987) showed that infants are especially attracted to the expanded intonation contours in child-directed, as opposed to adult-directed, speech. Mehler et al. (1988) demonstrated that four-day-olds are sensitive to prosodic features common to utterances in their mother's native language. Specifically, the infants sucked at higher rates when listening to utterances spoken in the mother's native language versus those spoken in a foreign language. What is striking about the infants' performance is that the utterances were not repetitions of a single phrase or even several phrases, but rather part of a continuously changing discourse. Moreover, the same pattern of responding occurred when most of the phonetic information was removed by low-pass filtering. This suggests that infants had extracted common features from the prosody, such as the characteristic stress and intonation, that hold across utterances in the language. It is also interesting that in a comparison involving utterances from two foreign languages (i.e., neither one being the mother's native language), there was no evidence that the infants differentiated the utterances. Consequently, the ability to extract the prosodic features that characterize utterances in the native language apparently requires some period of familiarization with the language.

Thus, the infant displays a sensitivity to prosodic features that may help to demarcate one language from another. Attention to such characteristics at this early age suggests that they may play an important role in how infants initially organize their knowledge about the sound structure of the native language.

DEVELOPMENTS IN SPEECH PERCEPTION
CAPACITIES DURING THE FIRST YEAR

The infants' perceptual capacities provide them with a first approximation of categories that potentially exist in utterances in their immediate environment. From this initial, and presumably nonlanguage-specific, categorization of speech, infants must arrive at the one that corresponds to the structure of the input language that they are learning. Of course, the infant's contact with the input language and its sound structure begins immediately after birth, if not sooner via intrauterine stimulation. Recent research has begun to investigate the effects of exposure to a particular language on speech perception capacities.

Discrimination of Foreign Language Contrasts

As noted above, young infants' capacities to discriminate speech contrasts are not limited to those that occur in the infants' immediate environment. For instance, Trehub (1976) showed that infants from English speaking homes were able to discriminate a contrast between [řa] and [ža] (such as occurs in Czech) as well as a nasalized versus non-nasalized vowel distinction between [pã] and [pa] (such as occurs in Polish or French). Similarly, Aslin et al. (1981) found that six-month-old American infants discriminated a prevoiced/voiced contrast that is not present in English. Evidence for discrimination of non-native contrasts also has been reported in studies with foreign infants listening to English speech contrasts. Research by Streeter (1976) with Kikuyu infants and by Lasky, Syrdal-Lasky, and Klein (1975) with Guatemalan infants revealed that both groups discriminated the English [ba]–[pa] contrast even though it does not occur in the language spoken in those infants' native environments.

These studies suggest that young infants have the capacity to discriminate phonetic contrasts in any of the world's languages. Nevertheless, no known human language requires its speakers to make every possible phonetic distinction. Instead, each language draws on a subset of the possible phonetic contrasts. Thus, in mastering a language, the infant must focus on those contrasts that mark meaningful distinctions between words in the native language. This is essentially a problem involving perceptual learning in the sense described by Gibson (1969). The infant needs to tune into some sources of information in the speech signal and to ignore others. Questions arise as to when infants begin to focus on the relevant contrasts for the native language and what happens to the ability to perceive contrasts not present in the language.

Evidently, the process of focusing on native language contrasts begins in the latter half of the first year of life. The pioneering research of Werker and her colleagues (see Werker, this volume; also Werker et al. 1981; Werker and Logan 1985; Werker and Lalonde 1988; Werker and Tees 1984a) demonstrates that, by 12 months of age, infants have taken some steps toward phonological categories. Certain phonetic contrasts falling within the same native language category are no longer readily discriminated, despite the fact that the same contrasts were discriminated by infants at 6 months of age. However, increased attention to native language contrasts may not preclude the discrimination of all non-native contrasts. Best, McRoberts, and Sithole (1988) examined the perception of Zulu click contrasts by infant and adult listeners from English-speaking homes. In contrast to Werker and her colleagues, Best, McRoberts, and Sithole (1988) found that the Zulu contrasts were discriminated at every age tested, even by 12- to 14-month-olds. Thus, there was no indication of decreased sensitivity to such contrasts despite their absence in English.

In addition to the research demonstrating influences from the native language on the perception of segmental contrasts during the first year, similar effects have been reported for the perception of prosodic cues. Thus, Jusczyk, Hirsh Pasek, Kemler Nelson, and Schomberg (in preparation; see also Jusczyk 1989) found that four and one-half-month-old American infants, raised in English-speaking environments, are sensitive to the location of interruptions in clauses in both

English and Polish utterances. Infants listened longer to utterances that were interrupted between successive clauses as opposed to ones that were interrupted in the middle of clauses.[1] However, by six months, the infants only showed such sensitivity for English language materials. For the Polish materials, there was no evidence that the utterances with the pauses between clauses were preferred over the ones with the pauses in the middle of clauses. One interpretation of these findings is that, as for certain segmental contrasts (e.g., Werker and Tees 1984a), infants focus on the features relevant to prosodic contrasts in the native language as opposed to ones relevant for other languages. The earlier age at which infants lock in to the native language in the case of prosody, as compared to segmental features, may reflect the fact that prosodic features are distributed much more globally throughout the utterance. Hence, they are more apt to capture infants' attention than are segmental cues.

Representation of Speech Sounds

Studies of speech discrimination provide an indication of infants' perceptual capacities. They demonstrate the kinds of distinctions infants can perceive under ideal circumstances. From these studies, it is clear that infants can detect very subtle distinctions between different speech sounds. Given the potential that infants have for attending to such detail in the speech signal, one might assume that any representation that they form of speech sounds is apt to be fine grained. Indeed, one might argue that infants' representations of speech should be more detailed than those of adults because the early representations might preserve phonetic distinctions not included in a phonemic description of native language utterances.

Although a case can be made for fine-grained representation of speech sounds by infants, there is reason to doubt that the representation is so detailed for speech heard in the natural environment. After all, the test environment for studying infant perceptual capacities is rather special in terms of its memory and attentional demands. Procedures like HAS provide massive repetitions of the sounds with little

---

[1]The reader might wonder whether there is some contradiction between the finding that four and one-half-month-old American infants are sensitive to prosodic markers of clauses in Polish, and the results of Mehler et al. (1988) where four-day-olds show a preference for the prosody of their native language. However, the data for Mehler et al. were obtained by directly pitting one language against the other. In contrast, the infants in the Jusczyk et al. study were tested on alternate versions of samples from the same language, either Polish or English. It is perfectly plausible that they could prefer the samples with pauses at the ends of clauses for each language, and, at the same time, preferred English to Polish. The latter was not an issue (and, hence not tested) in the Jusczyk et al. study.

variation or distraction. The speech sounds are at the very center of the infant's attentional focus. Repeated exposure to the sound may enable the infant to build up a much more detailed representation of the sound than would be possible in most natural settings where he or she is apt to hear a sound repeated only three or four times, and then usually in the context of a varied array of other sounds (as when one hears the same word repeated in different sentences). Given the circumstances, the infant may not be able to record the same degree of detail about the characteristics of speech sounds. In short, the kind of detail that infants represent about speech may not be equivalent to that permitted by their perceptual capacities in an ideal setting.

Information about infants' representation of speech sounds is crucial to understanding how phonological categories develop. Several recent investigations have explored this issue. Jusczyk and Derrah (1987) modified the HAS procedure in a way that required the infant to rely on a perceptual representation in order to detect the presence of a new item. Typically, to succeed in detecting a phonetic distinction with the HAS procedure, the infant needs only to recognize that the second stimulus is different in some way from the first stimulus. The infant need not register the precise locus of the difference between the syllables, only that they are different. Hence, the task amounts to a same-different discrimination problem. As such, it cannot reveal much about the organization of the infant's representation. However, if instead of a single stimulus during the familiarization phase of the experiment, a randomized series of different stimuli are presented, then detecting a novel item will require more than simply registering if two successive stimuli are the same or different. Because all of the syllables in the familiarization set differ from one another, the infant must encode information about each syllable and how it differs from the others in order to detect the presence of a new syllable in the test phase of the experiment.

Jusczyk and Derrah (1987) employed this modified HAS procedure in an investigation of whether infants' representation of syllables are structured in terms of sequences of phonetic segments. During the familiarization phase, the infants were presented with a randomized series of syllables that shared a common phonetic segment (e.g., [bi], [ba], [bo], [be]). After the infants habituated to this set, a new syllable was introduced which either shared (e.g., [bu]) or did not share (e.g., [du]) the common element with the other set members. Jusczyk and Derrah reasoned that if two-month-olds encoded the syllables as a sequence consisting of a particular consonant followed by a particular vowel, then they might recognize that [bu] shared a common segment with the other stimuli. If so, then higher sucking rates might occur for the more novel change, i.e., the one that did not include a common element, [du]. In fact, the infants did not respond in this way. Both types of changes were readily detected and there was no evidence of increased responding to the member from the novel phonetic category.

Subsequently, Bertoncini et al. (1988) replicated this basic finding concerning the infants' responsiveness to changes that either shared or did not share a common phonetic element with the familiarization set. In addition, they demonstrated that similar effects hold when the common element in the familiarization series is a vowel, (e.g., [bi], [si], [li], [mi]) and the test syllables either include (e.g., [di]) or do not include (e.g., [da]) the same vowel. Perhaps more important, for the present discussion, was a developmental difference between newborn and two-month-old infants. The amount of detail present in the representations appeared to increase with age. Thus, the newborns' representations apparently were not sufficiently detailed to differentiate between syllables when only consonantal information was changed. However, when the change involved vowel differences, the newborns performed as well as the two-month-olds.

Results of Bertoncini et al. (1988) raise an interesting possibility that changes involving vowel information are more salient for neonates than ones involving consonants. Considering that the vocalic portion of syllables serves as an important carrier of prosodic information, then the fact that it might be more likely to attract infants' attention is not surprising. Nevertheless, there are alternative ways of explaining these findings. One such account attributes the difference between the vowel and consonant cases to the nature of the familiarization sets in each experiment. The four-day-olds failed to discriminate the addition of a new syllable when they had been familiarized with a set of items that included consonants that were all perceptually very dissimilar to each other (e.g., [bi], [si], [li], [mi]) and the test item ([di]) perceptually was very similar to one of these (viz., [di]). Perhaps, the familiarization set served to focus infants' attention on coarse-grained distinctions between the syllables at the expense of finer distinctions, such as the one between [bi] and [di]. Jusczyk et al. (1990) explored this possibility by systematically manipulating the perceptual distance among items in the familiarization sets. In some instances, the items were perceptually highly similar (e.g., [pa], [ta], [ka]). In these cases, four-day-olds easily detected the addition of a new syllable even when it differed only in the consonantal information that it contained (e.g., [ma]). In other instances, the familiarization set was chosen to include syllables with very distinctive vowels (e.g., [bi], [ba], [bu]) and the new syllable contained a vowel (e.g., [bʌ]) that was perceptually similar to one in the familiarization set (viz., [ba]). Under these circumstances, the four-day-olds did not respond to the addition of the new syllable. Therefore, these results undermine the view that vowels are intrinsically more salient for neonates. Rather, they point up the critical role that attentional focus plays in determining the way that speech sounds are perceptually represented by infants.

Of course, for perceptual representations to have an impact on acquiring the sound structure of language or developing lexicon, they must be more than temporary. They must be encoded eventually in memory so that they can be accessed during speech recognition. To learn more about what infants retain about speech sounds, Jusczyk, Kennedy, and Jusczyk (in preparation) examined the effects of delayed testing on two-month-olds' responsiveness to changes in speech sounds. They used the modified HAS procedure, but introduced a two-minute delay period filled with distracting visual materials between the presentation of the original stimulus set and the test sequence. For example, one group of infants was exposed to a randomized series of the syllables [bi], [ba], and [bu] and then tested after the delay on the syllables [di], [da], and [du]. Had the infants' representation of the original series not contained sufficiently precise information about the original syllables, then the slight change in the test set (i.e., a single phonetic feature) might not have been detected. In fact, the infants gave evidence of retaining considerable detail about the syllables during the delay period. Even changes involving a single phonetic feature were detected.

Although Jusczyk et al.'s (1988) results indicated that infants preserve much detail in their representations, there was little evidence that these are structured in terms of phonetic segments. For example, performance was unaffected by whether the members of the familiarization set shared a common consonant (e.g., [bi], [ba], [bu]) or not (e.g., [si], [ba], [tu]). In contrast, a more recent study by Jusczyk, Jusczyk, Schomberg, and Koenig (in preparation) using a familiarization set of bisyllabic utterances that either included a common syllable (e.g., [ba'lo], [ba'zi], [ba'des], [ba'mɪt]) or not (e.g., [nɛ'lo], [pæ'zi], [ču'des], [ko'mɪt]), the presence of a common syllable did affect the detection of a new item in the test set. Specifically, the presence of the common syllable in the familiarization set apparently reduced the memory load for the infants during the delay period because only with the common syllable set were they able to detect the new item in the test set. Thus, there is some evidence that infants were sensitive to the presence of the common syllable in the familiarization series, and that their representations of the utterances were structured accordingly.

In summary, the picture that emerges concerning the representation of speech sounds during early infancy is that even newborns can encode rather detailed information into their perceptual representations, provided that their attention is drawn to such features. Furthermore, by two months, they can retain such information for at least a relatively brief interval. However, there is little evidence that the representations are structured in terms of phonetic segments at this stage of development. Instead, any matching between the input and perceptual representations seems to be on the basis of syllable-sized units.

Sensitivity to the Phonological Structure of the Native Language

Acquiring the phonology of a language requires knowing the elementary sound units from which the language builds its lexical items. In other words, one must learn the phones and how they map to phonological categories (i.e., the allophones corresponding to each category). In addition to knowing the elements, the learner also must be able to recognize what constitutes a lawful sequence of sounds in the language (i.e., the phonotactic, or ordering, constraints on the sequences of sounds the language permits). Both of these aspects, which concern the basic segments and their organization, are particular to the target language that the infant is acquiring. There is evidence that adults (e.g., Brown and Hildum 1956; Greenberg 1978; Greenberg and Jenkins 1964), and even children (e.g., Messer 1967; Pertz and Bever 1975) are sensitive to such features. Of course, in addition to their phonetic segments and phonotactic structures, languages differ in their prosodic features (stress, rhythm, intonation, etc.). Thus, one can ask when the infant becomes sensitive to the particular characteristics of typical utterances in the target language.

We have begun to explore this issue by investigating when the infant distinguishes words as belonging to either the native or a foreign language (Jusczyk, Friederici, Wessels, and Svenkerud in preparation). American infants at two ages (six and nine months) were tested using a headturn preference procedure (Fernald 1985; Hirsh-Pasek et al. 1987). A bilingual (English/Dutch) speaker recorded 16 lists of low-frequency two- and three-syllable words in each language. Many of the words recorded for each language contained phones and phonetic sequences that were unacceptable in the other language. For each infant, the English words were presented from a loudspeaker on one side of a test chamber and the Dutch words were presented on the opposite side. The infants' orientation times to the loudspeaker playing each type of list were used as an index of preference for the Dutch or English words. At six months, no clear preference for either the English or the Dutch words was found. However, by nine months, a clear preference for the English words was evident. The average orientation time for the English list was 8.93 seconds, whereas for the Dutch, it was only 5.03 seconds. Overall, 22 of 24 infants listened longer to the English lists. To determine whether infants were responding to the phonetic content of the utterances as opposed to their prosodic characteristics, a second experiment was conducted using low-pass filtered versions of the lists. With the phonetic content removed, the nine-month-olds now failed to show any preference for the English samples. Thus, these results suggest that the phonetic content was the major factor in determining the infants' preferences in this instance.

Further study is needed to separate the effects of phonetic content from those of phonotactic constraints. Thus, infants could have been responding either because of the presence of a sound unfamiliar to their native language, because of familiar sounds occurring in unfamiliar sequences, or because of some combination of the two. Regardless, the findings demonstrate that by nine months infants have picked up important information about the particular phonological properties characteristic of words in their native language. Thus, the reorganization of the basic speech perception categories around the sound patterns of the native language may begin between the sixth and ninth month of life. This may be the first step in the development of phonological categories.

However, sensitivity to other aspects of the sound structure of the native language may begin well before this point. For instance, as noted earlier, Mehler et al. (1988) found that four-day-olds preferred listening to extended passages in their mothers' native language as opposed to a foreign language. Moreover, in a separate experiment parallel to the English/Dutch experiment described above, Jusczyk et al. (in preparation) examined a pair of languages that are distinctive with respect to their prosodies, viz., English and Norwegian. They found that six-month-olds displayed significant listening preferences for lists of English, as opposed to Norwegian, words. Furthermore, the same pattern of preferences obtained even with low-pass filtered versions of the lists. Thus, there is sufficient information in the prosody to allow six-month-olds to distinguish English from Norwegian words. Taken together, the results of the English/Dutch and English/Norwegian experiments suggest that infants recognize utterances in the native language on the basis of prosodic cues before they become sensitive to its segmental characteristics.

OBSERVATIONS CONCERNING THE
DEVELOPMENT OF PERCEPTUAL CAPACITIES

To summarize, the picture that emerges concerning the development of speech perception capacities during the first year of life is a movement from universal categories to categories more narrowly attuned to the characteristics of the language spoken in the infant's environment. This trend is evident for both phonetic and prosodic aspects of language, although the process apparently is more accelerated with respect to prosody than to phonetics. Thus, during the first six months, when infants still display the capacity to discriminate phonetic distinctions outside the native language, they are beginning to focus on the prosodic structure of the native language. This is evident in neonates' preferences for native language passages. By six months, they seem to give greater attention to words conforming to the native language prosody, and become less attentive to prosodic markers of linguistic units in foreign languages. Sensitivity to the phonetic organization of the native language is apparent somewhere between six and nine months, when infants can distinguish native language words from foreign words on the basis of their phonetic content. Soon thereafter (between eight- and ten-months-of-age), a decline in sensitivity to certain phonetic contrasts outside the native language is observed. One speculation as to why sensitivity develops sooner to the prosody is that it extends over longer stretches in the utterances and, thus, may be more apt to capture the infant's attention.

In any event, the rapid development of knowledge about the sound structure of the native language is reminiscent of the way that complex behaviors, such as song learning in birds (Marler and Peters 1981), are acquired in other species (for discussion of the parallels, see Miller and Jusczyk 1989). Jusczyk and Bertoncini (1988) proposed that the development of phonological categories may be an example of what Gould and Marler (1987; Marler 1990) termed an "innately guided learning process." This term describes those situations in which organisms appear to be "preprogrammed" in their genetic makeup to learn particular things and to learn them in particular ways. Relatively complex patterns of behavior unfold in the presence of appropriate input during a sensitive period of development. For speech perception, the necessary capacities to discriminate, categorize, represent, and retain information about the sound structure of language seem to be in place at birth. During the months that follow, speech is an especially salient signal for the infant. The underlying capacities are rapidly tuned to the structural regularities present in the input, becoming specialized for dealing with the language that the infant is acquiring.

What Speech Production Data Indicate about the Development of Phonological Categories

Most theories concerning the development of phonological categories have been based heavily on data about the production of speech sounds. One difficulty in trying to relate work on perception and production is that there tends to be little overlap in the most frequently studied periods. As we have seen, there are abundant data concerning the perceptual capacities of infants during the first year of life (especially the first half of the first year). In the case of production, the most widely studied period is between the ages of two and four years (Ferguson 1986).

One reason the older age range traditionally has been favored in studies of production is that most vocalizations that occur during the first year of life are characterized as babbling rather than attempts at word production. Just what the relation is between babbling and word production has been disputed for some time by child phonologists. Jakobson (1941/1968), who based his arguments on observations reported by Gregoire (1933), claimed that babbling behavior is "prelinguistic" and not "the first genuine stage of language." Moreover, he suggested that during the prelinguistic stages, the child would produce a large variety of different sounds that were not found together in a single language or even a group of languages. Following this period, he claimed that a discontinuity occurred between babbling and speech, which might be filled by a so-called silent period, wherein the "child then loses nearly all of his ability to produce sounds" (p. 21). The true beginnings of language acquisition were hypothesized to begin at the end of this period. Velten (1943) also argued for a silent period intervening between prelinguistic and linguistic behaviors.

Thus, during the early stages of research on phonological development, there was a tendency to treat babbling as perhaps preparatory for language production, but not really as genuine linguistic behavior (e.g., Fry 1966). Hence, studies focusing on phonological development began at the point when the child was uttering words. In recent years, Jakobson's claims about distinct prelinguistic and linguistic phases have been challenged (e.g., Locke 1983). Careful examination of babbling in infants from different cultures suggests that Jakobson's claims about the infant's "astonishing . . . diversity of sound productions" (p. 21) were greatly overstated. Locke (1983) notes that data collected on twelve-month-old infants by Irwin (1947), by Pierce and Hanna (1974), and by Fisichelli (1950) indicate that the 12 most frequent consonants account for 95% of all the consonants heard in the infants' productions. By comparison, the 12 least frequent consonants, which were largely fricatives, affricates, and liquids, appeared in only about 5% of the infants' utterances. In addition, Cruttenden (1970) reported that two children he studied showed a number of important omissions with respect to the sounds included in their babbling repertoire. He concluded that contrary to the earlier claims, his subjects did not babble all the sounds of English.

More important, recent studies provide little evidence of any discontinuity between babbling and early word production. Thus, several researchers have noted that their subjects continued to babble even after they began producing their first words (e.g., Blount 1969; Elbers

1982; Labov and Labov 1978; Leopold 1947; Olmsted 1971). Moreover, early words often continue patterns prevalent in the child's babbling. Elbers and Ton (1985) conclude that words and babble are formed from the same pool of productive sound patterns. Similarly, other investigators (e.g., Stoel-Gammon and Cooper 1984; Vihman et al. 1985; Vihman and Miller 1988) have reported that the repertoire of sounds and sound combinations used by any given child in late babbling and in early word productions are closely related. Consequently, it seems reasonable to treat babbling behavior as a genuine stage of language development.

Language Input and Babbling

An important phonetic milestone is achieved at around seven-months-of-age when the infant begins to engage in so-called "reduplicated" (Roug, Landberg, and Lundberg 1989; Stark 1980) or "canonical" (Oller 1980) babbling. Prior to this time, most vocalizations are confined to isolated vowel-like sounds that are sometimes accompanied by nasalization or glottal consonants and velar/uvular fricatives (Roug et al. 1989). The period of reduplicated babbling occurs when the child begins to produce sequences of syllables usually consisting of a stop consonant combined with an open, central vowel (e.g., "babababa"). There is little variation in either intonation or constituent consonant and vowel segments. Similar tendencies have been noted for such languages as English (Oller 1980; Stark 1980), Dutch (Koopmans van Beinum and van der Stelt 1986) and Swedish (Roug et al. 1989). This period is the first point at which the child produces syllables that follow constraints associated with natural languages (Oller 1980).

Given that reduplicated babbling is observed cross-linguistically, one can ask about the impact of the native language on babbling. Brown (1958) suggested that babbling drifts in the direction of the target language. There has been much debate about this. For example, Weir (1966) argued that her data pointed to considerable differences in the babbling behavior of North American, Russian, and Chinese infants from six months onward. However, Atkinson, MacWhinney, and Stoel (1968) reported that adult listeners could not judge the language background of these infants from their babbling significantly better than chance. Olney and Scholnick (1976) improved on the test procedures used by Atkinson et al. but still found no evidence that their subjects could reliably distinguish samples from English and Chinese infants ranging from six to eighteen months. More recently, Boysson-Bardies, Sagart, and Durand (1984) reported that French adults distinguished the babbling of a French from an Arab infant, but not from a

Chinese infant. Thus, whatever native language influences are present in babbling during this period are not readily detectable for adults.

Another way of evaluating such influences is to examine babbling patterns cross-linguistically for significant differences in the repertoire of infants from various language backgrounds. In his survey of existing reports of babbling from a variety of different languages, Locke (1983) found little evidence of differences in phonetic repertoires related to language background. He also noted considerable variation in the phonetic repertoires of infants from the same language background. He concluded that there is little support for the view that babbling drifts toward the native language at this phase of development. However, much of Locke's review focused on the inventory of consonants found in babbling. Recently, Boysson-Bardies et al. (1989) noted that vowel production in ten-month-olds from four different language backgrounds (French, Arabic, English, and Chinese) tends to parallel differences found in adult productions of vowels in these languages. They conclude that "the build-up of language-oriented articulatory skills is already emerging at the end of the first year" (p. 15).

One possible explanation for the discrepancy between Boysson-Bardies et al. (1989) and Locke (1983) is that native language effects may show up sooner in the production of vowels than in consonants. Indeed, the estimates of the onset of consistent cross-linguistic differences in the production of consonants tend to correspond to the phase of vocalization referred to as "variegated" babbling. This is a form of babbling that is characterized by an alternation of consonantal segments rather than a reduplication of a consonant (Roug et al. 1989). The production of variegated babbling, which overlaps with reduplicated babbling, increases dramatically around twelve to fourteen months when the child begins to produce a variety of consonants overlaid on a sentence-like intonation pattern. During this time, word production is beginning and there is a marked increase in the number of word patterns imitated (Vihman and Miller 1988).

Therefore, although native language influences may affect vowel production toward the end of the first year, it seems that comparable effects on consonantal production are not present until several months into the second year. In view of the results from infant speech perception studies, it seems that influences from the native language are slower to emerge in production than in perception.

The Relation Between Perception and Production

A frequently debated issue is the extent to which discrepancies between the infant's productions and the adult target words are attributable to perceptual factors. Is the infant's representation of the sound structure of adult words a relatively accurate model of critical phonetic details? One problem in resolving the issue is that there are scant data on the perceptual capacities of individual infants at the moment when they begin to attempt to produce words. To visualize better the possible relations that exist in the development of perceptual and productive skills, table I summarizes important changes that have been discovered in each domain.

The primary reason for assuming that the perceptual representations of newly learned words must be relatively accurate comes from the infant speech perception literature. The fact that infants can discriminate such a wide range of subtle phonetic contrasts is taken as evidence that any discrepancy between infants' and adults' productions of the same word cannot be the fault of perception. If so, then discrepancies between the child's utterances and the adult's must stem from factors such as inadequate articulatory control, limitations in memory and attention, and the like.

However, there are problems in inferring from infants' performance on speech discrimination measures to the nature of the perceptual representations they use to recognize words (Jusczyk 1986; Locke 1988; Studdert-Kennedy 1986). Thus, the word learning situation imposes many demands on the infant's attention. Moreover, ordinary listening conditions are considerably noisier than those that prevail in a laboratory setting. Consequently, the perceptual representation that infants encode for particular words may not include all of the detail that they are capable of perceiving under ideal circumstances.

Although questions can be raised about the accuracy of the underlying perceptual representations for words, there is certainly no denying that important output constraints affect the accuracy of infants' productions of target words. For example, Ferguson and Farwell (1975) reported that the word "pen" received a number of phonetically different pronunciations by the same child in the course of a single observation period. This type of variability in pronunciation has been widely reported (e.g., Leonard et al. 1982; Menn 1976; Priestly 1976; Schwartz and Folger 1977; Waterson 1978). Although it is conceivable that variations in input to the child account for some of this variability, studies have shown that infants are variable with respect to timing of motor movements (e.g., Kent and Forner 1980; Macken and Barton 1980). In addition, Locke (1983) notes that many of the simplifications that appear in children's early words have been observed cross-linguistically (e.g., stopping, fronting, initial stop voicing, final obstruent devoicing, gliding, consonant harmony, cluster reduction, etc.). Finally, now it is reasonably well documented that even before eighteen months, children will avoid attempting to produce certain words. Specifically, chil-

Table I. Timetable for Developments in Perception and Production

Age	Perception	Production
0–1 mo.	Categorical discrimination of speech contrasts	
	Discrimination of utterances in foreign from maternal language	
	Discrimination of own mother's voice from another mother's	
	Some ability to represent speech contrasts when attending to relevant dimensions	
1–4 mo.	Ability to represent some speech contrasts over short delay periods	Cooing, laughter, some velar sounds
	Normalization for speaking rates and changes in talkers	
	Can switch attentional focus in detecting some speech contrasts	
	Ability to detect changes in intonation patterns	
	Recognition of same syllable in different utterances	
4–6 mo.	Detection of prosodic markers for clausal units in foreign and native language	Vowel sounds, squealing, growling
	Preference for infant-directed over adult-directed speech	
	Can match some vocalizations with appropriate facial shapes	
6–8 mo.	Can use prosodic features to distinguish foreign from native language words	Reduplicated babbling: rhythmic strings of alternating consonants and vowels
	Ability to use prosodic markers to clausal units in some foreign languages drops out	
8–10 mo.	Decline in ability to detect certain phonetic contrasts in foreign languages is noted	Babbling with more sentence-like intonation appears
	Ability to detect foreign from native language words on basis of phonetic cues is noted	Babbling of infants from different language backgrounds becomes discriminable

continued

Table I. *continued*

Age	Perception	Production
	Ability to detect prosodic markers of subclausal units in native language	First word may occur
10–12 mo.	Reorganization of perceptual categories to reflect structure of phonemes in native language begins	Variegated babbling is dominant—strings of alternating consonants, vowels, and contrastive stress patterns

dren are much less likely to attempt new words containing sounds not already present in the inventory of sounds they use in babbling (Ferguson and Farwell 1975; Leonard et al. 1981; Vihman et al. 1985). That such avoidances may have a source in factors relating to output is suggested by results demonstrating that children comprehend words with phonological characteristics that they do not produce (Schwartz and Leonard 1982; Schwartz and Pollock 1987).

The belief that infants' perceptual representations of speech are reasonably close approximations to phonetic descriptions has led to proposals of *two-lexicon* models (e.g., Ingram 1976; Menn 1983; Spencer 1986; Vihman 1982). The basic premise of these models is that an input lexicon is used in recognizing words and a separate output lexicon containing information derived from the input is used for word production. Among the arguments in favor of such models is the fact that children can perceive many more sound distinctions than they produce (Matthei 1989). Critics of this model, such as Wheeler and Iverson (1986), object to the redundancy it requires in storing information relevant to a word's use (e.g., syntactic, semantic, and morphological information). However, a reasonable alternative to the two-lexicon model is what has been termed a *two-entry* approach (Matthei 1989; Wheeler and Iverson 1986). Such a model has only a single lexicon containing relevant syntactic, semantic, and morphological information. However, it also includes separate access routes for perception and production to the information contained in the central store (similar to what Forster 1976, 1979 has proposed for the adult lexicon). Thus, a way of resolving some of the discrepancies in the development of phonological categories in perception and production is to view them in terms of a *two-entry* approach to the lexicon. Each type of access route might have a different developmental course. Furthermore, given the changing shape and dimensions of the vocal tract during infancy, plus the amount of coordination required to sequence the articulators properly, it would not be unreasonable to suppose that productive capacities might lag behind perceptual ones.

One implication of a two-entry approach to the lexicon is that perception and production develop relatively independently of each other. Their main point of contact comes through links to a common meaning in the lexicon. This means that perceptual and productive processes are more likely to influence each other after links to common meanings have been established. However, to rule out any mutual influences before this point seems to be too strong a claim in view of the findings indicating that four- to five-month-olds show some ability to match vowel sounds to appropriate mouth movements (e.g., Kuhl and Meltzoff 1982, 1984; MacKain et al. 1983).[2] Furthermore, sources of perceptual input available to infants include their own productions, and certainly one would expect that some play in producing sounds in babbling involves exploring the acoustic consequences of various articulatory gestures. The point here is that as *meaning* and the desire to be understood become the child's primary preoccupations, pressures arise to bring productive representations of words more closely in line with perceptual representations. Consequently, the language tuning that goes on in phonological development, once meaning becomes important, is likely to have more impact on production than on perception.

DEVELOPING PHONOLOGICAL CATEGORIES

How do phonological categories develop? One difficulty in formulating a sensible answer to this question is in assembling all the pieces of knowledge that we have accumulated about infant speech perception capacities into a coherent picture. We have rather extensive data from studies that involve the presentation of isolated contrasting syllables. These data suggest that from birth infants can perform some sort of rough categorization of speech sounds. During the earliest stages, the categorization does not seem to depend much on the input available in the native environment. However, a more language-specific type of categorization is obvious toward the end of the first year of life. Finally, recent studies using long samples of connected speech suggest that in-

---

[2]In addition, one wonders whether a *two-entry* account of lexical development would provide the most parsimonious explanation of certain phenomena associated with semantic development. For example, the phenomenon of overextension in early word meanings is much more common in production than in comprehension (Thomson and Chapman 1977). The notion that perception and production tap a common meaning in the lexicon would not offer a ready explanation for the difference in frequency of overextensions in these domains. On the other hand, it is not clear that any alternative conceptualization of the lexicon (e.g., separate lexicons for perception and production or a unified lexicon for both) provides a more natural account of the differential frequency of overextensions in perception and production.

fants are sensitive to language-specific features of the input at a much earlier age for prosodic features than for phonetic ones.

A MODEL OF THE DEVELOPMENT OF SPEECH PERCEPTION CAPACITIES

Previous discussions of this topic (e.g., Aslin et al. 1983; Eimas, Miller, and Jusczyk 1987; Jusczyk 1985, 1986), have stressed the importance of viewing this process in the context of developing the means to recognize words in fluent speech. To become an effective perceiver of fluent speech, the infant must be able to identify words in the speech stream rapidly. Because word recognition is held to be an endpoint of the developmental process, it is sensible to view the development of phonological categories not as an end in itself. Rather, phonological categories emerge in the process of developing a word recognition system. I proposed a tentative model of the way that speech perception capacities evolve to support this process. The model was basically a developmental version of the LAFS (Lexical Access From Spectra) model (Klatt 1979). However, it is now clear that there are certain difficulties with the original formulation of LAFS, many of which were acknowledged by Klatt (1988). For this reason, I have revised the developmental model considerably. The new model is called WRAPSA—Word Recognition And Phonetic Structure Acquisition (figure 1).

A guiding assumption behind WRAPSA is that the endpoint in the development of speech perception processes is the ability to recognize words in fluent speech. Because the flow of information in continuous speech is great, a premium is placed upon developing the means to identify words in the speech stream rapidly. An attractive feature of Klatt's LAFS model was that it attempted to access words directly from the input without an intermediate stage of deriving a phonetic representation during on-line word recognition. WRAPSA generally preserves this feature, although it delivers an input that is roughly segmented into syllables. A brief description of the word recognition process is the following. The input undergoes a preliminary stage of auditory analysis that extracts an array of basic properties from the signal. These properties are grouped into syllable-sized units and weighted as to their importance in signaling meaningful distinctions in the language, then the weighted representation is matched against lexical representations stored in secondary memory. Weighting the representation amounts to directing attention to certain properties in the signal. The weighting scheme that is developed is not only particular to a given language, but also, in all likelihood, to a particular dialect. Thus, mastery of the sound structure of the native language entails acquiring the appropriate weighting scheme. The main com-

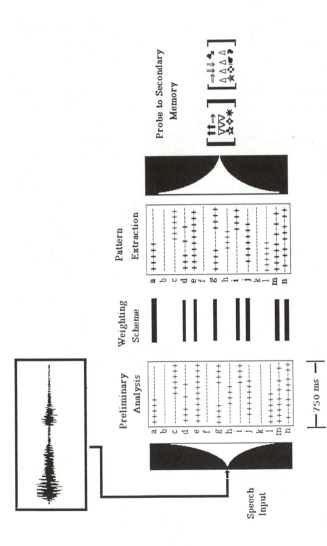

Figure 1.   Diagram of the WRAPSA Model. Input to the system is the wave form of the English utterance "baby." First stage of processing involves a preliminary analysis of the signal by the analytic processes, which for purposes of description are labeled from "a" to "n." Because the processes are constantly monitoring the input, a continuous reading of the presence of activity is available for a given timeslice, here 750 msec. Certain of these processes are more closely monitored than others due to the Weighting Scheme associated with the native language (designated by the bold bars). The sound pattern is extracted from the emphasized processes (in bold face) and then serves as a probe to secondary memory. The bold brackets indicate the stressed syllable, the symbols inside are meant to indicate that some featural description of the sound structure is present, but not one that is explicitly segmented into phones.

ponents of the model—their functions and their development—are elaborated in the remainder of this section.

Preliminary Analysis of the Signal

Processing at this stage involves passing the signal, transformed by the peripheral auditory system, through an array of analytic processes that yield decisions about the acoustic properties present. The analytic processes provide a description of the signal in terms of a number of spectral and temporal features. Following Sawusch (1986), I assume that extraction of these features occurs in particular frequency regions. In this sense, the analytic processes are spectrally specific. They record such information as: (1) the presence of noise in some spectral region; (2) whether it is periodic or aperiodic; (3) durations and intensities; (4) bandwidths; and (5) presence, direction, and degrees of spectral changes, etc. Although extraction of features takes place independently for the analytic processes, some temporal tagging of features as occurring within the same syllable-sized unit is also hypothesized to occur. In effect, the syllables are the elementary temporal slices for the input. This fits well with the key role given by many theorists (e.g., Goldsmith 1976; Liberman and Prince 1977; Selkirk 1984) to syllables in the organization of prosodic factors in speech, such as rhythm, stress, and tone.

In principle, the analytic processes provide a great deal of fine-grained information that could be used in discriminating different sounds. These processes constitute the sensory limits on the perception of speech and nonspeech sounds. They provide the dimensions along which acoustic signals ultimately can be arranged and classified. These analytic processes are an important part of the infant's innate endowment for speech perception. These capacities are those often tapped in experiments demonstrating that young infants are sensitive to distinctions even outside those of the native language spoken within their environment. Also, it is the existence of the analytic processes that makes it possible for adults learning foreign languages to acquire distinctions not present in their native language (e.g., Caramazza et al. 1973; Flege 1990; Flege and Eefting 1987). In addition, the sensitivity to within-category differences that shows up under certain conditions in categorical perception experiments (e.g., Carney et al. 1977; Pisoni and Tash 1974; Samuel 1977) can be attributed to this level of processing.

Pattern Extraction and the Interpretive Scheme

Because the analytic processes constantly are monitoring the input, any descriptions they provide are necessarily short-lived. Thus, some pattern extraction process is required to retain a representation of information present in the signal at a given moment. In principle, a number of different descriptive patterns could be extracted from the same input. Which pattern is selected to describe the input and undergo further processing depends upon attentional factors. During the first months of life, patterns extracted are apt to be very general and to apply to speech and nonspeech input alike. These patterns provide the infant with a preliminary categorization of the input. The role of experience is to refine the description selection process to yield a classification of the input that corresponds best to the structure of the native language. The application of descriptions to the input constitutes a critical stage in perception and representation of the speech signal. In fact, I would argue that the "speech mode" of perception is simply the application of certain kinds of descriptive patterns to the output of the analytic processes.

Just what does the descriptive pattern selection process involve? Elsewhere I have suggested that the key is in learning an interpretive scheme that weights the information returned by the analytic processes so as to give prominence to those dimensions that are critical in signaling meaningful distinctions in the language (e.g., Jusczyk 1981, 1985). Consequently, the interpretive scheme acts to constrain the possible patterns that could be used to describe the input. A critical juncture is reached when the infant starts to attach linguistic significance to speech. The operation of trying to assign meaning to a given set of utterance tokens is an important factor in encouraging the child to attend to similarities and differences that exist in the acoustic attributes of these tokens. As development proceeds, the infant begins to understand which properties furnished by the analytic processes are most relevant to signaling meaningful differences in the native language. Hence, learning the interpretive scheme is a matter of becoming most sensitive to these properties. What the interpretive scheme amounts to is a formula or automatic means of setting the focus of selective attention processes to these properties, rather than others.

The role of selective attention here is similar to one recently proposed by Nosofsky (1986, 1987; Nosofsky, Clark, and Shin 1989). Nosofsky's Generalized Context Model for category representation can account for a number of phenomena associated with classification behavior, including rule-based categorizations and recognition judgments. In the model, selective attention is represented in terms of the stretching and shrinking of distances in psychological space. Selectively attending to a particular dimension distorts the overall psychological space in certain ways. Distances between points along an attended dimension are *stretched* (making them more discriminable), whereas distances along unattended dimensions are *shrunk* (making them less discriminable). These notions of stretching and shrinking are equivalent to what I mean when I refer to weighting the information returned by the analytic processes. The purpose of interpretive scheme is to focus attention on these dimensions and to provide a description that best fits them.

One caveat needs to be added to this picture. It concerns which features go into the description that is sent on for further processing. Because my focus has been on word recognition, I have stressed attending to those features that serve to distinguish different words. Clearly, it is important that these be encoded in the perceptual representation in order for recognition to occur. However, as discussed in the next section, the encoding probably also includes properties other than those necessary to discriminate lexical items (e.g., characteristics relevant to distinguishing among talkers, their emotional states, the acoustic surrounds, etc). Therefore, besides the critical properties for distinguishing among words, I assume that the description contains some random selection of other properties available from the analytic processes.

There is good reason to take seriously the notion that the attainment of fluent word recognition involves the development of an interpretive scheme. First of all, the infant data suggest that early speech sound categories are universal in that they do not appear to vary from one language background to another. Moreover, many parallels have been noted in how young infants process speech and complex nonspeech sounds, suggesting that general auditory mechanisms underlie speech perception at these early stages (e.g., Jusczyk et al. 1983; Jusczyk et al. 1980; Jusczyk et al. 1989; Krumhansl and Jusczyk 1990). Yet, toward the end of the first year of life, sensitivity begins to decline to some speech contrasts outside of the native language (Werker and Lalonde 1988; Werker and Tees 1984a; Werker and Pegg this volume). Nevertheless, the decline is not irreversible because listeners can be retrained to perceive such distinctions (e.g., Flege 1990; Logan, Lively, and Pisoni 1989; McClasky, Pisoni, and Carrell 1980; Pisoni et al. 1982; Werker and Tees 1984b). Consequently, one interpretation of these declines in perception is that they are the result of shifts in attention away from the dimensions that distinguish the foreign language contrasts and the concomitant reorganization that occurs in the psychological spacing of the sounds.

Additional evidence suggesting that an interpretive scheme is involved in fluent speech perception comes from studies demonstrating that the same acoustic information can be perceived in more than one way. For example, Carden et al. (1981) demonstrated that merely changing the instruction set for listeners (telling them to label sounds as either stops or fricatives) was sufficient to induce shifts in the location of a perceptual category boundary. These shifts, which occurred both in identification and discrimination tests, were comparable to those observed when frication noises were actually added or subtracted from the stimuli. Similarly, studies using sinewave analogues to speech have shown significant shifts in how such stimuli are perceived depending on whether subjects are instructed to hear the sounds as speech or nonspeech (e.g., Bailey, Summerfield, and Dorman 1977; Grunke and Pisoni 1982; Remez et al. 1981; Schwab 1981). As Nusbaum and Schwab (1986) noted, the effect of engaging phonetic processing in such tasks is to induce changes in the perceptual sensitivity of listeners. Finally, it seems that bilingual speakers classify the same speech token differently depending on the language used in an accompanying carrier phrase. Elman, Diehl, and Buchwald (1977) reported that Spanish-English bilinguals changed the voicing category associated with a particular token according to whether the carrier phrase was in Spanish or English. In all cases just considered, the physical properties of the stimuli remain the same across the different instruction sets. Thus, the only reasonable explanation for the results observed is that subjects weight the available acoustic information differently in the various situations.

What, then, determines how the infant arrives at the correct interpretive scheme? As noted earlier, Jusczyk and Bertoncini (1988) proposed that the development of speech perception be viewed as an innately guided learning process wherein the infant is primed in certain ways to seek out some types of signals as opposed to others. Speech signals have an inherent importance for the infant and are apt to have a high priority for further processing and memory storage. The innate prewiring underlying the infant's speech perception abilities allows for development to occur in one of several directions. The nature of the input helps to select the direction that development will take. Thus, learning the sound properties of the native language takes place rapidly because the system is innately structured to be sensitive to correlations of certain distributional properties and not others.

Recognizing and Storing the Representation

Once a description has been assigned to the input, it can be compared to previously stored representations so that its meaning may be accessed. It is worth considering the nature of the representations that the infant is comparing to the processed input. Previously, I suggested that these representations take the form of prototypes (e.g., Jusczyk 1985, 1986). The notion was that the initial representations that infants develop for words are rather global. It was suggested that a sufficient number of highly salient features from the input are stored to distinguish each word from other words currently in the infant's recognition lexicon. Hence, developing a lexical entry involved selecting from the information that was available through the application of the analytic processes. The prototype that was formed as a result of this process was expected to undergo continual refinement as more and more entries were added to the lexicon.[3] The refinement was conceived to be a process of developing a more detailed representation that would be sufficient to distinguish among different lexical items. The interpretive weighting scheme was hypothesized to develop in conjunction with this process of forming and refining the prototypes.

Viewing lexical representations as prototypes implicitly assumes the existence of some sort of generic memory system wherein representations of categories are stored (e.g., Tulving 1983). Thus, the description of the sound structure of the lexical item in memory is a general one, as opposed to a particular one, that corresponds to an utterance that the child had actually encountered. Most cognitive models make this assumption that unitary, abstract representations of categories are stored in memory and matched to incoming signals during recognition. However, recently an alternative conceptualization of this process has been put forth. Accounts based on the storage of individual exemplars may provide a more accurate view of the way that category information is recognized and remembered (e.g., Hintzman 1986, 1988; Jacoby and Brooks 1984; Nosofsky 1988). The notion behind such models is that "only traces of individual episodes are stored and that aggregates of traces acting in concert at the time of retrieval represent the category as a whole" (Hintzman 1986, p. 411). Jacoby and Brooks (1984) argue that if the available representations are of specific episodes, then generality would come from treating similar situations analogously. What they have called "nonanalytic generalization" could be used to explain word recognition. "A word could be identified by reference to a previous occurrence of a word in a similar context, from a similar source, and in a similar format, rather than by reference to a generalized representation of the word . . . " (Jacoby and Brooks 1984, p. 3). Hintzman's Minerva 2 model (1986), which stores only descriptions of individual episodes, demonstrates that computing a local average from stored instances can serve as an effective recognition routine.

---

[3]The notion that global representations could suffice for word recognition during early stages of development with more detailed representations added as vocabulary grows receives some empirical support from a recent study by Charles-Luce and Luce (1990). They calculated the number of near neighbors (perceptually similar words) for words in children's lexicons at various ages. They found that a vocabulary typical for a seven-year-old contains a much lower proportion of highly confusable items than does that for an average adult.

Multiple-trace models of memory have much to recommend them. They can account for important findings that have been associated with prototypes (e.g., differential forgetting of prototypes and old instances, typicality and category size effects). In addition, these models can explain context-dependent effects reported in the memory and concept-learning literature (e.g., Craik and Kirsner 1974; Jacoby 1983; Osgood and Hoosain 1974; Potter and Faulconer 1979; Roth and Shoben 1983). Recently Logan (1988) has demonstrated that an instance-based model can provide an account of automaticity in skill learning. This last demonstration may have important ramifications for theorizing about fluent word recognition because, as Logan notes, automatic processing is defined as fast, effortless, autonomous, and unavailable to conscious awareness. These same properties are characteristic of fluent speech recognition. Hence, the demonstration that such automaticity can be derived from a system that stores only individual instances makes it reasonable to consider an instance-based account of word recognition.

The notion that the matching process during word recognition involves representations of previously encountered exemplars as opposed to an abstract prototype has certain advantages for the developmental model under consideration. It could provide a clearer account of how knowledge of the sound structure is modified by experience. To see this, consider what happens when a memory trace is stored. The trace itself preserves the overall organization of the properties in the perceptual representation. However, not every utterance that an infant hears will be recorded as an episodic trace. Although some random storage of the sound structure of the processed input may occur, in general, storage of sound patterns requires that some extra effort be given to processing the sounds. This may involve rehearsing the perceptual representation, an effort to associate it with the meaning or the context, or some other such process. The role of experience is not to modify previously stored traces; rather, new traces are added to those already in secondary (i.e., long-term) memory. The addition of a new trace modifies the way that the whole memory system behaves. The more a new trace differs from preceding ones, the greater is the change in the behavior of the memory system during subsequent efforts at identification of new items. Recognition in a system such as this occurs when a new input, or probe, is broadcast simultaneously to all traces in secondary memory. Each trace is activated according to its similarity to the probe, with traces having the greatest overlap being the most strongly activated. The reply that is returned from secondary memory to primary memory has been described as an *echo* (Hintzman 1986). All traces in secondary memory contribute to this echo. If several traces are strongly activated, then the content of the echo primarily will reflect their common properties. Traces most similar to the probe produce a more intense response and thus contribute more to the echo. This ensures that characteristics distinguishing one trace from the others tend to be masked in the echo. In comparing the echo to the probe, the echo might be used to fill in gaps that exist in the information supplied by the probe. Phenomena like phonemic restoration effects (e.g., Samuel 1981a,b, 1986; Warren 1970) might be explained in this way. In any case, should the particular instance be stored in memory, then the trace will take the form of the processed probe.

The structure of the probe in a system like this critically determines which combination of traces contribute most heavily to the echo. Depending upon how specific the probe is, the set of traces most strongly activated may be large or small. The interpretive scheme discussed earlier helps constrain the perceptual representation that serves as the probe. Prior to the time that the infant engages in any meaningful encoding of speech sounds, the configuration of properties selected for speech probes might be expected to vary more or less randomly. When the infant begins to establish an interpretive scheme, the configuration of properties appearing in the probe for a particular word should show considerably more stability. That is, features most likely to be included in the probe will be those suited to drawing meaningful distinctions in the target language. This is not to say that the probe faithfully includes all properties necessary to identify the item in any context. At the onset of the development of the lexicon, only a partial description of the word's sound structure (such as its stress pattern and a few of its key phonetic features) may make up the probe. Even three-year-olds may have such incompletely specified representations (e.g., Echols 1989; Peters 1977). A partial description of this sort may be sufficient for word recognition, if vocabulary is small and contains few items with highly similar sound structures (Charles-Luce and Luce 1990).

There is good reason to suppose that the perceptual representations that serve as probes are structured in terms of syllable-like units. As noted earlier, many of the most important prosodic features of language, including intonation, stress patterns, and tone, are organized in syllable-sized units (e.g., Goldsmith 1976; Halle and Vergnaud 1987; Hayes 1982; Liberman and Prince 1977; Selkirk 1984). Moreover, infants are attentive to prosodic features of the native language at an early age (e.g., DeCasper and Fifer 1980; Fernald 1985; Mehler et al. 1988). Thus, attention to the prosody could help to segment the input into syllable-sized chunks that would then serve as a basis for structuring the perceptual representation. Organizing the representations in terms of syllable-sized units may also have certain payoffs for achieving a correct segmentation of speech into words. For languages with regular stress patterns such as Czech or Polish, locating the main stress can provide information about location of word boundaries in the input (Gleitman et al. 1988). Furthermore, as knowledge grows of the syllable forms permitted by the language, this, too, can aid in segmenting fluent speech into words (Church 1987). For this reason, WRAPSA assumes that among the global properties included in both the probe and the representations encoded in secondary memory would be an indication of the number of syllable-sized units present and their relative prominence.

DO INFANTS ENGAGE IN PHONETIC SEGMENTATION?

To this point, the model has said little about phonological categories and their development. This is because, like Klatt (1979), we do not see the process of fluent speech recognition as requiring a description of the input in terms of phonetic segments. Nevertheless, even though the recovery of a phonetic description might be avoided in most instances of fluent speech recognition, phonetic representations are believed to be important to explain many other phenomena related to the sound structure of language. For example, accounts of speech production errors such as slips of the tongue assume that the speaker has available a phonetic description of an utterance (Fromkin 1973; Shattuck-Hufnagel and Klatt 1979). In addition, many linguistic accounts of the native speaker's understanding of the phonological features of language, including the ability to produce the correct phonetic realization of certain inflections, assume the availability of a phonetic description of the input (e.g., Baudouin de Courtenay 1972; Bromberger and Halle 1986; Chomsky and Halle 1968; Jakobson 1971; Trubetzkoy 1939). Finally, the ability to recover some sort of phonetic description is necessary to explain how listeners can identify unfamiliar words or nonwords in speech (Klatt 1979). Thus, the listener eventually can access a phonetic representation. But does access to a phonetic representation develop prior to the ability to recognize words? Moreover, is the computation of a phonetic representation a necessary stage in word recognition?

Some of the results discussed earlier seem to argue against the view incorporated in the WRAPSA model and in favor of young infants' representing speech as sequences of phonetic segments. One type of finding comes from the study by Jusczyk et al. (in preparation) where nine-month-olds could distinguish native language words from foreign language words. Infants apparently were able to discriminate English versus Dutch words on the basis of either phonetic or phonotactic cues. The second type of finding concerns the loss in sensitivity to non-native language contrasts toward the end of the first year (e.g., Werker and Lalonde 1988). One interpretation of these results is that the infant has learned the phonemic categories of the native language.

Such a development seems to require that infants perform some phonetic segmentation of the input to arrive at the correct phonemic classes. Finally, Greiser and Kuhl (1989) have reported that infants form prototypes for vowel categories. I am not convinced that any of these results demands that the infant perform some sort of phonetic segmentation of the input. To see why, let us examine the way in which each type of result might be explained by WRAPSA.

Discriminating Foreign from Native Language Words

As noted earlier, there is little evidence during the first few months that the infant's perceptual representations of speech are analyzed into phonetic segment-sized units (e.g., Bertoncini et al. 1988; Jusczyk and Derrah 1987). Nor is such a representation required to explain speech production during this phase of development. Is there a way of providing the necessary information for distinguishing native language words from foreign ones without invoking a phonetically segmented representation? In fact, the relevant information is also available simply by taking account of which syllables appear in the input. Syllables contain the necessary information about both the phones used in the language and the phonotactic constraints. Familiarity with the inventory of syllables used by speakers of the language allows the learner to detect those that violate the syllable structure that the language permits, either because of the appearance of certain phonetic segments or illegal sequences of segments. Once having gained access to syllable units, the child can begin analyzing their internal structure. Clements and Keyser (1983) have argued that

> . . . syllable structure provides an organizational principle which permits a significant degree of simplification in the task of the language learner. Syllable structure is a readily discoverable principle of classification which allows the formulation of phonological rules in terms of language-particular classes of sounds such as 'syllable-final consonant,' 'syllabic nucleus,' 'extrasyllabic consonant' and the like. Once the principles of syllabic organization have been worked out for a given language, many formally arbitrary rule statements can be replaced by internally motivated statements involving syllable-based categories such as these (p. 116).

Furthermore, many important prosodic features of language are defined with respect to syllable-units (e.g., Goldsmith 1976; Liberman and Prince 1977). The fact that infants are sensitive to such features and their organization soon after birth (e.g., Mehler et al. 1988) suggests that they have the capacity for some kind of syllabic segmentation of the input. Empirical support for this contention comes from studies by Jusczyk et al. (in preparation) and Goodsitt, Morgan, and Kuhl (submitted), which show that infants can gain a processing advantage when input includes invariant, recurring syllables.

The Decline in Sensitivity to Foreign Language Contrasts

One of the most remarkable findings concerning the development of speech perception capacities has to do with the decline in infants' responsiveness to contrasts outside of the native language. An implication of these results is that by 12 months, infants have already taken steps toward phonological categories in the native language. However, recall that any decline in sensitivity to foreign language contrasts is less than complete. Best et al. (1988) found that both adults and twelve- to fourteen-month-old infants from English speaking homes were able to discriminate Zulu click contrasts. There was no indication of any decreased sensitivity to these contrasts despite the fact that they do not occur in English.

Is there any way to explain the foreign language findings within the framework of WRAPSA? Recall that the model postulates that a special mode of speech perception only evolves when the infant starts to attach linguistic significance to speech. It is at this point that the development of the interpretive scheme for speech sounds begins. Prior to this time, processing of speech sounds relies on the analytic processes and whatever general schemes exist for processing acoustic signals. Hence, during the first months of life, foreign and native language contrasts are treated alike and processed in the same way as certain complex nonspeech contrasts (e.g., Jusczyk et al. 1980, 1983, 1989; also see Studdert-Kennedy 1986 for a similar suggestion concerning early speech discrimination abilities).

Once the speech mode of perception begins to develop, its interpretation scheme takes precedence over any general auditory processing schemes for speech sounds. Consequently, when foreign language contrasts drop out it is because they are distinguished along an unattended dimension. Because distances along such dimensions are shrunk, two previously discriminable points can no longer be resolved, therefore, the distinction between them is not detected. If at some point, the infant begins to attend once again to this dimension, such as when learning a foreign language that employs this distinction, then the distances will be stretched again allowing it to be detected. In this way, WRAPSA can handle those cases in which sensitivity to foreign contrasts declines. How does the model account for the Zulu click case? The argument is that such sounds fall outside the range of sounds that infants frequently hear in the context of conversations. Hence, these sounds are treated as nonspeech sounds. To the extent that sufficient information is available from the analytic processes to distinguish them, the infants will be able to discriminate them.

Demonstrations of Prototype Learning

A recent study with six-month-old infants by Greiser and Kuhl (1989) claims that infants form prototypes for vowel categories. In one experiment, infants were trained to discriminate good exemplars of two vowel categories, [i] and [ɛ]. The infants were then tested with 32 novel tokens from each of the two categories to determine whether they would sort the tokens into the appropriate categories. The infants correctly classified the novel tokens on first exposure to them over 90% of the time. In an additional experiment, Greiser and Kuhl compared the effects of training infants with good (i.e., prototypical) versus poor exemplars of the vowel categories. Correct generalization to new instances of each vowel category was significantly greater for infants trained on the good exemplars. Although Greiser and Kuhl interpret their findings as support for prototypes, an exemplar model makes very similar predictions in this situation. As noted earlier, Hintzman (1986) has shown that an exemplar model can account for effects usually associated with prototypes.

More to the point, however, is whether these results can be taken as a demonstration that infants are representing individual phonetic segments. At first glance, it might seem so because the test materials are phonetic segments (viz., vowels). However, the stimuli can also be described as syllables. One cannot say with certainty whether any prototypes that infants might have concern phonetic segments such as vowels or some larger units, such as syllables. The data simply are not definitive with respect to whether more complex syllables are represented in terms of sequences of phonetic segments.

HOW PHONOLOGICAL CATEGORIES DEVELOP

Eventually, the learner is able to derive a phonetic representation of utterances. Certainly, some such representation underlies the ability to read (Liberman et al. 1974; Morais et al. 1979; Rozin and Gleitman 1977; Treiman 1987; Walley, Smith, and Jusczyk 1986). Given a system like WRAPSA, how does phonetic representation come about? The nature of the word recognition process may play a role in this development. Specifically, there is an initial-to-final bias in processing in that speech is organized temporally. Systems such as LAFS take advantage of this in organizing the word recognition network to begin processing with

acoustic onset properties. Thus, words sharing common initial segments are grouped together by having similar acoustic characteristics
at onset. Common characteristics shared by a large number of nearby
items and not shared by more distant ones could serve as an initial
basis for developing representations corresponding to phonological
categories.

The notion that some general acoustic description exists for the
same phonetic segment in a particular position in a syllable regardless
of other segments with which it occurs is a central tenet of acoustic-
property-based models of speech perception (e.g., Kewley-Port, Pisoni, and Studdert-Kennedy 1983; Searle, Jacobson, and Rayment 1979;
Stevens and Blumstein 1981). There is also some evidence of perceptual
equivalents to such general acoustic descriptions—at least for adult listeners. Jusczyk, Smith, and Murphy (1980) found that adults could use
the information available in the first 30 msec at the onset of syllables to
form groups based on the identity of their initial segments. In a related
study, Ivry and Jusczyk (1985) reported a comparable finding when
only the last 30 msec before the offsets of the syllables were presented
and the task was to form groups based on the identity of the syllable-
final segments. Thus, a tendency to group items according to acoustic
similarities at onset could eventually support the development of phonological categories. Moreover, this process is compatible with an instance-based system, as Hintzman (1986) has demonstrated. If such an
abstraction were made the object of conscious reflection, then a trace of
the phonological category would be stored in secondary memory. The
system would converge on categories consistent with those in the native language simply because the frequency of utterances to which the
learner is exposed conform to these categories a much greater proportion of the time than they do not.[4]

A limitation of the present account is that it offers a solution for
only part of the story. Namely, it explains how phones that are in free
variation with one another (i.e., can be substituted for one another in
the same syllable position) could come to be linked to the same phonological category. In such a case, one can plead the fact that the meaning of the utterance does not change when one element is substituted
for the other. What is not explained is how elements occupying different positions in syllables (i.e., ones that are in complementary distribution with one another) could ever become linked to the same phonological category. How do infants learn that a phonetic segment in one

---

[4]I acknowledge MacKain's (1982) point that the input is likely to contain instances
that fall outside the bounds of phonemic categories as well (e.g., the inclusion of prevoiced /b/ along with voiced /b/ in English). However, it seems likely that these will occur
much less frequently than those that fall within the range for the category.

context is to be treated as a variant of another phone in an entirely different context? Appeals to perceptual similarity apparently will not suffice because which phones get assigned to the same phoneme varies from language to language (Fodor, Bever, and Garrett 1974). The response that I offer here is that, currently, there are no data that demonstrate that infants actually do perceive similarities between segments occurring in different positions. Thus far, what limited data there are showing that different phonetic segments are categorized together involve cases occupying the syllable-initial position (e.g., Werker and Lalonde 1988). Hence, there is no reason to assume that infants under one year of age do perceive similarities between segments in complementary distribution. In fact, as I have suggested previously (e.g., Jusczyk 1985), children may not make such associations much before they learn to read. As to what the basis could be for recognizing such similarities, I can only speculate that, perhaps, reference to articulatory gestures eventually provides the necessary link.

Finally, although phonetic representations might arise in the way described here, it does not necessarily follow that the word-recognition system is then reorganized to include phonetic representations in on-line speech recognition. Instead, a process involving a detailed phonetic representation of the input could evolve as a separate process employed in special circumstances (e.g., such as when a nonword or unfamiliar word is encountered).

The account just offered bears some similarities to one suggested by Lindblom (1986). It is worthwhile to indicate some of the similarities and differences in our views. Lindblom stressed the importance of viewing the development of the phonological system in the context of the communicative setting. He also took the position that syllables rather than phonetic segments form the elementary units of the child's sound system. The syllables are treated as holistic, without explicit internal segmentation. These assumptions are similar to those I have made. However, Lindblom's (1986) focus is on production, and he views the syllable primarily in gestural terms: "It is a gestalt trajectory coursing through the phonetic (articulatory/acoustic/perceptual) space . . . and represents an arbitrary closure-opening gesture in articulatory terms" (p. 502). For Lindblom, not only is a segmental representation of the input unavailable to the infant, but so is a featural description. This is a critical distinction with the assumptions made in the WRAPSA model. WRAPSA takes a description of the input in terms of a set of acoustic properties to be a given. The analytic processes that provide this description are a part of the innate biological endowment of the infant. They ultimately define the dimensions along which a categorization of the input can take place. It is only within these bounds that the distributional properties of the input can affect the way the system develops. In focusing exclusively on production, Lindblom views the developmental process as one of searching for distinctive sounds to represent different meanings. There is nothing in his account to indicate how the input is used in selecting the sounds to represent meanings. In contrast, WRAPSA holds that the perceived input is the target that the learner is trying to match in his or her productions.

In conclusion, I have posited a model of the way in which infant speech perception capacities may develop into phonological categories. Although the model focuses on the way that word recognition processes develop during infancy, it also attempts to deal with issues relating to the infant's knowledge of the sound structure of the native language. Much progress has been made in understanding the development of speech perception, and more detail has been added to the model to reflect this. Still, WRAPSA is basically a framework to test hypotheses about how such capacities develop with exposure to a particular language. Much remains to be learned before we can account for the way that speech perception capacities evolve into the knowledge system that deals with the sound structure of a native language.

REFERENCES

Aslin, R. N. 1987. Visual and auditory development in infancy. In *Handbook of Infancy, 2nd Edition*, ed. J. D. Osofsky. New York: Wiley.

Aslin, R. N., and Pisoni, D. B. 1980. Some developmental processes in speech perception. In *Child Phonology, Vol. 2: Perception* eds. G. H. Yeni-Komshian, J. F. Kavanagh, and C. A. Ferguson. New York: Academic Press.

Aslin, R. N., Pisoni, D. B., Hennessy, B. L., and Perey, A. J. 1981. Discrimination of voice onset time by human infants: New findings and implications for the effects of early experience. *Child Development* 52:1135–1145.

Aslin, R. N., Pisoni, D. B., and Jusczyk, P. W. 1983. Auditory development and speech perception in infancy. In *Handbook of Child Psychology: Vol. 2, Infancy and Developmental Psychobiology* eds. M. Haith and J. Campos. New York: Wiley.

Atkinson, K., MacWhinney, B., and Stoel, C. 1968. An experiment on the recognition of babbling. In *Language Behavior Research Laboratory Working Paper #14*. Berkeley: University of California.

Bailey, P. J., Summerfield, A. Q., and Dorman, M. F. 1977. On the identification of sine-wave analogs of certain speech sounds. *Status Report on Speech Research*, SR-51-52. New Haven, CT: Haskins Laboratories.

Baudouin de Courtenay, J. 1972. *Selected Writings of Baudouin de Courtenay* ed. E. Stankiewicz. Bloomington: Indiana University Press.

Bertoncini, J., Bijeljac-Babic, R., Blumstein, S. E., and Mehler, J. 1987. Discrimination in neonates of very short CV's. *Journal of the Acoustical Society of America* 82:31–37.

Bertoncini, J., Bijeljac-Babic, R., Jusczyk, P. W., Kennedy, L. J., and Mehler, J. 1988. An investigation of young infants' perceptual representations of speech sounds. *Journal of Experimental Psychology: General* 117:21–33.

Bertoncini, J., and Mehler, J. 1981. Syllables as units in infant speech perception. *Infant Behavior and Development* 4:247–60.

Bertoncini, J., Morais, J., Bijeljac-Babic, R., Mehler, J., MacAdams, S., and Peretz, I. 1990. Dichotic perception and laterality in neonates. *Brain and Language* 37:591–605.

Best, C. T., McRoberts, G. W., and Sithole, N. M. 1988. Examination of the perceptual re–organization for speech contrasts: Zulu click discrimination by English-speaking adults and infants. *Journal of Experimental Psychology: Human Perception and Performance* 14:245–360.

Bladon, R. A., Henton, G. C., and Pickering, J. B. 1984. Towards an auditory theory of speaker normalization. *Language and Communication* 4:59–69.

Blount, B. G. 1969. Acquisition of language by Luo children. Unpublished doctoral dissertation. University of California, Berkeley.

Boysson-Bardies, B. de, Sagart, L., and Durand, C. 1984. Discernible differences in the babbling of infants according to target-language. *Journal of Child Language* 11:1–15.

Boysson-Bardies, B. de, Hallé, P., Sagart, L., and Durand, C. 1989. A cross-linguistic investigation of vowel formants in babbling. *Journal of Child Language* 16:1–17.

Bromberger, S., and Halle, M. 1986. On the relationship between phonology and phonetics. In *Invariance and Variability in Speech Processes* eds. J. Perkell and D. H. Klatt. Hillsdale, NJ: Erlbaum.

Brown, R. 1958. *Words and Things*. Glencoe, IL: Free Press.

Brown, R., and Hildum, D. C. 1956. Expectancy and the identification of syllables. *Language* 32:411–19.

Buxton, H. 1983. Temporal predictability in the perception of English speech. In *Prosody: Models and Measurements* eds. A. Cutler and D. R. Ladd. Berlin: Springer-Verlag.

Caramazza, A., Yeni-Komshian, G., Zurif, E., and Carbone, E. 1973. The acqusition of a new phonological contrast: The case of stop consonants in French-English bilinguals. *Journal of the Acoustical Society of America* 54:421–28.

Carden, G. C., Levitt, A., Jusczyk, P. W., and Walley, A. C. 1981. Evidence for phonetic processing of cues to place of articulation: Perceived manner affects perceived place. *Perception & Psychophysics* 29:26–36.

Carney, A. E., Widin, G. P., and Veimeister, N. F. 1977. Noncategorical perception of stop consonants differing in VOT. *Journal of the Acoustical Society of America* 62:961–70.

Charles-Luce, J., and Luce, P. A. 1990. Similarity neighborhoods of words in young children's lexicons. *Journal of Child Language* 17:205–215.

Chomsky, N., and Halle, M. 1968. *The Sound Pattern of English*. New York: Harper & Row.

Church, K. 1987. Phonological parsing and lexical retrieval. *Cognition* 25:53–69.

Clements, G. N., and Keyser, S. J. 1983. *CV Phonology*. Cambridge, MA: MIT Press.

Craik, F. I. M., and Kirsner, K. 1974. The effect of speaker's voice on word recognition. *Quarterly Journal of Experimental Psychology* 26:274–84.

Cruttenden, A. 1970. A phonetic study of babbling. *British Journal of Disorders of Communication* 5:110–17.

Cutler, A., and Carter, D. M. 1987. The predominance of strong initial syllables in the English vocabulary. *Computer Speech and Language* 2:133–42.

Cutler, A., Mehler, J., Norris, D. G., and Segui, J. 1986. The syllable's differing role in the segmentation of French and English. *Journal of Memory and Language* 25:385–400.

Cutler, A., and Norris, D. G. 1988. The role of strong syllables in segmentation for lexical access. *Journal of Experimental Psychology: Human Perception and Performance* 14:113–21.

DeCasper, A. J., and Fifer, W. P. 1980. Of human bonding: Newborns prefer their mothers' voices. *Science* 208:1174–1176.

Echols, C. H. 1988. The role of stress, position and intonation in the representation and identification of early words. *Papers and Reports on Child Language Development* 27:39–46.

Eimas, P. D. 1974. Auditory and linguistic units of processing of cues for place of articulation by infants. *Perception & Psychophysics* 16:513–21.

Eimas, P. D. 1975. Auditory and phonetic coding of the cues for speech: Discrimination of the [r-l] distinction by young infants. *Perception & Psychophysics* 18:341–47.

Eimas, P. D., Miller, J. L., and Jusczyk, P. W. 1987. On infant speech perception and the acquisition of language. In *Categorical Perception* ed. S. Harnad. New York: Cambridge University Press.

Eimas, P. D., Siqueland, E. R., Jusczyk, P., and Vigorito, J. 1971. Speech perception in infants. *Science* 171:303–306.

Elbers, L. 1982. Operating principles in repetitive babbling: A case study. *Cognition* 12:45–64.

Elbers, L., and Ton, J. 1985. Play pen monologues: The interplay of words and babbles in the first words period. *Journal of Child Language* 12:551–67.

Elman, J. L., Diehl, R. L., and Buchwald, S. E. 1977. Perceptual switching in bilinguals. *Journal of the Acoustical Society of America* 62:971–74.

Fant, G. 1960. *Acoustic Theory of Speech Production.* The Hague: Mouton.

Ferguson, C. A. 1986. Discovering sound units and constructing sound systems: It's child's play. In *Invariance and Variability in Speech Processes* eds. J. Perkell and D. H. Klatt. Hillsdale, NJ: Lawrence Erlbaum Associates.

Ferguson, C. A., and Farwell, C. B. 1975. Words and sound in early language acquisition: English initial consonants in the first fifty words. *Language* 51: 419–39.

Fernald, A. 1985. Four-month-old infants prefer to listen to motherese. *Infant Behavior and Development* 8:181–95.

Fernald, A., and Kuhl, P. K. 1987. Acoustic determinants of infant preference for motherese speech. *Infant Behavior and Development* 10:279–93.

Fisichelli, R. M. 1950. An experimental study of the prelinguistic speech development of institutionalized infants. Unpublished doctoral dissertation, Fordham University.

Flege, J. 1990. Perception and production: The relevance of phonetic input to L2 phonological learning. In *Crosscurrents in Second Language Acquisition and Linguistic Theories* eds. C. A. Ferguson and T. Heubner. Philadelphia: John Benjamins.

Flege, J., and Eefting, W. 1987. The production and perception of English stops by Spanish speakers of English. *Journal of Phonetics* 15:67–83.

Fodor, J. A., Bever, T. G., and Garrett, M. F. 1974. *The Psychology of Language.* New York: McGraw-Hill.

Forster, K. 1976. Accessing the mental lexicon. In *New Approaches to Language Mechanisms* eds. R. Wales and E. Walker. Amsterdam: North Holland.

Forster, K. 1979. Levels of processing and the structure of the language processor. In *Sentence processing: Psycholinguistic Studies Presented to Merrill Garrett* eds. W. Cooper and E. Walker. Hillsdale, NJ: Erlbaum.

Fromkin, V. A. 1973. *Speech Errors as Linguistic Evidence*. The Hague: Mouton.

Fry, D. B. 1966. The development of the phonological system in the normal and the deaf child. In *The Genesis of Language* eds. F. A. Smith and G. A. Miller. Cambridge, MA: MIT Press.

Gibson, E. J. 1969. *Principles of Perceptual Learning and Development*. New York: Appleton-Century-Crofts.

Gleitman, L. R., Gleitman, H., Landau, B., and Wanner, E. 1988. Where learning begins: Initial representations for language learning. In *Linguistics: The Cambridge Survey, III, Language: The Psychological and Biological Aspects* ed. F. J. Newmeyer. Cambridge: Cambridge University Press.

Goldsmith, J. 1976. An overview of autosegmental phonology. *Linguistic Analysis* 2:23–68.

Goodsitt, J. V., Morgan, J. L., and Kuhl, P. K. (submitted). Contextual structure as a determinant of complexity in infant speech processing.

Gould, J. L., and Marler, P. 1987. Learning by instinct. *Scientific American* 256: 62–73.

Greenberg, J. H. 1978. Some generalizations concerning initial and final consonant clusters. In *Universals of Human Language, Vol. 2: Phonology* ed. J. H. Greenberg. Stanford, CA: Stanford University Press.

Greenberg, J. H., and Jenkins, J. J. 1964. Studies in the psychological correlates of the sound system of American English. *Word* 20:157–77.

Gregoire, A. 1933. L'apprentissage de la parole pendant les deux premieres annees de l'enfance. *Journal de Psychologie* 30:375–89.

Greiser, D., and Kuhl, P. K. 1989. The categorization of speech by infants: Support for speech-sound prototypes. *Developmental Psychology* 25:577–88.

Grunke, M. E., and Pisoni, D. B. 1982. Some experiments on perceptual learning of mirror-image acoustic patterns. *Perception & Psychophysics* 31:210–18.

Halle, M., and Vergnaud, J. R. 1987. *An Essay on Stress*. Cambridge, MA: MIT Press.

Hayes, B. 1982. Extrametricality and English stress. *Linguistic Inquiry* 13:227–76.

Hintzman, D. L. 1986. "Schema Abstraction" in a multiple-trace memory model. *Psychological Review* 93:411–28.

Hintzman, D. L. 1988. Judgments of frequency and recognition memory in a multiple-trace memory model. *Psychological Review* 95:528–51.

Hirsh-Pasek, K., Kemler Nelson, D. G., Jusczyk, P. W., Wright Cassidy, K., Druss, B., and Kennedy, L. 1987. Clauses are perceptual units for young infants. *Cognition* 26:269–86.

Ingram, D. 1976. *Phonological Disability in Children*. New York: Elsevier.

Irwin, O. C. 1947. Infant speech: Consonantal sounds according to place of articulation. *Journal of Speech Disorders* 12:397–401.

Ivry, R. B., and Jusczyk, P. W. 1985. Perceptual classification of information in vowel-consonant syllables. *Perception & Psychophysics* 37:93–102.

Jacoby, L. L. 1983. Perceptual enhancement: Persistent effects of an experience. *Journal of Experimental Psychology: Learning, Memory and Cognition* 9:21–38.

Jacoby, L. L., and Brooks, L. R. 1984. Nonanalytic cognition: Memory, perception, and concept learning. In *The Psychology of Learning and Motivation*, (Vol. 18) ed. G. H. Bower. New York: Academic.

Jakobson, R. 1941/1968. *Child Language, Aphasia, and Phonological Universals*. The Hague: Mouton.

Jakobson, R. 1971. *Selected Writings*. The Hague: Mouton.

Jusczyk, P. W. 1981. The processing of speech and nonspeech sounds by infants: Some implications. In *Development of Perception: Psychobiological Perspec-*

tives (Vol. 1) eds. R. N. Aslin, J. R. Alberts, and M. R. Petersen. New York: Academic.

Jusczyk, P. W. 1985. On characterizing the development of speech perception. In *Neonate Cognition: Beyond the Blooming, Buzzing Confusion* eds. J. Mehler and R. Fox. Hillsdale, NJ: Erlbaum.

Jusczyk, P. W. 1986. Towards a model for the development of speech perception. In *Invariance and Variability in Speech Processes* eds. J. Perkell and D. H. Klatt. Hillsdale, NJ: Erlbaum.

Jusczyk, P. W. 1989. Perception of cues to clausal units in native and non-native languages. Paper presented at the biennial meeting of the Society for Research in Child Development, Kansas City, April.

Jusczyk, P. W. In press a. How talker variation affects young infants' perception and memory of speech. In *Spoken Language* eds. J. Charles-Luce, P. A. Luce, and J. R. Sawusch. Norwood, NJ: Ablex.

Jusczyk, P. W. In press b. Infant speech perception and the development of the mental lexicon. In *The Transition from Speech Sounds to Spoken Words* eds. H. C. Nusbaum and J. C. Goodman. Cambridge, MA: MIT Press.

Jusczyk, P. W., and Bertoncini, J. 1988. Viewing the development of speech perception as an innately guided learning process. *Language and Speech* 31: 217–38.

Jusczyk, P. W., and Derrah, C. 1987. Representation of speech sounds by young infants. *Developmental Psychology* 23:648–54.

Jusczyk, P. W., and Thompson, E. J. 1978. Perception of a phonetic contrast in multisyllabic utterances by two-month-old infants. *Perception & Psychophysics* 23:105–109.

Jusczyk, P. W., Bertoncini, J., Bijeljac-Babic, R., Kennedy, L. J., and Mehler, J. 1990. The role of attention in speech perception by infants. *Cognitive Development*.

Jusczyk, P. W., Friederici, A. D., Wessels, J., and Svenkerud, V. In preparation. Infants' recognition of foreign versus native language words.

Jusczyk, P. W., Hirsh-Pasek, K., Kemler Nelson, D. G., and Schomberg, T. In preparation. Perception of acoustic correlates to clausal units in a foreign language by American infants.

Jusczyk, P. W., Jusczyk, A. M., Schomberg, T., and Koenig, N. In preparation. An investigation of the infant's representation of information in bisyllabic utterances.

Jusczyk, P. W., Kennedy, L. J., and Jusczyk, A. M. In preparation. Young infants' memory for information in speech syllables.

Jusczyk, P. W., Pisoni, D. B., and Mullennix, J. In press. Some consequences of stimulus variability on speech processing by two-month-olds. *Cognition*.

Jusczyk, P. W., Pisoni, D. B., Reed, M., Fernald, A., and Myers, M. 1983. Infants' discrimination of the duration of a rapid spectrum change in non-speech signals. *Science* 222:175–77.

Jusczyk, P. W., Pisoni, D. B., Walley, A. C., and Murray, J. 1980. Discrimination of the relative onset of two-component tones by infants. *Journal of the Acoustical Society of America* 67:262–70.

Jusczyk, P. W., Rosner, B. S., Reed, M., and Kennedy, L. J. 1989. Could temporal order differences underlie 2-month-olds' discrimination of English voicing contrasts? *Journal of the Acoustical Society of America* 85:1741–1749.

Jusczyk, P. W., Smith, L. B., and Murphy, C. 1980. The perceptual classification of speech. *Perception & Psychophysics* 30:10–23.

Kaplan, E., and Kaplan, G. 1971. The prelinguistic child. In *Human Development and Cognitive Processes* ed. J. Elliot. New York: Holt, Rinehart & Winston.

Kent, R., and Forner, L. 1980. Speech segment durations in sentence recitations by children and adults. *Journal of Phonetics* 8:157–68.

Kewley-Port, D., Pisoni, D. B., and Studdert-Kennedy, M. 1983. Perception of static and dynamic acoustic cues to place of articulation in initial stop consonants. *Journal of the Acoustical Society of America* 73:1779–1793.

Klatt, D. H. 1979. Speech perception: A model of acoustic-phonetic analysis and lexical access. *Journal of Phonetics* 7:279–312.

Klatt, D. H. 1988. Review of selected models of speech perception. In *Lexical Representation and Process* ed. W. Marslen-Wilson. Cambridge, MA: MIT Press.

Koopmans van Beinum, F. J., and van der Stelt, J. M. 1986. Early stages in the development of speech movements. In *Precursors of Early Speech* eds. B. Lindblom and R. Zetterstrom. New York: Stockton Press.

Krumhansl, C. L., and Jusczyk, P. W. 1990. Infants' perception of phrase structure in music. *Psychological Science* 1:70–73.

Kuhl, P. K. 1979. Speech perception in early infancy: Perceptual constancy for spectrally dissimilar vowel categories. *Journal of the Acoustical Society of America* 66:1668–1679.

Kuhl, P. K. 1983. Perception of auditory equivalence classes for speech in early infancy. *Infant Behavior and Development* 6:263–85.

Kuhl, P. K. 1987. Perception of speech and sound in early infancy. In *Handbook of Infant Perception*, Vol. 2 eds. P. Salapatek and L. Cohen. New York: Academic Press.

Kuhl, P. K., and Meltzoff, A. N. 1982. The bimodal perception of speech in infancy. *Science* 218:1138–1144.

Kuhl, P. K., and Meltzoff, A. N. 1984. The intermodal representation of speech in infants. *Infant Behavior and Development* 7:361–81.

Labov, W., and Labov, T. 1978. The phonetics of cat and mama. *Language* 54:816–52.

Lasky, R. E., Syrdal-Lasky, A., and Klein, R. E. 1975. VOT discrimination by four to six and a half month old infants from Spanish environments. *Journal of Experimental Child Psychology* 20:215–25.

Leonard, L., Rowan, L., Morris, B., and Fey, M. 1982. Intra-word variability in young children. *Journal of Child Language* 9:55–70.

Leonard, L., Schwartz, R., Morris, B., and Chapman, K. 1981. Factors influencing early lexical acquisition: Lexical orientation and phonological composition. *Child Development* 52:882–87.

Leopold, W. F. 1947. *Speech Development of a Bilingual Child: A Linguist's Record.* (Vol. 2: *Sound-Learning in the First Two Years*). Evanston, IL: Northwestern University Press.

Liberman, A. M., Cooper, F. S., Shankweiler, D. P., and Studdert-Kennedy, M. 1967. Perception of the speech code. *Psychological Review* 74:431–61.

Liberman, A. M., Delattre, P. C., and Cooper, F. S. 1952. The role of selected stimulus-variables in the perception of the unvoiced stop consonants. *American Journal of Psychology* 65:497–516.

Liberman, I. Y., Shankweiler, D., Fisher, F. W., and Carter, B. 1974. Explicit syllable and phoneme segmentation in the young child. *Journal of Experimental Child Psychology* 18:201–212.

Liberman, M., and Prince, A. 1977. On stress and linguistic rhythm. *Linguistic Inquiry* 8:249–336.

Lindblom, B. 1986. On the origin and purpose of discreteness and invariance in sound patterns. In *Invariance and Variability in Speech Processes* eds. J. Perkell & D. H. Klatt. Hillsdale, NJ: Erlbaum.

Locke, J. L. 1983. *Phonological Acquisition and Change*. New York: Academic.

Locke, J. L. 1988. The sound shape of early lexical representations. In *The Emergent Lexicon: The Child's Development of a Linguistic Vocabulary* eds. M. D. Smith and J. L. Locke. New York: Academic.

Logan, G. D. 1988. Toward an instance theory of automatization. *Psychological Review* 95:492–527.

Logan, J. S., Lively, S. E., and Pisoni, D. B. 1989. Training Japanese listeners to identify /r/ and /l/. *Journal of the Acoustical Society of America* 85:S137–138.

Macken, M. A., and Barton, D. 1980. The acquisition of the voicing contrast in English: A study of voice onset time in word-initual stop consonants. *Journal of Child Language* 7:41–74.

MacKain, K. S. 1982. Assessing the role of experience on infants' speech discrimination. *Journal of Child Language* 9:527–42.

MacKain, K. S., Studdert-Kennedy, M., Spieker, S., and Stern, D. S. 1983. Infant intermodal perception of speech is a left hemisphere function. *Science* 219:1347–1349.

Marler, P. 1991. The instinct to learn. In *The Epigenesis of Mind* eds. S. Carey and R. Gelman. Hillsdale, NJ: Erlbaum.

Marler, P., and Peters, S. 1981. Birdsong and speech: Evidence for special processing. In *Perspectives on the Study of Speech* eds. P. D. Eimas and J. L. Miller. Hillsdale, NJ: Erlbaum.

Martin, C. S., Mullennix, J. W., Pisoni, D. B., and Summers, W. V. 1989. Effects of talker variability on recall of spoken word lists. *Journal of Experimental Psychology: Learning, Memory, and Cognition* 15:676–84.

Matthei, E. H. 1989. Crossing boundaries: More evidence for phonological constraints on early multi-word utterances. *Journal of Child Language* 16:41–54.

McClasky, C. L., Pisoni, D. B., and Carrell, T. D. 1980. Effects of transfer of training on identification of a new linguistic contrast in voicing. In *Research on Speech Perception*, Progress Report No. 6, Indiana University, Bloomington, IN.

Mehler, J., Jusczyk, P. W., Lambertz, G., Halstead, N., Bertoncini, J., and Amiel-Tison, C. 1988. A precursor of language acquisition in young infants. *Cognition* 29:143–78.

Menn, L. 1976. Pattern, control and contrast in beginning speech: A case study of word form and word function. Unpublished doctoral dissertation. University of Illinois.

Menn, L. 1983. Development of articulatory, phonetic, and phonological capabilities. In *Language Production* (vol. 2) ed. B. Butterworth. New York: Academic.

Messer, S. 1967. Implicit phonology in children. *Journal of Verbal Learning and Verbal Behavior* 6:609–613.

Miller, J. L., and Eimas, P. D. 1979. Organization in infant speech perception. *Canadian Journal of Psychology* 33:353–67.

Miller, J. L., and Jusczyk, P. W. 1989. Seeking the biological bases for speech perception. *Cognition* 33:111–37.

Morais, J., Cary, L., Alegria, J., and Bertelson, P. 1979. Does awareness of speech as a sequence of phones arise spontaneously? *Cognition* 7:323–31.

Morse, P. A. 1972. The discrimination of speech and nonspeech stimuli in early infancy. *Journal of Experimental Child Psychology* 13:477–92.

Mullennix, J. W., Pisoni, D. B., and Martin, C. S. 1989. Some effects of talker variability on spoken word recognition. *Journal of the Acoustical Society of America* 85:365–78.

Nosofsky, R. M. 1986. Attention, similarity, and the identification-categorization relationship. *Journal of Experimental Psychology: General* 115:39–57.

Nosofsky, R. M. 1987. Attention and learning processes in the identification and categorization of integral stimuli. *Journal of Experimental Psychology: Learning, Memory & Cognition* 15:700–708.

Nosofsky, R. M. 1988. Exemplar-based accounts of relations between classification, recognition, and typicality. *Journal of Experimental Psychology: Learning, Memory & Cognition* 14:70–78.

Nosofsky, R. M., Clark,, S. E., and Shin, H. J. 1989. Rules and exemplars in categorization, identification and recognition. *Journal of Experimental Psychology: Learning, Memory & Cognition* 15:282–304.

Nusbaum, H. C., and Schwab, E. C. 1986. The role of attention and active processing in speech perception. In *Pattern Recognition by Humans and Machines, Vol. 1: Speech Perception* eds. E. C. Schwab and H. C. Nusbaum. New York: Academic Press.

Oller, D. K. 1980. The emergence of the sounds of speech in infancy. In *Child Phonology* (Vol. 1: *Production*) eds. G. H. Yeni-Komshian, J. F. Kavanagh, and C. A. Ferguson. New York: Academic.

Olmsted, D. L. 1971. *Out of the Mouths of Babes: Earliest Stages in Language Learning.* The Hague: Mouton.

Olney, R. L., and Scholnick, E. K. 1976. Adult judgments of age and linguistic differences in infant vocalization. *Journal of Child Language* 3:145–55.

Osgood, C. E., and Hoosain, R. 1974. Salience of the word as a unit in the perception of language. *Perception & Psychophysics* 15:168–92.

Pertz, D. L., and Bever, T. G. 1975. Sensitivity to phonological universals in children and adolescents. *Language* 51:149–62.

Peters, A. M. 1977. Language learning strategies: Does the whole equal the sum of the parts? *Language* 53:560–73.

Pierce, J. E., and Hanna, I. V. 1974. *The Development of a Phonological System in English Speaking American Children.* Portland, OR: HaPi Press.

Pisoni, D. B., Aslin, R. N., Perey, A. J., and Hennessy, B. L. 1982. Some effects of laboratory training on identification and discrimination of voicing contrasts in stop consonants. *Journal of Experimental Psychology: Human Perception and Performance* 8:297–314.

Pisoni, D. B., and Tash, J. 1974. Reaction times to comparisons within and across phonetic categories. *Perceptions & Psychophysics* 15:285–90.

Potter, M. C., and Faulconer, B. A. 1979. Understanding noun phrases. *Journal of Verbal Learning and Verbal Behavior* 18:509–21.

Priestly, T. M. S. 1976. One idiosyncratic strategy in the acquisition of phonology. *Journal of Child Language* 4:45–66.

Remez, R. E., Rubin, P. E., Pisoni, D. B., and Carrell, T. D. 1981. Speech perception without traditional cues. *Science* 212:947–50.

Repp, B. H., Liberman, A. M., Eccardt, T., and Pesetsky, D. 1978. Perceptual integration of acoustic cues for stop, fricative and affricate manner. *Journal of Experimental Psychology: Human Perception and Performance* 4:621–37.

Roth, E. M., and Schoben, E. J. 1983. The effect of context on the structure of categories. *Cognitive Psychology* 15:346–78.

Roug, L., Landberg, I., and Lundberg, L.-J. 1989. Phonetic developments in early infancy: A study of four Swedish children during the first eighteen months of life. *Journal of Child Language* 16:19–40.

Rozin, P., and Gleitman, L. R. 1977. The structure and acquisition of reading II: The reading process and the acquisition of the alphabetic principle. In *To-*

ward a Psychology of Reading eds. A. S. Reber and D. L. Scarborough. Hillsdale, NJ: Erlbaum.

Samuel, A. G. 1977. The effect of discrimination training on speech perception: Noncategorical perception. *Perception & Psychophysics* 22:321–30.

Samuel, A. G. 1981a. Phonemic restoration: Insights from a new methodology. *Journal of Experimental Psychology: General* 110:474–94.

Samuel, A. G. 1981b. The role of bottom-up confirmation in the phonemic restoration illusion. *Journal of Experimental Psychology: Human Perception and Performance* 7:1124–1131.

Samuel, A. G. 1986. The role of the lexicon in speech perception. In *Pattern Recognition by Humans and Machines: Vol. 1, Speech Perception* eds. E. C. Schwab and H. C. Nusbaum. New York: Academic Press.

Sawusch, J. R. 1986. Auditory and phonetic coding of speech. In *Pattern Recognition by Humans and Machines: Vol. 1, Speech Perception* eds. E. C. Schwab and H. C. Nusbaum. New York: Academic Press.

Schwab, E. C. 1981. Auditory and phonetic processing for tone analogs of speech. Unpublished doctoral dissertation. State University of New York at Buffalo.

Schwartz, R., and Folger, M. 1977. Sensorimotor development and descriptions of child phonology: A preliminary view of phonological analysis for Stage I speech. *Papers and Reports on Child Language Development* 13:8–15.

Schwartz, R., and Leonard, L. 1982. Do children pick and choose? An examination of phonological selection and avoidance in early lexical acquisition. *Journal of Child Language* 9:319–36.

Schwartz, R., and Pollock, K. 1987. A further examination of phonologically-based lexical selection. Unpublished manuscript. Purdue University, West Lafayette, IN

Searle, C. L., Jacobson, J. Z., and Rayment, S. G. 1979. Phoneme recognition based on human audition. *Journal of the Acoustical Society of America* 65:799–809.

Selkirk, E. O. 1984. *Phonology and Syntax: The Relation Between Sound and Structure*. Cambridge, MA: MIT Press.

Shattuck-Hufnagel, S., and Klatt, D. H. 1979. The limited use of distinctive features and markedness in speech production: Evidence from speech error data. *Journal of Verbal Learning and Verbal Behavior* 18:41–55.

Shillcock, R. C. 1990. Lexical hypotheses in continuous speech. In *Cognitive Models of Speech Processing* ed. G. T. M. Altman. Cambridge, MA: Bradford.

Spencer, A. 1986. Towards a theory of phonological development. *Lingua* 68:3–38.

Spring, D. R., and Dale, P. S. 1977. Discrimination of linguistic stress in early infancy. *Journal of Speech and Hearing Research* 20:224–32.

Stark, R. E. 1980. Stages of speech development in the first year of life. In *Child Phonology* (Vol. 1: *Production*) eds. G. H. Yeni-Komshian, J. F. Kavanagh, and C. A. Ferguson. New York: Academic.

Stevens, K. N., and Blumstein, S. E. 1981. The search for invariant acoustic correlates of phonetic features. In *Perspectives on the Study of Speech* eds. P. D. Eimas and J. L. Miller. Hillsdale, NJ: Erlbaum.

Stoel-Gammon, C., and Cooper, J. A. 1984. Patterns of early lexical and phonological development. *Journal of Child Language* 11:247–71.

Streeter, L. A. 1976. Language perception of 2-month-old infants shows effects of both innate mechanisms and experience. *Nature* 259:39–41.

Studdert-Kennedy, M. 1986. Sources of variability in early speech development In *Invariance and Variability in Speech Processes* eds. J. Perkell and D. H. Klatt. Hillsdale, NJ: Erlbaum.

Summerfield, Q. 1975. Acoustic and phonetic components of the influence of voice changes and identification times for CVC syllables. *Report of Speech Research in Progress* 2(4). Belfast, Ireland: The Queen's University of Belfast.

Summerfield, Q., and Haggard, M. P. 1973. Vocal tract normalisation as demonstrated by reaction times. *Report of Speech Research in Progress* 2. Belfast, Ireland: The Queen's University of Belfast.

Thomson, J. R., and Chapman, R. S. 1977. Who is "Daddy"? The status of two-year-olds' over extended words in use and comprehension. *Journal of Child Language* 4:359–75.

Trehub, S. E. 1976. The discrimination of foreign speech contrasts by infants and adults. *Child Development* 47:466–72.

Treiman, R. 1987. On the relationship between phonological awareness and literacy. *European Bulletin of Cognitive Psychology* 7:524–29.

Trubetzkoy, N. 1939. *Principes de Phonologie.* (J. Cantineau, trans. 1949). Paris: Klincksieck.

Tulving, E. 1983. *Elements of Episodic Memory.* New York: Oxford University Press.

Velten, H. V. 1943. The growth of phonemic and lexical patterns in infant language. *Language* 19:281–92.

Verbrugge, R. R., Strange, W., Shankweiler, D. P., and Edman, T. R. 1976. What information enables a listener to map a talker's vowel space? *Journal of the Acoustical Society of America* 60:198–212.

Vihman, M. 1982. A note on children's lexical representation. *Journal of Child Language* 9:249–53.

Vihman, M., and Miller, R. 1988. Words and babble at the threshold of language acquisition. In *The Emergent Lexicon: The Child's Development of a Linguistic Vocabulary* eds. M. D. Smith and J. L. Locke. New York: Academic.

Vihman, M., Macken, M., Miller, R., Simmons, H., and Miller, J. 1985. From babbling to speech: A re-assessment of the continuity issue. *Language* 61:397–445.

Walley, A. C., Smith, L. B., and Jusczyk, P. W. 1986. The role of phonemes and syllables in the preceived similarity of speech sounds for children. *Memory & Cognition* 14:220–29.

Warren, R. M. 1970. Phonemic restoration of missing speech sounds. *Science* 167:392–93.

Waterson, N. 1978. The growth of complexity in phonological development. In *The Development of Communication* eds. N. Waterson and C. Snow. Chicester: Wiley.

Weir, R. W. 1966. Some questions on the child's learning of phonology. In *The Genesis of Language* eds. F. Smith and G. A. Miller. Cambridge, MA: MIT Press.

Werker, J. F., and Tees, R. C. 1984a. Cross-language speech perception: Evidence for perceptual reorganization during the first year of life. *Infant Behavior and Development* 7:49–63.

Werker, J. F., and Tees, R. C. 1984b. Phonemic and phonetic factors in adult cross-language speech perception. *Journal of the Acoustical Society of America* 75:1866–1878.

Werker, J. F., and Lalonde, C. E. 1988. Cross-language speech perception: Initial capabilities and developmental change. *Developmental Psychology* 24:672–83.

Werker, J. F., and Logan, J. 1985. Cross-language evidence for three factors in speech perception. *Perception & Psychophysics* 37:35–44.

Werker, J. F., Gilbert, J. H. V., Humphrey, K., and Tees, R. C. 1981. Developmental aspects of cross-language speech perception. *Child Development* 52:349–55.

Wheeler, D., and Iverson, G. 1986. Hierarchical structures in child phonology. Paper presented at the Annual Meeting of the Linguistic Society of America.

Chapter • 2

The Biology of Phonological Development

Ray D. Kent

The biological study of spoken language has significant precedent even in the single book that Eric Lenneberg published in 1967. In fact, a biological perspective on spoken language is not rare; nor should it be, given that spoken language is the product of a living organism. Speech is heir to flesh. The biology of spoken language may recede in some of the abstract, mathematical studies of language. The rewrite rule of generative phonology does not look much like a biological proposition, but it is in fact underwritten by the biology of the language user.

This chapter sets forth a few biological principles that may account for several aspects of phonological development, particularly in the first two years of life. The developmental range of the inquiry is restricted not because biology fades away after the age of two, but because the biological story that unfolds in the first two years of life sets the stage for the remainder of the developmental process. The principles to be discussed are both narrow and broad. The narrow principles pertain to specific domains of structure, or time, or both. The broad principles embrace patterns that sweep across biological structures and across development itself. The biological perspective taken here is behavioral in its thrust, and might be termed ethological (*ethology* = the biology of behavior).

This work was supported in part by research grant DC00319 from the National Institute on Deafness and Other Communicative Disorders.

There is a shared tradition of investigation in motor development and phonological development that might be called *baby biography*, as it came to be known following the seminal work of Darwin (1877) and Shinn (1900). The study of language development has of course had its baby biographers; the names of Leopold (1939, 1947, 1949a,b), Piaget (1955), and Bloom (1970, 1973) come quickly to mind. But despite this common tradition, the two fields of motor and phonological development have not been particularly interactive. It seems reasonable that lessons learned in the general study of motor development should inform at least part of the investigation of phonological development. Phonology is not just motor science, but it is certainly underlain by motor processes. These processes, together with the sensory processes that mediate ambient language and feedback to the child, form the gridwork for phonological development. The motor and sensory processes, in turn, are part of a larger biological study, some broad principles of which are next addressed.

BROAD PRINCIPLES OF DEVELOPMENTAL BIOLOGY

1. The course of development is marked by reversals and revisions.
2. There is considerable variation in the development of individuals and individual structures.
3. For any given structure, there is typically an excess capacity or potential for development.

The principles listed above might be thought to have come from a textbook summary of early language development. In fact, they come from a summary of general biological development—the development of plant stomata, of insects, and of rats (Sachs 1988). These are broad principles that pertain to developmental biology. What happens in language development is not necessarily outside the general biological scheme of things. Language may be more subtle, more abstract, more cultural than other phenomena in developmental biology, but it may follow some of the same patterns.

Considering these general biological principles, Sachs proposed a developmental solution he called *epigenetic selection*, a process in which the final state, rather than a set of individual events leading to that state, is strictly specified. The process allows for the correction of developmental mistakes, which are thought to occur frequently in developmental biology. Sachs proposed some general developmental rules by which epigenetic selection would proceed. These rules are examined in detail later in this chapter, but three of them are listed here to provide a biological framework:

1. A negative correlation holds for the development of similar events; that is, one event will inhibit, but not necessarily prevent, the development of a closely related event. An example Sachs gives from biology is that Hydra heads inhibit the formation of similar structures. A similar inhibition seems to occur in phonological development (indeed, in language development generally).
2. A positive correlation holds for the development of events that are different or complementary. A biological example is that one tissue can induce the differentiation of another tissue. Similar phenomena occur in language. For example, the principle of maximal contrast in phonology involves the mutual reinforcement of complementary features.
3. An increasing positive feedback occurs during the development of complementary processes. For example, in botany, rapidly growing buds induce vascular differentiation and root initiation. In language, the growing lexicon of a very young child induces phonological contrasts and regularities by which the lexicon can be expressed.

These three general rules or mechanisms are a backdrop to the following discussion, which considers both particular and general phenomena in the biology of phonology. The first issue is that of the formation of vowel and consonant precursors, which are called *vocants* and *closants*, respectively (Martin 1981). Although there may be no real harm in using the terms *vowel* and *consonant* with respect to the sounds uttered by infants, the terms *vocant* and *closant* serve as a reminder that an infant's sounds may not be directly interpretable within an adult phonological system.

The Biological Mold for Vowels and Consonants: Remodeling of the Vocal Tract Anatomy in the Infant

A necessary point of departure is a brief consideration of the vocal tract anatomy of the human infant. As several writers point out, the human infant has a vocal tract that perhaps more closely resembles that of the nonhuman primate than that of the adult human. Figure 1 depicts infant and adult vocal tracts. Of course, they differ in size. Because of the difference in resonator length, the infant's vowels will have much higher resonance (formant) frequencies than those of adults. For example, whereas the midcentral vowel of an adult male typically has first, second, and third formant frequencies of 500, 1,500, and 2,500 Hz, respectively, the corresponding frequencies of a phonetically similar vowel produced by an infant are approximately 1,000, 3,000, and 5,000

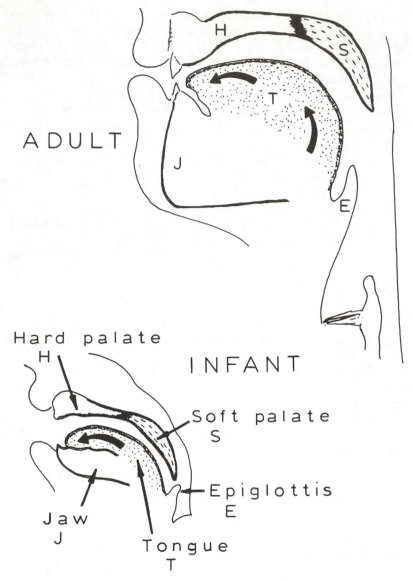

Figure 1.   Drawings of infant and adult vocal tracts. Abbreviated labels on adult vocal tract are identified on the sketch of the infant tract. The filled arrows within the tongue outlines indicate differences in orientation of the tongue in the vocal tract.

Hz (Kent and Murray 1982). How, then, can infants recognize the phonetic equivalence between their vowels and vowels produced by their adult caregivers? The answer may lie in a transformation of the linear formant frequency values to Bark differences (e.g., Bark F2–F1 and

Bark F3–F2). Hodge (1989) showed that this transformation was quite successful in normalizing the formant frequencies of phonetically equivalent vowels produced by adults, children, and infants. The Bark transform applied to differences between formant frequencies may model the process by which the human ear responds to vowel stimuli.

But in addition to the size difference, the infant vocal tract is unlike the adult vocal tract in other ways. Specifically, compared to the adult, the infant has: a broader oral cavity, a shorter pharynx, a gradually sloping oropharyngeal channel, a relatively anterior tongue mass, a closely approximating velum and epiglottis, and a relatively high larynx. The resultant vocal tract may well have articulatory and acoustic characteristics different from those of the adult (Bosma 1975; Kent 1981; Lieberman, Crelin, and Klatt 1972). Within the first year, but particularly around two to four months of postnatal life (Sasaki et al. 1977), the infant's vocal tract is remodeled so that it begins to resemble that of the adult human, an apparently unique biological apparatus that owes its form largely to the human characteristics of erect bipedalism, a modified oral apparatus, and an enlarged brain (DuBrul 1976, 1977).

Stages of Phonological Development *qua* Development Anatomy

With this anatomic remodeling in mind, we now can ask about the infant's phonetic capabilities. Several authors have proposed stage descriptions of phonetic development in the first year of life. A remarkable feature of these various descriptions is that they differ in both the terminology and chronology of stages (Kent and Hodge 1991). This variability can be due to several sources, including variability among the infants observed, variability in the observational methods and criteria of the investigators, and variability in classification schemes. Despite the variations, some overall alignments emerge from comparison of the stage descriptions. First, most authors note a transition from a very early stage (extending from birth to about two to three months postnatal) that is primarily phonatory but is marked by the occurrence of restricted closants (especially velars). Another stage, beginning at about three to four months and extending up to about six months, is one of marked accomplishment in supraglottal or articulatory actions. In this stage, phonation often is accompanied by supraglottal constrictions and releases, which impart to the acoustic product a fairly distinct syllabicity and an impression of consonant–vowel sequence (a CV syllable). Oller (1978) called this the *Expansion Stage* and described it in terms of the frequent appearance of "fully resonant nuclei" and a diversity of sites of supraglottal constriction. It is interesting that Camp et al. (1987) reported that individual differences among infants were most reliable during the interval of four to six months and recommended this period as the optimal time to assess vocalization with a minimal set of observations.

Is there a biologic accompaniment to this change in sound production? One particularly strong candidate is the remodeling of the vocal tract described earlier. At about the same time that the infant's vocal tract undergoes a significant remodeling, the infant's phonetic output also changes. (For further discussion, see Kent 1981, 1984.) For present purposes, it is sufficient to note an association of anatomic and behavioral change. The anatomic change may not be sufficient to produce the behavioral change, but it is an expedient, if not necessary, contributing factor. The infant entering the fourth or fifth month of postnatal life seems to be capable of a reliable velopharyngeal valving (hence, oral versus nasal resonance), diversity in supraglottal constriction (hence, closant articulation at different places and manners), and at least a gross coordination of phonatory and supraglottal adjustments.

Rhythmic Stereotypy of Infantile Movements

Around six months of postnatal life, the infant's sound patterns again change sufficiently, commanding the attention of stage-givers. Beginning at this time, investigators note the appearance of "reduplicated babble" (Stark 1979), "canonical babble" (Oller 1978), "reduplicated articulatory movements" (Holmgren et al. 1986), "repetitive babble" (Elbers 1982) and "multisyllable babbling" (Mitchell and Kent 1990). These descriptions have in common a recognition of the infant's production of syllable trains. Interestingly, the appearance of this vocal pattern coincides with the more general appearance of repetitive movement in sequences that Thelen (1981) has termed "rhythmic stereotypies" (figure 2). These stereotypies of the limbs, fingers, neck, and trunk typically reach their peak frequencies at around six to nine months. The phonological phenomenon of canonical or multisyllable babbling may, therefore, be a vocal manifestation of a general tendency toward repetitive or rhythmic movement patterns. Support for such an interpretation comes from the observation that reduplication as a phonological regularity is a feature of L1 but not L2 acquisition. (Additional comments are made on the sensory and motoric benefits of the repetitive movements in babbling later in this chapter.)

The Tongue as Muscular Hydrostat

Motor control of the tongue is a first-order concern for the child learning to make speech sounds. The tongue is a unique motor system in the human body, consisting of extrinsic muscles that connect the tongue with the hard and soft tissues of the head and neck, and of

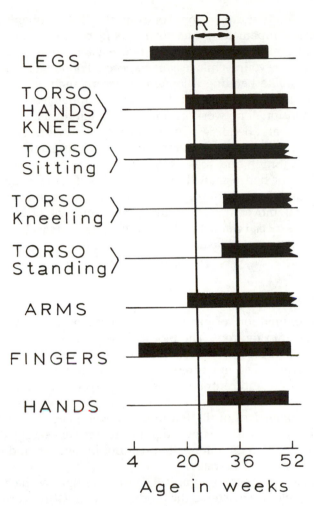

Figure 2.   Ages of appearance of "repetitive stereotypies" observed in infants (after Thelen 1981) compared to the emergence of repetitive babble (RB), which is typically said to begin between 24 and 36 weeks of life.

intrinsic muscles that have their origins and insertions within the tongue itself. The tongue does not have an internal bony or cartilaginous skeleton, but it does have a hydrostatic skeleton (DuBrul 1976, 1977; Kier and Smith 1985; Smith and Kier 1989). The tongue is a *muscular hydrostat*, a muscular organ that forms its own skeleton to support movement and then performs movements and shape changes relative to that skeleton. The tongues of various animals, the elephant's trunk and the octopus' tentacles, are all muscular hydrostats (Smith and Kier 1989). They are incompressible at physiological pressures and therefore can change in any one dimension only by making compensatory changes in another dimension. For example, protrusion of the human tongue is accompanied by a narrowing of its body.

Gaining motor control over a hydrostat presents some special problems to the young child learning speech. For one, bending the hydrostat is unlike bending a jointed structure such as a finger. The tongue has no joints per se; it flexes by appropriate contraction of its three-dimensional network of intrinsic longitudinal, vertical, and transverse fibers. Bending a hydrostat requires that muscle fibers be shortened on one aspect simultaneously with a resistance to a change in diameter (Smith and Kier 1989). If the diameter change is not resisted, then the hydrostat will shorten on one side but will not bend. To use the tongue in speech, the child must learn to control the tongue to meet skeletal, movement, and shaping requirements, often simultaneously. These special characteristics of the tongue may well play a role in vowel and consonant mastery.

Vocant/Vowel Development

The development of vocants/vowels is illustrated in the vowel quadrilateral plots in figure 3. The plot for one year reflects frequency of occurrence data for vocants in utterances produced near the end of the first year of life. The most frequently occurring vocants are the low-front, low-back, and central vowels. That is, vocant production might be diagrammed as an ellipse with its major axis running along the bottom (low dimension) of the traditional vowel quadrilateral. This pattern is consistent with a conception of the tongue as a hydrostat that moves primarily in an anterior-to-posterior dimension and with little elevation from a low carriage.

The data of Wellman et al. (1931) indicate that by the age of two years, the child has mastered the production of the three corner vowels [i u ɑ], the vowel [o], and the nonretroflex central vowels. This accomplishment results in a well-defined vowel triangle (because phonetic mastery is being imputed to the child, the term *vowel* will be used in preference to *vocant*). A principle of maximal contrast may be said to be at work, insofar as the vowels mastered are well separated in the quadrilateral plot. To say the same thing in terms of the biological principles outlined in the beginning of this chapter, the development of dissimilar or complementary events is positively correlated. The three corner vowels are maximally dissimilar in their acoustic and articulatory properties, and they are complementary in the sense that they define the acoustic-articulatory boundaries of vocant production. The corner vowel /æ/ is conspicuous by its absence. Although this vowel is frequently produced in babbling, it does not appear to be mastered at the

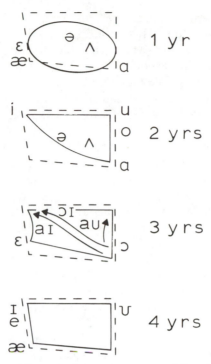

Figure 3. Vowel quadrilaterals drawn to represent the development of vo-cants/vowels in children. The phonetic symbols in each quadrilateral represent typical vowel development for the age shown (based largely on Wellman et al. 1931).

same time as the high vowels /i/ and /u/, which tend to be rare in bab-bling. This result suggests that the motoric experience in babbling is not totally predictive of the chronology of phonetic mastery. The lag in mastery of /æ/ compared to the other point vowels is reflected in the vowel errors of phonologically impaired children, who tend to produce frequent backing errors of /æ/ (Pollock and Keiser 1990).

By age three, the children studied by Wellman et al. (1931) had mastered the additional vowels /ɛ/ and /ɔ/ and the diphthongs /aɪ/, /ɔɪ/, and /au/. The mastery of /ɛ/ gives the child's vowel space a quadrilat-eral appearance, although the front dimension is truncated (because /æ/ is not mastered) relative to the adult quadrilateral. The mastery of /ɔ/ represents a differentiation of /ɑ/ and /ɔ/, which are highly confus-able vowel pairs in perceptual experiments (Sinnott 1989). The appear-ance of the diphthongs marks a kind of dynamic regulation. That is, by the age of three years, the child can move the tongue body with suffi-cient precision so that the gliding movements for diphthongs can be reliably performed.

The bottom drawing in figure 3 shows the additional vowels that are mastered by age four. This period is essentially one of differentiation. The children added the back vowel /ʊ/ and the remaining vowels /ɪ/, /e/ and /æ/ in the front series. The addition of the front vowels at this relatively late point in phonological development may indicate the difficulty of tongue-jaw synergy. Because of the hinge arrangement of the mandible, front vowels are affected to a greater extent by jaw articulation than are central or back vowels. Therefore, reliable production of the front vowels requires that the child make suitable adjustments in tongue articulation relative to the position of the mandible. The high-front /i/ is unlike the other members of the front series in that its extreme lingual elevation gives it a physiological distinctiveness that is likely accompanied by abundant tactile feedback through tongue contacts (with maxillary structures). Otomo (1988) has argued similarly for the distinctiveness of vowel /i/ in vowel acquisition.

The picture of vowel development is not complete in figure 3 because the retroflex vowels /ɝ/ and /ɚ/ have not been included. These vowels are the last to be mastered. They are difficult motorically because their articulation is one of retroflexion or bunching (Shriberg and Kent 1982), both of which involve a sophisticated bending of the lingual hydrostat. The motoric difficulty stands in constrast to the perceptual distinctiveness of the retroflex vowel. Of all the vowels, /i/ and /ɝ/ are the least likely to be confused with other vowels (Sinnott 1989). However, the high-front /i/ is mastered early (by two years), whereas /ɝ/ is mastered sometime after the age of four. Perceptual factors do not seem to account for this disparity, but motoric factors can.

Closant/Consonant Development

Closant/consonant production is summarized in table I. The earliest consonants to be mastered according to Sander (1972) are /p, m, h, n, w/, which are mastered by 90% of children by three years of age. The next consonants to be mastered are /b, k, g, d, f, j/, which reach the 90% mastery criterion by about four years. The consonants /t, n, r, l/ meet this mastery criterion by about six years. Finally, the consonants /s, tʃ, ʃ, z, ʤ, v, θ, ð, ʒ/ are mastered by 90% of the children at some time later than six years.

Considering the underlying motoric adjustments for these four developmental sets of sounds, the following analyses seem to apply:

Set One: Rapid ("ballistic") articulatory movement: /p, m, n/;
Slow ("ramp" movements characterized by constant velocity over a relatively long duration) articulatory movement: /w, h/;
Velopharyngeal valving: stops and nasals present;

Table I. Age of Mastery of Consonants of American English (Based Largely on Sander 1972). Consonants are Grouped According to the Age at which 90% of Children Demonstrate Mastery.

	Three years	Four years	Six years	Beyond six years
Stops	/p/	/b, d, g, k/	/t/	
Nasals	/m, n/		/ŋ/	
Glides	/w/	/j/		
Fricatives	/h/	/f/		/s, z, ʃ, v, θ, ð, ʒ/
Affricates				/tʃ, dʒ/
Liquids			/r, l/	

Voicing adjustment: voiced and voiceless items present, and
Primary places of articulation: bilabial, alveolar, and glottal.
Set Two: Additional items in the rapid or ballistic movement category:
/b, k, g, d/;
Additional items in the ramp movement category: /j/;
Fine force regulation for frication: /f/; and
Additional primary place of articulation: velar.
Set Three: Additional items in the rapid or ballistic movement category: /t, ŋ/;
Velopharyngeal valving to distinguish /m/–/b, p/ and /n/–/d, t/;
Voicing adjustment to distinguish /p/–/b/, /t/–/d/, and /k/–/g/; and
Tongue configuration (bending) for /r/ and /l/.
Set Four: Tongue configuration for dental, alveolar, and palatal fricatives; and
Fine force regulation for frication at each place of fricative articulation.

A similar motoric analysis can be made of the typology of phonetic inventories of 40 children with phonological disorders described by Dinnsen et al. (1990). (See also Dinnsen this volume). Dinnsen et al. (1990) identified five basic types of inventories, which they termed Levels A–E. Level A in their scheme, the simplest type of inventory, includes sounds in the categories of obstruent–stop, nasal, and glide. The motoric accomplishments at this level are regulation of velopharyngeal valving (stop versus nasal contrast) and regulation of the rate of articulatory movement (ballistic versus ramp). Level B introduces a voiced–voiceless distinction and an anterior–nonanterior distinction, which corresponds to the motoric achievements of regulation of laryngeal–supralaryngeal timing and a basic regulation of lingual articulation (basically apex versus body articulation). Level C is marked by the presence of fricatives and affricates. Fricative and affricate production requires regulation of lingual configuration and fine force control to generate frication. At Level D the system is expanded to include a liquid, either [l] or [r] (lateral or retroflex). The motoric developments pertain primarily to tongue shaping and fine force control, particularly involving a refined deformation of the lingual hydrostat. Finally, at Level E, the subjects were capable of either a stridency distinction or a lateral/retroflex distinction, either of which requires precise control of lingual configuration.

The motoric interpretation of the sound mastery data summarized by Sander (1972) and the phonological levels of Dinnsen et al. (1990) points to some common patterns. Although the two sources of data are not exactly congruent on all counts, they are consistent on some fundamental bases, including early regulation of velopharyngeal valving, voicing in at least syllable-initial position, and rate of lingual movement in respect to ballistic versus ramp articulations. The third of these also appears to be closely timed to the mastery of diphthongs (figure 3), indicating that at about three years of age, the child has achieved a significant degree of control over dynamic properties of lingual articulation. Remaining phonological accomplishments seem to be related largely to finer adjustments in lingual position and shape and to fine force control. Thus, a nearly final stage of phonological accomplishment lies in the mastery of fricatives (strident and nonstrident) and the liquids. The latter probably emerge from the motor patterns for glides, given the strong evidence for gliding of liquids in early periods of development (Haelsig and Madison 1986).

The liquids and lingual fricatives require a further refinement, a deformation of the lingual hydrostat. As noted earlier, bending a hydrostat requires two simultaneous adjustments, a shortening of one aspect or surface and a resistance to a change in diameter. It might be surprising, then, that apicals should be among the most frequently produced closants in babbling. Does this mean that the infant has mastered the supposedly difficult feat of hydrostat deformation? The answer is *not necessarily*. Hodge (1989) has presented acoustic evidence that apical articulations in repetitive babbling such as /dæ, dæ, dæ/ are performed largely by a passive movement of the tongue riding on an active mandible. As indicated earlier in the discussion of front vowels, motor control of tongue-jaw synergy appears to be a relatively late accomplishment. The difficulty of tongue-jaw synergy is shown in experiments in which children attempt to produce vowels under bite-block conditions (Edwards 1989). The bite block, which fixes the mandible, requires that the child reorganize lingual movements in accord with the fixed jaw position.

Integration and Differentiation in Babbling and First Words

Development involves processes of differentiation and integration. Differentiation is the isolation of dimensions or features, whereas integration is the combination of such isolated properties into functional ensembles or relations (Fentress 1984). Fentress pointed out that coordinated action involves both of these processes and a given observer's assumptions about how to segment actions for analysis will determine which of these will be emphasized. Progressive differentiation and integration are complementary and co-occurring processes during the development of coordinated action. Speech is a coordinated action, and the learning of its coordinations is one part of phonological development.

The Structured Vocalization and Canonical Babbling

One of the earliest vocal behaviors that invites analysis into differentiating and integrating processes is the CV syllable. Murphy et al. (1983) referred to this combination as a *structured vocalization*. Their term is interesting for it holds the essence of differentiation and integration. A structure is an ensemble of pieces. The CV syllable is noteworthy for its high frequency in infant vocalizations (Kent and Bauer 1985) and for its predictive relationship with subsequent events in language acquisition (Menyuk, Liebergott, and Schultz 1986; Murphy et al. 1983). This syllable is a unit that integrates movements into a pattern that adult listeners can segment into vowel and consonant components. Oller (1986, and this volume) assigns special developmental significance to the *canonical syllable,* which may be a precursor of the kind of motoric and sound pattern that constitutes adult speech.

The CV structure is elaborated at about six to nine months into sequences of repetitive or multisyllabic babbling. This kind of babbling has now been studied in some detail. What has been learned can be summarized in terms of differentiating and integrating processes. An analysis of babbling of one child by Elbers (1982) indicated a systematic progression of phonetic diversity. Stages of babbling were identified as follows: prerepetitive (nonrepeated or simple vocalizations), repetitive (repeated stereotypical syllables), concatenating (repeated syllables with place or manner variations), and mixing (combinations of the earlier forms). Elbers's study gives an intuitively sensible picture of babbling as a process of increasing differentiation. The infant moves from highly stereotyped syllable chains to phonetically diversified chains.

However, the pattern that Elbers described for her child may not be the general or modal pattern. Other investigators have reported that phonetic variation in syllable sequences is common at or near the beginning of multisyllable babbling (Mitchell and Kent 1990; Smith, Brown-Sweeney, and Stoel-Gammon 1988). Possibly, some children follow a progression like that described by Elbers (1982) whereas other children, presumably the majority, produce repetitive and variegated sequences close to the onset of multisyllabic babbling. In either pattern, the eventual course ensures differentiation in the form of phonetic diversity within syllable chains. At the same time, the chain is an integrative unit that possesses its own prosodic envelope defined in terms of fundamental frequency contour, intensity pattern, syllable rate, and other temporal features. Thus, the multisyllable chain is a motor pattern involving precursors of prosodic structure and phonetic (segmental) constituents.

The emergence of coordinated activity in the infant is viewed by some writers as a process of selection and not imposition (Edelman 1987; Thelen 1989). The process involves the infant's sensitivity to, and use of, the multiple sensory consequences of movement. This sensory information is the basis for a continuing selection and refinement of patterns of coordination. Edelman (1987, 1989) describes the process in terms of a gradual global mapping between a motor gesture and its sensory consequences. It is assumed that each motor ensemble produces simultaneous, multiple sensory inputs that are represented in local network maps. Such maps overlap substantially with one another and with the motor ensemble connections. From this overlap, the relationships of the input and output arrays are continuously and multiply correlated to generate the global mapping (cf. Stemberger this volume). As variants of a movement are performed in various contexts (even slightly dissimilar), the sensory input is integrated into the global mapping to refine and strengthen sensory and motor associations. The correlation of sensory and motor features apparently produces stable action categories even through repetition. Kuperstein (1988) indicates that a reentry procedure itself permits the system to learn and generalize. The multisyllabic, often repetitive, babbling of a child may be an instance of this process.

The process that Edelman (1987, 1988) calls *reentrant signaling* among maps may be the means by which phonemic organization emerges in the child. As sounds are produced, they are represented both in terms of the neuronal activity for the associated motor events and in terms of the neuronal activity in a number of receptor sheets (cutaneous, kinesthetic, auditory) and their associated local maps. Repeated productions of a sound in various contexts would allow correlations to be established among these various sheets and maps, in such a way that an eventual equivalence class is formed from the correlations among selected neuronal populations. Perhaps the phoneme may be defined at the level of a global map, which is a dynamic structure of local maps connected through reentry. Global mapping is an activity in which connections are made between neuronal groups selected in one set of local maps (perhaps involving feature detection) and other sets of maps (perhaps involving the correlation of features established by movement continuity and intention).

The Motor Substrate of Phonetic Organization and Representation

With the production of vocables and early words, the child begins to organize articulatory movements in linguistic units serving deictic referential, or other communicative functions. The stability of these early forms is questionable. Although vocables sometimes are called phonetically consistent forms, not all vocables meet this criterion (Kent and Bauer 1985). Ferguson and Farwell (1975) described a remarkable degree of phonetic variability in a young girl's production of the word *pen*. The phonetic transcriptions certainly do show substantial variability in the word productions but they also contain hints of an underlying similarity in the phonetic or motor patterns. For example, most have a movement involving the velopharynx (hence, nasalization of some part of the sound pattern). However, the relative timing of any given movement component varies within the movement sequence. Ferguson and Farwell (1975) described this variance in production in terms of misalignment of features with parent segments. For instance, the nasality feature often was present but it was not assigned to the correct segment in the sequence. Alternatively, an analysis by movement components is directed not so much to reveal a phonetic pattern as a *motor score* (cf. Lindblom this volume). The motor score is the temporal pattern of movement. As the coordinative skills of the child develop, the motor score is increasingly reliable. Segmental (phonetic) consistency is rooted partly, if not largely, in precision of motor performance. Stated differently, segmental consistency depends upon motoric consistency. The two accounts, feature-based phonetic pattern and motor score, might be unified in the conception of reentrant signaling between sensory and motor maps, from which phonemic organization emerges through global mapping, as discussed earlier. The apparent variable "floating" across the word of a feature such as nasalization would, in this view, reflect the presence of the feature in local maps but the lack of established correlations among the features in the total pattern.

Perhaps the most constant finding of studies of motor development is that children are more variable than adults. Thomas and Thomas (1988) described the developmental pattern of increasing consistency as "the most robust and interesting characteristic in movement" (p. 95). This finding of age- or skill-dependent variability has been amply demonstrated for speech. Compared to adults or older children, young children are more variable in repeated trials of a phonetic sequence (Chermak and Schneiderman 1986; Eguchi and Hirsh 1969; Kent and Forner 1980; Sharkey and Folkins 1985). The larger variability in children has been interpreted as an index of immaturity in motor control. But if nothing else, the variability means that the details of the movement are less predictable both by observers and by the child who produces the movement. It also means that the study of early speech should distinguish two kinds of variability: one, the variability in phonetic organization; and two, the variability in motor performance. Conceivably, motor variability can be so great as to result in an apparent variability in phonetic organization. For example, extreme mistiming of velopharyngeal opening and closure can alter the movement sequence so that listeners will hear an apparent shift of the nasality feature to another segment in the sequence.

This issue (distinguishing motoric error or variability from phonologic error or variability) has been discussed extensively in the literature on neurological speech disorders (McNeil and Kent 1990). An apparent substitution error (replacement of one phoneme by another) can result from a variety of motoric mechanisms, including uncoordinated synergistic muscle actions (Buckingham 1979; Itoh et al. 1980; Keller 1987; Rosenbek, Kent, and LaPointe 1984), gesture reduction (Keller 1984), or phoneme sequence simplification (Keller 1984). That is, any of a number of motor-level phenomena conceivably can result in an apparent phonologic error. If children have variable motoric systems (as the literature on motor development consistently demonstrates), then it seems reasonable, if not unavoidable, that some part of phonetic variability is to be explained at the motor level.

Figure 4 is a diagram of various levels implicated in the utterance of a word. Although future research may show that one or more of these levels is not essential in a model of the production process, it is difficult to exclude any of them on the basis of current evidence. That is, it is difficult to exclude any of them for the mature language user. But it is not necessarily the case that the young child learning language produces early words in a fashion that involves all of the levels shown in figure 4. Some writers on phonological development advocate the word as the early unit of phonological production. In such a view, at least two levels of organization would be required—the word and the motor sequence. The latter takes the form of a gestural score, or a prescription of the movements to be produced. Voluntary skilled movement is linked to a plan or pattern that determines the relationship among the movement components. A child just learning to produce words must relate an intended word to a motor plan, or gestural score. The score can be considered as the composite of a set of sensorimotor trajectories, where each such trajectory is a neural representation of a movement and its sensory consequences. The production of almost

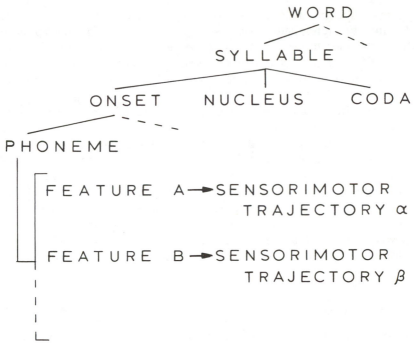

Figure 4.   Model of various levels involved in phonological organization, from the word to sensorimotor trajectories. The sensorimotor trajectories are combined into a gestural score for an utterance.

any word requires that several of these sensorimotor trajectories be combined in a gestural score. Because the child at the first word stage presumably is learning both words and the motor skills of speech that enable the utterance of words, an account of early word production demands consideration of at least the word level and the motor control level.

It seems possible, then, that a child in the very early stages of phonological development (say, a child with a vocabulary of fewer than 25 to 50 words) expresses these few words not with an adult-like phonetic specification but rather with stored motor scores, one score for each word. Variability in the actual realization of a given score is not unexpected, given the evidence for motoric variability in young children. It is doubtful that a stable prearticulatory representation could develop until such time as the child has a reasonably stable motor execution. The prearticulatory representation does not arise de novo, but rather from the coordination of perceptual and motor experiences. If first word production is a matter of relating word with gestural score, then major advances in subsequent phonological development would involve completion of the intervening levels of organization depicted in figure 4. The literature on phonological development has paid scant attention to motor patterns per se. However, Vihman (this volume) draws attention to vocal motor schemes as an influential factor in early word production. The formulaic nature of many vocables and first words may reflect the child's reliance on a small number of gestural scores.

What might be learned from work such as that presented by Vihman (this volume) is that certain motor patterns or schemes give the child a leverage into a quasiphonetic production capability. The term *quasiphonetic* is used here to denote a sound pattern that can be transcribed readily enough but does not necessarily reflect a true organization of phonetic units. Attribution of segmental composition is quite possible even when segmental organization is not yet present, and therefore most of the extant data on infant vocalizations are based on transcriptions. But the perspective here is that early motor patterns are the means to the kind of skilled performance from which phonetic production can emerge.

A Biological Model of Early Phonological Development

A biological model of perceptual and motor factors in phonological development is shown in figure 5. In the figure are the input channel (principally audition, but this input may be integrated with vision) and the output channel (motor regulation of the speech apparatus). Movements of the speech apparatus produce considerable sensory information, which is incorporated into the central nervous system representation of emerging speech motor control. Both input and output channels have a genetically determined potential. With respect to audition, the genetic potential is for an apparently universal (among human beings), multicategoried analysis of acoustic stimuli. An initial perceptual categorization is needed so that the organism can discriminate and identify salient aspects of the environment, but this initial categorization system must be subject to change as the organism adapts to the environment (Edelman 1987). Jusczyk (this volume) concludes that infants' speech sound categories are universal, being about the same in various language backgrounds. This universality is evidence of the genetic template by which the infant achieves an initial categorization of the auditory world. By the end of the first year of life, there is a decrease in sensitivity to some phonetic contrasts that are not part of the ambient language (Werker and Tees 1984; Werker 1989; Werker and Pegg this volume). The sensitivity can be regained, apparently with some effort (Werker 1989).

The genetic potential for output, as mediated by environmental factors, is expressed primarily in the form of predispositions to certain

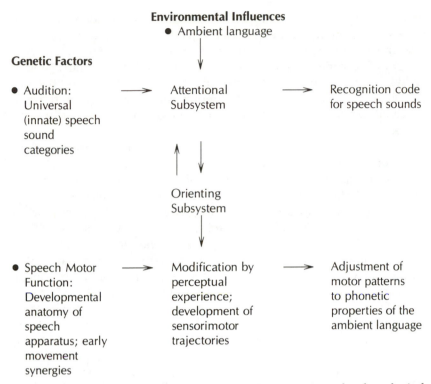

Environmental Influences
- Ambient language

Genetic Factors

- Audition:
  Universal
  (innate) speech
  sound
  categories

→ Attentional
  Subsystem

→ Recognition code
  for speech sounds

Orienting
Subsystem

- Speech Motor
  Function:
  Developmental
  anatomy of
  speech
  apparatus; early
  movement
  synergies

→ Modification by
  perceptual
  experience;
  development of
  sensorimotor
  trajectories

→ Adjustment of
  motor patterns
  to phonetic
  properties of the
  ambient language

Figure 5. A scheme of auditory-motor developments in early phonological acquisition. Genetic and experiential factors interact during development to produce the final observed behaviors.

sound patterns. These predispositions are evidenced by cross-language and cross-cultural similarities in early phonological behavior (Locke 1983) and by common tendencies across individual infants learning the same language (Vihman, Ferguson, and Elbert 1986).

Exposure to the ambient language selects some categories of auditory analysis for preservation, others for neglect. The mechanisms appear to involve both attentional and orienting processes (Carpenter and Grossberg 1987). These processes interact to produce a recognition that is stable for important events but also adaptive as environmental circumstances or behavioral demands change. Carpenter and Grossberg (1987) described a stability-plasticity dilemma. On the one hand, a system must demonstrate stability in the presence of irrelevant or frequently repeated events. On the other hand, the system must be plastic to deal with new or novel events, or changing circumstances. As a solution to this dilemma, Carpenter and Grossberg (1987) proposed a stable self-organizing neural recognition code that is formed by the interaction of an attention system and an orienting system. The former processes familiar events to maintain stable representations for these events and to effect learned expectations (top-down processing). The orienting system detects unfamiliar events so as to reset the attentional system. The combined action of these two systems would enable a child to adapt perceptual categories present at birth to those of the ambient language. Subsequent adjustment of the categories, as in the case of second-language learning, is possible but often with some difficulty (Werker 1989).

Motor control proceeds quite differently. A proper understanding of motor events may be clouded by a premature phonetic attribution to infants' sound productions. For example, the historic argument as to whether babbling drift reflects phonetic expansion (a increase in phonetic categories) or phonetic contraction (a decrease in these categories) begs the question of phonetic capability, or the very existence of segments. The infant in the babbling period may not possess a segmental prearticulatory representation that mirrors the ambient language. However, this is not to say that babbling is totally devoid of phonetic characteristics. Such characteristics can indeed be described, but care should be taken in the description of these characteristics. A conservative approach is to emphasize the nascent motor control functions rather than the apparent (but arguable) phonetic representations underlying infant sound productions. This does not mean that infants cannot detect auditory features in their own vocalizations. This capability is fundamental to the learning of a phonetic system and is the way in which auditory experience helps to mold the motor patterns of speech.

Quite early in life, as the infant gains motor regulation of the vocal tract and is exposed to the ambient language, articulatory adjustments will reflect the learning of a motor envelope. This envelope is to some degree language sensitive, and this sensitivity is revealed in cross-language studies of infant babble, which indicate that babbling becomes adjusted to the parent language in terms of features such as syllable structure and vowel articulation (Boysson-Bardies, Sagart, and Durand 1984; Boysson-Bardies, Halle, and Durand 1989; Boysson-Bardies et al. this volume). Additional evidence of the sensitivity of babbling to audition is that hearing-impaired infants differ from hearing infants in the phonetic and acoustic characteristics of their babble (Kent et al. 1986; Oller et al. 1985; Stoel-Gammon and Otomo 1986; Oller this volume).

Adjustments in the motor envelope presumably are precursors to phonetic mastery but they are not in themselves necessarily segmental in nature. A good part of what an infant does in babbling may be an adjustment in general motoric configuration or pattern. The accomplishment of this motor envelope should facilitate the mastery of phonetic elements compatible with the envelope. Phonetic regulation per se (that is, motor control that reflects a segmentally organized prearticulatory representation) would become evident as the infant continues to select and refine movement patterns in accord with the properties of the ambient language (cf. Lindblom this volume). Eventually, motor patterns are linked to the recognition code. Motor regulation, as the recognition code, is amenable to adjustment. Motor patterns become habitual but not inflexible.

The literature on phonological development has come to possess some specialized concepts and terminology that are not reconciled easily with other aspects of development. For example, largely through the influence of Stampe (1969), many studies of phonological development have relied on phonological processes, which Ingram (1979) defined as "a universal set of hierarchically ordered procedures used by children to simplify speech" (p. 133). Taken literally, this concept implies that children possess the adult phonological forms at least to the extent that they can subject these forms to the simplifying procedures. The processes are effectively imposed on underlying adult forms. Phonological maturity then comes with the disappearance of the simplifying operations.

At issue here is whether development is understood better as a process in which the child simplifies a fully comprehended version of the mature behavior or as a process in which the child progressively applies available resources (through selection and refinement) in attempting to emulate the mature behavior. The latter alternative is undergirded by much of the general developmental literature, one part of which is immediately relevant: the literature on motor development.

Children at various ages differ from adults in the kinematics of movement. Hay (1979) reported that the progression of skill in reaching movements was not monotonic. Reaching movements for five-year-olds were predominantly ballistic (movements of short duration, high velocity, and rapid acceleration and deceleration). Seven-year-olds were not much more accurate than the five-year-olds but their movements showed the emergence of ramp and step movements. *Ramps* are low, constant velocity movements of relatively long duration, and *steps* are a series of composite shifts to an end location. The predominant movements of the nine-year-olds were more mature, taking the form of medium speed, single-step responses with a positive correlation between accuracy and movement time. In a study of tapping movements, Schellekens, Kalverboer, and Scholten (1984) analyzed the movements into a distance covering phase and a homing phase. Total movement time decreased with age, and most of this developmental difference was explained by a change in the duration of the homing phase. With increasing age, the distance covering phase became more accurate and the number of movement elements (instances of accelerations and decelerations) decreased.

If the motor regulation of speech movements is similar to that of the limb movements just described, then certain implications for phonological development follow. First, the early tendency toward stopping may be associated with a tendency toward ballistic movements. When the term *ballistic* has been used to describe speech sounds, it usually is attached to the stops. These articulations typically have short duration, high velocity, and a steeply triangular velocity profile (rapid acceleration and deceleration). The canonical syllable of babbling may reflect the developmentally stable distance covering phase of movement in which both peak velocity and the time to peak velocity depend on the amplitude of movement. Ballistic movements suffice for this motor response.

Among the most vulnerable segments in early speech is the syllable-final consonant which, according to phonological process description, frequently is deleted. However, Weismer (1984) observed that some children who were judged to delete the final consonant in fact produced formant transitions consistent with the supposedly absent consonant articulation. Such a pattern could come about through execution of a poorly controlled homing phase that fails to generate adequate acoustic cues for the syllable-final consonant. Fricatives, for example, might have any one of three outcomes in a phonetic transcription: (1) deletion, if the relevant cues are absent or weak; (2) stop substitution, if the transition is intact but the frication noise is deficient; and (3) verified fricative production. Studies of limb movement have shown that the final phase of movement (the homing phase) is influenced by target size. With smaller targets, more time is given to the final phase (MacKenzie et al. 1987). If fricatives demand articulatory precision in the form of a critical constriction, then less skilled speakers might devote more time to the homing phase, thus risking the perceptual salience of the formant transition. These speakers also may fail to control the articulation adequately to ensure frication noise. However, in this motor perspective, they have not necessarily simplified an adult pattern; rather, they have used limited motoric resources to achieve a difficult goal.

SUMMARY

This chapter has presented a brief biological perspective on phonological development. In fact, the relevant biology is far beyond the scope of a short chapter. Special emphasis has been given to some fundamental principles of biological development, to anatomic change, and to sensorimotor coordination. Evidence has been presented to show the relevance of these factors to phonological development. These factors are by no means a complete account of the emergence of spoken language, but they are an important part of the story and a part that is increasingly open to investigation by noninvasive techniques.

REFERENCES

Bloom, L. 1970. *Language Development: Form and Function in Emerging Grammars.* Cambridge, MA: MIT Press.

Bloom, L. 1973. *One Word at a Time: The Use of Single Word Utterances before Syntax.* The Hague: Mouton.

Bosma, J. F. 1975. Anatomic and physiologic development of the speech apparatus. In *The Nervous System. Vol. 3. Human Communication and Its Disorders* ed. D. B. Tower. New York: Raven Press.

Boysson-Bardies, B., Sagart, L., and Durand, C. 1984. Discernible differences in the babbling of infants according to target language. *Journal of Child Language* 11:1–15.

Boysson-Bardies, B., Halle, P., and Durand, C. 1989. A crosslinguistic investigation of vowel formants in babbling. *Journal of Child Language* 16:1–17.

Buckingham, H. W., Jr. 1979. Explanation in apraxia with consequences for the concept of apraxia of speech. *Brain and Language* 8:202–226.

Camp, B., Burgess, D., Morgan, L., and Zerbe, G. 1987. A longitudinal study of infant vocalization in the first year. *Journal of Pediatric Psychology* 12:321–31.

Carpenter, G. A., and Grossberg, S. 1987. Discovering order in chaos: Stable self-organization of neural recognition codes. In *Perspectives in Biological Dynamics and Theoretical Medicine* eds. S. H. Koslow, A. J. Mandell, and M. F. Shlesinger. *Annals of the New York Academy of Sciences* 504:33–51.

Chermak, G., and Schneiderman, C. 1986. Speech timing variability of children and adults. *Journal of Phonetics* 13:477–80.

Darwin, C. 1877. A biographic sketch of an infant. *Mind* 2:285–94.

Dinnsen, D. A., Chin, S. B., Elbert, M., and Powell, T. 1990. Some constraints on functionally disordered phonologies: Phonetic inventories and phonotactics. *Journal of Speech and Hearing Research* 33:28–37.

DuBrul, E. L. 1976. Biomechanics of speech sounds. *Annals of the New York Academy of Sciences* 280:631–42.

DuBrul, E. L. 1977. Origin of the speech apparatus and its reconstruction in fossils. *Brain and Language* 4:365–81.

Edelman, G. 1987. *Neural Darwinism: The Theory of Neuronal Group Selection.* New York: Basic Books.

Edelman, G. 1989. *The Remembered Present.* New York: Basic Books.

Edwards, J. 1989. Compensatory articulation of normal and phonologically disordered children. Paper presented at the 1989 Annual Meeting of the New York Speech Language-Hearing Association, Monticello, NY.

Eguchi, S., and Hirsh, I. J. 1969. Development of speech sounds in children. *Archives of Otolaryngology* Suppl.:257.

Elbers, L. 1982. Operating principles in repetitive babbling: A cognitive continuity approach. *Cognition* 12:45–63.

Fentress, J. C. 1984. The development of coordination. *Journal of Motor Behavior* 16:99–134.

Ferguson, C. A., and Farwell, C. B. 1975. Words and sounds in early language acquisition. *Language* 51:419–39.

Haelsig, P. C., and Madison, C. L. 1986. A study of phonological processes exhibited by 3-, 4-, and 5-year-old children. *Language, Speech and Hearing Services in Schools* 17:107–114.

Hay, L. 1979. Spatiotemporal analysis of movements in children: Motor programs versus feedback in the development of reaching. *Journal of Motor Behavior* 11:189–200.

Hodge, M. 1989. Dynamic spectral-temporal characteristics of children's speech: Implications for a model of speech skill development. Ph.D. dissertations in progress, University of Wisconsin-Madison, Madison, WI.

Holmgren, K., Lindblom, B., Aurelius, G., Jalling, B., and Zetterstrom, R. 1986. On the phonetics of infant vocalization. In *Precursors of Early Speech* eds. B. Lindblom and R. Zetterstrom. New York: Stockton Press.

Ingram, D. 1979. Phonological patterns in the speech of young children. In *Language Acquisition* eds. P. Fletcher and M. Garman. Cambridge UK: Cambridge University Press.

Itoh, M., Sasanuma, S., Hirose, H., Yoshioka, H., and Ushijima, T. 1980. Abnormal articulatory dynamics in a patient with apraxia of speech. X-ray microbeam observation. *Brain and Language* 11:66–75.

Keller, E. 1984. Simplification and gesture reduction in phonological disorders of apraxia and aphasia. In *Apraxia of Speech: Physiology, Acoustics, Linguistics and Management* ed. J. C. Rosenbek, M. R. McNeil, and A. E. Aronson. San Diego: College-Hill Press.

Keller, E. 1987. Ultrasound measurements of tongue dorsum movements in articulatory speech impairments. In *Phonetic Approaches to Speech Production in Aphasia and Related Disorders* ed. J. H. Ryalls. Boston: College-Hill Press.

Kent, R. D. 1981. Articulatory-acoustic perspectives on speech development. In *Language Behavior in Infancy and Early Childhood* ed. R. E. Stark. New York: Elsevier/North Holland.

Kent, R. D. 1984. The psychobiology of speech development: co-emergence of language and a movement system. *American Journal of Physiology* 246:R888–R894.

Kent, R. D., and Bauer, H. R. 1985. Vocalizations of one year olds. *Journal of Child Language* 12:491–526.

Kent, R. D., and Forner, L. L. 1980. Speech segment durations in sentence recitations by children and adults. *Journal of Phonetics* 12:157–68.

Kent, R. D., and Hodge, M. 1990. The biogenesis of speech: Continuity and process in early speech and language development. In *Progress in Research on Child Language Disorders* ed. J. F. Miller. Austin, TX: Pro-Ed.

Kent, R. D., and Murray, A. 1982. Acoustic features of infant vocalic utterances at 3, 6 and 9 months. *Journal of the Acoustical Society of America* 72:353–65.

Kent, R. D., Osberger, M. J., Netsell, R., and Hustedde, C. G. 1986. Phonetic development in identical twins differing in auditory function. *Journal of Speech and Hearing Disorders* 52:64–75.

Kier, W. M., and Smith, K. K. 1985. Tongues, tentacles, and trunks: The biomechanics of movement in muscular-hydrostats. *Zoological Journal of the Linnean Society* 83:307–324.

Kuperstein, M. 1988. Neural model of adaptive hand-eye coordination for single postures. *Science* 239:1308–1311.

Lenneberg, E. H. 1967. *Biological Foundations of Language.* New York: Wiley.

Leopold, W. 1939, 1947, 1949a, 1949b. *Speech Development in a Bilingual Child: A Linguist's Record.* Vol. I-IV. Evanston, IL: Northwestern University Press.

Lieberman, P., Crelin, E. S., and Klatt, D. H. 1972. Phonetic ability and related anatomy of the newborn, adult human, Neanderthal man, and the chimpanzee. *American Anthropologist* 74:287–307.

Locke, J. L. 1983. *Phonological Acquisition and Change.* New York: Academic Press.

MacKenzie, C. L., Marteniuk, R. G., Dugas, C., Liske, D., and Eickmeier, B. 1987. Three-dimensional movement trajectories in Fitts' task: Implications for control. *Quarterly Journal of Experimental Psychology* 39A:629–47.

Martin, J. A. M. 1981. *Voice, Speech and Language in the Child: Development and Disorder.* New York: Springer-Verlag.

McNeil, M. R. and Kent, R. D. 1990. Motoric characteristics of aphasic and apraxic speech. In *Advances in Psychology: Cerebral Control of Speech and Limb Movements* ed. G. R. Hammond. Amsterdam: Elsevier Science Publishers.

Menyuk, P., Liebergott, J., and Schultz, M. 1986. Predicting phonological development. *Precursors of Early Speech* eds. B. Lindblom and R. Zetterstrom. New York: Stockton Press.

Mitchell, P. R., and Kent, R. D. 1990. Phonetic variation in multisyllabic babbling. *Journal of Child Language* 17:247–65.

Murphy, R., Menyuk, P., Liebergott, J., and Schultz, M. 1983. Predicting rate of lexical acquisition. Paper presented at the Biennial Meeting of the Society for Research in Child Development, Detroit, MI.

Oller, D. K. 1978. Infant vocalizations and the development of speech. *Allied Health and Behavioral Science* 1:523–49.

Oller, D. K. 1986. Metaphonology and infant vocalizations. In *Early Precursors of Speech* eds. B. Lindblom and R. Zetterstrom. Basingstoke: Macmillan.

Oller, D. K., Eilers, R. E., Bull, D. H., and Carney, A. E. 1985. Prespeech vocalizations of a deaf infant: A comparison with normal metaphonological development. *Journal of Speech and Hearing Research* 28:47–62.

Otomo, K. 1988. Development of vowel articulation from 22 to 30 months of age: Preliminary analyses. Paper presented at 1988 Child Phonology Conference, University of Illinois, Urbana-Champaign.

Piaget, J. 1955. *The Language and Thought of the Child.* Translated by M. Gabain. Cleveland: Meridian Books.

Pollock, K. E., and Keiser, N. J. 1990. An examination of vowel errors in phonologically disordered children. *Clinical Linguistics and Phonetics* 4:161–78.

Rosenbek, J. C., Kent, R. D., and LaPointe, L. L. 1984. Apraxia of speech: An overview and some perspectives. In *Apraxia of Speech: Physiology, Acoustics, Linguistics, Management.* San Diego: College-Hill Press.

Sachs, T. 1988. Epigenetic selection: An alternative mechanism of pattern formation. *Journal of Theoretical Biology* 134:547–59.

Sander, E. 1972. When are speech sounds learned? *Journal of Speech and Hearing Disorders* 37:55–63.

Sasaki, C. T., Levine, P. A., Laitman, J. T., and Crelin, E. S. 1977. Postnatal descent of the epiglottis in man. *Archives of Otolaryngology* 103:169–71.

Sharkey, S., and Folkins, J. 1985. Variability of lip and jaw movements in children and adults. Implications for the development of speech motor control. *Journal of Speech and Hearing Research* 28:8–15.

Schellekens, J. M. H., Kalverboer, A. F., and Scholten, C. A. 1984. The microstructure of tapping movements in children. *Journal of Motor Behavior* 16:20–39.

Shinn, M. 1900. *The Biography of a Baby.* New York: Houghton Mifflin.

Shriberg, L. D., and Kent, R. D. 1982. *Clinical Phonetics.* New York: Macmillan.

Sinnott, J. M. 1989. Detection and discrimination of synthetic English vowels by Old World Monkeys. *Journal of the Acoustical Society of America* 86:557–65.

Smith, B., Brown-Sweeney, S., and Stoel-Gammon, C. 1988. A quantitative analysis of reduplicated and variegated babbling. Paper read at the Child Phonology Conference, May 1988, University of Illinois-Champaign-Urbana.

Smith, K. K., and Kier, W. M. 1989. Trunks, tongues, and tentacles: Moving with skeletons of muscle. *American Scientist* 77:29–35.

Stampe, D. 1969. The acquisition of phonetic representation. In *Papers from the Fifth Regional Meeting, Chicago Linguistics Society* ed. R. Binnick, A. Davison, G. Green, and J. L. Morgan. Reprinted in D. Stampe, *A Dissertation in Natural Phonology.* New York: Garland Publishing Co.

Stark, R. 1979. Prespeech segmental feature development. In *Language Acquisition* ed. P. Fletcher and M. Garman. New York: Cambridge University Press.

Stoel-Gammon, C., and Otomo, K. 1986. Babbling development of hearing-impaired and normally hearing subjects. *Journal of Speech and Hearing Disorders* 51:33–41.

Thelen, E. 1981. Rhythmical behavior in infancy: An ethological perspective. *Developmental Psychology* 17:237–57.

Thelen, E. 1989. Evolving and dissolving synergies in the development of leg coordination. In *Perspectives on the Coordination of Movement* ed. S. A. Wallace. Amsterdam: North Holland.

Thomas, K. T., and Thomas, J. R. 1988. Perceptual development and its differential influence on limb positioning under two movement conditions in children. In *Advances in Motor Development Research* eds. J. E. Clark and J. H. Humphrey. New York: AMS Press.

Vihman, M. M., Ferguson, C. A., and Elbert, M. 1986. Phonological development from babbling to speech: Common tendencies and individual differences. *Applied Psycholinguistics* 7:3–40.

Wellman, B., Case, E., Mengert, I., and Bradbury, D. 1931. Speech sounds of young children. *University of Iowa Studies in Child Welfare* 5:7–80.

Werker, J. F. 1989. Becoming a native listener. *American Scientist* 77:54–59.

Werker, J. F., and Tees, R. C. 1984. Cross-language speech perception: Evidence for perceptual reorganization during the first year of life. *Infant Behavior and Development* 7:49–63.

Weismer, G. 1984. Acoustical analysis strategies for the refinement of phonological analysis. *ASHA Monographs* 22:3–15.

Chapter • 3

Vocal Learning and the Emergence of Phonological Capacity
A Neurobiological Approach

John L. Locke and Dawn M. Pearson

> . . . perceptual, central, and motor mechanisms are the building blocks
> out of which complex behavior is formed. . . . A developmental analysis
> requires looking for the factors causing the development of the building
> blocks themselves, as well as for the way connections among these build-
> ing blocks become established (Hogan 1988).

EMERGENCE OF PHONOLOGICAL CAPACITY

Like other phonologists, we are keenly interested in the development
of a linguistic sound system. In this chapter, however, we concentrate
on the question of how children come to possess the *capacity* for spoken
language and how they apply this capacity in vocal learning and early
phonological development. Why do infants seek to imitate speech?
How is it that when they do, infants are successful in carrying out the

The authors wish to acknowledge the very considerable assistance of Catherine
Best, John Fentress, Mark Hauser, and Michael Studdert-Kennedy, who read the manuscript and suggested changes in earlier drafts. Douglas Frost, Kaaren Bekken, James
Flege, and Nancy Hildebrandt also offered helpful comments. Some of the ideas expressed in this chapter have been developed into a more complete theory of the child's
development of spoken language in Locke (in press).

specific perceptual and motor operations required to reproduce the sounds of spoken language?

We believe that the infant is an active participant in the process whereby its brain comes fully to possess the capacity for spoken language. Wherever possible, we have sought inspiration from phylogenetic models and data from other species to support the plausibility of our view. The chapter begins with an examination of the human's evolved capacity for spoken language. First, we identify the general characteristics of sound production in the "prelinguistic" infant, tracing the source of ontogenetic patterning to larger phylogenetic constructs that govern the evolution of structure and function. Second, we ask how environmental factors collaborate with genetics to produce the brain's capacity for phonology, examining animal and human data that show that sensory stimulation challenges the brain to grow in developmentally adaptive ways, tuning genetically specified structure to meet the gross requirements of language. We discuss a special form of sensory stimulation, provided by the infant itself, which arguably encourages vocal-motor development and auditory-motor coordination. Assuming that phonological capacity is in place, we turn our attention to the exercise of this capacity. We argue that sound learning is set in motion by dispositions to vocal imitation that are species specific, present in human but not nonhuman primates. When coupled with phonological capacity, these dispositions enable the acquisition of spoken language. We think the development of linguistic cognition is best understood within a neurobiological framework. Species-characteristic perceptual biases and dispositions to motor action makes spoken language learnable and useable, and nudge the child toward certain paths in the development of a linguistic sound system.

Pattern and Variation in Phonological Development

Just as for other behaviors, children's imperfect productions of spoken language are patterned and not random. Variation usually occurs within limits that can be specified in phonetic terms. We believe a great deal more about phonological development will be understood when the reasons for children's speech patterns and phonetic variations have been identified.

Babbling, unlike the sounds of crying, shrieking, cooing, yelling, and fussing, is defined by the production of well-formed or *canonical* syllables that have many of the acoustic characteristics of adult speech. Canonical syllables are defined in specific physical terms relating to duration, as well as to frequency, amplitude, and their changes over time (Oller 1986). These syllables are the product of infants' natural tendency to alternately elevate and depress the mandible (MacNeilage and Davis in press). The elevation of the mandible, along with labial or lingual action, narrows and obstructs the vocal tract. This yield closants, which resemble consonant sounds. The depression of the mandible, with collateral oral adjustments, yields vocants, which sound like vowels (Kent and Bauer 1985).

The evidence suggests that babbling typically begins abruptly between six and ten months of age (with many infants at about six to seven months), regardless of whether the ambient language is American English (Smith and Oller 1981; Ramsay 1984), Dutch (van der Stelt and Koopmans-van Beinum 1986), Russian (Bel'tyukov and Salakhova 1973), or Swedish (Holmgren et al. 1986). Oller and Eilers (1988) place the onset at six to ten months, because it is between these ages that the ratio of canonical syllables per utterance first exceeds a level unsurpassed in the deaf until some time later (as detailed later in this chapter).

There is perceptual and instrumental evidence that indicates that syllables in multisyllabic strings often are produced rhythmically (Bickley, Lindblom, and Roug 1986); in the reduplicated strings of thirteen month olds, syllables tend to repeat every 200 msec (Kent and Bauer 1985), which approximates the average duration of syllables in adult conversational speech. MacNeilage and Davis (in press) have suggested that reduplicated babbling is responsible for the formation of phonological "frames" into which speech segments, when they become available, can be inserted.

Classical speculation (e.g., Jakobson 1968) notwithstanding, the empirical evidence suggests that phones—the content of phonological frames—are highly restricted in infants' babbling. Consonant-like closures typically are limited, by phonetic feature, to oral and glottal stops, nasals, and approximants. Babbling has an extremely low occurrence of liquids, affricates, and supraglottal fricatives. Among vocalic sounds, low central and low front vowels predominate (Kent and Bauer 1985). In babble, syllable-final obstruents occur rarely and consonant clusters are virtually nonexistent (Locke 1983a).

It follows from the above that infants produce a characteristic repertoire of oral movements and sounds. At about 12 months, [h, w, j, p, b, m, t, d, n, k, g] account for about 90% of all consonant-like segments in the babbling of infants exposed to American English. Infants reared in non-English linguistic environments produce a *similar repertoire* of consonant-like segments. The rather extensive evidence for this, which is reviewed elsewhere (Locke 1983a), includes phonetic diaries of infants reared in diverse linguistic environments, as well as perceptual and instrumental attempts to distinguish paired voice samples from two or more language environments. Such cross-linguistic similarities suggest that infants' phonetic forms may be configured by anatomical and physiological factors and, indeed, efforts to account for prelinguistic vocalizations in physical terms have met with some success (Kent 1981; Locke 1983a).

Phonetic Action Patterns

These findings suggest that over the first year, infants' sounds (and, therefore, sound-making *movements*) are relatively insensitive to specific ambient experience. Moreover, many of the sounds that appear frequently in babbling resemble phonemes that occur in the majority of the world's languages. According to our analyses, both the nasal and glide sounds that are so frequent in babbling are rostered, on an average, in over 90% of the languages of the world. The affricates and oral fricatives that are so rare in babbling occur in just 40 to 50% of the world's languages (*Handbook of Phonological Data from a Sample of the World's Languages* 1979).

The featural patterns of babbling are so robust as to survive congenital deafness and neonatal brain damage. Studies of deaf infants (Carr 1953; Smith 1982; Stoel-Gammon and Otomo 1986; Sykes 1940) reveal place, manner, and syllabic patterns that parallel trends observed in hearing infants. Marchman, Miller, and Bates (1991) analyzed the phonetic patterns of 10 neurologically normal infants and five infants with unilateral focal lesions. The authors observed that for both the control and the focal lesion groups, stops were more frequent than other manners of consonant production, e.g., fricatives, nasals, and liquids. Labials and dentals were more frequent in both groups than velars, and both groups were unlikely to produce final consonants or consonant clusters.

If there are natural categories of vocal activity that are so strong as to survive deafness and brain damage, their induction or stabilization may require little from the recognized mechanisms of *learning*. If so, we would expect certain phonetic movement patterns to "behave" somewhat like the modal action patterns of those animals in whom the role of postnatal learning remains to be demonstrated. According to Barlow (1977), a modal action pattern is "a recognizable spatiotemporal pattern of movement that . . . is widely distributed in similar form throughout an interbreeding population" (p. 99) and "can be performed in the absence of any apparent stimulation" (p. 108). An analogy to phonetic activity is possible because modal action patterns can be *disrupted* or *altered*, and because there is "a role for experience" in their emergence.

Barlow believes that some modal action patterns are "cleanly triggered" whereas others are "under stimulus control." Similarly, picking up Mayr's (1976) distinction between open and closed behavior programs, Tooby and Cosmides (1989) have suggested that "the more universal preferences are the product of more closed behavior programs, whereas the more variable are the expression of more open behavior programs" (p. 37). This relationship has evolved because open behavior programs are "open to environmental inputs, and hence variable in expression, [unlike] those that are closed to environmental input, and consequently uniform in expression" (p. 36).

If the more frequently operationalized *phonetic action patterns* are the product of relatively closed behavior programs, we might expect that "universal" phonemes would assume fewer different forms of expression than "nonuniversal" phonemes.[1] According to the *UCLA Phonological Segment Inventory Database* (1981), /m/ is the most frequent phoneme in the languages of the world, occurring in 97% of the systems in the sample. On the other hand, the American English type of /r/ is the least frequent phoneme, occurring in fewer than 5% of the languages. On purely statistical grounds, we should expect the more universal /m/ to have about 20 times as many variants as the less frequent /r/. On strictly biological grounds, we should expect universal phonemes to be more closed—and therefore to reveal fewer variants within and across languages—than the less widely distributed and more open ones. And sure enough, in strong support of the biological hypothesis, the *Handbook of Phonological Data from a Sample of the World's Languages* (1979) reveals only half as many types of bilabial nasals as /r/-like liquids.

Whether one observes infants, speakers, or languages, the threads of biology are everywhere to be seen, woven through the fabric of phonetic behavior and phonological structure. In table I, we have attempted with *m* and *r* to illustrate the weave of these threads. Sounds that are frequent in babbling, such as [m], are generally well represented in the world's languages, and also tend not to assume as many forms as the less restricted phonemes, either across languages or within them as dialectal variations. These same, "unmarked" sounds seem to have relatively more closed behavior programs and to require fewer exemplars in order to be mastered. Finally, /m/ is inclined to develop early, is less likely than /r/ to be disordered, and is articulatorily simpler.

We have discussed the patterning in infants' vocal behavior, but there also is variation in human utterances at all levels of mastery. It is implicit in the notion of idiolect that no two adults residing within a linguistic community speak in precisely the same way, and it is obvious from developmental studies that children take different paths to linguistic maturity (Ferguson and Farwell 1975; Nelson 1981). What theoretical importance attaches to such variations?

For reasons stated elsewhere (Locke 1988), we question the as-

---

[1]This follows only if segmental universals are largely based on production factors, as seems to be the case (Lindblom 1983; Ohala 1983), although there may also be a perceptual basis as well (Stevens and Keyser 1989).

Table I. Some Attributes and Distributional Characteristics of Two Phonetic Gestures

	/m/	/r/
Prominence in Babbling	Prominent	Restricted
Breadth of Linguistic Distribution	Universal	Restricted
Variation across Dialects	Narrow	Broad
Patency of Behavior Program	Closed	Open
Role of Linguistic Stimulation	Limited	Moderate
Developmental Schedule	Early	Late
Probability of Disorder	Low	High

sumption that interchild variation implies the operation of "cognitive factors" in phonological development (see also Studdert-Kennedy 1991). However, variation presents analysts with an important opportunity; in the effort to identify its source, we may learn how the sound system of a language is acquired. For example, we may attempt to distinguish environmental effects from perceptual and physiologic effects, and within the environmental domain, to distinguish maternal from paternal and sibling influences. In a particular child, we also may look to see if certain phonetic constructions are more variable than others.

Why, then, do children vary? What are the bases of attested phonological patterns? We think it is helpful to approach such questions from a phylogenetic perspective.

PHONOLOGICAL ORGANIZATION
IN THE SPECIES: PHYLOGENETIC FACTORS

In animals, Fentress and McLeod (1986) have identified several cases where movements displayed by mature animals appear prefunctionally during earlier stages of development. One example is the preening of young passerine birds prior to their development of feathers. Likewise, as though their utility in spoken language is "anticipated," the vocal movements of mature humans first appear in infancy, persisting into adulthood to form the sounds of established languages. Infants heavily favor stop consonants over fricatives, and there are languages that have stops and no fricatives but no languages that exemplify the reverse pattern. Infants produce consonant-like singletons but no clusters, and all languages have singletons but many lack clusters. These "phonologically universal" patterns, which cut across languages and speakers are, in effect, the phonetic properties of *Homo sapiens*.

The evolution of structure is built upon a series of successive individual ontogenies. Therefore, phylogenetic theories are able to inspire and inform theories of ontogeny (Tharp and Burns 1989). Additionally, observations on a variety of animals make possible insights about our own species, or at least provide a framework for more analytical thinking about humans. Let us begin with an observation by Thorpe (1961) on the function of birdsong. Thorpe outlined several characteristics necessary for birdsong to function optimally. These characteristics may apply to spoken language as well.

Monomorphic Design

First, Thorpe (1961) suggested that birdsong must be sufficiently stereotyped to characterize the species. Evidence of a human sound-making capacity is ubiquitous, and includes similarity of error pattern among children attempting to learn a variety of languages. Regardless of whether their exposure is to German, French, or a variety of other languages, children evince characteristic patterns of segment substitution and omission (Locke 1983a). What produces the patterning? The answer, we believe, lies in the gross physical similarity of vocal organs among individual members of a species. This "monomorphic design" of human anatomy and physiology (Tooby and Cosmides 1988) exists because in the thousands of years in the phylogeny of *Homo sapiens*, natural selection has reduced the range of genetic variation, generation after generation, until only a small amount of structural variation is left.

On a gross level, it is obvious that there is one basic architecture to the sound production system of humans. Every normal human's brain has two roughly similar hemispheres, with interconnecting pathways, and a vocal tract with common sets of resonating chambers and mechanisms. Presumably, it is this grossly monomorphic vocal design that has produced phonologically universal patterns (Greenberg, Ferguson, and Moravcsik 1978), as well as the central phonetic tendencies, described above, of infants reared in different linguistic communities.

Structural Variability

Thorpe (1961) also said that to function optimally birdsong must possess a second characteristic: it must be variable enough for individual recognition. Every species is composed of genetically diverse individuals. This genetic variation makes evolution possible, because natural selection cannot occur unless there is genetically transmitted variation across the individual members of a species. The general population of normal speakers includes individuals with extreme variations in vocal tract morphology from the brain (Geschwind and Levitsky 1968) to the tongue (Fletcher and Meldrum 1968). Observed differences in neonatal sound production may be caused by these physical variations. This is suggested by the presence of large individual differences in many of the seemingly unlearned motor action patterns by which various animals communicate. Much of the evidence comes from nonhuman primates (Kaplan, Winship-Ball, and Sim 1978; Lieblich et al. 1980), although individual differences occur in many other species (Petrinovich 1974; Poindron and Carrick 1976). Such variations are far from trivial, for in many species vocal uniqueness at birth may encourage parental nurturance (Gould 1975) and protection from predators (Waser 1977).

Furthermore, it is hard to attribute animals' unique vocal signatures to differences in environmental exposure because there is systematic variation in the vocalizations of songbirds even when they are exposed to identical (taped) sound patterns (Marler and Peters 1982) or to no vocal models at all (Marler and Sherman 1985), and there are individual differences in birds who are experimentally deafened at hatching (Marler and Sherman 1983).

Humans also have uniquely different voices from the age of earliest observation. At 16 hours postnatally, there is evidence that infants respond differently to tape recordings of their own voices than to those of other infants (Martin and Clark 1982). Later, at six months, infants still exhibit their own unique phonetic signatures, with some infants producing proportionately more tokens of a phonetic category than other infants (Oller et al. 1976). This is long before the earliest evidence of vocal assimilation (Boysson-Bardies et al. 1989; Boysson-Bardies et al. this volume). For these reasons, we think anatomical and physiological differences are the most likely basis of young infants' vocal differences.

Environmental Coding of Design Biases

Through the process of evolution as conceptualized by Darwin, information about the environment of living beings enters their genes. But reciprocally it also is true that "genetic information" enters the environment, and that organisms are exposed disproportionately to stimulation patterns that are compatible with their own constitutional "design biases." Tooby and Cosmides (1988) have written that:

> The environment of an animal—in the sense of which features of the world it depends on or uses as inputs—is just as much the creation of the evolutionary process as the genes are. Thus, the evolutionary process can be said to store information necessary for development in both the environment and the genes. Both are 'biologically determined,' if such a phrase has any meaning (pp. 5–6).

If these relationships also applied to language, there would be a measure of harmony between the child's linguistic environment and the child's physiologic dispositions. We think this is so, and have argued elsewhere (Locke 1983a) that the constitutional biases of adults, through their speech, tend to reinforce many of children's own behavioral predispositions. In spoken language, basis for this reinforcement lies in the fact that natural categories of phonetic activity never are subdued completely by linguistic convention or dissolved by physical maturation. For example, voiced stops in word-final position are perpetually "at risk" of devoicing, deletion, or other forms of weakening in the casual conversations of *normal adult speakers* as well as in the speech of children. This means that children are underexposed to precisely those sound patterns for which phonological mastery may require an unusually lucid and stable example. Whether this contributes to the later development of these constructions is unknown.

THE ROLE OF ENVIRONMENTAL STIMULATION AND INFANT ACTIVITY IN NEURAL DEVELOPMENT

Development of Information Storage Systems

Greenough, Black, and Wallace (1987) have proposed that mammalian brain development relies upon two different systems for the storage of environmental information, based on the type of information that is stored and the brain mechanisms that do the storing. One system is termed *experience expectant* and the other is considered *experience dependent*. In both systems the sensory environment plays an important role by maintaining or inducing neural capacity, or by not doing so. The modulations that occur in neural development include induction, stabilization, and atrophy (cf. Changeux and Danchin 1976; Cowan et al. 1984). These neural modulations seem analogous to certain functional effects in language: the development, maintenance, and loss of neonatal perceptual and motor operations related to speech (Aslin and Pisoni 1980; Burnham 1986; Locke 1980a, 1980b; Werker 1991).[2]

Experience-expectant Systems. Experience-expectant information systems develop early in the life of organisms, and include the activation of auditory and visual systems. Such systems store environmental information that is available to all individuals. During the devel-

---

[2]The analogy is imperfect, however. Experiments on the perception of Zulu click contrasts by English-reared infants and adults support a phonological rather than a psychoacoustic explanation for perceptual loss (Best, McRoberts, and Sithole 1988).

opment of experience-expectant systems, synaptic connections, pre-scribed by the genes, are overproduced. If appropriate stimulation is lacking, these connections are likely to atrophy. In a classic study, Wiesel and Hubel (1963) found that in kittens whose right eyelid had been sutured shut before the time of normal eye opening, there was "profound atrophy" in cell layers along the visual pathway receiving input from the covered eye. Anatomical changes within those areas of the brain also included a reduction in size of cell bodies and nuclei. The direct effect of visual experience on brain growth in the young cat is demonstrated further by the finding that monocular lid closure after about two months of visual experience showed less severe atrophic changes than in kittens deprived from birth. In mature cats, closing the right eye for three months produced no abnormal changes in the layers receiving input from the closed eye.[3]

Experience-dependent Systems. In most animals, brain devel-opment falls very heavily into the experience-expectant category de-scribed above. But there also are cases in which cellular structure that is absent at birth develops in response to appropriate stimulation. Ac-cording to Greenough et al. (1987), experience-dependent systems are less sensitive to the age of developing organisms, and involve storage of information that is unique to individuals. In the storage process, ex-perience stimulates changes in synaptic efficacy or dendritic morphol-ogy as well as by formation of new connections in regions associated with the information-processing activity that caused their formation (Knudsen 1985).

In some cases, it appears that early neural connections will be lost regardless of whether appropriate experience is available or not. In the case of *transient neural connections,* however, experience can slow the rate of atrophy or even permanently stabilize these connections that otherwise would be completely eliminated (Frost 1989). Frost and Inno-centi (1986) investigated the role of early postnatal visual experience in the development of visual callosal connections. They found that in cats, "binocular visual deprivation . . . accentuates the normally oc-curring loss of juvenile callosal axons" (p. 260). Frost and Innocenti concluded that normal visual experience has a stabilizing influence on certain axons crossing at the corpus callosum. That is, visual cortex un-dergoes a reshaping postnatally where a paring down process occurs, an elimination of certain callosal connections present at birth. The re-

---

[3]There is a behavioral instantiation of experience expectancy that may be somewhat relevant to the phonetic development of human infants. The ability to localize sounds in space under normal circumstances is present by at least seven months (Perris and Clifton 1988). If unsupported by appropriate (binaural) experience, however, localization accu-racy declines, perhaps between four- and eight-years-of-age (Beggs and Foreman 1980).

distribution of axonal connections as the kitten matures appears to be based in part on the experience of vision.

Neoteny and Plasticity. Brain development in humans is affected by the environment over a longer period than is neural development in animals. The reasons for this extended period of cortical plasticity are associated with neoteny, the retention of juvenile somatic characteristics (Gould 1977a). At birth, human infants are incapable of locomotion, hunting, or foraging, as many other animals are perfectly equipped to do. The "down side" of neoteny is that the protection and care required for survival may not in all cases be forthcoming. But there also are huge advantages to neoteny, for if, as Gould (1977b) says, human infants are born nine months too soon, then their central nervous system is in a highly malleable and absorptive state during exposure to a variety of experiences. This plasticity may be due to protein molecules such as MAP2 (Aoki and Siekevitz 1988) and GAP-43 (Benowitz and Routtenberg 1987; Fishman in press), whose concentrations are greater during neural development and axonal regeneration.

In humans, because of congenital sensory deficits and techniques for measuring cortical activity, it is possible to study indirectly the effects of sensory deprivation upon brain development. Neville, Schmidt, and Kutas (1983) found that over temporal cortex, a region normally associated with auditory processing, visual peripheral stimulation evoked larger brain responses in congenitally deaf subjects than in hearing subjects. This work suggests that auditory deprivation does not prevent development of auditory cortex because visual stimulation—without competing audition—usurps that region of the brain for itself.

It appears that multiple sources of stimulation compete for neural capacity. Following unimodal sensory deprivation, there are two types of change. There is "compensatory hypertrophy," increased growth and activity of remaining sensory systems, which do not have to compete with the "undernourished" system. There also is early growth (experience-expectant, in Greenough's terms) in the "disconnected" area that is maintained by sensory functions that normally are handled in adjacent brain regions. Among the congenitally deaf, according to Neville (1991), both the anterior expansion into areas normally used for auditory processing and the increased activity in posterior areas could be accounted for by early visual afferents that are stabilized by visual experience when there is no competing input from the auditory modality.

Neural Effects of Self-Produced Stimulation

Evidence from a variety of research populations and domains suggests that neonates' early sensory and motor experience challenges the brain to develop the capacity for more complex behavior. In several reports, Dodwell, Timney, and Emerson (1976) and Timney, Emerson, and Dodwell (1979) describe experiments in which kittens were reared in total darkness until the end of their third month. For an hour each day, the animals were placed in an apparatus in which visual stimulation (vertical stripes) was available at the press of a bar. The authors found that at about the end of the second month (during the critical period for visual development), kittens began to press the bar with great frequency, and to continue to do so until the end of the experiment at 100 days. Figure 1 reveals that normally reared kittens did not press the bar to illuminate the visual pattern, but dark-reared kittens did.

In a second experiment, kittens were reared in normal light for a period and were light-deprived thereafter. As before, they were given an opportunity each day to press the bar for visual stimulation. It was

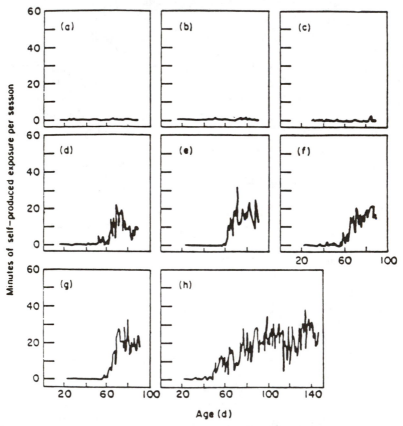

Figure 1.   Minutes of self-produced exposure per session (equal to minutes of bar pressing) by the normal (a–c) and dark-reared (d–h) kittens, as a function of age in days (from Timney, Emerson, and Dodwell 1979).

found that these kittens began bar pressing at about the same age as kittens in the first experiment. The stimulus seeking effect, then, was age dependent in these studies; it was not caused by previous deprivation but by the animals' maturational state and sensory experience at the time of test.

In an additional experiment in which stimulation involved either the visual display or several different types of auditory tones, dark-reared kittens pressed the bar selectively to obtain visual but not auditory stimulation. As is revealed by figure 2, the kittens rarely pressed the bar for tones, and because they had not been deprived of sound, their brains would not have needed any additional auditory stimulation. On some level, the kittens "seemed to know" what kinds of excitation their brains needed to develop; they worked only for the stimulation their brains required to reach capacity.

The infant's exposure to sound undoubtedly causes the elaboration of auditory cortical networks that will subsequently be needed for the processing of spoken language.[4] The effects of *vocal* stimulation upon brain development probably begin as early as vocalization is first experienced. On the purely receptive side, this may begin as early as the third trimester of pregnancy, when the mother's voice may be heard by the fetus (Birnholz and Benacerraf 1983; DeCasper and Spence 1986). On the expressive side, the first vocalization also is early, typically occurring at birth, but in some cases prior to birth.[5] What do neonatal and infant vocalization do for the development of vocal perceptual and motor capacity?

Do *humans* work for stimulation in order to "feed" developing areas of the brain; do human infants "know" what sensory nourishment their brains require to develop fully the capacity for behavior that evolutionary changes have provided for? If there is a human auditory parallel to the kitten's need for visual stimulation, we should expect hearing-deprived infants to work for auditory stimulation. If they do, we might be tempted to speculate that in vocalizing, infants foster the cerebral capacity to process auditory patterns; and that in babbling, infants develop the capacity of their brains to match ambient auditory patterns with those of their vocal tracts. According to this speculation, infants would *build* the capacity for spoken language with their own behavior.

---

[4]Confirming evidence for this is scarce; there seem to be no histological studies of congenitally deaf humans. On the behavioral side, there does exist a small amount of evidence suggesting that transient hearing loss in early childhood may impair later speech perception (Clarkson, Eimas, and Marean 1989).

[5]The very first vocalization may be produced by the fetus. Blair (1965) has reported that it is not uncommon, under certain circumstances, for the fetus to vocalize. This condition, termed *vagitus uterinus*, apparently comes about when the membrane ruptures and air suddenly rushes into the uterus.

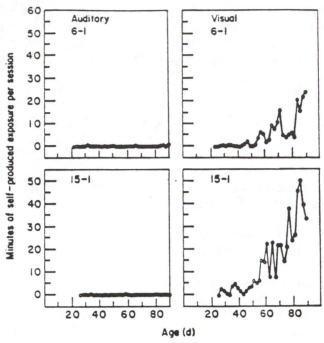

Figure 2.   Responses of two dark-reared kittens (6-1 and 15-1) for auditory (left panels) and visual (right panels) stimulation. Though the plots appear continuous, days on which visual input could be obtained alternated with "auditory" days (from Timney, Emerson, and Dodwell 1979).

One might guess that sound-deprived infants vocalize less than hearing infants, but this seems not to be the case. Lenneberg, Rebelsky, and Nichols (1965) taperecorded biweekly two small groups of infants over the first three months of life. One group consisted of 10 normally hearing infants being reared by their hearing parents. The other group contained six children whose parents were deaf. Five of these children had hearing, one was deaf. Two of the hearing children had an older, hearing sibling. Therefore, this second group contained three hearing children who were exposed mainly to their deaf (and essentially nonoral) parents, and their access to phonetic stimulation was documentably less than that of the children of hearing and speaking parents. Lenneberg, Rebelsky, and Nichols (1965) reported that the auditory deprived subjects cried, fussed, and cooed *just as frequently* as the children who were freely exposed to speech.

During at least the first year of life, deaf infants may *babble less*, i.e., produce fewer canonical syllables per utterance than normally hearing infants of the same age. However, there are indications that deaf infants may *vocalize more* than normally hearing infants, and perhaps that auditorily deprived humans do expend extra effort to get auditory stimulation. There are two relevant reports, although each contained just one auditory deprived subject. In Oller et al. (1985), it appeared that the congenitally deaf infant that was studied may have vocalized more freely than the 11 hearing infants, for in half-hour sessions, at 7 + months, the hearing infants produced from 33 to 68 utterances per session; in contrast, in four sessions at 8 + months, the deaf infant produced 76, 62, 75, and 90 utterances. The authors remarked that "we found no difficulty in obtaining a full sample from the deaf baby on each of four sessions" (p. 62).

Kent et al. (1987) studied twin boys from eight to twenty-four months of age. One of the twins had a measured hearing threshold of 45 dB at 250 Hz (with amplification) and wore amplification "during every waking hour." The hearing-impaired child, therefore, could hear the voices of other people as well as his own voice. The authors commented that " . . . he was a prolific vocalizer—sometimes producing more utterances within a recording session than the hearing twin" (p. 71).

These reports are suggestive. If infants vocalize to supply their brains with needed stimulation, we might expect at least a slight increase in the vocalization of hearing infants during times when environmental stimulation is merely less. In Jones and Moss (1971), two-week-old infants vocalized more frequently when alone than when an observer was present (even after "protest" vocalizations had been eliminated). Delack (1976) found that infants vocalized more frequently when they were alone than when their mothers or a stranger was in the room. This pattern was evident from the first observations at seven weeks. Both these ages precede the onset of vocal turn-taking, when infants might be expected to vocalize less in the presence of a speaking mother, but for different reasons. In future research of this kind, it will be interesting to see what differences in vocal structure or phonetic content occur in social and alone conditions.

Functional Effects of Self-Produced Stimulation

How do animals benefit "down the road" from the sight and sounds of their early motor activities? What harm is done when developing animals are *denied* the opportunity to hear the vocalizations of others, and of themselves? Several studies have deprived animals of self-hearing in an effort to investigate its role in vocal control or vocal learning.

First, we should note that both animals and neonatal humans *react* when their vocal feedback is tampered with. Buchwald and Shipley (1985) found that kittens deafened at the age of four weeks vocalized much more loudly than their hearing littermates. They also observed that 80 dB of white noise caused a 10 dB increase in the vocal intensity of kittens' vocalizations. Sinnott, Stebbins, and Moody (1975) found that in Old World monkeys, low-frequency noise (corresponding to the monkey's fundamental frequency range) increased vocal amplitude by about 2 dB for every 10 dB of masking noise, a magnitude that approximates the Lombard effect observed in humans. In humans, delayed auditory feedback causes significant reduction in cry duration at one week of age (Cullen et al. 1968).

In a study of vocal learning (Marler and Waser 1977), canaries were denied access to their own vocal output, as well as that of taped tutors, either temporarily (through intense masking noise) or permanently (through surgical deafening). Birds that received masking noise subsequently were exposed to taped songs; however they heard the songs at a reduced level, due to permanent threshold shifts caused by their earlier exposure to the masking noise. Birds receiving 40 days of masking (95 to 100 dB of continuous white noise) experienced threshold shifts of approximately 20 decibels; 200 days of noise shifted thresholds between 50 and 60 dB. It is relevant to the work on deaf human infants that the birds in this latter group still

> . . . had sufficient auditory feedback from their song to increase its complexity quite significantly. Whereas in the first season the syllable repertoire was not significantly different from that of deaf birds, in the second season it came close to matching the repertoire of birds reared in noise until weaning and then isolated from adult song. . . . It is intriguing that the *improvement was delayed until the second season*. The explanation for this is unclear (Marler and Waser 1977, p. 14, emphasis added).

Canaries are not the only animals whose vocal development is delayed by hearing loss. Hearing-impaired human infants do not begin to babble until one or more months after normally hearing infants do (Oller and Eilers 1988), and when they do babble, their repertoire of consonant-like sounds is much smaller than that of hearing infants (Stoel-Gammon and Otomo 1986). The literature also hints at a similar effect in children who cannot hear the voices of others because of environmental phonetic deprivation. Dennis (1941) reported on twin girls who were raised with reduced exposure to the voices of others, and their onset of babbling seemingly was delayed.

What happens to the vocal learning of an animal that has heard only its own vocalizations? Experimental manipulations in songbirds provide some clues. In the typical study, sparrows or canaries are reared in social isolation and exposed to no song (or deafened) or in the control case, to audiotapes of conspecific (or heterospecific) song. The evidence (Konishi 1965; Marler and Tamura 1964; Marler 1975; Marler and Waser 1977) suggests that while exposure to taped (conspecific) tutors produces well-formed syllables and organized melodies, no exposure to taped tutors produces small repertoires and anomalies (but still a very adult-like song). Moreover, total deafness is more deleterious to song learning than is isolation rearing (i.e., hearing of only one's own voice). In other words, self-hearing appears to facilitate vocal development. Konishi stated that "however the pattern of a song heard during the critical period is stored in the central nervous system, auditory feedback is indispensable for its reproduction in the corresponding vocal pattern" (1965, p. 772). If there are benefits to hearing one's own vocalization, what kind of phonological development might we expect of a child who can hear others vocalize but not herself?

We have reported elsewhere (Locke and Pearson 1990) the early vocal history and syllabic analysis of a girl who was aphonic from 5 to 20 months of age. When we first began to observe Jenny systematically at 17 months, she was able to vocalize for brief intervals (due to the growth of her trachea), and on rare occasions did so. Jenny was observed in eight sessions that occurred during the period of Jenny's tracheostomy and four sessions that took place within the month following decannulation.

Figure 3 shows the number of canonical syllables per utterance using Oller's (1986) measurement criteria. Note that in all sessions before and after decannulation the incidence of canonical syllable production approached zero. Even by the end of her 21st month, Jenny's ratio of canonical syllables to utterances still had not reached 0.2. This ratio—twenty syllables per hundred utterances—distinguishes hear-

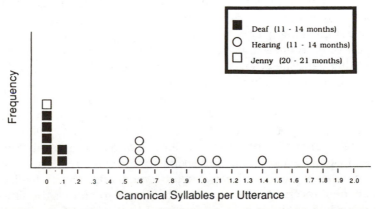

Figure 3. Ratio of canonical syllables per utterance in eleven- to fourteen-month-old deaf and hearing infants (adapted from Figure 2 in Oller and Eilers 1988); comparable data from Jenny at twenty to twenty-one months may be seen in the extreme lefthand corner. A cut-off of 0.20 effectively distinguishes hearing from deaf infants, and is used as the criterion for onset of babbling (from Locke and Pearson 1990).

ing persons from deaf persons, and it is considered the minimum criterion for the canonical babbling stage (Oller and Eilers 1988). Additionally, although Jenny knew many words, she did not plunge into speech, and for several months after decannulation this normally sociable child was linguistically inactive. We conclude that Jenny's inability to hear herself vocalize during the babbling period caused a sigthetic had worn off, the amphibians were slightly delayed in the develnificant delay in her production of canonical syllables and speech.

MOVEMENT-PRODUCED STIMULATION: DEVELOPMENT OF A VOCAL GUIDANCE SYSTEM

At least since the classic experiments by Carmichael (1926, 1927) there has been interest in the effect of the environment on the development of motor control. In an early stage of development, Carmichael temporarily anesthetized frogs and salamanders. Later, when the anesopment of swimming. This suggested to Carmichael that motor development was not entirely maturational, and that "the excitation and response of the elements of the neuromuscular system is itself a part of the growth process" (1926, p. 56). More recently, Changeux (1985) has summarized experiments in which chick embryos were peripherally paralyzed for a short time. These chicks later revealed a decreased number of motoneurons in the spinal cord. In other research, Johnson et al. (1972) found that if one leg of a baby opossum is cut off when the baby has just entered his mother's pouch, neural columns in the cortex that would control the digits on the amputated limb fail to develop. Greenough, Larson, and Withers (1985) trained rats to use one paw or both paws to reach for food. Postmortem brain studies revealed that dendrites were more highly branched in "both paw" animals; ipsilateral branching was less than contralateral branching in "one paw" animals. These studies suggest that simple levels of physical activity beget enhanced neural capacity for more complex forms of motor behavior. It appears, then, that early physical activity helps to expand the organism's capacity for movement, and that early exposure to speech fosters development of the capacity for perceptual processing.

But what of the *hook-up* between movement and sensory feedback? What benefits accrue to the organism that is able to process the sensory signals provided by his own movements? In a series of experiments, Held and his associates found that denying animals access to sensory feedback from their motor activity reduces the ability to use such information in the guidance of movements, and by inference, prevents the establishment of long-term storage of motor-sensory correlations. In one experiment (Held and Hein 1963) pairs of kittens were dark-reared for a period and then placed in a gondola situated at the center of a circular room with striped walls. By walking, the experimental or active kitten was able to rotate the gondola and thus to "produce" visual stimulation. The control kitten was pulled passively through the same space; this passive animal therefore received access to exactly the same visual stimulation. Motor coordination tests indicated that the active kittens were considerably more likely to predicate their movement upon available visual information than were the passive kittens.

In later experiments, fundamentally the same result was observed in other neonatally deprived kittens (Hein and Held 1967) and monkeys (Held and Bauer 1967), as well as adult humans participating in a variety of "rearrangement" experiments (where, for example, prisms would be used to alter visual-motor relations; Held and Bossom 1967). In an attempt to account for such findings Held (1961) offered a unified model that, after von Holst (1954), recognized the distinct contributions to motor activity of reafferent and exafferent sensation. Reafference refers to stimulation that varies with the natural movements of the organism; exafference denotes stimulation that is independent of such movements.

Held's model, reproduced in figure 4, works essentially as follows. Efferent signals from motor activity, and afferent signals from the visual (or other) sensations associated with that activity, are both referred to as Correlation Storage. The Correlation Storage

> retains traces or previous combinations of concurrent efferent and re-afferent signals. The currently monitored efferent signal is presumed to select the trace combination containing the identical efferent part and to activate the re-afferent trace combined with it. The resulting revived re-

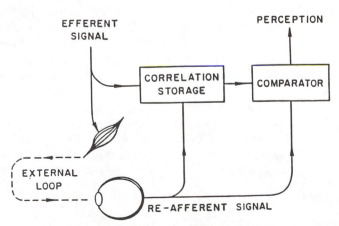

Figure 4.   Model of the process whereby efferent sensations are coordinated with self-produced afferent feedback in sensory motor learning (from Held 1961).

afferent signal is sent to the Comparator for comparison with the current re-afferent signal (Held 1961, p. 30).

We think vocalization may work approximately like other forms of self-produced stimulation, and we suggest later that babbling—beyond certain effects described previously (Locke 1986)—supplies the human infant with a phonetic guidance system that aids sound learning and facilitates the development of spoken language.

PHONOLOGY AS PHENOTYPE

We have been discussing the role of experience in neural and functional development, but what of genetic effects? Is there a demonstrable genetic basis for language learning ability, including developmental language disorders? The phenotype for *specific language impairment* includes a measurably below-age linguistic development in the face of normal (peripheral) speech and hearing mechanisms, intelligence, emotional adjustment, and exposure to language. Additionally, the profile of specific language impairment may include a high incidence of males and of nondextral laterality (Luchsinger and Arnold 1965). Although behavioral genetics studies are just beginning, there already is evidence of a significant aggregation of specific language impairment in families (Tallal, Ross, and Curtiss 1989; Tomblin 1989; Lewis, Ekelman, and Aram 1989; Parlour and Broen 1989). There also is evidence for genetic effects among normally developing children. In a word production study, Locke and Mather (1989) found a higher concordance for phonological pattern in monozygotic than dizygotic twins.

This work carries powerful neurological implications with regard to etiology of developmental language disorder. Consider for a moment the case of developmental dyslexia. This very focal problem with printed language is associated with underlying difficulties in *phonological* processing (Catts 1989). It is, therefore, of interest that dyslexia has a genetic (Smith 1986) and a neurologic basis, with evidence of more nearly symmetrical *plana temporalia* across the two hemispheres (Geschwind and Galaburda 1987). In light of these and other findings above, we would not be surprised if neuroimaging techniques were eventually to reveal a higher than population incidence of hemispheric symmetry in phonological areas of the brain among specifically language-impaired children.

The Neurology of Phonetic Action Patterns

We argued earlier that infants produce a repertoire of speech-like movements that have the characteristics of relatively closed, invariant, action patterns. We suggested that the capacity to control these move-ments was jointly produced by genetic and environmental factors, and that fetal and extrauterine environments play a role in the induction of neural capacity for *motor* control. Of course, if perception and produc-tion are controlled by the same neural structures, merely hearing speech could, in principle, stimulate development of motor command centers.

Several studies (Wada, Clarke, and Hamm 1975; Witelson and Pallie 1973) indicate that a structure associated with language, the left planum temporalis, is larger than the right planum at or prior to birth. The anatomical groundwork for left hemisphere superiority in lan-guage processing may, therefore, exist well before the acquisition of language. And, indeed, evoked potential studies have found exagge-rated left hemisphere responses to speech in preterm infants, tested at 36 weeks conceptional age, and at birth (Molfese and Molfese 1979, 1980). Similar effects have been found at three to four months, using dichotic listening procedures (Best, Hoffman, and Glanville 1982; Glanville, Best, and Levinson 1977). There seem to be no data, at this age, as to whether there is left hemisphere superiority in the *production* of speech sounds.

Presumably these early effects of activity upon motor cortex occur just before and after birth. What about later effects? We noted earlier that infants seem to begin babbling abruptly, typically between six and seven months of age. Significantly, this seems to coincide with the beginning of rhythmic hand activity and the onset of one-handed reaching (Ramsay 1984; Thelen 1981). Because in Ramsay's elicitation experiment the reaching hand was almost exclusively the right one, his results suggest that the onset of babbling may coincide with the first behavioral expression of left hemisphere control over motor activity. This suggests that babbling and speech are controlled by the same cere-bral hemisphere. A hint that this might be so may be found in Fogel and Hannan's (1985) naturalistic study of nine- to fifteen-week-old in-fants. These infants displayed significantly more right-handed "point-ing" following mouth movements, and significantly more left-handed "pointing" following vocalization (which at nine to fifteen weeks would contain few oral closures).

What neurological developments might account for the co-occur-rence of babbling, manual laterality, and rhythmic hand activity at ap-proximately the same age? Let us examine the relevant literature, some of it also reviewed in Locke (in press). Goldman-Rakic (1987) has found peaks of brain growth in monkeys that coincide with cognitive devel-opments, so it is reasonable to suppose that the human infant's brain also experiences growth spurts (perhaps at about six to seven months) that coincide with the onset of babbling.

At a gross level of analysis, data reported by Winick (1968) indicate that brain weight and several other measures increase sharply, in normally developing infants, between five and one-half and six and one-half months. In a detailed study of two infants over the first year of life, Lampl and Emde (1983) found that the last period of substantial increase in head circumference occurred at about six to seven months. Winick and Rosso (1969) report that increases in head circumference normally begin to taper off at about six months. Conel (1939–1967) reported cortical thickness data on humans from birth to 80 months of age. His data show sudden increases in the thickness of temporal cortex throughout the first year of life, and there is a distinct peak in the rate of growth of motor cortex at approximately six months. Data from Yakovlev and Lecours (1967 and Lecours 1975) suggest that intra- and interhemispheric cortical association bundles begin to myelinate at about five to six months postnatally. Neuroanatomy at this level is too gross to be related to specific patterns of phonetic behavior, of course, but synchrony of discrete "milestones" in the two domains promises that with additional research such interconnections eventually will be identified.

At a more specific level of analysis, Simonds and Scheibel (1989)—in a histological study—counted and measured the length of dendrites in the left and right speech-motor areas (*pars opercularis* and *triangularis*) and motor areas (the foot of the precentral gyrus; the orofacial zone of the primary motor area) bilaterally in 17 children from three months to seventy-two months. Dendrite location was categorized, along the dendritic spine, as proximal (the three dendrites closest to the soma) and distal (the three dendrites beyond the proximal ones). Simonds and Scheibel found that at three months, there were not differences in the number of left or right dendrites in motor and speech-motor areas. However, at five to six months, there were more distal dendrites in the left hemisphere both in motor and speech-motor areas. In length analyses, this trend toward left hemisphere superiority was first evident at twelve to fifteen months.

The development of these neural asymmetries heralds the emergence of phonological capacity. For during the same interval that dendrites become disproportionately longer in speech regions of the left hemisphere, infants' spontaneous behavior begins to evidence lateralized brain function in conjunction with language development. What facts support this? First, a recent report indicates that at thirteen to fourteen months, infants in a two-choice looking task began to gaze more often to the right than to the left (Mount et al. 1989). By itself, this fact might say little about the capacity for speech. But it has been observed that five- to six-month-olds look longer at filmed faces whose visible articulations match the utterance that is heard (e.g., [mama], [zuzu]) but *only if the infant is looking to the right* (MacKain et al. 1983).

Second, in Mount et al. the correlation between percentage fixation time to the right and mean length of utterance increased during sixteen to twenty-one months, reaching a peak at 20 months (r = .87).

These brain-behavior correlations suggest that cortical mechanisms for the control of speech develop just before the first expression of that control in babbling. Emergent control, of course, also is implied by behaviors themselves, as revealed in the developmental sequencing of vocal stages (Kent 1981) and the surface characteristics of vocalizations within each stage (Oller 1980). For example, in the child's transition from simple repetition (e.g., [dadadadada]) to variegated babbling, there is greater intermixing of movements with different articulatory sources (e.g., [badabepita]). As indicated earlier, we think babbling may stimulate some additional brain growth of the type that is needed for vocal learning.

VOCAL LEARNING: THE APPLICATION OF PHONOLOGICAL CAPACITY

Up to this point we have discussed the emergence of phonological capacity in human infants. This capacity can be revealed by the experimental procedures used in perception experiments, but it usually is expressed naturally for the first time when infants begin vocal learning. An early indication that vocal learning may be about to start is the occurrence of turn taking.

Turn Taking

Kuhl and Meltzoff (1982) reported the results of an experiment in which eighteen- to twenty-week-old infants watched a film of a woman producing isolated vowel sounds ([i] or [a]) at the rate of one every three seconds. To the experimenters' surprise, many of the infants joined in with the speaker on the film, responding echoically in almost perfect time. Such vocal turn taking between infants and their mothers has been observed under naturalistic circumstances by several investigators (Bateson 1975; Beebe et al. 1988; Stern et al. 1975). Significantly, Ginsburg and Kilbourne (1988) report that the cessation of vocal overlapping, and the beginning of vocal alternation with adult speakers may occur at twelve- to eighteen-weeks-of-age.

Congruent evidence for turn taking may be found in a report by Berger and Cunningham (1983). In normally developing infants, they found that vocalization decreased sharply between the sessions held at thirteen- to sixteen-weeks- and nineteen- to twenty-weeks-of-age. From this time on (observations continued until twenty-three to twenty-four weeks), infants decreasingly vocalized when their mothers spoke and increasingly vocalized when their mothers were silent.

Because retarded children typically do not develop language normally, it would be of interest to know whether their tendency to imitate vocally also is different, as one might expect. Fortunately, Berger and Cunningham also included in their study a group of infants with Down syndrome. These infants' vocal clashing very sharply *increased* during the interval when clashing declined in the normally developing infants. This finding, depicted in figure 5, is important for it suggests that vocal turn taking may facilitate development of spoken language.

It seems that when adults respond contingently (e.g., with a phonetically similar form), during the infant's turn, his vocal output may become more speech-like. Bloom, Russell, and Wassenberg (1987) found that contingent responding by adults increased the ratio of syllabic to vocalic sounds in three-month-old infants. Veneziano (1988) found that maternal echoing encouraged infants to repeat their own forms, or perhaps to accommodate slightly to the sounds of the mother.

Is Vocal Imitation "Innate"?

Vocalization and babbling can be *triggered*, and it seems that speech may well be the best trigger. First, there is now a fair amount of evidence that neonates imitate silent movements or configurations of the mouth (Meltzoff 1986; Meltzoff and Moore 1977). Some imitated move-

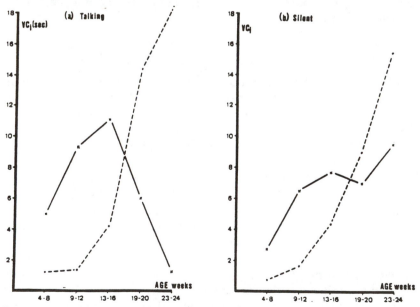

Figure 5. Total time spent vocalizing by normally developing (x——x) and Down syndrome (•----•) infants during sessions when the mother talked or was silent.

ments—protrusion of the lips and tongue, mouth opening—are exaggerations of movements associated with speaking. Second, there are the results of Kuhl and Meltzoff (1982). As indicated earlier, two groups of eighteen- to twenty-week-old infants watched a film of a woman repetitively articulating [i] and [a]. While the film played, one group of infants heard the same vowel that the woman visibly articulated in the film, or a different vowel. The other group of infants heard control stimuli that contained no formants but did have similar durations and amplitude contours. Interestingly, infants who heard the intact vowels echoed the woman in almost perfect time (i.e., at about the same rate) during the interstimulus intervals, and also seemed to imitate spectral properties of the vowels. However, infants who heard the degraded vowels remained silent during the film. In other words, at least while watching a film of a woman speaking, the sounds of speech triggered echoic behavior in young infants. This was confirmed in a later study that included additional data (Kuhl and Meltzoff 1988). In this study, moreover, when asked to identify echoic responses as [i] or [a], in the case of some infants the listeners' choices matched the stimulus on about 90% of the trials. It is not known, however, if the imitations were on target because infants' imitated aural cues that they heard or merely vocalized in synchrony with the woman while also imitating the oral configurations that they saw.

Dodd (1972) reported that social and vocal stimulation elicited more infant vocalization than social stimulation alone; these combined sources of stimulation also elicited more consonant utterances and more long utterances. Kagan (1970) found that eight-month-olds were unusually quiet when listening to a recording of a man reading sentences. "When it stopped," according to Kagan, "babbling began, as though the vocalizations were released by the processing of the sounds" (p. 338).

Except for isolated cases (Sweeney 1973), human infants show little tendency to imitate nonhuman sounds. What, then, motivates eighteen-week-old infants who see and hear a woman producing isolated vowels to chime in spontaneously, matching temporal and spectral properties of the stimuli? Why, in other words, do infants imitate conspecific sounds—human speech—and why do the sounds of speech, at certain points in the development of infants, seem to trigger vocal imitation?

Feedback

According to Fry (1966), the babbling of human infants is responsible for "the establishment of the auditory feedback loop. As sound-producing movements are repeated and repeated," Fry said, "a strong link is forged between tactual and kinesthetic impressions and the auditory sensations that the child receives from his own utterances" (p. 189). Kuhl and Meltzoff (1988) state that infants do two things when they imitate vocally:

> They compare the auditory results of their own vocal maneuvers with the auditory results . . . produced by someone else. That is, they make an intramodal auditory-auditory match; and second, they develop a set of auditory-articulatory mapping rules that allow them to make adjustments in production to get closer to the auditory target they wish to achieve (p. 254).

Babbling, then, arises in advance of speech and continues until a phonetic guidance system has begun to function. How does that guidance system work? We believe the Held model seen earlier (figure 4) may be treated as an *animal model for babbling*, and that with minimal adaptation it can account for infant vocal learning of the kind that occurs during and after the babbling-to-speech transition. In Held's model, as in the classic servomodel of Fairbanks (1954), motor commands are stored, along with their perceived sensory product, in a Comparator. In the speech case, when an infant engages in articulatory activity, the auditory correlates of his articulations are automatically retrieved from memory and compared to what actually is heard. As a consequence, the infant is able to use auditory information to guide vocal and articulatory activity, and to select the articulatory activity most likely to correspond to the sound patterns of perceived words. What is crucial to this model is a mechanism (Held's "Correlation Storage") that binds movements to their sensory feedback. We think reduplicated babbling helps to activate this mechanism, and that more complex phonetic forms represent a more elaborate application of the infant's vocal guidance system.

Consider, in this context, the study of Belmore et al. (1973). They studied the effects of delayed auditory feedback on several vocal parameters in an effort to estimate how closely infants monitored their voices auditorily. Preverbal infants in the sample, who were six- to ten-months-of-age, were placed in one of two categories according to their degree of vocal sophistication. In eight subjects, fewer than 25% of spontaneous utterances included CV sequences involving consonants other than [h] and glottal stops. In three subjects, 34 to 60% of utterances included CV syllables with these supraglottal characteristics. It is of interest to note that delayed feedback significantly altered utterance duration in only one of the eight less vocally sophisticated subjects, but in all three of the more vocally advanced infants. Although the number of subjects was small, these results support the hypothesized link between vocal monitoring and phonetic complexity.

To summarize, the infant may well have two complementary sources of information on the articulatory-auditory associations that are needed for phonetic learning. One source is supplied when the infant *observes* speech activity, and thereby learns associations between visible lip configurations and sound patterns in the speech of others, the infant already being aware of both types of cues at or soon after birth. It also is possible that information in this source is neonatally present and is triggered or activated by early sensory experience. The second source is supplied when the infant *participates* in the production of speech-like activity, hears the audible product of its movements, and learns associations between articulation and sound.

Vocal Imitation and Phonological Continuity

In structured elicitation tasks, Snow (1989) observed the frequency of vocal and verbal, gestural, and object-mediated imitation in one hundred normally developing infants. Observations were made at fourteen months and at twenty months. Snow found that at fourteen months, vocal imitativeness varied from child to child, but was not correlated with gestural or object-mediated imitativeness. This and other published findings of like nature suggested to Snow that vocal imitation is "domain specific."

It is of interest to note that vocal imitation at fourteen months was correlated moderately with verbal imitation at twenty months. Moreover, vocal imitativeness at fourteen months correlated significantly with the number of nouns and the number of verbs produced, the total productive vocabulary, and the ratio of words produced to words comprehended at twenty months. These correlations were specific to vocal imitativeness; no correlations of similar direction or magnitude were found for gestural and object-mediated imitation.

Snow's (1989) analysis of individual subjects suggested that children who were less vocally imitative at fourteen months also had smaller vocabularies at twenty months. It also seemed that infant "non-imitators may have more restricted phonological systems . . . " as child speakers (p. 87). Children's vocal imitativeness at fourteen months was correlated with maternal imitativeness of the child's words and vocalizations.

To what do imitative children apply their tendency to copy; what is *in* their phonetic environment? We suggested earlier that the child's linguistic environment contains "genetic" information inasmuch as adult speech preserves many of the same biases as the infant's developing vocal-motor system. Recently, Locke analyzed the initial consonants of, words spoken by five mothers to their children, whose ages ranged from eighteen to thirty months. A manner of articulation analysis of all consonant singles revealed that glides or voiced stops were the most frequent class of sounds produced by all mothers, and nasals and liquids were the least commonly produced classes of word-initial consonants. The coefficient of concordance was a highly reliable .95.

We suggested above that for physiological reasons, children may not *need* to hear very many productions of the developmentally early stops and glides in order to master their expression (relative to the developmentally late fricatives and affricates) but they will hear more of the early sounds in the speech of adults. Developmentally, these confounds between factors that are internal to the child and factors that are external to the child may facilitate the emergence of words. Theoretically, the "logical" distinction between phonological development and phonetic development is almost completely obliterated by these same confounds (for a broader discussion of this, see Locke 1983b).

Presumably, imitation is the process that turns vocal play into vocal learning. But the infant's inherent phonetic dispositions continue to hold sway. Qualitatively, there is topographic similarity in the phonetic patterns of early and more advanced stages of babbling (Oller et al. 1976; Emmorey 1985), which in turn resemble the patterns of child speech at the syllabic and segmental levels. Where syllable structure is concerned, there is an exceedingly strong relationship between babble and early speech. Kent and Bauer (1985) found that in the babble of five thirteen-month-old infants, CV syllables occurred with over 10 times the frequency of VC syllables. Stoel-Gammon (1985) found that in the speech of fifteen-month-olds, word-initial consonants were nearly six times more plentiful than word-final ones, a trend that weakens with chronological age but never completely disappears (Locke 1983a). The core of consonant-like sounds ([h, w, j, p, b, m, t, d, n, k, g]), which accounts for over 90% of the consonant-like segments in babbling (Locke 1983a), also accounts for about 90% of the sounds in children's first 50 words (Locke 1989). According to data in Stoel-Gammon (1985), all the repertoire sounds above were present in at least half of the two-year-olds in her study, except for [j], a finding confirmed generally by Vihman and her associates (Vihman 1986, 1988; Vihman et al. 1985).

There are quantitative relationships as well. Marler and Peters (1982) observed a positive correlation between repertoire size in infancy and adulthood in the swamp sparrow, and a similar relationship has been observed in human infants. Vihman (1986) found size of consonant inventory in the initial lexicon of twelve-month-olds to correlate positively with their phonological development at the age of three years. Likewise, Menyuk, Liebergott, and Schultz (1986) found positive correlations between degree of syllabicity in vocal play at twelve months and word-final consonant production in speech at twenty-nine months.

Several case studies suggest continuity between prelinguistic behavior and language development. Speidel (1989) anecdotally described two children, Sally and Mark: "Sally . . . began with repetitive babbling around 7 months and began to speak in words when she was a little over 1 year old. From the beginning her speech was fairly intelligible. . . . In contrast, Mark showed no repetitive babbling and spoke nearly unintelligibly until he was over 2 years old" (p. 202). In a more systematic investigation, Stoel-Gammon (1989) found that nested in a larger sample of thirty-four children were two whose early phonetic development was atypical. One child produced few canonical babbles from nine to twenty-one months. The other had an unusual pattern of sound preferences in his babbling. At twenty-four months, the words of both subjects were produced with a more limited phonetic repertoire and with simpler syllable shapes, compared to peers.[6]

FROM VOCAL LEARNING TO PHONOLOGY

Some phonologists believe that "biological models" depict the child as a passive organism. However, the child in our model is continuously active at every stage of the expansion and application of his neural capability for spoken language. This activity takes the form of attending to sensory stimulation, as infants evidently do when they exchange vocal "turns" with adults. It includes the production of vocal stimulation by the infant itself. From self-produced stimulation, the child derives production experience and a store of motor-auditory equivalences that enable the expression of internal representations and aural guidance of articulatory movements.

There are indications that Fry (1966) was right when he said babbling is a form of motor practice for speech. First, Thelen (1981) has observed that stereotypic, nongoal-directed repetitions of a motor act tend to decline as voluntary control over that movement is acquired. This general principle may apply to babbling, which is a repetitive motor activity (Bickley, Lindblom, and Roug 1986; Kent and Bauer 1985); occasionally, it is even practiced silently (Roug, Landberg, and Lund-

---

[6]Continuity has clinical implications, including the ability to predict abnormal or delayed development (and therefore to arrange for early intervention). Jensen et al. (1988) followed Danish infants longitudinally who were or were not developing normally (based on Apgar scores, birthweight, and presence or absence of neonatal cerebral symptoms). During the first year, at-risk subjects produced significantly fewer consonant-like sounds and reduplicated syllables than did the children who were judged to be without risk. Some five years later, a much higher proportion of the at-risk children also scored below age level on a language test.

berg 1989). Second, there is evidence that babbling continues into the second year of life, when young children are beginning to master speech articulation, and does not cease with the development of an initial lexicon (Locke 1983a).

Extrapolations from the animal evidence of Held and others, reviewed earlier, suggest that Kuhl and Meltzoff (1988) were correct in suggesting that babbling encourages development of articulatory-auditory mapping rules. Merely hearing others speak is worth something, merely engaging in oral-motor activity undoubtedly has developmental value, but the hearing of *one's own* articulations clearly is important to the formation of a phonetic guidance system. Our tracheostomized subject, Jenny, lacked this opportunity and paid a developmental price for her aphonia.

The development of cognition cannot be studied fruitfully outside a biological framework. "A 'blank slate,' " according to Cosmides and Tooby (1987), "will stay forever blank: Without innate cognitive mechanisms, learning is impossible" (p. 291). Mayr (1976) observed that even in open behavior programs, "certain types of information are more easily incorporated than others" (p. 698). Animal research suggests that "innate" predispositions (activated or maintained by environmental stimulation) bias organisms to pay especial attention to certain sensory patterns and, therefore, to learn particularly about those things (Locke 1990).

The developmentally more valid question, according to Marler (1990), is not whether some material is learned or "innate," but how "innate" mechanisms and experience produce learning. Where oral language is concerned, Marler (1975) suggested that there are "innate but modifiable templates for certain speech sounds [which] focus the infant's attention on a class of external stimuli appropriate for social responsiveness" (p. 390). This class of external stimuli includes, one must presume, vowels, consonants, syllable shapes, and patterns of loudness, pitch, and duration. Within that class, there are salience relations. Kuhl and Miller (1982) found that when infants are presented with contrasts between different pitch contours *or* different vowels, they discriminate each with relative ease. However, when confronted with contrasts involving pitch contour *and* vowel, the vocalic contrast overrides pitch contour. This suggests that infants are biased toward vocalic contrasts, which is adaptive because all languages have vowels, although fewer than half the world's languages systematically contrast pitch contour at the segmental level (Ruhlen 1976).

In these pages, readers will not encounter a new model of phonetic learning. However, we have presented a model of the *empowerment* of the child's capacity of phonetic learning. Infants may also come equipped with articulatory and auditory templates of a sort, the merger and modification of which may be fostered by observation of speech activity in others. But the learning of speech also is facilitated by active articulatory practice with auditory self-monitoring. As Studdert-Kennedy (1976) said, "it is precisely to exploration of its own vocal tract and to discovery of its own patterns of muscular action that the infant's motor learning must be directed" (p. 282). Presumably, this leads to modification of prelinguistic oral-motor targets, as well as the establishment of additional linkage between auditory and articulatory domains.

We leave the human infant with a faculty for phonology and a set of cognitive operations for vocal learning. He and she will go on to exercise that capability, and those operations, in the acquisition of at least one spoken language. As children they will gather up a lexicon, discover the phoneme and identify the organization of a sound system. They will learn morphological rules and acquire a syntax. But the possibility of this, and its nature, will be determined by the child's neural capacity for phonology, and therefore by the experiences and activities and constitutional biases that conspired to produce that capacity.

REFERENCES

Aoki, C., and Siekevitz, P. 1988. Plasticity in brain development. *Scientific American* 256:56–64.

Aslin, R. N., and Pisoni, D. B. 1980. Some developmental processes in speech perception. In *Child Phonology, Vol. II, Perception* eds. G. H. Yeni-Komshian, J. F. Kavanagh, and C. A. Ferguson. New York: Academic Press.

Barlow, G. W. 1977. Modal action patterns. In *How Animals Communicate* ed. T. A. Sebeok. Bloomington: Indiana University Press.

Bateson, M. C. 1975. Mother-infant exchanges: The epigenesis of conversational interaction. *Annals of the New York Academy of Sciences* 263:101–113.

Beebe, B., Alson, D., Jaffe, J., Feldstein, S., and Crown, C. 1988. Vocal congruence in mother-infant play. *Journal of Psycholinguistic Research* 17:245–59.

Beggs, W. D. A., and Foreman, D. L. 1980. Sound localization and early binaural experience in the deaf. *British Journal of Audiology* 14:41–48.

Belmore, N. F., Kewley-Port, D., Mobley, R. L., and Goodman, V. E. 1973. The development of auditory feedback monitoring: Delayed auditory feedback studies on the vocalizations of children aged six months to 19 months. *Journal of Speech and Hearing Research* 16:709–720.

Bel'tyukov, V. I., and Salakhova, A. D. 1973. Babbling in the hearing child. *Voprosy Psikhologii* 2:587–605.

Benowitz, L. I., and Routtenberg, A. 1987. A membrane phosphoprotein associated with neural development, axonal regeneration, phospholipid metabolism, and synaptic plasticity. *Trends in Neuroscience* 10:527–32.

Berger, J., and Cunningham, C. C. 1983. Development of early vocal behaviors and interactions in Down's syndrome and nonhandicapped infant-mother pairs. *Developmental Psychology* 19:322–31.

Best, C., Hoffman, H., and Glanville, B. 1982. Development of infant ear asymmetries for speech. *Perception and Psychophysics* 31:75–85.

Best, C. T., McRoberts, G. W., and Sithole, N. M. 1988. Examination of perceptual reorganization for nonnative speech contrasts: Zulu click discrimination by English-speaking adults and infants. *Journal of Experimental Psychology: Human Perception and Performance* 14:345–60.

Bickley, C., Lindblom, B., and Roug, L. 1986. Acoustic measures of rhythm in infants' babbling, or "All God's children got rhythm." *Proceedings of the 12th International Congress on Acoustics.*

Birnholz, J. C., and Benacerraf, B. R. 1983. The development of human fetal hearing. *Science* 222:516–18.

Blair, R. G. 1965. Vagitus uterinus: Crying in utero. *Lancet* 11:1164–1165.

Bloom, K., Russell, A., and Wassenberg, K. 1987. Turn taking affects the quality of infant vocalizations. *Journal of Child Language* 14:211–27.

Boysson-Bardies, B., Halle, P., Sagart, L., and Durand, C. 1989. A crosslinguistic investigation of vowel formants in babbling. *Journal of Child Language* 16:1–18.

Buchwald, J. S., and Shipley, C. 1985. A comparative model of infant cry. In *Infant Crying* eds. B. M. Lester and C. F. Z. Boukydis. New York: Plenum.

Burnham, D. K. 1986. Developmental loss of speech perception: Exposure to and experience with a first language. *Applied Psycholinguistics* 7:207–240.

Carmichael, L. 1926. The development of behavior in vertebrates experimentally removed from the influence of external stimulation. *Psychological Review* 33:51–58.

Carmichael, L. 1927. A further study of the development of behavior in vertebrates experimentally removed from the influence of external stimulation. *Psychological Review* 34:34–47.

Carr, J. 1953. An investigation of the spontaneous speech sounds of five-year-old deaf-born children. *Journal of Speech and Hearing Disorders* 18:22–29.

Catts, H. W. 1989. Phonological processing deficits and reading disabilities. In *Reading Disabilities: A Developmental Language Perspective* eds. A. G. Kamhi and H. W. Catts. Boston: Little, Brown and Company.

Changeux, J.-P. 1985. Remarks on the complexity of the nervous system and its ontogenesis. In *Neonate Cognition: Beyond the Blooming Buzzing Confusion* eds. J. Mehler and R. Fox. Hillsdale, NJ: Lawrence Erlbaum Associates.

Changeux, J.-P., and Danchin, A. 1976. Selective stabilization of developing synapses as a mechanism for specification of neuronal networks. *Nature* 264:705–712.

Clarkson, R. L., Eimas, P. D., and Marean, G. C. 1989. Speech perception in children with histories of recurrent otitis media. *Journal of the Acoustical Society of America* 85:926–33.

Conel, J. 1939–1967. *The Postnatal Development of the Human Cerebral Cortex.* Vols. I–VIII. Cambridge, MA: Harvard University Press.

Cosmides, L., and Tooby, J. 1987. From evolution to behavior: Evolutionary psychology as the missing link. In *The Latest on the Best: Essays on Evolution and Optimality* ed. J. Dupre. Cambridge, MA: MIT Press.

Cowan, W. M., Fawcett, J. W., O'Leary, D. D. M., and Stanfield, B. B. 1984. Regressive events in neurogenesis. *Science* 225:1258–1265.

Cullen, J. K., Fargo, N., Chase, R. A., and Baker, P. 1968. The development of auditory feedback monitoring: I. Delayed auditory feedback studies on infant cry. *Journal of Speech and Hearing Research* 11:85–93.

DeCasper, A., and Spence, M. 1986. Prenatal maternal speech influences newborns' perception of speech sounds. *Infant Behavior and Development* 9:133–50.

Delack, J. B. 1976. Aspects of infant speech development in the first year of life. *Canadian Journal of Linguistics* 21:17–37.

Dennis, W. 1941. Infant development under conditions of restricted practice of minimum social stimulation. *Genetic Psychology Monographs* 23:143–89.

Dodd, B. J. 1972. Comparison of babbling patterns in normal and Down-syndrome infants. *Journal of Mental Deficiency Research* 16:35–40.

Dodwell, P. C., Timney, B. N., and Emerson, V. F. 1976. Development of visual stimulus-seeking in dark-reared kittens. *Nature* 260:777–78.

Emmorey, K. 1985. The transition from early to late babbling. *UCLA Working Papers in Phonetics* 62:61–69.

Fairbanks, G. 1954. Systematic research in experimental phonetics. 1. A theory of the speech mechanism as a servosystem. *Journal of Speech and Hearing Disorders* 19:133–39.

Fentress, J. C., and McLeod, P. J. 1986. Motor patterns in development. In *Handbook of Behavioral Neurobiology*. Vol. VIII. *Developmental Psychobiology and Developmental Neurobiology* ed. Blass, E. M. New York: Plenum Press.

Ferguson, C. A., and Farwell, C. B. 1975. Words and sounds in early language acquisition. *Language* 51:419–439.

Fishman, M. C. In press. Genes and neuronal plasticity. In *Assembly of the Nervous System* ed. L. Landmesser. New York: Liss.

Fletcher, S. G., and Meldrum, J. R. 1968. Lingual function and relative length of the lingual frenulum. *Journal of Speech and Hearing Research* 11:382–90.

Fogel, A., and Hannan, T. E. 1985. Manual actions of nine- to fifteen-week-old human infants during face-to-face interaction with their mother. *Child Development* 56:1271–1279.

Frost, D. O. 1989. Transitory neuronal connections in normal development and disease. In *Brain and Reading* eds. C. von Euler, I. Lundberg, and G. Lennerstrad. London: Macmillan.

Frost, D. O., and Innocenti, G. M. 1986. Effects of sensory experience on the development of visual callosal connections In *Two Hemispheres—One Brain: Functions of the Corpus Callosum* eds. F. Lepore, M. Petito, and H. H. Jasper. New York: Liss.

Fry, D. B. 1966. The development of the phonological system in the normal and deaf child. In *The Genesis of Language* eds. F. Smith and G. A. Miller. Cambridge, MA: The MIT Press.

Geschwind, N., and Galaburda, A. M. (eds.). 1987. *Cerebral Lateralization: Biological Mechanisms, Associations, and Pathology*. Cambridge, MA: The MIT Press.

Geschwind, N. and Levitsky, W. 1968. Human brain: Left-right asymmetries in temporal speech region. *Science* 161:186–87.

Ginsburg, G. P., and Kilbourne, B. K. 1988. Emergence of vocal alternation in mother-infant interchanges. *Journal of Child Language* 15:221–35.

Glanville, B., Best, C. and Levinson, R. 1977. A cardiac measure of cerebral asymmetries in infant auditory perception. *Developmental Psychology* 13:54–59.

Goldman-Rakic, P. S. 1987. Development of cortical circuitry and cognitive function. *Child Development* 58:601–622.

Gould, E. 1975. Experimental studies of the ontogeny of ultrasonic vocalizations in bats. *Developmental Psychobiology* 8:333–46.

Gould, S. J. 1977a. *Ontogeny and Phylogeny*. Cambridge, MA: Harvard University Press.

Gould, S. J. 1977b. *Ever since Darwin: Reflections in Natural History*. New York: Norton.

Greenberg, J. H., Ferguson, C. A., and Moravcsik, E. A. 1978 (eds.). *Universals of Human Language*. Vol. 2. *Phonology*. Stanford, CA: Stanford University Press.

Greenough, W. T., Black, J. F., and Wallace, C. S. 1987. Experience and brain development. *Child Development* 58:539–59.

Greenough, W. T., Larson, J. R., and Withers, G. S. 1985. Effects of unilateral and bilateral training in a reaching task on dendritic branching of neurons in the rat motor-sensory forelimb cortex. *Behavioral and Neural Biology* 44:301–314.

Handbook of Phonological Data from a Sample of the World's Languages: A Report of the Stanford Phonolgy Archive 1979. Stanford University, Department of Linguistics.

Hein, A., and Held, R. 1967. Dissociation of the visual placing response into elicited and guided components. *Science* 158:390–92.

Held, R. 1961. Exposure-history as a factor in maintaining stability of perception and coordination. *Journal of Nervous and Mental Disease* 132:26–32.

Held, R., and Bauer, J. A. 1967. Visually guided reaching in infant monkeys and restricted rearing. *Science* 155:718–20.

Held, R., and Bossom, J. 1961. Neonatal deprivation and adult rearrangement: Complementary techniques for analyzing plastic sensory-motor coordinations. *Journal of Comparative and Physiological Psychology* 54:33–37.

Held, R., and Hein, A. 1963. Movement-produced stimulation in the development of visually guided behavior. *Journal of Comparative and Physiological Psychology* 56:872–76.

Hogan, J. A. 1988. Cause and function in the development of behavior systems. In *Handbook of Behavioral Neurobiology*. Vol. IX. *Developmental Psychobiology and Behavioral Ecology* ed. E. M. Blass. New York: Plenum.

Holmgren, K., Lindblom, B., Aurelius, G., Jalling, B., and Zetterstrom, R. 1986. On the phonetics of infant vocalization. In *Precursors of Early Speech* eds. B. Lindblom and R. Zetterstrom. New York: Stockton Press.

Jakobson, R. 1968. *Child Language, Aphasia, and Phonological Universals*. The Hague: Mouton (originally published, 1941).

Jensen, T. S., Boggild-Andersen, B., Schmidt, J., Ankerhus, J., and Hansen, E. 1988. Perinatal risk factors and first-year vocalizations: Influence on preschool language and motor performance. *Developmental Medicine and Child Neurology* 30:153–61.

Johnson, J. I., Hamilton, T. C., Hsung, J-C., and Ulinski, P. S. 1972. Gracile nucleus absent in adult opossums after leg removal in infancy. *Brain Research*, 38:421–24.

Jones, S. J., and Moss, H. A. 1971. Age, state and maternal behavior associated with infant vocalizations. *Child Development* 42:1039–1051.

Kagan, J. 1970. Continuity in cognitive development during the first year of life. In *Early Experience and Visual Information Processing in Perceptual and Reading Disorders* eds. F. A. Young and D. B. Lindsley. Washington: National Academy of Sciences.

Kaplan, J. N., Winship-Ball, A., and Sim, L. 1978. Maternal discrimination of infant vocalizations in squirrel monkeys. *Primates* 19:187–93.

Kenney, M. D., Mason, W. A., and Hill, S. D. 1979. Effects of age, objects, and visual experience on affective responses of rhesus monkeys to strangers. *Developmental Psychology* 15:176–84.

Kent, R. D. 1981. Articulatory-acoustic perspectives on speech development. In *Language Behavior in Infancy and Early Childhood* ed. R. Stark. Amsterdam: Elsevier North Holland.

Kent, R. D., and Bauer, H. R. 1985. Vocalizations of one-year olds. *Journal of Child Language* 12:491–526.

Kent, R. D., Osberger, M. J., Netsell, R., and Hustedde, C. G. 1987. Phonetic development in identical twins differing in auditory function. *Journal of Speech and Hearing Disorders* 52:64–75.

Knudsen, E. I. 1985. Experience alters the spatial tuning of auditory units in the optic tectum during a sensitive period in the barn owl. *Journal of Neuroscience* 5:3094–3109.

Konishi, M. 1965. The role of auditory feedback in the control of vocalization in the White-Crowned Sparrow. *Zeitschrift fur Tierpsychologie* 22:770–783.

Kuhl, P. K., and Meltzoff, A. N. 1982. The bimodal perception of speech in infancy. *Science* 218:1138–1141.

Kuhl, P. K., and Meltzoff, A. N. 1988. Speech as an intermodal object of perception. In *Perceptual Development in Infancy* ed. A. Yonas. Minnesota Symposia on Child Psychology. Hillsdale, NJ: Lawrence Erlbaum Associates.

Kuhl, P., and Miller, J. 1982. Discrimination of auditory target dimensions in the presence or absence of variation in a second dimension by infants. *Perception and Psychophysics* 31:279–92.

Lampl, M., and Emde, R. N. 1983. Episodic growth in infancy: A preliminary report on length, head circumference, and behavior. In *Levels and Transitions in Children's Development: New Directions for Child Development*, No. 21, ed. K. W. Fischer. San Francisco: Jossey-Bass.

Lecours, A. R. 1975. Myelogenetic correlates of the development of speech and language. In *Foundations of Language Development: A Multidisciplinary Approach*. Vol. I, eds. E. H. Lenneberg and E. Lenneberg. New York: Academic Press.

Lenneberg, E. H., Rebelsky, F. G., and Nichols, I. A. 1965. The vocalizations of infants born to deaf and to hearing parents. *Human Development* 8:23–37.

Lewis, B. A., Ekelman, B. L., and Aram, D. M. 1989. A family study of severe familial/phonological disorders. *Journal of Speech and Hearing Research.*

Lieblich, A., Symmes, D., Newman, J., and Shapiro, M. 1980. Development of the isolation peep in laboratory-bred squirrel monkeys. *Animal Behavior* 28:1–9.

Lindblom, B. 1983. Economy of speech gestures. In *The Production of Speech* ed. P. F. MacNeilage. New York: Springer-Verlag.

Locke, J. L. 1980a. The prediction of child speech errors: Implications for a theory of acquisition. In *Child phonology.* Vol. I. *Production*, eds. G. H. Yeni-Komshian, J. F. Kavanagh, and C. Ferguson. New York: Academic Press.

Locke, J. L. 1980b. Mechanisms of phonological development in children: Maintenance, learning and loss. *Papers from the Sixteenth Regional Meeting of the Chicago Linguistic Society* 220–38.

Locke, J. L. 1983a. *Phonological Acquisition and Change.* New York: Academic Press.

Locke, J. L. 1983b. Clinical phonology: The explanation and treatment of speech sound disorders. *Journal of Speech and Hearing Disorders* 48:339–41.

Locke, J. L. 1986. The linguistic significance of babbling. In *Precursors of Early Speech* eds. B. Lindblom and R. Zetterstrom. New York: Stockton Press.

Locke, J. L. 1988. Variation in human biology and child phonology: A response to Goad and Ingram. *Journal of Child Language* 15:663–68.

Locke, J. L. 1989. Babbling and early speech: Continuity and individual differences. *First Language* 9:191–206.

Locke, J. L. 1990. Structure and stimulation in the ontogeny of spoken language. *Developmental Psychobiology* 23:621–43.

Locke, J. L. In press. *The Child's Path to Spoken Language.* Cambridge, MA: Harvard University Press.

Locke, J. L., and Mather, P. 1989. Genetic factors in the ontogeny of spoken language: Evidence from monozygotic and dizygotic twins. *Journal of Child Language* 16:553–59.

Locke, J. L., and Pearson, D. M. 1990. Linguistic significance of babbling: Evidence from a tracheostomized infant. *Journal of Child Language* 17:1–16.

Luchsinger, R., and Arnold, G. E. 1965. *Voice-Speech-Language*. Belmont, CA: Wadsworth.

MacKain, K., Studdert-Kennedy, M., Spieker, S., and Stern, D. 1983. Infant intermodal speech perception is a left-hemisphere function. *Science* 219: 1347–1349.

MacNeilage, P. F., and Davis, B. In press. Acquisition of speech production: Frames, then content. In *Attention and Performance XIII: Motor Representation and Control* ed. M. Jeannerod.

Marchman, V. A., Miller, R., and Bates, E. A. 1991. Babble and first words in children with focal brain injury. *Applied Psycholinguistics* 12:1–22.

Marler, P. 1975. An ethological theory of the origin of vocal learning. *Annals of the New York Academy of Sciences* 280:386–95.

Marler, P. 1990. Innate learning preferences: Signals for communication. *Developmental Psychobiology* 23:557–68.

Marler, P., and Peters, A. 1982. Structural changes in song ontogeny in the swamp sparrow *Melospiza georgiana*. *Auk* 99:446–58.

Marler, P., and Sherman, V. 1983. Song structure without auditory feedback: Emendations of the auditory template hypothesis. *Journal of Neuroscience* 3: 517–31.

Marler, P., and Sherman, V. 1985. Innate differences in singing behavior of sparrows reared in isolation from adult conspecific song. *Animal Behavior* 33: 57–71.

Marler, P., and Tamura, M. 1964. Culturally transmitted patterns of vocal behavior in sparrows. *Science* 146:1483–1486.

Marler, P., and Waser, M. S. 1977. Role of auditory feedback in canary song development. *Journal of Comparative and Physiological Psychology* 91:8–16.

Martin, G. B., and Clark, R. D. 1982. Distress crying in neonates: Species and peer specificity. *Developmental Psychology* 18:3–9.

Mayr, E. 1976. Behavior programs and evolutionary strategies. In *Evolution and the Diversity of Life: Selected Essays* ed. E. Mayr. Cambridge, MA: Harvard University Press.

Meltzoff, A. N. 1986. Imitation, intermodal representation, and the origins of mind. In *Precursors of Early Speech* eds. B. Lindblom and R. Zetterstrom. New York: Stockton Press.

Meltzoff, A. N., and Moore, M. K. 1977. Imitation of facial and manual gestures by human neonates. *Science* 198:75–78.

Menyuk, P., Liebergott, J., and Schultz, M. 1986. Predicting phonological development. In *Precursors of Early Speech* eds. B. Lindblom and R. Zetterstrom. New York: Stockton Press.

Molfese, D. L., and Molfese, V. J. 1979. Hemisphere and stimulus differences as reflected in the cortical responses of newborn infants to speech stimuli. *Developmental Psychology* 15:505–511.

Molfese, D. L., and Molfese, V. J. 1980. Cortical responses of preterm infants to phonetic and nonphonetic speech stimuli. *Developmental Psychology* 16:574–81.

Mount, R., Reznick, J. S., Kagan, J., Hiatt, S., and Szpak, M. 1989. Direction of gaze and emergence of speech in the second year. *Brain and Language* 36: 406–410.

Nelson, K. 1981. Individual differences in language development: Implications for development and language. *Developmental Psychology* 17:170–87.

Neville, H. J. 1991. Neurobiology of cognitive and language processing: Effects of early experience. In *Brain Maturation and Cognitive Development: Comparative and Cross-cultural Perspective* eds. K. Gibson and A. C. Petersen. New York: Aldine de Gruyter Press.

Neville, H. J., Schmidt, A., and Kutas, M. 1983. Altered visual-evoked potentials in congenitally deaf adults. *Brain Research* 266:127–32.

Ohala, J. J. 1983. The origin of sound patterns in vocal tract constraints. In *The Production of Speech* ed. P. F. MacNeilage. New York: Springer-Verlag.

Oller, D. K. 1980. The emergence of the sounds of speech in infancy. In *Child Phonology.* Vol. I. *Production* eds. G. H. Yeni-Komshian, J. F. Kavanagh, and C. A. Ferguson. New York: Academic Press.

Oller, D. K. 1986. Metaphonology and infant vocalizations. In *Precursors of Early Speech* eds. B. Lindblom and R. Zetterstrom. New York: Stockton Press.

Oller, D. K., and Eilers, R. E. 1988. The role of audition in infant babbling. *Child Development* 59:441–49.

Oller, D. K., Eilers, R., Bull, D., and Carney, A. 1985. Prespeech vocalizations of a deaf infant: A comparison with normal metaphonological development. *Journal of Speech and Hearing Research* 28:47–63.

Oller, D. K., Wieman, L. A., Doyle, W. J., and Ross, C. 1976. Infant babbling and speech. *Journal of Child Language* 3:1–11.

Parlour, S. F., and Broen, P. A. 1989. Familial risk for articulation disorder: A 25-year follow-up. Paper presented at the Nineteenth Annual meeting of the Behavior Genetics Association, Charlottesville, Virginia, June.

Perris, E. E., and Clifton, R. K. 1988. Reaching in the dark toward sound as a measure of auditory localization in infants. *Infant Behavior and Development* 11:473–91.

Petrinovich, L. 1974. Individual recognition of pup vocalization by northern elephant seal mothers. *Zeitschrift fur Tierpsychologie* 34:308–312.

Poindron, P., and Carrick, M. J. 1976. Hearing recognition of the lamb by its mother. *Animal Behavior* 24:600–602.

Ramsay, D. S. 1984. Onset of duplicated syllable babbling and unimanual handedness in infancy: Evidence for developmental change in hemispheric specialization? *Developmental Psychology* 20:64–71.

Roug, L., Landberg, I., and Lundberg, L.-J. 1989. Phonetic development in early infancy: A study of four Swedish children during the first eighteen months of life. *Journal of Child Language* 16:19–40.

Ruhlen, M. 1976. *A Guide to Languages of the World.* Stanford, CA: Language Universals Project, Stanford University.

Simonds, R. J., and Scheibel, A. B. 1989. The postnatal development of the motor speech area: A preliminary study. *Brain and Language* 37:42–58.

Sinnott, J. M., Stebbins, W. C., and Moody, D. B. 1975. Regulation of voice amplitude by the monkey. *Journal of the Acoustical Society of America* 58:412–14.

Skinner, B. F. 1983. *A Matter of Consequences.* New York: Knopf.

Smith, B. L. 1982. Some observations concerning pre-meaningful vocalizations of hearing-impaired infants. *Journal of Speech and Hearing Disorders* 47:439–42.

Smith, B. L. and Oller, D. K. 1981. A comparative study of pre-meaningful vocalizations produced by normally developing and Down's syndrome infants. *Journal of Speech and Hearing Disorders* 46:46–51.

Smith, S. D. (ed.). 1986. *Genetics and Learning Disabilities.* San Diego: College-Hill Press.

Snow, C. E. 1989. Initiativeness: A trait or a skill? In *The Many Faces of Imitation in Language Learning* eds. G. E. Speidel and K. E. Nelson. New York: Springer-Verlag.

Speidel, G. E. 1989. A biological basis for individual differences in learning to speak. In *The Many Faces of Imitation in Language Learning* eds. G. E. Speidel and K. E. Nelson. New York: Springer-Verlag.

Stern, D. N., Jaffe, J., Beebe, B., and Bennett, S. L. 1975. Vocalizing in unison and alternation: Two modes of communication within the mother-infant dyad. *Annals of the New York Academy of Sciences* 263:89–100.

Stevens, K. N., and Keyser, S. J. 1989. Primary features and their enhancement in consonants. *Language* 65:81–106.

Stoel-Gammon, C. 1985. Phonetic inventories, 15–14 months: A longitudinal study. *Journal of Speech and Hearing Research* 28:505–512.

Stoel-Gammon, C. 1989. Prespeech and early speech development of two late talkers. *First Language* 9:207–224.

Stoel-Gammon, C., and Otomo, K. 1986. Babbling development of hearing impaired and normally hearing subjects. *Journal of Speech and Hearing Disorders* 51:33–41.

Studdert-Kennedy, M. 1976. Speech perception. In *Contemporary Issues in Experimental Phonetics* ed. N. Lass. New York: Academic Press.

Studdert-Kennedy, M. 1991. Language development from an evolutionary perspective. In *Biobehavioral Foundations of Language Development* eds. N. Krasnegor, D. Rumbaugh, R. Schiefelbusch and M. Studdert-Kennedy. Hillsdale, NJ: Lawrence Erlbaum Associates.

Sweeney, S. 1973. The importance of imitation in the early stages of speech acquisition: A case report. *Journal of Speech and Hearing Disorders* 38:490–94.

Sykes, J. L. 1940. A study of the spontaneous vocalizations of young deaf children. *Psychological Monographs* 52:104–123.

Tallal, P., Ross, R., and Curtiss, S. 1989. Familial aggregation in specific language impairment. *Journal of Speech and Hearing Disorders* 54:167–73.

Tharp, R. G., and Burns, C. E. S. 1989. Phylogenetic processes in verbal language imitation. In *The Many Faces of Imitation in Language Learning* eds. G. E. Speidel and K. E. Nelson. New York: Springer-Verlag.

Thelen, E. 1981. Rhythmical behavior in infancy: An ethological perspective. *Developmental Psychology* 17:237–57.

Thorpe, W. H. 1961. Bird-song. The biology of vocal communication and expression in birds. *Cambridge Monographs in Experimental Biology* 12:1–143.

Timney, B. N., Emerson, V. F., and Dodwell, P. C. 1979. Development of visual stimulus-seeking in kittens. *Quarterly Journal of Experimental Psychology* 31:63–81.

Tomblin, J. B. 1989. Familial concentration of developmental language impairment. *Journal of Speech and Hearing Research* 54:287–95.

Tooby, J., and Cosmides, L. 1988. Can non-universal mental organs evolve? Constraints from genetics, adaptation, and the evolution of sex. *Institute for Evolutionary Studies Technical Report 88-2.*

Tooby, J., and Cosmides, L. 1989. The innate versus the manifest: How universal does universal have to be? *Behavioral and Brain Sciences* 12:36–37.

UCLA Phonological Segment Inventory Database: Data and Index 1981. *UCLA Working Papers in Phonetics* 53:1–243.

van der Stelt, J. M., and Koopmans-van Beinum, F. J. 1986. The onset of babbling related to gross motor development. In *Precursors of Early Speech* eds. B. Lindblom and R. Zetterstrom. New York: Stockton Press.

Veneziano, E. 1988. Vocal/verbal interaction and the construction of early lexical knowledge. In *The Emergent Lexicon: The Child's Development of a Linguistic Vocabulary* eds. M. D. Smith and J. L. Locke. New York: Academic Press.

Vihman, M. M. 1986. Individual differences in babbling and early speech: Predicting to age three. In *Precursors of Early Speech* eds. B. Lindblom and R. Zetterstrom. New York: Stockton Press.

Vihman, M. M. 1988. Words and babble at the threshold of language acquisition. In *The Emergent Lexicon: The Child's Development of a Linguistic Vocabulary* eds. M. D. Smith and J. L. Locke. New York: Academic Press.

Vihman, M. M., Macken, M. A., Miller, R., Simmons, H., and Miller, J. 1985. From babbling to speech: A reassessment of the continuity issue. *Language* 61:397–446.

von Holst, E. 1954. Relations between the central nervous system and the peripheral organs. *British Journal of Animal Behavior* 2:89–94.

Wada, J. A., Clarke, R., and Hamm, A. 1975. Cerebral asymmetry in humans. *Archives of Neurology* 32:239–46.

Waser, P. M. 1977. Individual recognition, intragroup cohesion and intergroup spacing: Evidence from sound playback to forest monkeys. *Behaviour* 60:28–74.

Werker, J. F. 1991. The ontogeny of speech perception. In *Modularity and the Motor Theory of Speech Perception* eds. I. G. Mattingly and M. Studdert-Kennedy. Hillsdale, NJ: Lawrence Erlbaum Associates.

Wiesel, T. N., and Hubel, D. H. 1963. Effects of visual deprivation on morphology and physiology of cells in the cat's lateral geniculate body. *Journal of Neurophysiology* 26:978–93.

Winick, M. 1968. Changes in nucleic acid and protein content of the human brain during growth. *Pediatric Research* 2:352–55.

Winick, M., and Rosso, P. 1969. Head circumference and cellular growth of the brain in normal and marasmic children. *Journal of Pediatrics* 74:774–78.

Witelson, S. F., and Pallie, W. 1973. Left hemisphere specialization for language in the newborn. Neuroanatomical evidence of asymmetry. *Brain* 96:641–46.

Yakovlev, P. L., and Lecours, A. R. 1967. The myelogenetic cycles of regional maturation of the brain. In *Regional Development of the Brain in Early Life* ed. A. Minkowski. Oxford: Blackwell.

Chapter • 4

Phonological Units as Adaptive Emergents of Lexical Development

Björn Lindblom

THE DEVELOPMENT OF PHONEMES

Children learn new words at an extremely rapid rate. Miller (1977) quotes figures on vocabulary size (Templin 1957) indicating that the median six-year-old child knows 13,000 words (7,800 root words) and the median eight-year-old knows 28,300 (17,600 roots). He makes the conservative estimate that, between the ages of six and eight, the median child acquires about 20 words (15 roots) per day. He concludes "that children learn a lot more words than we teach them" (p. 157).

Studdert-Kennedy (1983, 1987) draws attention to the phonetic aspects of this spectacular development pointing out that in acquiring a vocabulary, every normal child puts into play the principle that sets human language apart from other systems of animal communication and that provides the key to acquiring a large lexicon: the principle of *phonemic coding*. He presents an account (1987, p. 67) suggesting that

This research was supported in 1985–86 by a Sloan Foundation grant to the Center for Advanced Studies in the Behavioral Sciences, Stanford, California and by a joint grant ("Joller II") from the HSFR (Humanistiska-Samhällsvetenskapliga Forskningsrådet) and the NFR (Naturvetenskapliga Forskningsrådet) of Sweden.

The author is particularly grateful to Ann Peters of the University of Hawaii at Manoa for fruitful suggestions and for generously sharing her insights and lecture notes with him.

under "pressure from an increasing vocabulary, recurrent patterns of sound and gesture crystallize into phonemic control units."

What is the nature of this process of "crystallization"? In 1980 Menn (p. 30) stated that ". . . no general adequate account exists of how children end up with phonemes. . . ." How much is known today? We mention three possible frameworks within which that question might be addressed.

During the past decade, several child phonologists have favored the so-called *cognitive* or *problem-solving model* (Macken and Ferguson 1983; Menn 1983). Macken and Ferguson (1983) review evidence that leads them to portray phonological development as a process during which the child actively selects, makes inferences, and forms and tests hypotheses. They propose the cognitive model as a replacement of previous universalist-linguistic models (e.g., Jakobson, Generative Phonology, and Natural Phonology). Menn (1983, p. 3): "Since about 1974 we have moved away from a model in which phonological development was considered to resemble the differentiation of an embryo. In its place we have evolved a notion of the young child as a creature of some intelligence who is trying to solve a problem: the problem of sounding like her companions when communicating with them. . . . " And further, on p. 23, in the context of discussing "natural processes": "To build a rigorous theory of the acquisition of phonology, one must be able to explain why children fall into those particular pits." She continues: "And that step would still be only a beginning, for physiology only dictates what articulatory goals are likely to be surrounded with what traps. To explain how children succeed in avoiding or climbing out of them, we need a problem solving theory, a cognitive theory."

Another approach has emerged from the last few decades of syntax-oriented work, the "parameter-setting" model or the "selective" theory of language acquisition (Lightfoot 1989). This paradigm is built around the theory of *Universal Grammar* (UG) formulated by Chomsky (1981). UG postulates innate parameters and principles that are set by exposure to a specific language. This linguistic experience is assumed to be highly impoverished in comparison with the grammar that eventually develops.

PHONOLOGICAL UNITS AS EMERGENTS

Let us consider a third possibility suggested by the insight underlying Studdert-Kennedy's term *crystallization* and by two generally recognized observations.

First, genetic information alone is insufficient to account for language acquisition. Language must be assumed to develop like other complex behaviors, that is, through an open, incomplete genetic program (Mayr 1974). Second, linguistic input by itself underdetermines adult grammar. This is the "poverty of the stimulus" argument convincingly advocated by proponents of UG.

If they are neither completely in the genes nor completely in the linguistic input, where, then, do grammatical complexities come from? It seems ineluctable to assume that it is the interaction between the two that shapes the end product. To take that conclusion one step further, we have strong reasons to consider the possibility that this interaction produces a result that is not merely the sum of its component parts but is more. The interaction is a source of novelty and complexity. In other words, it generates qualitatively new phenomena, *emergents*[1], whose complexity is not explicitly preformed, but arises as an automatic consequence of the interaction, that is by *self-organization*[2], and goes beyond that found either in the initial conditions or in the input.

The above approaches exemplify two distinct, more general views of language acquisition. They both assume that linguistic experience is limited in relation to what is eventually acquired. We can illustrate these views with their answers to the following question.

WHAT MAKES LANGUAGE LEARNABLE?

The *functionalist* answer comes from those who strive to place the study of language within the theory of evolutionary biology (Studdert-Kennedy 1986; see also Pinker and Bloom 1990 for extensive discussion). It claims that language is a product of emergence and functional adaptation. The evolutionary constraints that shape its complexities are also at play during acquisition and provide children with shortcuts to adult grammar. Processes of emergence and functional adaptation contribute significantly to making languages learnable.

The *formalist* answer comes from those who regard language as a challenge of evolutionary theory (Chomsky 1972), or even an embarassment for it (Premack 1985). Or from those who find it unproblematic to accept that ". . . language is much like mathematical formulas— These make up a world of their own—. . ." and the "obvious fact that so much in language is non-optimal for purposes of communicating

---

[1]Note that the term *emergence* is used in its narrow, technical sense, implying not merely appearance but also novelty and increased complexity.

[2]The modeling of emergent complexity by self-organizing processes has recently become a popular topic in a large number of disciplines ranging from physics and biology to behavioral and social sciences (e.g., the writings of Prigogine). Crystallization is an example of emergent states in a physical system. Literally it refers to a change that a set of molecules undergo in the presence of certain boundary conditions.

cognitive information" (Halle 1975, p. 528). A well-known formalist claim is that the complexities of adult grammar are largely determined by an idiosyncratic, genetically specified and autonomous language module (UG), which helps children find their way to adult linguistic competence. Processes of emergence and functional adaptation *do not* contribute significantly to making languages learnable.

MODELING—A HEURISTIC TOOL

Here we take the first view and apply it to phonology. One of the goals of this chapter is to sketch, in principle, a model of phonological development constructed along functionalist lines. Our primary purpose is to offer a framework to support predictions about lexical development that can, in due course, be derived and tested. No doubt child phonologists would want to base such predictions on assumptions about motoric, perceptual, and cognitive universals, the role of input language and the child's current perceptual representation of it, and so forth. The model permits us to plug in hypotheses about the quantitative definition of those factors and allows us to deduce their consequences for a hypothetical developing lexical system. It is a "plug-in" model not confined to the particular quantifications adopted in the applications presented below. Its ability to make predictions is guaranteed once a numerical interpretation of the constraints has been worked out.

The quality of the predictions is, of course, related to how well they match the facts to be explained, but moreover to the extent to which we succeed in basing the definitions of the constraints on *independently motivated explanatory principles*. Given a set of black boxes, it is tempting to "postulate" some particular condition merely because it improves the predictions. "Arguing from data" is a common, and initially an often necessary, procedure in model making and theory construction. But it is *not* an end in itself and, in the long run, it is nonexplanatory. The strength of the functionalist position is that it takes seriously the search for precursors and independent motivations. Within the UG paradigm that search is judged fruitless—prejudged in our opinion—and is programmatically abandoned.

When solid independent motivation for the model has been identified, we may find that it is, nevertheless, empirically inadequate. It makes partially or totally wrong predictions,[3] or it turns out that its

---

[3]A characteristic of models is their simplification of reality. The present case is no exception. In defense of simple models see Boyd and Richerson (1985, pp. 25–31). They write: "To substitute an ill-understood model of the world for the ill-understood world is not progress" (p. 25).

conceptualization is too unwieldy. As in any modeling attempt, we will then be faced with deciding whether to revise its structure, or to reject it and start from scratch. We should use models as throw-away heuristic tools, rather than possessively defended summaries of established facts. They offer a principled and rigorous way of evaluating assumptions and enable us to gain insights from assumptions even if they prove to be wrong. The point is that with a model, mistakes can be made in systematic, constructive, and easily detected ways.

For the moment we claim that the proposed framework achieves the following: It derives phonetic forms as adaptations to universal performance constraints as well as to language-specific and child-specific factors. And, as we shall see, it is set up in such a way as to give us phonological units and rules "free of charge," that is, as spontaneously assembled emergent consequences of lexical development. Consequently, it differs from traditional conceptions of phonology and distinctive feature theories in that it treats sound structure *deductively* (Lindblom 1990). Rather than "postulate" units and processes *axiomatically*, it explicitly aims at deducing them from starting points that are motivated by knowledge independent of the facts to be explained.

FUNCTIONAL ADAPTATION IN ADULT SOUND SYSTEMS

In this section we focus on what children finally acquire: adult sound systems. We do so simply because any complete model of child phonology will presumably describe a succession of stages, the fully developed system being one of the stages. Thus, the model must accommodate adult phonology also. What is its nature?

We shall demonstrate that significant cross-linguistic aspects of adult sound structure can be seen not as arbitrary and idiosyncratic reflexes of the autonomous language module, but as adaptations to universal constraints on the production and perception of speech. This demonstration is intended as background and partial justification for the model to be proposed. It also clarifies why the model takes the form it does, showing whence the computational format came.

We begin by making three points related to speech versus non-speech, phonetic alphabets, and co-occurrence restrictions within phonetic inventories. They all raise the same question: Languages sample the universal phonetic space in highly constrained ways. Why?

First, a cross-linguistic perspective on phonetic systems reveals an overwhelming number of place, manner, and phonation-type mechanisms (Ladefoged and Maddieson 1986). However, when the phonetic segments of the world's languages are compared with the total sound-producing capabilities of the human vocal tract—the *anthropophonic* space in Catford's terminology (Catford 1977)—a strong trend of convergence emerges (Chafe 1970; Lindblom 1990b). A core set of vowels and consonants recurs across all languages. Large phonetic inventories include this core set and attain their size by invoking various elaborations of it (Lindblom and Maddieson 1988). These elaborations create an impression of diversity but, as the anthropophonic perspective shows, it is a diversity that underexploits the total physical degrees of freedom of the speech production mechanisms.

Second, universal phonetic alphabets such as the IPA encode information coming essentially from two sources: phonological analyses of individual languages and cross-linguistic comparisons of the physical values of the postulated phonological segments. Within languages a single symbol is used to represent the variants of a given phoneme and across languages the same symbol is used to describe physically similar sounds (Ladefoged 1987). The fact that so far this procedure has not resulted in an unmanageably long list of sound types but has produced a relatively limited total set is significant. It too shows the tendency for languages to converge phonetically.

Third, we note that there are severe restrictions on how phonetic inventories select combinations of segments from the universal set. A single example is that a large percentage of the world's languages have five-vowel systems. According to typological studies, over 90% of five-vowel systems have the values /i, e, a, o, u/ (Crothers 1978; Maddieson 1984). There are more than 200 different vowel segment-types in the UPSID database, Maddieson's survey of 317 languages (Maddieson 1984). The probability of obtaining that particular set by choosing five vowels at random from the total set of 200 is $(200 - 5)! \times 5!/200!$, which is a very small number. The analogous reasoning applied to the distribution of consonant segments gives us similar results.

To sum up the three points, why are the possibilities of the anthropophonic space used so fastidiously? And why do the possibilities that *do* get used show such restricted patterns of co-occurrence? What are the constraints?

Before addressing those issues let us consider also a formal aspect of the combinatorial use languages make of their discrete segmental and featural building blocks. (The source of data to be discussed is Maddieson 1984.)

Consider the three-by-four system of Chipewyan affricates. The plain set (top row in the exhibit below) contains a dental with nonsibilant release, a dental/alveolar with sibilant release, a dental/alveolar with lateral release, and a palato-alveolar. An aspirated series (second row) and an ejective set (third row) parallel the plain set.

t̠θ	ts	tɬ	tʃ
t̠θʰ	tsʰ	tɬʰ	tʃʰ	Chipewyan
t̠θʼ	tsʼ	tɬʼ	tʃʼ

Alawa, like many other Australian languages, favors place of articulation and exhibits three series of stops: oral, prenasalized, and nasal at the same points of articulation.

b	d	d̲	ḍ	g	
ᵐb	ⁿd	ⁿd̲	ⁿḍ	ᵑg	Alawa
m	n	n̲	ṇ	ŋ	

Finally Sui (Kam-Tai) presents a nasal inventory with four places times three phonation types (voiced, voiceless, laryngealized):

m	n	ɲ	ŋ	
m̥	n̥	ɲ̥	ŋ̥	Sui
m̃	ñ	ɲ̃	ŋ̃	

Such *tightly packed matrices* are typologically very common. Restating the point with a hypothetical example, we do not expect to find stops and nasals to form the following matrix in which each segment has a unique place of articulation:

.	.	.	.	t̠	.	.	q	ʔ
b	.	d̠	.	.	.	g	.	.	Case 1
.	ɱ	.	n	.	ɲ	.	.	.

What we typically find instead is more like this arrangement:

p	.	.	t	.	.	k	.	.
b	.	.	d	.	.	g	.	.	Case 2
m	.	.	n	.	.	ŋ	.	.

Why is Case 2 the common pattern? Why do we not see a more diverse use of features as in Case 1? As pointed out by Ohala (1980), languages tend to obey the principle of maximum utilization of the available distinctive features.

Whence does that principle come? Should we assume that, in phonological development, it comes from the input? Children simply learn the sounds of the language around them. Or do children need a principle because perceptual experience underdetermines the sound structures to be learned? If so, is it the result of the "cognitive problem-solving" attributed to the child (Macken and Ferguson 1983; Menn 1983)? Or should we simply refrain from seeking its causes and relegate it to the machinery postulated for Universal Grammar? Note that, if we do the latter, we will eventually have to explain how it got into UG in the first place, or treat it as an inexplicable UG idiosyncrasy. Neither the cognitive nor the UG route is taken here.

CHOOSING THE FRAMEWORK:
DARWINIAN VARIATION AND SELECTION

The above observations exemplify substantive aspects of sound structure (restrictions on the range and combinability of phonetic values) as well as formal properties (phonemic coding, maximum utilization of the available distinctive features). How do we support the claim that those phenomena are adaptations to functional constraints? What should be the formal structure of the argument?

Our strategy is to adopt an "analysis-by-synthesis" approach and to perform simulation experiments with a model that implements the constraints to be investigated. The Darwinian principles of *variation* and *cumulative selection* are the main sources of the model's generative power. Very briefly stated, the motivation for this choice is as follows: Language is a product of biological and cultural evolution. Two major concepts in current accounts of evolutionary processes are *variation* and *cumulative selection*. That is true for models of biological (Mayr 1978) as well as of cultural evolution (Boyd and Richerson 1985). The main message conveyed by the contemporary neo-Darwinian paradigm is the unrivaled success and explanatory power of those principles (Dawkins 1986).[4] Darwinism is universal (Dawkins 1983). Consequently, a minimal and fundamental requirement on any explanatory linguistic theory aiming at compatibility with biological sciences is that it should at least be constructed with those key concepts as its foundation.[5]

In terms familiar to phoneticians, we can think of this variation-selection model as a "source-filter" theory. It assumes a set of research agenda structured in three steps (cf. Oster and Wilson 1978):

1. Definition of the *search space*, that is, the pool of variation, the phonetic raw materials from which linguistic selections can be made. A few paragraphs ago, this is what we called the anthropophonic space. Specifying the search space consists in establishing quantitative and independently motivated definitions of notions such as "possible utterance," "possible articulation," "possible gesture," etc.

---

[4]Dawkins's simulations of biomorphs in *The Blind Watchmaker* (Dawkins 1986) is an instructive and compelling demonstration of how extremely complex geometrical pattern can arise by utterly simple means: cumulative selection operating under iteratively applied constraints.

[5]This stance is, of course, controversial in linguistics but is, in our opinion, successfully defended by Pinker and Bloom (1990).

2. Definition of *performance constraints,* that is, factors pertaining to the use of spoken language hypothesized by the linguist to play a role in the shaping of sound patterns and linguistic structures. Presumably constraints assumed to facilitate the task of speaker, listener, and learner will be plugged in here, e.g., "discriminability," "articulatory complexity," "learnability." The goal here is to quantify the adaptive value of sounds and gestures. Note again that this needs to be done with maximum attention to anchoring definitions in independently known facts and principles.
3. Definition of *optimization criteria,* that is, the numerical conditions under which linguistic selections take place. For instance, the criteria that optimal, or sufficiently optimal, systems of speech sounds should meet.

The following section briefly summarizes research exemplifying this program. Its general theme is, *if phonological systems were seen as adaptations to performance constraints, what would they be like?* The examples can be said to constitute a feasibility demonstration. We touch upon three topics. First, the results of experiments on the simulation of vowel systems that provide evidence that "discriminability" is likely to be one of the constraints. For a second illustration, some consonant inventory data that shed further light on the nature of the functional constraints indicate that discriminability in consonant inventories interacts with a tendency to minimize "articulatory complexity." This becomes evident when consonant (and vowel) systems are examined as a function of size and suggests that a combination of production and perception constraints, "sufficient contrast," is at work shaping phonetic inventories. Third, we describe an attempt to apply the format of the vowel simulations to holistically defined syllables. These experiments use a quantitative measure combining discriminability and articulatory cost and provide preliminary clues to modeling phonological units as emergents of lexical development.

CONSTRAINTS ON SPEAKING
AND LISTENING: DISCRIMINABILITY AND PRONOUNCEABILITY

Vowel Systems

The computational experiments performed indicate that it is possible to predict significant aspects of the contents of the world's vowel inventories (Lindblom 1986). These simulations were based on a "vowel space" derived from a physiologically based numerical model of "possible vowels" (Lindblom and Sundberg 1971) and translated into acoustic and auditory dimensions using the acoustic theory of speech production (Fant 1960) and an implementation of an auditory model (Schroeder, Atal, and Hall 1979). A measure of "discriminability" was defined according to the results of psychoacoustic experimentation (Plomp 1970; Bladon and Lindblom 1981). This work suggests that vowel qualities are selected to be discriminable—a condition implicitly imposed by the on-line processes of speaker-listener interaction.

Role of Size in Phonetic Inventories

Discriminability seems to play a role in consonant systems also. Lindblom and Maddieson (1988) sorted the consonants of the 317 languages in the UPSID database (Maddieson 1984) into obstruents and sonorants. For the entire corpus they plotted the number of obstruents against size of total inventory. That number grew linearly as a function of size with a slope of approximately 0.7. Accordingly, languages seem to use about 70% obstruents and 30% sonorants. The authors point out that there is no a priori reason to expect a linear size-dependent relation and a slope that remains constant across languages, because UPSID contains enough obstruent and sonorant segment-types for even the largest systems to use any proportions between the extremes of 100% obstruents or 100% sonorants. They suggest that the linear size-dependence and the cross-linguistic constancy arise from a discriminability condition in interaction with a large perceptual space for obstruents and a smaller one for sonorants.

Lindblom and Maddieson (1988) also argue that discriminability is not the sole determinant of the contents of phonetic inventories. Working with the notion of "articulatory elaboration," they classified UPSID segments as *Basic*, *Elaborated*, and *Complex* articulations. An *Elaborated* segment is characterized by a single elaboration. A *Basic* segment has no elaborations. *Complex* articulations have two or more elaborations. Accordingly, a breathy [d̤] or a retroflex [ɖ] are *Elaborated;* breathy and retroflex [ɖ̤] is *Complex;* and the dental [d̪] is *Basic.*

Applying this classification to the segments of UPSID, Lindblom and Maddieson (1988) found evidence for a *Size Principle:* a very robust and typologically general relationship between the recruitment of these segment categories and the size of the inventory. Small systems use only the more elementary, "babble-like" Basic segments (e.g., [p, t, k, m, n, i, e, a, o, u . . .]). Medium-sized invoke Basic and Elaborated segments (e.g., clicks; ejectives; implosives; vowels with extra features, consonants invoking secondary manner, place, and phonation types such as aspiration, palatalization, creaky voice, etc.). Large systems exhibit all three types: Basic, Elaborated, and Complex (e.g., ejective affricates, nasalized diphthongs, long and pharyngealized vowels).

The following interpretation was offered: In small inventories, intrasystemic demands for distinctiveness are reduced. Basic, motorically elementary articulations are perceptually sufficient to maintain discriminability. In medium and large systems, however, there is greater perceptual competition within the vowel and consonant paradigms. For this reason languages need additional dimensions as a function of size. Witness the lawful linear relationships observed across the UPSID language groups.

The authors suggest that the phonetic mechanism associated with the Size Principle originates in the tug-of-war between production-based and perception-based conditions, which implicitly impose *"sufficient contrast"* as the selectional criterion shaping phonological patterns.

From Segments to Syllables

In Lindblom, MacNeilage, and Studdert-Kennedy (1983) the format of the vowel system simulations was extended to a set of CV-like syllables. Performance constraints were quantified in terms of a measure combining "discriminability" and "articulatory cost." Phonetically these syllables were *holistic formant trajectories* running between one of seven locus patterns (corresponding to complete closure at one of seven points, bilabial through uvular) to one of nineteen open-configuration formant patterns (the vowel space of Lindblom 1986).

Articulatory ease has long been invoked as an explanation for various phonetic phenomena. It has not been easy to quantify, a circumstance that may have contributed to its somewhat shaky theoretical status. Nevertheless, a common-sense die-hard, it keeps reappearing. At least the following two aspects of this dimension seem relevant: biomechanics and spatio-temporal motor coordination (Ohala 1989; Lindblom 1990).

Biomechanically, movements presuppose forces applied to structures with mass, damping, and compressibility. Physics teaches that the further and the faster a spring-mass system is displaced, the greater the energy needed per unit time, in other words the more "costly" the movement. Phonetic mechanisms are, of course, more complicated than simple physical analogies, but biomechanics is definitely part of the complex picture. Accordingly, we *do* see the consequences of biomechanical constraints in real speech. For instance, contextual assimilation of vowels (so-called articulatory or formant "undershoot") is commonly seen in many languages for short vowel durations (Lindblom 1963; Moon 1991). Biomechanical analyses of articulatory displacement and undershoot (Nelson, Perkell, and Westbury 1984) show two things. First, if speech motor control is biomechanically "cost-effective," undershoot behavior is natural and to be expected. Second, avoiding undershoot is possible within limits, but involves expending more "effort."

In Lindblom, MacNeilage, and Studdert-Kennedy (1983) each syllable was assigned an "articulatory cost" derived by applying bio-mechanical criteria to the syllable's parametric specification in terms of a production model (Lindblom and Sundberg 1971; Lindblom, Pauli, and Sundberg 1975). These numbers represented "penalty scores" that depended on the extent and rate of the given syllable's component movements. To exemplify the rate criterion, a trajectory from a palatal closure to a front configuration would score lower than a transition from a uvular place to the same front configuration. The extent criterion had the effect of penalizing extreme displacements, e.g., movements beginning from retroflex, but not dental, onsets. For each individual syllable, the final articulatory score was a linear combination of those two criteria.

In the work on vowels—which were steady-state formant patterns—*discriminability* was defined as:

$$D(i,j) = [c \int_0^{24.5} |E(i,x) - E(j,x)|^p \, dt]^{1/p} \qquad (1)$$

with $p = 2$ and where x is frequency calibrated in auditorily relevant Bark units and $E(x)$ is an "auditory spectrum" computed according to the method proposed by Schroeder, Atal, and Hall (1979).[6]

In the CV simulations, this measure was applied to a sequence of spectral time samples and computed sample by sample and summed over time following a suggestion by Klatt (1979). The general expression gives us the area under a given distance-time function:

$$d(i,j) = \int_0^T D(i,j) \, dt \qquad (2)$$

where T is the duration of the integration window.

This measure has some interesting properties that can be illustrated with the following simple problem. We begin with two imaginary parallel vertical line segments. Our task is to draw, say, nine straight lines running between arbitrary points on the two vertical segments in such a way that we maximize the areas enclosed by all the possible line pairs (more precisely, in such a way that the sum of the inverted and squared areas is minimized):

$$\sum_{i=2}^{9} \sum_{j=1}^{i-1} 1/(A(i,j))^2 \rightarrow \text{minimized} \qquad (3)$$

---

[6]The integration window 0–24.5 is the frequency range of human hearing in Bark units and c is a constant. When $p = 2$, Equation (1) is known as the Euclidean distance between two arbitrary spectra i and j. For experimental justification and evaluations of the parameters, see e.g., Bladon and Lindblom (1981).

It can be shown easily that Case R in figure 1 is better than Case S. It is, in fact, the optimal solution of the problem. Note how the lines in R converge on common onsets and endpoints—an effect that is not dependent upon the number of lines that have to be drawn.

The result in figure 1 raises the question of whether convergence of lines would be obtained also for a slightly more complicated situation. Suppose that in the geometric problem we replace the lines to be drawn by formant transitions represented as sequences of spectral slices. Would these spectral trajectories show similar convergence?

The answer is that, in fact, they do. They can be understood in terms of the convergence effect demonstrated by the preceding geometric exercise. This is shown by some results first reported in Lindblom, MacNeilage, and Studdert-Kennedy (1983), which is summarized below.

Equation (3) has the same form as the optimization criterion of the vowel simulations in Lindblom (1986). If we substitute $d(i,j)$ of equation (2) for $A(i,j)$ of equation (3) we obtain:

$$\sum_{i=2}^{n} \sum_{j=1}^{i-1} 1/(d(i,j))^2 \rightarrow \text{minimized} \qquad (4)$$

This formula defines a criterion for choosing the optimal set of k items (syllables) from a larger total inventory. If there is a total of n syllables, then there are $n!/(n-k)!k!$ ways of choosing k syllables from the

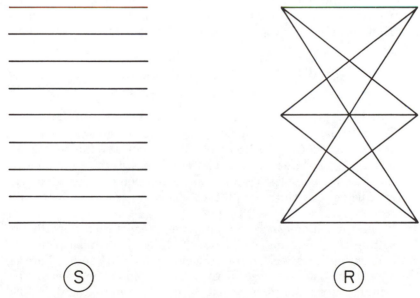

S
R

Figure 1.   A geometric optimization problem.

total set. One of those combinations meets the criterion of equation (4). That combination is the set of k syllables (formant trajectories) that are more separated in the auditorily calibrated space than any other combination. Thus, that is the set that optimizes the discriminability criterion.

Equation (4) paves the way for the final form of the criterion, which combines articulatory cost and discriminability in the following way:

$$\sum_{i=2}^{n} \sum_{j=1}^{i-1} 1/(d(i,j)/a(i,j))^2 \to \text{minimized} \tag{5}$$

Here the $d(i,j)$ term evaluates the discriminability of syllables i and j. The $a(i,j)$ term is the sum of the penalty scores for syllables i and j. High discriminability scores make the value of equation (5) small, whereas high articulatory costs make it large.

In Lindblom, MacNeilage, and Studdert-Kennedy (1983) simulations were run to generate optimal sets of 15 syllables selected sequentially according to equation (5). The procedure was initiated repeatedly using a different syllable each time. The results of $7 \times 19 = 133$ runs were pooled and the frequency of occurrence of each syllable was observed. The 15 syllables with the highest ranks were taken as the optimal set.

Figure 2 shows that set plotted as trajectories between closures (left) and open configurations (right). The most noteworthy points are:

1. The lines do not show unique, individual onsets and endpoints. They converge, repeatedly favoring four onsets and six offsets;
2. Those onsets and endpoints can be translated into phonetic labels:

bi	bɛ	ba	bo	bu
di	dɛ	da	do	du
g₊i	g₊ɛ	ga	go	gɨ

(where [g₊] refers to a palatal and [g] to a velar closure);
3. The articulatory and acoustic specifications of these syllables are *holistic*. Acoustically, each syllable can be seen as a transition from a "locus" to a "target" formant pattern. Articulatorily, it is a movement from a complete closure to a more open configuration. The articulatory descriptions of these syllables is examined more fully below;
4. When simulations are rerun removing articulatory factors (that is, setting all $a(i,j)$ terms of equation (5) to one), a similar pattern of converging lines is seen, but onsets such as [ɖ] and [G] are favored. This indicates that the source of the convergence is the discriminability criterion and that [b, d, g] are more highly valued than [ɖ] and [G] for articulatory reasons: Their configurations rep-

CLOSURES

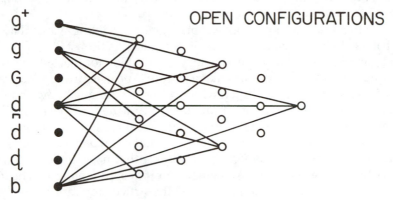

Figure 2.   Results of simulations: Trajectories in phonetic space.

   resent less extreme displacements, smaller departures from a neutral vocal tract;
5. Figure 2 and the exhibit in item 2 above show "assimilations" that are caused by the fact that higher penalties were assigned to g_+u g_+o and gi gɛ than to g_+i $g_+ɛ$ and go gu;
6. Because palatals group with front vowels and velars with back and central in complementary distribution, a "phonemic analysis" would give us three consonants /b, d, g/ and five vowels /i, e, a, o, u/.
7. Recall that there are no explicit "segments" in the phonetic description of the syllables. Nor are there explicit assimilation "rules." Cf. Menn's remarks that seem as appropriate to the present model derivations as to the rule use by children she discussed (1983, p. 15): "Rules are always to be regarded as the analyst's tentative hypotheses about the child's mental operations. And it is also important to remember that a rule is no more than a description of a hypothesized regularity of behavior. It is not an explanation of anything to say that a child has a deletion rule or a substitution rule. . . ." Our results show that her reminder should be taken seriously. In the sense of our introductory discussion the "segments" and "rules" of the present experiments are *emergents* of the simulated lexical development.

A MECHANISM OF LEXICAL SELF-SEGMENTATION
AND THE CONTINUITY OF MOTOR DEVELOPMENT

If the syllable selections are regarded as a simplified model of lexical development, we note that "selecting" means "acquiring," which in turn implies "committing to memory." Let us look at the derivations from the viewpoint of a hypothetical storage mechanism. How might the organization of such a memory develop?

When the learning device adopts a given syllable as a lexical item, what has to be remembered? Consider the acquisition of [ba]. The top of figure 3 shows stylized articulatory information for that syllable displayed in the style of an "articulatory score" (Browman and Goldstein 1985). Three panels are shown with lip closure, tongue body, and jaw movements. The lips move from closure to a neutral position. The tongue moves from a neutral to a pharyngeal configuration, and the jaw from high to low. The time variations of the top panels are the synthesis instructions ("production routines") that need to be placed in long-term storage and invoked whenever [ba] is pronounced. The format of the top display indicates that the articulators are to be synchronized as shown.

The panels of the bottom part show the same information, but the different format is used to emphasize the fact that the three activities are spatially and anatomically distinct. Here, synchronization is represented by the horizontal connecting lines. Let us assume that these control functions, along with their anatomical addresses and their common timescale, are what is remembered when the lexical item [ba] is acquired. They are stored as a unitary package labeled [ba].

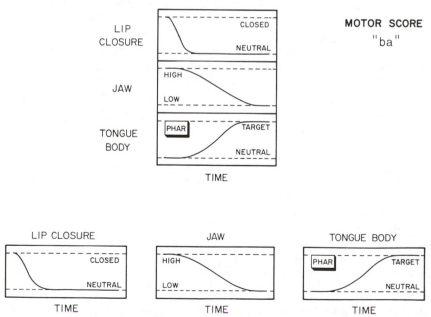

Figure 3.   Temporal and spatial aspects of motor score for syllable [ba].

Now consider four motor scores representing [ba], [bi], [da], and [di]. Their motor scores are shown in figure 4. The spatial format brings out the fact that the lip gestures of [ba] and [bi] are identical and that the tongue movements of [ba]–[da], and of [bi]–[di], are the same.

How does our learning device discover those facts without our telling it explicitly? If we stipulate that *anatomically and temporally identical control functions should be stored only once,* the left half of figure 4 can be reduced to the "network" in the right portion of the figure. Again we take the interconnecting lines to mean ". . . should be synchronized with. . . ".

To further illustrate this method of storage, suppose that a system develops containing 15 syllables with three distinct onset patterns and five different endpoint targets. The storing of that information would take the form shown in figure 5. In the general case of m onsets and n endpoints, $m + n$ rather than $m \times n$ patterns would be stored thanks to the spatio-temporal identity principle.

For this economy to work—and for the learning device to apply this storage method without explicit programming—the following three assumptions need to be made: (1) Articulatory scores must break down into anatomically distinct components (lips, tongue tip, tongue body, jaw, etc.); (2) The lexicon must contain motor scores that share anatomically distinct control functions (gestures). Linguistically speaking, this implies that there must be "minimal pairs"; (3) The activity pattern for each anatomical channel is stored separately—*somatotopically* in neurophysiological terms. And, if a given time function is already in somatotopic storage, it need not be stored again. The only thing that needs to be stored is the synchronization link to the rest of the motor score. When these conditions are met by the model, a "segmentation" will be automatically imposed on the stored motor scores.

Assumption (3) is neurophysiologically plausible. Assumption (1) seems anatomically inevitable for segmental aspects of normal speech. It, no doubt, applies to signed language also (Meier 1990). It is less obvious if it applies to the production of fundamental frequency contours.

Assumption (2) can be justified for early phonological development if we do not restrict "minimal pairs" exclusively to phonemic constrasts. Menn states that, ". . . the concept of phoneme is difficult to apply in the early stages of language development" because ". . . minimal pairs . . . are so rare as to make statements about the presence or absence of constrast impossible" (1983, p. 11). Many children described in the literature seem to develop contrastive phonetic forms that are constructed around a common core of fixed articulatory routines shared across the forms. Examples of such *production schemata* are the five types of prosodic structure discussed in Waterson (1971), the "tem-

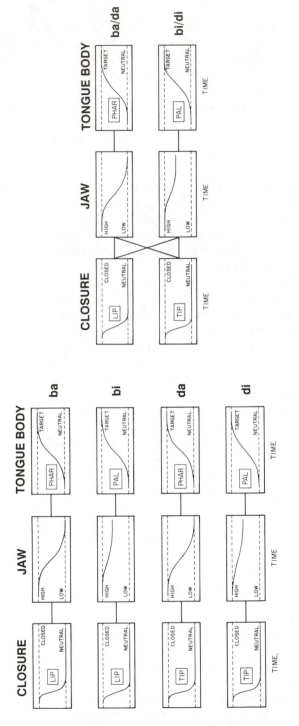

Figure 4. Motor scores for [ba], [bi], [da], and [di].

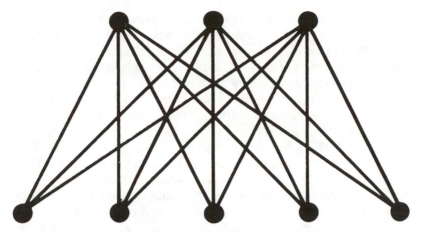

Figure 5.   Result of self-segmentation applied to 15 syllables with spatio-temporally distinct onset endpoint patterns.

plates" used by the children described in Vihman (1976), Priestly (1977), and Macken (1979), the "vocal motor schemes" of McCune and Vihman (1987) and the "locally modified frames" of MacNeilage and Davis (1990).

If, in line with the above considerations, we perform a segmentation on these databases, we sometimes see the possibility of phonemic chunks, sometimes larger segments. For her son P (at age 1.6) Waterson (1971) lists examples that are compatible with both smaller and larger units: According to the self-segmentaion procedure, [ɲeːɲe/ɲiːɲɪ] 'finger,' [ɲẽːɲẽ] 'window,' [ɲaɲa] 'another,' and [ɲaɲø] 'Randall' yield interleaving C_C_ and _V_V structures whereas 'fish' [ɪʃ /ʊ ʃ], 'fetch' [ɪʃ], 'vest' [ʊ ʃ], 'dish' [dɪ ʃ], and 'brush' [by ʃ] produce V_, CV_ and _C segments. The first 30 words recorded for Daniel Menn between 16 and 22.5 months contain contrasts that provide phoneme-sized segments (Menn 1976, 1987): [hæ] 'hi', [gæ] 'squirrel' or 'carry', [æ] or [æ–æ] 'airplane', [næ] 'banana', and [bæ] 'bread' the latter contrasting with [bu] 'boot' and [ba] 'bottle.'

It seems possible to conclude, then, that the above three conditions can be met rather naturally. Incorporating them into the model produces a mechanism of *self-segmentation*. No explicit programming is necessary for this process to take place. It is an automatic consequence of vocabulary growth and the presence of minimal pairs.

Next we consider another aspect of motor learning. Behavioral research on memory indicates that there is a "cost" attached to committing something to memory. The larger the piece of information to be stored, the more costly the operation.

In view of such findings let us stipulate that, everything else being equal, *the probability that a new word* (a new articulatory pattern) *will be added to the lexicon is inversely related to the amount of information that has to be committed to memory.* For our purposes, let "amount of information" be measured in terms of motor-score subunits defined by self-segmentation. We also know from behavioral research that establishing memory traces is facilitated by contextual cues. If two motor scores are partially similar—similarity being structured in terms of shared gestures—they will provide context for each other and increase each other's probability of being memorized.

The effect of self-segmentation and motor continuity should be to increase "the utilization of the available distinctive features" (cf. Ohala's principle). In other words, to make derived phonetic forms much more like Case 2 than Case 1 of the preceding discussion.

The idea of articulatory learning proceeding as if the child performs a *local search* around production patterns already mastered, is not new in the literature dealing with phonological development and its modeling. It is supported by various observations.

Continuity of development has been a strong theme in recent research on the transition from babbling to speech (Oller et al. 1975; Vihman et al. 1985). The child's mastery of motor skills proceeds gradually. Gestures become more differentiated in terms of the demands of both biomechanics and the fine details of spatio-temporal coordination. Thus, continuity seems to originate, at least in part, in the way the space of the production mechanism is explored by the child: first low-cost phenomena, later elaborations. As suggested here, another possible source of continuity is memorial constraints.

Menn's account of phonological development comes particularly close to the present proposal. Self-segmentation and continuity of motor learning could be seen as elaborations of her notion of "ease of articulation." She writes (1978): ". . . reliance on subroutines . . . also maximizes utilization of skills already acquired, for the child adding a new word to his/her lexicon can simplify that task if he/she can assimilate the word to existing subroutines" (p. 165). Waterson (1971) observes that "the child might be seeking out whole-word patterns in the adult language that were similar to whole-word patterns that the child had learned to produce" (p. 32). And Menn (1983, p. 21) extends "ease of articulation" to include production routines already acquired as a factor affecting the learnability of a new sound: ". . . physiological causes are only one factor in determining 'ease of articulation' for the individual child. The other factor, and I propose that it is the major factor, is the state of the child's knowledge at a given time . . . [l] is "easier" than [j] only because this child happens to have found out how to make an [l] first."

MacNeilage and Davis (1990) view variegation in babbling and the development of first words as a process of differentiating the basic carrier movement of speech, the open-close alternation of the mandible, the Frame of the Frame-Content theory. Under the rubric of *local modifications* they list five processes by which such differentiation could occur and four of which are compatible with continuity: relative timing, metrical variation, (new movement), temporo-spatial variation, and contextual restriction.

Summarizing the child's tendency to the "avoidance" (Schwartz and Leonard 1982) and "favorite sounds" strategies (Ferguson and Farwell 1975), Studdert-Kennedy (1987) remarks: "Initially, it exploits these (articulatory) routines by adding to its repertoire only words composed of gestural patterns similar to those it has already 'solved', and by avoiding words with markedly different patterns . . ." (p. 79).

PREDICTING THE FORMS OF LEXICAL DEVELOPMENT: MODEL OVERVIEW AND RESEARCH AGENDA

Our modeling began with vowel systems. Then we considered CV syllables. Now we take the third step, proposing a procedure for generating predictions about phonetic forms in lexical development. This proposal adds new components but preserves continuity with the vowel and syllable models. An overview is presented in figure 6.

The Input

The driving force of the model is at the center of the diagram: the *cognitive parameters*. In the present work we have limited their role to representing size of inventory and size of lexicon. In principle it is through the "cognitive parameters" that this phonetic model interacts with the rest of lexical and grammatical development.

This restricted use of cognitive factors is methodologically deliberate. Recall the theme of our research strategy: If lexical systems were seen as functional adaptations to the constraints of speaking, listening, and learning to speak, what would they be like? Focusing this formulation on phonetic constraints should make it possible to ascertain how far phonetic factors alone will take us toward modeling phonological structures. In other words, the present approach attempts to "inverse-filter away" phonetics so as to identify a residue of phenomena requiring nonphonetic explanation. Accordingly, the immediate goal is not a complete model but a heuristic one.

The search space, here labeled the *anthropophonic space* (Catford 1977), provides raw materials and input for the derivations. So far definitions of the space of "possible vowel" and "possible syllable" have

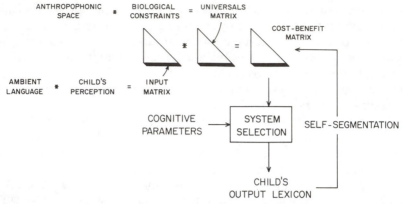

Figure 6. Overview of computational framework for predicting phonetic forms of lexical development.

been explored. As phonetic production models become more sophisticated, the scope should be widened to include both speech and nonspeech sounds, as well as neurobiological precursor mechanisms (MacNeilage 1987, 1991) and developmental changes.

Presumably the overt behavior of the child is like that of the adult speaker in that, in babbling and early speech, children's productions are already selective and constrained in relation to the total phonetic capacity defined by the neurophysical degrees of freedom of their vocal systems. An account of their vocalizations presupposes a specification of what they are *in principle* capable of doing (the developing but language-independent phonetic space) and what they are actually observed doing (the behaviors in that space that are *actually* selected under the influence of functional constraints).

The Output

The model enumerates phonetic specifications of lexical forms according to a rank order that is determined by the interaction of phonetic universals, language-specific factors, and the particular learning path taken during an individual run. Vocabulary growth is studied by inspecting more and more forms according to their rank order. The model consequently suggests hypotheses about "order of acquisition," but, as we shall see below, developmental paths can vary for various reasons. Hence, there is no single, fixed order of acquisition.

The Universal and Language-Specific Constraints

In figures 7 through 10 the format of the computations is outlined. The production constraints process "possible articulations" specified by

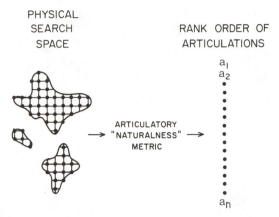

Figure 7. Left: The range of "possible articulations" (universal phonetic space, or the anthropophonic space). Note the subspaces; they indicate continuous variation within quantally separated and qualitatively distinct regions (cf. Stevens 1989). The grid patterns indicate quantization imposed for computational reasons.

the search space (or some fragment of it) and evaluate them with respect to "articulatory cost." We can think of the output of this stage as a rank-ordered list of favored articulations (figure 7).

The items on this list provide the rows and columns of the triangular matrix of figure 8. This notation is used at several levels in the present framework. The reason is the nature of "discriminability." It is a "systemic" parameter in that it presupposes a comparison between at least two elements. When n items are compared, the number of pair-

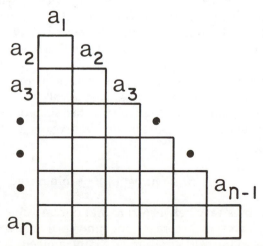

Figure 8. The triangular matrix as a method of representing information on the contrasting pairs formed by a set of n articulatory patterns.

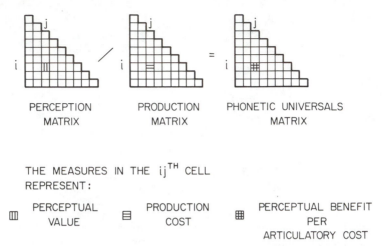

Figure 9.   The universals matrix containing measures of the adaptive values of a set of contrasting articulations as determined by biological production and perception constraints.

wise comparisons grows as $n(n-1)/2$. It then becomes convenient to use the "round-robin" notation of the triangular matrix as a reference to the pairwise comparisons made and to store information on these pairs as cell contents.

The model uses several such matrices. The values of the "universals matrix" are obtained by dividing the numbers of the "perception matrix" by those of the "production matrix" for the corresponding cells (figure 9). A cell entry in the universals matrix measures the functional value—the "perceptual benefit per articulatory cost"—of incorporating the contrast between articulations $a(i)$ and $a(j)$ in the derivations. The "perceptual advantage" and the "pronounceability" of that contrast are entered in the $a(i,j)$ cells of the perception and production matrices respectively.

Another matrix (figure 10) contains coefficients reflecting the contrasts that actually occur in the linguistic input. The interaction between the "input matrix" and the universal factors produces the matrix from which system selections are made, the "cost-benefit matrix." It is specified by:

$$\sum_{i=2}^{n} \sum_{j=1}^{i-1} s(i,j)/(d(i,j)/a(i,j))^2 \rightarrow \text{minimized} \qquad (6)$$

where $s(i,j)$ entries vary between zero and one. A value of one in the input-matrix leaves the score of the universal matrix unchanged, whereas zeros in the cells appropriate for the ambient language make the procedure converge on the adult system. Values between these ex-

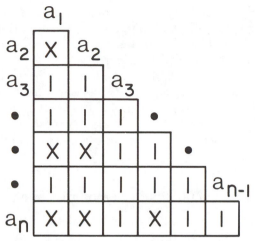

Figure 10.   The input matrix. Representation of the contrasts of the ambient language. The value of one signifies a nonoccurring contrast, an X is a number between zero and one that reflects the balance between universal language-specific factors.

tremes represent shifts in the balance between universal and language-specific factors. Systematic variations of this balance may have some interesting consequences for modeling developmental differences both between individuals and between stages.

An important source of weighting of the language-specific factors is the development of the child's perceptual system, which has been shown to progress from an initial state of relatively neutral sensitivity to a reorganization more tuned to the language spoken around it (Werker and Pegg this volume). The difference between the $d(i,j)$ matrix and the $s(i,j)$ matrix—which are both related to perception—is that the former captures biologically determined, developmental relations whereas the latter reflects the modulation of those relations by linguistic experience.

Systemic Selection

A key feature of the model is the systemic nature of the selection criterion. The equations handle that aspect by means of the double summation sign, which implies that it is the *sum of all possible contrast scores* that is calculated. Hence, entire systems are evaluated and compared with each other. The procedure selects phonetic forms that are optimal, not by themselves in isolation, but relative to the other members of the system. The functional value of an articulation is not context-free, but is defined only in relation to its system neighbors. This systemic criterion forces constituent elements to cooperate and is responsible for the quantal properties of the selections. (Cf. Stevens (1989) in which acoustic-auditory stability is the selection criterion. That criterion is nonsystemic yielding predictions of targets, not systems.)

If we assume that, in lexical access, the speech signal is compared in parallel with elements of the listener's lexical system and its role is to discriminate among the possible candidates of that system (Luce 1986), the percept is itself a product of a systemic process. Hence, the origin and the nature of discriminability can be traced to the processes of on-line speech perception.

Self-segmentation and Continuity of Motor Learning

To accommodate the gestural components defined by self-segmentation and their influence on the course of lexical development, we introduce a feedback loop that has the effect of recalibrating cell entries in the cost-benefit matrix. Menn's notion of "articulatory ease" (Menn 1983)—the idea that already acquired motor skills facilitate the learning of new related forms—implies that the functional values of all potential, not-yet-acquired contrasts invoking those skills undergo modification. We propose that, in the model, self-segmentation produces a set of coefficients that, everything else being equal, increase the probability of selecting new contrasts involving those already acquired routines. That set is denoted by $m(i,j)$ in equation (7).

$$\sum_{i=2}^{n} \sum_{j=1}^{i-1} s(i,j)m(i,j)/(d(i,j)/a(i,j))^2 \rightarrow \text{minimized} \qquad (7)$$

Through $m(i,j)$ new items with already mastered self-segmented gestures are allowed to perturb the hierarchy defined by phonetic factors (the a and d matrices) and by the input (the s matrix). The strength with which that happens can be adjusted in terms of a "gain control," that is by weighting the $m(i,j)$ coefficients uniformly in relation to the other matrices.

Sources of Individual Variation

Equation (7) states an optimization criterion. It defines the best system. A set of "sufficiently good" systems would be obtained by making a slight modification of equation (7). Instead of a single optimal system, we can ask for a whole collection of systems whose common denominator is that they are all better than a given threshold value:

$$\sum_{i=2}^{n} \sum_{j=1}^{i-1} s(i,j)m(i,j)/(d(i,j)/a(i,j))^2 < \text{threshold} \qquad (8)$$

This expression generates several solutions all compatible with the "sufficiently good" criterion and thus, would introduce the variety we need to study individual learning paths.

Another factor that could give rise to individual variation is the starting point of the derivations that can be set at random or in some principled way. Eventually the constraints would make two different initiations converge, but at first the processes will exhibit discrepancies. Self-segmentation could then conceivably take two different routes before reaching equifinality.

A third possibility has to do with statistical differences in the specification of the input and the rate at which individual children develop perceptual representations of its contents. Accordingly, the present model offers a number of ways in which individual variation could arise.

Role of Universals

The phonetic universals exert an indirect influence on the derivations. Their effects do not neccesarily appear on the surface in forms that remain constant across derivations. Their causal role is indirect and implicit.

The universals matrix is structured to reflect the conflicting demands of production and perception. At the top of the list of favored articulations (figure 7) the model would place phonetic gestures that are biomechanically low-cost and that put minimal demands on articulatory channel capacity in terms of temporal fine control and spatial precision. Provided that we quantify production constraints along such lines, we would expect the model to predict initial utterances with limited displacements and movement rates and requiring little spatio-temporal coordination. Canonical babbling seems to exhibit precisely those characteristics. Investigations of variegated babbling and first words show that there are strong preferences for certain co-articulatory patterns of vowel-consonant co-occurrence (MacNeilage and Davis 1990; Vihman this volume). Such findings suggest that reduced extents of movement are favored, which lends further support to a biomechanical component of production cost.

However, during the last few years it has become increasingly clear that from its onset the motor processes of babbling are already being shaped by the child's auditory (and visual) perception of the speech around it, as well as by its auditory perception of itself. That interpretation (Vihman 1988; Studdert-Kennedy 1989) is suggested by differences between groups of normal, deaf, blind, and tracheostomized children (Locke 1983; Locke and Pearson 1989; Mulford 1988; Stoel-Gammon 1988).

Thus, babbling may be a compromise that keeps articulatory costs down while nevertheless achieving some degree of auditory similarity with salient and discriminable properties of the input signal; for example, its gross amplitude envelope characteristics. The machinery that seems suitable for accommodating such compromise behaviors in the present model is the cost-benefit matrix.

Language-specific Effects

The instrument for representing the ambient language is the input matrix whose cell entries can be set according to experimental evidence on the state of the child's perceptual system. The development of perceptual phonetic categories is currently a dynamic research area (Jusczyk this volume; Kluender 1988; Kuhl 1989; Werker and Pegg this volume). However, before more detailed study can be made of how predicted systems depend upon the input matrix, we also need more information on the detailed acoustic nature of the speech that the children experience and use to build a perceptual representation of the input language. Preliminary evidence from our own laboratory (Davis and Lindblom 1991) indicates that, while baby talk to a six-month-old may contain instances of vowel and consonant segments that are prototypical (in the sense of Kuhl 1989) and relatively context-free, it also shows the variability and ambiguities typical of coarticulated and reduced adult-to-adult speech. Insofar as baby talk does not undo those phenomena, it, too, poses the problem of phonetic invariance (Perkell and Klatt 1986; Lindblom 1990a). Consequently, when addressing the nature of the child's perceptual representations, we also need to deal with the question of their acoustic bases.

CONCLUSIONS

According to the present account, children end up with phonemes for two reasons. They possess the necessary conceptual capacity and the communicative need to develop large lexicons. Given these cognitive pressures—whose origins pose a separate problem not addressed here (see Bates 1979)—they fortuitously hit upon the path toward phonemic coding aided by articulatory, perceptual, and memorial processes. One claim we can make is that *phonetic gestures* are *emergents, not primitives* of the theory. This is in line with the crystallization process envisioned by Studdert-Kennedy, but is clearly different from the premises of standard distinctive feature theory (Jakobson, Fant, and Halle 1969; Chomsky and Halle 1968). Thus, phonological emergence offers a spontaneous and unsupervised mechanism for supplementing the input speech which, we assume, presents the child with the "invariance problem." It illustrates how children can learn more than they experience or are taught.

There is no abrupt transition from "holistic" to "analytic" coding because the present account is a "have-your-cake-and-eat-it-too" scenario. Phonetically, acquired words remain continuous motor scores and unitary acoustic patterns. Phonologically, they gradually develop gestural overlap and, by self-segmentation, they cumulatively assemble a network of discrete structures. Blowing out a candle may be phonetically identical to a voiceless bilabial fricative but is functionally (and presumably neurophysiologically) different because it does not enter into a system of phonological relations (Sapir 1925; Studdert-Kennedy 1989). "System of phonological relations" here receives a preliminary concrete interpretation.

Also note that the problem of "psychological reality" does not arise here in its usual form, because "psychological reality" must be seen as the theory's starting point. Again, recall that if developing lexical systems were seen as adaptations to functional constraints, what would they be like? In the context of that theme, the problem of "psychological reality" becomes that of unpacking the "functional constraints," anchoring them in independently motivated behavioral knowledge, rather than that of justifying a postulated formalistic account post hoc.

One further advantage of undertaking a search for emergents is *methodological parsimony.* We avoid attributing too much to the child. Clearly children do not develop phonemes "in order to" solve the problem of acquiring a large lexicon at a rapid rate. In the parlance of ecological psychologists (Bellugi and Studdert-Kennedy 1981), the mechanism of emergence makes it unnecessary to "take loans on" cognition—a risk facing proponents of cognitive models. Nor is it necessary to take loans on evolution—a risk facing proponents of universal grammar.

Comprehensive predictions for detailed comparison with children's phonetic forms have not been attempted here. They presuppose major interdisciplinary investments and must await further developments of phonetic theory. We do not want to give the impression that there are quantitative universal phonetic production models ready to use for the articulatory and acoustic synthesis of some arbitrary portion of the anthropophonic space. Nor do we know how to quantify possible performance constraints in experimentally satisfactory ways. Current efforts in that direction are admittedly preliminary.

Do such circumstances make the present program premature? The answer is simply that the issues that have been discussed in this chapter deserve to be taken seriously. Unless they are explicitly raised, they are unlikely to be addressed.

REFERENCES

Bates, E. 1979. *The Emergence of Symbols.* New York: Academic Press.

Bellugi, U., and Studdert-Kennedy, M. 1980. *Sign Language and Spoken Language: Biological Constraints on Linguistic Form.* Dahlem workshop. Weinheim: Verlag Chemie.

Bladon, R. A. W., and Lindblom, B. 1981. Modeling the judgment of vowel quality differences. *Journal of the Acoustical Society of America* 69:1414–1422.

Boyd, R., and Richerson, P. 1985. *Culture and the Evolutionary Process.* Chicago: Chicago University Press.

Browman, C. P., and Goldstein, L. M. 1985. Dynamic modeling of phonetic structure. In *Phonetic Linguistics,* ed. V. A. Fromkin. Orlando, FL: Academic Press.

Catford, J. C. 1977. *Fundamental Problems in Phonetics.* Bloomington: Indiana University Press.

Chafe, W. L. 1970. *Meaning and the Structure of Language.* Chicago: Chicago University Press.

Chomsky, N. 1972. *Language and Mind.* Harcourt, Brace, and World (extended edition).

Chomsky, N. 1981. *Lectures on Government and Binding.* Dordrecht: Foris.

Chomsky, N., and Halle, M. 1968. *The Sound Pattern of English.* New York: Harper & Row.

Crothers, J. 1978. Typology and universals of vowel systems. In *Universals of Human Language.* Vol 2., eds. J. H. Greenberg, C. A. Ferguson, and E. A. Moravcsik. Stanford: Stanford University Press.

Davis, B. L., and MacNeilage, P. F. 1990. Acquisition of correct vowel production: A quantitative case study. *Journal of Speech and Hearing Research* 33:16–27.

Davis, B., and Lindblom, B. 1991. Prototypical vowel information in baby talk. *Current Phonetic Research Paradigms: Implications for Speech Motor Control. Perilus.* Stockholm University.

Dawkins, R. 1983. Universal Darwinism. In *Evolution from Molecules to Men,* ed. D. S. Bendall. Cambridge: Cambridge University Press.

Dawkins, R. 1986. *The Blind Watchmaker.* London and New York: Norton.

Fant, G. 1960. *The Acoustic Theory of Speech Production.* The Hague: Mouton.

Ferguson, C. A., and Farwell, C. B. 1975. Words and sounds in early language acquisition: English initial consonants in the first fifty words. *Language* 51:419–39.

Halle, M. 1975. Confessio grammatici. *Language* 51:525–35.

Jakobson, R., Fant, G., and Halle, M. 1969. *Preliminaries to Speech Analysis.* Cambridge: M I T Press.

Klatt, D. H. 1979. Speech perception: A model of acoustic-phonetic analysis and lexical access. *Journal of Phonetics* 7:279–312.

Kluender, K. K. 1988. Auditory constraints on phonetic categorization: Trading relations in humans in nonhumans. Doctoral dissertation, Department of Psychology, University of Texas, Austin.

Kuhl, P. K. 1989. Speech categories are represented by prototypes. *5th Annual Meeting of the Language Origins Society.* University of Austin, Austin, Texas.

Ladefoged, P. 1987. Revising the International Phonetic Alphabet. *Proceedings of the XIth International Congress of Phonetic Sciences.* Section 64.5.1, Tallinn, Estonia.

Ladefoged, P., and Maddieson, I. 1986. Some of the sounds of the world's languages. *UCLA Working Papers in Phonetics* 64.

Lightfoot, D. 1989. The child's trigger experience: Degree of learnability. *Behavioral and Brain Sciences* 12(2):321–75.

Lindblom, B. 1963. Spectrographic study of vowel reduction. *Journal of the Acoustical Society of America* 35:1773–1781.

Lindblom, B. 1986. Phonetic universals in vowel systems. In *Experimental Phonology,* eds. J. J. Ohala and J. J. Jaeger. Orlando, FL: Academic Press.

Lindblom, B. 1990a. Explaining phonetic variation: A sketch of the H&H theory. In *Speech Production and Speech Modeling,* eds. W. J. Hardcastle and A. Marchal. Dordrecht: Kluwer Publishers.

Lindblom, B. 1990b. On the notion of "possible speech sound." *Journal of Phonetics* 18:135–52.

Lindblom, B., and Maddieson, I. 1988. Phonetic universals in consonant systems. In *Language, Speech and Mind,* eds. L. M. Hyman and C. N. Li. London and New York: Routledge.

Lindblom, B., MacNeilage, P. and Studdert-Kennedy, M. 1983. Self-organizing processes and the explanation of phonological universals. In *Explanations of Linguistic Universals,* eds. B. Butterworth, B. Comrie, and Ö. Dahl. The Hague: Mouton.

Lindblom, B., and Sundberg, J. 1971. Acoustical consequences of lip, tongue, jaw and larynx movement. *Journal of the Acoustical Society of America* 50(4): 1166–1179.

Lindblom, B., Pauli, S., and Sundberg, J. 1975. Modeling coarticulation in apical stops. In *Proceedings of the Speech Communication Seminar,* Vol 2., ed. G. Fant. Stockholm: Almqvist & Wiksell.

Locke, J. L. 1983. *Phonological Acquisition and Change.* New York: Academic Press.

Locke, J. L., and Pearson, D. M. 1989. Linguistic significance of babbling: Evidence from a tracheostomized infant. *Report from the Neurolinguistics Laboratory at Massachusetts General Hospital.*

Luce, P. A. 1986. Neighborhoods of words in the mental lexicon. Doctoral dissertation, Department of Psychology, Indiana University.

Macken, M. A. 1979. Developmental reorganization of phonology: A hierarchy of basic units of acquisition. *Lingua* 49:11–49.

Macken, M. A., and Ferguson, C. A. 1983. Cognitive aspects of phonological development: Model, evidence and issues. In *Children's Language.* Vol 4., ed. K. Nelson. Hillsdale, NJ: Lawrence Erlbaum and Associates.

MacNeilage, P. F. 1987. The evolution of hemispheric specialization for manual function and language. In *Higher Brain Functions: Recent Explorations of the Brain's Emergent Properties,* ed. S. Wise. New York: Wiley.

MacNeilage, P. F. 1991. The "postural origins" theory of primate neurobiological asymmetries. In *Biobehavioral Foundations of Language Development,* eds. N. Krasnegor, D. Rumbaugh, R. Schiefelbusch, and M. Studdert-Kennedy. Hillsdale, NJ: Lawrence Erlbaum Associates.

MacNeilage, P. F., and Davis, B. L. 1990. Acquisition of speech production: Frames, then content. In *Attention and Performance XIII: Motor Representation and Control,* ed. M. Jeannerod. NJ: Lawrence Erlbaum Associates.

Maddieson, I. 1984. *Patterns of Sound.* Cambridge: Cambridge University Press.

Mayr, E. 1974. Behavior programs and evolutionary strategies. *American Scientist* 62:650–59.

Mayr, E. 1978. Evolution. *Scientific American* 239(3):39–47.

McCune, L., and Vihman, M. 1987. Vocal motor schemes. *Papers and Reports on Child Language Development* 26:72–79.

Meier, R. 1990. A psycholinguistic perspective on phonological segmentation in sign and speech. Ms thesis, University of Texas at Austin.

Menn, L. 1976. Pattern, control and contrast in beginning speech. Unpublished doctoral dissertation, University of Illinois.

Menn, L. 1978. Phonological units in beginning speech. In *Syllables and Segments*, eds. A. Bell and J. B. Hooper. Amsterdam: North Holland.

Menn, L. 1980. Phonological theory and child phonology. In *Child Phonology*, Vol 1. eds. G. H. Yeni-Komshian, J. F. Kavanagh, and C. A. Ferguson. New York: Academic Press.

Menn, L. 1983. Development of articulatory, phonetic and phonological capabilities. In *Language Production* vol II., ed. B. Butterworth. London: Academic Press.

Menn, L. 1987. Two kids, two stories: Problems in relating early lexical and phonological development. *Stanford Child Language Research Forum*, April 1987.

Miller, G. A. 1977. *Spontaneous Apprentices.* New York: Seabury Press.

Moon, S.-J. 1991. An acoustic and perceptual study of undershoot in clear and citation-form speech. Unpublished doctoral dissertation, University of Texas.

Mulford, R. 1988. First words of the blind child. In *The Emergent Lexicon*, eds. M. D. Smith and J. L. Locke. New York: Academic Press.

Nelson, W. L., Perkell, J. S., and Westbury, J. R. 1984. Mandible movements during increasingly rapid articulations of single syllables: Preliminary observations. *Journal of the Acoustical Society of America* 75(3):945–51.

Ohala, J. J. 1980. Chairman's introduction to the symposium on phonetic universals in phonological systems and their explanation. In *Proceedings of the Ninth International Congress of Phonetic Sciences*. 1979, Institute of Phonetics, University of Copenhagen.

Ohala, J. J. 1989. The phonetics and phonology of aspects of assimilation. In *1st Conference on Laboratory Phonology*, eds. M. Beckman and J. Kingston. Cambridge: Cambridge University Press.

Oller, D., Wieman, L. A., Doyle, W. J., and Ross, C. 1975. Infant babbling and speech. *Journal of Child Language* 3:1–11.

Oster, G. F., and Wilson, E. O. 1978. A critique of optimization theory in evolutionary biology. In *Caste and Ecology in the Social Insects*, eds. G. F. Oster and E. O. Wilson. Princeton, NJ: Princeton University Press.

Perkell, J., and Klatt, D. 1986. *Invariance and Variability of Speech Processes.* Hillsdale, NJ: Lawrence Erlbaum Associates.

Pinker, S., and Bloom, P. 1990. Natural language and natural selection. *Behavioral and Brain Sciences* 13:707–784.

Plomp, R. 1970. Timbre as a multidimensional attribute of complex tones. In *Frequency Analysis and Periodicity Detection in Hearing*, eds. R. Plomp and G. Smoorenburg. Leiden: Sijthoff.

Premack, D. 1985. 'Gavagai!' or the future history of the animal language controversy. *Cognition* 19:207–96.

Priestly, T. M. S. 1977. One idiosyncratic strategy in the acquisition of phonology. *Journal of Child Language* 4:46–65.

Sapir, E. 1925. Sound patterns in language. *Language* 1:37–51.

Schroeder, M., Atal, S., and Hall, J. L. 1979. Objective measure of certain speech signal degradations based on masking properties of human auditory perception. In *Frontiers of Speech Communication Research*, eds. B. Lindblom and S. Öhman. London: Academic Press.

Schwartz, R., and Leonard, L. 1982. Do children pick and choose? An examination of phonological selection and avoidance in early lexical acquisition. *Journal of Child Language* 9:319–36.

Stevens, K. N. 1989. On the quantal nature of speech. *Journal of Phonetics* 17(1/2):3–45.

Stoel-Gammon, C. 1988. Prelinguistic vocalizations of hearing-impaired and normally hearing subjects: A comparison of consonantal inventories. *Journal of Speech and Hearing Disorders* 53(3):302–315.

Studdert-Kennedy, M. 1983. On learning to speak. *Human Neurobiology* 2:191–95.

Studdert-Kennedy, M. 1986. Chapter 1 in B. Lindblom, P. MacNeilage, and M. Studdert-Kennedy (in preparation): *Evolution of Spoken Language.* Orlando, FL: Academic Press.

Studdert-Kennedy, M. 1987. The phoneme as a perceptuomotor structure. In *Language, Perception and Production* eds. A. Allport, D. MacKay, W. Prinz, and E. Scheerer. New York: Academic Press.

Studdert-Kennedy, M. 1989. The early development of phonology. In *Neurobiology of Early Infant Behavior,* eds. C. von Euler, H. Forsberg, and H. Lagercrantz. New York: Stockton.

Templin, M. C. 1957. *Certain Language Skills in Children: Their Development and Interrelationships.* Minneapolis: University of Minnesota Press.

Vihman, M. M. 1976. From prespeech to speech: On early phonology. *Papers and Reports on Child Language Development* 12.

Vihman, M. M. 1988. The ontogeny of phonetic gestures: speech production. In *Modularity and the Motor Theory of Speech Perception,* eds. I. Mattingly and M. Studdert-Kennedy. Hillsdale, NJ: Lawrence Erlbaum Associates.

Vihman, M. M., Macken, M. A., Miller, R., Simmons, H., and Miller, J. 1985. From babbling to speech: A reassessment of the continuity issue. *Language* 61(3):395–443.

Waterson, N. 1971. Child phonology: A prosodic view. *Journal of Linguistics* 7:179–211.

Chapter • 5

A Connectionist View of Child Phonology
Phonological Processing without Phonological Processes

Joseph Paul Stemberger

Children's pronunciations of words often are quite different from the pronunciations of adult native speakers of the language. One of the goals of child phonology is to account for these differences, and a number of approaches have been taken. Usually, the researcher first determines how the child's pronunciation of words differs from that of adults.[1] In one common approach, the differences between the adult form and the child form are encoded as phonological processes (Smith 1973; Ingram 1976; Macken 1987). These processes take the form of the word as the child has perceived it as input and change it into the child form. The processes apply on-line during language production to derive the child's pronunciation every time the

---

[1]Some researchers focus on the child's system and ignore its relation with adult phonology (Ferguson and Farwell 1975; Dinnsen and Elbert 1984; Stoel-Gammon 1985). This approach is incomplete, because the relation to the (perceived) adult pronunciation is what drives the child to alter his or her phonological system.

This work was supported in part by NSF Research Grant #BNS-8710288. At various points in the paper, I introduce unpublished diary data from my two oldest children, Gwendolyn and Morgan. For details of procedure, see Stemberger (1988).

child attempts to say a given word. A second common approach is the two-lexicon approach (Menn 1983; Dinnsen and Elbert 1984). The child has a special lexicon used only for language production that stores those pronunciations that are very close to the child's actual pronunciations. There is also a perceptual lexicon, in which the form of the word as perceived by the child is stored. The child has processes that convert the pronunciation in the perceptual lexicon into a form the child can actually produce, which is then stored permanently in the production lexicon. The processes apply only once for a given word (to create the entry in the production lexicon), not each time the child uses the word.

These two approaches agree on one very fundamental point: the existence of explicit procedures (processes) for deriving the child's actual pronunciation from the perceived form (whether the changes are made on-line or off-line). I believe that this point of agreement between the approaches is incorrect. The child has no overt procedures for adapting perceived forms to a form that he or she can produce, but instead attempts to reproduce the perceived form faithfully. All changes are accidental; they are true errors, in which the child's system produces a result that it was not designed to produce. As the child's pronunciation changes over time, the improvements derive from increased accuracy in the access of phonological information.

I am attempting to do away with explicit procedures for deriving the child's pronunciations for several reasons. First, I do not feel that they give a psychologically plausible picture of young children. It is unlikely that children alter their output goals or output targets for pronouncing words in the way that processes assume.[2] Second, the process approach assumes that specific aspects of the child's system are needed only to produce errors. Pinker (1984) objects to such schemes and argues for a Continuity Hypothesis, holding that the same basic things are going on at all stages of development. We must treat adult and child behavior as being fundamentally the same. Rumelhart and McClelland (1986) object to explicit rules of any sort. I do not feel that we have enough information to object to all rules, but child phonology processes should be eliminated because they are not based on data in the input language and are not needed in adult speech. Because it is convenient to refer to particular changes in pronunciation, it is necessary to coin a more neutral term for them; I will use the term *warp*.

The child's phonological warps are true errors, deriving from the same processing characteristics that underlie true phonological speech errors in the speech of children and adults (as well as phonological paraphasias in aphasia). There are obvious differences in frequency (every time versus rare), but this difference is both superficial and pre-

---

[2]The word *goal* as used here has no implication of consciousness or intentionality.

dictable. Vihman (1978, 1981) and Locke (1983) also view the child's warps as errors, but do not discuss how the errors occur. In this paper I explicitly address how errors (at all ages) arise.

What goes on in language development is exactly the same as in other areas of development. It seems easy to think about the child's phonological errors as involving a change of goals on the part of the child (via processes). However, we rarely attribute motor errors to a change in goals. When a child attempts to walk and instead falls down, we do not assume that the child has modified the (impossible) goal of walking into falling down, which the child is capable of doing.[3] The child's language errors should be viewed in the same way.

FUNDAMENTAL CONCEPTS

The most promising approach for explaining human cognitive behavior is *connectionism*. The more traditional symbolic approaches are plagued by a theory that is too powerful, that in principle can *describe* all imaginable types of language systems (and that hence can *explain* none). The usual strategy in symbolic models is to determine empirically what actually happens and then to build in constraints on the system's power so that it can no longer handle things that never happen. Although these constraints are empirically motivated, they are arbitrary from the standpoint of the theoretical framework in which they are stated. Connectionism has a quite different goal: to account for characteristics of cognitive processing in a theory-internal fashion, starting from simple units and processing characteristics. To be sure, we are far from reaching the stated goal, but even with "cheating"— where the characteristics are partly assumed in such a way as to be useful (Lachter and Bever 1988)—we can learn a great deal about what is needed to describe a given phenomenon. Macken (1987) has suggested that a symbolic level that includes overt processes is needed, in addition to a stochastic level such as connectionist models represent; one goal of this chapter is to argue that the stochastic level adequately accounts for warps, with no need for a higher level of representation.

There are two main approaches within connectionism: *local* connectionism, in which units have a functional value (an apparent symbol such as the word *dog* or the phoneme /p/),[4] defined in terms of how

---

[3]Note that a child may, however, decide to avoid entirely a certain activity such as walking—consciously avoiding the activity rather than altering the low-level goals of the activity.

[4]I say "apparent symbols" because local connectionist models are made nonsymbolic by the existence of gang effects, which distribute the representation of any given unit across a set of units.

they interact with other units in the system and in relation to input from and output to the external world; and *distributed* connectionism, where ideally no unit (except very low-level ones) have any functional value. The two variations behave in similar ways and show similar sets of properties. In this chapter I generally use a local model, but switch to distributed models when the need arises (generally, because only distributed models have a well-defined learning component).

The local connectionist model I use is based on the reading model of McClelland and Rumelhart (1981), as extended to language production by Stemberger (1985, 1990). There are strong similarities with the models of Dell (1986) and MacKay (1987). None of the applications to child phonology here have yet been simulated on a computer. However, because simulations must be vastly oversimplified given the state of computer technology today, so that all researchers disavow the verisimilitude of their models, I do not view this as a problem.

In this model, all information is encoded in terms of *units* with an *activation level,* which is a measure of the amount of activity in that unit; low levels denote inactive units, whereas very high levels denote that the unit currently is being produced. Each unit has a basic *resting level* to which it returns when it is not being used. Units can differ in terms of how high their resting levels are; units with high resting levels (generally of high frequency) can be accessed more rapidly and more accurately than units with low resting levels (generally of low frequency). There is always some *noise* in the system, i.e., random fluctuations in resting levels and the amount of activation being passed between different units. This noise can result in the wrong unit having the most activation, in which case it is erroneously accessed. Units are organized into different functional levels: the feature level, the phoneme level, the word level, etc.

Some units are in a complementary relationship, so that only one can be produced at a given point, e.g., *dog* versus *cat,* /t/ versus /d/, or [+ voiced] versus [− voiced]. A unit contributes *inhibition* (essentially negative activation) to decrease the activation level of the competing unit. The most activated unit usually inhibits competing units so that they can only reach low levels of activation. The effectiveness of this depends on how activated the winner eventually becomes; the greater the activation of the winner, the less the activation of the competitors.

Language production begins at the semantic and pragmatic levels, proceeds to the word and syntactic levels, then to the syllable and phoneme levels, then to the feature level, and then to the motor programming system (figure 1). However, processing is not entirely top-down. As processing begins on each level, partial information is passed to the next level down in a phenomenon known as *cascading.* As the activation level of lower-level units rises, activation gets passed back up to

MEANING:

WORDS:

PHONOLOGICAL:

FEATURE:

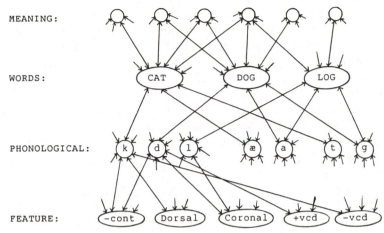

Figure 1.   Fragment of the system, showing levels and interconnections.

higher levels (as *feedback*) and can influence the activity at those higher levels. Any given unit receives activation from a number of sources at various levels, which it sums. The outcome is determined by the total amount of activation present in each unit, regardless of source. The system tends to wind up at a stable state with compatible units accessed at all levels.

One of the most important characteristics of connectionist models is *superpositional memory*: the representations of different words overlap; that is, use partially overlapping sets of units. In a local model this is not true of the lexical level, but is true of units at the semantic and phonological levels. Superpositional memory automatically causes different words to interact with each other, so that generalizations across words occur. This allows the system to show very regular behavior without explicitly discovering or extracting such generalizations. None of the main properties of connectionist models (desirable or undesirable) would be present without superpositional memory. One consequence of superpositional memory is that lower level units must be selected actively from a competing set of phonemes and features, on the basis of activation from higher-level units; accessing a word does not give easy access to the word's component phonemes.

Whenever a unit is activated, it sends activation out to all other units to which it is connected. Activation is scattered to incorrect units that are similar to the intended *target* unit, because such incorrect units are connected to target units at other levels—for example, when accessing /f/, /v/ becomes partially activated due to feedback from the features that /v/ shares with /f/. Feedback can lead to errors; for example, if /v/ is already activated for some reason, feedback may make it the most activated phoneme and allow it to inhibit (and thereby replace) /f/.

When many units at a given level are similar, they mutually rein-force shared information. Such a grouping of units is called a *gang* (fig-ure 2). For example, if most words in the lexicon start with a /b/, all these words will reinforce /b/, and the system will tend to access a /b/ at the beginning of the word regardless of whether the target word be-gins with a /b/ or not.

The key concept in discussing what happens during processing is the *accessibility* of a unit. A highly accessible unit will show few errors. An inaccessible unit will show a 100% error rate. Accessibility varies with context, depending on how much competition (inhibition) is present from other units. It is probable that accessibility is related partly to how difficult it is to produce the sound (aerodynamically, bio-mechanically, etc.; cf. Kent this volume; Lindblom this volume), but it is at least partly a function of frequency (type *and* token). A unit may be inaccessible because (a) it has too low an activation level (due to a low resting level or to too little activation coming through the connections with higher units), or (b) a similar competitor has too much activation (and hence inhibits it too much).

Learning has two instantiations in the model. First, resting levels increase with each access of a unit, so high-frequency targets become more accessible. Second, the mapping between units on adjacent levels must be learned. Each connection has a *weight* that determines how much activation is passed. For /v/, the weights should be high on the connections with [Labial], [+continuant], and [+voiced], and low on the connections with [Coronal], [−continuant], and [−voiced]. The proper weights are learned by attempting to say something and eval-uating how well it worked. If it worked all right, nothing is changed. If there was something wrong (determined by comparing the perceived form of what was produced to the perceived form of adults' pronuncia-tions), the child alters the weights so that the correct pronunciation will be more likely the next time (e.g., Rumelhart, Hinton, and Williams 1986). Inherent in this process is error; in order to tune the system cor-rectly, the child must produce forms with errors to find out where the system is set up inaccurately. If /v/ is mispronounced as [d], the weights on connections to [Labial] and [+continuant] are increased, and those to [Coronal] and [−continuant] are decreased. Changes in

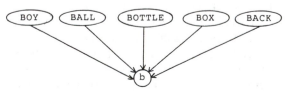

Figure 2. Top-down gangs.

weights are small, in order not to upset the entire system; it may take a long time before weights are changed enough to have an effect. Due to noise, there is usually a period of variation where the target output is sometimes accessible and sometimes not. This period may be very brief or quite long, depending on how much competition there is from other output states and on the size of the weight changes.

It is necessary to take a stand on fundamental characteristics of phonological representations. There is presently insufficient information to determine reliably what representations are like. I will assume features; segments; syllable units, which parse the string into syllables and syllable constituents; and a coarse phonological representation (like the CV tier in phonological theory) that codes only the number of segments involved. The coarse representations can be viewed as "slots" to which each phoneme must be associated in order to be produced (Shattuck-Hufnagel 1979; Dell 1986; Stemberger 1990); without a slot, the phoneme cannot attain enough activation and is "deleted" (i.e., is not accessed). There must be a way to access the same element, e.g., the feature [+voiced], several times in a single word, and this is probably done with multiple sets of features that, nonetheless, can interfere with each other.

I assume that the child's representations are composed of segments (/b/, /a/, /u/) rather than undifferentiated syllables (/ba/, /bu/) (cf. Lindblom this volume). It is clear that segmental representations are present in adult speech (e.g., Stemberger 1990). Segmental representations also work best to account for basic properties of phonological warps at most ages: (a) most warps treat consonants and vowels as independent; (b) warps often affect particular segments rather than features (so that /v/ is affected although /f/ and /z/ are not); (c) consonants in clusters often are subject to deletion, but they are much less commonly fused into a single segment (e.g., /sp/ → [f]), suggesting that they are strongly differentiated; and (d) it is very rare to split a single segment into two segments (e.g., Fey and Gandour 1982). Most of these arguments do not hold for the child's first words, however, because first words are so restricted phonologically and so few output states are accessible. There are no compelling arguments *against* segmental representations from the beginning, however. One argument is that some children have difficulty binding individual features together (e.g., *pin* in Ferguson and Farwell 1975), but such scrambling of features (a) is uncommon across children, and (b) can be viewed as a problem with serial ordering, not with segmentation. A second argument against early segmentation is the lexical explosion that is assumed to take place at about 50 words, which has been attributed to the discovery of the segment by the child (Macken 1979). Because it is now recognized that few children show a lexical explosion, this is not a compelling argument (Stoel-Gammon 1987). Dell (1986) includes both segment units (/b/) and syllable units (/ba/) in his simulations of adult behavior; it is possible that data may be found that require syllable units, but I will take them as currently unproven; and evidence *for* syllable units cannot be construed as evidence *against* the additional presence of segments.

I assume that the child's representations are identical to those of adults (barring occasional misperceptions). The difference from adult language production falls into three realms. First, connections between the units on different levels do not have the proper weights. All possible output states are present from the beginning, but most are inaccessible because of the incorrect weights. Second, the inhibition of nontarget units may be more (or less) efficient than in adult speech. Third, the parameters underlying some of the basic characteristics of processing, such as the amount of feedback from the phonological to the lexical levels, may be set differently than in adult speech.

I explore the ramifications of these proposals for child phonology, organizing the discussion around particular phenomena. Error effects can be divided into basic effects on the accessibility of a unit and interference effects from other units being accessed.

NONINTERFERENCE PHENOMENA

Phenomena that do not involve interference from other units that are being processed reflect pure difficulties with the access of phonological elements. The most common type of speech error made by adults (both normal and aphasic) is substitution of some sound for the target sound, followed by loss of segments, and last by addition of segments where none occurred in the target (Blumstein 1973; Stemberger 1982). If the target element attains a high enough activation level, it is processed correctly. Somewhat lower levels of activation make the element prone to substitution by competing elements. If the activation level is too low, then even nontarget segments have too little activation, and nothing is accessed. In adult speech, activation levels are high enough that loss is relatively uncommon. In child speech, activation levels are in general lower; the target unit often receives so little activation that nothing is accessed, and deletion results.

Some types of loss errors derive from a limited set of coarse representations in the child's speech. At the beginning, there is at most a single consonant at any given position in the word, with clusters being impossible. Because only one consonant position is provided, at most one will be accessed; generally, the other consonant is deleted (but see below). Deletion of word-final consonants may be due to the lack of a slot in some children. However, if the child can produce some final consonants but deletes others, the necessary slot structure is present, and the loss errors have other sources.

Loss versus substitution errors highlight how accurate and fine-tuned a system can be. A system can be so fine-tuned that it either gets the right answer or no answer at all; or set up more sloppily, so that elements that come close to the right answer are accessed. The first approach gives loss errors. The second approach gives substitutions. Adult language systems take the second approach. Young children vary in terms of how fine-tuned the system is. While all children do some deletion and some substitution, some children use more of one than the other. A child who begins as a deleter must alter the system to be sloppier and more gradient, so that elements can be accessed with intermediate levels of activation.

To correct a loss error, the originally low levels of activation on the target unit must be raised. In the process of correction it is likely that there will be a stage where activation is at an intermediate level. This predicts a developmental progression: loss errors, then substitution errors, then correct forms. This progression will appear if the activation is increased gradually enough, but a very swift increase will skip the substitution phase. A developmental pattern where the child first substitutes, then deletes, then gets it right should be uncommon.

Loss and substitution are always both potentially possible in the access of a segment. One important determinant of which option is taken is the degree of *phonetic similarity* between the target segment and other segments. Substitutions are possible only if there is another pattern that is similar enough, or if some pattern is of such high strength that it will tend to be accessed given *any* input. Otherwise, deletion occurs.

In adult speakers of a language, the main reason that errors occur is simple accessing failure. In all cases the right output state is potentially accessible. Early speech is quite different. All output states are present, but the speaker has not yet learned the proper connection weights to access them. There are three things that influence which states are accessible. First, connection weights are initially random. This means that different children will show different patterns of errors. Even the most difficult sound might show up correct on the first attempt by a particular child (Menn 1983). Second, the system is tuned during the babbling stage (as has been traditionally assumed; cf. Kent this volume). During this period of "play," the child produces sounds "randomly." The child perceives the results, and can use them to alter the weights between perceived units and output states, so that, eventually, the perceived unit reliably can activate the proper output state. This learning phase using babbling produces a system with a small number of learned mappings between perception and production, which can then be used to realize words that the child has learned from adults. This accounts for the continuity between the child's babbling and first words (Locke 1983; Vihman, Ferguson, and Elbert 1986). Third, there are the changes to the system made in attempting to correct errors, that alter connection weights and hence the degree of similarity between two input patterns. These three factors, along with the fine-tuning that determines the likelihood of loss and substitution errors, provide the underpinnings for the child's phonological warps.

Once a mapping between levels has been learned, the new output state begins to act as an attractor for related states. High-frequency elements have higher average resting levels; they are more accurately produced (because they need less activation from higher levels to be accessed), but they are more likely to inhibit similar states and substitute for them. Once strong output states are present, they make it more difficult to process anything that is at all similar to them, and the system tends to get into those states erroneously (e.g., Jordan 1986).

Errors probably occur at a combination of levels. First, errors may be at the phonological level (as they are in adult speech). Second, feedback from lower levels to higher levels propagates lower-level errors to higher levels. Incorrect states at, for example, the motor level would cause a scattering of activation at the phonological level, activating the incorrect phonological units that are associated with the erroneous motor state, to a degree dependent on the amount of feedback from the lower level. In a system that mostly functions accurately (such as the adult system), this is advantageous, as it ensures that the output of adjacent levels is compatible. However, in a system that is highly inaccurate, it may not be advantageous: a level that is highly inaccurate will interfere with the proper functioning of earlier levels, causing many more errors to occur than would otherwise be present.

Gang Effects

In local connectionist systems, the words that are stored in the lexicon interact: words that are similar reinforce all information that they have in common (McClelland and Elman 1986; Stemberger and MacWhinney 1986a). Gang effects involve the activation of a number of units at the lexical level, which then contributes to a particular output at the phonological level. There are two distinct ways in which these gangs can arise: in a meaning-based fashion and in a sound-based fashion.

Meaning-based gangs arise in a purely top-down fashion. On the basis of activated semantic units, words are activated at the lexical level, as a function of the number of connections with the semantic units. If the system is finely tuned, only one lexical item will be activated. But if it is sloppy, there will be low-level activation on other words that are semantically similar. If these words are similar phonologically, they all reinforce the same phonological outcome. How much effect meaning-based gangs have depends (a) on how dense the lexicon is (i.e., on how closely lexical items, especially semantically related items, resemble each other phonologically), and (b) on how sloppy access is. Meaning-based gangs can account for the productivity of suffixes such as -ing, for example, with a large number of progressive forms all ending in the same sounds and causing them to be accessed at the phonological level even for nonce forms (e.g., stigging).

In general, the correlation between meaning and sound is low: words that are similar in meaning tend to be different in sound. A meaning-based gang of words will not tend to have much effect, at least in large, diverse adult lexicons. With very small lexicons, it is possible for meaning-based gangs to have more effect, if the lexicon is phonologically dense. Some children select which words they want to use in language production on the basis of whether they can pronounce the sounds in them (Ferguson and Farwell 1975; Schwartz and Leonard 1982). This leads to a lexicon in which all the words bear strong phonological resemblances to each other. Thus, to the degree that non-target words are accessed, they reinforce certain phonological patterns more than others. The system can tolerate several of these gangs, reinforcing a small number of output patterns differentially, and interfering with other output patterns.

Note that this explanation resembles a two-lexicon approach to phonology. It assumes that the child has a clear mapping from word to sound only for words that have been attempted in production, not for all words that can be recognized in speech perception. It draws a distinction between different channels in the system, with a perceptual channel and a production channel. The lexical level is shared for both, but the mappings in the different channels will depend on which words have actually been learned, separately, for each channel.

It is possible to get meaning-based gang effects even in a sparse lexicon, as long as there are relatively few phonological output states that are of high strength. The activated gangs of words would contribute activation to a large number of output states. However, if most of the output states are so weak as to be functionally absent, most of the gangs will have no effect at the lower level, and the remaining gangs will have more effect.

Meaning-based gang effects underlie *canonical forms* (Menn 1983; Vihman 1981): particular phonological patterns shared by large numbers of words. They are prevalent in the speech of many (but not all) children for the first fifty words. Words that do not fit the canonical form but come close are altered so that they fit. Words that are quite different from the canonical patterns are often avoided. For example, Leonard and Brown (1984) discuss a case where the child's only final consonants were [p] and [s], which were a part of many words. Other final labial consonants were changed into [p], while all other final consonants were replaced by [s]; [s] was also added to words that should have ended in a vowel. However, as the lexicon becomes larger and less dense, canonical forms disappear.

Sound-based gang effects arise due to feedback from the phonological level (figure 3). As phonological units are activated, they feed activation back to lexical units, causing a secondary scattering of activation to nontarget words. These secondarily activated words can form gangs, based purely on their similarity to the target word in sound, which can then alter phonological processing. In large lexicons, or in small lexicons that are phonologically diverse with large numbers of output states available, this is the only way in which phonologically coherent gangs can form.

Feedback from the phonological level to the word level underlies not only sound-based gangs, but the Repeated Phoneme Effect in speech errors as well (Dell 1986). Stemberger (1989a) found that this effect did *not* appear in the speech errors produced by his two children, and argued that there was a lesser degree of feedback from the phonological to the lexical level in child speech. Interestingly, neither child showed extensive use of canonical forms in early speech. Furthermore, the number of words in the lexicon had little effect on the child's substitution warps for /v/, /z/, /θ/, /ð/, or for stops after /s/. For example, Morgan realized word-initial /v/ as a labiodental glide [ʋ], merging it with /w/, /f/, and /r/, even though there were more words beginning with /b/ ($n = 15$) than with the other three phones combined ($n = 7$). It was noted above that such feedback may not be desirable in a child's early speech, because it would propagate phonological errors back to the lexical level and cause errors to occur there. Leonard (this volume) discusses the possible role of sound-based gangs in the output of children with articulation disorders. It is possible that an adult-like level of feedback may actually underlie their disorder. How general sound-

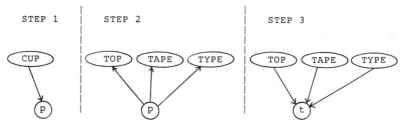

Figure 3. Formation and effects of bottom-up gangs.

based gangs are in the speech of young children needs further investigation.

Regressions

Regressions are regarded as one of the more important phenomena in a child's development of phonological skills. The child gives up a pronunciation that may be completely accurate and begins to make errors. This is odd-looking in process models where the processes are assumed to be solutions by the child for altering perceived forms into something that can be pronounced. Macken (1987) suggests that regressions come about through the generalization of processes needed elsewhere, but has not made clear *why* this should occur.

In previous work (Stemberger 1989b) I have discussed phonological regressions in the approach taken here. I divide regressions into two basic types: trade-offs versus simple regressions. In trade-offs the sound, or sequence of sounds, is accurate at neither stage, but one aspect improves while another gets worse. Small changes in connection weights are made to correct the output. These changes alter the similarity between the target and other output states; similarity may be altered enough that the system begins substituting a different thing for the target, which will be correct where the previous substitution had been wrong (because the connection weights made that aspect of the sound more accessible), but incorrect where before it had been right. In attempting to correct the new error, the system sometimes returns to the original substitution. Stemberger (1989b) presents one case where the child realized /ð/ as either [l] or [d], and swung back and forth between the two pronunciations over a period of a year or two, in an attempt to correct (alternately) the features [continuant] and [sonorant].[5]

In one trade-off regression an [m] was added after final vowels that should have been rounded, after previously being vowel-final, as a way to express vowel rounding (e.g., [nɤ:m] 'no'). The entire system of vowel-final words was destabilized, undergoing two other regressions: addition of /h/ after /i/ (at the same time that final /s/ began to be realized as [h] rather than [ʔ]), and addition of a final shwa. All three characteristics were then eliminated together within two months. The elimination of the final [m] also led to the substitution of [t] for word-final /p/ in a few words. This instance involved a complex interaction between four distinct warps, where a change in one area destabilized

---

[5]Macken presents an interesting trade-off regression, where /kr/ was originally realized as /k/, with the /r/ entirely deleted, but later was realized as [f], which is a fusion of the /k/ (obstruence and voicelessness) with the /r/ (continuance and labiality). The activation of the /r/ was increased (to overcome loss), which led to a fusion.

other similar areas and led to further changes. They follow naturally from the assumption that low-level aspects of the connections between units underlie the phenomena.

Regressions can result from overgeneralizing some change to the system that is needed to improve production elsewhere (Macken 1987). A model must be able to account not only for the existence of such changes, but also for their rarity. Stemberger divides such changes into two types: *crossfire* (where the two sounds were previously not neutralized; illustrated in the previous paragraph) and *overshoot*. In overshoot, A and B had originally been neutralized as A, but were then neutralized as B. For example, Gwendolyn originally simplified word-initial consonant clusters by deleting a liquid or glide. When deletion was eliminated at 3;3, the glide was variably overgeneralized to other words: e.g., *stop* [tʰwa:p] and *book* [bwət]. Overshoot is a byproduct of the changes made to connection weights: if the changes are too large, they can reverse the biases of the system and thereby reverse the errors. Interestingly, most of Stemberger's examples of overshoot involve sequences of segments, where a segment is first deleted and then added where it should not be; this results from an *addition bias*, whereby the addition of a segment is a more likely error type in certain circumstances (Stemberger and Treiman 1986; Stemberger 1990). Overgeneralizing regressions should also be more likely when the segment that regresses was earlier inaccurate in another way or was accurate but accessed at a relatively low activation level.

The model sketched here predicts the types of regressions fairly well. Because all regressions are viewed as errors like all other phonological warps, there is no conceptual problem with why the child would create a process to eliminate the correct production of a sound and replace it with an incorrect one. Because the correct form has often been present in the system for a while and may be of high strength, we predict the uncommonness of regressions.

Idioms and Lexical Diffusion

Particular words in a child's phonological system often are advanced beyond the rest of the child's system (progressive idioms) or less accurate than the rest of the child's system (regressive idioms). Regressive idioms can have several sources. First, they might involve a word of exceptionally low strength; the low amount of activation given to the word's component segments makes substitutions more likely than in other words (Stemberger and MacWhinney 1986b; Dell 1991; Ellis, Miller, and Sin 1983). In words of higher frequency, however, we must assume that the child has misperceived the word early on and never noticed the mistake (Smith 1973), or learned his or her own mispronunciation or that of another child (Butler Platt and MacWhinney 1983).

Progressive idioms involve the access of a marginal output pattern under the right circumstances: the word is of particularly high strength, or the child places a particularly large amount of attention on producing it. A progressive idiom can disappear (a) through a phasing out of the special attention given to the word, or (b) if the competing pattern that dominates most other words increases in strength to the point where it is able to overcome even the great levels of activation from the target word.

Extreme cases of idioms are rare. Far more common are cases where a number of words are advanced or late relative to other words (*lexical diffusion*), reflecting the same factors that underlie idioms. Some researchers argue that lexical diffusion and idioms imply whole-word motor programming rather than programming specific to individual segments (MacNeilage, Hutchinson, and Lasater 1981; Studdert-Kennedy 1987). Note that the phenomenon has no such implication here. Because the strength of a lexical item propagates to all lower levels of the system, differences in strength at a lexical level are reflected by differences in the accuracy of phonological and motor processing. Lexical factors underlying errors are a required aspect of the model.

Chain Shifts

There is another rare but well-documented phenomenon that shows that a pattern can be only marginally inaccessible. In *chain-shifts* a sound /B/ is realized as [C], while a sound /A/ is realized as [B]. Leopold (1947) gives one example where /ǰ/ is deaffricated to [d], while /č/ is voiced to [ǰ]. Morgan provided another example; she added [m] to the end of many vowel-final words (*shoes* [suː:m]), while also showing Labial Backing of any underlying /m/'s in that position (*zoom* [zuː:n]).

Chain-shifts occur when an output pattern is barely accessible; either the output pattern is of too low strength to be accessed, or the input pattern is of too low strength to access it, or both, *given the presence of a similar output state that may act as an attractor* (figure 4). In the example from Morgan's speech, a final [m] cannot be accessed when a nonlabial consonant occurs earlier in the word, and the system winds up in another, similar, very strong output pattern ([n]). The pattern [m] can be accessed erroneously by a rounded vowel, however, because the feature of labiality is strong enough to get it into that state; [n] does not result, because the rounding of a vowel is simply not similar enough to a final [n] to lead to such a substitution.

Chain-shifts are a clear illustration that substitutions can occur

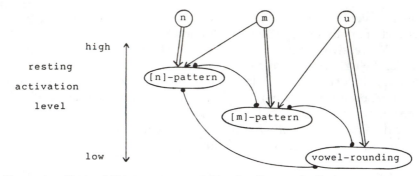

Figure 4.   Chain shifting; pattern substitution due to similarity.

even when an output pattern is present. Output patterns can be inaccessible in certain contexts, where they are overridden by similar but stronger patterns. However, it is likely that the conditions under which chain-shifts occur (a barely accessible output state; a much stronger similar output state; a third output state confused with that marginal output state without being similar enough to be confused with the strong output state) are uncommon, so that chain-shifts are rare.

Fusions

While most warps are simple substitutions or deletions, there is a more complex category of error in relation to consonant clusters in particular: fusions, where the two consonants combine into a third segment that takes some features from both sounds, e.g., [f] for /sp/. Fusions occur because the child is trying to access both sounds, thereby giving activation to both. In most cases the strongest phoneme or output pattern will win. However, it is possible for the two patterns to interact, so that a compromise pattern is accessed, one that shares features with both target segments.

Perhaps the most common type of segment fusion involves fusing a voiceless fricative and a sonorant into a voiceless sonorant (e.g., [m̥] for /sm/). In sonorants the larynx is independent of the supralaryngeal vocal tract in aerodynamic terms, so that either voicing or voicelessness can be combined with the supralaryngeal spatial configuration with no further changes. If the strongest output pattern is for [m] (Ringo 1985 suggests that children usually produce a voiced sonorant at an earlier stage, before the fusion arises), but there is also a weak response for [s], the larynx may spread slightly, possibly enough to prevent voicing; this becomes more likely as the /s/ is increased in activation to overcome deletion. Few other possible blends could arise from such small articulatory changes, for reasons of phonetic distance or aerodynamic difficulty. For example, an [f] resulting from an /s/ and a /p/ involves a very different (and differently controlled) gesture with the lips than does [p]. This illustrates the low-level activation of a competing output state.

In general, low-level activation of competing output states should lead to subtle articulatory alterations (Weismer 1984; Dinnsen and Elbert 1984). Substitution of one sound for another does *not* entail acoustic identity. When a substitution occurs, the resulting pattern generally is not activated as greatly as when it is the correct pattern, and alternative patterns are not as well inhibited. This leads to a weaker motor response, altered to some degree to be similar to other patterns. Even when there is so little activation that a consonant is "deleted," there may still be a very low activation response that may be able to faintly activate the articulators.

Interference Effects

The phenomena discussed so far involve the access of an element without interference from any other element in the word or sentence. A number of other phenomena involve interactions between two or more elements processed at the same time, whether within a single word or in two words that are near each other. The bulk of errors in adult speech are due to contextual interference.

There is a basic average level of activation that a given unit will be accessed with, which can be affected by interference from other segments. There are three basic environments: a neutral one in which there are no competing segments, an intermediate one in which the target segment is repeated elsewhere, and a hostile one in which there is another competing consonant (with the degree of interference a function of the degree of similarity). A segment is most accessible when there are no competing segments, least when there is a competing one, and intermediate when it is repeated elsewhere (Shattuck-Hufnagel 1979; Stemberger 1989c; Lecours and Lhermitte 1969).

This hierarchy can be seen in one warp from Morgan at 1;8. /p/ became a velar before a syllabic /r/ or /l/: never if the word began with a glottal (*apple* [ʔapo]), variably if the word began with a labial (*people* [pʰiːpo] ~ [pʰiːko]), and always otherwise (*nipple* [niko]). Glottals are neutral and do not interfere with true consonants, because they involve no specification for movements in the oral cavity, as true consonants do (e.g., Keating 1988). The greater interference from competing consonants could also be seen with word-final bilabials at this same period, which were realized as bilabial after a glottal (*hop* [hapʰ]) or a bilabial (*bump* [bʌpʰ]), but as a dental elsewhere (*flap* [fatʰ]). This hierarchy makes testable predictions. The data would be problematic if the final bilabial was possible only after a bilabial ([bʌpʰ]) but *not* after a (neutral) glottal (*hop* [hatʰ]), i.e., if repetition made access easier than in a neutral environment.

Word-medial [k] had two interesting regressions associated with it. Word-medial [k] was the first intervocalic consonant to arise in non-harmonic environments, and it acted as an attractor to /p/, as just noted. There was one word in which it acted as an attractor to /p/ even though it began with a glottal: *open*. Originally, the final /n/ was deleted, and the /p/ was correct: [ʔapʰ]. Interference from the /n/ was originally too weak to prevent access of [p], but at this period, [k] became a strong enough output that it replaced [p]: [ʔoːkʰ]. After a month or so, [k] became a weaker output state (whether from attempts to correct errors or from the appearance of more intervocalic consonants to act as competitors). The substitution of [k] for /p/ disappeared. This allowed [p] to surface before syllabic /r/ and /l/ (e.g., *nipple*). The [k] disappeared from *open*, to be replaced by [t]: [ʔoːtʰ] (because connection weights had been changed to make the syllabic /n/ more accessible), followed soon by [ʔoːtən]. In addition, word-medial [k] disappeared from two environments in which it had previously been correct: when the word ended with a /t/ (e.g., *pocket* [pʰatətʰ]), and where the word began with a /k/ (e.g., *cracker* [tʰato]). This last regression illustrates the fact that the repetition of a segment makes it more prone to error, and also illustrates that harmony can be restricted to occurring between very similar elements (because /g/ did not undergo harmony when the word ended in /t/, and [n] did not trigger harmony in /k/).

Interference is, in general, observed from segments that are lost. In every consonant cluster, there are two or more consonants competing for a similar position in the word. This causes the activation levels of the consonants to decrease. This decrease is greatest when competition is the most intense: either because of greater similarity or because only one consonant is accessible. If slots are provided for both consonants, competition seems to be less. Word-initial velars give a good illustration of this interference (Dyson 1986). The likelihood of the [k] output is greatest with singleton consonants, as in *key* (a neutral environment). It is less likely in *queen*, where there is competition between /k/ and /w/; this is true whether one member of the cluster is deleted or not. Competition between the members of a cluster can allow velar fronting, which had earlier been found in all velars, to continue to operate in clusters. The competition can also lower activation levels enough that both consonants become inaccessible, and the whole cluster is deleted (Ingram 1976).

Competition can also make itself felt from consonants that are part of word-initial unstressed syllables that are deleted (Stemberger, Pollock, and Salck in preparation). In most cases the syllable is lost and one of the two consonants is accessed. The two target consonants are in competition, and it is the most accessible that wins. The competition between the two consonants is essentially the same as in the processing of consonant clusters, and the result is predicted to be similar. For example, the competition between the /b/ and /l/ of *ballóon* is usually resolved as [b], just as it is in the cluster in *black;* even if the consonants are in the opposite order (/ləbówm/). There is, however, some tendency for the second consonant to win out, as it belongs to the same syllable as the vowel that is accessed. When the initial unstressed syllable *is* produced, both consonants are not always accessed. There is sometimes a period during which one of the two consonants is still lost, either the consonant of the first (word-initial unstressed) syllable or the consonant of the second (stressed) syllable. In some children's speech the second consonant is deleted (*ballóon* [bu:ú:n]), but the first consonant is deleted for most children who show this pattern (/nəsǽt/ [əsǽt]). Competition lowers the activation level of the consonant and prevents access, even though an extra syllable is present in which the consonant might be produced.

As noted above, the degree of interference between two segments is partly a function of similarity and partly one of accessibility. It is for this reason that most observed interference is between two consonants. Interference between two vowels is unlikely, because vowels are more accessible (as shown by the fact that they are mastered earlier and involved in fewer speech errors; e.g., Stemberger 1989a). Interference between a vowel and a consonant is less likely, because vowels and consonants are not very similar. However, interference between vowels and the most similar consonants (glides and /l/) is possible. For example, in Morgan's speech, sequences such as /il/ were realized as back vowels (*milk* [mo:k], with [o] realizing the velarization of the /l/), and the /l/ in the onset in *play* combined with the diphthong /ey/ ([pʰoy]). Second, interference might be observable if consonants are only marginally accessible, so the small perturbations caused by the vowel can make themselves felt. This may be what lies behind the facts observed by Stoel-Gammon (1983), where labials are not accessible before front vowels. Accessibility problems of this magnitude are rare, and most children do not show such effects.

Interference effects are also observed between two consonants that occupy different positions in the word, such as word-initial versus word-final. Sometimes, nonassimilatory substitutions result. An example was given above where noninitial bilabials became dentals in the environments with the most interference. Regressions are also occasionally seen, with a word-initial consonant rendered accurately when a word-final consonant is deleted but inaccurately if a word-final consonant is accessed (Leonard this volume).

A further effect of interference can be observed after children begin to produce sentences with two or more words. In a single-word utterance, the only interference comes from within the word. In multi-word utterances, there is *additionally* interference from the other words, and accessibility can be expected to suffer. As a result, children's pronunciations are often less accurate in multiword sentences than in single-word sentences (e.g., Scollon 1976; Donahue 1986).

The most conspicuous example of interference between elements is harmony: assimilation between noncontiguous elements, e.g., [gak] for *duck*. The two consonants are usually in the same word and differ in syllable position. Harmony has been observed in two-word combinations (e.g., Donahue 1986; Matthei 1989), in which case the two consonants are in parallel syllable positions (two onsets or two codas). Harmony generally involves consonants, much more rarely involving vowels (which are in general more accessible). Harmony most often involves word-initial consonants, which are also the most prone to being mispronounced in slips of the tongue in both adult and child speech (Stemberger 1989a).[6] Consonants that are being accessed at low activation levels (e.g., because they have only recently appeared in the child's system) are prone to harmony (Vihman 1978), e.g., in Morgan's speech [l] (which had realized both /l/ and /y/) was replaced by [y] (for /y/) and [ʤ] (for /l/), except when there was an [l] later in the word, as in *yellow* [lɛlo] and *lilac* [laylak].[7] Last, alveolars are most likely to undergo place harmony and stops are most likely to undergo manner harmony, just as in speech errors (Stemberger and Stoel-Gammon 1991).

The exact organization of the access of segments is not yet clear, but we can assume that there are a limited number of copies of any given segment, perhaps (as Dell 1986 assumes) coded to position in the syllable. Access to any copy of a given segment will activate every other copy to some extent, through feedback from the feature level to the phoneme level. Thus, in the activation of the word *top*, the activation of syllable-initial /t/ leads to some activation on syllable-final /t/, and the activation of syllable-final /p/ gives some activation to syllable-initial

---

[6]Vihman (1978) stated this last fact in a different fashion, noting that harmony generally involves the *anticipation* of material from a later point in the utterance, just as in adult speech errors. However, Stemberger (1989b) reports that young children are more likely to *perseverate* in between-word phonological speech errors, which seems to conflict with the harmony tendencies. Both types of errors do preferentially involve word-initial phonemes.

[7]Because /l/ was pronounced correctly when /l/ was repeated later in the word, but incorrectly when no /l/ was present, one might ask whether the /l/ is a counter example to the claim above that repetition leads to warps when neutral environments do not. Unfortunately, there are few words in English that contain /l/ in a neutral environment, i.e., with only vowels and glottals as in *lie* and *low,* and none were recorded explicitly during this period. It is, thus, unclear whether these data were a counter example.

/p/. When the features of the two segments are similar, feedback also gives activation to the other segment. Thus, initial /t/ and final /p/ must inhibit initial /p/ and final /t/ that are both gaining a fair amount of activation from several sources. If the activation accruing to the nontarget segments is greater than that of the target segments, harmony results: /pa:p/ or /ta:t/.

Although harmony is usually between two phonetically similar segments, there are exceptions. When we have a similar but weak output state along with a distant but very strong output state, the distant output state sometimes wins (figure 5). This often involves fricatives as targets, with a change to stops combined with a change of place of articulation, while corresponding stops do not undergo harmony: *sleep* [pʰi:p] versus *stop* [tʰap]; *sock* [gak] versus *stick* [dik]. A distantly related segment is changed, but not a closely related segment. What underlies this phenomenon is the accessibility of the different segments; if [s] is a weaker output state than [t], then the following [p] might outcompete it but not the stronger [t].[8]

When unstressed syllables are added initially to a child's system, they have low activation levels and may show interference between dissimilar elements. Both consonants and vowels are in error, and the phenomenon is termed *reduplication: monkey* [mama]. The consonant and vowel errors derive from the same cause but are independent substitutions. The model predicts that reduplication will be replaced by consonant harmony and/or vowel harmony as activation levels increase; and that there will be an increasing role for phonetic similarity as the system improves.

CONCLUSION

I have discussed the main phenomena involved in children's acquisition of phonological skills in language production. I have shown how most phenomena can be described as on-line changes based on the adult form as the child has perceived it. The changes are not by design, but result from errors of access.

During the development of the model presented here, one thing has become clear: far too little information is available about the commonness of particular warps across children. In most cases where the model makes predictions about the relative frequencies of two things,

---

[8]Distant substitutions occasionally are observed in noninterference phenomena as well. In Morgan's speech /f/ was realized as [t], not as (the occurring) [p], because [p] was a weak output state. The model predicts that this will be less common in noninterference warps than in harmony, just as similarity is more important in noncontextual than in contextual speech errors (Stemberger 1982).

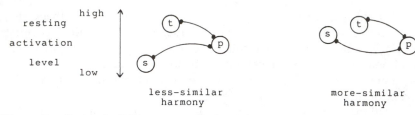

Figure 5. Strength differences underlying harmonies that are sensitive to segment similarity, with only /s/ (less similar) or /t/ (more similar) harmonizing as [p]; greater feedback from the features of [t] to [p] is not shown.

no data are available to evaluate the claim. In a process approach, where most anything is possible, quantitative predictions seem relatively unimportant. There need be no tendencies across children, but if there are, we can stipulate them. In contrast, this model relates the child's warps to other characteristics (such as true speech errors and how well nontarget units are inhibited), and the ability to evaluate quantitative predictions becomes crucial. If progress is to be made, more longitudinal and cross-sectional studies of large numbers of children will have to be performed to increase our data base.

I would like to end with a comment on the usefulness of research that assumes overt processes. I believe that this is still a worthwhile endeavour. The child's system does not actually contain explicit procedures to change the adult pronunciation into the child's pronunciation, but in terms of its output, it behaves *as if* such procedures were present. Processes provide a useful summary of what is going on. We must simply recognize them for the useful abstraction that they are, and not imbue them with any direct psychological status.

REFERENCES

Blumstein, S. 1973. *A Phonological Investigation of Aphasia.* The Hague: Mouton.

Butler Platt, C., and MacWhinney, B. 1983. Error assimilation as a mechanism in language learning. *Journal of Child Language* 10:401–414.

Dell, G. S. 1986. A spreading activation theory of retrieval in sentence production. *Psychological Review* 93:283–321.

Dell, G. S. 1991. Effect of frequency and vocabulary type on phonological speech errors. *Language and Cognitive Process* 5:313–49.

Dinnsen, D. A., and Elbert, M. 1984. On the relationship between phonology and learning. In *Phonological Theory and the Misarticulating Child* eds. M. Elbert, D. Dinnsen, and G. Weismer. (*ASHA Monographs, #22.*)

Donahue, M. 1986. Phonological constraints on the emergence of two-word utterances. *Journal of Child Language* 13:209–218.

Dyson, A. T. 1986. Development of velar consonants among normal two-year-olds. *Journal of Speech and Hearing Research* 29:493–98.

Ellis, A. W., Miller, D., and Sin, G. 1983. Wernicke's aphasia and normal language processing: A case study in cognitive neuropsychology. *Cognition* 15:111–44.

Ferguson, C. A., and Farwell, C. B. 1975. Words and sounds in early language acquisition. *Language* 51:419–39.

Fey, D., and Gandour, J. 1982. Rule discovery in phonological acquisition. *Journal of Child Language* 9:71–81.

Ingram, D. 1976. *Phonological Disability in Children*. New York: Elsevier.

Jordan, M. 1986. Serial order: A parallel distributed processing approach. *Institute for Cognitive Science Report 8604*. San Diego: University of California, San Diego.

Keating, P. A. 1988. Underspecification in phonetics. *Phonology* 5:275–92.

Lachter, J., and Bever, T. G. 1988. The relation between linguistic structure and associative theories of language learning—A constructive critique of some connectionist learning models. *Cognition* 28:195–247.

Lecours, A. R., and Lhermitte, F. 1969. Phonemic paraphasias: Linguistic structures and tentative hypotheses. *Cortex* 5:193–228.

Leonard, L. B., and Brown, B. L. 1984. Nature and boundaries of phonologic categories: A case study of an unusual phonologic pattern in a language-impaired child. *Journal of Speech and Hearing Disorders* 49:419–28.

Leopold, W. F. 1947. *Speech Development of a Bilingual Child: A Linguist's Record. Vol. II: Sound Learning in the First Two Years*. Chicago: Northwestern University Press.

Locke, J. 1983. *Phonological Acquisition and Change*. New York: Academic Press.

MacKay, D. G. 1987. *The Organization of Perception and Action*. New York: Springer-Verlag.

Macken, M. 1979. Developmental reorganization of phonology: A hierarchy of basic units of acquisition. *Lingua* 49:11–49.

Macken, M. 1987. Learning and constraints on phonological acquisition. In *Models of Language Acquisition*, ed. B. MacWhinney. Hillsdale, NJ: Lawrence Erlbaum Associates.

MacNeilage, P. F., Hutchinson, J., and Lasater, S. 1981. The production of speech: Development and dissolution of motoric and premotoric processes. In *Attention and Performance IX* ed. J. Long and A. Baddeley. Hillsdale, NJ: Lawrence Erlbaum Associates.

Matthei, E. H. 1989. Crossing boundaries: More evidence for phonological constraints on early multi-word utterances. *Journal of Child Language* 16:41–54.

McClelland, J. L., and Elman, J. L. 1986. The TRACE model of speech perception. *Cognitive Psychology* 18:1–86.

McClelland, J. L., and Rumelhart, D. E. 1981. An interactive activation model of context effects in letter recognition: Part 1. An account of basic findings. *Psychological Review* 88:375–407.

Menn, L. 1983. Development of articulatory, phonetic, and phonological capabilities. In *Language Production. Volume 2: Development, Writing, and Other Language Processes* ed. B. Butterworth. London: Academic Press.

Pinker, S. 1984. *Language Learnability and Language Development*. Cambridge, MA: Harvard University Press.

Ringo, C. C. 1985. The nature of change in phonological development: Evidence from the acquisition of /s/ + stop and /s/ + nasal clusters. Ph.D. diss., Brown University, Providence, RI.

Rumelhart, D., and McClelland, J. 1986. On learning the past tenses of English verbs. In *Parallel Distributed Processing: Explorations in the Microstructure of*

Cognition, vol. 1, ed. D. E. Rumelhart and J. L. McClelland. Cambridge, MA: Bransford Books.

Rumelhart, D. E., Hinton, G., and Williams, R. 1986. Learning internal representations by error propagation. In *Parallel Distributed Processing: Explorations in the Microstructure of Cognition,* vol. 1, ed. D. E. Rumelhart and J. L. McClelland. Cambridge, MA: Bransford Books.

Schwartz, R., and Leonard, L. 1982. Do children pick and choose? An examination of phonological selection and avoidance in early lexical acquisition. *Journal of Child Language* 9:319–36.

Scollon, R. T. 1976. *Conversations with a One-Year-Old.* Honolulu: University of Hawaii Press.

Shattuck-Hufnagel, S. 1979. Speech errors as evidence for a serial-ordering mechanism in sentence production. In *Sentence Processing* ed. W. E. Cooper and E. C. T. Wales. Hillsdale, NJ: Lawrence Erlbaum Associates.

Smith, N. V. 1973. *The Acquisition of Phonology.* Cambridge: Cambridge University Press.

Stemberger, J. P. 1982. The nature of segments in the lexicon: Evidence from speech errors. *Lingua* 56:43–67.

Stemberger, J. P. 1985. An interactive activation model of language production. In *Progress in the Psychology of Language,* vol. 1 ed. A. W. Ellis. London: Lawrence Erlbaum Associates.

Stemberger, J. P. 1988. Between-word processes in child phonology. *Journal of Child Language* 15:39–61.

Stemberger, J. P. 1989a. Speech errors in early child language production. *Journal of Memory and Language* 28:164–88.

Stemberger, J. P. 1989b. Regressive overgeneralizations in child phonology. Unpublished manuscript: University of Minnesota.

Stemberger, J. P. 1989c. Morphological processing and the Repeated Phoneme Effect. Unpublished manuscript: University of Minnesota.

Stemberger, J. P. 1990. Wordshape errors in language production. *Cognition* 35:123–57.

Stemberger, J. P., and MacWhinney, B. 1986a. Form-oriented errors in inflectional processing. *Cognitive Psychology* 18:329–54.

Stemberger, J. P., and MacWhinney, B. 1986b. Frequency and the lexical storage of regularly inflected forms. *Memory and Cognition* 14:17–26.

Stemberger, J. P., Pollock, K., and Salck, J. In preparation. Initial unstressed syllables in young child speech. University of Minnesota.

Stemberger, J. P., and Treiman, R. 1986. The internal structure of word-initial consonant clusters. *Journal of Memory and Language* 25:163–80.

Stemberger, J. P., and Stoel-Gammon, C. 1991. The underspecification of coronals: Evidence from language acquisition and performance error. In *The Special Status of Coronals,* ed. C. Paradis and J.-F. Prunet. Dordrecht, Holland: Foris.

Stoel-Gammon, C. 1983. Constraints on consonant-vowel sequences in early words. *Journal of Child Language* 10:455–57.

Stoel-Gammon, C. 1987. The relationship between lexical and phonological development in young children. Workshop at the Stanford Child Language Research Forum, Stanford University, April 1987.

Studdert-Kennedy, M. 1987. The phoneme as a perceptuomotor structure. In *Language Perception and Production* ed. A. Allport, D. MacKay, W. Prinz, and E. Scheerer. London: Academic Press.

Vihman, M. M. 1978. Consonant harmony: Its scope and function in child language. In *Universals of Human Language, Vol. 2: Phonology* ed. J. H. Greenberg. Stanford, CA: Stanford University Press.

Vihman, M. M. 1981. Phonology and the development of the lexicon: Evidence from children's errors. *Journal of Child Language* 8:239–64.

Vihman, M. M., Ferguson, C. A., and Elbert, M. 1986. Phonological development from babbling to speech: Common tendencies and individual differences. *Applied Psycholinguistics* 7:3–40.

Weismer, G. 1984. Acoustic analysis strategies for the refinement of phonological analysis. In *Phonological Theory and the Misarticulating Child* ed. M. Elbert, D. A. Dinnsen, and G. Weismer. (*ASHA Monographs #22.*)

Chapter • 6

Variation in Developing and Fully Developed Phonetic Inventories

Daniel A. Dinnsen

A minimum requirement of any linguistic theory is that it must account for the full range of variation permitted in the world's languages. Language-specific differences across fully developed languages have constituted the principal source of variation for linguistic theorizing. Variation also has been observed in developing systems during the process of acquisition. This latter type of variation has, however, played a lesser role in the formulation and testing of linguistic theories. This is somewhat surprising, because the study of developing systems could be expected to contribute most directly to a theory of language that is also a theory of acquisition:

> The problem for the linguist, as well as for the child learning the language, is to determine from the data of performance the underlying system of rules . . . (Chomsky 1965, p. 4).

The problem seems to have been that the facts about developing systems do not fit well with the facts about fully developed systems. The numerous reports of variation across, and individual differences in,

I am especially grateful to Steven B. Chin for his many valuable contributions to this paper and to the overall project from which it derives. I would also like to thank Phil Connell, Judith Gierut, and Mary Elbert for their many helpful comments. This work was supported in part by grants to Indiana University from the National Institutes of Health (NS 20976 and DC 00260).

developing systems would seem to be in conflict with any universal or even language-specific constraints that have the effect of limiting variation. It is difficult to imagine why this should be, because even a developing system is a system of some sort at any point in time. One possibility is that researchers may have been focusing on the wrong properties of linguistic systems. That is, the disparities and variation that have been observed within and across systems may not be as unconstrained as has been suggested but may instead be the expected superficial effects of general and defining principles of language compatible with both fully developed and developing systems.

An illustrative parallel presents itself from botany. There are many different species of bamboo (although, of course, all such woody or arborescent plants are members of the tribe *Bambusae* within the family *Gramineae*, that is, the "grasses," and are all species within a highly constrained number of genera, for example, *Bambusa, Arundinaria,* or *Dendrocalamus*). The identification of a species is very difficult due to the variation that occurs within a species. For any given species, readily accessible structures such as leaves, stems, and roots all vary in their appearance. Environmental factors such as the type of soil, amount of sunlight, temperature, and so forth affect the appearance of these structures. There is, however, one structure that allows for the unambiguous identification of bamboo, and that is its blossom. Certain properties of the blossom remain invariant within a species despite variation in other structures and in the environment.

The problem is that this defining characteristic reveals itself only once in a century immediately preceding the death of the plant. Thus, what is most crucial to the correct identification of bamboo is the least accessible. Also, the variation that occurs within a species represents the superficial effects of environmental factors in more accessible structures. The parallel for us suggests that we need to turn our attention to the "blossoms" of language.

The purpose of this chapter is to identify some defining principles of language that are consistent across the facts of variation and the facts of acquisition. The specific focus is variation in the phonetic inventories of developing and fully developed phonological systems. Specifically, cross-sectional and longitudinal data are reported from young children, both normally acquiring and functionally disordered, acquiring English (and to a more limited extent other languages), and these data are compared with cross-linguistic variation in phonetic inventories of fully developed primary languages.

One way in which languages differ is by the set of sounds that constitute the phonetic inventory. Also, in the course of language acquisition, a child's phonetic inventory changes by adding certain sounds

and eliminating certain others. The variation that exists across phonetic inventories and in the order of acquisition of sounds has rendered
untenable absolute universals or even implicational universals formulated in terms of specific sounds. There is, thus, no universal phonetic
inventory, all sounds of which occur in all languages. Not even the occurrence of some specific sound will predict necessarily the occurrence
of some other specific sound. We are left with weaker statements that
can only be expressed as trends or general tendencies. For example,
the sound [s] is estimated to occur in 86% of the world's languages
(Maddieson 1984). The fact remains that it does not occur in all languages. Similarly, the sound [θ] is usually, but not always, acquired
after [s] (Jakobson 1968; Prather, Hedrick, and Kern 1975; Stoel-Gammon
and Dunn 1985). Nevertheless, the phonetic inventory of a language is
such a basic property of the sound system and the tendencies associated with the composition of phonetic inventories are so strong that it is
difficult to imagine that there would not be principles that underlie the
nature and development of phonetic inventories.

In a recent study Dinnsen et al. (1990) examined the phonetic
inventories of 40 young children with moderate to severe functional
(nonorganic) disorders of speech. The inventories differed widely in
the occurrence of specific sounds. Despite this variation, the inventories could be typologized in such a way that each inventory could be
uniquely assigned to one of five distinct sets or levels of complexity.
The sets were defined not by the sounds per se but rather by a limited
set of phonetic features that distinguished the sounds. The five sets of
inventories were moreover implicationally related in a subset relation
by the feature distinctions. That is, the occurrence of a particular feature distinction in one set implied necessarily the occurrence of all
other distinctions characteristic of all simpler sets of inventories. Table I
summarizes these findings by presenting example inventories for each
of the five sets arranged in order of increasing complexity.

All inventories included vowels, glides, obstruent stops, and nasals. The specific sounds associated with these general classes varied
across the inventories. Level A inventories were limited to these general classes of sounds. There was, thus, no voice or manner distinction
among the obstruents, and non-nasal sonorant consonants (liquids)
did not occur. Several distinctive features thus are relevant to the characterization of such inventories. The feature [syllabic] distinguishes the
vowels from all other occurring sounds. The feature [consonantal] distinguishes the glides from all other nonsyllabic sounds (i.e., the obstruents and nasals). The feature [sonorant] distinguishes the obstruents from the nasals. Given these features for distinguishing among
basic classes of sounds, certain laws can be formulated that further

Table I. Typology of Pretreatment Phonetic Inventories for Forty Functionally Misarticulating Children

Level	Contrastive Features	Example Inventories	
A	[syllabic] [consonantal] [sonorant] [coronal]	b d m n w	ŋ j ʔh
B	[voice]	pb td m n w	kg ŋ j ʔh

C	[continuant]
	[delayed release]
		1) pb td
		      fv sz
		      m n
		      w
			2) pb td kg
			      fv sz ʃ t͡s d͡z t͡ʃ ǰ
			      m n ŋ
			      w j h

D	[nasal]	1) pb td
		      fv θð
		      m n ʃ t͡ʃ ǰ
		      w l j kg ŋ ʔh
			2) pb td kg
			      fv sz ʃ
			      m n ŋ
			      w j h

E	[strident]
	[lateral]
		1) pb td
		      fv θð sz
		      m n l ʃ t͡ʃ ǰ
		      w j kg ŋ ʔh
			2) pb td kg
			      fv sz ʃ t͡s t͡ʃ ǰ
			      m n ŋ r
			      w l r j ʔ

194

specify the sounds in those classes: (1) all consonants are stops; (2) all obstruents are voiceless and unaspirated (particular transcription biases notwithstanding); and (3) all sonorant consonants are nasals.

Level B inventories were limited to the same basic classes of sounds with the addition of a voice distinction among the obstruents. Level B inventories thus elaborated Level A inventories by introducing the feature [voice] to distinguish the voiced from the voiceless stops.

Level C inventories included the same classes of sounds found in Levels A and B with the addition of fricatives and/or affricates. The manner features [continuant] and/or [delayed release] thus characterized Level C inventories.

Level D inventories added to the classes of sounds by introducing one liquid consonant, either an [l]-sound or an [r]-sound. Since for all simpler inventories all sonorant consonants were predictably nasals, the feature [nasal] was necessary to distinguish among the sonorant consonants and define a separate class of nasals and a class of liquids.

Level E inventories included all classes of sounds characteristic of simpler inventories and extended a distinction in either or both the class of liquids or the class of obstruents. The class of liquids could be extended by the inclusion of both [l] and [r]. The feature [lateral] was thus necessary to distinguish among the liquid consonants. The class of obstruents could be extended by the inclusion of both strident and nonstrident sounds at the same place of articulation, e.g., [s] and [θ]. The feature [strident] was thus necessary to distinguish these sounds.

The description of phonetic inventories in terms of a limited set of necessary but general feature distinctions rather than specific sounds allows inventories to vary in terms of specific sounds within a class but limits variation across classes of sounds. The limits are reflected in a typological characterization of the inventories and are expressed as a series of unidirectional implicational laws. For example, the presence of a stridency distinction implies necessarily the presence of a liquid consonant, which in turn implies a voice and manner distinction among obstruents. No claim is made about which liquid will occur, only that a liquid must occur if a stridency distinction occurs. Similarly, no claim is made about which specific fricatives will occur or which specific stops will be voiced or voiceless. Thus, given a feature distinction characteristic of a relatively complex inventory, all feature distinctions required of simpler inventories should also be present. Because the implication is unidirectional, the reverse does not follow. For example, then, the presence of the feature [voice] does not imply necessarily the presence of a manner distinction, a liquid consonant, or a stridency or laterality distinction.

These constraints seem to govern cross-sectional variation in the phonetic inventories of young children with functional speech disorders. To claim that these constraints also govern acquisition, it would be necessary to examine changes in phonetic inventories. Consequently, in a follow-up study, Dinnsen, Chin, and Elbert (in press) examined the post-treatment phonetic inventories for the same children to determine whether changes in these inventories were governed by the same constraints. There are, of course, any number of logically possible ways that inventories might change that could violate the constraints on cross-sectional variation, especially after treatment. For example, a Level B inventory might add a laterality distinction but fail to evidence a manner distinction among the obstruents. Similarly, a Level C inventory might add a stridency distinction but fail to include a liquid consonant.

Each child received conventional minimal pair contrast treatment (this procedure is described in Elbert and Gierut 1986) on one to three sounds until a predetermined performance criterion was achieved. All inventories changed by either adding or eliminating sounds. The sounds added were not always those treated, and the sounds treated were not always added. Despite variation in specific changes, all inventories changed in conformity with the constraints on pretreatment inventories. That is, each post-treatment inventory could be uniquely assigned to one of the five previously established levels of complexity. Table II summarizes the results from that study by presenting representative inventories for each of the available levels.

There were no examples in this study of post-treatment inventories consistent with Level B. Their absence was likely attributable to the limited number of pretreatment inventories associated with Levels A and B.

The constraining effect of these laws was especially evident in those relatively simple inventories that changed to a complex inventory and acquired implied distinctions without direct treatment on sounds reflecting those distinctions. Instances of this were seen in the various Level C inventories that changed to Level E, acquiring a liquid consonant without treatment on that class of sounds.

These results suggest that the constraints governing cross-sectional variation also hold in the acquisition process for this sample. Thus, the acquisition of a manner distinction depended on the presence of a voice distinction. The acquisition of a liquid consonant depended on the presence of both manner and voice distinctions. Finally, the acquisition of a stridency or laterality distinction depended on the presence of a liquid consonant along with voice and manner distinctions among the obstruents.

While these constraints were first established to account for variation in the phonetic inventories of young children with functional speech disorders, they also account for cross-sectional and longitudinal variation in younger normal acquirers. Several studies (i.e., Leopold 1947;

Table II. Typology of Post-Treatment Phonetic Inventories for Thirty-Four Functionally Misarticulating Children

Level	Contrastive Features	Example Inventories

A	[syllabic]
	[consonantal]
	[sonorant]
	[coronal]
		`b d      g            ʔh`
		`m n      ŋ`
		`w      j`

B	[voice]	(NO EXAMPLES)

C	[continuant]
	[delayed release]
		1)
		`p b  t d    k g          ʔh`
		`f v  θ ð  s z  ŋ`
		`m    n`
		`w         j`
		
		2)
		`p b  t d    k g          ʔh`
		`f    s z  ʃ`
		`          č ǰ`
		`m    n      ŋ`
		`w         j`

D	[nasal]	`p b  t d            k     h`
		`f v`
		`m    n      ŋ`
		`w         j           ʔh`

E	[strident]
	[lateral]
		1)
		`p b  t d    k g          ʔh`
		`f v  θ ð  s z  ʃ`
		`          č ǰ`
		`m    n      ŋ`
		`w         j`
		
		2)
		`p b  t d    k g          ʔh`
		`f v  s z  ʃ`
		`          č ǰ`
		`m    n      ŋ`
		`     l`
		`w    r    j`

197

Macken 1978, 1979; Moskowitz 1970; Pye, Ingram, and List 1987; Stoel-Gammon and Cooper 1984; Vihman, Ferguson, and Elbert 1986) report the facts about individual children's systems in sufficient detail to allow a reanalysis of their phonetic inventories using the same methodologies. The phonetic inventories of these twenty children at one to three points in time could each be uniquely assigned to one of the five previously established levels of complexity. Table III summarizes the results of the reanalysis by noting the level of complexity to which representative phonetic inventories could be assigned.

Table III. Typology of Phonetic Inventories of Normal Language Acquirers

Level	Names	Age	Source
A	Si (Spanish)	1;7	Macken (1979)
	J (Spanish)	1;9	Macken (1978)
	Hildegard	1;2	Ingram (1989); Leopold (1947)
B	Timmy	1;3	Vihman et al. (1986)
C	Deborah	1;2	Vihman, Ferguson, and Elbert (1986)
	Daniel	1;2	Stoel-Gammon and Cooper (1984)
	Will	1;5	Stoel-Gammon and Cooper (1984)
D	Sean	1;2	Vihman et al. (1986)
	Si	1;9	Macken (1979)
	Hildegard	2;0	Moskowitz (1970); Leopold (1947)
	Five Quiché children	1;7–3;0	Pye, Ingram, and List (1987)
	Sarah	1;3	Stoel-Gammon and Cooper (1984)
E	Si (Spanish)	1;11	Macken (1979)
	Erica	2;0	Moskowitz (1970)
	Mackie	2;0	Moskowitz (1970)

Phonetic inventories for children with extremely small lexicons (10–20 words) may evidence slight apparent anomalies. For instance, the 15-word-state inventory for Emily, reported by Vihman, Ferguson, and Elbert (1986) lacks semivowels, in apparent violation of the requirements for a Level D inventory. However, Emily in fact did not attempt any semivowels, and further, her inventory includes [ʔ], which is characterized as [−cons, −syl], and whose presence in the inventory, thus, fulfills the requisite distinction between glides and true consonants.

A somewhat more subtle example is reported for Daniel in Menn (1971). The emergence of obstruents in the order [b]/[g], [F] (a [+tense, +acute] fricative), [dž], [v], [p] seems to violate the constraint that a voice contrast emerges before manner contrasts. It is important, however, to remember that not all differences are contrastive differences. In this case, the voicing and manner of articulation for [F] are redundant, that is, entirely predictable from its place of articulation (prior to the appearance of [F], there were no [+acute] obstruents). Thus, at this point, if an obstruent was [+acute], it was also redundantly [−voice] and [+continuant]. When [dž] was added to the inventory, voicing was no longer redundant, because there now existed both [+voice] and [−voice] segments that were both [+acute]; however, manner features for this place of articulation were still redundant, predictable from the voicing of the segment. That is, [+voice, +acute] was redundantly [−continuant], and [−voice, +acute] was redundantly [+continuant]. The result was that at this point, voicing was contrastive, but manner of articulation was not. A true manner contrast ([v] versus [b]) did not develop until just after the voicing contrast had. This way of viewing data of this sort underlies the conception of an inventory as a set of distinctions rather than merely a set of sounds.

Hildegard's inventory showed a development from Level A at age 1;2 to Level D at 2;0 years of age. The majority of the inventories relate to the development of English; however, some also relate to other languages, e.g., Spanish and Quiché. In fact, one of the children acquiring Spanish, Si, had a consonantal inventory at age 1;7 that was limited to nasals and obstruent stops with no voice distinction, i.e., Level A. Subsequently, a voice and manner distinction were added within the obstruents along with a liquid consonant to achieve a well-formed Level D inventory at age 1;9. Finally, the inventory expanded even further to achieve a well-formed Level E inventory by age 1;11.

The findings from developing inventories, whether normal or disordered, whether English-based or not, reflect the effects of a common set of constraints that narrowly defines the composition and development of inventories. These constraints also yield a typology of implicationally related inventories. Given these effects, the form and representation of the constraints must specify those feature distinctions common to all inventories, the implicational relationships among feature distinctions, and the order in which feature distinctions are acquired. Furthermore, because there are substantial individual differences across inventories, the constraints must also underdetermine certain other properties. That is, any lack of specificity in the constraints should predict variation in association with those unspecified properties. These requirements can be satisfied if phonetic inventories are derived from a system of hierarchically related feature distinctions and associated default principles. Figures 1A through 1E present a series of hierarchical tree structures from which each type of inventory would derive.

Each tree structure incorporates the three major class features ([syllabic], [consonantal], and [sonorant]) to allow for the occurrence and differentiation of sounds in major classes. The feature [syllabic] was common to all types of inventories, defining vowels as a class and differentiating them from all other nonvowel sounds (i.e., glides and consonants). The feature [consonantal] was necessary as a subordinate distinction for all sounds specified as [− syllabic], in order to define the

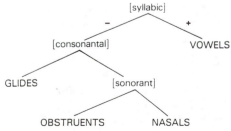

Figure 1A.   Level A.

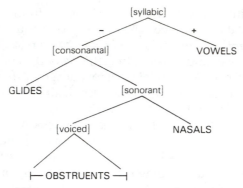

Figure 1B.   Level B.

class of occurring consonants and differentiate them from the other occurring nonvowels (glides). Finally, the feature [sonorant] was necessary as a subordinate feature distinction for all sounds specified as
[+consonantal] because two fundamentally different classes of consonants occurred in all the inventories; namely, a class of obstruents
([-sonorant]) and a class of sonorant consonants. Level A inventories
were limited to these general classes of sounds, represented as the terminal elements in figure 1A.

Default principles associated with the tree structures further specify the sounds that can occur in a particular class of terminal elements.
For example, the relevant default principles for Level A (figure 1A) are:

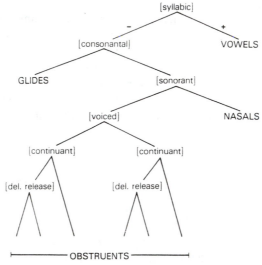

Figure 1C.   Level C.

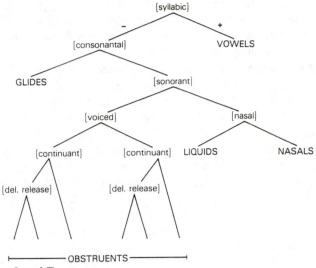

Figure 1D.   Level D.

Principle 1.   All consonants are stops.
Principle 2.   All obstruents are voiceless and unaspirated.
Principle 3.   All sonorant consonants are nasals.

Because Principle 1 is defined on a superordinate feature, [+con-sonantal], it holds for all subordinate distinctions, thus guaranteeing that the sonorant consonants will be (nasal) stops and that there will be

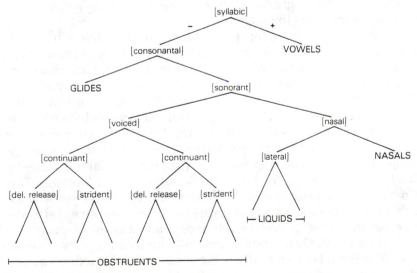

Figure 1E.   Level E.

no manner distinction among the obstruents. Principle 2 further restricts the class of obstruents in such a way that there will be no voice distinction. Principle 3 accounts for the fact that if there are sonorant consonants in a system, they must be nasals.

Level B inventories (figure 1B) are characterized by the same features in the same hierarchical configuration, except that the class of obstruents is further elaborated by the introduction of the subordinate feature [voice] to allow for the occurrence and differentiation of both voiced and voiceless obstruents. Default Principles 1 and 3 still hold for Level B inventories, but Principle 2 is replaced by a feature distinction.

Level C inventories (figure 1C) maintain the distinctions of simpler levels but extend them by the introduction of a subordinate manner of articulation distinction among the obstruents. The features [continuant] and [delayed release] account for the occurrence and differentiation of fricatives and/or affricates as distinct from stops. Either or both features are required for such inventories because no implicational relationship between fricatives and affricates can be established. For illustration purposes, figure 1C characterizes a system with both fricatives and affricates, all of which are both voiced and voiceless. Clearly, not all of these distinctions are necessary for Level C inventories. A system with stops and affricates but no fricatives would not need the feature [continuant]; alternatively, a system with stops and fricatives but no affricates would not need the feature [delayed release]. Any features not needed to distinguish classes of sounds would be predictable from other features. The fact remains that the necessity of either [continuant] or [delayed release] introduces a manner distinction. The scope of Principle 1 is accordingly limited to sonorant consonants when a manner distinction enters the system.

It should be noted at this point that the features in the hierarchy and in the default principles make no reference to, for example, place of articulation features. This is an instance of underdetermination. That is, these constraints purposely fail to specify which particular places of articulation will be associated with these features, leaving the specifics to be determined by other general principles or by constraints specific to a particular system. This means that systems are free to vary in terms of underdetermined properties. For example, then, while fricatives and/or affricates may occur in a system, no claim is made by these constraints about the place of articulation they will occupy. This is not to say that place of articulation features are without constraints. In fact, there are probably rather severe constraints on place of articulation, but they seem to be relatively independent of these constraints (cf. Dinnsen et al. 1990). Another underdetermined property of inventories at this level of complexity is the stridency of the occurring fricatives. That is, stridency is fully predictable in these inventories. The result is that all fricatives will be strident, or all will be nonstrident, or some places of articulation will be strident and other places of articulation will be nonstrident. The occurrence of strident and nonstrident fricatives with the same place of articulation is excluded in inventories with this level of complexity (but cf. Level E below).

Level D inventories (figure 1D) maintain all necessary feature distinctions and relationships characteristic of simpler inventories but extend the class of sonorant consonants beyond nasals to include a liquid consonant as well. The feature [nasal] is, thus, necessary as a subordinate distinguishing feature of sonorant consonants in order to differentiate nasals from other occurring sonorant consonants such as either [l] or [r], both of which are specified as [− nasal]. For Level D inventories, then, the introduction of the feature [nasal] replaces Principle 3. Another aspect of underdetermination is illustrated by the absence of any specification for the laterality of the liquid consonant. That is, some inventories include the lateral liquid [l] but not [r]; others include the nonlateral liquid [r] but not [l]. Consequently, because the constraints through this level of complexity underdetermine laterality, inventories are free to vary on this property.

Level E inventories (figure 1E) maintain the feature distinctions and hierarchical relationships of simpler inventories while also extending distinctions among the liquids and/or sounds specified as [+ delayed release] (fricatives and affricates). The introduction of the feature [lateral] as a subordinate distinction among non-nasal sonorant consonants accounts for the occurrence and differentiation of [l] and [r]. The introduction of the feature [strident] as a subordinate feature of fricatives accounts for the occurrence and differentiation of both [s] and [θ]. For illustration purposes, figure 1E characterizes one of the possible instances of a Level E inventory which includes both a stridency and laterality distinction. Both features need not co-occur in Level E inventories because there are some inventories with a laterality distinction and no stridency distinction, and there are others with a stridency distinction and no laterality distinction.

It can be seen that this structural representation of inventories places the various types of inventories in subset relationships with the increase in complexity deriving from the replacement of a default specification by the elaboration of a terminal node of a simpler inventory.

Three important facts derive from this characterization. First, the hierarchical dominance relationships among features directly represent certain implicational relationships and orders of acquisition. For example, the fact that fricatives are acquired after the acquisition of a voice distinction follows from the dominance relationship between the voice nodes and the manner nodes ([continuant] and/or [delayed release]). Likewise, the occurrence of a stridency distinction implies the

occurrence of a manner distinction, because the manner node dominates the stridency node. The occurrence of a laterality distinction implies the occurrence of a liquid consonant, which in turn implies the
occurrence of nasals, as reflected in the dominance relationships and
associated default principles. Liquids are, thus, acquired after nasals.

Second, the hierarchical structures also account for the absence of
implicational relationships and an absence of strict orders of acquisition in certain other cases. For example, there is no implicational relationship between, or strict order in, the acquisition of stridency and
laterality although both are characteristic of Level E. This is, however,
precisely what would be expected given that stridency is immediately
dominated by a feature unrelated to the feature that immediately dominates laterality.

Third, there are certain other implicational relationships and orders of acquisition that obtain but are not obviously predicted from the
structure of the hierarchy alone. For example, why should liquids be
acquired after a manner distinction because there is no dominance relationship between nasality and manner features? This lack of a dominance relationship also fails to explain the implicational relationship
that apparently exists between these two classes of sounds. Similarly,
the occurrence of a stridency distinction implies the occurrence of a
liquid consonant, yet the hierarchical structures specify no dominance
relationship between the relevant features.

This final point suggests either that this geometry of feature distinctions is wrong or that some constraint beyond the hierarchical
structuring of feature distinctions may be operating. An examination
of phonetic inventories in fully developed languages of the world
would provide a further test of these constraints and may distinguish
between constraints on the nature of phonetic inventories and constraints on the acquisition of those inventories.

Fully developed languages can be identified that have phonetic inventories corresponding with the typology of developing inventories
represented in figure 1. Table IV presents some examples of languages
with inventories corresponding to the different levels of complexity.

It is interesting that while the sounds associated with Level A

Table IV. Typology of Phonetic Inventories for Fully Developed Languages (Inventories according to Maddieson 1984)

Level	Example Language(s)
A	Unattested
B	Dera, Auca
C	Efik, Birom, Amoy
D	Senadi, Garo
E	English, Ewe

(vowels, glides, obstruent stops, and nasals) are quite common, surveys of the languages of the world (Maddieson 1984; Ruhlen 1976) have failed to identify any language with an inventory limited to Level A. It is unclear whether the absence of such languages is systematic or the result of inadequate sampling. Clearly, a Level A inventory would be quite simple with very few sounds. The majority of the world's languages include a substantial number of consonant sounds, the mean number in Maddieson's sample being approximately 23 (Maddieson 1984). There are, however, languages with as few as 6 consonant sounds, e.g., Rotoka (Maddieson 1984). Even with such a limited number of sounds, such inventories include enough feature distinctions to be assigned to levels more complex than A. Despite the absence of fully developed languages limited to Level A, all the other levels of complexity find fully developed languages that are in conformity with the constraints of that level.

In addition to the types of languages noted above, there are also phonetic inventories of fully developed languages that do not obviously fit this characterization. First, contrary to what might have been expected based on Level A inventories (and for that matter all other inventories), there are languages without nasals or any sonorant consonants, e.g., Mura (Maddieson 1984) and Puget Sound Salish (Maddieson 1984). In these languages, then, all consonants are obstruents. This suggests that there may be a more basic, simpler structure than that represented in figure 1A. That is, the consonantal node would not branch to dominate sonorant and nonsonorant nodes, but rather would specify all consonants to be [− sonorant] by a default principle (formulated below). It happens that there is also developmental evidence for this simpler or more basic structure in the phonetic inventory of Hildegard at 10 months (Leopold 1947). Her consonantal inventory at that point included only obstruent stops. The first nasal was acquired subsequent to the appearance of the obstruents. Languages may, thus, have no sonorant consonants; but if they do, they will be acquired after at least one obstruent. These facts about fully developed and developing inventories allow default Principle 1 (above) to be revised as follows:

Principle 1': All consonants are obstruent stops.

Second, contrary to what might be expected from Level C inventories, there are languages with a manner distinction among obstruents but no voice distinction, e.g., Maori (Maddieson 1984) and Hawaiian (Maddieson 1984). The default specification for the feature [voice] in obstruents can evidently be maintained as required by Principle 2 (above) even if other subordinate features such as manner features are elaborated. The introduction of a manner distinction does, nonetheless, replace or limit one of the other default specifications for the continuancy of all consonants as provided by Principle 1 (or its revision, Principle 1'). Apparently, then, default specifications are relatively resistant to being replaced. While the replacement of a default principle may be optional, the fact remains, at least for developing systems with both a voice and manner distinction, that the voice distinction is acquired before the manner distinction. In other words, if the default Principles 1 and 2 are both replaced, Principle 2 is replaced before Principle 1. This ordering restriction is a constraint on acquisition that excludes the logical possibility of acquiring a manner distinction before a voice distinction.

Third, contrary to what might be expected based on Level D inventories, there are languages with liquid consonants but no manner distinction among obstruents, e.g., Diyari (Maddieson 1984). Thus, while developing systems provide evidence of an implicational relationship between liquids and manner such that the presence of a nasal/nonnasal distinction in the sonorants implies the presence of a manner distinction in the obstruents, there is no dominance relationship between these classes of sounds as represented in figure 1D that would explain this apparent implication. The absence of a dominance relationship would, however, correctly predict that there could be languages like Diyari. Moreover, in addition to languages like Diyari, the existence of developing and fully developed languages consistent with Level B (no manner distinction in obstruents and no nasal/nonnasal distinction in the sonorant consonants), Level C (a manner distinction but no nasal/nonnasal distinction), and Level D (both a manner and nasal/nonnasal distinction) establishes that all the logical possibilities obtain relative to these two classes of sounds. This is, however, precisely what would be expected from the absence of a dominance relationship in the hierarchy. The fact remains, however, that there is a strict order in the acquisition of these distinctions, at least in the acquisition of English (and possibly other languages, such as Spanish). Thus, if a language has a manner distinction in the obstruents and a nasal/nonnasal distinction in the sonorants, the obstruent distinction will be acquired before the sonorant distinction. This result is achieved by ordering the replacement of Principle 1 before the replacement of Principle 3. Because this limitation does not follow from the dominance relations in the hierarchy, the ordered replacement of default principles would appear to derive from a constraint on acquisition rather than a constraint on inventories per se.

The facts about developing and fully developed phonetic inventories are, thus, highly compatible and suggest that all inventories follow from a single universal hierarchical structure with associated default principles and the ordered replacement of those principles. Figure 2 presents the structure from which these various types of inventories could derive.

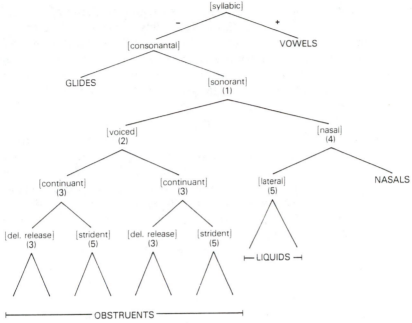

Figure 2.   Universal hierarchy.

The numbers in the hierarchy correspond to an ordered set of questions that must be asked and answered by the language learner. The ordering of some of the questions derives from the dominance relations in the tree structure itself, with others following from constraints on acquisition. The specific questions that a learner must ask and answer are as follows:

1. Does the language include sonorant consonants (i.e., distinguish between obstruent and sonorant consonants)?
2. Does the language include both voiced and voiceless obstruents (i.e., distinguish voicing)?
3. Does the language include fricatives or affricates (i.e., distinguish manner of articulation)?
4. Does the language include a liquid consonant (i.e., distinguish between nasal and nonnasal sonorant consonants)?
5. Does the language further distinguish either the liquid consonants or the obstruents (in terms of laterality and/or stridency)?

The process of acquisition is, thus, viewed as a series of questions that the learner asks and answers about the surrounding language. The substance of the questions is predetermined from the universal hierarchy (figure 2), with the questions being asked and answered in the order noted above. The facts of the surrounding language determine the answers to the questions. The answers result in successive approximations of the target system. Because of the underdetermined nature of the hierarchy, the sounds acquired at any given time may not necessarily be exactly those of the target system; but they will at least contain features of the target language sounds as required by the universal hierarchy.

To illustrate the implementation of these constraints, consider, for example, a language like Western Desert (Maddieson 1984), which includes nasals, liquids, and obstruent stops with no voice or manner distinction. For the learner of that language at the earliest stage of development, Principles 1' and 2 are operative and, thus, limit the consonantal inventory to obstruent stops with no voice or manner distinction. When the child asks the first question, the facts of the language require that Principle 1' be replaced (or modified as Principle 1), resulting in the elaboration of the consonantal node (or figure 1A). At this point, Principles 1 and 2 restrict the obstruents to stops with no voice or manner distinction. Principle 3 becomes apparent and restricts the sonorant consonants to nasals. When the second and third questions are asked, the facts of the language allow Principles 1, 2, and 3 to be retained. When the fourth question is asked, the facts of the language require that Principle 3 be replaced through the elaboration of sonorant consonants. If the last question is asked, the facts of the language would not motivate any further elaboration of the inventory.

Under this proposal, languages can vary in the composition and development of their phonetic inventories within certain limits. The variation derives from either underspecification or options to replace default principles. Variation is limited, however, by the substantive properties of the default principles, the ordered replacement of those principles, the specific features in the hierarchy, and the dominance relations among the features. The consequence is that no two learners of a given language will vary in the order in which these feature distinctions are acquired. Similarly, no two languages with the same feature distinctions will vary in the order in which they are acquired.

While languages and learners can vary in the replacement of default principles and, thus, in the presence/absence of certain feature distinctions, there are limits on this variation as represented in the constraints that derive from the hierarchy and the associated default principles. For example, the hierarchy establishes an implicational relationship such that the occurrence of liquids implies the occurrence of nasals, which implies the occurrence of obstruents. Thus, while languages and learners may vary on the presence or absence of liquids, they will not vary on the occurrence of nasals and obstruents if liquids do occur.

In sum, while individual differences can be observed in develop-

ing systems, those differences exist within the limits of certain specifiable constraints. That is, certain lawful uniformities emerge about
classes of sounds that allow for a typological characterization of those
inventories. Each inventory can be uniquely assigned to one of a limited and implicationally related set of inventories. Moreover, the typological characterization can be shown to correspond with distinct stages
of acquisition that are themselves strictly ordered. In addition, these
typological characterizations of developing inventories can also be
shown to properly characterize cross linguistic variation in the world's
languages.

The typological characterization of all inventories and the order of
acquisition are argued to follow from a universally specified feature geometry and associated default principles. All phonetic inventories may
be described as systems of distinct oppositions derived from a highly
limited set of features that are hierarchically related. The relationships
among features are fixed for all phonological systems. Each feature in
the hierarchy has an associated set of (universal) default specifications
that limit the range of sounds associated with that feature. Default values can, however, be replaced by the introduction of a feature distinction to account for cross-linguistic differences and changes in developing inventories. This is achieved by elaborating a subordinate feature in
terms of a more subordinate binary feature. For example, there are
some developing systems and fully developed languages in which all
consonants are obstruents. Therefore, the default value for [+conso-
nantal] is [−sonorant]. There are, of course, systems that include both
sonorant and obstruent consonants. To account for such systems, the
feature [+consonantal] must be elaborated to dominate the subordinate features [+sonorant] and [−sonorant]. Because all languages
with sonorant consonants include nasals, a default principle specifies
sonorant consonants as [+nasal]. This default may also be overridden
in a similar manner to account for inventories with both nasal and non-
nasal (liquid) sonorant consonants. To account for such systems, the
[+sonorant] node would be elaborated to dominate a [+nasal] and
[−nasal] node. Such a characterization accounts for typological properties of phonetic inventories and acquisitional orders. Thus, as illustrated above, any language with liquid consonants includes nasal consonants, and any language with nasal consonants includes obstruents.
Likewise, the order in which these classes of sounds is acquired corresponds with the dominance relationships and defaults represented in
the hierarchical structure; that is, obstruent stops are acquired before
nasals, and nasals are acquired before liquids.

Finally, the constraints that govern phonetic inventories, whether
developing or fully developed can be expressed as substantive linguistic principles that interact with constraints on acquisition to further

limit variation. Returning to the bamboo parallel noted at the beginning of this chapter, the "blossoms" (or defining characteristics) of phonetic inventories are not to be found in the occurrence or nonoccurrence of specific sounds. The variation associated with specific sounds is extensive and can be attributed to other factors, much like the variation of the other structures of bamboo. The "blossoms" are instead abstract linguistic structures and principles formulated in terms of feature distinctions and relationships as set forth here.

REFERENCES

Chomsky, N. 1965. *Aspects of the Theory of Syntax*. Cambridge, MA: MIT Press.

Dinnsen, D. A., Chin, S. B., and Elbert, M. In press. On the lawfulness of change in phonetic inventories. *Lingua*.

Dinnsen, D. A., Chin, S. B., Elbert, M., and Powell, T. W. 1990. Some constraints on functionally disordered phonologies: Phonetic inventories and phonotactics. *Journal of Speech and Hearing Research* 33:28–37.

Elbert, M., and Gierut, J. 1986. *Handbook of Clinical Phonology: Approaches to Assessment and Treatment*. San Diego, CA: College-Hill Press.

Jakobson, R. 1968. *Child Language, Aphasia, and Phonological Universal*, trans. A. Keiler. The Hague: Mouton.

Leopold, W. F. 1947. *Speech Development of a Bilingual Child: A Linguist's Record. Vol II: Sound Learning in the First Two Years*. Evanston, IL: Northwestern University.

Macken, M. A. 1978. Permitted complexity in phonological development: One child's acquisition of Spanish consonants. *Lingua* 44:219–53.

Macken, M. A. 1979. Developmental reorganization of phonology: A hierarchy of basic units of acquisition. *Lingua* 49:11–49.

Maddieson, I. 1984. *Patterns of Sounds*. Cambridge: Cambridge University Press.

Menn, L. 1971. Phonotactic rules in beginning speech: A study in the development of English discourse. *Lingua* 26:225–51.

Moskowitz, A. I. 1970. The two-year-old stage in the acquisition of English phonology. *Language* 46:426–41.

Prather, E. M., Hedrick, D. L., and Kern, C. A. 1975. Articulation development in children aged two to four years. *Journal of Speech and Hearing Disorders* 40: 179–91.

Pye, C., Ingram, D., and List, H. 1987. A comparison of initial consonant acquisition in English and Quiché. In *Children's Language*, Volume 6, ed. K. E. Nelson and A. van Kleeck. Hillsdale, NJ: Lawrence Erlbaum.

Ruhlen, M. 1976. *A Guide to the Languages of the World*. Stanford, CA: Language Universals Project, Stanford University.

Stoel-Gammon, C., and Cooper, J. 1984. Patterns of early lexical and phonological development. *Journal of Child Language* 11:247–71.

Stoel-Gammon, C., and Dunn, C. 1985. *Normal and Disordered Phonology in Children*. Baltimore, MD: University Park Press.

Vihman, M. M., Ferguson, C. A., and Elbert, M. 1986. Phonological development from babbling to speech: Common tendencies and individual differences. *Applied Psycholinguistics* 7:3–40.

Chapter • 7

The "Two-Lexicon" Account of Child Phonology
Looking Back, Looking Ahead

Lise Menn and Edward Matthei

Apologia: Science does not exist in a vacuum; it exists in a culture and is created by the interaction of many individuals.[1] This chapter is a history of a model and a projection for its future, and so we will set it firmly in its era, with attention to the people who have been involved. We also follow Margaret Bullowa's rule: use the active voice; take responsibility for what you say. Come along; we intend this ride to be fun—well, anyhow, if you like child phonology.

LOOKING BACK

The "two-lexicon" model of child phonology must have acquired its name in the early 1970s. Ferguson, Peizer, and Weeks (1973) put the notion into a general linguistic context, talking about their subject, Leslie:

---

[1]We are grateful to A. Katherine Baldwin, William Bright, Charles A. Ferguson, Clayton Lewis, K. P. Mohanan, Michael Mozer, and Ronnie Silber for their comments and suggestions at many stages of preparation of this manuscript, as well as to participants in the 1989 Child Phonology Conference, including fellow contributors to this volume.

. . . it seems likely that she has an internal representation of many adult vocables which she "understands" but does not produce. . . . On the other hand, it also seems likely that she has an internal representation for items which she can produce but which have no adult model. . . . In a way, this split seems plausible for adults too, since we may have words in our "passive" vocabulary which we have heard or read but have never used in speech and we may even be quite uncertain about details of their pronunciation; and we occasionally produce nonce forms which follow our phonological pattern but have no exact counterpart in the language around us (p. 56).

Ingram (1974) used the terms *input representation* and *output representation* in dealing with child phonology; this seems to be the first time that the basic idea appeared in print. A more personal memory: in 1975, Paul Kiparsky was getting LM to make her ideas about rules in child phonology explicit, as they were beginning work on the conference paper that appeared as Kiparsky and Menn (1977; see p. 61). LM was using such terms as *underlying forms, recognition forms,* and *production forms,* in trying to distinguish rules of child phonology (or *regularities,* if you prefer) from SPE-type (Sound Pattern of English) phonological rules, and Kiparsky got up and drew some boxes on the blackboard: "You mean like this?" Enlightenment, satori. See figure 1.

By the following year (Menn 1976 [1979:120–122]), LM was invoking this model in explaining the frequent delay in the spread of new rules to old forms (a topic we discuss below). In 1977, with the help of some tutorials by Nick Clements, the output lexicon received an autosegmental recasting, and the most elaborately set-out versions of the model appeared in Menn (1978, 1983). Well, what's the matter with it? Why are we reviewing it now?

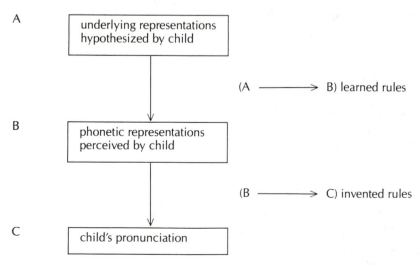

Figure 1.   Two-lexicon model as presented in Kiparsky and Menn (1977).

First, we would like to get rid of a relatively trivial level of misunderstanding (Wheeler and Iverson 1986). Figure 1 and its terminology were concerned only with the forms of words; we assumed that both input and output lexical entries were connected to the same semantic information, not that there were two full and independent lexical entries corresponding to each adult word. Matthei (1989) suggests that the terminology might be clearer if one referred to input and output "access files" instead. That's true, especially because the lexicon is a much more formidable construct now than it was in the 1970s. (But one could imagine that a child's recognition knowledge of, say, the syntactic privileges of a verb might exceed his or her production knowledge. See also the quote above from Ferguson, Peizer, and Weeks [1973] and note 5. Perhaps we needn't change the terminology quite yet; it might have its uses.)

What were the data that Ingram, Ferguson, and Menn intended to capture by separating the young child's knowledge about the sounds of words into two "lexicons"? And why is it that some researchers, such as Lawrence Leonard and Richard Schwartz, have felt totally at home with this move, whereas others, such as Marlys Macken and Neil Smith, have been quite sure that it represented an unnecessary complication?

The linguistic data: When children display regular correspondences between the sounds of the adult words they attempt to say and the sounds they actually produce, we can write rules to describe those regularities. That much can be done with one lexicon plus a set of "production rules." But there is a very common type of nonregularity that emerges in longitudinal studies: words that a child has learned to say at a later date may be subject to different rules than words that he or she learned to say at an earlier time. In other words, there is often a lag in the application of new rules to existing words. An example from Daniel (Menn 1971) makes this clear: fairly early on, Daniel produced "down" and "stone," both very frequent words, as [dæwn] and [don], respectively. Sometime later, he began to show a nasal harmony rule, producing "beans" as [minz] and "dance" as [næns]. For a while after this point, "down" and "stone" were maintained in their nonassimilated forms; then the forms [næwn] and [non] began to appear, in free variation with them. Finally, [næwn] and [non] were triumphant—[dæwn] and [don] disappeared.

At this point, standard phonologies give us one option: we have to mark the words "stone" and "down" as exceptions to the nasal assimilation rule until they catch up with the rest of the nasal-final words. Such use of exception markings can be regarded as a notational variant on the use of two lexicons (Menn 1983). But it is not a "mere" notational variant—though notation is important too. (Would you like to balance your checkbook with Roman instead of Arabic numerals?) If your goal goes beyond descriptive adequacy, you choose the notation that fits best with where you think your explanations will come from. Elegance and parsimony are secondary criteria, trivial by comparison: they only loom large when one limits oneself to working within a Saussurean model of language as a self-contained system, because then there is little else to go on. So we look for acquisition explanations in psychological and physiological terms as a matter of methodology (for further discussion, see the Methods overview).

The two-lexicon model, then, in our usage, is intended to hook onto psychology. This means that its constructs refer to hypothetical entities in the child's mind. To claim "psychological reality" for any model is too much; but this model tries for, let us say, psychological responsibility. We quote Ferguson, Peizer, and Weeks (1973) again (p. 56, f.n. 15): " . . . the position taken here is that linguistic theory is to be regarded as behavioral theory, subject to the same kind of empirical testing and fraught with the same risks as any other kind of behavioral theory." This is our essential disagreement with Spencer (1986), who complains that in a psycholinguistically motivated model, "the relationship between linguistic constructs and psycholinguistic constructs would become very obscure" (p. 29). Close! On our view, if we ever get it right, the difference between them will disappear entirely!

Our constructs are not, therefore, only "about" linguistic notions, such as abstract underlying forms; they are "about" the particular child's more-or-less fragmentary knowledge of the adult language. And the model must be modifiable as we make better guesses as to what children know about language, just as it must be modifiable to reflect changes in an individual child's "guesses" about the adult language (or rather, about the varieties and registers of the ambient language). In the final part of this chapter, we will in fact suggest some major modifications in the model; but first, we continue to review its excuses for being.

The "input" or "recognition" lexicon is supposed, by definition, to contain all the child's knowledge that permits him or her to recognize a word. It may very well be wrong or incompletely specified with respect to the adult form (Ingram 1974). We have no direct access to the child's recognition knowledge, but we do our best to approximate it. To test the correctness of this approximation directly, we have to test the child's abilities to distinguish between words. For example, suppose we want to test whether Daniel's recognition representation of the word for "stone," once he began saying it [non], should be notated as [ston], [don], or [non] (or possibly, following Ingram, as [Xon], where X is "some unknown speech sound"). To do this, we should have data as to whether he was able to distinguish among such syllables, and to tell which of them referred to "stone"; but we don't. All we know for sure is that he had a contrast between the onset of "no" and the onset of "down" and "stone" *before* he began to say [næwn] and [non].

Now, if we have psychological interpretations of linguistic primitives for *two* competing models, they may become testably distinct even if they would have been notational variants in purely linguistic terms. Macken (1980) has a single-lexicon model that also is interpreted psychologically, and so such a comparison is possible. First, we should review Macken's excellent reasoning in support of her model; then, of course, we will argue that it's better to keep the two-lexicon model because we can incorporate the strengths of her analysis into it.

In her reanalysis of Smith (1973), Macken (1980, this volume) was concerned with modeling the spread of new rules that improved the child's output accuracy. Smith's son, Amahl, had some sets of words to which such new rules applied swiftly, "across the board." But there would be an occasional hold-out word, a regressive phonological idiom, that retained his earlier pronunciation. The star example was [gʊk] for "took," which retained this form after velar harmony had completely disappeared elsewhere—or rather, had been completely replaced by rules giving more accurate productions in such words. These words were clear exceptions to the general pattern of rule spread to all members of some phonologically defined class of words. It was as though Amahl, in these special cases, did not have an accurate internal representation of the adult word to apply his new rules to.

Macken's model equates "child's underlying form" (i.e., the form that his rules apply to) with "perceptual representation," and so she suggests that these events can be explained by the hypothesis that Amahl had learned his own output form (by hearing himself talk) and had replaced [tʊk] by [gʊk] in his lexicon—that is, in his list of underlying forms. This seems quite reasonable; similar learning from one's own incorrect forms has been suggested by Butler Platt and MacWhinney (1983) and by Vihman (1982). Because we have no relevant data on Amahl's perceptual confusions, Macken cannot test her hypothesis, but it could be checked in principle on any child who shows such a regressive idiom.

The problem is applying this explanation to the other kind of phonological idiom, a "progressive idiom," such as Daniel's [don], whose pronunciation is *better*, at least temporarily, than pronunciation of other words of a similar pattern. During those few weeks when the nasal assimilation rule applied to all nasal-final words except the well-practiced "down" and "stone," what kind of representations do we need to postulate? Clearly, we need a non-nasal onset for these words in whatever we take to be the lexicon, and we need to exempt them from the nasal assimilation rule that was taking "beans" into [minz] and "dance" into [næns]—unless we claim that this assimilation rule was due to a misperception of the oral onsets in all other adult words with nasals somewhere in them. This is of course conceivable,[2] but for Daniel we do not have the precondition—the child's earlier output error—that makes Macken's "took" example from Amahl so plausible. This time, the postulated misperception could not be the result of the child's learning his own incorrect forms, because no such forms existed prior to the onset of the nasal assimilation rule.

Another argument for having some form of stored output representation comes from the Jacob data (Menn 1976). The first consonant that Jacob mastered was /d/, and the first to contrast with it was /g/ (or /k/); /b/-initial words were avoided for many months after his family and LM could demonstrate that he understood quite a few of them ("box," "ball," "bib" . . .). The one /b/ word that Jacob occasionally produced, under social pressure, was "bye-bye," as [dædæ]. (By the way, this is a rare clear counterexample to Jakobson's claim that an anterior /b–d/ contrast will appear before an anterior/posterior contrast. His claim does hold if it is taken as a weak rather than as a strong universal.)

When Jacob did learn to produce bilabials, many of the old /b/ words that we knew he understood made their first appearances with /d/, and then were immediately revised to a correct /b/. One old word, "ball," which he had never before attempted in anyone's hearing, now

---

[2]It is, however, extremely unlikely. Such errors would have to be independent random errors, but the probability that a random error process would produce all of Daniel's new nasal assimilations is essentially zero. Consistent misperception (as in some sort of perceptual filtering) could lead to correct pronunciation; if Daniel had consistently heard stops as the corresponding nasals, e.g., [binz] as [minz], then he might have had to produce a stop in order to hear himself say a nasal. But a stop versus nasal *confusion* should have resulted in a roughly 50/50 distribution of correct and assimilated forms. Incidentally, although LM did not try to check his recognition abilities with [non], she did get an accomplice to ask Daniel for a /gʌk/ at a time when "stuck," "duck," and "truck" were all produced as /gʌk/. He looked puzzled, and glanced neither at his "truck" nor his "duck"; if he had been confused, it seems likely that he would have looked at both of them and then back at the speaker for clarification. His variable productions of "boot" [bup—dut] and of "boat" [bop—dot], which are discussed again below, also make a perceptual explanation unlikely for his errors on stop positions. Of course, this does not bear on the question of the explanation of his nasality errors.

Can output homonymy be caused by perceptual confusion? Yes, certainly, for unconditioned collapses of distinctions, such as between all instances of /f/ and /θ/ (see Velleman 1988), as well as for the "learning one's own error" cases such as the one described by Macken (1980). But no one really knows if conditioned sound-errors can be caused by true confusion—as opposed to misidentification of a particular conditioned allophone, a phenomenon which Macken has convincingly demonstrated for Amahl Smith. For a pattern such as Daniel's consonant harmony, the child would have to be able to hear, say, a /d/ accurately when all stops in a word were alveolar, but to be unable to hear it when a labial or a velar was present in the word—a sort of "perceptual overload" phenomenon. This is logically possible, but it seems that it has not been looked for.

appeared as [da]; however, unlike the other /b/ words, "ball" remained [da] for about 10 days before being corrected to [ba]. (There is no possible perceptual explanation for these events—i.e., no way to argue that /b/ was ever misperceived as /d/, with the possible exception of "bye-bye"—because then the systematic avoidance of /b/ words would be unexplainable. If Jacob had "confused" /b/ and /d/, he would have tried to say the /b/ words as cheerfully as he tried to say the /d/ words.)

What can we say about this? It is hard to deal with, unless there was a /b/-percept-to-[d]-output connection that Jacob created during the period where [d] would have been his closest available approximation to /b/. If we say that it was a rule but keep to a single lexicon model, we have to have the older words marked as lexically undergoing the rule and the newer ones as not doing so. This linguistic device "works" —but how is it to be interpreted psycholinguistically? *Something* has been stored about pronunciation that is connected to the particular lexical items and that is not a matter of misperception.

So the two-lexicon model was designed to handle both these kinds of irregularities of rule propagation: slow propagation of a rule that improves production accuracy (or, if you prefer, slow loss of a rule that reduced production accuracy), as in the Amahl example, and slow propagation of a rule that reduces production accuracy, as in the Daniel and Jacob examples. The output lexicon is defined as the collection of stored "ways to say" words; more precisely, the collection of stored information that is required to produce the child's words. (This qualification and its rationale are discussed later.) The motivation here is that slow spread of rules makes sense if "the way to say a word" is something that is also stored and held onto, something that has a reality separate from the input representation plus the rules. This idea is supported to the extent that we can show that new rules seem to show up first on new lexical items, and then spread to established ones. (But sufficiently fine-grained data are not abundant—rule-spread can happen within hours.) As the two-lexicon model is revised, its ability to handle events like these should not be lost.

Now, about the qualification just mentioned, which involves a minor revision of the original model. Following the generative linguistics model closely, and armed with the then-new autosegmental formalism, Menn (1978) attempted to remove as much redundancy from the lexicon as possible. This gave rise to the information in the figure 2 diagram.

Rules were now broken into two groups depending on how they seemed to function. (There was never any independent evidence for this assignment—it just seemed to make general sense.) The upper set of rules were *selection rules*, which characterized those aspects of the adult word that the child preserves. These could be seen as off-line "fil-

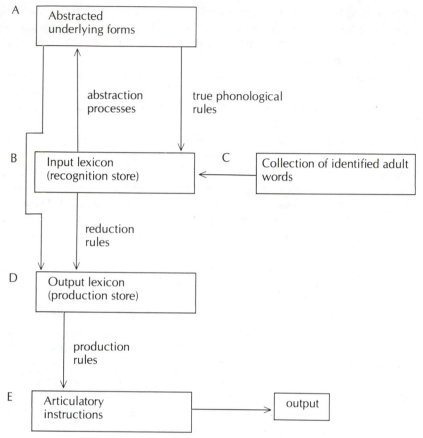

Figure 2.   Revised two-lexicon model, from Menn (1978).

ters," mapping the input lexical entry onto the output lexical entry. The lower set of rules were *production rules*, filling in the redundant aspects of the output word on-line, during output. The production rules were considered to be motor execution rules (analogous to allophonic/phonetic detail rules). In this version, what is stored in the output lexicon is just the information required to keep the child's output words distinct from one another; patterns that can be described by generally applicable rules are supplied as the automatic finishing touches in production. So, for example, if a child voices all initial stop consonants, this voicing is not specified in the output lexicon. Instead, the stored forms of words are treated as having the voicing of initial consonants unspecified. The voicing is supplied by the lowest level rules, the production rules. This model requires, then, that initial nasalization was specified in the lexicon when Daniel's "down" and "stone" were not yet undergoing his nasal harmony rule; it also suggests that when this rule became exceptionless, the nasality of initial consonants was no longer specified in the lexicon (being now predictable), but rather that it was supplied by the production rules when the next consonant in the word was nasal.

This was very cute, but it is not, on the face of it, "psychologically responsible." If we do think that there is a change in the lexicon and the production rules when a rule has spread to the last hold-out form, what is the mechanism for this change? How does it happen? How could we show that it had happened—what empirically testable consequences would it have? And for that matter, what psychological evidence is there for the absence or presence of redundancy in either the input or the output lexicon? Issues like this are discussed further below; they are part of the continuing tension between models motivated by the assumptions of generative phonology versus models motivated by the desire for maximally plausible psycholinguistic interpretation.

Here's another story—a girl, *A*, of 4;6, whose family EM knew well, had, up to a certain point, produced all noninitial /l/'s as [w], e.g., "sled" [swɛd], "yellow" [jéwow], although initial /l/ and /w/ were produced correctly. Her mother then became sensitized to the change to accurate pronunciation of these forms after she observed her daughter, on two separate occasions, apparently practicing previously mispronounced forms. The child would sit by herself and carefully articulate long lists of words that contained noninitial /l/ (her old [w]). Does this sound like a typical across-the-board change, so far? What is interesting is that she also changed all the previously correct noninitial /w/'s to [l], both in her practice sessions and in spontaneous speech. The most notable example, probably due to frequency and salience, was [halájʔɛn pʌntʃ] "Hawaiian Punch." The over-correction lasted for about two months.

What explanations are available here? This is an across-the-board change, so the corrections and hypercorrections were not made on a case-by-case basis. Once the child noticed that her [w] output did not match her parents' [l], there must have been a rule change. It also looks as if she did not distinguish between noninitial /l/ and /w/ in her lexical representation. But which lexical representation: input or output? Once again, perceptual confusion data are not available. But it seems that this may have been an output lexicon conflation of /l/ and /w/, because the perceptual cues for /l/ and /w/ in intervocalic position are probably at least as clear as in initial position. In terms of the model, we could say that the selection rules omitted the feature [lateral] from noninitial glides, and that the rule change consisted of the addition of a [+ lateral] specification to these segments.

As with many other box-and-arrow models, the two-lexicon model was forced to undergo a fair amount of proliferation to deal with additional circumstances—in this case, with additional types of variability in behavior (Ferguson 1986). The most important case is the need to model the frequent (although unreliable) superiority of imitated forms over those drawn from long-term memory. An extreme Daniel example, where it is likely that the child failed to identify the adult word without context: during the apparently iron grip of his velar assimilation rule, LM asked Daniel if he wanted his toy duck, which was invisible to him from where he stood. Daniel said, to her astonishment, "[dʌk]?" He then moved to where he could see what she was pointing to, looked at the duck, and shook his head, saying "[gʌk]." Clearly, it is necessary for any model to be able to bypass some of the rules when the influence from immediate auditory memory is maximal, and where, conversely, the influence from any long-term information store is minimal. The situation seems fully parallel to what happens to any of us attempting to master a foreign pronunciation.[3]

It is, of course, also necessary to be able to deal with a good many other kinds of variation—some linked to attentional variables, and some to the gradual replacement of older by newer forms. After all, the child's system is, in its very essence, a developing system and, therefore, unstable.

PROBLEMS AND PSEUDO-PROBLEMS FOR THE TWO-LEXICON MODEL

We have tried to argue that the two-lexicon approach has some real advantages over a single-lexicon model. Menn (1983) argued that the two-lexicon model handled some of the phenomena that we have just reviewed "more gracefully"; we have extended that argument here, and have claimed that there are at least some characteristics of the model that make it more "psychologically responsible," as well.

We have also acknowledged that the model has had its critics. We have addressed some of the criticisms above, in our discussion of psychological responsibility and notational variants. Before we continue with our defense, let us restate our basic premise: we want to account for the behavior—the productions and the indications of comprehension—of little talkers. So we must concern ourselves with both the child's fragmentary and developing knowledge of the adult language *and* the developing (and also fragmentary) mechanisms that the child uses in

---

[3]Ferguson reminds us that the rule-bypass account by no means exhausts the subtlety of the relations between imitation and spontaneous production. Sometimes pronunciation of a nonsense or unfamiliar item is more accurate than spontaneous production of a comparable familiar word, as here, but sometimes the reverse is true. He adds the suggestion that this latter phenomenon may be related to Berko's well-known finding (1958) that plurals on known words (e.g., "glasses") are mastered before plural endings can be added to unknown or nonsense words (e.g., "tasses").

employing that knowledge. In a way, the old competence/performance problem is rearing its ugly head here. (If the current adult psycholinguistic literature is any indication, mechanisms for recruiting linguistic knowledge may not be the ones that would be considered the most parsimonious if they were looked at in purely linguistic terms; see, e.g., Seidenberg et al. 1982.)

Considerations of parsimony also may have led to the resurrection (Pinker 1984) of another perennial problem/criticism, the "continuity problem." Continuity in development is an assumption verging on dogma among developmentalists. After all, as Roger Brown (1973) has remarked, we don't expect Mother Nature to build cul-de-sacs.[4] But natural selection does not have to produce perfect systems; if we blunder our way into a workable end-state without too much cost, that is adequate until a competing organism does it better (see almost any general book by Stephen J. Gould). LM (in the Models overview) argues that there is no inherent evil in postulating an immature system that differs from a mature one—as long as we also discharge our responsibility for showing how and why the metamorphosis from one system to the other takes place.

We clearly can see one type of developmental cul-de-sac in the U-shaped curves of overgeneralizations, not to mention Daniel's "-rs rule," discussed below. And surface discontinuity may be a result of an underlying continuous development (see Models overview for further discussion)—it is a question of where and how you look for your explanations. Some of the continuity "problems" may have arisen because so-called "phonological regressions" have formed the bases of many arguments for the two-lexicon model. But let's note that these are *behavioral* regressions, not massive backward steps in the child's system. It is quite common to observe such behavioral regressions in child language—we have already mentioned some above—as well as in other areas of development (see, e.g., Strauss 1982).

The two-lexicon model has been criticized, then, for introducing a discontinuity (Stemberger this volume). But one-lexicon models, which still need sets of rules that convert adult forms (or perceptual forms) to child productions, have similar continuity problems: those rules still have to be eliminated—or, in phonological process models, suppressed. In the two-lexicon model, this problem is absolutely no different, except that it has two aspects, each of which has a direct psychological interpretation.

---

[4]An aside: the occasional side trip there-and-back-again may still be quite interesting and informative. An old logician friend and teacher of EM's at Chicago once remarked that he didn't quite see why all his fellow logicians hated tautologies. "After all," he said, "every time you go around the circle you usually notice something new."

First, in the terms of figure 2, the selection rules (the ones specifying which aspects of the recognition form the child will attempt to reproduce) are expected to relax over time, regressions aside. In other
words, the child gradually will become more willing and able to attempt to reproduce all the sounds of the adult word, with the end stage
being adult competence. Selection rules are, thus, reduced to zero (or
near-zero; many adults have some problem words, perhaps words of
foreign origin with non-English phones, which they recognize but
whose strange sounds they do not even try to say). Second, the production rules become increasingly more adequate, to the point where
they can be identified with the low-level (phonetic specification) rules
of English phonology in the adult—rules that are needed anyway. In
the end state, input and output lexicons (almost) coincide, and the output representation becomes whatever "phonemic" representation we
think is best in the light of adult psycholinguistic research.[5]

A related criticism is that this model claims that the child "has his
own system" (Spencer 1986, p. 5) rather than having an incomplete adult
system. We cannot see how a psychologically responsible model could
claim anything else: each child must construct his or her own version
of the adult system, because there is no other way in which it can be
transmitted. Inevitably, it will be incomplete in some ways, and inaccurate in others, as it develops. Even in its end state, it will have some
idiosyncrasies (see Mohanan this volume for a much fuller exposition
of this position).

REAL PROBLEMS FOR THE MODEL: WHY WE CANNOT STOP HERE

There are, nevertheless, some real problems for the two-lexicon model.
Recently, a number of investigators have presented evidence that certain word-level phonological constraints in the speech of children may
also operate on children's early word combinations, i.e., across word
boundaries (Donahue 1986; Matthei 1989; Stemberger 1988).

The evidence that some word-level constraints may apply on-line

---

[5]A number of colleagues, e.g., K. P. Mohanan (personal communication), have independently noted that adult input-output asymmetries are quite substantial when we
compare our rather good ability to understand other "accents" and dialects—and specialized speech registers—with our very limited (and variable) ability to produce them.
Our models need not only two lexicons, they also need, in some sense, two of everything. As our approaches move toward closer approximations of human language use
and knowledge, such asymmetries belong in our models. Cf. the quote above from Ferguson, Peizer, and Weeks (1973) on active versus passive vocabularies. To quote from
Ferguson and Farwell (1975, p. 437): "Our approach is to try to understand children's
phonological development in itself in order to improve our phonological theory, even if
this requires new theoretical constructs for the latter."

to word combinations presents a real problem for the two-lexicon model. Why so? Why can't we just put two words together from the output lexicon and then run them through the production rules as a sequence, treating them as a single phonological word? We cannot do this because some of the rules involved are (if we take the model seriously) selection rules, the rules that derive the output lexicon. And the mechanisms for combining words (i.e., the syntax) *use* lexical representations, but do not *derive* word combinations within the lexicon.

Scollon (1976) observed what he interpreted as regression to earlier phonological forms when the first word combinations appeared in his subject's speech. So, we might argue that the "added effort" required to produce word combinations results in the child's returning to earlier, well-established output forms or something like that. But evidence from Matthei's (1989) subject, E, indicates that this is not generally the case. Word combinations in E's speech appeared only after she began to produce polysyllabic forms, and all of E's early word combinations were limited to two syllables, as were her polysyllabic forms. Among the first combinations EM observed (at 17 months) was [bei bʊ] "baby's book." At the time that this example appeared, both words had well-established CVCV forms ([béjbi] "baby" and [búkə] "book"), and both had appeared in these full CVCV forms in the same recording session as the combination. However, these forms cannot be described as true regressions to earlier forms. The dominant form in E's earlier production was a simple CV pattern, all right: but the forms in her early word combinations are more appropriately described as truncations of existing forms, for "baby" had been consistently [bi] until the CVCV forms appeared. In addition, forms that had always had the shape CVCV, e.g., "mama" [mɔ́mɔ], from 11 months on, were not immune to this truncation: "mama's key" shows up as [mɔ ki] at 17 months and again at 18 months.

If we grant that these forms are not true regressions, then we must assume that the same constraints are operating both within and across words. We might, as Matthei (1989) proposed, move the output constraints from the output lexicon to somewhere else—but where? And, if we do that, how do we specify the way that those constraints will interact with the lexicon to create the child's output representations? (The problem is perhaps even stickier in one-lexicon models, where the child's forms are derived directly from representations of adult forms, because output constraints have much less direct representation in those models.) In the two-lexicon model, some of the effects of output constraints are explicitly represented by having the production rules "fill in" underspecified feature values, but these require a particular input, namely, the underspecified representations to be found in the output lexicon. And the underspecification is supposed to be produced by the action of the selection rules. Are we now going to let the selection rules work in real time? Can we specify (and motivate!) a route for two-word phrases from either the input lexicon or the output lexicon, having them take a sort of side-trip to the pronunciation rules? Is there any good reason to prefer one of these routes over another? Is there any set of predictions that we can derive that would distinguish one of these proposed routes from the other? And do we really feel comfortable cycling what seem to be the first bits of syntax through the lexicon? (Now, that might be a more serious continuity problem!) Finally, if we cycle two-word phrases through the lexicon via some route or other, how will we keep imitations, which do not show the same amount of reduction, from traveling the same route?

Admitting the seriousness of this problem has caused us to notice another one—which LM, with chagrin, acknowledges that she should have seen years ago. In the autosegmental version of the two-lexicon model (Menn 1978), the output lexical entry for a fully harmonized word like [gʌk] for "duck" is supposed to be CVC plus a specification for the vowel and a specification for the velar; the selection rules have done the job of stripping away the unrealizable alveolar specification of the initial [d] of the input lexical entry. Also, in general, output lexical entries are supposed to be fully specified. Variations at a given time, as in the [gʌk] story above, are ascribed to "bypassing the output lexicon" when the child is imitating a model or for some other reason attending to the form of his or her production, and are handled by drawing another arrow (Menn 1979). Other types of variation are supposed to be due to developmental changes in the selection rules, producing competing stored forms. (The production rules are supposed to apply on line—i.e., their outputs are not stored—so changes in them over time should produce irreversible changes in the output forms, not random variation.)

Now, LM has described Daniel's unstable consonant harmony forms [bup–dut] "boot" and [bop–dot] "boat" more times than she cares to admit (starting with Menn 1971). These two cases have to be described, within the model, as arising from competition among contemporary stored output forms produced by the operation of two rival selection rules: (a) delete the position of articulation specification for the alveolar if another stop position of articulation is present; (b) delete the specification of position of articulation for the initial consonant if a final consonant is present. Competition between ways to say a word, though, is a strange notion for a linguist's lexicon; the field has not really even assimilated Labov's variable rules very well. (That isn't to say that linguists dealing with adult language are absolved from dealing with the problem, at least not if [bop–dot] is analogous to an adult's variable use of [íðɾ–ájðɾ].)

There's more. T. M. S. Priestly's child (1977) seemed to have a couple of different ways of mapping certain adult words into his [CVjVC] canonical form, e.g., [májos] and [méjan] for "monster," [tájak] and [tájaŋ] for "tiger." Examination of the range of forms he produced does not encourage one to think in terms of well-defined selection rules at all, and that means no well-defined forms in the output lexicon to compete with one another. Although we have no real test of this, it looks very much as though many of the output forms were made by taking that stable [CVjVC] skeleton "from the output lexicon" and then adding in the unstable consonant specifications on line "from the input lexicon." Elaine Paden's data (unpublished) on hundreds of children's attempts to produce the word *flower* give one the same impression. The two-lexicon model here begins to feel like a bunch of clunky machinery forcing the data into a mold. It is not graceful any more.

Whatever tack we take now, we run into problems; we multiply boxes and paths until we get loops and alternatives and exceptions and specifications of which path is to be taken, ending up with a maze that starts to lose its reason for existence, namely, the proud claim to testable "psychological responsibility." It is reminiscent of the growth of the "multitude of logogens" that caused John Morton's splendid ideas (see Morton 1979) to lose their initial appeal.

Where can we go from here? Consideration of a few more problems will help to motivate the direction we have taken. Missing from formal linguistics and from child language since Chomsky pronounced anathema upon Skinner is any consideration of frequency, although psychologists and psycholinguists of course must consider it all the time (see Hasher and Zacks 1984). To mention the word is to invoke (shudder, whisper) *behaviorism*. But now that we have proven to each other again and again that frequency cannot explain a large set of linguistic phenomena, it is time to face the fact that there is another set of linguistic phenomena that it *can* explain. For example, there is the fact that only the most frequent verbs appear in correct forms ("came," "went") before becoming over-regularized; the next batch of irregular past tenses make their first appearances with zero change, or with the regular past ending. And of course the standard argument for the persistence of suppletive and irregular past (and plural) forms in English, in the face of general child over-regularization, is again their frequency.

In child phonology, consider the regressive and progressive idioms, discussed above. A major characteristic of such forms is that these forms are used very frequently by the child; they seem to resist assimilation into the child's general patterns or rule system because they are used often, and are older and well established. The idioms seem to be, in an intuitive sense, stronger than less frequently used words, for it is generally the newer and less frequent forms that undergo immediate

Table I.   [eij] To [ij] Rule (Entries in parentheses were imitations of words in comprehension vocabulary; others were spontaneous utterances. Forms marked "Summer report" were relayed by Jacob's mother, Judith Aissen.)

Age	Tea	Tape	Key	Gate	Egg	Away	Cake	"A"	Play	"E"	Table
16;16	ti										
16;30		ʔtæ									
17;2		dæ									
17;16		ej									
17;18	di dɛj	(tɛj) (tɛj) (dɛ)	kʰj			(ʌɣɛ)					
17;23		te	kʰj								
17;25	ti	ʔtxi	xiɛ								
17;27		ti di tujʌ	xɛ								
18;2		gej	kʊ								
18;4	tʷi	tej	(kʰj) ki								
18;9	uti					(wɛ)					
18;13			ki	(gi)		(wɛʔ) (awe)					
18;18		ti dʒɛ	ki								
18;20	ti di	taj (dɛj)				we	(ki) (ke)				
18;23		kʌ			(ejʰ)						
18;25		daj									
18;27		ti	ki								
18;30		di				owʔɛj					

Table I. *continued*

Age	Tea	Tape	Key	Gate	Egg	Away	Cake	"A"	Play	"E"	Table
19;9						(wʌj) (wɛj)					
19;10		(tʰi)	ki								
19;17		(di)	ki				(ʌk)		(pɛj)		
19;22								(ej)			
19;22								(i)			
19;27					ɩk						
19;29	ti	ti	ki		ʊk						
20;1					ɛkʔ				(pɛj)		
20;8		(ti)	ki								
20;15			kʰiç		(eʔk)						
20;18–19		kʰi	kiç			kek			(i)		
20;20			ti ki xi							(ej)	
20;22	ti						(kʔejk) (gi:k)				
Summer report				ik						ti	

change. But our generative-based boxologies are deterministic, and there is no straightforward way to graft probabilistic processes onto them. How, in a generative-model lexicon, can we possibly motivate or formalize a claim that phonological idioms are stronger than other words?

The final kind of problem is that of unruly data. Such data from Menn (1976) and from the Daniel diary have been in search of a theory for over fifteen years; they show fuzzy-boundary "cross-talk" interactions that are totally indescribable with box-and-arrow models. And, to let the cat out of the bag, it is these phenomena that impelled LM to start looking for connectionist colleagues to work with after hearing a lecture by Jay McClelland at MIT in 1986. (Satori no. 2.) In connectionist models, we expect fuzzy boundaries, we expect forms to interact with each other, we expect frequency effects—and, crucially, we also expect both input and output forms to be stored in some linked way. We also have instance-based learning, the "phonic core of remembered lexical items and articulations which produce them," suggested by Ferguson and Farwell (1975, p. 36). If we have storage for both input and output forms, we at least have the potential for modeling all of the good things that the two-lexicon model buys us, and we may be able to get rid of the aspects of the model that were getting oppressive. Stemberger (this volume) outlines one connectionist approach; after we describe our fuzzy data, we sketch another, focusing somewhat more on its design principles and their motivation.

We don't know, of course, that a connectionist model could actually account for these data. Perhaps it would have serious inadequacies of its own. The thesis of this section is not, then, a simple pro-connectionist argument. But it is intended to disturb even further those who feel that a working model of child phonology already exists. Data like these had to be treated as noise originally, but now it is time to try holding our theories accountable to them as well as to the better-behaved data that we all know and love.

UNRULY PATTERNS FROM JACOB AND DANIEL

"Tea"—"Tape"

Jacob imitated "tea" for the first time at 16;16 (we deal here, by the way, only with imitations of words for which there is prior evidence of comprehension, and therefore at least some gross internal phonological representation). He produced it spontaneously twice at 17;18, once as [di] and once as [dɛj], with a lowered nuclear vowel. "Tape" is first attested at 16;30, with a low nuclear vowel, and spontaneously with a mid nuclear vowel at 17;16 and 17;23. "Key" was produced correctly at 17:18, once correctly and once as [xiɛ] at 17;23, and as [xɛ] at 17;25. So one might suggest, in conventional terms, that a rule taking adult [i] into output [ɛ] was forming; see table I.

Unfortunately for this account, we also have the reverse change happening simultaneously: we have "tape" produced as [ʔtxi], [ti], [di], [tʊjʌ] on 17;25 and 17;27. "Tea" also reverts to correct spontaneous [ti] on 17;27, and the vowel remains correct thereafter.

One might think that things were getting sorted out around 18;2—in other words, that an accurate production of both sounds was coming under control—because "tape" reappears with the low nuclear vowel on 18;2 and 18;4, with "key" and "tea" correct. Alas, no. At 18;18, "gate" is *imitated* as [gi], and all occurrences of "tape" revert to [ti]. A rule changing [ei] to [i] before adult stop consonants seems to have been established, and it remains in place for several more months. In summary, the words "tape," "tea," and "key" seem to have been *influencing one another* as they became part of Jacob's spontaneous production vocabulary. There was some kind of cross-talk going on.

Kaká—"Cracker"

The *kaká*—"cracker" story is similar, but simpler—simple enough so that the problems it poses are not at the level of description, but of motivation of that description. This story involves stress patterns rather than segmental phonemes. Both *kaká* and "cracker" were established as distinct and correctly stressed lexical items [kaká, káka] prior to 18;27. (*Kaká* is a nursery word for "feces," learned from a Greek babysitter.) Jacob also had the word "cookie," produced correctly as [kúki]; he used it interchangeably with [káka] "cracker," apparently not yet having worked out the semantic distinction between them. *Kaká* was notable as the only consonant-initial word in Jacob's vocabulary that had stress on the second syllable, and these three words were the only ones of the form [k(X)VkV]; see table II.

On 19;24 and 19;27, "cookie" showed up in spontaneous speech with final stress, as [kʌkí] (the "cracker" variant did not appear in the corpus). As this was happening, [kaká] started to appear with initial stress, becoming potentially homophonous with the unattested form [káka] "cracker." "Cookie" had reverted to the correct initial-stress pattern by the next attestations, on 20;18. The final configuration (attested for both words on 20;22) leaves Jacob with all his CVCV words stressed on the first syllable, smoothing out his system nicely. But a model of rule origin that has to do with the child attempting to find a way to produce new and difficult sounds will not suffice here. There has been a *consolidation* of patterns, first the small [káka—kaká] set (variably) as

Table II.   Kaká And "Cracker." (Imitations in Parentheses)

Age	Kaká	Cookie/Cracker
Prior to 18;27	kaká	kúki/káka
18;27	(kaká)	
19;10		kʌ́ki
19;17	gakʔ	
19;24	káka	kʌkí
19;27	káka	(kúki)
	kaká	kʌkí
19;29		kúki
20;18		kúkʲi
		kʌ́kw
20;22	káka	kúki
		kʌ́ki

[kaká], and then a submergence of this small pattern into the more general [CV́CV].

"Bus"—"Bike"

At 20;8, Jacob imitated the word for his new kiddie car very well as [bajk], less well as [bek], and produced it spontaneously as [bʌj]. After this, the off-glide was always present in imitation, and by 20;22 it was there in spontaneous production as well. But the off-glide spread to words that had monophthongs even in the speech of Jacob's Texas-born father, the linguist Jorge Hankamer: on 20;18, "box" was produced twice spontaneously as [bakts] and as [bajtç], and on 20;20 and for a long time thereafter, the previously monophthongal "bus" was produced as [bajs]. "Horsie," "boy," "umbrella," and perhaps "toys" were also at least briefly touched by this rule, and it became stable, apparently, for words of the form [CVs] where the vowel is [−high, −round]. The positive instances were "bus," "grass," "and "mess," produced as [bajs], [rajs], and [majs] respectively. In addition, "bag" and "bang" showed the diphthong, but here the model provided by Jacob's father may have been influential; see table III.

Daniel's -rs Rule

Some newly-analyzed diary data from Daniel present the same unruly picture from much later in phonological acquisition. Menn (1973) described the onset-rule changes below in terms of a "crystal-growth" model, but re-examination of the data suggests that this metaphor is much too optimistic. We expect the crystal—at least, the idealized crystal—to grow along defined axes, from well-defined nuclei, but well-defined axes are hard to spot in the data below.

Table III.   "Bice" Shift Rule

Age	Bike	Ice	Nice	Bus	Box	Bang	Boy	Bag	Umbrella
20;8	bʌj (bajk) (bek)	(æx) ajç			(bakʰ)	(bajŋ) (bæ)			
20;13			nʌjs	bʌ bæˢ	(bakh)				
20;15	abakʰ (bajk)				(bakh)				
20;18	(bɛjk) (bakʰ)	ajç		bas	bajtç bakts				
20;19						bajŋ (baŋ)			
20;20				baɨs	bakʰ bak	bæ bajŋ	(baj)	(bajg)	(baj) (ʌbʌ:)
20;21						(bajn) (bæŋ)	(baj)		
20;22	bajk				(baᵏ) ʌbak	baŋ bajŋ			
summer[a]					(bajs)				

[a]Summer data also include the forms "grass" [rajs] and "mess" [majs].

continued

Table III.   *continued*

Age	Horsie, Horse	Toys	Book	Bucket	Block	(Your) Back	Broke(n)	Ball	Bark
20;8	(hʌs) as			(bækʰ)				bo (ʌw)	
20;13			(bʌpʰ)	(bʌk) (dʌtɨ)	bwæ			bɔ ba	
20;15				(bʌk)				bɔ ba	bʌk
20;18							(bʷɔk)	bɔ ba	
20;19	hɔjs hɔši	(tʰʌis) (tʰɔis)				ʌbɛk			
20;20	hajçi ɔçi				ak		bɛkʰ bwok	bɔ	
20;21	hʌši haš								
20;22	haši hʌjsi			(ʌbʌkɨ) (mpʷʌkɨt)			bʌ bʷʌk (boki) (bokņ)	bɔ	

Daniel was one of those children who notices the frequent appearance of the {Z} morphemes /s–z–əz/ at the ends of nouns and verbs in English long before deciphering the semantics behind them. (It's a wonder to us that there aren't more such children, given that this single set of allomorphs represents six morphemes: the noun plural, the possessive, the 3rd singular present of verbs, the contracted 3rd singular present copula "is," the contracted 3rd singular present auxiliary "is," and the contracted 3rd singular perfect auxiliary "has"). He apparently took it to be a phonological rather than morphological pattern: starting at about 25 months, an [s] (or occasionally a [z]) started to appear on a large subset of his words, regardless of whether they were used in situations that could be interpreted as calling for the plural, the possessive, or one of the contracted functor verb forms. About ten of these words (first group, table IV) had been previously produced without the extraneous [s], but most of them showed up with it from their first appearance.

The first recorded word to show the extraneous [s] was "butter," which appeared on 7/8 after "horse" and "Mr. Rogers" [ars] had been established, and also after "berry/berries" ([beiz] was being used indiscriminately for singular and plural). The [s] then spread to "water" (7/10), "dirty" (7/18), "pillow" (7/18), "bottle" (7/20), and "Daddy" (7/23).

The words that had the extraneous [s] formed a rough phonological grouping: they included about half of Daniel's two- or three-syllable words with initial stress, plus three or four /r/-final monosyllables. The [s] appeared sporadically on some of these words, quite reliably on others. The problem is that the domain of the rule is not well-defined. For the monosyllables, this is not serious; the rule applied regularly to "pear," "bear," and "hair," which have a rather syllabic final [r], to "chair" and "door" sometimes, but not to "floor," and never to "car," "bar," or "jar." It applied sporadically to one word not ending in [r], "bird," but not to "beard." And all three of his sibilant-final words "brush," "trash," and "push" were assimilated to the [rs] output type, as [bʌrʃ], [garʃ], and [prʃ] (there was no [s - ʃ] contrast). Here, at least, one can imagine a prototype structure at work.

Table V groups the bisyllabic words by medial consonant, which seems to be the best available predictor of the appearance of the [s], and within group by final syllable type (syllabic liquid, [i] vowel, CVC). Appearance of the [s] seems to be entwined with other aspects of the treatment of polysyllables, for example, whether the word was of the form C_iVC_iV.

The sampling density is, of course, a limiting factor in any attempt to model these data. (Sampling bias is undoubtedly toward the recording of errors and subsequent corrections of established errors, but it is

Table IV. Time-Sequence of Rule Spread: Order of Appearance of the Attested Polysyllabic Forms that Fell into the Eventual Domain of the *-rs* Rule (15 July = Age 25 Months: 15 September = 27 Months)

		Showing Rule Onset	Variable Onset	"Regression" After Onset	Not Showing Rule
July	8	Berry/s S Butter S			
	10	•Water S			
	14				Mommy +Coffee
	18	Dirty S Pillow S			
	19	Barb'ra S			
	20	•Bottle S			
	23	•Daddy S Slipper S			
	24		'Copter (S)		Marker +Button
	25	+Pacifier Trixie S			+Cover Shower
	26	Cel'ry S	Chicken (S)		
	27	Sweater S (Re)corder S Pepper S •Pacifier S Caterpillar S +Baby			
	28	Sprinkler (S) Table S Peter S			
	29	Ladder S •Baby S		Slipper	
	31	Lady S		Baby Cel'ry	
Aug.	2				Melon
	4	Danny S			Toilet
	6	•Cover S +Hamper			
	7	+Button			
	8				Pocket Apple
	11	•Squirrel S			
	12		Hamper (S)		
	13	•Button S			
	14			Trixie	
	16				(De)flector
	20	Honey S			
	21	Ginny S			
	29	Shovel S			

Table IV. *continued*

		Showing Rule Onset	Variable Onset	"Regression" After Onset	Not Showing Rule
	30	Granny S			
		Gleny S			
				•Coffee S	
Sept.	2	Cucumber S			
	4	Record S			
	6	Flower S			
		Baloney S			
	10	Gerbil S			
	11	•(Ba)nana			
	13			Record	
	15			Danny	
				Granny	
	16			Hamper	
				Baby	
				Button	
	17				Dinner
	20	Counter S			
		Hamper S			
		Powder S			
	21	Nana S			Bigger
		Heavy S			
	22	•Cracker S			
	28	Cereal S			
		Mixer S			
	29	Robin S		Pepper	
		Ready S			
Oct.	8[a]	Many S			
	14				Stroller
	20			Hammer	
	23			Ladder	
	24			Recorder	
	26			(Ba)loney	
	29			Pillow	
Nov.	1			Counter	
				Gerbil	
	4			Water[b]	
	23			Cucumber	
	24			Nana	
	27[c]			Candy	
				Cracker	

S indicates that Daniel produced the word with final [s] or [z] on the date indicated. (S) in parentheses indicates that the word was pronounced both with and without the final sound on the indicated date.

+Marks forms that will later undergo the -rs rule.

•Marks onset of [s/z] in forms previously attested without the -rs rule.

Unmarked words have their first attestation showing the -rs form, or have variable forms on the first day of attestation.

Words in rule domain attested prior to 8 July: "apple," +"(ba)nana," +"bottle," +"coffee," +"cover," +"cracker," +"daddy," "kittens" (plural model), +"pacifier," +"squirrel," +"water."

ᵃBecause no new forms showed the rule after October 8, forms that failed to show the rule were also not tabulated after this date.

ᵇThe word 'water' alternates between forms with and without S from November 4 to 21; thereafter, forms without S are stable.

ᶜThe last words attested as regressing to correct form were: December 6, "banana;" December 8, "pacifier;" January 15, "Robin" and "cereal."

not clear how to correct for this.) With sufficient ingenuity, no doubt some strange rules could be written to describe this history, but it is not easy to see how to allow for such factors as the frequency of plurals in the input (high for "slipper," nonexistent for "butter").

After this bombardment with intractable data, we hope some readers are willing to concede that a connectionist approach may offer a way out. But that does not mean that everything that we have done with the two-lexicon model is to be discarded; we are not trying to start a revolution. On the contrary, we need to salvage all of the insights that we have achieved so far; and we need to make sure that they are properly represented in any new model that we adopt.

LOOKING AHEAD

What are the essential insights or claims of the two-lexicon model, the core of information that we want to preserve regardless of the formalism and/or mechanisms that we may choose to adopt? In review, we group the phenomena under three headings.

Reduction of information:

a. Children (and adults!) recognize more words than they can say, and usually can do this in phonetic variants (e.g., regional accents) that they don't produce.

b. Young children recognize more phonemic contrasts than they can honor in production.

c. The total set of output forms consists largely—but not entirely—of clusters of closely related forms, which can be described formally in terms of prosodies or canonical forms in autosegmental representation.

d. These forms in general contain fewer independently specified elements (less information) than corresponding adult forms.

Mapping:

e. Many children have systematic ways of reducing adult words to

Table V. "Extraneous -rs" Rule on Disyllables, Organized by Medial Consonant: Attestations From July 8 to September 15

	Almost Always [s/z]	Sometimes [s/z]	Never [s/z]
Medial Labials			
[p]	#Papers [pejpʌz] 1 #Diapers [barpɛrs] 6 #Copies [kapʌz] 1 Slippers(s) [lʌpʌz] 7/8 Zipper [ɪpʌz] 1 Pepper [pɛpɾs] 1	Leopard [ɛpɾ] 1/3ᵃ Copter [kapɾ] 2/5	Floppy [ap-pi] 1 Puppy [pʌp-i] 2 Poppy [papi] 1 Sleepy [ipi] 2 Apple [æpḷ] 10
[b]	Barb'ra [bɾs] 5 Gerbil(s) [gɾs] 1 Table [bɾs] 1 Robinᵇ [aʊns] 1	Baby(s) [beibi, beiz] 4/6	Frisbee [bi] 1
[m]	#Thermos [öʊs] 1 (Cu)cumber [kʌrs] 1 Flower [æwɾs] 1	Hamper [hærs, hæmpʊm] 1/4	Mommy [mami] 10
[w]			Weewee [wiwi] 1 Shower [æa] 1
[f]	Shovel [öʊs] 1	Coffee [kʌpi, kɔis] 2/3	
[v]		Cover [gʌv] 1/2	Clover [kov] 2
Medial Coronals			
[t]	#Asters [æt-tüs] 2 Lobster(s) [at-tüs] 2	Button [mʌnt] 1/5	Curtain [kɔrtṇ] 1 Newton [nutṇ] 2 Pretzel [bartsḷ] 5 Kitchen [kit-sin] 3
[D]	Water [ɔrs] 7/8 Peter [pirs] 3 Sweater [ɛʌrs] 2 Butter [bʌrs] 7		

Table V. continued

	Almost Always [s/z]	Sometimes [s/z]	Never [s/z]
	Bottle [baz] 3		
	Dirty [dö-ʊs] 1		
	(Re)corder [kɔɛrs] 3		
	Lady [eis] 4		
	Daddy [dæis] 10		
	Pillow [bwʌz] 9/9		
	Jello [ʔr̩s] 1		
[l]			Toilet [tɔjt] 2
			Melon [meʔen] 2
			Salad [æd] 1
[n]	(Ba)nana [næs] 2	Nana[c] [nana] 1	
	(Ba)loney [mois] 1		
	Honey [hʌis] 2		
	Granny [gæeis] 2		
	Gleny [gɛis] 2		
	Ginny [giis] 2		
	Danny [næis] 1		
	Candy [kæis] 1		
[r]	Berry [beiz] 4	Cel'ry [öi] 2/4	Carry [kæi] 1[d]
	Squirrel [grs] 2		Carrot [kart, æk] 2
Medial [k]		Cookie [gʊki] 2/3	(Ken)tucky [gʌki] 1
		Cracker [garkr̩] 3/4	Marker [garkr̩] 1
		Record [rɪkr̩] 1/3	Pocket [gak] 1
		Trixie [gukɪrs, giki] 1/2	(De)flector [ɛkɛr] 1
		Chicken [gukɪrs, uŋkuŋ] 1/3	Napkin [ŋækuŋ] 1
		Sprinkler [uŋkɛr, uŋk-i, uŋk-ös] 1/3	Charcoal[e] [gar-kol] 1

continued

Table V. continued

Almost Always [s/z]	Sometimes [s/z]	Never [s/z]
		Doggie [gɔgi] 1

Adult words always modeled on plural or s-final input are marked with * and cited in the s-final form; their final [s/z] in Daniel's speech is not "extraneous," but they may have played a role in reinforcing the pattern. Other adult words especially likely to be heard in the plural are given with final (s). In phonetic transcriptions, a hyphen marks open transition.

Numbers after words indicate the number of attestations per word from July 8 through September 14; a fraction such as 3/4 indicates that, of 4 recorded instances, 3 showed the [s/z]. Imitations and spontaneous utterances are not separated in this count.

[a]Produced without -s on 1st imitation; corrected from -s on 9/13.

[b]Possessive target.

[c]Appeared with -s after 9/15.

[d]It is interesting that this verb form did not appear with -s. It was the only verb form to which the rule might have applied; all other two-syllable verb forms were -ing forms, and -ing was one of Daniel's three available post-tonic syllable patterns (the others being [i] and [r̥s]; cf. the entries for "chicken," "sprinkler," "napkin," and "Trixie"). For discussion, see Menn (1971).

[e]This heavy second syllable clearly had a major effect on the form of Daniel's imitation. "Grandpop" [bap] and "lipstick" [gʌk] also showed attempts at the full second syllable, though without the first syllable.

forms that fit within their production capacities, i.e., have rules or regularities. These rules reduce the information contained in each word.

Inertia of the system:

f. Some of the very early words are likely to be "progressive phonological idioms," containing relatively complex sequences of segments. (They are called "idioms" because the knack of producing such sequences apparently does not generalize to other similar words.)

g. Changes in rules frequently are seen first in new lexical items; spread to frequent, established words may be slow, and this slow change may not be a matter of misperception. The child seems, therefore, to have stored something about the way-to-say at least some of his or her words.

PLAUSIBLE "CONNECTIONS" AND
INITIAL SETTINGS FOR A PSYCHOLOGICALLY RESPONSIBLE MODEL

Suppose we stand back and try to organize all the kinds of language learning opportunities that we think exist in the first year or so of life, and those innate and early-learned abilities for which we have direct evidence, to date.[6] What kinds of associations does a normally developing child have the opportunity to develop from birth to the onset of speech? Whatever they are, a good psycholinguistic model, connectionist or other, ought to reflect them.

First, let's consider the connections that can be made across and within the child's perceptual and motor modalities, and that presumably arise from hearing and feeling him or herself babble (see especially Locke and Pearson this volume). These do not involve responses from other people, so let's call them "internal loop" associations (cf. Mattingly 1976). In babbling, the child has the opportunity to link kinesthetic sensation, motor commands, and traces of percepts of his or her own sounds across these three modalities. These links can be of two kinds. The first kind consists of *simultaneous* links, which connect the three modalities at a given instant (though the notion of "instant" is likely to be problematic for motor commands)—for example, the motor, auditory, and kinesthetic experiences of producing a [b]. The second consists of *sequential* links, within each of these three modalities (motor–motor, auditory–auditory, kinesthetic–kinesthetic)—for example, the complete sequence of auditory sensations involved in hear-

---

[6]This section developed during extensive conversations of LM with computer scientists Clayton Lewis and Michael C. Mozer, whom we thank heartily. It is also informed by many other papers in this volume.

ing a syllable like [bej] or [pʰa]. We would expect the formation of cross-modal sequential links as well—for example, feeling the sensation of producing the beginning of a consonant will become linked with the motor commands and the sound of its eventual release as well as with the kinesthetics of that release.

So a rich web of cross-modal and within-mode redundancies are available for learning. We will refer to these as motor/auditory/kinesthetic (MAK) patterns. In the connectionist model that we have been designing, which draws on the work of Jordan (in press) and Mozer (1988), these internal loop MAK patterns are essential, because they are what later gives the child the ability to figure out how to modify a faulty articulation to bring it closer to a target. We speak of them as giving the system its "predictive" or "feed-forward" capabilities, and we assume that they develop gradually, over time, but always leading the rest of the connections listed below. Innate predispositions of the system can be modeled very naturally, e.g., by hard-wiring some connections or adjusting certain firing thresholds. Such an introduction of "biases" may lead to more psychologically responsible/plausible models.

Second, as the child listens to adult speech (still without adult-child interaction), there are sequential connections that can be built up within sound-percepts, reflecting the phonotactic redundancies of the ambient language. (Are initial voiceless stops aspirated? Do certain vowels have on-glides or off-glides?) Looking at other speakers also is likely to be involved in developing links between some auditory inputs and motor patterns, because infant imitation of lip and jaw movements indicates an innate link between seeing movements of other persons and executing those movements oneself. Kuhl and Meltzoff (1988) have established that there is an astonishingly early link between hearing and seeing vowels produced (see also the chapters in this volume by Jusczyk and by Locke and Pearson).

Third, as the child attempts to imitate adult speech, some adult sound patterns will become linked with his or her own motor/auditory/kinesthetic patterns (Vihman 1991, 1993). To the extent that the child recognizes adult imitations of his or her babbling (see Locke and Pearson this volume), these links can be made even stronger. (But how does this recognition happen? Extensive pitch normalization, in particular, is required. And note that in order to embody this in a model, the term "recognize" must be given an interpretation: what would a computer model do that corresponds to "recognizing?")

Fourth, the beginning of comprehension means, by definition, that the child starts to link recurring adult sound patterns ("bye-bye," "cookie") with associated recurring real-world states. Also, by definition, if the child develops her own proto-words, then she is linking her own internal motor/acoustic/kinesthetic patterns with recurrent real-world states. We don't know how these get started, but maybe the link is initially kinesthetic/motor-to-situation, with the auditory link developing secondarily as the child hears him or herself.

Fifth, the onset of meaningful speech should be—by definition, again—equivalent to a strengthening of these connections between internal MAK patterns and some world state, to the point where the recurrence of that real-world state (a departure, a desire for a cookie) makes it possible for the child to retrieve the motor commands associated with it. Each use of such a set of motor commands will build further linkage with the acoustic and kinesthetic sensations produced by saying the word. Nothing succeeds like success!

External feedback again comes into play here. Imitation by the adult will further strengthen the links of all of these MAK elements to the memory of the sound of the adult's voice, although the effect of imitation-with-correction will undoubtedly differ from the effect of literal imitation.

Let's consider the effects of adult responses to babble and early speech in more detail. One of the major phenomena of speech perception is normalization: the fact that certain acoustically different signals may be treated as equivalent representatives of phonetic categories. A classic example is the treatment of "the same" word spoken by a male adult, a female adult, and a child as being the same word in spite of huge differences in absolute formant value and smaller differences in the ratio of the formants (Ladefoged and Broadbent 1957). Because a purely sound-based imitation of the child by the adult (Veneziano 1981; Velleman et al. 1989) will produce links between the child's internal MAK associations and the sound of the adult's voice, the child's innate normalization abilities (Kuhl and Miller 1982) should be enhanced. Furthermore, this scenario offers the opportunity for language-particular (i.e., phonemic) equivalences to be established as well, independent of the development of word meanings. Assuming that parental imitations are influenced by the allophonic patterns of their language to some extent, the auditory feedback to the child will be more or less consistently biased toward those patterns. So we assume, although we have no data on hand (somebody should get some!), that an English-speaking parent imitating a child's prevoiced [ba] babble is likely to shorten the duration of the prevoicing or to eliminate it entirely, producing the typical short-lag initial [b]. In contrast, a Spanish-speaking parent should be likely to maintain the prevoicing and perhaps spirantize the sound. Note that nothing so far in this scenario influences the child's *production* to move toward the ambient variety of /b/; so far only the perceptual equivalence of the adult /b/ phone(s) with the child's internal MAK representation of [b] is being established. This scenario might also be appropriate for modeling some part of the loss of sensitivity to a potential contrast that is not present in the ambient language, such as [l - r] in Japanese (see Jusczyk and Werker and Pegg this volume).

To move the child toward matching the adult production, we must introduce a social factor (in some guise or other), as has long been recognized. We must assume some mechanism that makes the child prefer to produce a sound that is more like the adult sound, to the extent that she can. When the operation of such a mechanism might start to have a detectable effect is of course the topic of studies of "babbling drift," such as the work of Boysson-Bardies and her associates (1984, 1989). It is also implicated in the child's use of lower voice pitch with adult-based forms in protolanguage (Halliday 1975; Painter 1984; Menn 1976).

As Snow (1977) and others have shown, semantically contingent responses to the normal child's babbling increase in number as the child approaches the age of 10 months or so; obviously, this external feedback loop affords the opportunity for word learning. It apparently also can have some rather interesting effects on the child's phonology if the adult makes a wrong guess in responding to the child's apparent intended target. Waterson (1971) reports that her subject, P., created the word [fiẽfiẽ], which seemed to be a hybrid of "hymn" and "angel," with reference to a child's hymnal with a picture of an angel on the cover. In Menn (1971), Daniel appeared to have a hybrid of "snap" and "button," produced as [næt] (his consonant harmony rule would only have made "snap" into "map," had it applied here). Furthermore, this formation generalized to a minor rule: "lap" became [æt]. Priestly (1977) has some examples as well.

Working out a complete model of how hybrid words arise would occupy too much space for the present paper, but it is an excellent challenge, especially because the model must not produce hybrids every time a child's label for an object gets some other word (such as "Yes!" or "Pretty!") as a response.

CONCLUSION

In early tries at producing utterances that match particular stored (adult-speech) auditory patterns, the child links those patterns with the sound of his or her own voice in producing them, and with the feeling and commands of the articulatory movements that were used. Repetitions of the child's utterances by adults strengthens those links further. (Okay, it *is* reinforcement.) These are the kinds of information and the connections that we had assigned to "input lexicon," "output lexicon," and "rules;" the compartments are gone. Unfortunately for our intuitions, to quote Mozer (personal communication), they have been "replaced by much vaguer concepts."

The development of an autosegmental structure must be due in some way to priming-type interactions among similar nonadjacent articulatory gestures. Modeling this presents a considerable challenge, because it seems that doing so will require a rich representation of auditory and articulatory axes of similarity. (The need for a vowel height tier, consonant place tier, and nasalization tier are all implied by the harmony and other phonotactic constraints of early child language data—see Menn 1978; Spencer 1986). Mozer comments (personal communication) to us that "judging similarity and acting on the basis of similarity are things that connectionist models do well, but it's most likely going to be up to us (the modelers) to design an appropriate representation" so that the similarity judgements of the model mirror those of the human child.

Similar motor/kinesthetic patterns like Jacob's "tea"—"tape" forge connections with and interfere with one another, increasing regularity and decreasing accuracy. Similar sequential auditory patterns must also connect to one another, developing perceptual schemata (Schwartz et al. 1987; Waterson 1981), and possibly inducing some misperceptions. (These are well known to be typical behaviors of connectionist models.)

All this can, at least potentially, go on without segmentation below the word level. Some sort of segmentation, however, seems to be involved in the development of what we notate as rules (for models of the development of segments, see Lindblom's and Jusczyk's chapters in this volume). Rules that operate on-line arise through the association of part of a sound pattern for a word with part of the motor/kinesthetic information, independent of the word meaning. Under "rule," we include both error-producing rules and correct links of target sounds with the articulatory gestures needed to produce them. They are both auditory-motor linkages, and do not differ in kind.

What, now, has become of the two-lexicon model? We originally needed two lexicons because of all the evidence that recognition and production forms are both stored, and we needed the selection rule/ production rule division in order to adhere to two fairly standard principles: (a) The lexicon is minimally redundant; (b) Rules that do very different jobs (discarding information versus spelling out predictable information) belong in separate components.

We still have stored input and output forms, but they are no longer in hard-walled "boxes;" instead, as Mozer points out, they are differentiated by being represented by different sets of connections. The selection rule/production rule division has been swallowed up; instead we have postulated an intricate interconnection of all the information associated with a word, with the connections being strongest when they are most frequent and reliable. Redundancy is not removed at all, because rule-governed behavior arises from connections among repre- sentations of instances. This purely linguistic application of the par- simony principle has no place in instance-based models, connectionist or other.[7] This conception agrees in many ways with Stemberger's con- nectionist model (this volume), and either could be modified toward the other; the most substantive difference is probably our explicit atten- tion to the strengthening of sequential (within-word) connections and the use of the Jordan (in press) feed-forward component to model the way in which babbling "tunes" the system for speech. The overlaps with Jusczyk's and Lindblom's conceptions are also obvious.

Our computer science friends, Michael Mozer and Clayton Lewis, however, warn us that there are going to be problems with implemen- tation of these "models" as real computer simulations. Some available types of computer devices are basically designed to predict what comes next in a sequence, which is not an appropriate model for learning to speak. Also, the typical connectionist device trains a network to match a target set of correctly specified features. However, the central aspect of learning phonology is that the child does not know at the beginning what the feature specifications are. That's what the adult knows and the child has to find out, by the trial-and-error cross-modal linking pro- cess that we have described here. Our colleagues say that they are really enjoying the challenge of devising an implementation of this learning model, which will eventually require not only the simulation of (devel- oping!) motor, auditory, and kinesthetic topologies, but also attention and, in a full-blown model, real-world knowledge.

On the other hand, basic aspects of "standard" connectionist mod- els already give us things we want, e.g., interaction/crosstalk among rules, gradual pattern extraction (rules can start out as whole-word in- put-to-output patterns, and then get more segmental), a predisposi- tion to build autosegmental structures, and a lag in propagation of new rules to existing words (assuming we can get this lag to vary appropri- ately). Simulating these properties ranged from ad-hoc to hopeless in the box-and-arrow model that we have been so fond of.

So is the two-lexicon model to be abandoned? As a cutting-edge research-level model, yes, we think so; there are too many things wrong with it. But as a teaching-level model, and as a way of organizing many

---

[7]The parsimony principle was originally brought from linguistics into psycholin- guistics with the justification that mental storage space is costly, and computation cheap. Now we have much evidence that storage is cheap, and computation is costly (e.g., Sei- denberg et al. 1982); we also have evidence that psycholinguistic processes are redun- dant, e.g., if you accept the arguments of Menn and MacWhinney (1984) that inflectional endings are both represented in the lexicon and added on-line during speech.

kinds of data, we probably have to keep using it, perhaps for a long while, because there is no working, intuitively satisfying replacement. And Leonard's proposed test of the two-lexicon model versus a basic/generic connectionist model (this volume) may very well favor the two-lexicon model. If it does, the connectionist model will need more elaboration to simulate the child's behavior adequately. Well, has being psychologically responsible ever been easy?

REFERENCES

Berko, J. 1958. The child's learning of English morphology. *Word* 14:150–77.
Boysson-Bardies, B. de, Sagart, L., and Durand, C. 1984. Discernible differences in the babbling of infants according to target language. *Journal of Child Language* 11:1–15.
Boysson-Bardies, B. de, Hallé, P., Sagart, L., and Durand, C. 1989. A crosslinguistic investigation of vowel formants in babbling. *Journal of Child Language* 16:1–18.
Brown, R. 1973. *A First Language.* Cambridge, MA: Harvard University Press.
Butler Platt, C., and MacWhinney, B. 1983. Error assimilation as a mechanism in language learning. *Journal of Child Language* 10:401–414.
Donahue, M. 1986. Phonological constraints on the emergence of two-word utterances. *Journal of Child Language* 13:209–218.
Ferguson, C. A. 1986. Discovering sound units and constructing sound systems: It's child's play. In *Invariance and Variability in Speech Processes* ed. J. Perkell and D. Klatt. Hillsdale, NJ: Lawrence Erlbaum Associates.
Ferguson, C. A., and Farwell, C. B. 1975. Words and sounds in early language acquisition. *Language* 51:419–39.
Ferguson, C. A., Peizer, D. B., and Weeks, T. A. 1973. Model-and-replica phonological grammar of a child's first words. *Lingua* 31:35–65.
Halliday, M. A. K. 1975. *Learning How to Mean.* London: Edward Arnold.
Hasher, L., and Zacks, R. T. 1984. Automatic processing of fundamental information. The case of frequency of occurrence. *American Psychologist* 39: 1372–1388.
Ingram, D. 1974. Phonological rules in young children. *Journal of Child Language* 1:49–64.
Jordan, M. In press. Indeterminate motor skill learning problems. To appear in *Attention and Performance XIII* ed. M. Jeannerod. Cambridge, MA: MIT Press.
Kiparsky, P., and Menn, L. 1977. On the acquisition of phonology. In *Language Learning and Thought* ed. J. Macnamara. New York: Academic Press. Reprinted in *Interlanguage Phonology: The Acquisition of a Second Language Sound System* eds. G. Ioup and S. H. Weinberger. Cambridge, MA: Newbury House, 1987.
Kuhl, P. K., and Meltzoff, A. N. 1988. Speech as an intermodal object of perception. In *Perceptual Development in Infancy* ed. A. Yonas. Hillsdale, NJ: Lawrence Erlbaum Associates.
Kuhl, P. K., and Miller, J. 1982. Discrimination of auditory target dimensions in the presence or absence of variation in a second dimension by infants. *Perception and Psychophysics* 31:279–92.
Ladefoged, P., and Broadbent, D. E. 1957. Information conveyed by vowels. *Journal of the Acoustic Society of America* 29:98–104. Reprinted in *Readings in*

Acoustic Phonetics ed. I. Lehiste. Cambridge, MA: MIT Press, 1967.

Macken, M. A. 1980. The child's lexical representation: The 'puzzle-puddle-pickle' evidence. *Journal of Linguistics* 16:1–17.

Matthei, E. 1989. Crossing boundaries: More evidence for phonological constraints on early multi-word utterances. *Journal of Child Language* 16:41–54.

Mattingly, I. 1976. Phonetic prerequisites for first-language acquisition. In *Baby Talk and Infant Speech* eds. W. von Raffler-Engel and Y. Lebrun. Amsterdam: Swets and Zeitlinger.

Menn, L. 1971. Phonotactic rules in beginning speech. *Lingua* 26:225–41.

Menn, L. 1973. On the origin and growth of phonological and syntactic rules. *Papers from the Ninth Regional Meeting of the Chicago Linguistic Society.* Chicago: Chicago Linguistic Society.

Menn, L. 1976. Pattern, control, and contrast in beginning speech: A case study in the development of word form and word function. Ph.D. diss., University of Illinois, Urbana. Published, Bloomington: Indiana University Linguistic Club, 1979.

Menn, L. 1978. Phonological units in beginning speech. In *Syllables and Segments*, eds. A. Bell and J. B. Hooper. Amsterdam: North-Holland.

Menn, L. 1979. Transition and variation in child phonology: Modeling a developing system. *Proceedings of the Ninth International Congress of Phonetic Sciences*, Vol. II. Copenhagen.

Menn, L. 1983. Development of articulatory, phonetic, and phonological capabilities. In *Language Production*, Vol. II, ed. B. Butterworth. London: Academic Press.

Menn, L., and MacWhinney, B. 1984. The repeated morph constraint: Towards an explanation. *Language* 60:519–41.

Morton, J. 1979. Word recognition. In *Psycholinguistics: Series 2, Structures and Processes* eds. J. Morton and J. Marshall. London: Elek.

Mozer, M. 1988. *A Focused Back-Propagation Algorithm for Temporal Pattern Recognition.* (Technical Report CRG-TR-88-3.) Toronto: Dept. of Computer Science, University of Toronto.

Paden, E. P. Unpublished. Communication Disorders Department, University of Illinois, Champaign-Urbana.

Painter, C. 1984. *Into the Mother Tongue.* London: Frances Pinter.

Pinker, S. 1984. *Language Learnability and Language Development.* Cambridge, MA: Harvard University Press.

Priestly, T. M. S. 1977. One idiosyncratic strategy in the acquisition of phonology. *Journal of Child Language* 4:45–66.

Schwartz, R. G., Leonard, L. B., Frome Loeb, D. M., and Swanson, L. A. 1987. Attempted sounds are sometimes not: An expanded view of phonological selection and avoidance. *Journal of Child Language* 14:411–18.

Scollon, R. 1976. *Conversations with a One-Year-Old: A Case Study of the Developmental Foundations of Syntax.* Honolulu: University of Hawaii Press.

Seidenberg, M. S., Tanenhaus, M. K., Leiman, J. M., and Bienkowski, M. 1982. Automatic access of the meanings of ambiguous words in context: Some limitations of knowledge-based processing. *Cognitive Psychology* 14:489–537.

Smith, N. V. 1973. *The Acquisition of Phonology: A Case Study.* Cambridge: Cambridge University Press.

Snow, C. E. 1977. The development of conversation between mothers and babies. *Journal of Child Language* 4:1–13.

Spencer, A. 1986. Towards a theory of phonological development. *Lingua* 68:3–38.

Stemberger, J. P. 1988. Between-word processes in child phonology. *Journal of Child Language* 15:39–62.

Strauss, S. (ed.). 1982. *U-Shaped Behavioral Growth*. New York: Academic Press.

Velleman, S. L., Mangipudi, L., and Locke, J. L. 1989. Prelinguistic phonetic contingency: Data from Down syndrome. *First Language* 9:159–74.

Veneziano, E. 1981. Early language and nonverbal representation: A reassessment. *Journal of Child Language* 8:541–63.

Vihman, M. M. 1982. A note on children's lexical representations. *Journal of Child Language* 9:249–53.

Vihman, M. M. 1991. Ontogeny of phonetic gestures: Speech perception. In *Modularity and the Motor Theory of Speech Production*, eds. I. G. Mattingly and M. Studdert-Kennedy. Hillsdale, NJ: Lawrence Erlbaum Associates.

Vihman, M. M. 1993. Variable paths to early word production. *Journal of Phonetics*.

Waterson, N. 1971. Child phonology: A prosodic view. *Journal of Linguistics* 7: 179–211. Reprinted in *Prosodic Phonology: The Theory and its Application to Language Acquisition and Speech Processing* by N. Waterson. Newcastle-upon-Tyne: Grevatt & Grevatt, 1987.

Waterson, N. 1981. A tentative developmental model of phonological representation. In *The Cognitive Representation of Speech* eds. T. Myers, J. Laver, and J. Anderson. Amsterdam: North-Holland. Reprinted in *Prosodic Phonology: The Theory and its Application to Language Acquisition and Speech Processing* by N. Waterson. Newcastle-upon-Tyne: Grevatt & Grevatt, 1987.

Wheeler, D., and Iverson, G. 1986. Hierarchical structures in child phonology. Paper presented at 61st Annual Meeting of the Linguistic Society of America, December 1986, New York.

Chapter • 8

Where's Phonology?

Marlys A. Macken

The results in the field over the last ten years have been almost entirely concerned with the phonetics of acquisition. Does this mean that there is no abstract phonology learned? No autonomous phonological generalizations or rules? Is the acquisition of "phonology" in fact the acquisition of phonetics? Several current theories of acquisition would answer "yes" to each of these questions. Much of the data in the literature is compatible with such theories, though this is in large part due to the dual nature of the phonology-phonetics interface and to the virtual absence of research on languages with complex morphology. The premise of this chapter is that there is an autonomous phonological component. To distinguish this "phonology" from its phonetic substance even in early stages and morphologically simple data, I present evidence of distinctly phonological rules and arguments for a particular theory of phonological rules, representations, and acquisition. The answers to these questions pose a challenge to current phonetics-oriented acquisition theories and return in spirit to the theory of Jakobson (1941/68).

I begin by focussing on the nature of rules. I present a model of acquisition, and a theory of change that distinguishes rules types. The model says that phonology is a cognitive domain acquired like other cognitive domains. Thus, the central acquisition mechanism is a constrained hypothesis formation mechanism where patterns are discovered and generalizations, or rules, are created and where the linguistic constraints are not so restricted as to result in invariance but, rather, so closely replicate the formal constraints on languages in general as to render any set of ten or twenty learners (of even the same language) a virtual typological study of language parameters. Clearest evidence for the generalization of a rule is a nonlinearity, a step backwards, a point where the learner gets better "phonologically" by getting worse "phonetically." The theory of change claims that the nature of structure is most evident when structures change and that different properties of change reflect different underlying structures. I then apply my model and theory of change to the problem of distinguishing phonetics from phonology, developmentally, arguing that a particular rule type and associated nonlinearity show the relative autonomy of phonology from phonetic content. I further argue that this rule type appears to lie outside the explanatory scope of acquisition self-organizing models and similar evolutionary models from biology, both of which are canonically phonetics models of acquisition.

After analyzing types of rules, I turn to what I believe is the central representation issue concerning the early phonological stages. According to the leading theories on the first acquired phonological constituent, the earliest phonological grammars are organized around the segment, syllable, or prosodic word. Here, I present data on the structure and content of learner's lexical representations and propose that the phonology of these representations is the phonology of "lexical templates." I show that there are two broad types of grammars, harmony and melody types (where individual learners use basically one or the other), that representations in both types are controlled by constraints across nonadjacent consonants in polysyllabic words, that these constraints closely resemble adjacency restrictions in adult languages like the typical content of linked structures and minimal distance constraints on tautosyllabic clusters, and that there is little or no evidence, at this stage, of fixed consonant-vowel (CV) syllabic units where the vowel is other than a default vowel. I argue that these facts and others show that these first grammars are built on templates with CV planar segregation and that the first constituent is the prosodic word, and not the syllable. I conclude with a discussion of the syllable and other prosodic constituents and the role of templates in later stages.

RULE TYPES AND CHANGE

This section focuses on a developmental puzzle, a case of "getting better by getting worse." For many kinds of development, change or learning is continuous—a series of steps that lead forward to skilled performance, mastery, or greater knowledge. This puzzle, in contrast, involves the learner temporarily going in reverse: it is then a developmental discontinuity, a nonlinearity. What I think this nonlinearity shows us is that there is a distinct difference between the learning of phonetics and the learning of phonology—or, to put it differently, that the phonology is relatively autonomous or independent of the substantive content of phonetics.

This conclusion will depend on a reasonable model of the domain of phonetics and a convincing model of what kind of learning and development is most compatible with the constructs and principles of phonetics, as well as on assumptions about phonology and its associated acquisition model. Specifically, what I argue is that phonetics is, at a minimum, the learning of "segments," the objects of perception and production, and that phonology, at a minimum, is the learning of superordinate principles that govern segments but are not reducible to the individual properties of individual segments. Phonetics certainly involves more units than segments alone. Similarly, phonology involves more than principles involving segments. The crucial difference here is whether or not there is a segmental phenomenon that is not the sum of its individual parts. The crucial data is seen in table III, where something happens to three different segments that is not the result of three independent changes affecting each of the segments individually.

Second, I assume that a developmental model subserving phonetics is one of continuous differentiation and integration where change is largely or wholly continuous: once a learner acquires a particular feature of a segment, she or he will not lose it except, perhaps, in particular contexts (given that segments always occur in particular words). For example, sometimes harmony stabilizes new sounds, at the expense of other sounds in the word. When this happens, clearly a local process is operating on the word, and such a process is one of the kind of local processes that are easily explained by the phonetics model, for example, from Macken 1978: *tasa* 'cup' [tata] at Time 1 (T1); [tasa] very briefly at T2; [sasa] at T3; [tasa] at T4; and many other similar words. If, in contrast, we find the *loss* of success on a particular segment and that loss is not a result of phonetic constraints on segments or a consequence of the local context of the segment, then we have a preliminary candidate for a phonologically driven phenomenon. If then, the theory of phonology can explain the change, then we have a case of "getting better *phonologically*" by "getting worse *phonetically*," where the learner has learned a principle of the grammar at the expense of segments and particular words.

Given that the developmental model for phonetics, as I have sketched it, is highly compatible with self-organizing models in biology and evolutionary models of differentiation and integration, the question is: Can data of rule Type 3 (table III) be explained in some other way by these biological and evolutionary models without invoking abstract principles, or a "grammar"?

After discussing briefly the relationship between phonology and phonetics, I turn to the problem of how we figure out what the learner knows at a given point, T1, so that we can be sure about what changes at a later point, T2, and why. My approach is to view "change" as a window on representations, specifically that where properties of change are different, the structures undergoing those changes are different also. I have analyzed three basic types of change and, hence, types of rules: Type 1, perceptually based rules (Macken 1980); Type 2, articulatory based rules (Macken 1980); and Type 3, phonologically based abstract rules and principles, the grammar at work (see also Macken and Ferguson 1983). My conclusion is that Types 1 and 2 fall within the purview of phonetics, while Type 3 is one of the earliest manifestations of phonologically based acquisition.[1]

On Phonetics and Phonology

If we say that phonetics involves learning the objects of perception and production, like "segments," and we recognize the considerable segment and category learning that takes place in the child's first year, then phonetic learning is most compatible with theories that say that development is a continuous process of differentiation and integration. During the second year, when the child begins using words, the first year process proceeds. Simply put, words are broken down into segments, and categories for individual segments, across all contexts, are learned. The process of learning a phonology could then be accounted for by the interaction of general principles of phonetics and the language particular patterns of segments, under the control of a general pattern recognizer mechanism. Is the transition to language continuous?

As is well known, the first phonological theory on this issue took the discontinuous view. Jakobson (1941/68) advanced the view that the phonology is an autonomous system independent of its phonetic content. Thus, if language acquisition mirrored the theoretical account in a principled way, the phonetics of the first year should be highly discontinuous with the phonology of the language proper. Literally dozens of studies have shown this view of the transitional period (between babbling and language) to be at least wrong in specifics. Thus, one issue seems solved for phonology: the transitional system is a continuous development of the earlier babbling stage, babbling continues throughout the earliest stages of lexical development, there is no sudden or

---

[1]For similarly phonological models and additional data, see in particular Smith (1973), Kiparsky and Menn (1977), Macken and Ferguson (1983), and Fey and Gandor (1982).

dramatic loss in abilities at the end of the first year or so, and the same sounds and sound patterns characterize both babbling and words. What this body of research tells us about is the firm foundation of early phonology upon the phonetic skills and abilities developed during the first year and onward. Unless we take the view that it's all turtles up or down (to borrow a phrase), meaning that it's all phonology or all phonetics, the data from the first year-and-a-half do not decide the issue of the relation of phonology and phonetics, of the end state to this now more broadly construed "initial" state.

Is there a discontinuity later that signals phonological as opposed to phonetic learning? Certainly we know that if we look beyond segments there must be phonological rule learning that involves underlying representations and rules. And that is because we know that it is unlikely that speakers memorize whole words or paradigms. Take two simple examples. There, first, are languages with complex phrasal phonologies, like Chaga, an African tonal language: tones on Chaga words vary by syntactic position and tonal environment; as a consequence of the eight or so phrasal tone rules, most words have about a dozen tonal variants. The memorization problem gets quite a bit more problematic when we come to languages with highly productive morphologies, which in turn have highly complex phonologies: take Shona, another African language, which is estimated to have more than 8 trillion possible forms of verbs (Odden 1981). This number is so high because there are several morphemes that can be permuted. However, virtually no acquisition work has been done on such languages, so we do not have evidence about how complex phonologies are acquired, but surely the data when they come in, will show discontinuities that correspond to the acquisition of truly phonological rules.

At hand, however, are data on just such a discontinuity and one that applies to the simple task of learning segments. Before evaluating the data, we need a way to determine what a child's underlying representation is, in order to know exactly what is learned. We need a "window" on the mind.

Change as a Window on the Mind and Acquisition

Within linguistics, interest in language acquisition originally was motivated by the belief that research here would reveal the mental processes underlying the interpretation of linguistic input and the formation of grammatical rules. The promise of language acquisition was to be its unique "window" on language. Yet much of literature is purely descriptive statements of what learners do, specifically of what they produce. And these descriptions of production have typically failed to illuminate the process of acquisition or the nature of the representational symbol structures that underlie language. The reasons for this state of affairs are many, but a central problem is that such descriptions, say the transcriptions of what children produce, are always compatible with many different analyses and explanations.

In order to model acquisition, we need to know several things. First, we need to know what the child "knows," independently of what the child "produces." This is really the problem of determining what the child's mental representation is. Second, we must know what is in fact changing in a fundamental way. My approach to this indeterminacy problem is to turn it around a bit. Rather than looking for the structure of the internal grammar in the linguistic descriptions of performance per se, or even in the order in which particular structures are acquired, I look at the properties of change itself, under the assumption that the characteristics of diachronic change differentiate linguistic (synchronic) structure. In this way, change itself can be the illuminating window we seek: the nature of linguistic structure becomes clear during change, much the same way that objects, that appear interlocked when still, separate into distinct forms when one of them moves.

Three Types of Developmental Change and Three Rule Types

Consider, the statement of Rule Type 1 and table I. (The data in tables I and II are from one child, from about 2;0–2;5 [years; months].) For Rule Type 1, two segments x and y that are distinct in the adult language are neutralized as y in the child's speech, at Time 1 (T1) in table I. Does the child know that x and y are different, but can only say y? Or does she not know they are different, and in fact has both represented as y in her mental lexicon? To take the first set, English contrasts velar and coronal stops before syllabic, velarized /l/ in words like *puddle* and *pickle*. However, the child producing the data in both table I and table II produced both types of these words initially with a medial velar stop, as shown under T1 of table I. Thus, we might say that this child has a "rule" at T1 that velarizes coronal obstruents before a syllabic lateral.

Table I. Type 1: Underlying Representations at T1 Are the Same as the Surface Representations; No Phonological Neutralization Rule at T1

	puddle	pickle	train	chalk	hand	bran
T_1	[pəgəl]	[pɪkəl]	[tʃen]	[tʃak]	[hæn]	[bræn]
T_2	[pədəl]	[pɪtəl]	[tren]	[trak]	[hænd]	[brænd]

Type 1: (i) Two segments x and y are neutralized as y, (ii) a phonological change x' spreads slowly through the learners lexicon (iii) word-by-word (with some consistent lexical exceptions) and (iv) appears in the correct x and incorrect y environment, resulting in error on y.

But look what happens at Time 2: when /d/ is added to some of the *puddle* words, some of the previously correct /k/'s and /g/'s in *pickle*-type words regress—an error occurs.

Similarly, for the other two sets of data shown in table I. So, for /tr/ and *ch*, as in *train* and *chalk*, the child first produces both as the affricate [tʃ], then later at T2, when /tr/ is correctly produced as [tr], some ch-initial words are incorrectly produced as tr-initial also. At this same time, no /t/-initial words, like *ten* (the number) or *talk* ('to speak') are produced incorrectly. With respect to the *hand-bran* type words, initially, all final /nd/ clusters are produced as /n/. Later, when the child learns that these words also have a [d] at the end, the child mistakenly adds [d] to words that end only in [n]. Thus, when *hand*-type words change from [haen] to [haend], *bran*-type words change incorrectly from [braen] to [braend].

The description of this type of change is given here:

> Type 1. (i) Two segments *x* and *y* are neutralized as *y*, (ii) a phonological change *x'* spreads slowly through the learner's lexicon (iii) word-by-word (with some consistent lexical exceptions) and (iv) appears in the correct *x* and incorrect *y* environment, resulting in error on *y*.[2]

What the data in table I show is that at Time 1, the child does not actually make a distinction between *x* and *y*. Rather, the child's productions directly reflect her underlying representations, as indicated by the figure caption. The loss of ability at T2 is a direct reflection of the problem, namely that the child has not separated out fully the velar and coronal phonetic segments in this environment. We can also infer, then, that the merger of *x* and *y* seen at T1 is the result of a perceptual confusion over the nature of two phonetic segment categories. Moreover, the perceptual rather than articulatory nature of the rule can be seen in a close inspection of these rules and their plausible acoustic base and also, by inference, from the slow rate of change and number of exceptions: the lexical representations of these words must be changed individually.

Let us now turn to Type 2 rules. Again, we find that at Time 1 a contrast between two segments in the adult language is neutralized in the child's speech. But in contrast with the situation for the data in table I, when a change occurs here at T2, only one of the two segments is changed. Consider, the /s/ and /t/ examples in the first two columns of table II. Across-the-board, the adult fricative /s/ is produced as [t] at Time 1, and thus there are many homophonous pairs like *bus* and *but*.

---

[2]Type 1 change is an acquisition analogue of lexical diffusion sound change (Wang 1969). Elsewhere I examine whether substantive phonetic content of features (cf. Chomsky and Halle 1968, Chapter 9) plays a role in distinguishing Rule Types 1 and 2 (cf. Labov 1981).

Table II. Type 2: Underlying Representations Are the Same at T1 as They Are at T2. Phonological Rules at T1, e.g., [+ cont, − son] → [− cont], *bus*

	bus	*but*	*pretty*	*pip*	*rain*	*den*
T₁	[bət]	[bət]	[bɪdi]	[bɪp]	[ḍein]	[ḍən]
T₂	[bəs]	[bət]	[prɪdi]	[pɪp]	[rein]	[ḍən]

Type 2: (i) Two segments x and y are neutralized as y, (ii) a phonological change x spreads rapidly through the learners lexicon (iii) in all and only the correct environments (ATB, across-the-board) (iv) with no errors on y.

At Time 2, when /s/ is produced correctly for the first time, only words that should have an /s/ are changed. No words that should have a /t/ are incorrectly changed.

And similarly for the other examples of table II. The second pair of words on this table illustrate what happens with initial /pr/ and /p/: at T1, /r/ is not produced in words like *pretty*; at T2, when the child begins to produce /r/, the /r/ is added to only what would be the correct environments from the adult point of view. For words like *rain* and *den*, the third set on table II, /r/ and /d/ are neutralized, but when /r/ is correctly produced for the first time, there are no errors produced in words that should have a /d/.

This type of change is described as:

Type 2. (i) Two segments *x* and *y* are neutralized as *y*, (ii) a phonological change *x'* spreads rapidly through the learners lexicon (iii) in all and only the correct environments (across-the-board ATB) (iv) with no errors on *y*.[3]

From the properties of change described here and illustrated in table II, we can infer that the child did have a contrast between /t/ and /s/ at Time 1, that this contrast was encoded in her underlying representations, and that the problem at Time 1 was an inability to pronounce [s]. As I have noted above, the learner's underlying representations are the same at T1 and T2, namely correct, with respect to the adult language at both times, and a rule of some kind operates at T1 to derive the surface representation. Type 2 rules are then articulatorily based segmental rules, and accordingly could be handled by our phonetic model. The key property of this rule type is that the change is rapid and across-the-board, meaning that the change applies in all and only the correct environments. This shows that the change applies to an underlying, well-defined category.

The two types of change that we have seen thus distinguish two types of rules. Type 1 rules are perceptual encoding rules that operate "upstream" of the lexical representation. In figure 1 we have a model of

---

[3]Type 2 change is a type of Neogrammarian change (e.g., Osthoff and Bruggman 1878).

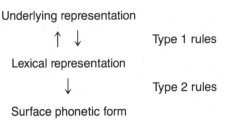

Figure 1.   Model of representational system.

the necessary representational system. What's listed as "lexical representation" is the child's phonemic representation; it is psychologically real for the child and is the level accessed on line. As the child learns to unravel perceptual confusions, she creates correct underlying forms. These underlying forms will ultimately encode morphophonemic information, but that occurs late in the second year and onward. Type 2 rules are production output rules that operate "downstream" of the lexical representation.[4] In figure 1 they are shown as mapping between the lexical representation and the surface phonetic level. The surface level likely has no psychological reality, meaning that the children generally are not aware of how they "mispronounce." Children older than two (and sometimes younger) can be made aware of how they mispronounce, and on occasion some children can be so aware of their inability to pronounce a particular segment that they will systematically avoid saying words containing that segment. In spite of these cases, I hold that what I have labelled the "surface phonetic form" in figure 1 is not a separate, psychologically real representation, and in this respect in particular, my model differs from the Menn 1983 "two-lexicon" model. Moreover, the representational format in figure 1 is necessary for other reasons that we need not go into here. But we can say at this point that nothing so far precludes a simple "learning of segments" analysis for Type 1 and Type 2 rules.

Let's turn now to the problem. In table III there is representative data on stop + /r/ clusters from another child. Table III shows the development of these clusters in this child's speech from about 1;6 to 2;2. At Time 1 (from 1;6 to 1;10), this child reduced initial stop + /r/ clusters by

---

[4]The terminology here "upstream" and "downstream" from the lexical representation is taken from Macken (1980) and reflects the attempt there to integrate the developmental, processing aspects of the two rule types with the derivational structure of underlying representations in standard generative phonology. Rule Types 1 and 2 resemble the distinction in Lexical Phonology between lexical rules, which like Rule Type 1 operate above the phonemic representation and have exceptions, and postlexical rules, which like Rule Type 2 operate below the lexical representation and apply across-the-board (see Kiparsky 1982). The two rule types may thus be an early reflex of the organization of the grammar.

Table III. Type 3: Underlying Representations Are the Same at T1 as They Are at T3. Phonological Rule Applies at T3: [− cont, − voice] → [f] /— [r]. At T1–T4 URs Contain an /r/ that Is Deleted by Rule

	pretty	tree	drink	cradle
T₁	[pʰɪtʰi]	[tʰi]	[t ɪŋkʰ]	[kʰedəl]
T₂	↓	[fi]	[fiŋkʰ]	↓
T₃	[fɪtʰi]	[fi]	[fiŋkʰ]	[fedəl]
T₄	[pʰɪtʰi]	[fi]	[fiŋkʰ]	[fedəl]

Type 3: (i) Two segments *x, y* (,z) are distinct, (ii) a phonological change *x'* spreads through the learner's lexicon in the correct environment and (iii), some time (typically, weeks) later spreads rapidly and ATB to the incorrect *y* (,z) environment(s), (iv) resulting in errors on *y* (,z).

deleting the /r/. Place of articulation was correct for all three places of articulation. Voicing is contrastive at the labial and velar places, but not clearly so for /tr/ versus /dr/. At Time 2 (from 1;11.0 to 1;11.14), initial /tr/ and /dr/ are produced, not as [t], but as [f], *tree* is [fi:], *drinking* is [fiŋkɪŋ], while /pr/-initial and /kr/-initial words remain the same as during Time 1. Phonetically, the coalescence of /tr/ into /f/ makes sense. The strong aspiration in this cluster and the labiality of English /r/ in adult pronunciations combine into a labial voiceless fricative in the child's form. To this point, the rule operates on a simple segment class in a phonetically straightforward way. But look what happens at the next stage, Time 3: from 1;11.28 to 2;1.16, this child uses [f] for all initial /pr/, /tr/, /dr/, and /kr/, and we find words like [fɪti], [fi:], [fiŋkɪŋ] and [fedl], along with lots of other examples. Phonetically, of course, this too is not aberrant, in that the [r] is partly devoiced after all aspirated stops, and most rules are phonetically coherent (cf. Postal's natural-ness condition). Throughout Time 3, [f] was never produced in place of adult /br/, /gr/, /r/ or stops in any other environment.

The properties of this kind of change can be summarized as:

Type 3. (i) Two or more segments *x, y* (,z) are distinct, (ii) then a phonolog-ical change *x'* spreads through the learner's lexicon in the correct environ-ment and (iii), some time later (typically, weeks) spreads rapidly and ATB to the incorrect *y* (,z) environment(s), (iv) resulting in errors on *y* (,z).

What can we determine about this type of rule? The first change at T2 affects /tr/ and /dr/, and not initial /t/ or /d/ words. Obviously, the change is related to the feature composition of phonological coronal + r clusters. This first change looks like it could be either a Type 1 or a Type 2 rule: if it were a Type 1 rule, then when the /tr/–[f] confusion were unlearned, some errors on true /f/-initial words (like *feel*) would be ex-pected. The child's corpus does not provide the data needed to solve this question about the status of the T2 /tr,dr/ → [f] Rule. At T3, the change occurs that I am calling Type 3: a Type 3 rule is the *generaliza-*

tion, one might say *overgeneralization*, of an initial segmental rule to different *categories* of segments. In the example, the initial /tr,dr/-to-[f] rule spreads rapidly and across-the-board to initial /pr/ and /kr/ words. This clearly is an error, but not like the errors seen in Type 1 rules. The nature of this change, namely that the generalization to /pr/ and /kr/ takes place very fast (within days) and in an across-the-board manner, tells us something very important: as with Type 2 rules, whenever a change has these properties, we know that the change is operating on underlying, well-defined categories, probably the same ones that adults have. Thus, we can conclude that the child has correct underlying representations for /pr/ and /kr/ initial clusters. To be absolutely precise, we don't know that the child's representation is identical to an adult's, e.g., that both have a fully segmented /pʰ + r/ representation. What we know is that, like adults, the child's representation encodes sufficient information to separate /p/, /p-r/, /f/, etc., distinctly.

What can we learn about the error created at T3? Why is it different from the error seen in Type 1–perceptual-coding rules? When at T4, the overgeneralization is pulled back in /pr/ initial words (and possibly) in /kr/ initial words), *pretty* is correctly produced with an initial [pʰ] and there are no errors on initial [f] words, like *feel*. The absence of further errors at T4, as with the speed and across-the-board manner of change at T3, confirms that throughout T1-T4, the child's underlying representations correctly distinguish among all stop + /r/ clusters and encode the contrast between these clusters and singleton /p/, /t/, and /k/ words. The Type 3 rule is then not a perceptual encoding rule.

The conclusion we have just derived from these facts about change is that the underlying representations are the same at T1, T2, and T3, that these representations correctly distinguish among the relevant places of articulation and presence/absence of /r/, and that phonological rules apply to these underlying forms to produce the surface forms.

Is the Type 3 actually an articulatory-based segmental rule, a Type 2 rule that just happens to have been independently generated in each of the three clusters? First, we must note that the data in table III do not fully resemble Type 2 rules either, but more crucial is the following: to claim that the data in table III show three separate Type 2 rules, one would have to claim that the substitution of [f] for each of the three clusters is an independently motivated, phonetically natural rule. Phonetically, a strong argument for naturalness can be made for /tr/, a weak argument might be made for /pr/, and an even weaker or nonexistent argument for /kr/. With respect to acquisition data, a number of English-speaking children use [f] for /tr/, there are isolated examples of a child using [f] for /pr/ on a few words (but no case of an ATB rule), and no other case in what is a very large literature of a child using [f] for /kr/. Finally, it is extremely unlikely that three such formally similar rules would spontaneously arise independently at the same time. I conclude that the data in table III, and other examples like these, illustrate a third type of rule: one that is not strictly speaking segmentally motivated, but rather is a generalization over different classes of segments, a more abstract rule and one that shows the child constructing a relatively abstract, autonomous phonological grammar. We could discuss at length how much of a grammar and what kind of grammar such data reveal, but the crucial point for the present discussion is that here we have a phenomenon that lies outside the range of individual segments. This is then a case of getting better *phonologically,* by getting worse phonetically.

Conclusions

Why is Rule Type 3 a problem for phonetics models of self-organizing systems from biology, and for evolutionary models of differentiation and integration? The interest of self-organizing systems for a theory of language acquisition is that such systems show ways in which complex systems may be the outcome of simple, local actions that are not under the control of a grand scheme or blueprint. Thus, we might find that language acquisition can result in a language, indeed a grammar, but not be driven by an abstract "Universal Grammar." Thus, for example, termites build termite nests without a goal or *a priori* blueprint for the shape, height, etc., of nests. Similarly, bees build honeycombs without any intention or knowledge, however primitive, of hexagons. Hexagonal shapes are simply what happens to circles when uniform pressure is applied on all sides, and the circles are simply the imprint of the bee's head in the wax. The bee does not have a "grammar" of hexagons and honeycombs, but something quite a bit simpler, an instruction for a highly local behavior.

For these models to work for phonology acquisition, first, the complex outcome that linguists think looks like a "grammar" must be the result of similarly local operations. Certainly, rules like the Type 1 and Type 2 rules that operate on individual segments count as "local" in the requisite sense. However, Rule Type 3 is not strictly segment-based nor "local" in this sense. Thus, the Type 3 rules are not principled phonetics types rules, and further, they fall outside the scope of self-organizing systems.

Most generally, the problem faced by such models is to account for how learners arrive at, not just any grammar, but essentially a single grammar. This is the "hill-climbing problem" for purely local discovery algorithms. It is what Chomsky has called "the logical problem of acquisition" or "Plato's problem." That learners succeed in this sense and succeed on so complex a task so relatively quickly must, I believe, be explained by the operation of an innate, highly specific phonological grammar. Though this innate grammar must accommodate variation and exceptions better than the classical Chomskyan model and may in fact utilize mechanisms like those of self-organizing systems, it remains the heart of the explanation (cf. Macken 1987). For phonology, post-1968 parameterized rule systems and enriched theories of representations provide better and more explanatory coverage for the variation seen among individual learners within and across languages. I turn now to these representational issues.

LEXICAL TEMPLATES

Representational Units

In most studies of phonological acquisition, a segment-sized unit is assumed or explicitly hypothesized to be the unit of acquisition. Such studies describe the learner's output in terms of segment-to-segment rules that derive a child surface form from an underlying segment typically assumed to be the adult phoneme or in terms of processes (or descriptive statements) that associate the child surface form with an adult segment (without implying a direct derivation between the two). In generative studies where the feature is assumed to be basic, segments still function centrally (e.g., Jakobson 1941/68; Smith 1973).

One of the earliest counterproposals to the segment as the basic building block of the phonology was Moskowitz (1971), which focused on the role of the syllable. Moskowitz noted the descriptive validity of the syllable (e.g., the predominance of CV syllables in early stages) and in addition posited the syllable as an autonomous unit of generalization: stages were identified through the development of an inventory of syllables that combine across time in specific ways in words, from monosyllables to full reduplication to "partial reduplication," say from [ki] to [kiki] to [kiti]. Whereas in segment or feature models, the difference between [ti] and [ki] is the contrast [t:k] or [+/− coronal], in the syllable model, phonetic distinctions are syllable features, such as a difference in syllable onset. Moskowitz saw development in terms of the acquisition of successively smaller units: after the "sentence" unit, initially only an intonation contour and a string of sounds (the major achievement of the babbling period), the learner discovers the syllable; only after the partial reduplicaton phase does the learner discover the phone or segment as a unit. For example, a child of 1;5 used words of two different syllables. Several weeks later, he acquired an [1]-onset syllable which was used in *Emula* (proper name), [lala]. Although this child already had the syllable [mu] in his inventory, the new element first functioned at the primitive level of full reduplication.

Few studies have found evidence that the syllable drives acquisition in the ways predicted by Moskowitz, and in general, languages do not exhibit the kinds of co-occurrence constraints between onsets and rhymes and/or between syllables (except in reduplication) that are at the center of this theory. A unit larger than the syllable does, however, play a significant role during early acquisition stages.

Ferguson and Farwell (1975) were among the first to suggest that words are identified and, perhaps, contrasted as whole units. These authors presented "phone trees" that group together similar segments that occur in the same position across several words and suggested that contrastive segments are differentiated through the changes that occur in this network of associations between similar sounding words. Various aspects of development that show the importance of the phonological word have been identified (see, in particular, Waterson 1971; Menn 1978; Chiat 1979).

In Macken (1979), I identified the entire word as a phonological unit, the "prosodic word," where each target word was assigned to a particular "word pattern" (or "template") based on its general features: words, not segments or syllables, were the building blocks of the early period. I proposed that learners start out with the prosodic word as the basic unit and form phonotactic and accentual 'generalizations' that take the form of a set of templates encoding the structure and content of representations at the "word" level. Initially the learning of segments is partially determined by the development of rules at the word level. The "word" as a phonological unit thus both specifies the domain of constraints and phonological processes and also forms an autonomous, psychologically real level of representation. The child formulates hypotheses on the bases of global similarity between words, then abstracts templates, and expands and generalizes these templates to handle new words. The word patterns or templates in these data showed that the consonant constraints were separate from the vowel constraints. Without considering the word as the basic organizational unit, some phonological phenomena, particularly at the segment level, would have appeared quite arbitrary and the patterning of other phonological phenomena could not be explained. The learning of templates, segments, and features occurred simultaneously from 1;7 to 2;1. The evidence for the centrality of the word largely disappeared by the age 2;1, and the data from 2;2 to 2;5 could be adequately described in terms of traditional segment and, secondarily, feature rules. I argued that the prosodic word, segment, and feature form a hierarchy of basic representational units of acquisition.

If we assume that this hierarchy is the same as what is now known as the "prosodic hierarchy" (see Nespor and Vogel 1986), we expect that the syllable is at the very least an autonomous unit of representation and in addition may be developmentally positioned in the hierarchy. We might further expect that other units like the metrical foot, the phonological phrase or clitic group may play a role as well. Separate developments in phonological theory show that "word patterns" are lexical "templates" as in Semitic (McCarthy 1979, 1981) and that the separate patterning of consonant as opposed vowels in word patterns corresponds to the "planar segregation" of consonants and vowels (e.g., McCarthy 1979, 1981; Archangeli 1985). Planes and higher prosodic units are linked through the "CV skeleton" (e.g., Clements and Keyser 1981). I will from this point use the terminology and theory of post-1968 nonlinear phonology in discussing the prosodic word and templates and the relationship between two different types of lexical templates, the harmony grammars (cf. Macken 1978) as opposed to the melody grammars (Macken 1979, 1988, 1989).

Harmony and Melody Templates

Most children, during the earliest stages, use rules of consonant harmony and vowel harmony. Such productions can be analyzed as segment based assimilation rules (Smith 1973), the concatenation of identical syllables (Moskowitz 1971) or rules implementing templates (Macken 1978). Data like those given in table IV (taken from Macken 1978) are typical of such harmony forms.

Children differ in the extent to which they imploy harmony rules (e.g., Vihman 1978), the direction of assimilation left-right or right-left (cf. also what is referred to in the acquisition literature as "initial position focuser" versus "final position focuser"), and the nature of the dominant segment (e.g., the strength hierarchies for manner in Macken 1978, and place in Macken 1978, Macken 1979—where labial is

Table IV.   Consonant Harmony. Corals Assimilate to Noncorals

	peine 'comb' *pelota* 'ball' *mesa* 'table'		*sopa*	'soup'	*casa* 'house' *carro* 'car'		*troca* 'truck' *chango* 'monkey'	
T1*	[pepe] [popa] [mefe]		[popa]		[kaka] [kaku]		[koka] ([kaŋo])	
T2**	[pene] [pota] [mesa]		[fopa]		[kasa] [karo]		[koka] [xaŋo]	(2;5)

*Ages 1;10–1;11.
**Primarily ages 2;1–2;2.

stronger than velar, and in Menn 1976—where velar is stronger than labial). Consonant harmony is considerably more widespread than vowel harmony, and in individual children who use both, consonant harmony persists longer in time than do rules of vowel harmony. The domain is the word (and in early stages, the utterance). Coronal consonants are overwhelmingly the "weak," nondominant segments (modulo some variation in acquisition order). Harmony itself can be an argument for the planar segregation of consonants and vowels (cf. the no-line-crossing constraint of autosegmental phonology; Archangeli 1985), as can the independent development of the consonant versus vowel systems.

Some children, however, use consonant harmony only minimally. Such children show lexical constraints of a very different kind (Macken 1979; Macken and Ferguson 1983; Macken 1988, 1989). Their templates show rigid co-occurrence constraints in the sequencing of place and manner types of consonants—what I will call *melody templates* as distinguished from *harmony templates*. Data like those in table V (based on Macken 1979) illustrate melody templates and development. The data in table V show the [labial + coronal] and [velar + coronal] templates.

The dominance relations seen in the harmony systems show up in melody systems also, but in a different way: in the former, coronals undergo harmony, particularly when they precede noncoronals; in melody templates, coronals are sequenced to the right of noncoronals. The linear order requirements of the melody templates are met by the operation of a variety of different, and sometimes uncommon rules, such as metathesis, dissimilation, and template-driven deletion and

Table V. Acquisition Order of CVCV Harmony and Melody Templates, 1;7 – 2;1

	$C_1V \ \ C_1V$		e.g.	$C_1V \ \ C_2V$		e.g.
T_1	$\begin{bmatrix} +ant \\ -cor \end{bmatrix}$	$\begin{bmatrix} +ant \\ -cor \end{bmatrix}$	p_p_	$\begin{bmatrix} +ant \\ -cor \end{bmatrix}$	$\begin{bmatrix} +ant \\ +cor \end{bmatrix}$	m_n_
	$\begin{bmatrix} +ant \\ +cor \end{bmatrix}$	$\begin{bmatrix} +ant \\ +cor \end{bmatrix}$	n_n_			
T_2				$\begin{bmatrix} +ant \\ -cor \end{bmatrix}$	$\begin{bmatrix} -ant \\ -cor \end{bmatrix}$	p_k_
T_3	$\begin{bmatrix} -ant \\ -cor \end{bmatrix}$	$\begin{bmatrix} -ant \\ -cor \end{bmatrix}$	k_k_			
T_4				$\begin{bmatrix} +ant \\ +cor \end{bmatrix}$	$\begin{bmatrix} -ant \\ +cor \end{bmatrix}$	n_ɲ_
T_5				$\begin{bmatrix} -ant \\ -cor \end{bmatrix}$	$\begin{bmatrix} +ant \\ +cor \end{bmatrix}$	k_t_
				$\begin{bmatrix} +ant \\ -cor \end{bmatrix}$	$\begin{bmatrix} -ant \\ +cor \end{bmatrix}$	b_ɲ_

substitution rules. It is in part through the "conspiracy" effect of this variety of formally dissimilar rules that the template is shown most clearly, table VI (based on Macken 1979).

A particularly unusual melody template is reported in Priestley (1977) where all disyllabic words are produced as [CVjVC]. Several melody templates implement the basic skeletal template. Table VII contains the four templates used for eight or more words each. (Templates are arranged in descending order of productivity.) Association of melody units to templatic skeletal position is edge-in or left-right, and examples of both are given in the table. A few words show exceptional association and/or the operation of exceptional pre-association rules: e.g., *sucker* [fajak], *streamer* [mijat], *tomorrow* [pajom], *chocolate* [kajak]. In only four of seventy words does a coronal consonant occur before a noncoronal. The primary vocalic templates are [i-a], [a-a] and [E-a]; only two words violate the basic constraint that V1 is higher than or equal in height to V2.

In CVC (V) melody templates where the two consonants differ in place of articulation, noncoronal consonants occur in C1 position and coronals in C2 position to the right of either labial or velar consonants.[5] Learners who use harmony grammars also show the right edge positioning of coronals. This can be seen in later stages when harmony rules become optional and/or when consonant clusters are acquired. When harmony becomes optional, typically, [− cor][+ cor] words will not undergo harmony at a point where [+ cor][− cor] words still do (e.g., Macken 1978, table IV). When words with two string-adjacent consonants are produced, a common metathesis rule moves the coronal to the right of a noncoronal. Table VIII gives a few of the 80 or so exam-

Table VI.   Variety of Template-Controlled Rules: Deletion, Metathesis, Substitution

First C_1VC_2V melody template

		$\begin{bmatrix}+\text{ant}\\-\text{cor}\end{bmatrix}$	$\begin{bmatrix}+\text{ant}\\+\text{cor}\end{bmatrix}$			
(i)	*manzana* 'apple'	[mana]		(ii)	*pelota* 'ball'	[pata]
	Fernando	[mano]			*zapato* 'shoe'	[pato]
	Ramon	[mon]			*sopa* 'soup'	[pota]
	comiendo 'eating'	[mino]			*elefante* 'elephant'	[pate]
					libro 'book'	[pito]
					vestido 'dress'	[pitl]
					perro 'dog'	[pedo]
					reloj 'watch'	[bUdo]

[5]One source (Stern 1924) provides a case where the consonantal melody template is further restricted to permit only velar consonants in C1 position; this consonant is either [k] or [h/x].

Table VII.   CVjCV Melody Templates, 1;10 – 2;2

(1)	$\begin{bmatrix} +\text{ant} \\ -\text{cor} \end{bmatrix}$	$\begin{bmatrix} +\text{cor} \end{bmatrix}$	*breadman* [bijan]	*bison* [bajas]
(2)	$\begin{bmatrix} -\text{ant} \\ -\text{cor} \end{bmatrix}$	$\begin{bmatrix} +\text{cor} \end{bmatrix}$	*cupboard* [kajat]	*coaster* [kajows]
(3)	$[+\text{cor}]$	$[+\text{cor}]$	*records* [rejas]	*Jennifer* [dʒejɛn]
(4)	$\begin{bmatrix} +\text{ant} \\ -\text{cor} \end{bmatrix}$	$\begin{bmatrix} -\text{ant} \\ -\text{cor} \end{bmatrix}$	*finger* [fijak]	

ples from one child documented in Smith (1973). Lexical constraints in languages like Tagalog place coronals to the right of noncoronals; and [+ cor][– cor] metathesis is very common cross-linguistically (Bailey 1971).

In CVC(V) melody templates where the two consonants differ in manner of articulation, the predominant linear order is [– cont][+ cont] (e.g., tables IV and V; the full data in Priestly 1977). This left-right dominance relation is found in harmony systems also where fricatives assimilate to stops (e.g., the manner hierarchy in Macken 1978), in the context-free substitution of stops for fricatives (Jakobson 1941/1968) and the earlier acquisition of fricatives in final and medial positions of the word. Other manner templates also predominantly linearize true consonants left-right from strongest to weakest (cf. strength hierarchies) or less sonorous to most sonorous (cf. the sonority hierarchy).

Most cases of melody templates thus far reported are consonantal templates or cases where the learner uses both consonantal templates and vocalic templates, as in Priestly (1977). The data on vocalic templates is much more incomplete. Data in Grammont (1923) show a vocalic template operating that requires the first vowel to be lower than the second; identical vowels undergo dissimilation, as in *pipi* [pepi] and *cu-cul* [cocu]. In Vihman (1976), the template for vowels of differing height required the lowest vowel in the first position; violations were reordered, as in /ema/ 'mother' [ami] or [ani] and /isa/ 'father' [asi]. A different kind of template, a syllable template, is also occasionally reported. For a period of time, the child in Smith (1973) used [ri –] as a general-purpose unstressed syllable: *attack* [ritæk], *exhaust* [rirɔst], *enjoy* [ridɔi], *thermometer* [rimɔmitə], etc. The child in Menn (1976) used [tim –] in a similar way: *balloon* [timbun], *baloni* [timboni], *banana* [timdana], *piano* [timpano], etc.

Table VIII.   [+ cor] [– cor] Metathesis, 2;2 – 3;3

ask	[a:kt]	whisk	[wiktə]	difficult	[gipətul]
bulb	[bʌbl]	helping	[ɛplin]	music	[mu:gi:]
film	[flim]	alligator	[ægəleɪtə]	galloping	[gæpəlin]
wolf	[wufl]	animal	[æmələn]	bicycle	[baɪəsəl]

Conclusions

The evidence we have on the structure and content of learners' lexical representations shows, I propose, that there are two broad types of grammars, harmony (e.g., ClVClV) and melody e.g., C1VC2V), and that individual learners may primarily use one or the other. In both types, representations are controlled by constraints across non-string-adjacent consonants in polysyllabic words that closely resemble strict adjacency restrictions in adult languages like minimal distance and place/manner sequencing constraints on tautosyllabic clusters and the typical content of linked structures. Finally, there is little evidence of generalized use of an inventory of fixed CV syllabic units (where V is other than a default vowel). These facts suggest that these first grammars are built on the basic unit of "prosodic word" and that representations at this level are structured by lexical templates with CV planar segregation. The melody grammars most clearly instantiate the diagnostics for phonological planar segregation: (1) rigid CVC(V) constraints, (2) strict CV(CV) syllables, and (3) metathesis (McCarthy 1989).

Although implemented differently, the constraints on harmony and melody grammar are very similar. When viewed from the perspective of parameters made available by universal grammar, the variation in different individual systems can be seen as a typology of template systems much the way stress systems result from the parameters of prosodic unit, directionality, left-right dominance and iterativity. From such a perspective, the difference between harmony and melody types is a difference on the iterativity parameter (where the noniterative type, the melody type, employs the default coronal consonant in C2 position) or on a binarity parameter (where monovalence in the non-binary, harmony type triggers automatic spreading).

I began with the question, "where's phonology?" Given the state of the field, an answer cannot yet be given. I believe that the data thus far show that "phonology" is in each grammar constructed by each individual learner and in the changes over time in each of those grammars. The constraints on those learners are no more and no less than the constraints on the formal system itself, and it is the formal system that explains the form, the variation, and the process.[6]

---

[6]Other obligations prevented me from completing this chapter. The chapter is, by necessity, brief, particularly section two (representation). Section one (rules) was to include a major section on other rule types and the onset of phonological rules. I believe the latter co-occurs with and is cognitively linked with the simultaneous emergence of first syntactic rules and with the (first) qualitative and quantitative change in the lexicon. It appears that categorical, 'abstract,' rule-based thinking emerges about the same time in three components of the grammar, the phonology, syntax, and lexicon.

REFERENCES

Archangeli, D. 1985. Yokuts harmony: Evidence for coplanar representation in nonlinear phonology. *Linguistic Inquiry* 16:335-72.

Archangeli, D. 1988. Aspects of underspecification theory. *Phonology* 5:183-207.

Bailey, C. J. 1971. Towards specifying constraints on phonological metathesis. *Linguistic Inquiry* 1:347-49.

Chiat, S. 1979. The role of the word in phonological development. *Linguistics* 17:591-610

Chomsky, N., and Halle, M. 1968. *The Sound Pattern of English*. New York: Harper and Row.

Clements, G. N., and Keyser, S. J. 1983. *CV Phonology.* Cambridge MA: The MIT Press.

Ferguson, C. A., and Farwell, C. B. 1975. Words and sounds in early language acquisition. *Language* 51:419-39.

Fey, M., and Gandour, J. 1982. Rule discovery in phonological acquisition. *Journal of Child Language* 9:71-81.

Grammont, M. 1923. L'assimilation. *Bulletin de la Societe de Linquistique de Paris* 24.

Jakobson, R. 1941/1968. *Child Language, Aphasia and Phonological Universals.* Mouton: The Hague.

Kiparsky, P. 1982. Lexical morphology and phonology. In *Linguistics in the Morning Calm*, ed. I. S. Yang. Seoul: Hanshin.

Kiparsky, P., and Menn, L. 1977. On the acquisition of phonology. In *Language Learning and Thought*, ed. J. MacNamara. New York: Academic Press.

Labov, W. 1981. Resolving the Neogrammarian controversy. *Language* 57:267-308.

Leopold, W. F. 1947. *Speech Development of a Bilingual Child*. Vol 2. Chicago: Northwestern University Press.

Macken, M. 1978. Permitted complexity in phonological development. *Lingua* 44:219-53.

Macken, M. 1979. Developmental reorganization of phonology. *Lingua* 49:11-49.

Macken, M. 1980. The child's lexical representation. *Journal of Linguistics* 16:1-17.

Macken, M. 1987. Representation, rules and overgeneralization in phonology. In *Mechanisms of Language Acquisition*, ed. B. MacWhinney. Hillsdale, NJ: Lawrence Erlbaum Associates.

Macken, M. 1988. Melody and harmony. Paper given at Cornell University, Department of Modern Languages and Linguistics, February.

Macken, M. 1989. Lexical templates. ms. University of Texas, Austin.

Macken, M., and Ferguson, C. A. 1983. Cognitive aspects of phonological development. In *Children's Language*, ed. K. E. Nelson. Vol 4. Hillsdale, NJ: Lawrence Erlbaum Associates.

McCarthy, J. 1979. Formal problems in Semitic phonology and morphology. Ph.D. dissertation. MIT.

McCarthy, J. 1981. A prosodic theory of nonconcatenative morphology. *Linguistic Inquiry.* 12:373-418.

McCarthy, J. 1989. Linear order and phonological representations. *Linguistic Inquiry* 20:71-99.

Menn, L. 1971. Phonotactic rules in beginning speech. *Lingua* 26:225-51.

Menn, L. 1976. Pattern, control and contrast in beginning speech. Unpublished Ph.D. dissertation. Univ. of Illinois.

Menn, L. 1978. Phonological units in beginning speech. In *Syllables and Segments*, eds. A. Bell and J. Hooper. Amsterdam: North Holland.

Menn, L. 1983. Development of articulatory, phonetic and phonological capabilities. In *Language Production*, Vol. 1, ed. B. Butterworth. London: Academic Press.

Moskowitz, B. A. 1973. The acquisition of phonology and syntax. In *Approaches to Natural Language*, eds. J. Hintikka et al. Dordrecht: Reidel.

Nespor, M., and Vogel, I. 1986. *Prosodic Phonology.* Dordrecht: Foris.

Odden, D. 1981. *Problems in tone assignment in Shona.* Ph.D. diss. University of IL–Champaign-Urbana.

Osthoff, H., and Brugmann, K. 1878. *Morphologische Untersuchungen.* Leipzig.

Priestley, T. M. S. 1977. One idiosyncratic strategy in the acquisition of phonology. *Journal of Child Language.* 4:45-66.

Smith, N. V. 1973. *The Acquisition of Phonology.* Cambridge: Cambridge University Press.

Vihman, M. 1976. From prespeech to speech. *Papers and Reports on Child Language Development.* Stanford University 3:51-94.

Vihman, M. 1978. Consonant harmony. In *Universals of Human Language.* Vol 2, ed. J. Greenberg. Stanford: Stanford University Press.

Wang, W. S.-Y. 1969. Competing changes as a cause of residue. *Language* 45:9-25.

Waterson, N. 1971. Child phonology: A prosodic view. *Journal of Linguistics* 7:179-211.

PART · II

Research

Overview

Research on Phonological Development
Recent Advances

Carol Stoel-Gammon

In his concluding remarks at the child phonology conference sponsored by the National Institutes of Health in 1978, Jenkins stated that the field of child phonology was "fresh, young, and rapidly expanding" (Yeni-Komshian, Kavanagh, and Ferguson 1980). He went on to note that the rapid rate of development places a "staggering burden" on investigators because, ideally, they should be well versed in a diverse set of disciplines ranging from voice science, acoustics, and instrumentation, to child development and behavioral management techniques, to psycholinguistics, psychometrics, and statistics, among others. Although it is doubtful that any single investigator is fully knowledgeable in all the areas encompassed by the field of child phonology, it is clear from the chapters in this volume that many researchers are reaching beyond traditional, narrowly defined domains to incorporate methodologies and findings from a variety of disciplines. I believe Jenkins must be impressed.

The International Conference on Phonological Development held at Stanford in 1989, a decade after the meeting at which Jenkins spoke, presents a field that is not quite so young or so fresh, but a field that has become increasingly sophisticated as it "comes of age." It remains, however, a field that would still be described as "rapidly expanding." The expansion has proceeded in several directions, most notably in the areas of crosslinguistic studies of development, infant speech perception, prelinguistic development, and the transition from babbling to speech; in addition, increasing attention has been given to atypical phonological development and how it contributes to (and benefits from) our understanding of normal phonological development. The past decade has also been marked by increased sophistication in the techniques used in data collection and data analysis. Each of these themes is represented by the research of one or more investigators in this book.

PRELINGUISTIC AND EARLY LINGUISTIC DEVELOPMENT

In the 1978 Child Phonology Conference (Yeni-Komshian, Kavanagh, and Ferguson 1980), the work of Oller (1980) and Stark (1980) represented the cutting edge of research on the nature of vocal development in the prelinguistic period. Both researchers highlighted two themes: (1) infant vocalizations develop in an ordered sequence of stages from birth to the onset of meaningful speech and (2) the speech sounds and syllable structures characteristic of the later babbling period closely resemble the sounds and syllable structures of first words. Investigations carried out in the past decade on infants raised in diverse language environments have indicated that, regardless of language community, infants proceed through the stages outlined by Oller and Stark. Moreover, there appears to be a high degree of regularity across languages in terms of the repertoire of sounds produced in babbling (see Locke 1983 for a review; also chapters by Kent, and Locke and Pearson this volume). For example, in all studies to date, the consonantal repertoires of infants in the later babbling period (after 9 months) typically include a high proportion of front (i.e., labial and dental/alveolar) consonants, of stops and nasals, and of open syllables.

In spite of the commonalities that are readily apparent, the research has also shown that babbling patterns are not the same for all infants. Crosslinguistic studies carried out since the 1978 conference have yielded a small but growing body of evidence that prelinguistic vocalizations show effects of the ambient language as early as 10 months (e.g., Boysson-Bardies et al. 1989). The chapters by Boysson-Bardies and colleagues and by Vihman in this section add considerable support for this view. Interestingly, it seems that the crosslinguistic effects are evident not so much in the types of sounds and syllable structures produced but in the frequency of occurrence of particular types (i.e., in the number of tokens). The findings of crosslinguistic investigations have led to a growing awareness that some questions cannot be answered on the basis of data from a single language; only crosslinguistic data can reveal which aspects of acquisition are universal and which are due to language-specific characteristics (e.g., Leonard et al. 1988). In this volume, for example, Ingram uses a crosslinguistic approach to test hypotheses regarding children's acquisition of phonological representations.

Another source of variation in early vocal development can be attributed to individual differences. In the past decade, several studies have revealed the presence of such differences in the babbling of infants learning the same language, and longitudinal data focusing on the transition from babbling to speech has shown that differences apparent in babbling are carried forward to the period of meaningful speech (Stoel-Gammon and Cooper 1984; Vihman, Ferguson, and Elbert 1986). This theme is explored further in Vihman's chapter, which documents individual differences in the occurrence of practiced syllables in babbling and then traces their occurrence in meaningful speech. My chapter reviewing investigations that show correlations between measures of prelinguistic vocalizations in infancy and measures of speech and language in early childhood also highlights individual differences.

With the increase in the number and range of studies devoted to the prelinguistic and early linguistic period, it has become clear that phonological acquisition in the "real word" stage is directly tied to patterns in the preceding period. Moreover, there is evidence to show that there are multiple variables that must be considered, including (1) the universal aspects of early acquisition; (2) the effects of the environment, particularly the phonological system of the ambient language, on speech perception and production; and (3) individual differences in both rate and style of learning.

METHODOLOGICAL ADVANCES

In the 1970s much of the data in the field of child phonology was obtained through naturalistic, unstructured data collection sessions in which children were observed while interacting with a caregiver or experimenter. This research resulted in the creation of rich longitudinal databases and the publication of many descriptive studies of phonological acquisition; in some cases, it yielded findings that had not been anticipated and could not be easily explained. For example, the Stanford Child Phonology Project followed the prelinguistic and early linguistic development of a group of young subjects, by recording the children's vocalizations on a weekly basis for seven to ten months. The recordings were then phonetically transcribed by members of the project. When analyzed, some unexpected findings emerged; particularly intriguing was "the seeming great selectivity of the child in deciding which words he will try to produce" (Ferguson and Farwell 1975, p. 429). Ferguson and Farwell viewed this selectivity as phonologically based, hypothesizing that subjects chose to include certain words in their vocabulary because these words contained certain sounds or sound classes while avoiding (i.e., excluding from their vocabulary) words that contained other sounds or sound classes.

Subsequent research, using similar research methodologies, supported this finding and showed, further, that selection and avoidance were tied to the child's phonological abilities. In general, words that were selected for inclusion in the productive lexicon contained sounds that the child could produce relatively accurately, whereas words that were avoided contained sounds that the child failed to produce accurately (e.g., Ferguson, Peizer, and Weeks 1973; Menn 1976). The notion of phonological selectivity was an intriguing one, but given the unstructured methods used in collecting the data, the possibility that the differences in early vocabularies were due to differences in input rather than to preferences related to the child's developing phonology could not be ruled out. That is, perhaps Child A showed a preference for labial sounds because she heard more labials in the speech directed toward her, while Child B "preferred" velars because his mother frequently used words like *cookie, cracker,* and other words with /k/. The only way to test the "differences in input" explanation was to control input and this was not possible using a naturalistic, observational paradigm.

EXPERIMENTAL APPROACHES

To solve the problem, Schwartz and Leonard (1982) designed an experimental procedure that allowed them to control both amount of input and the phonological form of the words to which the child was exposed. In their study they examined the productions of a group of subjects with small vocabularies to determine the consonantal inventories and syllable structures in the words of each child and then constructed a set of new words (nonsense or unfamiliar forms) corresponding to unfamiliar referents (objects and actions). The phonological composition of the word sets was individualized for each subject: half the words contained consonants that had been evidenced in the child's productions (IN words) and half contained consonants that had not (OUT words). IN words and OUT words were then presented to the subject an equal number of times in playlike sessions over a number of weeks. Schwartz and Leonard reported that subjects produced a significantly greater number of IN words during the sessions and acquired (i.e., produced spontaneously) IN words more rapidly than OUT words, thus confirming the hypothesis of phonologically based selectivity. Interestingly, comprehension probes showed that there were no differences in the comprehension of IN and OUT words, in spite of the differences in production (see Schwartz 1988 for a review of these studies). Subsequently, other researchers have developed experimental procedures to test other hypotheses about the organization and processing of children's phonological systems (e.g., Smith 1990). The use of experimental procedures in the study of child phonology allows us to test hypotheses in ways that are not possible using naturalistic paradigms. Together, naturalistic and experimental approaches provide data essential for hypothesis testing and theory construction.

MULTIDIMENSIONAL APPROACHES

Although the theme of each chapter in this volume centers around phonological development, all contributors recognize that the child's early linguistic development arises from interactions among a complex array of factors, including sensorimotor, phonological, semantic, syntactic, and communicative/functional. These interactions are afforded particular attention in the chapter by Elbers and Wijnen, who demonstrate that *effort* and *skill*, two aspects of acquisition that typically are ignored by theoretical linguists and child phonologists, play important roles in the language learning process. Their fine-grained longitudinal study of the transition from babbling to words and from single words to word combinations in one child adds to our understanding of the interactive processes that underlie language acquisition. Such an approach also sheds light on variables that could contribute to individual differences in the course of development.

McCune's chapter describing a dynamic systems approach also emphasizes the importance of interactions among aspects of cognitive, psychosocial, and motor development. Analysis of children's performance on a set of variables ranging from object permanence and representational play to vocal motor schemes, communicative grunts, and word use revealed strong individual differences across her subjects. She concludes that the key to understanding the transition from the premeaningful stage to the period of meaningful speech lies in "close examination of the systematicity inherent in the relevant variables along the path for each child." Thus, like Elbers and Wijnen, she advocates a multifaceted approach that incorporates many sources of data and multiple levels of analysis.

MEASUREMENT

Since the last conference, significant advances have been made in methodologies aimed at creating a usable scale of phonological development. Although measures of grammatical development have been available for some time now (e.g., MLU), comparable measures for phonology have been lacking. There are presently a number of proposed indices that assess particular aspects of the system; for example, Shriberg and Kwiatkowski's (1982) index of *percent consonant correct*, a measure of the proportion of correct consonantal productions in a sample, or Ingram's (1981) *articulation score*, based on the size of a child's consonantal inventory in word initial, medial, and final position, or Hodson's (1980) *phonological severity score*, derived from analyses of error patterns (phonological processes).

The particular measure one adopts depends on the goal of the study and in some cases a single metric may be sufficient. However, in order to obtain a relatively complete profile of a child's phonological system, multiple measures are needed. In particular, the following seem important: (1) a measure of the size and composition of the child's phonetic repertoire including an inventory of syllable shapes as well as speech sounds; (2) a measure of accuracy of production; and (3) a measure of the types and frequency of errors. As noted by Grunwell in her chapter, measures that allow us to assess a child's phonological system and compare his performance with that of other subjects are particularly important in the clinical context, so that children who are not developing normally can be identified and given appropriate remedial services.

The need for measurement of vocal development in the prelinguistic period also has been recognized and a number of indices have been developed; my chapter provides a review of many of the indices that are currently available. These include both stage-based measures (e.g., Oller 1980; Stark 1980) and a variety of inventory measures based on the sounds or syllable structures of the child's vocalizations.

FUTURE RESEARCH

Although research in the past decade has advanced our knowledge-base considerably and resolved many of the issues raised in the 1978 Conference on Child Phonology, some questions have remained unanswered and additional questions have arisen. A major area where there is an obvious gap in our knowledge is in the relationship between speech perception and production. Exciting advances have been made in each of these areas independently, but much of the research has centered around nonoverlapping age ranges. In speech perception, investigators have focused on early infancy, documenting the presence of a remarkable, and apparently universal, range of abilities for discriminating and categorizing speech sounds in the first few months of life. Interestingly, longitudinal cross-linguistic studies show a loss of discriminative abilities for some non-native speech sounds between 6 and 12 months (see Werker and Pegg this volume). In contrast, production studies have tended to look at the transition from babbling to speech in babies 9 months and older. To date, there has been little effort to integrate findings in these two areas, despite their obvious potential for interdependence. Thus, advances in each area notwithstanding, questions regarding the relationship between production and perception remain largely unanswered.

A major obstacle in studying the relationship between perception and production in infants and toddlers is the lack of techniques for testing perceptual abilities in the period of early meaningful speech. Recent efforts have centered around developing procedures in which visual displays are paired with acoustic stimuli (see Werker and Pegg this volume). While this technique has the potential for telling us something about phonemic discrimination and the nature of underlying representations in the young child, it has proved difficult to use with subjects younger than 18 or 19 months of age. At this point, it is not possible to determine if the failure is due to a child's inability to discriminate between phonemes of his language (perhaps words are perceived and produced as unanalyzed wholes rather than segments in the early stages) or to testing techniques that are not appropriate for children younger than 18 months.

Two other areas of phonological development that recently have been recognized as deserving of attention are suprasegmental development and the acquisition of vowels. With regard to the first area, it is of interest that theoretical phonologists have recently moved from a linear approach in which phonological representations consist of strings of segments to nonlinear approaches that stress the hierarchical nature of phonological representations, using a system of parallel tiers to represent both suprasegmental and segmental features (Goldsmith 1990). This emphasis on prosodic aspects provides a possible framework for investigating prosodic development in the young child and relating suprasegmental and segmental information. Although a few researchers have attempted to apply this framework to child phonology (e.g., Menn 1978; Spencer 1986), they have tended to focus on particular aspects of a child's phonology, looking exclusively at assimilatory patterns or syllable structures for example, with relatively little attention to general patterns of stress and timing in multisyllabic words or multiword utterances. Cross-linguistic studies of languages that differ in their stress and timing features would be particularly revealing in this regard—both for models of phonological development and for phonological theory. Because vowels form the syllabic nucleus and are the prime carriers of prosodic information, studies of vowels would seem to be a natural spin-off of research in the area of prosody (see Davis and MacNeilage 1990 for a recent case study of early vowel development).

Finally, there are several areas of research that, in my view, should become topics of focus in the coming decade. First, the shift in emphasis toward phonological development of the prelinguistic and early linguistic period coincided with a marked decline in research on the older child, ages three and up. While the move to younger subjects expanded our knowledge base considerably and raised questions that will undoubtedly be pursued in the years to come, the later stages of phonological acquisition should not be neglected. We know almost nothing about later stages of acquisition in languages other than English, or about how and when children acquire the allophonic and morphophonemic patterns of their language. In the last decade, these topic has received very little attention (see MacWhinney 1978 for a summary). Second, although phonological development in bilingual children has been a topic of study for some time, much of the research has been limited to descriptive case studies done by linguistically trained parents (e.g., Major 1977). Given the current theories regarding parameter setting, it would be of interest to investigate patterns of acquisition in a child learning two languages that differ on basic phonological parameters. Last, it has been shown that infants as young as six months attend to both auditory and visual aspects of speech input (Kuhl and Meltzoff 1982). In view of this finding, research directed toward phonological acquisition in blind babies would be a natural means of examining the role of vision in early phonology (see Mulford 1989 for a review of this topic).

These suggestions for future research are diverse, targeting a range of subject populations, e.g., older children, blind babies, children raised bilingually. Successful completion of these studies will require investigators who have a good understanding not only of phonological acquisition, but also of perceptual and cognitive development, phonological theory, and experimental design, at a minimum. This brings us back to the statement by Jenkins (cited introductory paragraph) regarding the wide range of skills needed for successful research in this area in the 1980s. Obviously, this need has not diminished in the 1990s.

REFERENCES

Boysson-Bardies, B. de, Hallé, P., Sagart, L., and Durand, C. 1989. A crosslinguistic investigation of vowel formants in babbling. *Journal of Child Language* 14:211–27.

Brown, R. 1973. *A First Language.* Cambridge: Harvard University Press.

Davis, B., and MacNeilage, P. 1990. Acquisition of correct vowel production: A quantitative case study. *Journal of Speech and Hearing Research* 33:16–27.

Ferguson, C. A., and Farwell, C. 1975. Words and sounds in early language acquisition: English initial consonants in the first fifty words. *Language* 51: 419–39.

Ferguson, C. A., Peizer, D. B., and Weeks, T. E. 1973. Model-and-replica phonological grammar of a child's first words. *Lingua* 31:35–65.

Goldsmith, J. A. 1990. *Autosegmental and Metrical Phonology.* Oxford: Basil Blackwell, Ltd.

Hodson, B. 1980. *The Assessment of Phonological Processes.* Danville, IL: Interstate Press.

Ingram, D. 1981. *Procedures for the Phonological Analysis of Children's Language.* Baltimore: University Park Press.

Jenkins, J. 1980. Research in child phonology: Comments, criticism, and advice. In *Child Phonology,* Vol. 2. *Perception,* eds. G. H. Yeni-Komshian, J. F. Kavanagh, and C. A. Ferguson. New York: Academic Press.

Kuhl, P. K., and Meltzoff, A. N. 1982. The bimodal perception of speech in infancy. *Science* 218:1138–1141.

Leonard, L. B., Sabbadini, L., Volterra, V., and Leonard, J. L. 1988. Some influences on the grammar of English- and Italian-speaking children with specific language impairment. *Applied Psycholinguistics* 9:39–57.

Locke, J. 1983. *Phonological Acquisition and Change.* New York: Academic Press.

MacWhinney, B. 1978. The acquisition of morphophonology. *Monographs of the Society for Research in Child Development* 43, serial no. 174.

Major, R. 1977. Phonological differentiation of a bilingual child. *Ohio State University Working Papers in Linguistics* 22:88–122.

Menn, L. 1976. Pattern, control and contrast in beginning speech. Unpublished doctoral dissertation, University of Illinois.

Menn, L. 1978. Phonological units in beginning speech. In *Syllables and Segments,* eds. A. Bell and J. B. Hooper. Amsterdam: North Holland.

Mulford, R. 1988. First words of the blind child. In *The Emergent Lexicon,* eds. M. D. Smith and J. L. Locke. San Diego: Academic Press.

Oller, D. K. 1980. The emergence of the sounds of speech in infancy. In *Child Phonology,* Vol. 1. *Production,* eds. G. Yeni-Komshian, J. F. Kavanagh, and C. A. Ferguson. New York: Academic Press.

Schwartz, R. G. 1988. Phonological factors in early lexical acquisition. In *The Emergent Lexicon,* eds. M. D. Smith and J. L. Locke. San Diego: Academic Press.

Schwartz, R., and Leonard, L. 1982. Do children pick and choose? *Journal of Child Language* 9:319–36.

Shriberg, L., and Kwiatkowski, J. 1982. Phonological disorders III: A procedure for assessing severity of involvement. *Journal of Speech and Hearing Disorders* 47:256–70.

Smith, B. L. 1990. Elicitation of slips of the tongue from young children: A new method and preliminary observations. *Applied Psycholinguistics* 11:131–44.

Spencer, A. 1986. Towards a theory of phonological development. *Lingua* 68:3–38.

Stark, R. 1980. Stages of speech development in the first year of life. In *Child Phonology,* Vol. 1. *Production,* eds. G. Yeni-Komshian, J. Kavanagh, and C. A. Ferguson. New York: Academic Press.

Stoel-Gammon, C., and Cooper, J. 1984. Patterns of early lexical and phonological development. *Journal of Child Language* 11:247–71.

Vihman, M. M., Ferguson, C. A., and Elbert, M. 1986. Phonological development from babbling to speech: Common tendencies and individual differences. *Applied Psycholinguistics* 7:3–40.

Yeni-Komshian, G., Kavanagh, J. F., and Ferguson, C. A. (eds.) 1980. *Child Phonology,* Volume 1: *Production,* Volume 2: *Perception.* New York: Academic Press.

Current Research

Chapter • 9

Infant Speech Perception and Phonological Acquisition

Janet F. Werker and Judith E. Pegg

The story that has emerged from our laboratory over the past ten years has been summarized in previous papers (Werker 1989; Werker 1991). We have provided confirmatory evidence in support of four main points:

1. Young infants can discriminate nearly every phonetic contrast on which they have been tested–including those that do not occur in their language-learning environment (Aslin et al. 1981; Best, McRoberts, and Sithole 1988; Eimas 1975; Lasky, Syrdal-Lasky, and Klein 1975; Streeter 1976; Trehub 1976; Werker et al. 1981; Werker and Tees 1984a; Werker and Lalonde 1988; but see Eilers, Wilson, and Moore 1979; and Eilers, Gavin, and Oller 1982 for contradictory findings).

2. There is a profound change across age in the ease with which people discriminate some non-native contrasts (MacKain, Best, and Strange 1981; Lisker and Abramson 1970; Polka 1991; Trehub 1976; Werker et al. 1981; Werker and Tees 1984a; Werker and Lalonde 1988), although this developmental change does not apply to every non-native contrast (Best, McRoberts, and Sithole 1988; Polka in press; Strange 1986; Werker et al. 1981).

3. This developmental change is evident within the first year of life (Best and McRoberts 1989; Werker and Tees 1984b; Werker and Lalonde 1988).

4. The change involves a reorganization in perceptual biases rather than a loss of initial auditory capabilities (Werker and Tees 1984a; Werker and Logan 1985).

In an early experiment we compared English-learning infants aged 6 to 8 months, English-speaking adults, and Hindi-speaking adults on their ability to discriminate two non-English Hindi contrasts: a place-of-articulation distinction between retroflex and dental voiceless stop consonants, /ṭa/–/t̪a/ and a voicing distinction between voiceless aspi-rated and breathy voiced dental stops, /tʰa/–/dʰa/. All stimuli were pro-duced by a native Hindi speaker. Subjects were tested in a category change procedure involving a head turn response for infants and a but-ton press for adults. Results revealed that the 6- to 8-month-old English-learning infants and the Hindi-speaking adults could discrimi-nate both Hindi contrasts, but the English-speaking adults had diffi-culty particularly with the retroflex/dental place-of-articulation distinc-tion (Werker et al. 1981). This finding was replicated using the Interior Salish, Nthlakapmx (or Thompson[1]) glottalized velar/uvular contrast, /ḱi/–/q́i/ (Werker and Tees 1984a). Both studies provided evidence of broad based phonetic discrimination abilities in young infants, and evi-dence of language-specific tuning in adults.

Even in the initial report it was evident that for adults some non-native distinctions are perceptually more difficult than others. Without any training, 4 out of 10 English-speaking adults were able to discrimi-nate the Hindi voicing contrast, /tʰa/–/dʰa/, whereas only 1 out of 10 English-speaking adults reached discrimination criterion on the retro-flex/dental place-of-articulation contrast, /ṭa/–/t̪a/. Twenty-five training trials improved the performance of 7 out of 10 adults on the voicing contrast, but had no measurable effect on the retroflex/dental distinc-tion (Werker et al. 1981).

In an attempt to ascertain when in development the reorganiza-tion in non-native sensitivities might be apparent, we tested English-speaking children ages 12, 8, and 4 and found they perform as poorly as English-speaking adults on the Hindi non-English contrasts (Werker and Tees 1983). This indicated that the reorganization occurs before age 4. In fact, we found that the reorganization is evident by 10 to 12 months of age.

Evidence for a developmental change by 10 to 12 months of age was provided in a series of cross-sectional and longitudinal studies with infants. In the first study, English-learning infants aged 6 to 8, 8 to

---

[1]In our early work we referred to this Interior Salish language as Thompson because that is the name given it in the literature. However, the correct (native) name for the language is Nthlakapmx.

10, and 10 to 12 months were compared on their ability to discriminate the Hindi retroflex/dental and the Nthlakapmx (or Thompson), glottalized velar/uvular contrasts (Werker and Tees 1984a). Almost all of the infants aged 6 to 8 months could discriminate both non-English contrasts, but among the infants aged 10 to 12 months, only 2 out of 10 could discriminate the retroflex/dental contrast, and only 1 out of 10 the velar/uvular. These results were replicated in the same procedure using synthetically produced voiced retroflex/dental stimuli (Werker and Lalonde 1988). Best and McRoberts have also replicated this finding for the /ki/–/qi/ contrast by testing infants in a habituation/ dishabituation looking procedure rather than in a head turn task (Best and McRoberts 1989). Taken together, these replications provide strong confirmation of a developmental reorganization in non-native speech perception within the first year of life.

DEVELOPMENTAL CHANGES IN SPEECH PERCEPTION DO NOT INVOLVE LOSS

As noted in the previous section, English-speaking adults have difficulty discriminating the Hindi retroflex/dental contrast. We have shown, however, that English-speaking adults can discriminate this non-native contrast if tested in a sensitive enough procedure (Werker and Tees 1984a; Werker and Logan 1985; Morosan and Werker, in preparation). In fact, adult listeners can use one of three different processing strategies—phonemic, phonetic, or acoustic—depending on testing conditions.

Evidence of three different processing strategies was provided in several studies (see also Mann 1986). In one study we showed that performance on the retroflex/dental contrast varies as a function of both interstimulus interval (ISI) and number of testing trials (Werker and Logan 1985). When tested with an ISI over 500 msec, subjects appeared to use a phonemic processing strategy and were unable to discriminate the non-native contrast. At shorter ISIs, subjects showed evidence of using both a phonetic and an acoustic strategy. Evidence for a phonetic strategy was provided by subjects who could discriminate retroflex from dental exemplars, but could not discriminate among the several exemplars within either phonetic category. Evidence of acoustic processing was provided by subjects who could discriminate between the several retroflex or the several dental exemplars. By the fifth block of 80 trials, subjects in all ISI conditions were showing evidence of acoustic processing. These findings indicate that adult listeners can discriminate between tokens on the basis of phonetic and acoustic information if the task requires it. The most readily available strategy, however, is to perceive speech stimuli in terms of native-language phonemic categories.

This pattern of results has been replicated using a new contextual manipulation, and using the synthetic tokens from the Werker and Lalonde (1988) study rather than the natural tokens from our earlier work (e.g., Werker et al. 1981). The synthetic tokens were used to ensure that the acoustic variability within categories was equivalent to that between categories. The contextual manipulation involved varying the kinds of pairings used in the stimulus set. In the first contextual condition, there were four kinds of pairings: phonemically different (bilabial/dental), phonetically different (retroflex/dental), acoustically different (two different bilabial, dental, or retroflex stimuli), and physically identical (the same token paired with itself). The results from an analysis of the proportion "Different" responses indicated that, in this first condition, English listeners could easily discriminate the phonemically different (English bilabial/dental) pairings, but did quite poorly on all other pairing types. However, the results from an A' analysis (which corrects for false alarms[2]) indicated that English listeners also discriminated the phonetically different pairings significantly better than chance. Thus, in this first contextual condition, there was evidence of both phonemic and phonetic processing.

In the second contextual condition, the phonemically different pairings were eliminated. Results from the proportion "Different" analysis indicated that in this second condition subjects responded "Different" significantly more often to the phonetically different and the acoustically different pairings. However, the results from the A' analysis indicated that this was entirely accounted for by an increase in false alarm rate as the A' values were not significantly greater than chance for either the phonetically or acoustically different pairings.

In the third contextual condition, only within phonetic category and physically identical pairings were presented. There was a (nonsignificant) increase in the proportion "Different" responses to the acoustically different pairings. Moreover the A' analysis also indicated a slight (but nonsignificant) improvement in A' scores to the acoustically different pairings in this contextual condition (Morosan and Werker, in preparation).

Taken together, the results from the three contextual conditions are consistent with our previous finding that adults can use at least three different processing strategies depending upon testing condition. Again, there was evidence that phonemic processing is privileged, but even stronger evidence that phonetic processing is more

---

[2]False alarm rate is obtained by noting the proportion of "Different" responses to physically identical pairings.

privileged than acoustic. In reminder, phonemic and phonetic processing were evident in the first contextual condition, indicating that the
presence of a functional phonemic contrast facilitates linguistic processing in general, thus, elevating performance on the phonetically different pairings. Performance on the phonetically different pairings fell
to the level of performance on the acoustically different pairings in the
second contextual condition, and there was only marginal improvement on the acoustically different pairings in the third condition.

The evidence of three different processing strategies is just one example of research illustrating that the developmental change in cross-
language speech perception involves a reorganization of initial sensitivities and not a loss in auditory sensitivities. Studies showing that
adults can be trained to discriminate nearly any non-native contrast
(Logan, Lively, and Pisoni 1991; MacKain, Best, and Strange 1981; Morosan and Jamieson 1989; Pisoni et al. 1982; Tees and Werker 1984) made
it clear that the developmental change is not irreversible. Studies showing that adults can discriminate the acoustic cues differentiating non-
native contrasts even without training (Werker and Tees 1984b) show
that this sensitivity is maintained, making it unlikely that the developmental change in cross-language speech perception results from an absolute loss in auditory sensitivities.

Our work with 4-, 8-, and 12-year-old children also led us to suspect
that the reorganization in cross-language speech perception might be
explained more adequately by considering something other than loss.
English-speaking children of all three ages had difficulty discriminating both the retroflex/dental and the voiceless aspirated/breathy voiced
Hindi contrasts. However, the 4-year-olds had the greatest difficulty.
Whereas 30% to 40% of English-speaking adults and older children
could discriminate the Hindi voicing contrast /tʰa/–/dʰa/ with no training, none of the 4-year-old children could (Werker and Tees 1983). In
addition, our earlier work showed that nearly all 6- to 8-month-old infants can discriminate this contrast. This data pattern is perplexing if
one believes that it is due to a loss in auditory sensitivities. The only
conclusion that is possible with an auditory loss explanation is that
4-year-olds are somehow less able than both younger and older children to hear some non-native phonetic differences. Because this is
clearly unlikely, we began to consider alternative explanations.

One possible explanation is that by 4 years of age the child will
have structured some phonological rules, and may be following them
quite rigidly. Older children and adults have the flexibility to switch
between phonologically based performance and alternative processing
strategies (acoustic, phonetic) when required by task conditions. Young
children, however, may lack this flexibility, and instead adhere strictly
to a phonemic processing strategy. This would preclude discrimination

of even acoustically salient non-native contrasts, such as /tʰa/–/dʰa/. Although this hypothesis requires further empirical verification, it led us to consider the influence of phonology on phonetic perception both in childhood and throughout the rest of the life span. Other researchers have also begun to argue that developmental changes in phonetic perception may be related to phonology (Best, McRoberts, and Sithole 1988; Burnham 1986; MacKain 1988; Strange 1986). Before focusing on the possible influence of phonology, however, we would like to consider other types of mechanisms that might help explain the developmental changes we have identified.

UNDERSTANDING THE DEVELOPMENTAL REORGANIZATION

Several possible models for understanding developmental changes in cross-language speech perception have been proposed in the literature. These mechanisms include (1) perceptual tuning (e.g., Aslin and Pisoni 1980), (2) modular recalibration (Mattingly and Liberman 1989), (3) articulatory mediation (e.g., Vihman this volume; Locke 1991), (4) self-organization and, (5) cognitive mediation (e.g., Lalonde 1989; McCune this volume). In this section we briefly outline each model and the mechanism that is proposed to explain developmental changes in speech perception. We then comment on the ability of each of these models to account for the data.[3]

Perceptual Tuning

In 1976 Gottlieb outlined five different roles experience can play in the development of any perceptual system. These include: no effect (maturation), maintenance/loss, facilitation, attunement, and induction. This inclusive model served to organize and direct work in perceptual development in a number of fields, including our own work in cross-language speech perception (Werker 1989).[4]

The results from early work in cross-language speech perception were interpreted as suggesting that maintenance of the auditory ability

---

[3]In an earlier paper (Werker 1991) we presented a preliminary outline of these possibilities. In that paper, self-organization was not presented and phonological acquisition was considered along with the other alternatives. Because this chapter focuses on the relationship between speech perception and phonology, phonological processes are considered in a separate section in this paper.

[4]Also see Aslin and Pisoni 1981 and Gottlieb 1981 for an elaboration of how this model applies to speech perception.

to discriminate non-native contrasts required experience in hearing those particular phones. The change between infancy and adulthood in the ability to discriminate non-native contrasts was attributed to a lack of relevant listening experience. The evidence reviewed above, showing that adults can (under some testing conditions) discriminate non-native contrasts, has made it clear, however, that the maintenance/ loss explanation must be supplemented. Research showing that lack of listening experience does not necessarily lead to loss challenges this explanation. In illustration, Best and colleagues have shown that English-learning infants and adults can maintain the ability to discriminate non-English (Zulu) click contrasts even without any listening experience (Best, McRoberts, and Sithole 1988).

These results suggest that if a maintenance/loss process is occurring, it operates at a linguistic rather than auditory level. Because maintenance at a linguistic level may require a different kind of explanation than maintenance of auditory sensitivities, it may be useful to consider the other possibilities presented below.

Modular Recalibration

It has also been suggested that age-related changes in cross-language speech perception can be explained directly by a resetting of the parameters in the phonetic module (Mattingly and Liberman 1989). According to this interpretation, the initial broad-based phonetic sensitivities represent the default option in the phonetic module. At some point in development, this module becomes sensitive to the effects of linguistic experience, and can be reset directly in accordance with the phonetic parameters that have functional significance in the child's language environment. To use an analogy, phonetic sensitivities in the developing child are seen to be recalibrated in much the same way that sound localization is recalibrated as the head grows. According to this line of reasoning, the developmental change in discrimination of non-native contrasts results from a direct resetting of the initial phonetic sensitivities to reflect the parameters of the linguistic environment.

Two important characteristics of the modular recalibration view serve to distinguish it from the perceptual tuning alternative: first, that speech perception cannot be understood by general purpose auditory mechanisms, and second, that the phonetic module is impenetrable to the influence of other systems. Because the system is modular, phonetic sensitivities change without cognitive mediation. Nevertheless the "output" of the phonetic module can be acted on by other developing systems, making it possible that cognition, or some other mechanism, can influence the use of changing phonetic sensitivities.

Articulatory Mediation

One hypothesis for which there is increasing support is that the reorganization in cross-language speech perception is mediated by the child's emerging productive abilities (Locke 1991; Vihman and Miller 1988; Vihman this volume). According to this interpretation, perception is filtered through intentional production. The characteristics of babbling at 10 months include the ability to produce nonreduplicated and intentional CV and CVC utterances (Kent this volume; Oller this volume; Stark 1980). This developing articulatory control provides a sensorimotor mechanism through which ambient speech can be filtered. For this hypothesis to be considered viable, we would expect to see some evidence of language specific influences on babbling by 10 to 12 months of age—the age at which the reorganization in cross-language speech perception is first apparent.

Until recently, most of the research in early vocal development indicated a high degree of regularity across languages in the repertoire of sounds produced in babbling, with little evidence of language-specific influence until after the acquisition of the first word (see Locke 1983). There is now evidence that the child's babbling repertoire may show the influence of the ambient language environment by as early as 10 months of age (Boysson-Bardies, Sagart, and Durand 1984) both for vowels (Boysson-Bardies et al. 1989) and for global features of consonants (Boysson-Bardies et al. this volume). These data increase the likelihood that developmental changes in babbling and in cross-language speech perception are related in some way. It is not yet known whether the sensorimotor filter explanation is feasible, or whether the relationship is merely correlational. A challenge for further research is to attempt to specify the nature of this relationship.

Self-Organizing Systems

It is also possible that the reorganization in cross-language speech perception is the result of the dynamics of self-organizing systems (e.g., Lindblom and Engstrand 1989; Fogel and Thelen 1987). While this alternative has not yet been developed with respect to our data, it has been considered with respect to phonological development (Lindblom, MacNeilage, and Studdert-Kennedy 1983). According to our understanding of how this mechanism might apply to the case at hand, the interactions between the properties of the child's initial auditory/phonetic space and the input from the linguistic environment would be expected to yield a highly predictable set of changes in phonetic perception culminating in the appearance of language-specific phonetic sensitivities. In other words, language-specific phonetic sensitivities would be an emergent property. If all the factors contributing to the reorganization in phonetic sensitivities were identified, it should be possible to explain why the reorganization occurs around 10 to 12 months of age rather than some other point in development. The focus in this approach would be to identify each of the many contributing factors and to trace their development. The interactions between the developmental trajectories of each factor should result in a coalescence of overall change toward the 10 to 12 month time period for phonetic reorganization.

According to this view, there is no single causal mechanism accounting for the developmental reorganization in cross-language speech perception. The final maturing factor is seen as the "rate limiting" factor because it is only after it has reached a criterial level of functioning that the emergent reorganization will be evident. Nevertheless, each of the several related factors is viewed as contributing to the emergence of the reorganization.

Cognitive Recategorization

Finally, it has been suggested that the reorganization in cross-language speech perception could be brought about through the application of general developing cognitive abilities to the phonetic domain (Lalonde 1989; Lalonde and Werker in revision; McCune this volume). According to this line of reasoning, the reorganization in cross-language speech perception is an instance of an initial, biologically based categorization ability coming under the mediation of cognitive control in such a way that initial perceptual categories are reorganized to map onto those categories that have either functional significance or occur with some kind of systematic regularity in the baby's language learning environment. Although several models of speech perception follow a general cognitive approach (e.g., Jusczyk this volume), our specific concern is with developmental changes in cognition that occur at around 10 to 12 months of age. Thus, we focus on cognitive changes that occur during this developmental period (see also McCune this volume).

At around 8 to 10 months of age many important changes occur in the young infant's cognitive abilities. Lalonde (1989) has argued that many of these changing abilities, including the developmental reorganization in cross-language speech perception, require similar underlying cognitive abilities: specifically, the ability to coordinate present information with previously experienced information, and to implement this coordination in the service of a particular "action" or "goal." In an initial test of this hypothesis, we (Lalonde 1989; Lalonde and Werker in revision) recently completed a study comparing the developmental emergence of three skills. Forty infants (19 male and 21 female) aged approximately 9 months (range 8.25 to 10.09) were tested on three tasks: object search, visual categorization, and non-native speech perception. In the object search (AB) task the infant is required to search for an object hidden at a new location, after successfully searching at the first location (Piaget 1952). In our implementation of this task, a 3-second delay precedes the second search (Diamond 1985). The visual categorization task requires the infant to form perceptual categories based on the correlation of visual features in two-dimensional novel animals (Younger and Cohen 1983). The speech perception task involves asking infants to discriminate the Hindi retroflex/dental contrast used in our previous work. These three tasks were chosen because performance on all three changes in robust and replicable ways at around 8 to 10 months of age. As mentioned above, it can be argued that all demand a similar underlying prerequisite coordination ability.

The results of this study are provocative and suggest a developmental dependence among the three tasks. As shown in figure 1, of the 14 infants who passed the object search task, 9 also passed both the visual categorization and the speech perception tasks (note that *passing* the speech perception task means *failing* to discriminate the non-native contrast). Of the 14 infants who failed the object search task, 8 also failed both other tasks. Chi-square analyses suggest a stronger dependence between the speech perception and the object search task than between the speech perception and visual categorization task. A Prediction Analysis, however, indicates that the "best" model is one in which all three tasks are linked developmentally. It is important to note that this dependency maintains even when age is partialled out. These data are consistent with the possibility that the reorganization in cross-language speech perception is related to, if not dependent on, emerging cognitive abilities.

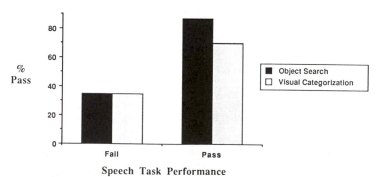

Figure 1. Proportion of subjects passing the AB and the visual categorization task as a function of performance on the cross-language speech perception task.

Summary of the First Five Models

Each of the preceding alternatives provides a framework for explaining the developmental reorganization in cross-language speech perception. We would argue, however, that individually, none is sufficient to account for the data. A truly adequate explanation needs, at the very least, to account for all of the following:

1. why the developmental change occurs by 10 to 12 months of age,
2. why the reorganization conforms to native-language phonemic categories, and
3. why adults are able to use different processing strategies (phonemic, phonetic, and acoustic) depending upon task conditions.

The first two models, perceptual tuning and modular recalibration, can account for the adherence to native-language phonemic categories, but fail to explain both the timing of the reorganization in infancy and the continued availability of different processing capabilities in adults. The articulatory mediation and self-organization models, on the other hand, may address the issues of timing and language specificity, but cannot provide an explanation of how and why an adult listener might adopt one or another processing strategy under different testing conditions.

The cognitive explanation also can easily address the issue of timing and language specificity, but in its present form, cannot fully explain continued adult competence. That is, this model would suggest that by 10 to 12 months of age the infant has the cognitive capabilities to reconstruct initial categories on the basis of the statistical distribution of variability in the input. We know from other work on the development of categorization skills that as children develop they become increasingly flexible in their ability to categorize information at different levels. It is, thus, possible that the continued development of cognitive categorization skills would result in a listener who could apply phonetic, phonemic, or even acoustic strategies for categorizing speech sounds. However, empirical work has not yet been done comparing the ontogeny of flexible categorization strategies in general to the specific application of these strategies in speech perception. Because no one mechanism outlined above can adequately explain all aspects of the data, we move to a consideration of the influence of phonological influences and processes.

Finally, we would suggest that these five models also make assumptions about the kind of input that could influence speech perception abilities. The perceptual tuning, self-organizing, and cognitive models all assume that it is the statistical distribution of variability in the input that is important for development change. On the other hand, both the modular recalibration and articulatory mediation alternatives require linguistically relevant input. In the case of modular re-calibration, the system is seen to be sensitive to not just any acoustic variability, but specifically to the phonetic variability in the input. In the case of articulatory mediation, it is self-produced articulations that function to modify perceptual/phonetic categories. It remains to be seen whether general acoustic or specifically linguistic input is primarily responsible for developmental change. However, because we cannot yet adequately quantify acoustic variability, but can systematically study phonological regularities in the input, it is at this level of analysis that consideration has to begin.

EVIDENCE FOR PHONOLOGICAL PROCESSES

The finding that infants of 10 to 12 months of age only discriminate phonemically relevant phonetic contrasts clearly illustrates the strong influence of native language input. In previous work we argued that this reorganization may only be possible if the infant has a rudimentary phonological system (Werker 1989; Werker 1991; Werker and Lalonde 1988). There is considerable evidence, however, that a phonological system is constructed only gradually across the first several years of life (Ferguson 1986; Ingram 1986, this volume; Menyuk, Menn, and Silber 1986; Stoel-Gammon 1985). Thus, it is possible that the infant 10 to 12 months old may not yet have even a rudimentary phonological system. Nevertheless, we would argue that the reorganization in phonetic sensitivity evident by the end of the first year of life serves as the foundation for the eventual acquisition of a phonological system. If this is the case, one would expect there to be evidence that developmental changes in phonetic sensitivity are intimately related to phonology. This suggestion is strengthened by recent experiments with young infants.

The work of Best and her colleagues provides one source of evidence. English-learning infants aged 6 to 8, 8 to 10, and 12 to 14 months were compared to English-speaking adults and Zulu-speaking adults on their ability to discriminate a voiceless unaspirated lateral versus apical Zulu click contrast, /ʇ/ /ʖ/ (Best et al. 1988). This contrast was used because the sounds are strikingly dissimilar from any phone in the English inventory and English-learning infants are unlikely to have heard them. In contrast to our results, subjects of all ages (including adult English speakers) evidenced the ability to discriminate the Zulu click contrast. These results led Best et al. to conclude that the absence of listening experience will not necessarily lead to a developmental reorganization in the ability to discriminate a contrast (see also MacKain 1988). They speculate that a reorganization in cross-language speech perception may only be evident if the non-native stimuli resemble native phones and can, thus, be assimilated to native-language phonological categories (see Flege 1987 and Wode 1977 for discussions of this issue in speech production). The fact that the Hindi retroflex/dental contrast is difficult for English listeners to discriminate may, therefore, be due to its assimilability to English alveolar consonants.

This interpretation was quite exciting, but a direct comparison of Best's results with our previous findings was necessary before it could be seriously considered. Because Best and her colleagues used a different testing procedure (habituation/dishabituation), it was possible that infants were discriminating the Zulu click contrast not because of its phonological status, but because it might be easier to reveal discriminatory capabilities in a habituation procedure. To address this possibility, Best and McRoberts (1989) compared English-learning infants aged 6 to 8 and 12 to 14 months of age on their ability to discriminate both the Zulu click contrast and the Nthlakapmx (Thompson) glottalized velar/uvular contrast /k̓i/–/q̓i/ used in our previous work (Werker and Tees 1984a). Results were as predicted. The 6- to 8-month-old infants could discriminate both non-English contrasts. As in our previous work, the 12- to 14-month-old English-learning infants no longer discriminated the velar/uvular distinction, but, consistent with Best's previous findings, they were able to discriminate the Zulu click contrast (see figure 2). Thus, discriminability may depend on the extent to which the contrast in question is assimilable within the subjects' native phonology.

In a further test of the hypothesis that phonetic reorganization is influenced by phonological status, Best (1989) tested infants of 6 to 8 and 10 to 12 months of age on three additional Zulu contrasts. These contrasts include phones that are assimilable to English phonetic categories, and should, thus, be likely candidates to reveal evidence of a reorganization in phonetic sensitivity by 10 to 12 months of age. Preliminary data are consistent with this prediction, and indicate that a developmental change in sensitivity to these contrasts occurs between 6 and 12 months of age. These results show why it is important to consider the kind of experience infants have had when attempting to understand developmental changes in speech perception (see MacKain 1982, 1988 for further discussion). It is not simply the case that auditory experience maintains sensitivity and lack thereof leads to loss; rather it seems that only linguistically relevant input (or lack thereof) influences speech perception. Although this does not require that infants are guided by an internal phonological system, it does indicate that infants are sensitive to the phonological regularities of the ambient language.

Further support for the suggestion that the developmental changes in linguistic/perceptual sensitivity evident by 10 to 12 months of age serve as the foundation for the eventual acquisition of a phonological

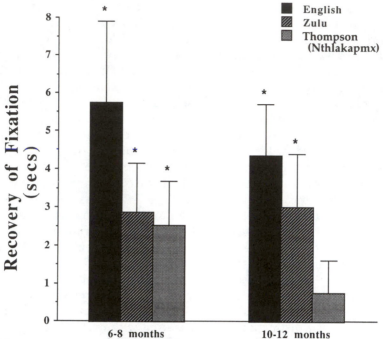

Figure 2. Discrimination scores for the two age groups of infants on the control English contrast, the Zulu click contrast, and the Nthlakapmx (Thompson) ejective contrast. (Reprinted with permission from Best and McRoberts 1989).

system comes from work by Jusczyk and his colleagues. Jusczyk, Friederici, and Wessels (in preparation) compared English-learning infants aged 6 and 9 months on their preference for two lists of low-frequency abstract words. One list contained words that conformed to English phonological rules and one contained words that conformed to Dutch phonological rules. The younger infants were equally interested in both sets of words, but the 9-month-old infants showed a clear preference for English over Dutch words. When the phonetic information was removed by low-pass filtering, the preference for English stimuli disappeared, confirming that there were no significant prosodic cues contributing to the preference. In a final manipulation, Jusczyk, Friederici, and Wessels ran a control study in which all the stimuli containing non-English phones were removed so that the only remaining differences between the English and the Dutch words were phonotactic. As before, English-learning infants 9 months of age showed a clear preference for the English words. Taken together, these results provide strong evidence that infants are influenced by native-language phonological regularities before 10 months of age.[5]

It should be noted that the language environment may exert an influence on the more global aspects of language perception at even earlier ages. For example, Jusczyk and colleagues have also tested English-learning infants on their preference for English versus Norwegian low frequency abstract words. The English/Norwegian comparison represents an important extension of the English/Dutch data because unlike English and Dutch, English and Norwegian have substantial prosodic differences. English-learning infants as young as 6 months of age showed a preference for the English words, presumably because the large prosodic differences between Norwegian and English provided more global cues on which to base their preference (Jusczyk this volume).

There is also some indication that infants show a preference for speech samples with periods of silence inserted at native (rather than non-native) clausal boundaries by 6 months of age (Hirsh-Pasek et al. 1987). Infants show a similar sensitivity for native phrasal boundaries by as early as 9 months of age (Jusczyk 1989), but not to word boundaries until about 11 months of age (Kemler Nelson 1989). Perhaps most surprising is the finding that infants show a preference for speech samples of their native language within days after birth (Mehler et al. 1988).

The research reviewed above reveals that infants' perceptual biases are influenced by the ambient language environment, beginning at birth with the most global aspects of speech and progressing to the syllabic (and potentially the segmental) level by 10 to 12 months of age. Although some of the infancy data reviewed above could be explained by perceptual tuning of one kind or another, with no need to resort to specifically linguistic factors, a formidable stumbling block to this interpretation is posed by the work of Best et al. showing that lack of listening experience does not lead to a reorganization when the contrasts cannot be mapped onto native speech sounds. Thus it must be concluded that infants have a bias to being influenced by structured linguistic input—a bias that could provide a foundation for phonology. The research involving older children and adults clearly indicates that internal phonological processes guide perception at some time after the infancy period. We are now interested in trying to understand the relationship between the sensitivity to phonological regularity during infancy and the eventual construction of a phonological system during early childhood.

---

[5]The question of whether infants make use of featural information (as implied by the term *phonetic*) or syllabic information is still unresolved. Infants may use both kinds of information to process language, use syllabic phonological rules before segmental phonological rules, or rely on other contextual cues. On the basis of the numerous experiments with young infants, however, we must assume that featural information is among the infants' repertoire (see Kuhl 1979, 1983 for corroborative evidence).

Current Infant Research

We have recently undertaken a research program investigating the actual use to which young infants put their changing perceptual sensitivities. We began by asking how words are represented in the infant's receptive lexicon. Our reasoning was that if developmental changes in perceptual sensitivity are related to the acquisition of a phonological system, there should be some evidence that infants use their new-found perceptual categories for segmenting and representing meaningful aspects of speech. In other words, the perceptual reorganization should have predictable effects on the structure of a receptive vocabulary.

The strongest evidence for the functional (phonological) use of perceptual categories would be provided if it could be shown that infants differentiate real words on the basis of minimal pair contrasts. Although the current zeitgeist favours a holistic representation, with the syllable or the overall word shape being the primary unit of analysis (Ferguson and Farwell 1975; Ferguson 1986; Jusczyk this volume; Mehler, Dupoux, and Segui 1990), we feel the strong alternative hypothesis should be fully tested before it is dismissed (see also Ingram this volume). By 2½ years of age children know, and can reliably discriminate some minimal pairs of words (Barton 1980; Oller and Eilers 1983; Strange and Broen 1980). Although there is little or no evidence that any of the words in the receptive lexicon of children younger than this age are represented in terms of minimal pair contrasts, it should be possible to chart the developmental emergence of this ability.

We decided to investigate this question by testing children between 12 and 20 months of age by looking at their ability to discriminate minimal pair nonsense words and known real words. If the child understands the word "dog," and is asked to find a "bog," will that child treat "bog" as an instance of the word "dog" or as something different? We reasoned that children who treat "bog" as nonequivalent to "dog," must, at the very least, include the difference between a bilabial and alveolar consonant in their lexical representation of "dog." Such results would be clear and interpretable. The difficulty is that if the child treats "bog" as equivalent to "dog," we don't know why. It could be that the child's lexical representation is simply not sufficiently detailed. On the other hand, it could be that the child can hear the difference but does not consider it critical, or even that the child suspects the object "dog" can have two names[6] (as a dog named Bog). We have run a number of different experiments to try to make these possibilities unequivocal.

---

[6]Considerable interest revolves around the question of whether young children use *mutual exclusivity* biases in early word learning (Markman 1991).

In our first series of experiments we tested children 14 to 16 and 18 to 20 months of age in a modified version of a two-choice looking procedure (see Golinkoff et al. 1987). In this procedure, children were seated in front of two television monitors, each showing a picture of a different moving object, while a recorded voice said "Where's the X? Find the X." The object on one of the monitors matched the label, while the object on the other did not. In a pretest session, subjects were tested on three pairs of phonetically dissimilar real words, all reported to be within the receptive vocabulary of an average 18-month-old and all reported to be understood by the children who participated. Following this pretest, infants were presented with five known words and five corresponding minimal pair nonsense words. One of the visual displays used on each trial matched the real-word referent, and the other was selected to be an equally interesting, but unnamed object. It was held that if the representation of real words in the receptive lexicon is sufficiently specified, subjects would look longer at the familiar object when the correct label was used than when the minimal pair nonsense word was used.

All subjects were tested first in the real-word condition to make sure they could (and would) perform the task, and were then tested in the word/nonsense word experimental condition. In both conditions, the side with the correct answer was counterbalanced across trials and across subjects, and each visual stimulus served as its own control to eliminate a possible visual preference confound. Unfortunately, although subjects in both age groups looked significantly longer at the matching video displays in the pretest real-word condition, their performance in the word/nonsense word testing condition was virtually equivalent to chance, making the data uninterpretable. The children looked equally long at both the known object and the novel object regardless of whether the acoustic stimulus was the real-word referent or the minimal pair nonsense word.

As outlined above, negative findings are hard to evaluate in this study. To rule out the possibility that the confusion resulted from phonetic similarity, we ran a control study with real and nonsense words, but used phonetically less similar nonsense words. Again, the results were uninterpretable, with subjects looking at each display about 50% of the time regardless of the label given. They did this in spite of the fact that they could clearly perform in this procedure when tested on pairs of real words and displays of known objects. Thus, we concluded that the demand characteristics of a two-choice procedure might be too difficult for addressing this particular question.

Pollock and Schwartz (1990) also used a similar procedure to investigate the detail of representation in children's early receptive lexicon. Instead of studying minimal pairs, however, Pollock and Schwartz manipulated the amount of information present by testing real words and nonsense words missing either the first phone, the final phone, or vowel, and so forth. Two experiments were reported. In the first experiment, there was some indication that children aged 18 to 20 months would treat various incomplete renditions of "dog" as correct, however this pattern was not obtained in the second experiment. For this reason, Pollock and Schwartz also conclude it is difficult to extract meaningful information from children of this age using a two-choice procedure with real- and nonsense-word stimuli.

More recently, we have been testing children in a procedure with simpler demand characteristics. In this procedure, children are shown only a single picture.[7] All children are first presented with a training trial in which a picture of a boat accompanied by the word *boat* in several different carrier phrases is presented. This is followed by four testing trials in which the child is shown a picture of a dog, accompanied by one of four target syllables in carrier phrases. On one trial the target word matches the picture. The other three trials include a minimal pair nonsense word ("bog"), a phonetically dissimilar nonsense word ("luf"), and a phonetically dissimilar real word ("car"). The order of presentation of the four subsequent trials is counterbalanced across children. In this procedure children need not choose between a matching and a novel object; they simply choose to either look or not look at the object being displayed.

The results to date are encouraging. Children over 19 months of age looked longest at the object when the matching word was presented, and significantly less in all other conditions. This indicates that they are sensitive to incorrect versus correct pronunciations of known words. Children under 19 months of age, however, show no evidence of different looking times in the expected directions (Werker and Baldwin 1991).

Although we are excited by the data from our 19-month-old subjects, we feel caution is warranted when interpreting this first result and we are currently rerunning the study with a larger sample of 18- and 19-month-old children. It is important to note that although we might have evidence for the beginnings of access to segmental information by 19 months of age, there is as yet no reliable evidence that younger children can respond to words on the basis of such fine detail. Even if the above results with 19-month-olds are replicated, further research is required to identify the factors that allow for the transformation between the infant of 10 to 12 months and the infant of 19 months of age. To facilitate this endeavor, we now propose a model of speech per-

---

[7]This procedure was suggested by Richard Aslin.

ception that differs slightly from our own past descriptions. Specifically, we now believe it is misleading to use the label *phonemic* to characterize the speech perception performance of infants aged 10 to 12
months, and instead we propose another term. This results in a four-
factor model of speech perception.

A FOUR FACTOR MODEL OF SPEECH PERCEPTION

As reviewed in the previous section, the developmental change in
cross-language speech perception during infancy may show that the
infant has a special sensitivity to the phonological structure of the
adult input. The resulting perceptual categories that are in place by 10
to 12 months of age may serve as the initial building blocks for the construction of a phonological system. We also made it clear, however, that
the reorganization evident by this age does not presuppose even a
rudimentary phonological system. Rather, the developmental change
may reflect only one of many variables that underlie the eventual construction of a phonology. Thus, we conclude that it is inappropriate to
characterize the modifications in infant speech perception evident by
10 to 12 months as phonemically mediated. Nevertheless, speech perception *is* different in infants aged 10 to 12 months than it is in infants
aged 6 months, and probably different again sometime after 19 months
of age, and the status of these abilities remains unaccounted for in the
speech perception models we have discussed. In this section we examine the implications of this finding for our previously proposed three
factor model of speech perception.

In the past we proposed a three factor model of human speech
perception including acoustic, phonetic, and phonemic factors (Werker
and Logan 1985). This model was extrapolated from the results obtained from speech perception experiments with adults, and then
used to characterize infant speech perception. Following this line of
reasoning, it seemed logical to attribute the emergence of phonemic
processing to the developmental change evident by 10 months of age.
As argued above, it may be presumptuous to credit infants this young
with phonemic processing.

We now suggest that there are at least *four* factors that have to be
considered to understand fully the data reviewed above (see figure 3).
These factors can be tentatively labeled acoustic, broad-based phonetic, language-specific phonetic, and phonemic. Previously, we defined
acoustic as the ability to discriminate the non-phonetic variability that
occurs even within phonetic categories; *phonetic* as a sensitivity to phonetic differences that have functional (phonemic) status in some language other than the native language; and *phonemic* as the privileged

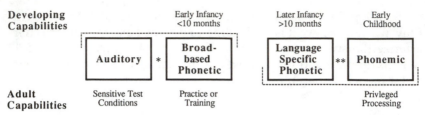

Figure 3. The four factors hypothesized to be relevant to understanding cross-language speech perception. (*Confirmatory evidence lacking for the independence of these two factors in adult speech perception. **Confirmatory evidence lacking for the independence of these two factors in adult speech perception.)

sensitivity to those phonetic contrasts that have functional significance within the native language.

We now advocate replacing the term *phonetic* with two terms. The first, *broad-based phonetic,* would describe more accurately the sensitivity shown by young infants from many different language environments to a broad range of phonetic contrasts. As previously stated, we would argue now also that it is misleading to use the term *phonemic* to refer to the changes in sensitivity evident by the end of the first year of life, and, thus, recommend the use of a second phonetic term— *language-specific phonetic*—to describe the decrease in sensitivity to nonfamiliar versus familiar phonetic contrasts evident by 10 to 12 months. This term captures the influence of native-language phonology on phonetic perception, but stops short of attributing even a rudimentary phonological system to the infant. Finally, hereafter our use of the term *phonemic* will be restricted to refer only to the perception of linguistically meaningful contrasts (Trubetzkoy 1969). In other words, the litmus test for phonemic processing is that the child/adult be able to apply their reorganized phonetic sensitivities to the task of distinguishing meaning in language. Although we once thought infants of 10 to 12 months of age might possess this ability, we have relinquished that expectation on the basis of our recent experimentation, which indicates the first appearance of this skill at 19 months. Much of our research effort is now directed at mapping the course of the transition from language-specific phonetic sensitivity to phonemic processing in early childhood, and to determining the nature of each of these distinct factors in later adult speech processing.

It is useful to note that studies of speech perception in adults as yet clearly reveal three independent processing factors only. According to the criteria outlined in the four-factor model, we would now label these three factors acoustic, broad-based phonetic, and phonemic. However, on the basis of research in speech production (Keating 1984), it is likely that evidence for a language-specific phonetic factor will also be found (see also Flege 1991). Furthermore, although we can separate clearly universal phonetic, language-specific phonetic, and phonemic factors during development, the issue of whether acoustic perception can be separated meaningfully from broad-based phonetic during early infancy is also still unresolved.[8] These unresolved issues need to be addressed in further research. Nevertheless, we are confident that the demarcation of the phonetic factor into *broad-based* and *language-specific* during infancy will foster the search for a more complete understanding of phonological acquisition.

SUMMARY

Our aim in writing this chapter has been to advance the notion that certain developmental changes in speech perception skills exert an influence on the course of phonological acquisition. Our work has shown that there is a reorganization in cross-language speech perception evident by the end of the first year of life, but this rather clear phenomenon is difficult to understand for a number of related reasons. First, the reorganization in perceptual sensitivities is in accordance with native language phonemic categories, showing that the ambient phonology can influence infant perceptual biases. This is emphasized by the finding that the reorganization seems to be most pronounced for phones that are assimilable to native-language categories. Second, it is now clear that infants' initial sensitivities are not simply lost. Adults can discriminate non-native phonetic contrasts under certain testing conditions. In fact, they have access to different processing strategies, depending upon testing conditions. Our search for plausible explanations of this data pattern led us initially to propose a three-factor model of adult speech perception. Recent findings have forced us to modify this model. Although we still contend that the infants' abilities do, in fact, become reorganized, and that adults have at their disposal strategies that allow them to discriminate non-native speech contrasts, we are now persuaded that there is a more fruitful way to delineate the developmental progression.

In the preceding pages we have tried to answer three questions: (1) why are developmental changes evident as early as 10 to 12 months of age? (2) why do the changes in phonetic perception conform to native-

---

[8] The meaning of initial infant speech perception biases is still not fully understood. There is disagreement concerning whether categorical-like perception in infancy evidences specifically phonetic factors, general psychoacoustic sensitivities, or direct perception of articulatory gestures.

language phonemic categories? and (3) why are adults able to show sensitivity to non-native phonetic, and even within-category acoustic differences under certain testing conditions? Following the section on phonological processes, we would now add a fourth question: (4) why are the changes evident only for speech sounds that are assimilable to native phones? In attempting to answer these questions, we considered several potential explanations that have been offered, i.e., perceptual tuning, modular recalibration, articulatory mediation, self-organization, cognitive mediation, and phonological processes.

We found several of these explanations useful for understanding some portion of the data presented, but each insufficient for explaining the complete pattern of results. To review, we argued that while perceptual tuning serves as an important theoretical construct within which to consider why the changes in non-native speech perception correspond to native-language categories (question 2 above), it cannot really account for the issue of age (question 1), alternative processing capabilities (question 3), or assimilability (question 4). Modular recalibration might also readily explain question 2, but would have to be developed quite a bit more in order to account for questions 3 and 4 above, and could not, to our understanding, ever adequately explain question 1 (timing). On the other hand, articulatory mediation might be particularly useful for explaining why the reorganization is evident by 10 to 12 months of age, and could potentially contribute to our understanding of the other three questions as well. We would argue, however, that in and of itself articulatory mediation also is not enough. Rather, it is critical to specify how the organism deals with the information obtained through articulatory experience. For example, articulatory experience could have a direct impact on the settings in a phonetic module (modular recalibration), or it could serve as an initial sensorimotor base for the eventual construction of more abstract phonological categories. With respect to the latter alternative, it is possible that developing cognitive abilities might facilitate the construction of such phonological categories. Thus, a certain level of cognitive development might be required for this to be possible.

For similar reasons, it is clear that the cognitive mediation hypothesis is not complete in and of itself. Rather, it is necessary to specify the source of information that the cognitive system uses. It might use the sensorimotor information available from increasingly coordinated and language-specific babbling output, or it could operate on the information the infant receives from listening to people speak. Finally, it was noted that the idea of self-organizing systems has not been well developed with respect to cross-language speech perception. Thus, it is not clear at this time whether it should be viewed as a competing explanation, or rather simply as an equivalent but alternate framework within which to consider the potential impact of all the other influences mentioned above.

Throughout this chapter, we explored how phonological processes might contribute to, or be reflected in, the reorganization in cross-language speech perception. However, the confusion between the influence of structured phonological input and the impact of internal phonological categories on phonetic perception was unavoidable within a three-factor model of speech perception. We are hopeful that the articulation of a four-factor model will alleviate this problem and facilitate the search for a more adequate understanding of developmental changes in speech perception. Efforts can now concentrate on explaining two transitions: the transition from broad-based to language-specific phonetic perception during infancy, and the transition from language-specific phonetic perception to phonemic processing at some point in later infancy or early childhood. Most certainly some of the mechanisms involved in each of these transitions will be different, but we hope the search for an adequate explanation will be easier now that the two transitions have been conceptually separated. In the final analysis, however, it will be necessary to consider the interdependency between the first and the second transitions in order to achieve a complete picture of the steps involved in phonological acquisition.

REFERENCES

Aslin, R. N., and Pisoni, D. B. 1980. Some developmental processes in speech perception. In *Child Phonology: Vol. 2: Perception,* eds. G. H. Yeni-Komshian, J. F. Kavanagh, and C. A. Ferguson. New York: Academic Press.

Aslin, R. N., Pisoni, D. B., Hennessy, B. L., and Perey, A. J. 1981. Discrimination of voice onset time by human infants: New findings and implications for the effect of early experience. *Child Development* 52:1135–1145.

Barton, D. 1980. Phonemic perception in children. In *Child Phonology: Vol. 2: Perception,* eds. G. H. Yeni-Komshian, J. F. Kavanagh, and C. A. Ferguson. New York: Academic Press.

Best, C. W. 1989. Phonologic and phonetic factors in the influence of the language environment on speech perception. Paper read at the International Conference on Event Perception and Action, July, 1989, Miami University, Miami, OH.

Best, C. W., and McRoberts, G. W. 1989. Phonological influences in infants' discrimination of two nonnative speech contrasts. Paper read at the Society for Research in Child Development, April 1989, Kansas City, MO.

Best, C. W., McRoberts, G. W., and Sithole, N. N. 1988. The phonological basis of perceptual loss for non-native contrasts: Maintenance of discrimination among Zulu clicks by English-speaking adults and infants. *Journal of Experimental Psychology: Human perception and Performance* 14:345–60.

Boysson-Bardies, B. de, Halle, P., Sagart, L., and Durand, C. 1989. A cross linguistic investigation of vowel formants in babbling. *Journal of Child Language* 16:1–17.

Boysson-Bardies, B. de, Sagart, L., and Durand, C. 1984. Discernible differences in the babbling of infants according to target language. *Journal of Child Language* 11(1):1–15.

Burnham, D. K. 1986. Developmental loss of speech perception: Exposure to and experience with a first language. *Applied Psycholinguistics* 7:207–240.

Diamond, A. 1985. Development of the ability to use recall to guide action, as indicated by performance on A not B. *Child Development* 56:868–883.

Eilers, R. E., Gavin, W. J., and Oller, D. K. 1982. Cross-linguistic perception in infancy: Early effects of linguistic experience. *Journal of Child Language* 9:289–302.

Eilers, R. E., Wilson, W. R., and Moore, J. M. 1979. Speech perception in the language innocent and the language wise: The perception of VOT. *Journal of Child Language* 6:1–18.

Eimas, P. D. 1975. Developmental studies in speech perception. In *Infant Perception: From Sensation to Perception*, Vol. 2, eds. L. B. Cohen and P. Salapatek. New York: Academic Press.

Ferguson, C. A. 1986. Discovering sound units and constructing sound systems: It's childs play. In *Invariance and Variability of Speech Processes*, eds. J. S. Perkell and D. H. Klatt. Hillsdale, NJ: Lawrence Erlbaum Associates.

Ferguson, C. A., and Farwell, C. B. 1975. Words and sounds in early language acquisition. *Language* 51:419–39.

Flege, J. E. 1987. The production of "new" and "similar" phones in a foreign language: Evidence for the effect of equivalence classification. *Journal of Phonetics* 15:47–65.

Flege, J. E. 1991. Age of learning affects the authenticity of voice-onset time (VOT) in stop consonants produced in a second language. *Journal of the Acoustical Society of America* 88(1):395–411.

Fogel, A., and Thelen, E. 1987. Development of early expressive and communicative action: Reinterpreting the evidence from a dynamic systems perspective. *Developmental Psychology* 23:747–61.

Golinkoff, R., Hirsh-Pasek, K., Cauley, K. M., and Gordon, L. 1987. The eyes have it: Lexical and syntactic comprehension in a new paradigm. *Journal of Child Language* 14:23–45.

Gottlieb, G. 1976. The roles of experience in the development of behavior and the nervous system. In *Studies on the Development of Behavior and the Nervous System, Vol. 3*, ed. G. Gottlieb. New York: Academic Press.

Gottlieb, G. 1981. Roles of early experience in species-specific perceptual development. In *Development of Perception, Vol. 1*, eds. R. N. Aslin, J. R. Alberts, and M. R. Petersen. New York: Academic Press.

Hirsh-Pasek, K., Kemler Nelson, D. G., Jusczyk, P. W., Wright Cassidy, K., Druss, B., and Kennedy, L. 1987. Clauses are perceptual units for young infants. *Cognition* 26:268–86.

Ingram, D. 1986. Phonological development: Production. In *Language Acquisition: Studies in First Language Development*, 2nd ed., eds. P. Fletcher and M. Garman. New York: Cambridge University Press.

Jusczyk, P. W. 1989. Perception of cues to clausal units in native and non-native languages. Paper presented at Society for Research in Child Development. April, 1989, Kansas City, MO.

Jusczyk, P. W., Friederici, A. D., and Wessels, J. In preparation. Infant's recognition of foreign versus native language words.

Keating, P. 1984. Phonetic and phonological representation of stop consonant voicing. *Language* 60:286–319.

Kemler Nelson, D. G. 1989. Developmental trends in infants' sensitivity to prosodic cues correlated with linguistic units. Paper presented at the Biennial meeting of the Society for Research in Child Development, Kansas City, MO, April.

Kuhl, P. K. 1979. Speech perception in early infancy: Perceptual constancy for spectrally dissimilar vowel categories. *Journal of the Acoustical Society of America* 66:1168–1179.

Kuhl, P. K. 1983. Perception of auditory equivalence classes for speech in early infancy. *Infant Behavior and Development* 6:263–85.

Lalonde, C. E. 1989. An investigation of the relations among object search skills, cross-language speech perception, and visual categorization in infancy. Unpublished Thesis, University of British Columbia.

Lalonde, C. E., and Werker, J. F. 1990. Cognitive/perceptual integration of three skills at 9 months. Abstract in *Infant Behavior and Development* 13:464.

Lalonde, C. E., and Werker, J. F. In revision. Cognitive influences on cross-language speech perception in infancy.

Lasky, R. E., Syrdal-Lasky, A., and Klein, R. E. 1975. VOT discrimination by four to six and a half month old infants from Spanish environments. *Journal of Experimental Child Psychology* 20:215–25.

Lindblom, B., and Engstrand, O. 1989. In what sense is speech quantal? *Journal of Phonetics* 17:107–121.

Lindblom, B., MacNeilage, P., and Studdert-Kennedy, M. 1983. Self-organizing processes and the explanation of language universals. In *Explanations of Linguistic Universals*, eds. G. Butterworth, B. Comrie, and Ö Dahl. Mouton: The Hague.

Lisker, L., and Abramson, A. S. 1970. The voicing dimension: Some experiments in comparative phonetics. In *Procedings of the 6th International Congress of Phonetic Sciences*. Prague: Academia.

Locke, J. 1983. *Phonological Acquisition and Change*. New York: Academic Press.

Locke, J. 1991. Structure and function in the ontogeny of spoken language. *Developmental Psychobiology* 23(7):621–43.

Logan, J. S., Lively, S. E., and Pisoni, D. B. 1991. Training Japanese listeners to identify /r/ and /l/: A first report. *Journal of the Acoustical Society of America* 89:874–86.

MacKain, K. S. 1982. Assessing the role of experience on infants' speech discrimination. *Journal of Child Language* 9:527–42.

MacKain, K. S. 1988. Filling the gap between speech and language. In *The Emergent Lexicon: The Child's Development of a Linguistic Vocabulary*, eds. M.D. Smith and J. Locke. New York: Academic Press.

MacKain, K. S., Best, C. T., and Strange, W. 1981. Categorical perception of English /r/ and /l/ by Japanese bilinguals. *Applied Psycholinguistics* 2:368–90.

Mann, V. A. 1986. Distinguishing universal and language-dependent levels of speech perception: Evidence from Japanese listeners' perception of English "l" and "r." *Cognition* 24:169–96.

Markman, E. M. 1991. The whole object, taxonomic, and mutual exclusivity assumptions as initial constraints on word meanings. In *Perspectives on Language and Cognition: Interrelations in Development*, eds. J. P. Byrnes and S. A. Gelman. Cambridge: Cambridge University Press.

Mattingly, I. G., and Liberman, A. M. 1989. Speech and other auditory modules. In *Signal and Sense: Local and Global Order in Perceptual Maps*, eds. G. M. Edelman, W. E. Gall, and W. W. Cowan. New York: Wiley.

Mehler, J., Dupoux, E., and Segui, J. 1990. Constraining models of lexical access: The onset of word recognition. In *Cognitive Models of Speech Processing*, ed. G. Altman. Cambridge: MIT Press.

Mehler, J., Jusczyk, P. W., Lambertz, G., Halsted, N., Bertoncini, J., and Amiel-Tison, C. 1988. A precursor of language acquisition in young infants. *Cognition* 29:143–78.

Menyuk, P., Menn, L., and Silber, R. 1986. Early strategies for the perception and production of words and sounds. In *Language Acquisition: Studies in First Language Development*, 2nd ed., eds. P. Fletcher and M. Garman. Cambridge: Cambridge University Press.

Morosan, D. E., and Jamieson, D. G. 1989. Evaluation of a technique for training new speech contrasts: Generalization across voices, but not word-position or task. *Journal of Speech and Hearing Research* 32:501–511.

Morosan, D., and Werker, J. F. In preparation. Further evidence for three factors in adult speech perception.

Oller, D. K., and Eilers, R. E. 1983. Speech identification in Spanish and English-learning two year olds. *Journal of Speech and Hearing Research* 26:50–53.

Piaget, J. 1952. *The Origins of Intelligence in Children*. New York: Norton.

Pisoni, D. B., Aslin, R. N., Perey, A. J., and Hennessy, B. L. 1982. Some effects of laboratory training on identification and discrimination of voicing contrasts in stop consonants. *Journal of Experimental Psychology: Human Perception and Performance* 8:297–314.

Polka, L. In press. Characterizing the influence of native experience on adult speech perception. *Perception and Psychophysics*.

Polka, L. 1991. Cross language perception in adults: Phonemic, phonetic, and acoustic contributions. *Journal of the Acoustical Society of America* 89(6):2961–2977.

Pollock, K., and Schwartz, R. G. 1990. Phonological perception of early words in 15-20 month old children. Unpublished manuscript.

Stark, R. E. 1980. Stages of speech development in the first year of life. In *Child Phonology: Vol 1. Production*, eds. G. H. Yeni-Komshian, J. F. Kavanagh, and C. A. Ferguson. New York: Academic Press.

Stoel-Gammon, C. 1985. Phonetic inventories, 15–24 months: A longitudinal study. *Journal of Speech and Hearing Research* 28(4):505–512.

Strange, W. 1986. Speech input and the development of speech perception. In *Otitis Media and Child Development*, ed. J. F. Kavanagh. Parkton, MD: York Press.

Strange, W., and Broen, P. A. 1980. Perception and production of approximant consonants by 3-year-olds: A first study. In *Child Phonology: Vol. 2. Perception*, eds. G. H. Yeni-Komshian, J. F. Kavanagh, and C. A. Ferguson. New York: Academic Press.

Streeter, L. A. 1976. Language perception of two-month old infants shows effects of both innate mechanisms and experience. *Nature* 259:39–41.

Tees, R. C., and Werker, J. F. 1984. Perceptual flexibility: Maintenance of recovery of the ability to discriminate nonnative speech sounds. *Canadian Journal of Psychology* 38:579–90.

Trehub, S. E. 1976. The discrimination of foreign speech constrasts by infants and adults. *Child Development* 47:466–472.

Trubetzkoy, N. S. 1969. *Principles of Phonology*. Trans. Christiane A.M. Baltaxe. Berkeley and Los Angeles: University of California Press.

Vihman, M. M., and Miller, R. L. 1988. Words and babble at the threshold of language acquisition. In *The Emergent Lexicon: The Child's Development of a Linguistic Vocabulary*, eds. M. D. Smith and J. L. Locke. New York: Academic Press.

Werker, J. F. 1989. Becoming a native listener. *American Scientist* 77:54–59.

Werker, J. F. 1991. Ontogeny of Speech Perception. In *Modularity and the Motor*

Theory of Speech Perception, eds. I. G. Mattingly and M. Studdert-Kennedy. Hillsdale, NJ: Lawrence Erlbaum Associates.

Werker, J. F., and Baldwin, D. A. 1991. Speech perception and lexical acquisition. Paper presented at the Society for Research and Child Development, April, Seattle, WA.

Werker, J. F., and Lalonde, C. E. 1988. Cross-language speech perception: Initial capabilities and developmental change. *Developmental Psychology* 24(5): 672–83.

Werker, J. F., and Logan, J. S. 1985. Cross-language evidence for three factors in speech perception. *Perception and Psychophysics* 37:35–44.

Werker, J. F., and Tees, R. C. 1983. Developmental changes across childhood in the perception of non-native speech sounds. *Canadian Journal of Psychology* 37(2):278–86.

Werker, J. F., and Tees, R. C. 1984a. Cross-language speech perception: Evidence for perceptual reorganization during the first year of life. *Infant Behaviour and Development* 7:49–63.

Werker, J. F., and Tees, R. C. 1984b. Phonemic and phonetic factors in adult cross-language speech perception. *Journal of the Acoustical Society of America* 75:1866–1878.

Werker, J. F., Gilbert J. H. V., Humphrey, K., and Tees, R. C. 1981. Developmental aspects of cross-language speech perception. *Child Development* 52:349–53.

Wode, H. 1977. The L2 acquisition of /r/. *Phonetica* 34:200–217.

Younger, B. A., and Cohen, L. 1983. Infant perception of correlations among attributes. *Child Development* 54:858–67.

Chapter • 10

First Words
A Dynamic Systems View

Lorraine McCune

As the field of psycholinguistics developed, theoretical fashion with respect to child language acquisition has, in the past several decades, emphasized behaviorist, nativist, cognitive, pragmatic or functional, and perhaps most recently, biological views. Each perspective contributed to understanding of language acquisition, but the shifts from one perspective to the next occurred without development of a unifying theoretical framework. Sameroff (1983) suggested that general systems theory might offer a comprehensive context for understanding development. According to MacNeilage (1980) "action theory" (Bernstein 1967; Turvey 1977; Fowler 1980) provided the basis for "radical reformulation of the theory of speech production" (p. 16). Thelen and others (e.g., Thelen, Kelso, and Fogel 1987) have progressed in developing the dynamic systems approach as a descriptive structure useful in highlighting what is known about language acquisition and posing new modes of investigation. Bates, Bretherton, and Snyder (1988) assume a componential structure for language that can be elucidated by study of individual differences. In this chapter longitudinal data from the period of initial word acquisition are interpreted from a dynamic systems perspective that emphasizes individual patterns of development to demonstrate the interaction of variables contributing to the development of first words. I offer examples to show how this framework can be used in relation to (1) the developmental organization of complex domains of behavior contributing to language acquisition, (2) the interpretation of children's initial articulatory control strategies, and (3) the conceptualization of adult-child cooperation in lexical acquisition.

The dynamic systems approach addresses problems involving complex organism/environment interactions. For example, until recently the waning of the stepping reflex was attributed to suppression or incorporation of brainstem activity with the growing influence of the central nervous system (CNS), and the relationship of the reflex to later voluntary steps was unknown. In a series of studies of organic and contextual determinants of these developments, Thelen and Fisher (1982, 1983) demonstrated that, although the stepping reflex ceased to be observed when the infant was held erect, infant kicks in the supine position maintained the movement properties exhibited in reflex steps. Furthermore, stepping could be "reinstated" by immersing the infant's legs in water. Detailed study of independent locomotion at one year of age indicated that the leg movements matched those of early reflex steps and supine kicks. As a result of this work, the stepping reflex is now thought to wane because of (a) CNS changes, (b) infant physical maturation and growth in the first two months that leads to a rapid deposit of fat in relation to development of leg musculature, and (c) the differential effects of gravity on an organism with heavier limbs (which can be compensated by immersion of the infant's legs in water).

Reflex steps and later independent upright locomotion may rely on preferential functional linkages among muscle groups (*coordinative structures*, Thelen, Kelso, and Fogel 1987). Such structures could allow integrated reactions to task demands, without discrete commands to individual muscles or hierarchical CNS coordination. Additional systems that develop and contribute to walking in the one-year-old include muscular strength, balance, the ability to shift weight to the lead foot, and psychological readiness. It should also be noted that, prior to independent walking, infants who are becoming motivated to walk accept contextual support from adults and objects to compensate for strength and balance limitations.

It can be inferred from this example that in dynamic systems theory behavioral and developmental outcomes depend upon the cooperative interactions of many subsystems. Dynamic stability is maintained as the system tends to exhibit one phase of organism-appropriate behavior until some instability potentiates another. These preferred phases, termed *attractor states* (Abraham and Shaw 1982) derive from the nature of the organism in the context in which it develops.

A phase of canonical babbling is potentiated by vocal tract characteristics and the active exercise of movement capacities characteristic of human infants. The infant's own sounds, as well as the sounds of others, are contextual contributors to this process. Verbal language, as the social coin of the human community, is an attractor that is strongly influenced by context. One question for this chapter is, "What motivates the infant's shift from a phase of babbling and prelinguistic communication to a phase of lexical acquisition?"

Development may be continuous (such as the transition from babble to speech—Vihman et al. 1988) and yet exhibit *discontinuous phase shifts* leading to qualitatively different modes of functioning that may be recognized as stages. This process is analogous to the tendency of physical systems toward certain forms of dynamic equilibrium. Data concerning human development have been similarly characterized using the concept of canalization (e.g., McCall 1981; Sameroff 1983; Waddington 1966). While various subsystems may appear divergent, a self-righting capacity tends toward appropriate developmental outcomes. This approach may be particularly useful in describing language acquisition that is characterized by strong individual differences in the early phase followed by universal similarity within language groups.

A subsystem may act as a *control parameter* in the sense that (given readiness in other subsystems) a new phase may emerge only when that component reaches a critical value. In development of a given skill the same subsystems may contribute in all cases, while those acting as control parameters may differ by child and circumstance. For example a retarded child might exhibit the vocal capacity for speech by one year of age, but not develop appropriate mental representation for language until age two, at which point language becomes evident. In this case, development of representation is the control parameter. A child with a structural difficulty caused by tracheostomy might exhibit representation in play for many months before vocal capacity permits development of a productive vocabulary. In this case, vocal capacity acts as a control parameter. In each case, the shift from a less mature to a more mature phase (prelanguage to language) is initiated when the status of contributing variables leads to instability.

General systems theories, including dynamic systems theory can be considered as "metatheory" in the sense that they suggest frameworks and properties that theories might exhibit, rather than providing detailed content applicable to a particular domain. Thus, Sameroff (1983) found Piaget's theory of cognitive development compatible with a general systems approach. Piaget's ideas are also helpful in explicating certain aspects of language acquisition. Piaget (1952) described universal processes of development (assimilation and accommodation, which together constitute adaptation), and described structural organizations of thought characteristic of various stages of development. Piagetian theory acknowledges that development is the product of a variety of factors (maturation, action by the subject, social transmission, and adaptation) but does not attempt to specify how these factors interact in a system (Piaget and Inhelder 1969).

The Piagetian notion of decalage allows that cognitive performance may vary across domains of functioning and contexts. Such acknowledgment entails acceptance of cognitive development as a continuous process, despite the fact that stages are recognized. Beginning in the 1970s the Genevan School has considered functional aspects of cognition that complement the continued focus on cognitive structure (Bullinger and Chatillon 1983). Recent "challenges" to the Piagetian position, such as skill theory (Fischer 1980), depend upon Piagetian formulations regarding structure, while shifting emphasis from cognitive structure to context of performance. The dynamic systems approach seeks to strike a balance among the variables contributing to development and performance by assuming equipotentiality of all aspects of the system to contribute to development. Research is then designed to specify the contributions of the subsystems. This approach may provide links among theoretical formulations that might, together, contribute to a more holistic understanding of the issues at hand.

DOMAINS OF DEVELOPMENT CONTRIBUTING TO LANGUAGE ACQUISITION

Cognitive Development

Cognitive development in infancy is evident in (a) increasing complexity of voluntary action in control of the physical and social world, and (b) emergence of mental representation that is demonstrated primarily in representational play and language. As early as 1975 Bates and colleagues (Bates, Camaioni, and Volterra 1975) identified tool use or means-end skills (which exemplify increasing control of the physical world) as a significant prerequisite for language. They reasoned that language is used as a communicative tool, and that children capable of using this "tool" should be able to use tools outside language as well. In subsequent studies (e.g., Bates et al. 1979; Harding and Golinkoff 1978) this relationship has been confirmed by correlational analysis.

Bloom (1973) suggested that object permanence should be related to language acquisition on representational grounds. Corrigan (1978) and Bates et al. (1979), who investigated this hypothesis by casting object permanence as a continuous variable and evaluating the correlation of numbers of items passed with vocabulary acquisition, found no significant relationships. Zachry (1978) studied onset of Stage 6 across domains of functioning and found them to be ordered so that entry into Stage 6 for object permanence always precedes entry for means/ ends skills. Because language continues to develop beyond Stage 6, it is reasonable to expect stronger correlations with a later sensori-motor skill.

Stage 6 of sensorimotor intelligence is of particular salience to language acquisition because it marks the transition to mental representation. McCune-Nicolich (1981a) proposed that the contribution of representation to language be evaluated by examining the timing of transitions between forms of language and nonlanguage behaviors considered to be equivalent in representational status. Reasoning from a Piagetian (1962) perspective, she assumed that onset of mental representation was required for language of any sort. With Werner and Kaplan (1963) she believed that words refer through the medium of internal representation of both word (symbolic vehicle) and object (internal referent). She reviewed previous literature and found that children who spoke early exhibited entry into Stage 6 of object permanence either before or within a short time after producing first words. Later talkers might show considerable delay between attaining Stage 6 and language onset. Object permanence is attained when language is just beginning, or will not begin for some months. (Stage 6 entry can be inferred from the child's retrieval of a toy, which is first hidden in a container, then deposited under a screen out of the child's view.)

Prior to the development of mental representation the child's conscious experience is thought to reflect immediate perceptual and motor activity. Memories involve "re-creation" of the child's own past sensorimotor experience in relation to present experience that "reminds" them of past events. Thus Rovee-Collier and her associates (e.g., Rovee-Collier, Griesler, and Early 1985) assess memory in two- to six-month-old infants by first training them to kick to operate a mobile, then examining the frequency of the baby's foot-kicks after a time-lapse when the baby re-experiences the training situation. Such directed kicking and its reinstatement weeks or months after training can be understood as sensorimotor memories. That is, motoric circular reactions are elicited by the babies' experience of the context in which they previously occurred. Onset of Stage 6 representation indicates that the child can experience mental representation separate from and possibly conflicting with present perceptual and motor experience. Thus, 11-month-olds who had attained Stage 6, but not those remaining at Stage 5, expressed surprise and continued to search when the toy they found in a search task was different from the one they had seen hidden (Ramsay and Campos 1978).

Bates and colleagues (e.g., Bates 1976; Bates et al. 1979; Bretherton et al. 1981) have found a correlational relationship between lexical development and symbolic play maturity and variety. Unlike object permanence in which the final critical acquisition is the onset of representation, representational skill as expressed in play continues to grow hand-in-hand with language throughout the second year. It is this rough equivalence in the timing of ongoing development of the skills that yields the positive correlation.

Psychosocial Development

It is apparent that language is a social phenomenon that emerges between child and caregivers (Bruner 1983). Werner and Kaplan (1963) proposed a strong hypothesis that the motive for representation and communicative development was the child's effort to maintain intersubjectivity with the mothering one in the course of self-other differentiation. Many detailed studies of individual child-caregiver dyads demonstrate the interactive, bidirectional nature of the structuring of early communication. However, the large number of conflicting and null findings that emerged in their comprehensive review of studies examining the relationship between mother-child interaction and language led Bates et al. (1982) to conclude that for normally developing children psychosocial variables represent a basic threshold rather than a useful explanation for individual differences in particular language variables. The high incidence of language delay accompanying disorders of the parent-child relationship suggests that when the appropriate threshold of psychosocial support is unavailable, children's capacity for language acquisition is severely affected.

Biological Constraints

Although psychologists and linguists tend to emphasize behavioral and conceptual variables, all movement, including speech, and all mental activity, including mental representation, is expressed in the biology of the organism. There is a maturational trajectory of both the central nervous system and the peripheral organs used in language production. Coordinative structures may contribute to early oral motor control in a manner analogous to their role in early leg movements. The nervous system undergoes growth that yields extreme functional changes during the first year of life, the developmental effects of which are not yet completely understood. For example, laying down of the myelin sheath and increased interconnectedness among neurological structures have a strong impact on transmission speed and efficiency for neurological information. While certain neurological dysfunctions are associated with particular biological configurations, it remains unclear what sorts of detailed biological developments or organization underlie the onset of language.

MacKain (1988) argues persuasively for the influence of hemispheric specialization and a perceptuomotor perspective on the part of the child from birth, but does not suggest developmental milestones potentiating speech production. Ramsay (1984) found evidence that certain levels of hemispheric specialization, indicated by development of handedness for various tasks, accompany babbling onset and development. Kent (this volume) emphasizes the biological aspects of phonology. He notes in particular that the structure of the oral cavity and articulators suggests certain propensities for development that are borne out in developmental data. Of special interest is the timing of the restructuring of the infant vocal tract toward the adult form (2–4 months) in relation to the "expansion stage" (Oller 1980), which entails enhanced accomplishment of "supraglottal or articulatory actions" (4–6 months, Kent this volume). Literature concerning oral-motor skills in feeding indicates six to nine months as a period that sees progressive differentiation of tongue movements from jaw movements and increased control of the extrinsic tongue musculature (Evans-Morris 1987).

Kent also remarks on the coincidence of reduplicated babbling with other repetitive rhythmic movements in infancy beginning around six or seven months. Thelen (1981) indicated that such voluntary rhythmic behaviors might be the developmental initiators of more precise control of the motor systems involved. Such a position emphasizes a close linkage of biological transition with motor development. We consider later how cognitive capacities arising during this period might provide some behavioral links between biological transitions and learned motor control.

Motor Development

Speech production requires intricate motor control of the vocal tract and articulatory structures. It is not known how such control is learned. However, the child's voluntary movements both utilize and influence physiological development. To the extent that phonetic transcription can be taken as a description of movement, the character of motor control in an individual baby's oral productions can be specified. However, motor components of speech development remain controversial, both because of inherent difficulties in investigating them and because of theoretical arguments concerning the linguistic units on the basis of which infants perceive and produce language. The position to be taken here is that segmental or syllabic regularities observable in the infant's surface productions do not necessarily entail their psychological reality as elements of a behavioral repertoire. However, regularities in phonetic transcription serve as a first step in understanding regularities in motor control of production.

THE DATA BASE

This report is based on collaborative work with Drs. Marilyn Vihman and Charles Ferguson of Stanford University. Subjects were 10 Stanford area infants and their mothers and 10 Rutgers area dyads who were visited at home on at least a monthly basis from 9 to 16 months of age. Stanford babies were visited weekly, with follow-up at three and five years of age while Rutgers babies were visited monthly until 24 months, also with follow-up at three and five. Monthly tapes from 9 to 16 months were phonetically transcribed for both samples, as described in Vihman (this volume). Descriptive profiles of the Rutgers sample provide the basis for inferences regarding the transition to words.

VOCAL AND REPRESENTATIONAL VARIABLES

Object Permanence

A measure designed by Corman and Escalona (1969) was administered monthly to the Rutgers sample. The criterion for Stage 6 entry in this study was success on two trials at finding a toy that was first hidden in a container, then deposited, out of the baby's view, under a small pillow.

Representational Play

The approach developed by McCune (McCune 1982; McCune-Nicolich 1981a; Nicolich 1977) was used to monitor representational development beyond entry into Stage 6 of object permanence. The earliest behavior assessed is representational play with real objects, which involves brief gestures and no apparent distinction between "pretend" and "real" actions (McCune 1987). For the present study, two levels of play were investigated: onset of single pretend acts and onset of play combinations. Criteria for single pretend is awareness on the part of the child of the representational quality of the act. This is indicated by elaborations such as sound effects when pretending to eat or move a small vehicle, or the pretend smile to the mother, asking her to share in the representational experience. This awareness indicates the child's ability to contemplate a representational meaning that is separate from, but related to, the present perceptual situation. Pretend combinations involve two acts in sequence, such as feeding the self, then a doll or combing the doll's hair, then feeding it. Such combinations indicate a capacity to maintain representational attention for a longer time, and reference representational meanings with more than one act.

Words

Words were identified by applying a set of criteria indicating the specificity of the phonological match with an adult target word and the security of the evidence for a consistent semantic range of application (Vihman and McCune in revision). See table I for the categories observed. In the present study we distinguish between lexically flexible words (including nominals and relationals) and all other forms. The lexically flexible words indicate semantic extension that can be related, in principle, to adult meanings. The more restricted character of the

Table I. Categories of Words Observed

Context Flexible Nominals. Nominal forms used with reference to a range of entities, suggesting awareness of the type/token relationship.

Context Limited Nominals. Nominal forms where use is limited to a routinized context, such as labeling animals during book-reading.

Specific Nominals. Forms used to refer to specific persons or entities (Nelson 1973), including nominals that typically have a broader extension in the language, but are restricted by the child to a single individual (e.g., "mommy," "daddy").

Relational. Words referring to reversible temporal or spatial transformations in the environment (e.g., "allgone," "back," "up"). Criteria established by McCune-Nicolich (1981b) require occurrence in two or more contexts (cf. also Sinclair 1970; Bloom 1973). Forms limited to a single context would be considered event words, social expressions, or routine/games as appropriate.

Event. Words occurring in the context of an event, but not apparently making reference to an entity, person, or action. In the course of pretend play these include both primitive words such as the conventionalized lip-smacking "yum," and conventional words that play a variety of grammatical roles for adults, such as "clean," restricted to play mopping, or "tea" restricted to accompanying a pouring gesture. Nonpretend examples include "ow" showing a hurt finger to mother and "walk-walk" used only to accompany the child's progress across the room.

Social Expression. Words used in social interaction ("thank you," "hi").

Routine/Game. Words that occur only in verbal rituals taught by adults such as animal sounds in response to "What does the doggie say?"

Deictic. Words indicating a person, entity or event ("this," "that") or marking interest ("aha," "look," "oh") often accompanied by pointing.

other, sometimes earlier, forms provides less evidence that the child has made the transition from preword vocalizing to word use.

Vocal Motor Schemes

In examining the transcripts for potential words we identified additional interesting nonword regularities. "Vocal Motor Schemes" (VMS) were identified as longitudinally stable forms of vocal production, without reference to semantic extension (McCune and Vihman 1987). These action patterns are sensorimotor schemes organized on the basis of habitual and variable articulatory movements.

While the simplest sensorimotor schemes are derived from reflexes, the more complex acquisitions develop through repetition and elaboration in activities termed "circular reactions" (Piaget and Inhelder 1969, p. 10). Such schemes, as the child develops a representational capacity and desires to express meaning, can shift function and be used in communication and play. For example, sucking is at first a reflex applied to any appropriate material. It differentiates and becomes an efficient means of taking food (breast or bottle) and comfort (thumb or pacifier). The child will eventually play at placing a bottle in the mouth, accompany this with abbreviated sucking motions, and finally use the lip-smacking sounds derived from sucking to indicate that a doll is drinking a toy bottle.

As sensorimotor schemes VMS are capable of integration, differentiation and combination. For example, the subject Alice, described by Vihman (this volume) showed an idiosyncratic preference for the segment [j] in the earliest transcriptions. Her development of a varied and flexible capacity to use palatal articulations contributed to both rapid lexical acquisition and an increasing tendency to deform adult forms to match her pattern. Transcribed consonants can facilitate identification of VMS patterns of production although they do not necessarily indicate linguistic control of the segment. A pattern may be as simple as [b] followed by a variable vowel or as complex as Alice's palatal pattern.

Thus far, group analyses have involved consonant-based VMS because of the relative ease of identifying consonant preferences. Although VMS need not involve a consonant, the aspects of motor control exhibited in early words suggest that a consonant-based VMS measure should provide a convenient shorthand for measuring the phenomenon in a fairly large sample. The criterion for VMS in the present study is sustained use (at least ten occurrences) of a given consonant over three monthly vocal samples. Glottals and glides are omitted from the overall analysis.

Communicative Grunts

Ongoing analyses of the data sets also include attention to protowords, following from earlier work by the Stanford group (Ferguson 1984; Vihman and Miller 1988). The term *protoword* has been applied to various word-like phenomena in the early language literature. In the present report I include analysis of stylized grunt-like forms that were apparently child-invented. The phonetic shape used by each child was related to his or her phonological system (e.g., Alice used a palatalized form [ʔeɪ]) and the range of communicative functions was also idiosyncratic.

DEVELOPMENTAL SEQUENCES

Description of the simple sequence of developments of the cognitive and vocal behaviors of interest as these emerged for individual children in the Rutgers sample provides the starting point for the analysis.

Words

We begin by considering the time of emergence of words (figure 1) in relation to the other variables. The solid line begins with the onset of flexible word types. The broken line indicates onset and use of more contextually limited words. Children continued to include such words in their repertoires after beginning to use strong nominals and relationals. We used total flexible types as an index of linguistic maturity, and the children are ranked in figure 1 in that order. A useful comparison throughout is that of the top five children (Total Flexible Types range from 5 to 27) and the bottom five (range 0 to 2).

Among the top five children we can see that Alice and Aurie both began flexible words at 14 months, although Alice was using other adult-based words from 9 months and Aurie's initial word activity was at 14 months. Ronnie, the sixth ranking child, used words early, but did not develop flexible words until 16 months. If we compare Aurie, the second-ranked child, with Danny, the last, neither of them showed any words between 9 and 13 months. Yet Aurie began with flexible words at 14 months and Danny did not begin using any words until 28 months. What can account for these differences? One might wonder whether the referential/expressive distinction (Nelson 1973) is implicated, but the subjects in this study all met published criteria as referential speakers.

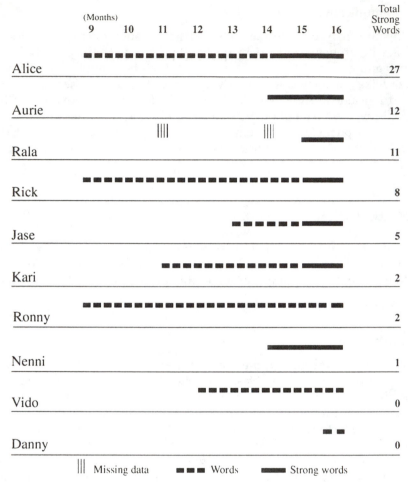

Figure 1. Word development.

Mental Representation

Figure 2 adds information about representation assessed using entry into Stage 6 of Object Permanence and onset of single pretend and combinatorial pretend play behaviors. For children who showed early word activity (broken lines) before developing flexible types, this tended to occur close in time to Stage 6 onset. Among the top five children who did show such early word activity Rala (third rank) and Jase (fifth rank) attained Stage 6 later than the other children and began word activity later as well.

Onset of pretend combinations varied from 9 months of age for Alice (first ranking subject) to 20 months (beyond the data in this

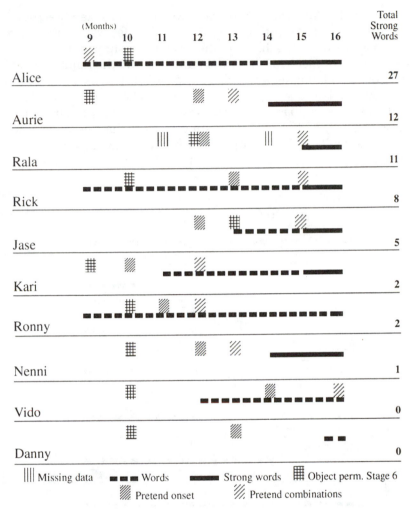

Figure 2.   Play and object permanence in relation to words.

study) for Danny, the last ranking. Flexible types began after this attainment for children who developed them in the course of the study.
Four of the top five children began flexible word use within a month of
showing play combinations, but for some children there were long sep-
arations in time between these events.

Vocal Motor Schemes

Children who were competent talkers at 16 months had developed
VMS earlier, included two or three VMS types based on different con-

sonants in their repertoire, and used VMS more consistently across the months of the study. Although glottals and glides were omitted from the analysis, we noted that 18 of the 20 children studied used [h] with frequency that met VMS criteria. Figure 3 shows the number of VMS developed and months where they occurred, as well as months where vocalizations based on [h] occurred at least ten times. (Note the shaded and cross-hatched bars where the shaded section represents [h], the cross-hatched, VMS.) It is interesting to note that the early talkers based their initial VMS on [p] or [t]. Children who demonstrated two VMS used both of these, while Alice (three VMS) added [n] (in keeping

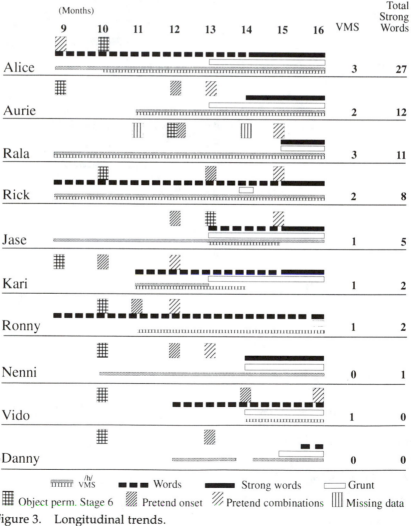

Figure 3. Longitudinal trends.

with the gestures of her palatal pattern), and Rala (three VMS) included [s]. The later talkers showed at most one consonant-based VMS sustained for at most four sessions.

The five earlier talkers and Nenni showed VMS level use of [h] across many sessions in contrast with the other later talkers. Netsell (1981) suggested that certain laryngeal muscles act as "an articulator" (p. 130), and noted the importance of the abduction/adduction of the vocal folds as a critical component in syllable repetition and the rhythmic aspects of speech. Ladefoged (1975) describes the position of the vocal folds for [h] as pulled apart so they cannot be set into vibration by the airstream, a position in which the air from the lungs escapes very rapidly (pp. 122–123). Apparent [h] in the transcripts may represent the child's development of control of the abduction/adduction of these muscles. Thus, it contributes to the sensorimotor foundation of the vocal capability without a necessary relation to word learning. Vihman's finding (this volume) of high frequency [h] in children learning French (which does not use /h/) supports this. The low occurrence of [h] in four of the five children showing few or no flexible words might be taken as a limitation in laryngeal control.

Data on total flexible types and VMS were available for both the Stanford and Rutgers samples. Because VMS might depend upon volubility, we performed correlational and stepwise regression analyses of these variables for the 20 subjects. VMS scores were derived by dividing total VMS for each child by number of observation sessions to correct for missing sessions. VMS was more highly correlated with development of flexible words than was volubility and entered first in the stepwise regression (table II).

Table II. Relationship between Total Vocal Motor Schemes, Total Flexible Word Types and Volubility

	Spearman Correlation Coefficients Stanford and Rutgers Samples—N = 20		
	Words	VMS	Volubility
Words		.85**	.51*
VMS			.76*

Stepwise Regression Predicting Total Flexible Word Types from VMS and Volubility	
Variable Entered	Partial R 2
Step 1 VMS	.57**
Step 2 Volubility	.10+

**Significance Level = 0.0001
*Significance Level = 0.02
+Significance Level = 0.03

Communicative Grunts

The onset of a communicative function for grunts was marked by a sharp increase in frequency of this type of vocalization and concommitant reduction in the frequency of other vocal forms for one or more months. The clear bars in figure 3 show onset and continued use of communicative grunts. It can be seen that regardless of the status of the other variables, of the seven children who both used communicative grunts and developed flexible word types, onset of flexible types followed or accompanied onset of communicative grunts.

Identifying Control Parameters

A dynamic systems approach to development allows for variation in the timing and means by which individuals approach mature behavior. Therefore, we consider the temporal development of representation (as indexed by play), vocal motor control as indexed by VMS, and grunt-based proto-words in relation to the onset of contextually flexible words. The five early talkers demonstrated VMS, play combinations, and communicative grunts prior to or in the same session as flexible words. For Alice, who showed VMS and play combinations for many months, communicative grunts appear as a control parameter. For Aurie and Rala, play combinations and communicative grunts first occurred in the same session, appearing together as potential control parameters for flexible words. For Rick and Jase as well as Kari and Ronny (later talkers), communicative grunts appear as the control parameter. Nenni showed one flexible word while not demonstrating VMS. Vido, with all parameters in place, appears ready to begin strong words, while Danny appears to need more progress in both vocal motor control and representation to facilitate flexible word acquisition. The limited repertoire and less stable use of VMS in the later talking group probably represents a limitation in sensorimotor control, which limits word acquisition when other parameters are in place.

DEVELOPMENT OF WORDS IN CONTEXT

Vocal Control

Kent's model of articulatory development (this volume) suggests that the child must, over the early years of language acquisition, develop ever finer control of the vocal apparatus. How might the motor abilities of VMS and the cognitive capacities at the transition to speech "explain" babies' ability to articulate typical early words? The simplest of these involve one or two CV syllables, where the several exemplars of a target may vary in phonetic shape.

These productions involve management of motor components in relation to the intention to say "X." Dynamic systems theory suggests placing a minimum of motor information in that intention. Rather, we are free to consider potential coordinative structures unifying the movement variables as largely "explanatory" of the apparently organized character of the phonetic realizations.

Suppose the intention to say "X" arises in a manner similar to the re-instatement of foot-kicks in a setting where this behavior was learned. The context-dependent early words may utilize a VMS vocal pattern as part of a frequently occurring situation. At 9 months Timmy (Vihman this volume) produced [b] initial one-syllable words in response to "What's this" if the object was a box, a ball, or a block. In response to a key, he was interested, but silent. This behavior may reflect his previous experience of seeing [b] objects while he and/or his mother produced [b] vocalizations. Piaget (1962) considered such early words as verbal schemes, intermediary between sensorimotor schemes and conceptual schemes (p. 218). Each word "participates" with the event referenced rather than indicating the object as an exemplar of a concept.

The phonetic variety across productions would reflect variety in the child's motor recreation of the prior event, just as foot-kicks may vary in amplitude. Earliest word productions may depend upon well-practiced sensorimotor schemes (VMS) instantiated in relation to the intention to produce a given word. The intention itself arises based on events that remind the child of a related prior situation. The present situation perceived, as well as the sensorimotor production (VMS-based word), serve to maintain the child's representational consciousness of a meaning to be shared, just as replicating the sounds of eating serves to maintain representational consciousness and express meaning in pretend play. This view does not require the inference of a stored lexicon for which we, as observers, have no external evidence.

From Kent's description, both lingual movement and shaping of the vocal tract for speech involve necessarily continuous rather than discrete movement, while jaw opening and closure and onset of an air flow for phonation are more discrete. It may be that the form of VMS developed is influenced by individual maturational trajectories. Earlier differentiation of lingual from jaw movements may potentiate a palatal articulation such as that demonstrated by Alice, while closer tongue-jaw synergy at the outset may characterize Timmy's initial pattern. Flexibility of the available pattern (e.g., palatalized articulation versus skill with the closant segment /b/) would allow broader differentiation of the VMS pattern as the range of targets expands.

Sensorimotor schemes are inferred to exist on the basis of regularity and systematic variation in behavior. The physiological and neurological basis of such schemes is not addressed. The concept is compatible with the position of Browman and Goldstein (1989), suggesting that articulatory actions be considered as specifiable gestures capable of organization into a score. It is difficult to determine the form that data should take to provide empirical validation for this rather attractive proposal.

If early vocalizations are influenced by pre-existing coordinative structures, the existence of such structures should influence any proposal for the initial production units in infancy. The consonant-vowel relationships reported by Vihman (this volume) suggest a synergistic relationship for vocant and closant properties at the onset of speech, possibly reflecting the tongue-jaw linkages of the early months. The variability across individuals in this analysis highlights the role child vocal activity must play in shaping the regularities observable within a given child's early productions. The high incidence of neutral vowels that require minimum tongue adjustment, along with individual consonant preferences suggests greater attention to the closant (more discrete) segments of speech production in the early period. Kent distinguishes between "ballistic" and "ramp" qualities of articulation. A similar distinction is made in the development of reaching and grasping. It may be that control of more discrete (rather than continuous) aspects of movement develops first, associated with a ballistic quality, to be followed by finer control of gradations of movement, yielding the eventual continuous quality of heard speech.

Cognitive and Social Influences

Maturation, social context, and cognitive development interact to allow the child to develop VMS during the sensorimotor and early symbolic period. The rhythmic stereotypies described by Thelen (1981) as peaking at seven months of age are primary circular reactions, where one movement is potentiated by and follows another like movement. Rhythmic behavior is taken as an indication of beginning readiness for voluntary control of the organs involved. Canonical babbling exemplifies a primary circular reaction, while the variety of execution in VMS exemplifies secondary circular reactions.

Imitation of sounds in the environment that are similar to the infant's sounds entails tertiary circular reaction because of the apparent guidance of the behavior by an external goal. Thus, the tendency to vocalize provides the opportunity for children to develop VMS that exemplify the sensorimotor circular reactions of Stages 4 and 5, and potentiate incorporation of adult sounds that are similar to infants' own sounds into the infant repertoire. Such adult-like sounds have potential to be identified as words. Stage 6 mental representation provides the cognitive basis for vocal forms to "represent" meaning.

The children in this study who spoke early all produced a repertoire of VMS, although the consonants used and the structure of the resultant utterances differed by child. The availability of VMS provides an opportunity for the parents to respond to the child's consistent vocal forms as if they were words, and to attribute meaning to them in relation to objects or events that appear to be the focus of the child's interest. For example, an infant who has the organic capacity and behavioral propensity to say [ba] is in an excellent position to produce words such as "ball" and "block" if his mother presents and names such objects, then welcomes [ba] as a name for the object. In this case aspects of the social and nonsocial context interact with developmental characteristics to initiate a phase-shift from "babble" to "word." A child who infrequently produces [b], or whose mother neither expects words nor presents them for imitation is unlikely to exhibit first words in this manner. This system can be considered self-organizing because the elements might interact in this way with no prior intentionality or direction. The parent who labels objects for the child may initially do so to enhance interest, with little expectation that the child is ready to speak. The child who emits a familiar repeated vocalization under appropriate circumstances may initially do so with no intention or awareness of the goal of "speech." Finally, the parent who accepts a child vocalization as a word may believe the child has somehow learned the word, although production of the pattern may be only accidentally related to the apparently appropriate context. In this example systematic relationships between child organic status and elements of context interact, leading to (apparent) word production (Veneziano 1988). Even without the knowing intention of both parties, this situation tends toward development of words.

Semantic Development

The child's development of meaning apart from sensorimotor action is demonstrated in representational play as well as in words. A child who feeds a doll with a toy bottle, or rolls a small car across the floor with appropriate sound effects, shows semantic understanding of a type of event (McCune 1987). Such play is much more frequent in the presence of the mother than in her absence (Dunn and Wooding 1977; Slade 1987), suggesting that these displays function communicatively to create shared meanings between mother and child. Combinatorial symbolic play often shows this directly, as the children induce the mothers to produce play acts related to their own. Bates et al. (1979) report that the "vocabularies" expressed in play during the second year of life include many of the same meanings as the early verbal lexicons. The early talkers in this study demonstrated such combinatorial play prior to flexible word acquisition. A range of different situations elicit a given play act, just as the child using language flexibly extends meanings beyond a single familiar context. According to Piaget (1962) verbal recall of past events is the first indication that the child's verbal schemes are becoming more representational. Bloom (1973) provides the charming example of Allison at about 16 months, coming in from an evening walk with her mother and surprising her father with the comment, "moon." Flexible words, by occurring in a variety of contexts, suggest that a mental state linking past and present is evoked for the child, rather than a sensorimotor behavior closely linked to a specific context or routine.

The Intention to Produce Words

The development of communicative grunts exposes a critical link between physiology and meaning. The sound we perceive or experience as a grunt occurs when sudden opening of the glottis releases air from the lungs. This occurs spontaneously when effortful behavior causes momentary closing of the glottis, and a subsequent physiological requirement for oxygen leads to involuntary expiration from the lungs. When we examined the children's transcripts to determine the environmental context of transcribed grunts, we discovered the following sequence of developments for children with frequent grunts and slow onset of communicative function for them.

The earliest occurrences were infrequent in a given month and occurred when the babies made postural adjustments, such as moving from a sitting to crawling position. Next we observed stronger grunt sounds that accompanied effortful behavior, such as attempts to force in a puzzle piece, or open a closed container. A subtle shift was subsequently noted when the child developed a stylized grunt-sound that seemed to be emitted intentionally in the course of means-ends activities, whether requiring physical effort or not. Finally, this stylized form was used specifically for communicative purposes that differed by child. It is this communicative form that is plotted in figure 3. The elaboration of such organically based sounds toward the lexicon is reminiscent of the dynamic structuring activity suggested by Werner and Kaplan (1963) as the manner in which vehicle (word) and referent (meaning) developed together based on their intrinsic relationship.

First the child experiences a consistent sound (his or her own grunt) in a related series of contexts (means/end behavior). Later more stylized grunts may be the child's vocal marking of these contexts. The occurrence of effort accompanied by effortful vocalization is likely to elicit comment or help from an adult present, whether or not the child's intention was communication. The child then experiences shared meaning with an adult. This experience may suggest this vocalization as a potential "means" toward the "goal" of communication. Its application then expands to a variety of communicative contexts. The tendency of children to develop a grunt-based protoword is based on a "shift of function" for the grunt (Werner and Kaplan 1963), (1) from a physiological response to effort, (2) to marking a sensorimotor category for self, and finally, (3) to the social goal of communicating with another.

Relationships to Flexible Word Development. Stylized grunt communications, once established, were accompanied by an expanding repertoire of flexible words in those children who previously showed VMS development and the representational milestones. To interpret this relationship it is helpful to consider the communicative grunts as defining a personal category of communicative events, historically derived from effortful action. The existence of such a category suggests a capacity on the part of the child for constructing such categories in relation to events unified by a common vocal pattern. This capacity may render the child sensitive to potential categories of meaning represented by adult-based words. This could be one route for attaining the naming insight that is credited with leading to a lexical burst. Availability of VMS then allows shaping of vocalizations toward targets.

CONCLUSION

The search for the developmental sources of language is hampered by uncertainty as to the best way to identify its true beginning. The vocal kinds described here include various levels of sound-meaning correspondence. Others might decide differently about where use of the term *word* is appropriate. If we consider the transition from nonverbal to verbal status as a phase-shift, where any time-point in the sequence allows only a probabalistic judgment of the child's status as "verbal," the definitional problem is recognized as endemic to the process of language acquisition. It also becomes obvious that a full range of data is necessary for rendering the probabalistic judgment.

If paths toward language are characterized by strong individual differences in how and when the critical variables express themselves, the general problem of how language is acquired will only be solved by close examination of the systematicity inherent in the relevant variables as they interact developmentally for each child. Such post hoc analysis of a sufficient number of cases should, in theory, permit predictive studies describing the status of the collective variable *in individual cases* a few months ahead. This would be a significant empirical feat with broad clinical and theoretical implications.

In the data described here it seems likely that the first five subjects in figure 3 have made the phase-shift from nonverbal to verbal by 16 months, with the exact point of that transition unknown. Judgment concerning the remaining subjects is less secure. Placing the case analyses in a dynamic systems framework is helpful in clarifying the relationships of the variables displayed in figure 3. On functional grounds, we assume that the child intends to vocalize and to communicate. The coincidence of these intentions, along with additional constraints, describes the task of producing words. The child, thus, tends toward language learning as a result of certain organic propensities and relationships with the environment.

It is possible that the paths to language suggested here characterize successful early talkers, while children who establish language rapidly, following a somewhat later start (e.g., beginning at 20 to 24 months), may use entirely different strategies. However, it seems evident that the sorts of contributing subsystems described here, although interacting in different ways, are influential in the transition to words even if the transition occurs later in development.

REFERENCES

Abraham, R. H., and Shaw, C. D. 1982. *Dynamics—The Geometry of Behavior.* Santa Cruz, CA: Aerial Press.

Bates, E. 1976. *Language in Context.* New York: Academic Press.

Bates, E., Benigni, L., Bretherton, I., Camaioni, L., and Volterra, V. 1979. *The Emergence of Symbols: Cognition and Communication in Infancy.* New York: Academic Press.

Bates, E., Bretherton, I., and Snyder, L. 1988. *From First Words to Grammar: Individual Differences and Dissociable Mechanisms.* New York: Cambridge University Press.

Bates, E., Bretherton, I., Beeghly-Smith, M., and McNew, S. 1982. Social bases of language development: A reassessment. In *Advances in Child Development and Behavior,* eds. H. Reese and L. Lipsitt. 8–68. Vol. 16. New York: Academic Press.

Bates, E., Camaioni, L., and Volterra, V. 1975. The acquisition of performatives prior to speech. *Merrill-Palmer Quarterly* 21:205–66.

Bernstein, N. 1967. *The Coordination and Regulation of Movements.* London: Pergamon.

Bloom, L. 1973. *One Word at a Time.* The Hague: Mouton.

Bretherton, I., Bates, E., McNew, S., Shore, C., Williamson, C., and Beeghly-Smith, M. 1981. Comprehension and production of symbols in infancy. *Developmental Psychology* 17:728–36.

Browman, C., and Goldstein, L. 1989. Articulatory gestures as phonological units. *Phonology* 6(2):201–251.

Bruner, J. S. 1983. *Child's Language: Learning to Use Language.* New York: Norton.

Bullinger, A., and Chatillon, J. F. 1983. Recent theory and research of the Genevan school. In *Handbook of Child Psychology,* Vol. 3, eds. P. H. Mussen, J. Flavell, and E. Markman. New York: Wiley.

Corman, H. H., and Escalona, E. 1969. Stages of sensorimotor development: A replication study. *Merrill-Palmer Quarterly* 15:351–61.

Corrigan, R. 1978. Language development as related to Stage 6 object permanence development. *Journal of Child Language* 5:173–89.

Dunn, J., and Wooding, B. 1977. Play in the home and its implications for learning. In *The Biology of Play,* eds. B. Tizard and D. Harvey. Philadelphia: Lippincott.

Evans-Morris, S. 1987. *Prefeeding Skills.* Tucson: Therapy Skill Builders.

Ferguson, C. 1984. Infants' talk before words. Paper presented at the 4th Biennial International Conference on Infant Studies. New York, April.

Fischer, K. W. 1980. A theory of cognitive development. *Psychological Review* 87:477–525.

Fowler, C. 1980. Coarticulation and theories of extrinsic timing. *Journal of Phonetics* 8:113–33.

Harding, C., and Golinkoff, R. 1978. The origins of intentional vocalizations in prelinguistic infants. *Child Development* 49:33–40.

Ladefoged, P. 1975. *A Course in Phonetics.* New York: Harcourt, Brace Jovanovitch.

MacKain, K. S. 1988. Filling the gap between speech and language. In *The Emergent Lexicon: The Child's Development of a Linguistic Vocabulary,* eds. M. D. Smith and J. L. Locke. New York: Academic Press.

MacNeilage, P. 1980. The control of speech production. In *Child Phonology: Vol. I, Production,* eds. G. H. Yeni-Komshian, J. F. Kavanagh, and C. A. Ferguson. New York: Academic Press.

McCall, R. B. 1981. Nature-nurture and the two realms of development: A proposed integration with respect to mental development. *Child Development* 52: 1–12.

McCune, L. 1982. A manual for analyzing symbolic play. Rutgers University.

McCune, L. 1987. The complementary roles of differentiation and integration in the transition to symbolization. In *Symbolism and Knowledge,* eds. J. Montangero, J. Tryphon, and S. Dionnet. Geneva: Foundation Archives Jean Piaget.

McCune, L. 1981. Toward symbolic functioning: Structure of early pretend games and potential parallels with language. *Child Development* 52:785–97.

McCune, L., and Vihman, M. 1987. Vocal motor schemes. *Papers and Reports in Child Language Development* 26:72–79.

McCune-Nicolich, L. 1981a. The cognitive basis of relational words. *Journal of Child Language* 8:15–36.

McCune-Nicolich, L. 1981b. Toward symbolic functioning: Structure of early pretend games and potential parallels with language. *Child Development* 52: 785–97.

Nelson, K. 1973. Structure and strategy in learning to talk. *Monograph of the Society for Research in Child Development* 1 & 2, Serial #49.

Netsell, R. 1981. The acquisition of speech motor control: A perspective with directions for research. In *Language Behavior in Infancy and Early Childhood,* ed. R. E. Stark. New York: Elsevier/North-Holland.

Nicolich, L. McC. 1977. Beyond sensorimotor intelligence: Assessment of symbolic maturity through analysis of pretend play. *Merrill-Palmer Quarterly* 23: 89–101.

Oller, K. 1980. The emergence of speech sounds in infancy. In *Child Phonology*, Vol. 1, *Production*, eds. G. H. Yeni-Komshian, J. F. Kavanagh, and C. A. Ferguson. New York: Academic Press.

Piaget, J. 1952. *Origins of Intelligence*. New York: Norton.

Piaget, J. 1962. *Play, Dreams and Imitation*. New York: Norton.

Piaget, J., and Inhelder, B. 1969. *The Psychology of the Child*. New York: Basic Books.

Ramsay, D. 1984. Onset of duplicated syllable babbling and unimanual handedness in infancy: Evidence for hemispheric specialization? *Developmental Psychology* 20:64–71.

Ramsay, D., and Campos, J. 1978. The onset of representation and entry into stage 6 of object permanence development. *Developmental Psychology* 52: 785–97.

Rovee-Collier, C., Griesler, P. C., and Early, L. A. 1985. Contextual determinants of retrieval in three-month-old infants. *Learning and Motivation* 16:139–57.

Sameroff, A. J. 1983. Developmental systems: contexts and evolution. In *Handbook of Child Psychology, Vol. 1, History, Theory and Methods*, 4th ed., ed. P. H. Mussen Series Editor and W. Kessen Volume Editor. New York: Wiley.

Sinclair, H. 1970. The transition from sensorimotor to symbolic activity. *Interchange* 1:119–26.

Slade, A. 1987. A longitudinal study of maternal involvement and symbolic play during the toddler period. *Child Development* 58:367–75.

Thelen, E. 1981. Rhythmical behavior in infancy: An ethological perspective. *Developmental Psychology* 17:237–57.

Thelen, E., and Fisher, D. M. 1982. Newborn stepping: An explanation for a "disappearing reflex." *Developmental Psychology* 18:760–77.

Thelen, E., and Fisher, D. M. 1983. From spontaneous to instrumental behavior: Kinematic analysis of movement changes during very early learning. *Child Development* 54:129–40.

Thelen, E., Kelso, J., and Fogel, A. 1987. Self organizing systems and infant motor development. *Developmental Review* 7:39–65.

Turvey, M. T. 1977. Preliminaries to a theory of action with reference to vision. In *Perceiving, Acting and Knowing: Toward an Ecological Psychology*, eds. R. Shaw and J. Bransford. Hillsdale, NJ: Erlbaum.

Veneziano, E. 1988. Vocal-verbal interaction and the construction of early lexical knowledge. In *The Emergent Lexicon: The Child's Development of a Linguistic Vocabulary*, eds. M. D. Smith and J. Locke. New York: Academic Press.

Vihman, M. M., and McCune, L. In revision. When is a word a word?

Vihman, M. M., and Miller, R. 1988. Words and babble at the threshold of language acquisition. In *The Emergent Lexicon: The Child's Development of a Linguistic Vocabulary*, eds. M. D. Smith and J. Locke. New York: Academic Press.

Vihman, M. M., Macken, M. A., Miller, R., Simmons, H., and Miller, J. 1985. From babbling to speech: A reassessment of the continuity issue. *Language* 61:395–443.

Waddington, C. H. 1966. *Principles of Development and Differentiation*. New York: Macmillan.

Werner, H., and Kaplan B. 1963. *Symbol Formation*. New York: Wiley.

Zachry, W. 1978. Ordinality and interdependence of representation and language development in infancy. *Child Development* 49:681–87.

Chapter • 11

Effort, Production Skill, And Language Learning

Loekie Elbers and Frank Wijnen

> . . . language is learned in early childhood, and adults have few memories of the intense effort that went into the learning process . . . (Moskowitz 1978, p. 82)

Developmental psycholinguists are adults and adults have few memories of how they acquired their first language. How might the field look if children were capable of doing the theorizing? It seems almost certain that research accents would be quite different. Possibly, two aspects of language learning that tend to be ignored in present adult approaches would be strongly emphasized in children's theories. These two aspects are *effort* and *skill*.

As to effort, influential contemporary views of language acquisition hold that it plays no role whatsoever. In learnability theory, for instance (Wexler 1982; Borer and Wexler 1987), the effortlessness of learning is axiomatic. It is proposed that language development is essentially due to (maturation of) innate linguistic knowledge. The following quote is illustrative " . . . language acquisition is not really something that the child does, it is something that *happens* to the child"

This chapter presents a synthesis of the ideas developed in our respective theses (Elbers 1989a; Wijnen 1990a). Both were written under the supervision of Willem Levelt. We thank him for inspiring discussions, and for his encouraging comments. Part of the research reported here (the transition from *semantic* to *syntactic* speech) was supported by the PSYCHON foundation, which is funded by the Netherlands Organization for Scientific Research (NWO). Without the assistance of Herma Veenhof-Haan this research would never have been completed.

(Chomsky 1988, p. 134, italics ours). What self-respecting child would subscribe to such a passive view of him or herself?

As to skill, a similar attitude seems to prevail in the field. Although children are daily engaged in practicing the skills of speaking and comprehending, adult investigators typically assume that these skills do not, in fact, develop in any fundamental way. They are held to be in place from the beginning, and the cognitive mechanisms involved in the production and perception of language are assumed to be identical in children and adults. MacNamara (1982) calls this the "null-hypothesis of developmental psychology." Pinker (1984) argues that explanatory accounts of language acquisition presuppose this null-hypothesis. Again, what child would be inclined to consider his or her own skill as essentially stationary?

The two postulates of nonexistence just described (there exist no effort and no skill development) seem to derive from the theoretical emphasis on linguistic *knowledge* (competence) that is characteristic for the field of developmental psycholinguistics. Notions such as *effort* and *skill* do not characterize aspects of structural knowledge but of performance. Thus, the postulates of nonexistence seem to reflect a need for denying that children's language *behavior* may, in any significant way, be implicated in the growth of their competence.

In this chapter, we adopt a less restrictive and more child-friendly[1] point of view. Our central assumption is not only that what children know (competence, knowledge) will influence what they do (performance, skill, ability), but also that what children do will influence what they may eventually *come* to know. Given this assumption, learning a language comprises the development of both competence *and* performance, and it will be especially the developmental interplay between these two that becomes the focus of research. In the following we argue for and illustrate the feasibility of such an interactive approach to language learning.

We start with expounding on the notion of effort. What is effort? Why is it mistaken to hold, a priori, that there is no effort involved in acquisition? What may be the relationship between effort, production skill, and learning? What aspects of children's performance are indicative of language-oriented effort? And how should we investigate these aspects and their role in language learning?

After this, we sketch a model of the development of the skill of speaking, that is, of language production. In this model, the cognitive mechanisms underlying production are held to change in the course of

---

[1]In using this expression we want to impart our concern for the "ecological validity" (Neisser 1976) of theories of development, i.e., for how well they account for what children actually do and experience "in the course of their everyday lives" (Claxton 1989, p. 23).

development. Two major transition points are identified that involve a reorganization of the cognitive structures and processes underlying performance. These are the transition from babbling to first words, around the first birthday, and the transition from *semantic* to *syntactic* speech during the third year of life.

Levelt, Sinclair, and Jarvella remark:

> It may be especially worthwhile to investigate which aspects of early speaking and listening activities do receive *explicit attention* during acquisition, and which do not—knowing this might tell us something about the procedures by which the child acquires linguistic skill, and about how speaking and listening are organized at different ages (1978, p. 13, italics ours).

Taking this for a lead, and considering language-oriented effort as, in the present context, synonymous with explicit attention, we proceed to trace the role played by this effort in each of the two transitions in the development of production skill. To this end, two case studies are reported, one for each transitional period. Because in our interactive approach, effort is not only supposed to play a role in the development of skill but also in that of linguistic knowledge. In the final section implications for knowledge acquisition will be discussed.

THE EFFORT OF LANGUAGE LEARNING

Why We Should Not Assume that Acquisition Is Effortless

A well-known contention from Chomsky is that in language learning " . . . a rich and complex system of rules and principles is attained in a uniform way, rapidly, effortlessly, on the basis of limited and rather degenerate evidence" (1981, p. 356). In recent years, several components of this contention have come under considerable attack. Children do not seem to acquire language in a uniform way. On the contrary, individual differences in nearly every area tend to be large (Nelson 1981; Wells 1986; Mills 1989). Also, the evidence presented to children typically is not limited and degenerate, but instead appears to be finely tuned (Snow and Ferguson 1977; Bohannon and Stanowicz 1988). As to acquisition being rapid, it has been pointed out that this is not a matter of fact but of taste (Gleitman, Landau, and Wanner 1988). Children need no less (or, alternatively, no more) than about 1500 days to learn the fundamentals of their language!

The only constituents of Chomsky's contention that do not seem to have invited much criticism are the claim that language knowledge consists of "a rich and complex system of rules" and the claim that language acquisition is effortless. Yet, it is precisely in the conjunction of these two claims that a confusion of professional and nonprofessional reasoning is evident. The rich-and-complex-system claim is a professional judgment, based on detailed and extensive linguistic investigation. The no effort claim, however, is a layman's contention, based on casual and superficial impression rather than on careful observation and research. But propositions of such a differing status should not be combined; it seems just as mistaken to hold that development *is* effortless because it *seems* effortless, as it would be to hold that language itself *is* simple because it *seems* rather simple to the ordinary speaker who is not a professional linguist. So what is evidently needed is a professional view on what, in fact, is "effort." For this, we can turn to the experimental psychological research on mental functions and faculties.

Effort in Psychological Research

In *Attention and Effort*, Kahneman states: "The effort that a subject invests at any one time corresponds to what he is doing, rather than to what is happening to him" (1973, p. 4). According to Kahneman, effort is the intensive, energetic aspect of attention (the other aspect being selectiveness). Effort is that part of general arousal that is task-induced, i.e., that is evoked by the activity the subject is currently engaged in. This task-induced arousal appears to vary as a function of task-difficulty rather than motivation, emotional state, etc. (Kahneman, Peavler, and Onuska 1968). Task-induced arousal can come about more or less voluntarily, as a result of the intentional selection of some task or activity, but it can also come about involuntarily, when a task contains features that are intrinsically arousal-inducing. This typically occurs when features are *new and unfamiliar* to the subject.

The most sensitive test of whether an activity demands effort is whether it can be easily disrupted, for instance, by intense involvement in another activity (Kahneman 1973, p. 189). Because perception and recognition generally are less easily disrupted than production and reproduction/recall (p. 191) we may conclude that, although perceptual activity may demand effort, these demands tend to be slight when compared to those of production.

A final point that should be made is as old as psychology itself and is best phrased in the words of William James, over a century ago: " . . . we cannot deny that an object once attended to will remain in the memory, whilst one inattentively allowed to pass will leave no traces behind" (1890, p. 427). Thus, what is processed with effort tends to be well retained.

Experiments illustrating the points made above about effort, production, and retention abound in psychology. For example, an experiment by Treisman (1964) illustrates that (re)production leaves stronger traces in the system than does perception per se. She performed a sha-dowing experiment in which subjects had to repeat a message on-line, while it was being presented to one ear. The same message was also presented (with a certain time-lag) to the other ear. Subjects were not informed beforehand about the two messages being identical. Treis-man found that when the unattended message leads, identity can only be recognized spontaneously when the time-lag between both presen-tations does not exceed 2 seconds. When the shadowed message leads however, identity may still be recognized after an interval of 5 seconds. These results show that the trace of an attended and reproduced mes-sage persists longer than that of a "merely perceived" message, even in the earliest phases of processing.

To sum up these professional answers: effort can be interpreted as the intensive, energetic aspect of attention. It can be allocated volun-tarily to some task but it can also be "drawn out" involuntarily by the new and unfamiliar features of a task. Effort seems to be implicated in production to a larger extent than in perception. It facilitates learning, in that what is processed with effort tends to leave relatively strong traces in the system.

What should we make of these notions in the context of children's first language learning? It seems that some rather unconventional hy-potheses can be based on them. For instance, one hypothesis might be that a child will, in general, learn more from his or her own production processes and their output than from perception of input (see R. Clark 1974, 1982; E. Clark 1982; Elbers 1988a, 1989a; Vihman 1987, in press; Wijnen 1990a, for relevant research and theorizing; see also Leonard, Locke and Pearson, and McCune this volume). A related hypothesis would be that this prediction will hold most clearly for the early stages of development, when production skills have not yet been automated and demand more effort than they do in later stages. These hypotheses mainly serve an illustrative purpose here.[2] In this article, it is not our intention to spell out all implications of introducing the notion of effort into developmental psycholinguistics. Here, we focus on suggesting answers to the basic questions of how effort can be identified in chil-dren's naturalistic linguistic performance and of what general func-

---

[2]Note however, that a "production-based" approach has the important advantage of bringing together language learning and other kinds of learning that occur in childhood. For instance, no one would seriously defend the idea that a child learns how to build with blocks primarily by analyzing the block constructions produced by *others*. Rather, one would assume that the child learns from his or her own constructive operations and their outcome (see for instance Karmiloff-Smith and Inhelder 1974). Yet theories of language acquisition, of whatever signature, mainly acknowledge the role of input in the learning process, not that of children's constructive production. A notable exception is Vihman (1982), who recognizes that a child's output may function as a privileged kind of input (see also Locke 1988).

tions it seems to have for the development of skill and knowledge. Taking the primary importance of production as given, we will concentrate on production performance.

Effort as Reflected in Children's Spontaneous Performance

One possibility that suggests itself is that disruptions of production performance (disfluencies such as hesitation pauses, speech errors, self-corrections, etc.) may be taken to reflect effort. Such performance errors constitute quite a general and valuable source of evidence. However, in children especially, these errors may reflect in principle *either* insufficient mobilization of effort *or* insufficient development of skill. Thus, performance errors cannot be used as *specific* indicators of the effort associated with a child's orientedness on language and learning. So it seems sensible to look for other operationalizations of language-oriented effort. Kahneman's distinction between voluntary and involuntary effort may be useful here, because it suggests what specific *categories* of children's language behavior might, a priori, be regarded as clear cases of linguistic effort. Voluntary linguistic effort might be reflected in those productions in which children seem to select language as a task to work on. This is often the case in the complex of behaviors that we will refer to as *language work*. Language work includes metalinguistic behavior as well as language play, exploration, and practice. Common to such behaviors is that language itself seems to be in the center of the child's attention, either as an object of reflection, or as something that is produced for its own sake and not primarily for communicating some message. In early childhood, metalinguistic utterances are scarce and language work may be generally identified with noninteractive speech (linguistic play, exploration, and practice, see Kuczaj 1982). This kind of speech is not uncommon at early ages; it may be produced while children are alone (crib speech), but it may also occur in social settings, interwoven with interactive speech (Kuczaj 1982, 1983). While language work represents voluntary linguistic effort, involuntary linguistic effort, in Kahneman's sense, might be present when children produce new and unfamiliar linguistic forms. This is most evidently the case in those productions that tend to be designated as *peak performances*. In peak performances children are performing at an advanced linguistic level, as compared to their usual production. Involuntary peak performances are externally motivated, for instance, by communicative pressure. Effort then is oriented on language as the means to an external goal. However, peak performances may also occur more or less unnecessarily and voluntarily, for instance in children's language work. These are the strongest instances of effort that can be identified (Elbers 1989a).

In summary, the potentially innovative conclusion that can be based on Kahneman's distinctions is that language work and peak performance have something important in common, even though language work may not always consist of peak performances and peak performances may be produced outside language work. What they share is *cognitive* effort (Elbers 1989a): the child's investment of language-oriented, attentive energy in linguistic performance. In child language research, average performance tends to be investigated rather than peak performance, and language work tends to be treated as a marginal epiphenomenon (see Ferguson and Macken 1983, who make the same complaint). Thus, the approach to linguistic effort proposed here brings two neglected kinds of behavior (language work and peak performance) together and emphasizes their relatedness and their importance for learning.

What Kind of Studies to Perform?

Because our primary interest does not concern effort itself but the role it plays in development, research focus should be on the interactions between aspects of general linguistic development on the one hand and aspects of the development of effort on the other. Focusing on developmental interactions calls for longitudinal studies. Moreover, because instances of effort may occur relatively rarely (as compared to ordinary performance), children's output should be sampled rather intensively. Therefore, fine-grained, intensive, longitudinal case studies seem indicated. In such studies, generalizability of results will often be sacrificed to in-depth analysis. However, this need not detract from the value of these studies. For example, in the linguistic investigation of Universal Grammar (UG), important insights about general principles and constraints are attained, not by studying as many languages as possible, but by studying a few, or even just one, in considerable detail. So why not study a child as if she or he were a language? This may shed light on the general principles of performance and on the various ways in which these might possibly interact to yield a range of individual differences between children. In this sense, the approach suggested here is quite linguistic in its method, even though it primarily focuses on process rather than structure. The "language" we report on is Thomas (Th), son of the first author. The case studies presented concern transition periods in his language (production) development. But before going on to this, we discuss the general development of production skill itself.

LANGUAGE PRODUCTION AS A DEVELOPING SKILL

The Mature Language Production Mechanism

If, as we assume, effort is manifested in and through production performance especially, then one should try to achieve some insight into the development of production skill. We start with briefly discussing the end state of development: the mature production mechanism. Research on adult production ability has converged in a three-part division of the underlying cognitive apparatus. Levelt's recent model (Levelt 1989) reflects the major characteristics of earlier, related proposals (Garrett 1975, 1980; Fromkin 1971, and others), and is taken for a starting point here (see Wijnen 1990a for a more extensive discussion of this model). In Levelt's system, the three main parts of the adult speech production mechanism, as portrayed in figure 1, are labelled *Conceptualizer*, *Formulator*, and *Articulator*. The Conceptualizer creates preverbal messages in what is presumed to be some sort of propositional format. These messages are input to the Formulator, which is a lexically driven device that consists of two sub-processors, the Grammatical Encoder, and the Phonological Encoder. The Grammatical Encoder em-

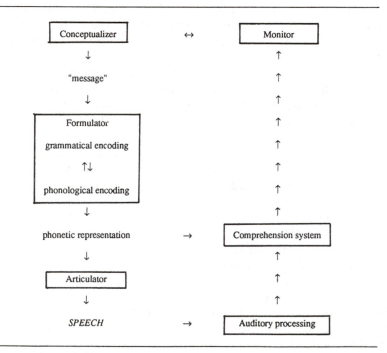

Figure 1.   A rough blueprint for the speaker (after Levelt 1989).

ploys message fragments, generated by the Conceptualizer, to access lexical representations of appropriate words via a semantic route. These lexical representations ("lemmata") incorporate information concerning the lexical item's meaning as well as its syntactic properties, e.g., syntactic category and associated grammatical arguments. This last information is used to build syntactic structures, which are input to the Phonological Encoder. This processor associates the end nodes (the lemmata) of the syntactic structures with the appropriate phonological forms (the lexemes) and computes the overall phonetic plan for the utterance, which is transmitted to the final component of the system, the Articulator. This processor employs the phonetic plans to construct motor programs for the articulatory apparatus.

The mature speech production system has certain processing characteristics: *modularity* (each of the processors depicted in figure 1 works in a relatively specialized and autonomous way); *hierarchy* (information-flow within the system is largely top-down); and *parallel operation* (all processors are simultaneously active in processing different parts of the utterance to be produced).

The system as sketched above is necessarily simplified (for details, see the 500 pages of Levelt's monograph), but conveys an impression of how the skill of speaking is organized in adults. It seems obvious that we should not impute this system, ripe and ready, to the beginning speaker. There are two reasons for this. In the first place, certain components of the system are dependent on (the development of) linguistic knowledge. For instance, as long as there is no knowledge of syntax there can be no Formulator such as the one described above. In the second place, certain processing characteristics are dependent on aspects of performance. For instance, as long as production processes are not yet automated (i.e., not yet sufficiently practiced) there will be little parallel operation of processors in the system. Wijnen (1990a) takes account of this in his theorizing about the development of the system described above.

The Development of the Language Production Mechanism

In Wijnen's approach (which we adopt here in a slightly adjusted form) the development of speaking is, in essence, the development of the interface between Conceptualizer and Articulator, i.e., of the Formulator. During the first year of life, i.e., the *prelinguistic* period, Conceptualizer and Articulator develop more or less independently. Children's conceptual representations in this stage are *event representations* (Golinkoff 1981; Nelson 1983). These are representations of complete action schemes, together with associated participants and contexts. At the same time children acquire, through their babbling, a repertoire of syllabic articulatory routines, and a cognitive map relating these articulatory gestures to their consequent acoustic features (see Wijnen 1988 on the continuing importance of syllabic units in articulatory development). The appearance of the first words implies that certain articulatory-acoustic patterns have become associated with certain concepts, i.e., with event representations or elements thereof. What particular concepts can acquire names depends to a large extent upon the articulatory routines that have been established in prior babbling (Elbers 1982; Vihman in press).

In the beginning lexicon there is little horizontal organization (i.e., semantic organization *within* the set of meanings and phonetic/phonological organization *within* the set of forms). So the organization is mainly vertical; particular *concepts* are directly tied to particular forms (see van Loon-Vervoorn and van der Ham-van Koppen 1988 for some interesting consequences concerning the mature lexicon). For the speaking process this means that the child is producing *names* rather than words and that speaking is mainly a question of *lexicalization*, i.e., of selecting which particular (part of a) concept to name. We assume that this primarily depends on the cognitive saliency of some conceptual element in comparison to other conceptual elements at a particular moment (Braine 1974), but it also necessarily depends on the availability of a name. Thus, the first interface between Conceptualizer and Articulator may be christened *Lexicalizer*. The Lexicalizer is still a long way from the mature Formulator because it takes care of lexicalization only, which is but a part of grammatical encoding in adult formulating.

In our view, the situation stays essentially like this for quite some time. Of course, the lexicon expands and its two levels of horizontal organization start developing (see Bowerman 1978; Elbers 1988b on child "errors" reflecting early semantic organization; Menn 1983; Ferguson 1986 on the character of early phonological organization). Also, eventually the child is able to produce two or more words connectedly. But word order in these early sentences seems still to be largely dependent on the same cognitive/semantic factors that also determine lexicalization per se (Brown 1973; Schlesinger 1971; Schaerlaekens 1973; Berman 1988). These may be factors like perceptual saliency, or universal cognitive primitives such as humanness, change-of-state, and unexpectedness (which play a role in adult sentence generation, too; see Sridhar 1988). Golinkoff (1981) argues that the semantic relations that are traditionally held to underlie early multiword utterances reflect the event structure of conceptual representations.

Near age 2;6 however, qualitative changes begin to occur again in the speech production mechanism. Particularly conspicuous in the child's output is the appearance of function words and grammatical morphemes. Furthermore, productive morphology and morphosyntax emerge. There are also some changes that are not directly visible. For instance, Valian (1986) suggests that syntactic categorization is achieved around or just before age 2;6. In particular, closed class words are differentiated from the open class (Wijnen 1990b). There are indications that surface structures change from flat into hierarchical (Hill 1983; Peters 1986). In summary, it seems that around age 2;6 syntax emerges and enters into speech. Henceforth, we speak of the transition from semantic to syntactic speech.

In the model of speech development adopted here, this second qualitative change (the first one being the appearance of the Lexicalizer) is not interpreted as a discontinuity in the sense that a conceptual/ semantic system is *replaced* by a new, syntactic, system (as is argued in certain competence approaches, e.g., Gleitman 1981; Pinker 1984), but as a discontinuity in the sense that something new is *added* to the production mechanism (without chucking out what was already there). As the child acquires syntactic properties of words (syntactic class and associated grammatical functions), planning routines are developed and added to the production mechanism. Lexicalizer plus planning routines are eventually to become what is known as the Grammatical Encoder. In the developing lexicon, the acquisition of the syntactic properties of lexical items defines the final step in the gradual differentiation of its two different levels of horizontal organization. These two levels now can be characterized as those of the *lemmata* and *lexemes,* respectively (see Elbers 1985 for evidence that lemmata and lexemes have indeed achieved independent representation around age 3). This implies that phonological encoding will become a more separate and independent process than it used to be. Thus, more or less simultaneously, Grammatical Encoder and Phonological Encoder begin to develop, together constituting a rudimentary Formulator.[3]

In summary, in this model of the development of production skill, two major transitions are assumed. Both concern the interface between conceptualizing and articulating. The first transition (from babbling to speech proper) consists of the emergence of the Lexicalizer. The second transition (from semantic to syntactic speech) consists of its expansion into something like a Formulator. In both transitions the developing lexicon plays an important part; in the first by making available names for concepts, in the second by making available syntactic properties of

---

[3]As soon as phrase building subroutines are added to the sentence construction process, many words belonging to the closed class are accessed and selected on the basis of syntactic specifications generated by phrase structure subroutines. Consequently, some of the function words that, presumably as a result of their relatively clear semantic content, had already been acquired (for instance, prepositions), are now degraded to a secondary role in sentence construction. This is one of the processing sides of closed class differentiation.

words. Thus, the model recognizes relationships between knowledge acquisition and skill development. By itself, however, the model does not specify what might be their meeting ground in development. What makes it possible for knowledge and skill to touch and so to develop interdependently? Our conjecture is that cognitive effort is such a meeting ground. If effort facilitates retention (see above), then we would expect this to hold for both the *representations* (knowledge) and the *processes* (skill) involved in a particular language behavior (though a certain amount of trade-off between both is conceivable). Thus, effort may be thought to stimulate the growth of knowledge and skill simultaneously. If this general idea is correct, we should find that peak performances and language work (our operationalizations of language-oriented effort, see above) tend to focus on those linguistic elements or distinctions that are in the process of being acquired *and* are of crucial importance for the particular kind of interface that is being installed in the developing production mechanism. In the transition from babbling to first words these would be the first "word shapes," in the transition from semantic to syntactic speech this would be the distinction between syntactic categories, in particular that between open class and closed class items.

THE TRANSITION FROM BABBLING TO EARLY WORD PRODUCTION

Introduction and Method

As indicated above, our investigations consist of case studies of the speech development of one boy, Th, who acquired Dutch as his native tongue. The first study concerns the relationship between Th's first word acquisition and the development of his contemporaneous babbling. The main results of this study were published in Elbers and Ton (1985). Here, we present some additional observations that were not included in the 1985 paper but that highlight the character of Th's effort in this transitional stage. From the results of the 1985 study it may be concluded that when the Lexicalizer emerges in the production mechanism, a continuous developmental interplay is launched between two modes of speech production: *babbling* (the Articulator is functioning independently from the Conceptualizer) and *talking* (the Lexicalizer mediates between Conceptualizer and Articulator). Elbers and Ton say it like this:

> We credit the child with two speech "systems": an already developed and further developing "babbling system" and a budding "talking system."
> . . . there is an interplay between both systems: words acquired by the talking system may influence and shift the course of babbling, whereas

babbling in its turn may predispose the talking system towards selecting words of a certain form (i.e., towards developing "phonological preferences") (1985, pp. 562–63).

It is not only because of its focus on the interactions between the development of (lexical) knowledge and of (babbling) performance that the Elbers and Ton study is illustrative for an effort-oriented approach, but also because of its methodology. First, it is a very intensive case study; a large number of babbles, collected over a period of only six weeks, was analyzed for microdevelopmental trends. Second, all babbles were recorded, not while the child was communicating, but while he was playing alone in his playpen. So we can interpret these playpen monologues to represent the language work of the first words period.

Results

At the end of the six weeks Th had acquired a productive repertoire of four words (see table I, which is based on Elbers and Ton 1985). The six weeks were divided into four periods: periods 1 and 4 each comprise two weeks; periods 2 and 3, one week. Period 1 starts when the child was 1 year, 3 months, and 18 days old, and had just acquired his first word, [ap(ə)] (adult meaning: 'a bite of food'). During period 2 he acquired a second word, [at(ə)] (adult meaning: 'car'), and during period 3 a third word, [paːt(ə)] (adult meaning: 'horse'). During period 4 the form [bəx] or [bux] (adult meaning: 'cat') was for the first time noted to be used in a referential way during interactive speech. As is evident from table I, all four word shapes (and their variant forms) were produced during solitary babbling. During period 1, the first word, [ap(ə)], was produced most frequently, and during period 2, the second word, [at(ə)]. During period 3, the third word, [paːt(ə)], is slightly

Table I.   Word Repertoire and Number of Babbled Word Shapes per Period[a]

	Period 1	Period 2	Period 3	Period 4
Word repertoire	[ap(ə)]	[ap(ə)] [at(ə)]	[ap(ə)] [at(ə)] [paːt(ə)]	[ap(ə)] [at(ə)] [paːt(ə)] [b(ə)x]
Word shape [ap(ə)]	88 (.08)	24 (.02)	20 (.02)	101 (.06)
Word shape [at(ə)]	8 (.01)	87 (.07)	43 (.03)	87 (.05)
Word shape [paːt(ə)]	1 (.00)	5 (.00)	49 (.04)	117 (.07)
Word shape [b(ə)x]	13 (.01)	11 (.01)	22 (.02)	34 (.02)
Total word shapes	110 (.10)	127 (.10)	134 (.11)	339 (.20)
Total babbles	1156	1235	1256	1674

[a]Percentages per period are between parentheses.

predominant. In all three periods, however, the total percentage of babbled word shapes remains about the same, that is, 10% to 11% of all the babbles produced. There is a clear discontinuity between these periods and the subsequent period 4. In period 4, babbled word shapes make up 20% of the output. This is about twice as much as before. So, while Th seems to attend mainly to his most recently acquired word shape (and its "differentiating features," o.c.) during the periods 1 to 3, in period 4 he seems to have discovered that he truly has a repertoire.

Certain phenomena add support to the idea that period 4 represents a kind of discontinuity in development. In this period the child not only rehearses *all* the words of his repertoire (instead of mainly the most recently acquired one), but he also seems to start asking himself the general question of "What can I do *to* a word shape?" This is suggested by the emergence of certain "peak performances involving word shapes." Because these peak performances occurred during language work (solitary monologues) they may be regarded as strong instances of effort. There are three such phenomena. Although in themselves infrequent, each mainly occurs in period 4.

The first phenomenon is that of *chaining different word shapes.* Sometimes the child produces a babble in which two different word shapes are concatenated. Examples are presented in table II. There are sequences in which such a chaining seems to be the end result of alternating between word shapes (see sequences a. and c.), but the chainings may also occur relatively independently (as in sequences b., d., and e.). So here is a child whose productive repertoire is not yet larger than four words but who is, in a sense, already occasionally producing two word utterances.

The second phenomenon is the chaining of word shapes and what we will call *positional vocables.* These are short, phonetically consistent forms that are prefixed to word shapes. Table III shows sequences of babbles in which a positional vocable and a word shape are chained (sequences a. to c.). Such babbles were not only produced in sequence, but could also occur as incidental productions (sequences d. to g.). A relevant observation was noted by the mother in her diary in the week following period 4: once, during noninteractive speech, the child produced sequences of positional vocable/word shape chainings in which

Table II.   Chainings of Word Shapes[a]

a) kx-'at, wx, a, at, bux, *at'bux*
b) aut, pu, ph, pfx, *at'bux*
c) pa:jt, bəx, ba:t, *bəx'ba:jt*
d) 'pa:tədətə'pa:tə, 'bato, *buxwə'ba:t*
e) a:pə-xə-'a:pə, w:, p, *pəx-a-'a:pə*

[a]In tables and text, '-' indicates a syllabic boundary; chainings are in italics.

Table III.   Chainings of a Positional Vocable and a Word Shape[a]

a) *tə-'auto, tə-'aːtə*, aːtə, utə, *tə-auʼtə*
b) *tə-'ætə, tə-'ətə*, t-aːtə-'auto
c) *kx̩-'baːdə, kx̩-'paːtə, kx̩-paːtə*
d) *kx̩-'at*, wx̩, a, at, bux, atʼbux
e) aːpə-xə-'aːpə, wː, p, pəx-a-'aːpə, *tə-'aːpə*
f) jaː'beː, jaː'beː, biːjə'wiːjo, (ʔ), *kx̩-'aːpə*
g) u-da-dl̩ːʼdetjə-'aːty, 'apaːt, tə-'oːt

[a]Chainings are in italics.

all word shapes of the repertoire were used in succession ([kx̩-apə], [kx̩-paːtə], [kx̩-auto], etc.). In the babbling monologues, there were two different positional vocables: [kx̩] and [tə]. Each could occur alone or could precede different word shapes. It should be noted that the child restricted their positional use to *word* shapes. Although he frequently produced certain canonical babbling forms (such as [baba] and [kaka]), he never prefixed these with one of the two positional vocable. It should also be noted that, although the positional vocables [tə] phonetically resembles a Dutch determiner ([də]), the positional vocable [kx̩] does not resemble any Dutch closed-class item.

The third phenomenon is that of the so-called *extended word shapes*, i.e., word shapes to which variable syllables are added. In table IV examples of extended word shapes are presented. All of these contain (variants of) the word shape [paːt(ə)] in final position. Vihman and Miller (1988) remark that the distinction between extended word shapes and word shapes embedded in jargon is sometimes difficult to make. This is also the case in our data. See for instance sequence g. in table III, in which /aty/ (a variant form of [at(ə)] appears at the end of a complex but prosodically coherent babble.

Discussion

Although the phenomenon of chaining two word shapes seems not to have been noticed often, the phenomena of adding positional vocables and producing extended word shapes have been observed by other authors as well (Dore et al. 1976; Vihman and Miller 1988, among others). What is new here is the fact that they emerge more or less simultaneously at a very early time (when the child has only a handful of words),

Table IV.   Extended Word Shapes

a) mː'baːt	e) təːtə-oː'pat	i) 'kɛkpaːjt
b) zɪxəw'baːt	f) pu'paːtə	j) bɛbɛ'baːt
c) bom'baːt	g) tum'paːjtjə	k) bɪ-'pæt
d) dzjəw'bæt	h) wɛtɛ'pajt	l) 'bujbaːt

and that their appearance coincides with a considerable general increase in the spontaneous production of word tokens per se. In earlier studies, Elbers (1982, 1988a) has argued that Th used the general strategies (or operating principles) of *chaining* babbles and *varying* babbles, for producing increasingly complex and variegated prelinguistic speech. In the present study, operations like these (chaining word shapes, chaining word shapes and babbles, successively varying these chainings, etc.) begin to be applied to the first word shapes. In this way, the sound and syllable play of prelinguistic babbling seems gradually to give way to the word play of so-called noninteractive speech. What we see here is continuity as well as discontinuity. There is continuity as to the general character of the operations performed. In other words, there is continuity in the *forms* of effort (see Elbers 1988a for a discussion of the apparent universality of these forms). But there is discontinuity in that they begin to be applied to word shapes rather than to categories of babble that have no lexical meaning. In other words, there is discontinuity as to the *focus* of effort. Apparently, this shift of focus may occur as soon as a few words are acquired and sufficiently practiced.

In the terms of our model of skill development, we conclude that the establishment of a few connections between Conceptualizer and Articulator may have immediate consequences for the direction of effort in speech production. Effort turns toward the elements of the interface, i.e., toward those speech forms that can be used by the Lexicalizer. This, probably, is not only important for automating and further developing production skill, but may also affect the interaction between production and perception and the character of early phonological representation (see, among others, Menn 1983; Schwartz and Leonard 1982; Schwartz et al. 1987; Jusczyk this volume). We return to this in the Discussion section.

THE TRANSITION FROM SEMANTIC TO SYNTACTIC SPEECH

Introduction

For the one-word and the early two-word utterance stage, there is yet no convincing evidence of syntactic mediation during sentence production (Peters 1986; Berman 1988; Braine 1988). However, around age 2;6 this seems to change. The closed class emerges. Determiners, pronouns, prepositions, copulas, auxiliaries, and so on either make their first entry in speech, or are used more frequently than before and with a specifically syntactic function. As Roger Brown poetically puts it, closed class morphemes start to "grow up, like an intricate sort of ivy, between and upon the major construction blocks of nouns, verbs, and adjectives" (1973, p. 289). The differentiation of open class and closed class is a well-known phenomenon in the development of linguistic competence. Less well known is a concurrent phenomenon in the development of linguistic performance. Between ages 2 and 3 children pass through a shorter or longer phase of increased disfluency (Yairi 1981, 1982; Wijnen 1990b). Children's utterances then contain many more incomplete sentences, self-corrections, hesitations, and repetitions of sounds, syllables, and larger units, than in either earlier or later stages. Some children may even develop what is known as *developmental stuttering* in this period (Bloodstein 1974; van Riper 1971; Elbers 1983). Is there a causal relationship between the differentiation of open and closed class and the temporary increase in disfluency?

Method

We analyzed records of Th's spontaneous speech between age 2;4 and age 3;0, in order to find an answer to the preceding question. In the period indicated, one hour of tape was collected weekly (with the exception of four weeks between 2;6 and 2;7). The tapes contain conversations between the child and his mother during ordinary routines such as breakfast and book reading (for details concerning transcription and coding see Wijnen 1990b). The child's mean utterance length in words increased from approximately 1.5 at age 2;4 to approximately three words at age 3;0. Thus, the period investigated covers Brown's stage II completely (Brown 1973). The data were analyzed in two separate investigations, each concentrating on a different aspect of performance. One study (Wijnen 1990b) focuses on those instances where skill fails, i.e., on the character, frequency, and distribution of *performance errors* (disfluencies) in Th's speech at different points of time. The other study focuses on the relationship between Th's general sentence development and the development of his language-oriented effort, i.e., of his *peak performances* and *language work* (Elbers 1989b). In the following, we present and discuss the results of the second investigation, after first having summarized the main results of the first one.

Performance Errors

Wijnen (1990b) observed that during the observation period, function words not only increase in number but also change status. For instance, prepositions evolve from being used as unspecific modifiers or verbs (one-place predicates) to a full-fledged relational use (two-place predicates). Wijnen also notes that a significant increase in the child's disfluency rate occurs between age 2;4 and 2;9, and is followed by a decline (see table V for examples of disfluencies). This increase cannot

Table V. Examples of Disfluencies

Repetitions in Sentences
K . . . kerstboom/(Ch . . . christmas tree/)
Ik . . . ik ben ook pap gegeten/(I . . . I am also porridge eaten/)
Heb je . . . heb je hier hand?/(Have you . . . have you here hand?/)
Gaan we I . . . lezen/(Go we r . . . read/)

Incomplete Sentences
Eh . . . dat is . . . /(Ah . . . that is . . . /)
Dan gaat de kapper . . . /(Then will the hairdresser . . . /)

Self-corrections
Ik wil hijs . . . een hijskraan hebben/(I want cra . . . a crane have/)
Zij lig . . . blijft liggen/(She lie . . . remains lying/)

simply be ascribed to increasing sentence length because it occurs across the board. For instance, two-word utterances are produced more disfluently at age 2;9 than at age 2;4. The bulk of disfluency is formed by repetitions (of sounds, syllables, words, and phrases), self-corrections, and incomplete sentences. Concurrently with the increase in the frequency of disfluencies, their distributional pattern changes. This is especially clear in the repetitions. These begin to concentrate themselves in the closed-class items (function words), and to start shifting toward sentence- and phrase-initial positions. Also, length of utterance comes to affect the proportion of sentence-initial disfluency, in that the later ages show a positive correlation between sentence length and amount of sentence-initial disfluency, which is not present at earlier ages. Moreover, the number of self-corrections involving "retraced" restarts (i.e., restarts at the syntactic boundary preceding the speech error, rather than at the error point itself) shows an increase. Thus, the patterns of disfluency that emerge in the later half of the observation period are remarkably similar to the hesitation patterns manifested by adults, whereas in the first half this is not yet the case. The decline of disfluency after age 2;9 coincides with a significant increase in the use of a particular sentence frame (pronoun + verb/auxiliary + minimally one other word). Over a quarter of all the child's sentences then fit this frame, so fluency seems to be bought at the price of a certain monotony.

Wijnen concludes that the type of speech planning that is developing in Th over the age range studied seems to be that of computing serially ordered representations in accordance with the demands of a developing morphosyntax. In this interpretation the distributional shifts of disfluencies toward clause-initial positions are due to the fact that speech is beginning to be planned in syntactically defined units, whereas the relative increase in the amount of disfluency is due to the unusualness of producing speech via a new and not yet smoothly operating processing step, i.e., grammatical encoding.

Peak Performance and Language Work

In the investigation to be reported now we compare and interpret the quantitative relationships between open-class and closed-class items in over-all sentence development, in the development of sentences that can be regarded as peak performances, and in the development of sentences that represent a particular kind of language work (i.e., utterances that are complete and communicatively superfluous self-repetitions). From the available transcriptions, two hours of spontaneous speech were analyzed at the ages of 2;4, 2;6, 2;7, 2;8, 2;9, and 2;11, constituting six periods of two weeks each. Open-class words (content words) were considered: nouns, main verbs, adjectives, and those adverbs that may, in principle, also be used as adjectives. All other words were considered to be closed class items (function words). Interjections were disregarded.

Peak Performances and Grammatical Encoding

In figure 2a the mean number of closed-class and open-class items per sentence is presented for each of the six periods. These means were computed over all complete and fully interpretable sentences; ±600 for each period. Two things are striking in figure 2a. First, the increase in mean sentence length is caused by the increase in mean number of function words per sentence. Chi-square tests show that the differences in the proportions of function words between periods II and III, and between periods V and VI are significant at $p = .001$. In contrast to

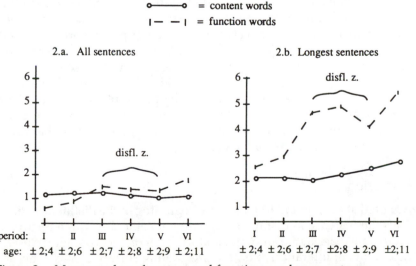

Figure 2. Mean number of content and function words per sentence.

Table VI.   Mean Number of Disfluencies per 100 Words

Period I —4.92	
Period II —4.62	
Period III—6.78 ⎫	
Period IV—6.46 ⎬ disfluency zone	
Period V —9.55 ⎭	
Period VI—5.73	

this, mean number of open-class items remains about the same over the whole age range. Secondly, there is a plateau phase during the periods III, IV, and V. These are precisely the periods in which disfluencies are the most frequent (see table VI). This so-called "disfluency zone" is indicated with a brace in figures 2, 3, and 4. In figure 2b a subcategory of the data from figure 2a is presented, i.e., the 25 *longest* sentences (not containing routine phrases) of each period. In table VII a few examples of such sentences can be found. Because sentence length and syntactic complexity tend to be positively correlated at this age (Brown 1973), we may interpret these longest sentences as peak performances that are indicative of a concentration of effort in syntactic planning.

Figure 2b clearly shows that syntax-oriented effort is spent on closed-class rather than open-class items. In all periods, the two earliest included, the longest sentences contain more closed-class than open-class items. Thus, peak performance is generally ahead of average performance. However, the significant increase in the frequency of closed-class items in period III, which occurs in average performance, simultaneously occurs in peak performance also (χ^2 is significant at $p = .05$ for the difference between period III and period II in figure 2b). This means that period III represents a true discontinuity in development, in that there is a relatively sudden preoccupation with the closed class that seems to be quite general. This conclusion is supported by certain subjective impressions; in this period Th often seemed to almost avoid open-class items and to produce unnecessarily context-dependent speech (see for example the longest sentences in Table VII) in an apparent attempt to "say it with function words" (in a sense, such utterances are the opposite of the telegraphic speech that is characteristic for the earlier two-word stage).

Discussion

As noted above, period III marks the beginning of the disfluency zone. Thus, an increase in disfluency apparently coincides with a relatively sudden increase in the amount of effort spent on incorporating closed-class items in utterances, i.e., on effectuating surface syntax. This ac-

Table VII.   Examples of Peak Performance and Language Work*

Peak Performance (longest sentences from period III)
   a) Kan niet meer d + ditte op doen/(Can no more th + this on do/)
   b) D + die moeten dees allemaal . . . op school/(Th + those must these all . . .
   on school/)
   c) En de eend . . . gaat er ook in/(And the duck . . . goes there also in/)
   d) Is hier nog niet op ə gaatje/(Is here still no on ə hole/)

Language Work (repeated sentences from period III)*
   e) datısəmeis/(Dutch: Dat is een muis. English: That is a mouse)
   f) patısəmœ˞ys/

   g) ɪmaxtRa:jə/(Dutch: Ik mag draaien. English: I may turn)
   h) ɪ̄gmaxtRa:jə/

   i) ma:nsıs:t-axtpədəvɔɪək/(Dutch: Maan zit achter de wolk. English: Moon sits
   behind the cloud)
   j) ma:nzıt-axtədəvɔɪək/

---

*Segments that are improved upon sentence repetition (or, in the case of improvement by deletion, segments that improve the articulation of the repeated sentence by being deleted) are printed in *italics*. Segments that are changed but not improved upon repetition (or, in the case of change by deletion, segments that change the articulation of the repeated sentence by being deleted) are *underlined*.

cords well with Wijnen's finding (see above) that disfluencies begin to cluster at the syntactic boundaries within sentences. Thus, both the peak performances *and* the distributional characteristics of performance errors suggest that disfluencies are correlated with doing something new and unfamiliar (i.e., grammatical encoding).

Language Work and Grammatical Encoding

While period III marks the beginning of the disfluency zone, period V marks its end. Is something special happening in period V that may be responsible for this? This question was investigated by looking at all utterances that were complete and communicatively superfluous self-repetitions. These are repetitions that do not occur *within* sentences (as the repetitions scored as disfluencies do) but *over* sentences (see table VII for a few examples), and that do not seem to have some particular communicative function (repetition not requested by mother, child not obviously claiming mother's attention, etc.). Such self-repeated sentences are a kind of language work and, therefore, they represent language-oriented effort. But in this case effort may be expected to have a *familiarizing* rather than an innovative function because, by definition, a repeated sentence is old and familiar in its meaning and syntax. In other words: this would not be the effort of installing a new component in the production mechanism but that of making it perform smoothly. In figure 3b the mean numbers of function words and content words are presented for the self-repeated sentences. Figure 3a reproduces figure 2a (general performance), for ease of comparison. Figures 3a and 3b are virtually identical up to period V. In the repeated sentences (figure 3b), however, function words score higher in period V than in the preceding period IV (χ^2 significant at $p = .05$), whereas in over-all performance (figure 3a) there is no difference between these two periods.

Discussion

As of period V, but not earlier, the child opts for the spontaneous self-repetition of sentences that contain a higher than average number of function words. The most plausible interpretation is that he now starts practicing and consolidating what, in earlier phases, he had been creating and installing, i.e., surface syntax and planning routines. This may be one of the factors contributing to the subsequent decline of disfluency. Another factor might be the child's tendency to make abundant use of one particular sentence frame in his production (see above), which is also a kind of repetition (though at a more abstract level than literal rehearsal). In other words, while doing something new and unfamiliar (peak performances) is associated with a rise in disfluency, familiarizing operations (language work) are associated with a decline. Thus, the results yield a coherent picture. However, if what is new and

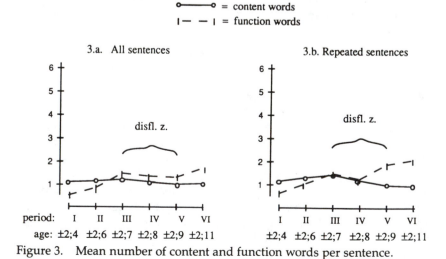

Figure 3. Mean number of content and function words per sentence.

unfamiliar in this period is the emerging Formulator, then a question arises about what aspect of this new processing component is most responsible for the disfluencies. What would be most unfamiliar? Grammatical encoding? Phonological encoding? Or, rather, their *co-ordination*? The next section addresses this question.

Language Work and Phonological Encoding

Communicatively superfluous self-repetitions of complete utterances might, conceivably, also reflect a kind of effort that is different from that of familiarizing syntactic planning. Because repetitions of utterances do not require any *novel* syntactic planning, effort might become free to be allocated to phonological encoding and/or articulation rather than to grammatical encoding. This was investigated by checking whether the articulation of words in the (last) repeated instance of a sentence was the same as in its first production or whether it was different. In the "different" category, a distinction was made between "improved" articulations (closer to adult model) and "different but not clearly improved" articulations (changed, but not unambiguously closer to adult model).[4] Examples of self-repeated sentences from period III can be found in table VII. For instance, in sentences e. and f. (Ik mag draaien/I may turn), the pronoun /ɪk/ is first pronounced as [ɪ] but later as [ɪg]. This is definitely closer to the adult model and therefore it is scored as an improvement. In sentences g. and h. however (Maan zit achter de wolk/moon sits behind the cloud), the preposition /axtəR/ is first produced as [axtə] and later as [axtRə]. It is debatable whether [axtRə] should be considered as closer to the adult model ([axtəR]) than /axtə/, therefore it is scored as "changed but not clearly improved." The results of the analysis are presented in figure 4: in 4a for the open class items, in 4b for the closed class items. It is clear from figure 4a that, once again, something is happening in period III, i.e., at the start of the disfluency zone. From this period onward, the articulation of the content words is improved upon repetition rather than merely changed (χ^2 for the difference between periods III and II is significant at $p = .01$). For the function words (figure 4b) there is no such effect in these periods (and the apparent tendency in period VI is not statistically significant).

---

[4]If the adult model of a certain item in a certain articulatory context permits several allophones in the same position, then the child's substitution (upon sentence repetition) of one allophone for another was scored as "same articulation." Note, furthermore, that the described method of scoring articulatory change in repetitions yields a *relative* measure. In itself, this measure tells nothing about the child's general level of articulatory skill or phonological knowledge.

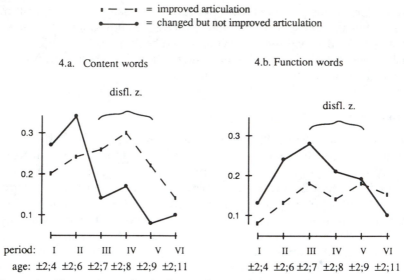

ı — —ı = improved articulation
•——• = changed but not improved articulation

4.a. Content words

disfl. z.

4.b. Function words

disfl. z.

period: I II III IV V VI
age: ±2;4 ±2;6 ±2;7 ±2;8 ±2;9 ±2;11

I II III IV V VI
±2;4 ±2;6 ±2;7 ±2;8 ±2;9 ±2;11

Figure 4.   Proportions of articulatory changes in repeated sentences.

Discussion

We may conclude that Th is, indeed, spending effort on phonological encoding and/or articulating. The remarkable thing, however, is that this effort seems to be concentrated on open-class rather than closed-class items. In a separate investigation of the immediate (within-sentence) self-corrections produced by Th and by one other boy, Wijnen (1990a) finds that when content words are corrected by means of substituting a different word, *correcting* items tend to be similar in phonological structure to *corrected* items. However, when function words are corrected by substitution, this phonological similarity is lacking. A plausible explanation for this result, as well as for the present findings, is that the *phonemization* (the development of phonological organization in the lexicon) of content words precedes that of function words. For the speaking process this would imply that during the lexicalization phase, content words may be confused phonologically (so that a wrong but target-similar phonological representation is selected), but function words may not. At the same time, this would also imply that during the monitoring of the output, content words can be checked more extensively than function words (because their phonological representation is more complete). Another variable that might be important here is the development of sentence prosody. This still awaits investigation.

Altogether, our results show a curious and suggestive pattern. At exactly the same time that disfluencies begin to peak in production (period III), function words in overall performance increase to equal content words, function words in peak performance show a dramatic further increase over content words, and in language work a tendency for improving articulation begins to emerge which is restricted to content words. Thus, period III seems to represent some sort of reorganizational phase in production development. Our conclusion is that when the closed class and the open class are being differentiated from each other, planning effort is drawn toward the closed class, while articulatory effort is simultaneously drawn toward the open class. Thus, the concurrent increase in disfluency may be interpreted as a manifestation of temporary imbalance in a system that has to adapt itself to conflicting claims on effort allocation which are the result of word class differentiation.

In conclusion, it seems clear that amount of disfluency need not only be related to the simple unusualness of certain new operations (grammatical and/or phonological encoding), but may also be due to their initially problematic coordination. Our subject's strategy for solving his fluency problems apparently consists in reducing the effort of planning new structure and increasing the effort of familiarizing such structure. Conceivably, other children might develop other strategies. This may be expected to depend on what specific aspect of formulating is most problematic for a particular child.

DISCUSSION

Jill de Villiers has remarked: "The only evidence from which to reach conclusions about underlying knowledge comes from performance, and the hard lesson is that performance in young children is inconsistent" (1988, p. 55). In our view, what this hard lesson teaches us is that attention should be paid to the essentially nonlinguistic, behavioral aspects of performance, such as effort. In the foregoing, we have used the term *performance* in the more or less ambiguous way in which it is commonly used, i.e., sometimes to indicate a child's actual language behavior at a particular moment, sometimes for referring to the more abstract processing mechanisms underlying this behavior. From now on, we will explicitly restrict *performance* to the first sense, and will use the term *skill* for referring to the last. *Knowledge* of course also refers to an abstract underlying system; the child's knowledge of the structure of language. Thus, language learning implies the development of two underlying entities; linguistic knowledge and linguistic skill.[5] For both,

---

[5]Chomsky, who originally coined the terms *competence* and *performance* (1967), now prefers to speak of *knowledge* and *ability* instead (1986, 1988). At first sight, this seems to be an improvement but in fact little is changed, for now the term *ability* is used in the

development presupposes performance, i.e., *behavior* (perception *and* production).

Although knowledge and skill may attain relatively independent status in adults, it is highly improbable that they develop independently in young children. This interdependency is (implicitly) acknowledged in even the strongly nativist views. For instance, Chomsky contends that the answer to the question of how knowledge of language is acquired, is given "by a specification of UG along with an account of the *ways* in which its principles *interact* with experience to yield a particular language" (1986, p. 3, italics ours). But in what way might *experience* (linguistic input) and *UG* (linguistic endowment) interact if not by way of perceiving and producing language? Also, recent investigations show that the development of articulation interacts with lexical and syntactic development (see Schwartz 1988 for an overview). Thus, an interactive approach that stresses both the interplay between the development of knowledge and that of skill as well as their shared dependency on performance, not only has an a priori plausibility but is also supported by research. To this we have added the contention that *effort*, as a variable of performance proper, plays an important role in the interplay just mentioned. To put it most strongly, effort may be regarded as the developmental meeting ground for knowledge and skill, or, to use a different metaphor, as the common source in performance that feeds both the development of knowledge and of skill and thus is responsible for their interrelated growth.

We have based this article on research and theory from experimental psychology for distinguishing two kinds of language-oriented effort in children's naturalistic production: peak performances and language work. Subsequently, we sketched a model of the development of production skill, and presented two case studies that illustrate the role of effort in the development of this skill. Rather than summarize all this (see the discussions on pp. 351–2; 358–9), we now prefer to speculate about its implications for the acquisition of linguistic knowledge.

In the two case studies, discontinuities in the development of lin-

---

same ambiguous way that was hitherto reserved for *performance*, i.e., sometimes for referring to language behavior itself, sometimes for referring to the abstract skill underlying it. "Two people may share exactly the same knowledge of language but differ markedly in their ability to put this knowledge to use" (Chomsky 1986, p. 9). Here ability is a kind of underlying *trait*, i.e., something that determines *potential* as well as actual behavior. However, the next quote only makes sense if we do *not* interpret ability as the general underlying trait itself, but as its specific realization in behavior at a particular moment: ". . . ability may be impaired . . . , with no loss of knowledge, a fact that would become clear if injury leading to impairment recedes and lost ability is recovered" (Chomsky 1986). One would not expect an underlying trait, if truly lost, to be re-acquired that automatically. So the more correct formulation seems to be that *performance* may be impaired, with no loss of *either* knowledge *or* general ability (skill).

guistic characteristics in over-all performance are interpreted as reflecting discoveries at the level of knowledge, whereas discontinuities in the development of the same characteristics in the subcategories of peak performance and/or language work are taken to reflect tendencies in the child's language-oriented effort. The first study (the transition from babbling to first words) shows that a sudden increase in the over-all production of the four word shapes acquired by the child, is accompanied by the emergence of certain peak performances involving these word shapes. Thus, a development in knowledge (the child's discovery that he has a *repertoire*) seems to give rise to a development in effort (the child's occasional production of chainings of two word shapes, or of a [canonical] babble and a word shape). In itself, this case study does not directly show in what way effort influences the subsequent development of further linguistic knowledge. However, it is tantalizing to speculate that the shift of effort's focus toward word shapes, which occurs in production, may, in its turn, have consequences for the focus of effort in *perception*. If, at this very early age, children already produce combinations involving word shapes (which combinations, being the product of effort, may be expected to leave relatively strong traces in their system, see p. 352), this might sensitize their perception mechanism to instances of such combinations in the input, i.e., to those parts of the input where a word from their own repertoire is preceded or followed by some other (acoustically salient) item. This might lead to *analysis* of these combinations, and thus, to the acquisition of new knowledge. Of course, this hypothesis of production guiding perceptual segmentation and analysis still has to be tested, but we do wish to mention it here because it illustrates the kind of interactive theorizing that goes with an effort-oriented approach.

The second case study (the transition from semantic to syntactic speech around age 2;6) does provide relatively direct evidence concerning the possible functions of effort for the acquisition of knowledge. In this study, over-all production performance manifests two discontinuous leaps; the first in period III, when function words evolve from being produced relatively infrequently to being produced about as frequently as content words, and the second in period VI, when function words clearly outnumber content words in sentence production (see figures 2a and 3a). This suggests that knowledge of the open-class/closed-class distinction is acquired in two more or less separate steps. The first step may be interpreted as the general discovery that certain words are somehow special, i.e., that there exists something like a closed class (class discovery). This interpretation is corroborated by the observation that the child in this stage often seems actively to prefer producing function words rather than content words (and so to produce the reverse of telegraphic speech, see p. 352). The second step may be interpreted as the more specific discovery of how particular kinds of function words should be incorporated in syntactic structures (structure discovery). This interpretation is supported by the finding that, for instance, prepositions evolve from being used as if they were main verbs to being used in a purely relational way (see p. 355). It should be noted that *before* the supposed class discovery is made, function words already outnumber content words in the peak performances (the longest utterances), and that *before* the supposed structure discovery is made, function words already outnumber content words in language work (self-repetitions of utterances). If we are correct in assuming that over-all performance generally reflects the state of a child's knowledge (which seems to be a common assumption in the field) then these results suggest that developments in effort may be conducive to the acquisition of knowledge. In our framework, the following chain of events may be hypothesized: at first, function words mainly figure in the child's peak performances. These utterances, being the product of effort, leave relatively strong traces in the child's memory (see p. 355) and so remain available for post hoc processing. This kind of processing leads to the discovery that certain words are somehow special (class discovery),[6] and, thus, are *interesting*. This causes still more function words to be packed into the peak performances and also causes a general increase of function words in over-all production. At the same time, class discovery stimulates attention to be paid to the articulation of the (phonemized) content words, which are now beginning to be recognized as the true carriers of sentence content. A period of linguistic upheaval follows (which also affects *skill*, see above) during which effort turns, among other things, toward grasping the specific properties of function words. This is done by way of recycling (repeating in language work) sentences that contain a relatively high number of function words (for skill development, recycling seems to have a familiarizing function, but for knowledge acquisition its function may be that of analysis). The result is structure discovery and a more adult way of incorporating function words in general production.

This sketch of how effort might influence knowledge acquisition is compatible with the data presented, but raises questions of its own. For instance, what would be the role of perception of input and of imita-

---

[6]Children might, for example, become aware of the fact that certain words do not seem to have a (stable) referential meaning and that there often are *choices* to be made between, for instance, producing a name or a pronoun. This would be a global discovery of the possibility of class *existence* (comparable to the equally global discovery of "having a repertoire" in the transition from babbling to speech) that might trigger an exploratory strategy of simply producing the nonreferential and/or unstable words as often as possible and "see what happens."

tion[7] in this production-based and -biased account of learning? Not to mention that of innate linguistic knowledge (if there is such a thing). These issues are important, but discussing them would lead us too far afield here. Furthermore, input and endowment already receive ample attention in the literature. In this article, we have emphasized two aspects of language learning that tend to be neglected: effort and skill. Our main aims have been (1) to argue that language learning comprises the development of *skill* as well as knowledge, (2) to show that there *is* effort involved in the learning process, (3) to suggest *how* this effort may be investigated in naturalistic performance, and (4) to make plausible that this effort is *bifunctional*, i.e., that it simultaneously serves the acquisition of linguistic skill and that of linguistic knowledge.

REFERENCES

Berman, R. A. 1988. Word class distinctions in developing grammars. In *Categories and Processes in Language Acquisition*, eds. Y. Levy, I. M. Schlesinger, and M. D. S. Braine. Hillsdale, NJ: Lawrence Erlbaum Associates.

Bloodstein, O. 1974. The rules of early stuttering. *Journal of Speech and Hearing Disorders* 39:379–94.

Bohannon, J., and Stanowicz, L. 1988. The issue of negative evidence: Adult response to children's language errors. *Developmental Psychology* 24:684–89.

Borer, H., and Wexler, K. 1987. The maturation of syntax. In *Parameter Setting*, eds. T. Roeper and E. Williams. Dordrecht: Reidel.

Bowerman, M. 1978. Systematizing semantic knowledge: Changes over time in the child's organization of word meaning. *Child Development* 49:977–87.

Braine, M. D. S. 1974. Length constraints, reduction rules, and holophrastic processes in children's word combinations. *Journal of Verbal Learning and Verbal Behavior* 13:448–56.

Braine, M. D. S. 1988. Modeling the acquisition of linguistic structure. In *Categories and Processes in Language Acquisition*, eds. Y. Levy, I. M. Schlesinger, and M. D. S. Braine. Hillsdale, NJ: Lawrence Erlbaum Associates.

Brown, R. 1973. *A First Language: The Early Stages*. Cambridge, MA: Harvard University Press.

Chomsky, N. 1967. The formal nature of language. In *Biological Foundations of Language*, ed. E. Lenneberg. NY: John Wiley.

Chomsky, N. 1981. Discussion of Putnam's comments. In *Readings in the Philosophy of Psychology, Vol. II*, ed. N. Block. London: Methuen and Co.

Chomsky, N. 1986. *Knowledge of Language: Its Nature, Origin, and Use*. NY: Praeger Publishers.

---

[7]Note that imitation may be interpreted as a kind of effort, and a very special kind at that. Imitation is a form of language behavior that shares characteristics with both peak performance and language work, because it is often communicatively superfluous (language work) and also often implies producing something that is new and unfamiliar (peak performance). In imitation however, language work and peak performance are concerned with elements of the input rather than of self-produced output. Investigating imitation in relation to the other variants of effort in development may prove to be a promising line of research.

Chomsky, N. 1988. *Language and Problems of Knowledge: The Managua Lectures.* Cambridge, MA: MIT Press.

Clark, E. 1982. Language change during language acquisition. In *Advances in Developmental Psychology, Vol. 2*, eds. M. E. Lamb and A. L. Brown. Hillsdale, NJ: Lawrence Erlbaum Associates.

Clark, R. 1974. Performing without competence. *Journal of Child Langauge* 1: 1–10.

Clark, R. 1982. Theory and method in child language research: Are we assuming too much? In *Language Development Vol. 1: Syntax and Semantics*, ed. S. Kuczaj. Hillsdale, NJ: Lawrence Erlbaum Associates.

Claxton, G. 1989. How do you tell a good cognitive theory when you see one? In *Growth Points in Cognition*, ed. G. Claxton. London: Routledge.

de Villiers, J. G. 1988. Faith, doubt and meaning. In *The Development of Language and Language Researchers: Essays in Honor of Roger Brown*, ed. F. S. Kessel. Hillsdale, NJ: Lawrence Erlbaum Associates.

Dore, J., Franklin, M. B., Miller, R. T., and Ramer, A. L. H. 1976. Transitional phenomena in early language acquisition. *Journal of Child Language*, 3:13–29.

Elbers, L. 1982. Operating principles in repetitive babbling: A cognitive continuity approach. *Cognition* 12:45–63.

Elbers, L. 1983. Ontwikkelingsstotteren: Wat ontwikkelt? *Gedrag* 11:28–43.

Elbers, L. 1985. A tip-of-the-tongue experience at age two? *Journal of Child Language* 12:353–65.

Elbers, L. 1988a. How children actively create their own language development: A basic cycle of cognitive operations. In *Children's Creative Communication*, ed. R. Söderbergh. Lund: Lund University Press.

Elbers, L. 1988b. New names from old words: Related aspects of children's metaphors and word compounds. *Journal of Child Language* 15:591–617.

Elbers, L. 1989a. The cognitive effort of developing a first language: Studies on children's active contributions to language learning. Ph.D. diss., Katholieke Universiteit Nijmegen.

Elbers, L. 1989b. Two transitions in the development of speech: An 'effort'-oriented approach. Paper read at the Conference on Phonological Development, September 1989, Stanford University, Stanford.

Elbers, L., and Ton, J. 1985. Play pen monologues: The interplay of words and babbles in the first words period. *Journal of Child Language* 12:551–65.

Ferguson, C. A. 1986. Discovering sound units and constructing sound systems: It's child's play. In *Invariance and Variability in Speech Processes*, eds. J. Perkell and D. Klatt. Hillsdale, NJ: Lawrence Erlbaum Associates.

Ferguson, C. A., and Macken, M. A. 1983. The role of play in phonological development. In *Children's Language. Vol. 4*, ed. K. E. Nelson. Hillsdale, NJ: Lawrence Erlbaum Associates.

Fromkin, V. A. 1971. The non-anomalous nature of anomalous utterances. *Language* 47:27–52.

Garrett, M. F. 1975. The analysis of sentence production. In *The Psychology of Learning and Motivation (Vol. 9)*, ed. G. H. Bower. NY: Academic Press.

Garrett, M. F. 1980. Levels of processing in sentence production. In *Language Production (Vol. 1): Speech and Talk*, ed. B. Butterworth. NY: Academic Press.

Gleitman, L. R. 1981. Maturational determinants of language growth. *Cognition* 10:103–114.

Gleitman, L. R., Landau, B., and Wanner, E. 1988. When learning begins: Initial representations for language learning. In *Linguistics: The Cambridge Survey*, ed. F. Newmeyer. Cambridge: Cambridge University Press.

Golinkoff, R. M. 1981. The case for semantic relations: Evidence from the verbal and nonverbal domains. *Journal of Child Language* 8:413–37.

Hill, J. A. C. 1983. A computational model of language acquisition in the two-year-old. Ph.D. diss., University of Massachusetts.

James, W. 1890. *The Principles of Psychology.* New York: Holt.

Kahneman, D. 1973. *Attention and Effort.* Englewood Cliffs, NJ: Prentice-Hall, Inc.

Kahneman, D., Peavler, W. S., and Onuska, L. 1968. Effects of verbalization and incentive on the pupil response to mental activity. *Canadian Journal of Experimental Psychology* 22:186–96.

Karmiloff-Smith, A., and Inhelder, B. 1974. "If you want to get ahead, get a theory." *Cognition* 3(3):195–212.

Kuczaj, S. A. 1982. Language play and language acquisition. In *Advances in Child Development and Behavior. Vol. 17*, ed. H. W. Reese. NY: Academic Press.

Kuczaj, S. A. 1983. *Crib Speech and Language Play.* NY: Springer-Verlag.

Levelt, W. J. M. 1989. *Speaking: from Intention to Articulation.* Cambridge, MA: MIT Press.

Levelt, W. J. M., Sinclair, A., and Jarvella, R. J. 1978. Causes and functions of linguistic awareness in language acquisition: Some introductory remarks. In *The Child's Conception of Language*, eds. A. Sinclair, R. J. Jarvella, and W. J. M. Levelt. NY: Springer.

Locke, J. L. 1988. The sound shape of early lexical representations. In *The Emergent Lexicon: The Child's Development of a Linguistic Vocabulary*, eds. M. D. Smith and J. L. Locke. San Diego: Academic Press.

MacNamara, J. 1982. *Names for Things: A Study of Child Language.* Cambridge, MA: Bradford Books/MIT Press.

Menn, L. 1983. Development of articulatory, phonetic and phonological capabilities. In *Language Production. Vol. 2*, ed. B. Butterworth, London: Academic Press.

Mills, A. E. 1989. Variatie en taalontwikkeling: Psammetichus revisited. Inaugural address. Amsterdam, November 1989.

Moskowitz, B. A. 1978. The acquisition of language. *Scientific American* 5:82–96.

Neisser, U. 1976. *Cognition and Reality.* San Francisco: W. H. Freeman.

Nelson, K. 1981. Individual differences in language development. *Developmental Psychology* 17:170–87.

Nelson, K. 1983. The derivation of concepts and categories from event representations. In *New Trends in Conceptual Representation: Challenges to Piaget's Theory?*, ed. E. K. Scholnick. Hillsdale, NJ: Lawrence Erlbaum Associates.

Peters, A. M. 1986. Early syntax. In *Language Acquisition: Second Edition*, eds. P. Fletcher and M. Garman. Cambridge: Cambridge University Press.

Pinker, S. 1984. *Language Learnability and Language Development.* Cambridge, MA: Harvard University Press.

Schaerlaekens, A. M. 1973. *The Two-word Sentence in Child Language Development.* Den Haag: Mouton.

Schlesinger, I. M. 1971. The production of utterances and language acquisition. In *The Ontogenesis of Grammar*, ed. D. I. Slobin. NY: Academic Press.

Schwartz, R., and Leonard, L. 1982. Do children pick and choose? An examination of phonological selection and avoidance in early lexical acquisition. *Journal of Child Language* 9:319–36.

Schwartz, R., Leonard, L., Loeb, D., and Swanson, L. 1987. Attempted sounds are sometimes not: An expanded view of phonological selection and avoidance. *Journal of Child Language* 14:00.

368 / Elbers and Wijnen

Snow, C. E., and Ferguson, C. A. (eds.) 1977. *Talking to Children: Language Input and Acquisition*. Cambridge: Cambridge University Press.

Sridhar, S. N. 1988. *Cognition and Sentence Production: A Cross-linguistic Study.* NY: Springer.

Treisman, A. M. 1964. Monitoring and storage of irrelevant messages in selective attention. *Journal of Verbal Learning and Verbal Behavior* 3:449–59.

Valian, V. 1986. Syntactic categories in the speech of young children. *Developmental Psychology* 4:562–79.

van Loon-Vervoorn, A., and van der Ham-van Koppen, M. 1988. The importance of age of word acquisition for imageability in word processing. In *Cognitive and Neuropsychological Approaches to Mental Imagery*, eds. M. Denis, J. Engelkamp, and J. T. E. Richardson. Dordrecht: Martinus Nijhoff Publishers.

van Riper, C. G. 1971. *The Nature of Stuttering*. Englewood Cliffs: Prentice-Hall.

Vihman, M. M. 1982. A note on children's lexical representations. *Journal of Child Language* 9:239–64.

Vihman, M. M. 1987. The interaction of production and perception in the transition to speech. Paper read at the Twelfth Annual Boston University Conference on Language Development, October 1987, Boston University, Boston.

Vihman, M. M. In press. Ontogeny of phonetic gestures: Speech production. To appear in *Modularity and the Motor Theory of Speech Perception*, eds. I. G. Mattingly and M. Studdert-Kennedy. Hillsdale, NJ: Lawrence Erlbaum Associates.

Vihman, M. M., and Miller, R. 1988. Words and babble at the threshold of language acquisition. In *The Emergent Lexicon: The Child's Development of a Linguistic Vocabulary*, eds. M. D. Smith and J. L. Locke. San Diego: Academic Press.

Wells, G. 1986. Variation in child language. In *Language Acquisition: Second Edition*, eds. P. Fletcher and M. Garman. Cambridge: Cambridge University Press.

Wexler, K. 1982. A principle theory for language acquisition. In *Language Acquisition: The State of the Art*, eds. E. Wanner and L. R. Gleitman. Cambridge: Cambridge University Press.

Wijnen, F. 1988. Spontaneous word fragmentations in children: Evidence for the syllable as a unit in speech production. *Journal of Phonetics* 16:187–202.

Wijnen, F. 1990a. On the development of language production mechanisms. Ph.D. diss., Katholieke Universiteit Nijmegen.

Wijnen, F. 1990b. The development of sentence planning. *Journal of Child Language* 17:651–75.

Yairi, E. 1981. Disfluencies of normally speaking two-year-old children. *Journal of Speech and Hearing Research* 24:490–95.

Yairi, E. 1982. Longitudinal studies of disfluencies in two-year-old children. *Journal of Speech and Hearing Research* 25:155–60.

Chapter • 12

Material Evidence of Infant Selection from the Target Language
A Cross-Linguistic Phonetic Study

Bénédicte de Boysson-Bardies,
Marilyn May Vihman,
Liselotte Roug-Hellichius,
Catherine Durand, Ingrid Landberg, and
Fumiko Arao

Phonetic segmentation and the phonological representation of units are not generally assumed to underlie infants' perceptual capacities within the first year. Such empirical evidence of "phonological representations" as the appearance of a rule system in word production is found only when the child already has acquired some 50 words (Macken and Ferguson 1983; Menn 1978, 1981). However, well before this stage infants produce speech-like syllables and

The work reported in this study reflects the collaborative efforts of the Cross-linguistic Project on Infant Vocalizations, which includes C. A. Ferguson (U.S.), B. Lindblom, O. Engstrand, and F. Lacerda (Sweden), and P. Hallé (France), in addition to the authors. We would like to express our gratitude to the other members of this team for their stimulating suggestions and ideas. We also thank the parents and the infants for their kind help. This work was supported in part by a grant from NSF (BNS 85-20048) to C. A. Ferguson with the participation of B. de Boysson-Bardies, B. Lindblom, and M. Vihman.

sequences of syllables. By 11 to 12 months of age some of these sound sequences can be recognized by adults as words.

Babbling has been shown to be a genuine stage in language development, with a repertoire and a syllable structure related to the repertoire and the structure of the first words (Oller et al. 1975; Woods and Stockman 1982; Leonard et al. 1981; Ferguson and Macken 1983; Vihman et al. 1985; Vihman and Miller 1988; Elbers and Ton 1985). However, it is sometimes assumed that neither babbling nor first word production is relevant to the later acquisition of phonology (Locke 1983).

TEN-MONTH-OLD INFANT CAPACITIES

At about 7 months of age, infants begin to produce "canonical" babbling. The notion of the "canonical" syllable has been defined by Oller (1986); these syllables are largely restricted to the most commonly occurring syllable types in languages. The productions of infants at the beginning of babbling are often composed of sequences of reduplicated CV syllables (Oller 1980; Stark 1980; Roug, Landberg, and Lundberg 1989). The articulatory gestures underlying such productions consist in cyclic alternation of open and closed vocal tract, with a clearly syllabic quality to the productions (MacNeilage, Studdert-Kennedy, and Lindblom 1985). These gestures are "maturationally given" and involve extensive coarticulation between vowel and lingual consonants. An explanation in terms of vocal tract maturation has been proposed to account for the evolution of babbling productions. The constraints on motor control and articulatory compatibility factors (Kent and Murray 1982; Kent and Bauer 1985) ensure considerable similarity between the first babbling sounds of all infants. However, by 10 months the infant's articulatory capacities allow for a variety of sounds. At this age infants more often vary the types of syllables they produce in a sequence: reduplication is less frequent, and variegation is achieved by the chaining of different syllables within a single utterance. The simple consonant-vowel types become less dominant. Also inter-infant variability can be considerable.

Around this same time the perceptual capacities of infants are evolving. Genetically encoded perceptual capacities narrow, and phonetic discrimination may become more dependent upon the phonemic organization of the language of the environment (Werker and Tees 1984). Evidence for selective attention to specific experience at the word level is found in infants' preference for words of their own language as against words of a different language (Jusczyk in press) and in infants' preference for samples that preserve words as units (Woodward 1987). The data show that infants' attention is focused on those aspects of language most relevant to categorization or recognition in the target language. Unfortunately, very little is known about the weight of different cues in speech perception, and these cues are not necessarily the same for different languages. However, epigenetic evolution of perceptual capacities allows the 10-month-old infant to weight specific aspects of input that are important in processing the language spoken in the environment. The special mode of perception evolves when infants start to attach linguistic significance to speech (Jusczyk in press). Although experimental data are few in this domain, there is strong empirical evidence of word comprehension at this age (Lewis 1936; Leopold 1939; Huttenlocher 1974).

Visually and acoustically, 10-month-old infants are capable of exemplar-based generalizations that allow them to respond to "prototypes" (Grieser and Kuhl 1989) even though they have never been exposed to them during familiarization. Capacities for recurrence and temporal organization of behavior, dependent upon frontal cortex maturation, emerge at this age (Goldman-Rakic 1981).

In order to produce words, infants have to relate an acoustic representation of a word to a set of articulatory gestures aiming to reproduce it. At the very least, the production of the first words indicates that the process of building a representation of speech has begun.

However, for most infants, babbling production continues to coexist with the first words for four or five months (Elbers 1982; Vihman and Miller 1988). There is a lag of four to five months between the first words and the time when the vocabulary increases rapidly in such a way as to suggest the beginning of a phonological organization in segmental units. A number of key issues arise in connection with the transition from babbling to the 50-word point in production. Among these are the organization of infant production and the nature of speech processing revealed by concurrent babbling.

CROSS-LINGUISTIC STUDIES

Cross-linguistic studies may help to determine whether the stage of variegated babbling and first words is constrained mainly by the universal motor level of organization, or whether the selection and organization of sound production reveals a "linguistic" processing of speech, and if so how (Boysson-Bardies, Sagart, and Bacri 1981).

A first cross-linguistic study was carried out on vowel production of 10-month-old infants (Boysson-Bardies et al. 1989). The vocalic space of the infant develops in a continuous and consistent way during the first year of life (Lieberman 1980; Buhr 1980), and at around 9 or 10 months there is a stabilization of the anatomical configuration of the vocal tract. Thus, the study of vowels in babbling should be particularly relevant to hypotheses concerning the early influence of the linguistic environment. The finding that differences in the vocalic spaces of 10-month-old infants reflected some of the systematic differences between the vocalic spaces of their target languages led to the hypothesis that setting loose articulatory limits to tongue and lip movements in vowel production could be the first step toward acquiring the vowel system, and that speech sounds in the surrounding language provide material for building the internal representations that infants use to try out articulatory patterns.

During the last two years we have undertaken another cross-linguistic study to investigate the phonetic/phonological organization of infant production in different linguistic environments from the age of 9 months until 25 words were produced in a session. The goal was to see when and how the influence of the target language becomes apparent in infant production.

INFLUENCE OF THE TARGET LANGUAGE

To support the hypothesis of an influence of perceptual processing of the target language on early production, two points must be ascertained. First, the infants' production has to exhibit tendencies specific to a group definable in terms of the linguistic background (i.e., intergroup differences have to override intragroup differences). Second, these tendencies have to reflect characteristics of the infants' linguistic background.

With regard to the first point, we have investigated universal and language-specific characteristics of the consonantal repertoire of late babbling and first words of 20 infants in four language groups. We examined the similarities and differences in the distribution of place and manner categories across the different language groups and their evolution during the transition period. A comparison of the distribution of manner and place categories in babbling production and in first words has been carried out, as well as the plotting of the distribution of manner categories for final consonants in babbling and words across the language groups. Finally, intergroup comparison has been carried out on the length of vocalizations in syllables.

With regard to the second point, we related these distributions to the distribution of place and manner categories in the sample of adult words used as targets by the infants. We chose not to follow the tradition of relating infant consonant repertoire to consonantal computations based on average media speech (radios, newspapers) because we do not view such a repertoire as representative of the child's environment. On the one hand, the assumption that the language of the environment influences infant productions does not mean that infants passively compute the frequency of sounds produced in their environment. On the other hand, fluent speech includes uncommon words rarely occurring in the infants' environment, as well as function words that are acoustically less salient and pragmatically less relevant for infants. Selective attention processes may underlie the organization of speech processing. Therefore, we decided to select a subset of adult words that are relevant for children. For that purpose we chose to compare the distribution of manner and place categories in infants' productions with the distribution of manner and place categories in the sample of adult words that served as targets for the infants. For each language group, measures of interest were computed on the basis of the phonetic transcription of the adult words attempted at least once by one infant in the group. The subset of adult words found to serve as targets included approximately 105 prototype words for each group. The distribution of place and manner categories in babbling and early words is thus compared to corresponding categories in words that are recognized as belonging to the children's environment in each language group.

TARGET-WORD DISTRIBUTION

The distribution of manner and place categories in the prototype target words shows clear-cut differences across four language groups: French, English, Japanese, and Swedish (figures 1 and 2).

The distribution of consonants at the onset of the target words in the four language groups differs markedly from the total distribution of consonants. One main attractor (for the infants) seems to be the onset of the signal. Some acoustic characteristics (such as the burst of energy of the stop) and some visual characteristics, (such as lip closure for labials) may help to form a global organization of perceptually rich forms that are particularly relevant acoustically and visually to indicate place or manner category (Stevens, 1972, 1980; Blumstein 1986; Lindblom 1986). Furthermore, in English and in Swedish the first syllable of a dissyllable is often stressed, reinforcing the weight of the onset. Consonantal production in the transition stage has been shown to be related to the position of the consonant in the word: deletion of the final consonant is frequent (Vihman and Ferguson 1987).

Swedish and American infants have a higher percentage of stops in target words than do the French and the Japanese. However, the percentage of initial stops is similar for Swedish, American, and Japanese infants. In all groups stops represent more than 60% of initial

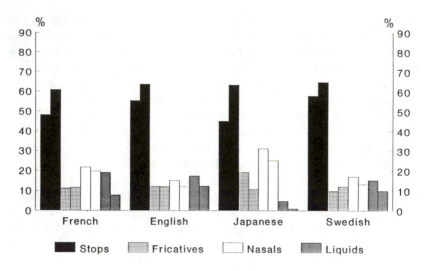

Figure 1.   Distribution of manner categories in French, English, Japanese, and Swedish. 1st column: All consonants in target words. 2nd column: Initial consonants in target words.

consonants in target words. The percentage of labials is higher in initial position for the four groups. In French, initial labials are far more numerous than in English, Japanese, or Swedish. These last groups share close distribution of place categories in initial position, but there is a higher percentage of initial velars in Swedish.

CROSS-CULTURAL DATA

Twenty infants (5 French, 5 American, 5 Japanese, and 5 Swedish) were recorded in their homes under similar conditions starting at the age of 9 to 10 months, when only babbling was present, and continuing until they produced 25 words during a half-hour session. The French, American, and Swedish infants were recorded in their country of origin. The Japanese infants were recorded in the San Francisco area in Japanese monolingual homes. Six sessions were transcribed in IPA: the first, a session in which only babbling was produced, the second and third when the child produced about 4 words, the fourth and fifth when the child produced 15 words, and the last when he or she produced 25 words. Most of the infants produced 4 words between 11 and 12 months, while the 25-word session was tape-recorded between 15 and 19 months, except for Japanese infants for whom the word sessions occurred later.

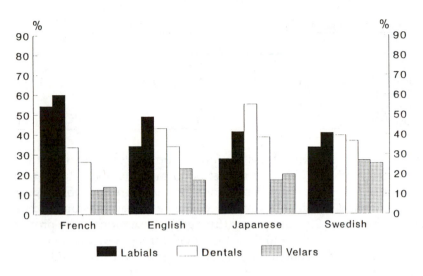

Figure 2.   Distribution of place categories in French, English, Japanese, and Swedish. 1st column: All consonants in target words. 2nd column: Initial consonants in target words.

The lag between the first 4 words and first 25 words was about five months for the majority of the infants (table I).

A subset of all transcriptions was cross-checked by two transcribers of different linguistic backgrounds. The reliability study resulted in more than 80% agreement and no systematic bias.

Consonantal productions were classified according to manner and place categories. Only "true" consonants have been considered in this study: glides and glottals were excluded from the count. For manner categories, consonants were classified according to five categories: stops, affricates, fricatives, nasals, and liquids. For ease of presentation, affricates and fricatives are grouped together. For place of articulation, consonants were classified into three categories: (1) labial (including labiodental), (2) dental (including alveolar and palatal), and (3) velars (including uvular).

DEVELOPMENT IN THE COURSE OF THE PERIOD STUDIED

There is considerable stability within each language group in the mean frequency distribution throughout the period studied for the manner categories. Developmental effects are revealed more by a drop in standard deviation than through changes of the mean. Standard deviations

Table I.   Mean Age of Subjects at Lexical Levels (in Months)

	0	4	15	25
Language				
French	10	12	15	16–17
English	9–10	11–12	14	16
Japanese	13	14	17–18	19
Swedish	9	11–12	15–16	16–17

(SD) are homogeneous across the four groups. Development is, thus, consistent with the idea of a reduction of individual variability reinforcing the specific tendencies in each language group. Table II gives the means and standard deviations for the percentage of stops and nasals at the 0- and 25-word points (first and last sessions). The proportion of fricatives and liquids is too small throughout this period to allow longitudinal comparison, especially given the wide individual variability (table II).

The evolution of the percentage of stops in all productions during the period studied is strikingly similar for the four groups. There is an increase in stop production between the 0-word session and the 4-word session, and a slight decrease from the 4- and 15-word sessions to the 25-word session. The similarity of this evolution suggests general tendencies (figure 3).

For place categories, intersubject variability in the first sessions is very strong. Figure 4 gives the means and standard deviations for labials. The dramatic SD drop from the first session to the 25-word session confirms the main trends found for place distribution. The drop of SD is the same for each group except Swedish. There are only four infants in session 0 for Swedish because one of the five children had no 0-word session.

Table II.   Percentage of Stops and Nasals: Mean and Standard Deviation for 0 and 25 Words Sessions

	Stops		Nasals	
	0	25	0	25
	(months)		(months)	
Language				
French	43.8	48.3	36.3	27.3
	(14.07)	(12.5)	(14.11)	(2.8)
English	64.9	67.7	16.8	16
	(16.12)	(11.78)	(20.82)	(6.91)
Japanese	58.7	61.3	26.8	21.2
	(8.54)	(3.88)	(12.43)	(6.01)
Swedish	66.5	71	16.6	8.1
	(23.85)	(11.69)	(7.31)	(6.46)

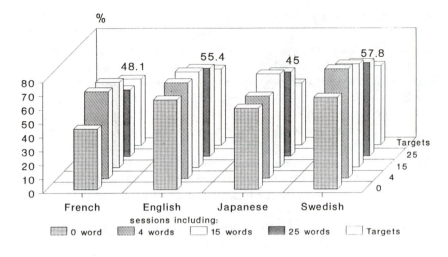

(The value labels indicated are
those of the targets)

Figure 3. Evolution of the percentage of stops.

For French and Swedish infants, the mean for labial productions is stable throughout the period studied, but there is a regular decline of labials in the American and Japanese infants' productions (see figure 6). Mean percentage of velar productions is also stable from the 4-word session onward (see figure 8).

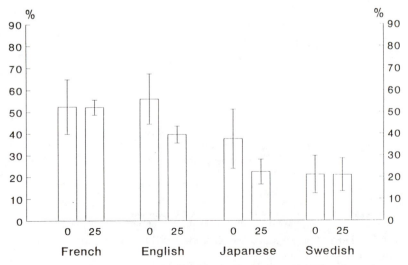

Figure 4. Mean percentage and *SD* of labials for 0- and 25-word sessions.

INTER-GROUP COMPARISON

The distribution of manner and place categories is different for the four infant groups. As predicted by "universal" tendencies, stops represent more than 50% of the consonants for all the groups (except French in the first and last sessions); however, there is a clear and significant difference between the groups $(F(3,16) = 3.88\,p = .05)$. Pair-wise comparison of the percentage of stops shows a significant difference for Swedish $(F(1,8) = 6.02\,p < .06)$ and French infant productions. A systematic difference in the percentage of nasals is also found between French and Japanese on the one hand and Swedish on the other $F(3,16) = 5.616\,p < .02$ (figure 5). English does not differ significantly from the other language groups (figure 6).

The percentage of fricatives and liquids is stable across the sessions for each group. These percentages are too small to allow informative group comparisons. However, liquids are less frequent in Japanese infants from the first session on. French and Swedish 10-month-old infants produce 12% and 10% liquids respectively, while the percentage of liquids is only 2% for the Japanese infants at the same age.

There are significant differences $(F(3,16) = 5.32\,p < .005)$ in labial distribution in the four groups: French and American infants produce

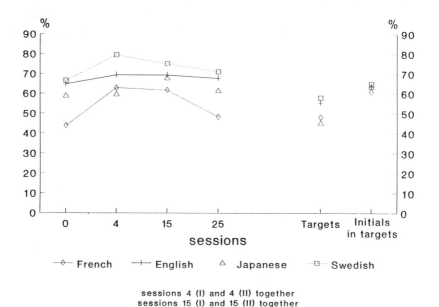

—◇— French   —+— English   △ Japanese   ⋯▢⋯ Swedish

sessions 4 (I) and 4 (II) together
sessions 15 (I) and 15 (II) together

Figure 5.   Percentage of stops by sessions for the four language groups (all productions).

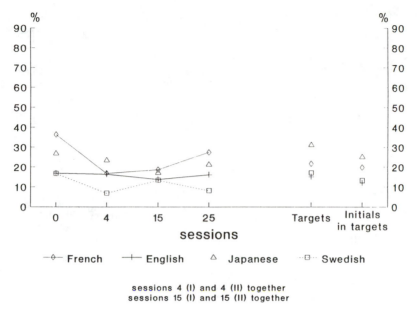

Figure 6.   Percentage of nasals by sessions for the four language groups (all productions).

more labials than Swedish and Japanese. The difference between the two groups is clear from the first session (figure 7).

Dentals are more numerous than labials in Japanese and Swedish from the first session on. For Japanese, dentals are mostly nasals. Labials and dentals together account for 75% to 80% of consonants according to place categories for English, Swedish, and Japanese groups, and 90% for French.

The French infants produce fewer velars from the first session on. In contrast, velar production for Japanese is relatively high and stable. From the first session until the last, the Japanese infants produce a mean of 25% velars and the French a mean of 9% ($F(1–8) = 6.44\ p < .05$) (figure 8).

SENSITIVITY TO PHONETIC
FREQUENCIES OF THE LINGUISTIC ENVIRONMENT

The comparison of the manner distribution categories of target words with the distribution of consonants in infant production (babbling and words or babbling only) shows the following:

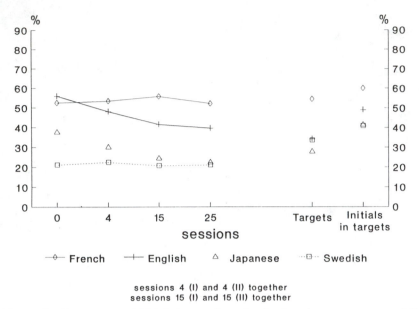

Figure 7.   Percentage of labials by sessions for the four language groups (all productions).

1. The patterns of manner distribution in infant productions (total productions or babbling productions only) do agree with the manner distribution patterns of target words in each group. The higher frequency of stops in Swedish and American infants as of the first sessions reflects the higher percentage of stops found in the adult words later chosen as targets by the infants. The distribution of consonants according to manner in the target words predicts the ranking to be Swedish > English > Japanese > French for stops. The ranking of stop percentage in infant production is indeed Swedish > English > Japanese > French. The higher frequency of nasals in French and Japanese infant productions reflects the higher percentage of nasals in the input languages. However, in babbling, French nasal production (mostly [m]), surpasses that of the Japanese (mostly [n]), although the adult distribution is the reverse. This may be related to the fact that in Japanese target words, weak final nasals are often realized as nasalized vowels. French target words frequently ended in nasalized vowels that are not counted here. The influence of targets and of the strong phonological characteristics of the adult language can be seen for liquids, in spite of the relatively low percentage of liquids in infant productions in all four groups. From the 0-word session onward, French infants produce about 10% liquids, but the percentage of liquids

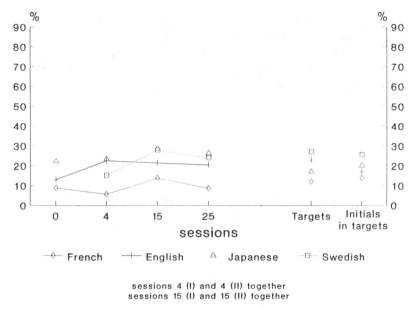

Figure 8.   Percentage of velars by sessions for the four language groups (all productions).

does not exceed 5% for Japanese infants (in target words, 19.3% and 4.8%, respectively).

2.   There is a far greater number of stops in the infants' productions than in targets in all four linguistic groups. The percentage of stops in infant productions more closely reflects the high frequency of stops as initial consonant in the target words.

The distribution of place of articulation in targets also is relevant in accounting for the distribution of place categories in the infant productions. The distribution of target initial consonants predicts the ranking of the percentage of labials, dentals, and velars found in the four groups (as shown in figure 3).

As might be predicted by the structure of the adult target words, French infants produce the highest percentage of labials and the lowest percentage of velars. Swedish and Japanese produce the lowest percentage of labials and the highest percentage of velars.

In spite of some common or "universal" tendencies (the high percentage of stops, the high percentage of labials and dentals), a selection of articulatory gestures in late babbling and first words can be seen to arise from phonetic patterns traceable to the linguistic environment of the child. The target words in the different groups often have the same meaning (toys, animals, food), but their sound patterns are different (e.g., 18% of target words in Swedish begin with a cluster, as against 5% in French). Infants do not systematically choose their target words from among the simplest phonetic forms. However, the target words for the different language groups have common characteristics, such as a high percentage of stops at the onset (more than 60% for all groups).

COMPARISON OF BABBLING REPERTOIRE AND INFANT WORD REPERTOIRE

The babbling repertoire and the first word repertoire have been shown to be closely related. For each individual infant a definite relationship has been found between the preference for some consonants in babbling and the speech gestures employed in the first words (Vihman et al. 1985; Vihman 1991). Vihman states that the differences in the use of phonetic categories in the prelinguistic stage predicts the use of phonetic categories in words for the individual child. However, interinfant variability decreases as the lexicon increases, and a pattern of increasing uniformity emerges across infants.

In this study, the comparison between babbling repertoire and infant word repertoire, independent of sessions, is very revealing of the motoric consequences arising from constraints on sequencing and combinations of segments. Differences are found in the distribution of manner and place categories between babbling productions and first word productions. They reveal a universal tendency favoring stops and labials in word production.

If we consider the totality of productions, the percentage of stops increases between the 0-word and 4-word sessions, is high at the 4- and 15-word sessions and then decreases at the 25-word session. This evolution holds for all four language groups. In contrast with a slight decrease at the 25-word session, the percentage of stops increases dramatically (more than 10%) in the word production of French, American, and Swedish infants. The increase in stops reflects the high frequency of stops in the initial consonants of target words. As speech is organized temporally, there is a bias toward the acoustic characteristics of the onset. First-syllable stress enhances the salience of the initial consonant: in American and Swedish infant productions, the percentage of stops is even higher than the percentage of initial stops in target words. At the same time, initial consonants require less motoric control, because the contextual constraints are minimal (figure 9).

The distribution found for fricatives is quite the reverse of that for stops. The production of fricatives increases or is stable overall for the four language groups from the first session to the 25-word session; however, the percentage of fricatives drops dramatically in word pro-

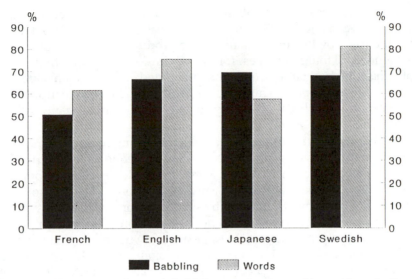

Figure 9. Percentage of stops in babbling production and in word production for the four languages.

duction. Continuants in babbling and in the target words represent about 10% of consonants. In infant words this percentage is reduced by half. The amount of control required for producing continuants in a target leads to strategies of substitution or avoidance when the infant must produce them under contextual or output constraints (Kent, this volume). In French, voiced fricatives are particularly avoided or missed when they appear in target words. This systematic and general difference between the babbling repertoire and the first word repertoire for the reciprocal distribution of stops and fricatives allows us to predict the phonological rules of substitution or deletion found in the productions of older children.

Japanese word production demonstrates an increase in the production of nasals accompanied by a decrease in that of stops. The generally high percentage of nasals and the low percentage of stops in target words fit well with these data. The percentage of fricatives in Japanese does not decrease between babbling and word production. On the one hand, Japanese infants are older, as a group, when 15 and 25 words are first produced in a session, and this may entail a decrease in the weight of motoric constraints on the articulatory process. On the other hand, affricates and fricatives are much more numerous in target words. Finally, affricates account for the stability of the fricative percentage. In Japanese motherese, fricatives are often produced as affricates, as an affect marker.

For place, the same phenomenon of reorganization in words is found. The percentage of labials decreases dramatically between the 0-word session and the 25-word session in babbling (except for French), but increases by 10% in infant first word production. The rise of labials is found in all four languages. It is in part linked to the high frequency of initial labials in target words. As mentioned earlier, not only are the acoustic onset properties more salient for the organization of input representation, but labials at the onset are also particularly visually salient (figure 10).

We interpret the differences between babbling repertoire and first word repertoire as reflecting the constraints of sequencing the articulatory gestures to produce a target word. The motor level has important implications for the shape of first word productions. The obligatory sequentiality of segments and syllables required for word production interacts with coarticulatory tendencies. Selection of articulatory gestures and free production of these gestures do not imply that the segments thus produced are independently manipulable (MacNeilage and Davis in press). The obligatory sequentiality also interacts with infant programming capacities. A limited resource assumption may account for a tendency to "return" to more basic adjustments when the infant tries to approximate a complex target.

FINAL CONSONANTS

Babbling and first words are characterized by a high proportion of open syllable production (Jakobson 1941; Oller et al. 1975). Languages differ widely on this point. In adult English, 32% of consonants occur in word-final position (Mines, Hanson, and Shoup 1978) as against only 18% in French (Malécot 1974). Because English is characterized by a high proportion of word-final stops and nasals, we made the assumption that we should find a higher percentage of final consonants in the vocalizations of American infants. Ranking on target words matches this assumption, with number of final consonants decreasing steadily in the order English, Swedish, French, and Japanese (table III).

For the total ratio of final consonants, our hypothesis for English is borne out. Japanese infants, as we predicted, produce a lower proportion of final consonants, but the difference between groups is too small to be interpreted. However, the distribution by manner categories is more revealing. In babbling, nasals represent 44% of final consonants in French compared with 45% in Japanese, 34% in Swedish, and only 8% in English. Final stops are more than twice as frequent in English (48%) as in French (21%), partly reflecting the percentage of final stops in target words, 41% versus 6% respectively. This trend is even more marked for infant word production, with 64% final stops in English,

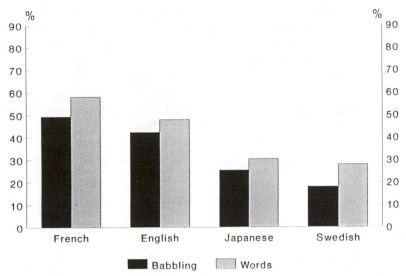

Figure 10. Percentage of labials in babbling and in words.

58% in Swedish, but only 5% in French, and 8% in Japanese. At the same time, nasals represent only 11% of final consonants in American infants' word production, and 88% of final consonants in Japanese infants' word production. Over 95% of final consonants in our target

Table III. Percentage of Final Consonants Babbling, in Infant Words and Target-Words According to Manner

	French (%)	English (%)	Japanese (%)	Swedish (%)
Babbling				
Stops	23	48	40	22
Fricatives	21	32	11	30
Nasals	44	8	45	34
Liquids	11	12	3	14
Total of final consonants	5	9	5	6
Words				
Stops	9	64	8	58
Fricatives	10	18	3	20
Nasals	77	11	89	17
Liquids	4	6	—	5
Total of final consonants	7	11	5	6
Target-words				
Stops	6	41	0	37
Fricatives	6	14	0	13
Nasals	35	11	100	15
Liquids	52	29	0	34
Total of final consonants	15	32	7	20

sample were nasals, since almost 5% of the sample might have been subject to the colloquial pattern of deleting final voiceless high vowels.

Here universal motoric proclivities appear clearly to interact with the influence of target words. For instance, the percentage of fricatives as final consonants is relatively high in babbling for all languages, as predicted (Oller et al. 1975). However, from the first session onward, the percentage of final fricatives is already lower in Japanese and French infants, in accord with the low frequency of final fricatives in these languages. The reverse is found for nasals. The under-representation of final liquids in French infant productions is the exception to the global fit with target word distribution of final consonants.

VOCALIZATION LENGTH

We predicted that both the complex affixing of Japanese and the phrasal phonotactic organization of French would lead to relatively longer surface phonological units for French and Japanese. Infant data show that Japanese and French infants indeed produced more di- and polysyllabic vocalizations than American infants, but only beginning with the 15-word sessions. From that point on, there is a strong difference between the mean number of multisyllabic vocalizations and words for American infants and other groups. The large number of monosyllables found in American infant productions reflects the high percentage of monosyllabic target words in this language (figure 11).

The length of target words has no influence on the length of babbling productions. However, when infants produce words they tend to maintain the syllable count of the adult word. The syllable count seems to provide the structure or "frame" for the organization of infant production, independently of the segmental content (which can be, and often is, variable). No systematic strategies of reduction or reduplication are found, although examples of such processes are found in all groups and are more frequent in the behavior of some infants.

DISCUSSION

Comparative analyses were carried out on the consonantal repertoire, although we did not assume that selection from the ambient language was based on prior phonetic segmentation by the infants. Indeed, acoustic patterns of syllable unit size or "a system in which the word is a unitary whole which has a general prosodic shape" (Macken 1979, p. 163) could lead to the same results as far as the distribution of consonants is concerned. A segmentally unanalyzed auditory representa-

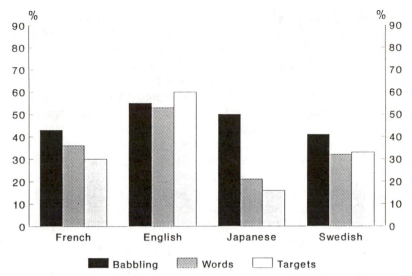

Figure 11. Percentage of monosyllabic productions in babbling, infant words, and target words for the four languages.

tion may provide a target for a motor plan sufficient to initiate an epigenetic selection of articulatory gestures.

The data confirm universal trends in the distribution of place and manner categories. Labials and dentals are more frequent than velars, and stops and nasals are more frequent than fricatives and liquids. In comparison with babbling, the repertoire of the first words shows a systematic bias in favor of stops and labials. However, in general there is a fair stability in the distribution of consonant categories over time within each language group.

Infants are sensitive to the sensory consequences of articulatory movements as well as to auditory information (Jusczyk, this volume; Werker and Pegg, this volume). During babbling, a selection can arise from gradual matching between motor gesture, its sensory consequences, and information selected from ambient speech (Locke 1986; Vihman 1991, this volume). The main point of this study, however, is the evidence of a selection process on general articulatory capacities when the infant starts to attach linguistic significance to speech. Near 10 months of age, in spite of individual differences between infants, babbling distribution (at least according to place and manner) already reflects a selection of the speech sounds in the words that are the most relevant in the infants' environment.

The data fit well with the assumption that words as sound units play an important role in organizing the child's early production (Vihman 1981; Waterson 1971). They also fit with the fact that, at about 9 to 10 months of age, infants begin to show signs of recognizing or under-standing some words. The onset of understanding that things or events can be referred to by name leads infants to pay attention to sounds or patterns of sounds that refer to objects or people in their immediate environment. Selection based on the salient features of acoustic repre-sentation of meaningful units leads to a higher frequency of some pat-terns already available in infant production. The infants' capacity to extract relevant acoustic information does not imply that infants seg-ment the stimuli into constituent units or categorize them in the same way as adults. However, from the kind of word representation they have at this age, the infants are able to derive a selection of the main articulatory gestures that will be necessary to produce (or to repro-duce) a small relevant basic lexicon.

It has been suggested that infants choose their first words from among the babbling sounds they prefer (Vihman, Ferguson, and Elbert 1986). We would say now that children derive their first words from babbling because the pool of productive sound patterns in integrated and concurrent babbling already is shaped by patterns derived from the words meaningful to them.

The results of our comparison of babbling and word production confirm the difficulty infants encounter in organizing and sequencing the articulatory configurations required to produce words. Word pro-duction is constructed by a progressive process: target selection fol-lowed by organization of a set of articulatory gestures. It involves asso-ciation and activation of different perceptual and motoric components. The perceptual representation that controls the infants' first produc-tions must be specified in terms of articulatory gestures in a temporal arrangement. Our data on late babbling show that the system is capa-ble of extracting and reproducing information about manner of artic-ulation and place of closure, while the data on first words indicate that the infant has trouble with temporal organization and the coarticula-tion process when producing sequences of articulatory gestures under output constraints. Overgeneralization of stops and labials, omissions, and reduplications, as well as free variation in item production show that motoric and sequencing programs are not yet well established. The setting and the control of these programs involves a level of organi-zation beyond the mere selection of sounds and context-free produc-tion of these sounds.

Lindblom (1986) proposes that the "precursors of featural and pho-nemic coding can in principle arise in a self-organizing way from an interaction between semantic development (vocabulary growth) and performance constraints" (p. 510). Between the first word and the 25-word sessions there is a lag of four to six months. This is a relatively long time, especially if one considers the rapid growth of the lexicon following this period. A basic reorganization has to occur in perception from "unanalyzed" word forms to phonemically represented words. Word recognition and word production at the end of the first year and the beginning of the second year contribute to the genesis of higher-order programs that are sooner or later expressed by a spurt in the lexicon and the evidence of phonological rules. Both reorganization of speech coding and progressive control of speech motor functions are needed for the construction of a mental lexicon and its expression in speech production.

REFERENCES

Blumstein, S. 1986. On acoustic invariance in speech. In *Invariance and Variability in Speech Processes*, eds. J. Perkell and D. Klatt. Hillsdale, NJ: Lawrence Erlbaum Associates.

Boysson-Bardies, B. de, Sagart, L., and Bacri, N. 1981. Phonetic analysis of late babbling: A case study of a French child. *Journal of Child Language* 8(3):511–24.

Boysson-Bardies, B. de, Hallé, P., Sagart, L., and Durand, C. 1989. A cross-linguistic investigation of vowel formants in babbling. *Journal of Child Language* 16:1–17.

Buhr, R. D. 1980. The emergence of vowels in an infant. *Journal of Speech and Hearing Research* 23(1):62–94.

Elbers, L. 1982. Operating principles in repetitive babbling: A cognitive continuity approach. *Cognition* 12:45–63.

Elbers, L., and Ton, J. 1985. Play pen monologues: The interplay of words and babbles in the first words period. *Journal of Child Language* 12:551–64.

Ferguson, C. A., and Macken, M. A. 1983. The role of play in phonological development. In *Children's Language*, vol. 4, ed. K. E. Nelson. Hillsdale, NJ: Lawrence Erlbaum Associates.

Goldman-Rakic, P. S. 1981. Development and plasticity of primate frontal association cortex. In *The Organization of Cerebral Cortex*, eds. F. O. Schmitt, F. G. Worden, S. G. Dennis, and G. Adelman. Cambridge, MA: MIT Press.

Grieser, D. A., and Kuhl, P. K. 1989. Categorization of speech by infants: Support for speech-sound prototypes. *Developmental Psychology* 25(4):577–88.

Huttenlocher, J. 1974. The origins of language comprehension. In *Theories in Cognitive Psychology*, ed. R. L. Solso. The Loyola Symposium, Potomac, MD. Hillsdale, NJ: Lawrence Erlbaum Associates.

Jakobson, R. 1941. *Kindersprache, Aphasie und allgemeine Lautgesetze.* Uppsala: Almqvist & Wiksell.

Jusczyk, P. W. In press. Infant speech perception and the development of the mental lexicon. In *The Transition from Speech Sounds to Spoken Words*, eds. H. C. Nusbaum and J. C. Goodman. Cambridge, MA: MIT Press.

Kent, R. D., and Bauer, H. R. 1985. Vocalizations of the one-year-old. *Journal of Child Language* 12:491–526.

Kent, R. D., and Murray, A. D. 1982. Acoustic features of infant vocalic utterances at 3, 6, and 9 months. *Journal of Acoustical Society of America* 72:353–65.

Leonard, L. B., Schwartz, R. G., Chapman, K., and Morris, B. 1981. Factors influencing early lexical acquisition: Lexical orientation and phonological composition. *Child Development* 52:882–87.

Leopold, W. E. 1939. *Speech Development of a Bilingual Child: A Linguist's Record*, vol. 1. Evanston, IL: Northwestern University Press.

Lewis, M. 1936. *Infant Speech: A Study of the Beginnings of Language*. NY: Harcourt Brace.

Lieberman, P. 1980. On the development of vowel production in young children. In *Child Phonology*, Vol. 1, *Production*, eds. G. H. Yeni-Komshian, J. F. Kavanagh, and C. A. Ferguson. NY: Academic Press.

Lindblom, B. 1986. On the origin and purpose of discreteness and invariance in sound patterns. In *Invariance and Variability in Speech Processes*, eds. J. Perkell and D. Klatt. Hillsdale, NJ: Lawrence Erlbaum Associates.

Locke, J. L. 1983. *Phonological Acquisition and Change*. NY: Academic Press.

Locke, J. L. 1986. Speech perception and the emergent lexicon: An ethological approach. In *Language Acquisition* (2d ed.), eds. P. Fletcher and M. Garman. Cambridge: The University Press.

Macken, M. A. 1979. Developmental reorganization of phonology: A hierarchy of basic units of acquisition. *Lingua* 49:11–49.

Macken, M. A., and Ferguson, C. A. 1983. Cognitive aspects of phonological development: Model, evidence and issues. In *Children's Language*, Vol. 4, ed. K. E. Nelson. Hillsdale, NJ: Lawrence Erlbaum Associates.

MacNeilage, P. F., and Davis, B. L. 1990. Acquisition of speech production: Frames, then content. In *Attention and Performance*, XIII Motor representation and control, ed. M. Jeannerod. Hillsdale, NJ: Lawrence Erlbaum Associates.

MacNeilage, P. F., Studdert-Kennedy, M. G., and Lindblom, B. 1985. Planning and production of speech: An overview. In *Proceeding of the Conference on Planning and Production of Speech in Normally Hearing and Deaf People*, ed. J. Lauter. *ASHA Reports*, 15–21.

Malécot, A. 1974. Frequency of occurrence of French phonemes and consonant clusters. *Phonetica* 29:158–70.

Menn, L. 1978. Phonological units in beginning speech. In *Syllables and Segments*, eds. A. Bell and J. B. Hooper. Amsterdam: North Holland.

Menn, L. 1981. Theories of phonological development. In *Native Language and Foreign Language Acquisition*, ed. H. Winitz. NY: Academic Press.

Mines, M. A., Hanson, B. F., and Shoup, J. E. 1978. Frequency of occurrence of phonemes in conversational English. *Language and Speech* 21:221–41.

Oller, D. K. 1980. The emergence of the sounds of speech in infancy. In *Child Phonology*, Vol. 1, *Production*, eds. G. H. Yeni-Komshian, J. F. Kavanagh, and C. A. Ferguson. NY: Academic Press.

Oller, D. K. 1986. Metaphonology and infant vocalization. In *Precursors of Early Speech*, eds. B. Lindblom and R. Zetterström. NY: Stockton Press.

Oller, D. K., Wieman, L. A., Doyle, W. J., and Ross, C. 1975. Infant babbling and speech. *Journal of Child Language* 3:1–11.

Roug, L., Landberg, I., and Lundberg, L. J. 1989. Phonetic developments in early infancy: A study of four Swedish children during the first eighteen months of life. *Journal of Child Language* 16:19–40.

Stark, R. E. 1980. Stages of speech development in the first year of life. In *Child Phonology*, Vol. 1, *Production*, eds. G. H. Yeni-Komshian, J. F. Kavanagh, and C. A. Ferguson. NY: Academic Press.

Stevens, K. N. 1972. The quantal nature of speech: Evidence from articulatory acoustic data. In *Human Communication: A Unified View*, eds. E. E. David Jr. and P. B. Denes. NY: McGraw Hill.

Stevens, K. N. 1980. Acoustic correlates of some phonetic categories. *Journal of Acoustical Society of America* 68(3):836–42.

Vihman, M. M. 1981. Phonology and the development of the lexicon: Evidence from children's errors. *Journal of Child Language* 8:239–64.

Vihman, M. M. 1991. Ontogeny of phonetic gestures: Speech production. In *Modularity and the Motor Theory of Speech Perception,* eds. I. G. Mattingly and M. Studdert-Kennedy. Hillsdale, NJ: Lawrence Erlbaum Associates.

Vihman, M. M., and Ferguson, C. A. 1987. The acquisition of final consonants. *Proceedings of the 11th International Congress of Phonetic Sciences.* Institute of Language and Literature. ESSR Academy of Sciences, Tallinn, Estonia.

Vihman, M. M., and Miller, R. 1988. Words and babble at the threshold of language acquisition. In *The Emergent Lexicon,* eds. M. D. Smith and J. L. Locke. NY: Academic Press.

Vihman, M. M., Ferguson, C. A., and Elbert, M. 1986. Phonological development from babbling to speech: Common tendencies and individual differences. *Applied Psycholinguistics* 7:3–40.

Vihman, M. M., Macken, M. A., Miller, R., Simmons, H., and Miller, J. 1985. From babbling to speech: A reassessment of the continuity issue. *Language* 61:395–443.

Waterson, N. 1971. Child phonology: A prosodic view. *Journal of Linguistics* 7: 170–211.

Werker, J. F., and Tees, R. C. 1984. Cross-language speech perception: Evidence for perceptual reorganization during the first year of life. *Infant Behavior and Development* 27:49–63.

Woods, D., and Stockman, I. 1982. Dominant consonant in non-language vocalization as a preparation for the first words of language. In *Proceedings of the Second International Congress for the Study of Child Language,* eds. C. E. Johnson and C. L. Thew. Lanham, MD: University Press of America.

Woodward, A. 1987. In the beginning was the word: Infants' early perception of word-units in the speech stream. Honors thesis, Swarthmore College, May 1987, unpublished.

Chapter • 13

Early Syllables and the Construction of Phonology

Marilyn May Vihman

Phonology can be said to begin with the child's first production of adult-like syllables. This important milestone, embedded in an emergent motoric rhythmicity (Thelen 1981; Bickley, Lindblom, and Roug 1986), is auditorily and developmentally striking enough to be identifiable by the untrained parental ear (Koopmans van-Beinum and van de Stelt 1986). The reduplicated or *canonical* syllables, the first child units to exhibit the timing characteristics of adult consonant and vowel sequences (Oller 1980), typically appear at about 6 to 8 months for normally hearing infants, whatever the ambient language (Stark 1980; Koopmans van-Beinum and van der Stelt 1986; Roug, Landberg, and Lundberg 1989). Whether deaf or hearing, children begin to produce adult-based words only some months after the achievement of this milestone, which thus appears to be a necessary first phonetic step for oral language production (Oller and Eilers 1988). The first identifiable syllables can be seen as the critical entry-point into language, since they make available to the child, within his or her own productive repertoire, the sound and feel of an adult-like syllable. Thus, the syllable—"a kind of atom in the formulation of speech"

Support from the National Science Foundation is gratefully acknowledged (BNS 7924167 to C. A. Ferguson and D. A. Huntington; BNS 8520048 and BNS 8318757 to C. A. Ferguson; and BNS 8319753 to L. McCune).

(Kent and Bauer 1982, p. 517)—is the raw material out of which a phonology may begin to be built.

Despite the evidently central status of syllable production, phonetic or phonological investigations of the period of transition into speech have heretofore concentrated largely on consonantal production (e.g., Oller et al. 1976; Stoel-Gammon and Cooper 1984; Vihman et al. 1985; Vihman, Ferguson, and Elbert 1986), with rare attention to vowels and consonant-vowel association (Davis and MacNeilage 1990; Stoel-Gammon 1983). The biological or ecological approach of Kent and Bauer (1985) is exceptional in its even-handed consideration of vowel- and consonant-like utterances as well as of periodicity, intonation, and syllable shapes in the vocalizations of five 13-month-old children. The present study contributes further to the correction of the imbalance by analyzing syllable use in the transition period across five samples of four to five children, each recorded under highly similar conditions at four sites, and with exposure to four different ambient languages.

A decade of relatively intensive work on the period of transition from babbling into speech has provided ample evidence to support at least three distinct conclusions regarding the factors involved in this transition. To begin with, babbling production is clearly rooted in a biological base common to all children (Locke 1983; Kent 1984). However, another line of research has shown conclusively that the child's phonetic production has in some respects begun to be shaped by the particular ambient language to which he or she is exposed even before the first words are attempted (Boysson-Bardies et al. 1989). Finally, there is equally strong support for the proposition that individual children follow individual paths, drawing their early lexicon largely from the phonetic repertoire which they have established in the course of the babbling period (Stoel-Gammon and Cooper 1984; Vihman et al. 1985; Vihman, Ferguson, and Elbert 1986). Using syllable production as a basis for analysis, this study will explore the relative contributions to early vocal production of biological constraints, the phonetic characteristics of particular languages, and the child's individual creativity or initiative in the construction of patterns.

The following specific issues will be tested against the syllable data:

1. *Cross-linguistic similarity* across the samples. To what extent do the same syllables dominate early production data for the children? Are *within-group* differences greater or less than differences across ambient-language groups?

2. *Consonant-vowel association.* Are there "privileged" associations between certain consonants and vowels in the data, or do CV combinations simply reflect the frequencies of the individual consonants and vowels?

3. *Continuity.* Can the syllables used in the early words be said to be drawn primarily from the repertoire of most-used syllables established in the preceding months?
4. *Basic units.* What is the status of *syllables, segments,* and *articulatory gestures* in vocalizations and early word patterns? Can the children be said to be learning syllables, particular consonant or vowel segments, or articulatory movements (or motor programs underlying such movements)? Are there clues in the data that might allow us to infer that one or another unit is "basic" to phonetic learning in this period?

DATA COLLECTION

The data analyzed in this study were collected as part of three separate studies, one centered at the Child Phonology Project at Stanford University, the second at Rutgers University, and the third based at Stanford, Paris, and Stockholm.

In the first Stanford study (under the direction of C. A. Ferguson and M. M. Vihman) 10 children aged 9 to 16 months were visited weekly in their homes for a half-hour of audio and video recording of an unstructured play session with the mother. The observer sometimes interacted with mother and child, much like a visiting relative. Mothers were asked to keep a diary of the child's lexical, communicative, and symbolic development, and discussed this diary with the observer each week, thereby maintaining a certain focus on aspects of development of interest to the study.

In the Rutgers study (under the direction of L. McCune) 10 English-learning children were followed monthly from 8 to 24 months, with a half-hour video-recording of unstructured play sessions with the mother, using a standard toy set. The mothers kept a list of the children's words, but there was otherwise no discussion of language development. Two observers attended each session but avoided interacting with mother or child during the recording. Word identification procedures were developed for the analysis of the two sets of English data by Vihman and McCune; these procedures were applied in analysis of the data of the international study as well.

The Cross-linguistic Project on Infant Vocalizations extended the research design of the Stanford study to five children learning different languages at each of three sites: French in Paris, France (under the direction of B. de Boysson-Bardies), Swedish in Stockholm, Sweden (under the direction of B. Lindblom, O. Engstrand, and L. Roug), and Japanese in the homes of Japanese businessmen training for two or three years in the area around Palo Alto, California (under the direction of

F. Arao). Based on observations and questions that had already arisen out of analyses completed for the English data, two changes were introduced into the research design: (1) the children were seen every two weeks, because that was found to allow optimal monitoring of lexical and phonological development for most children in this period; and (2) the new groups of infants were followed up to the point where they had a cumulative lexicon of about 50 words according to the mother's diary, or were producing 25 or more different spontaneous word types in a session, because this allowed comparison of relatively stable word patterns and their possible origins in babbling. In addition, a standard toy set was used at one or more sessions each month.

Phonetic transcription of the children's vocalizations was carried out at Stanford for all the English data. (Only the 9- to 16-month Rutgers sessions were used, corresponding to the data available for the Stanford sample.) The Japanese data also were transcribed at Stanford, while transcription of the French and Swedish data was undertaken independently at Paris and Stockholm and coordinated with Stanford procedures, including cross-linguistic reliability checks. The initial transcription of all sessions was completed by native speakers. (For further detail regarding reliability procedures and results, see Boysson-Bardies and Vihman 1991).

Sessions were identified for each child in which about 4, 15, and 25 words were first produced spontaneously, corresponding to a cumulative lexicon of about 8, 30, and 50 or more words, by maternal record (Vihman and Miller 1988). Because the English data were available only up until 16 or 17 months, only the five most advanced English-learning children from each project, those who had produced close to 15 or 25 words in a session by that time, are included in the present chapter.

IDENTIFICATION OF SYLLABLES FOR ANALYSIS

We sought to analyze three monthly sessions in the pre-linguistic period for each child. For this basic analysis of syllable use no distinction was made between "babble" or unidentifiable vocalizations and the few adult-based words used in these sessions. In order to be included in the analysis, a session had to provide about 40 or more consonant-vowel syllables. The first three months of data collection (a 9-, a 10-, and an 11-month session) were generally used; however, some sessions were missing for some children and several failed to provide sufficient data for analysis. The actual chronological distribution of the sessions used is detailed on table I. One Japanese child and one Swedish child had to be excluded from the study due to insufficient data in the early months of the study.

Table I.   Subjects and Numbers of Syllables Analyzed

		Sessions							
		I			II			III	
		A	B	C	A	B	C	A	B	C
I.	American (Rutgers)									
	Alice	9	93	34	10	149	93	11	105	33
	Aurie	9	48	23	11	111	63	12	94	43
	Jase	11	169	94	12	49	25	13	97	50
	Rala	10	50	29	12	120	60	13	114	35
	Rick	9	68	35	10	151	101	11	194	115
	(Stanford)									
	Deborah	9	233	128	10	276	116	11	219	70
	Emily	10	81	53	11	153	87	12	97	61
	Molly	9	468	263	10	145	42	11	193	99
	Sean	9	148	70	10	141	60	11	220	121
	Timmy	9	106	52	10	120	64	11	280	221
II.	French									
	Carole	10	85	40	10.5	259	191	11	206	141
	Charles	10	147	77	11	106	43	12	162	104
	Laurent	9	92	53	10	234	121	11	183	70
	Marie	10	92	61	11	271	142	13	386	180
	Noël	10	48	26	11	113	73	12	280	118
III.	Japanese									
	Haruo	13	257	97	14	242	61			
	Kazuko	12	36	26	13	242	117	14	352	227
	Kenji	12	277	151	12.5	129	26	13	320	142
	Taro	14	141	45	15	219	31			
IV.	Swedish									
	Hanna	9	68	58	10	192	154	11	332	218
	Kurt	9	169	124	10	113	85	11	96	70
	Lina	9	421	223	10	318	124	11	202	118
	Stig	9	227	141	10	137	77	11	36	29

Key: I, II, III = sessions analyzed.
A = Child's age in months
B = Total syllables produced
C = Raw number of syllables analyzed ("practiced syllables": syllables that constituted over 5% of the data for a given session).

The children produced 11,684 CV syllables (excluding [ʔ] as an onset consonant as well as syllabic nuclei containing no oral vowel), or a mean of 174 consonant-vowel combinations per child per session. The high-use syllables for each session, defined as those that accounted for

5% or more of the CV syllables used in the session, were identified as "practiced" syllables and those syllables constitute the data to be explored here. There were 6,100 practiced syllables, which amounted to 52% of the CV-syllables transcribed. The first session analyzed for each child preceded the first spontaneous use of four or more words for all but one child; no child was using more than seven or eight words by the last session analyzed for practiced syllables. For the continuity analysis, discussed below, a single session was analyzed for the syllables used in word tokens only.

In charting the syllables transcribed, adjacent tense/lax vowel pairs were combined ([i/ɪ]), as well as central [a]/front [æ] and central [ə]/[ʌ], in an effort to base the analysis on only the most reliably transcribed distinctions. In the case of consonants, voicing distinctions were disregarded, and alveolar was combined with palatal for both sibilants and affricates.

ANALYSES AND RESULTS

Cross-Linguistic Similarity

Table II charts the distribution across the five groups of the most commonly occurring syllables: those that account for 5% or more of the practiced syllables for at least one group (for those languages for which these syllables account for less than 5%, the frequencies are enclosed in parentheses; both words and babble are included indiscriminately in these data). Striking differences between the two American groups are in evidence here. In fact, in some respects the profile for the Stanford children has more in common with the profile for the French or Japanese than with that for the Rutgers children (cf. [ba], [ha]), while the profile for the Rutgers children more closely resembles that of the Swedish children ([di], [də]). In short, within-language differences seem to be as great as cross-language differences as far as the overall selection of practiced syllables is concerned.

The six top-ranked syllables were [da], [ba], [wa], [də], [ha], and [hə] (in that order). These account for half of the practiced syllables (50.3%). In general, the very high occurrence of practiced syllables involving [d] and [h] is evident. [da] is the most common syllable produced in every data set except Stanford, where it is a close second to [ba]. If all practiced syllables involving [d] are included, this consonant occurs in over one-fifth of all the syllables analyzed for each of the four language groups (Swedish 59%, English and French 30% each, and Japanese 20%). If the Rutgers and Stanford data are treated separately, [d] occurs in 40% and 25%, respectively.

Table II.   Group Profiles for Practiced Syllables Making Up 5% or More of the Total for At Least One Group

	English		French	Japanese	Swedish	Total
	(Rutgers)	(Stanford)				
T	833	1507	1440	923	1421	6100
C + a						
ba	(18)	163	284	126	79	670
da	140	158	286	140	475	1199
ga	(4)	150	(7)	(44)	(44)	249
na	(13)	(−)	(−)	116	(−)	129
wa	(9)	(6)	119	78	118	330
ha	(20)	77	122	(45)	(28)	292
C + e						
be	(28)	(−)	78	(−)	(−)	106
je	64	(48)	(−)	(−)	(−)	112
he	62	(48)	(25)	(9)	53	197
C + i						
di	51	(41)	(−)	(−)	104	196
hi	48	(−)	(−)	(−)	(−)	48
C + ə						
də	79	(66)	(40)	(14)	101	300
hə	67	110	(16)	(2)	82	277
C + o						
do	(9)	(12)	58	(33)	81	193
go	(−)	57	(−)	85	(−)	142
C + œ						
gœ	(−)	(−)	(−)	(−)	74	74

Key: T = Total practiced syllables/sample.

Raw number of occurrences for each sample are indicated after each syllable type. Syllables constituting less than 5% of the practiced syllable total for a language or site are in parentheses. Syllables that constitute 5% (or more) of the total for no single group are excluded here.

The next most commonly occurring consonant in the combined English practiced-syllable data is [h] (21%) (Rutgers 24%, Stanford 19%), which accounts for 12% of the Swedish data and 10% of the Japanese. Most interestingly, it also accounts for 11% of the French data, in spite of the fact that adult French lacks an /h/.

Every American child makes high use of one or more hV syllable, usually from the first session on (8/10 subjects). Eight of the children make high use of two or three hV syllables in one session or another. For two children, hV syllables become important in the third session, when lexical production is already underway, while for five children there is no high-use hV syllable in the last session. In Swedish, two of the children never make high use of an hV syllable, while the other two use three or four different hV syllables in one session and one or two hV syllables in another session. In Japanese, one or more hV syllable occurs in the practiced-syllable data for all four children, with no particular longitudinal pattern.

In the French data, [ha] (and in two cases [he]) are among the high-use syllables for every child in the first session analyzed. However, [ha] occurs for just one of the five children at the second session and for one other child at the third session. One does not expect the French child to organize a lexicon around the production of hV syllables, and indeed they do not—though [ha] does occur in the French children's word productions, as [hə] does in English, as either a start-up syllable or a stand-in for missing function words (cf. [hamɛ̃] *la main* "the hand"). In short, there is a pattern of loss of hV in the French data, which agrees with the fact of no /h/ in the adult system (/h/ does occur marginally in adult French, e.g., in the baby-talk word *ham* "to eat," as well as in certain interjections and, rarely, recent loan words).

Consider the cross-linguistic distribution of [h], based on all consonantal production in all sessions analyzed in the international study (only data from the five English-learning subjects included in the cross-linguistic study are used for English here [see table III]. All groups make moderate use of [h] at 0 words (16%–24%). The French and Swedish children drop to a low level of use by the 15-word point, while the American and Japanese children, despite individual fluctuations, continue at a moderate level of use which agrees closely with the adult target levels of 13% for English and 14% for Japanese (based on analysis of the adult-target forms of the words the children produced over the entire study). This change in use is characteristic of many pho-

Table III. Cross-linguistic Occurrence of [h]: Longitudinal Trends

	0 words	4 words	15 words	25 words	(Target)
English	18%	13%	16%	13%	(13%)
	4–42%	8–18%	3–28%	2–26%	
French	19%	8%	3%	6%	(0%)
	8–43%	2–23%	1–4%	1–11%	
Japanese	24%	20%	15%	11%	(14%)
	9–57%	3–49%	6–33%	3–45%	
Swedish	16%	7%	3%	4%	(8%)
	0–52%	2–13%	0–7%	0–8%	

Means and ranges for the distribution of [h] in words and babble at four data points (and distribution in adult target words). All data drawn from the Cross-linguistic Project on Infant Vocalizations.

netic parameters examined in the cross-linguistic project: Early within-group variation and between-group commonality gives way, as words are learned, to greater within-group commonality and between-group differences.

The prominence of hV syllables in early French babble production, at the same level as in the other languages, suggests that these are 'default' articulations or motor plans. The production of [h], which involves no fine motor adjustments, in fact no supraglottal activity at all, seems to be among the most accessible of speech articulations for infants.

With regard to the vowels used in the practiced syllables, [a/æ] and [ə/ʌ] occur the most commonly overall. [a/æ] is the top-ranked vowel type in all five groups. The neutral vowels [ə/ʌ] are ranked second in the Stanford English and Swedish data and third in the remaining groups; [e/ɛ] is ranked second in the Rutgers and the French data, while [o/ɔ] is second for Japanese. In syllables with [h], the syllable [hə] is the most common for American English and Swedish (see table IV), while for French and Japanese, [ha] is the most common. These differences in the frequency of occurrence of vowels could be taken as evidence of a difference in the "base of articulation" of these languages (Boysson-Bardies et al. 1989).

Consonant-Vowel Association

If vocal events depend upon "coordinative structures" (groups of muscles performing as functional units), as suggested by action theory (Fowler et al. 1978; MacNeilage 1980), systematic relationships should be apparent between consonantal and vocalic articulations early in the development of vocal control (McCune this volume). As part of an ongoing investigation of regularities apparent in the two English samples (McCune and Vihman 1987), L. McCune and I have been exploring the evidence for such systematic relationships. The charting of the children's practiced syllables was the first step in this investigation.

Specific hypotheses were suggestd in a recent article by Davis and MacNeilage (1990) who found three consonant-vowel associations in the word productions of a single English-learning subject aged 14–20

Table IV. Practiced Syllables Including [h]

	ha	he	hi	hu	hə	ho	hœ	hw	T
Rutgers	20	62	48	0	67	0	0	0	197
Stanford	77	48	0	53	110	0	5	0	293
French	122	25	0	0	16	0	3	0	166
Japanese	45	9	0	9	2	0	0	28	93
Swedish	28	53	0	0	82	0	9	0	172

months. Davis and MacNeilage reported that the central vowels [a] and [ə] occurred most often in a labial environment, high front vowels occurred in an alveolar environment, and high back vowels, though rare, occurred most in a velar environment. They suggest that there are good "mechanical" reasons to expect an association between velars and high (or non-low) back vowels (both involve raising of the back of the tongue), while alveolars may be expected to co-occur preferentially with non-low front vowels (cf. Kent and Murray 1982). Because there is no mechanical reason for lip closure to be followed by a central vowel, Davis and MacNeilage speculate that "perhaps the necessity to change the locus of control between tongue for the vowel and lips for the consonant prevents the tongue from gaining an articulatory advantage in utterances with labial consonants" (p. 26). In that case, the preference for [a] or [ə] in that environment would seem to reflect the status of these vowels as *default* choices, involving little or no movement of the tongue from a neutral or resting position.

We devised an analysis to test whether these three associations would also be displayed by the 23 subjects in our cross-linguistic sample. We plotted the distribution of each combination of the categories suggested by Davis and MacNeilage, with the addition of the high-use glottal [h]. We used a chi-square model to determine the "expected" frequency of each combination. For example, we multiplied the number of alveolars and of front vowels in our data and divided by the total practiced syllables. We then compared the expected with the observed (occurring) combinations of alveolar + front vowel. The full matrix of expected versus observed C + V categories could not appropriately be tested for significance, because the many (and unequal) repeated observations, or syllable incidences, for each subject would lead to a grossly inflated score for the matrix as a whole. Instead, an analysis of variance (ANOVA) was run to test whether consonant-vowel interaction could truly be said to obtain in these data. Appendix A describes that analysis and the results for each of the factors—Language (or group), Consonant and Vowel. The Consonant-Vowel interaction was found to be significant at $p < .001$.

The finding of a significant interaction means that the consonants and vowels cannot be taken to occur fully independently of one another in the children's productions. Some significant associations obtain. However, given the uneven distribution in the children's vocalizations of alveolars versus velars, for example, or of central versus back vowels, the analysis of variance can yield only a general and indirect impression of the actual associations underlying the overall significance of the CV interaction. But the specific interactions involved were of the greatest interest to us. In order to obtain a clearer picture of those interactions, separate chi-square analyses were performed on the data from each individual subject with regard to four possible associations of interest: the three that Davis and MacNeilage found in the word data from their English-learning subject, and the combination of [h] plus central vowel, suggested by the very common occurrence of the syllables [ha] and [hə] in our data, as described above. Table V summarizes the results of these analyses. In effect, what we are reporting here are 23 case studies, which we offer by way of comparison with the single Davis and MacNeilage case study.

None of the hypotheses tested was unequivocally supported, but a majority of the subjects with relevant data showed the predicted association between labials and central vowels and velars and back vowels. The other two categories showed no clear trend. Taking the combinations tested one at a time:

1. All but two of the children used both labials and central vowels; eleven showed positive associations between labials and central vowels, but three showed an equally strong negative association (or a tendency to use labials with other vowels or other consonant categories with central vowels, or both).
2. All but one of the children could be tested for the alveolar/front vowel association, but no clear conclusion could be drawn from our results, in which eight children showed the predicted positive association while seven showed a negative association. Even the ten English-learning children split five to three between positive and negative association, with two showing a chance distribution.
3. Of the six children whose practiced syllables included both velars and back vowels, four showed the predicted association, one showed a chance distribution, and one showed a (relatively weak) dissociation ($p < .05$).
4. The results for [h] plus central vowel were equivocal, but comparison of the results for the two consonant categories tested for an association with central vowels—labials and [h]—on a subject-by-subject basis reveals the inverse relationship to be expected from the logic of a two-by-two chi-square test. No subject showed either positive or negative association on both; four subjects (Alice: Rutgers; Timmy: Stanford; Haruo and Taro: Japanese) showed strong complementary dependencies, while 15 of the remaining 19 children showed either positive or negative association for only one category and a chance distribution on the other.

The categories that reflect significant CV association in these data are not distributed equally over all five data sets.

1. The association between labials and central vowels is supported by three groups, Stanford, Japanese, and Swedish, while the French

Table V.   Consonant/Vowel Association

		Labial/central	Alveolar/front	Velar/back	[h] /central
I.	American English:				
	(Rutgers)				
	Alice	−	−	(no V)	+
	Aurie	+	ns	ns	ns
	Jase	ns	−	(no C)	− (*)
	Rala	ns	+ (*)	(no V)	ns
	Rick	ns	−	(no C; no V)	−
	(Stanford)				
	Deborah	+	+ (*)	(no V)	ns
	Emily	+	+	(no C)	ns
	Molly	+	ns	+	ns
	Sean	ns	+	(no C; no V)	+
	Timmy	+	+	− (**)	−
II.	French				
	Carole	ns	ns	(no V)	+ (*)
	Charles	ns	+	(no C)	+
	Laurent	(no C)	−	(no C)	+
	Marie	+	ns	(no C)	ns
	Noël	−	ns	(no C; no V)	ns
III.	Japanese				
	Haruo	−	− (*)	(no C)	+ (**)
	Kazuko	+	+	+	ns
	Kenji	+	(no V)	+	ns
	Taro	+	ns	+	−
IV.	Swedish				
	Hanna	ns	−	(no C; no V)	−
	Lina	+	+	(no V)	(no C)
	Stig	(no C)	− (**)	(no V)	(no C)
	Kurt	+	ns	(no C; no V)	ns
	Total	11 +	8 +	4 +	6 +
		3 −	7 −	1 −	5 −

Key: Chi-square results for consonant and vowel categories for each subject individually. + = positive association, − = negative association, ns = nonsignificant.
No C or no V means that consonant or vowel category was not used in the practiced syllables for that subject. All results are significant at $p < .001$ unless otherwise noted (** = $p < .01$, * = $p < .05$).

C categories: labial = [p/b], [m], [ɸ/β, f/v], [w/μ]; (palatal/)alveolar = [t/d], [n], [s/z,
ʃ/ʒ], [tʃ/dʒ], [l], [j]; velar = [k/g], [ŋ].

V categories: front = [i/ɪ], [e/ɛ], [ɸ/œ]; (low/)central = [a/æ], [ə/ʌ]; back = [u/ʊ],
[o/ɔ], [ɯ].

and Rutgers data are divided. The association of [h] and central vowels obtains clearly only for French.

2. The chief source of the negative association of alveolars (and palatals) and front vowels is the data from three Rutgers and two Swedish children. The Swedish children all made use of [t/d] with a wide range of vowels. Four of the Rutgers children showed the same usage, while one child—Alice—used only [de] (20 instances), but balanced this with even greater use of both [ja] (22) and [na] (13). In contrast, the Stanford children showed the expected positive association, while the French and Japanese children were divided.

3. The association of [k/g] with back vowels is most evident in the Japanese data, but was also exhibited by one Stanford subject. For the Japanese subjects the relevant syllable is [ko/go]; [ku/gu] does not figure in the practiced syllable data for Japanese. The one Stanford subject with a significant association of velar with back vowels—Molly—used both [ku/gu] (47 instances) and [ko/go] (57). In the case of Davis and MacNeilage's subject, the single word *cookie* accounted for most uses. We consider the role of back-tongue activity in early word production when we discuss the individual English-learning children in more detail below.

In general, the strong role played by the individual child, which was apparent in the gap between the Stanford and Rutgers profiles on table II, is very much in evidence in the conflicting results displayed on table V. Davis and MacNeilage wonder whether the pattern of consonant-vowel interaction which they found " . . . is present at the initiation of babbling or whether it develops later" (p. 26). The mixed results found for different children in our data suggest that an equally appropriate question is whether the association would be clearly confirmed for a range of subjects (learning the same or different languages) if the data tested derived from the very earliest stage of syllable production, or whether it characterizes the development of only a subset of children, because the individual differences across the children at the outset of lexical use (as in our sample) seem to outweigh any underlying biological or physiological factor, which might give a more uniform or *universal* look to the results at a point somewhat closer to the "initiation of babbling" in these subjects. Let us turn now to a consideration of the status of the syllables favored by individual children as they make the transition from babble into speech.

Continuity

A specific relationship of continuity has been established in earlier studies between the shape of a given child's early words and his or her concurrent babbling repertoire (Vihman et al. 1985), based on analyses of place and manner in consonants, vocalization length, phonotactic shape, and most recently, for one child only, vowel production (Davis and MacNeilage 1990) (as these authors point out, the vowels favored in babbling did not lead to correct vowel production in words for this child, but were rather used for a wide range of targeted vowels, in monosyllables and in the first syllable of disyllabic productions). The analysis presented here was intended to discover whether the finding of continuity would also emerge from a comparison of early practiced syllable use and later word use.

For each child, the inventory of practiced syllables was established according to the procedure described above, based on total syllable production in the two or three sessions analyzed (regardless of probable communicative status—nonword, protoword, or word). The inventories thus established were then compared with the phonetic shapes of word tokens in the month in which four or more words were first produced spontaneously (a milestone we take to reflect the establishment of word use: see the discussion of the choice of this criterion in assigning a "word-acquisition point" to the child in Vihman et al. 1985). Imitative productions were included in the scoring; protowords (reflecting idiosyncratic sound-meaning links that function for a time for individual children [Vihman and Miller 1988]) were not.

In order to avoid the possible confound of comparing word shapes with syllables used concurrently for words and babble, we used for comparison with word shapes only those practiced syllables derived from earlier sessions. Just one child (Kurt, Swedish sample) had already begun using four or more words when he was first seen at 9 months. In that one case we used the next session analyzed for words. Table VI shows each child's age in months at the time of the last practiced-syllable session and at the time of the first four-word session and also indicates the number of practiced-syllable sessions included in the comparison.

Words were examined to determine whether half or more of the tokens of a word type included as CV-syllables one or more of the practiced syllables. Word tokens lacking a consonant were not included in the scoring. Table VI shows the results of this analysis. A minus sign (−) marks those cases in which less than half of the word types included practiced syllables.

As expected from previous research, the syllables used in early words are here primarily drawn from the repertoire of practiced syllables for at least some subjects in every group. Eight of the 23 subjects fail to show the correspondence, however. Recall that previous demonstrations of continuity involved concurrent production of words and babble (cf. Elbers and Ton 1985, who detail the ongoing interaction or

Table VI. Practiced Syllables and Syllables Used in Early Words

Language				Age in Months	
I. American English					
(Rutgers) Group total: 10/24				(1)	(2)
Alice	3/8	(2)	(−)	11	11
Aurie	4/6	(3)		12	14
Jase	1/3	(3)	(−)	13	15
Rala	0/3	(3)	(−)	13	15
Rick	2/4	(3)		11	15
(Stanford) Group total: 20/29					
Deborah	3/5	(2)		11	11
Emily	4/6	(3)		12	13
Molly	2/4	(1)		11	10
Sean	4/7	(3)		11	12
Timmy	7/7	(3)		11	11
II. French Group total: 9/21					
Carole	3/6	(1)		11	10
Charles	2/4	(1)		12	11
Laurent	2/4	(2)		11	10
Marie	1/4	(2)	(−)	13	13
Noël	1/3	(2)	(−)	12	12
III. Japanese Group total:9/26					
Haruo	1/6	(1)	(−)	14	14
Kazuko	4/8	(1)		14	13
Kenji	3/5	(1)		13	12
Taro	1/7	(1)	(−)	15	15
IV. Swedish					
Hanna	5/6	(2)		11	11
Kurt	3/6	(1)		11	9
Lina	3/7	(1)	(−)	11	10
Stig	5/6	(3)		11	15

Key: The number of CV-word-types with half or more tokens including practiced syllables from earlier sessions is given over the total word types produced. The number
of practiced-syllable sessions used for comparison is indicated in parentheses.
Age in months is indicated for (1) last session analyzed for practiced syllables and
(2) first session in which four or more word types were produced spontaneously
(= session analyzed for word shapes). Exceptions to the continuity hypothesis—
i.e., children less than half of whose word-types included earlier practiced syllables—are marked (−).

mutual influence of babble on words and words on babble in this
period for one Dutch child). Thus, it is not surprising that a prospective analysis—and one that in some cases spans more than one
month—should yield less striking evidence of continuity. In fact, the

exceptions include two of the five cases in which over a month elapsed between last prelinguistic session analyzed and first word session.

Considering the exceptions further, we find that only one involves a child whose first word session fell early (Lina—10 months, Swedish sample). Furthermore, of the five children who began to make use of four or more words only at 15 months, the "latest bloomers" among these relatively fast-developing children, three are among our exceptions. Out of the remaining 18 children, only 5 failed to base at least half of their word types on practiced syllables. Table VII outlines the correspondence between age at 4-word use and failure to exhibit continuity in syllable use in this analysis.

Why might children developing relatively more slowly be less likely to draw their early words from the syllables used frequently in earlier months? Vihman (1991) suggested a mechanism for the acquisition of a productive lexical repertoire based on the child's identification of adult sequences similar enough to his or her own babbling productions to trigger a "circular reaction" (Piaget 1952). Once an auditory feedback "loop" (Fry 1966) based on the child's own babbling is well-established, the child may begin to be particularly sensitive to the occurrence of the same sound patterns with which he or she has become familiar (in both the auditory and the kinesthetic modes) from self-monitoring. The child who is inclined to respond vocally to familiar vocal input will then begin to produce adult-like patterns based on his or her own repertoire of syllables (or *stable action categories*: Kent this volume)—and as the recognition of meaningful words is established, at roughly the same time, the child will begin to form a productive lexicon of adult-based words.

But this model may be appropriate only for those children who actively explore vocal possibilities in response to adult input (Vihman 1987). Analyses of consonant use have shown that establishment of a critical minimum of *vocal motor schemes*, or "motor acts . . . performed intentionally and . . . capable of variation and combination to form larger units" (McCune and Vihman 1987, p. 20) is necessary for early progress in lexical acquisition (cf. also McCune 1989, this volume). Some children, whose comprehension may be on a par with that of the

Table VII. Correspondence of Age at Four Words and Match Between Early Word Shapes and Practiced Syllables ("continuity")

Age at Four Words (in months)	9	10	11	12	13	14	15
Number of subjects showing continuity	1	3	4	2	2	1	2
Number of subjects failing to show continuity	0	1	1	1	1	1	3
Total		1	4	5	3	3	2	5

more voluble babblers, vocalize less abundantly and may be less inclined to respond vocally to adult input, possibly resulting in less rapid mastery of a range of vocal motor schemes. In the latter case the mechanism of early word production—which may be offset, in comparison with precocious word-users, by several months—may be quite different, because the internal representational abilities of children at this age are known to be in the process of dramatic change. Slower children may develop a repertoire of possible phonetic production-sequences internally; their early lexicon, when it finally emerges, need bear no particular resemblance to the syllables "practiced" some months earlier.

This interpretation might account for the pattern of exceptions to the continuity hypothesis found in this study, although of the children examined here, all but one had achieved a 50-word vocabulary by the age of 19 months and thus could not ultimately be characterized as "slowly developing." (The most slowly developing child included in this study, the Japanese child Taro, achieved 50 words at 23 months.) More appropriately, the hypothesis receives support from a rare study of the babbling patterns of two slowly-developing children (Stoel-Gammon 1989). Compare also Peters' (1986) suggestion that in the acquisition of syntax, slow versus rapidly developing children may differ qualitatively, or in the actual process of acquisition, as well as quantitatively, or in the rate of advance.

Finally, we should note that previous demonstrations of continuity in vocalizations across babble and speech have not been based on full syllables. It is possible that although the syllable is important as the first adult-like production unit, it does not play an organizing role for all of the children. That is, even if early practiced syllables had been compared with word sessions following within a month for all 23 children, it is possible that a certain number of those children would fail to show word types based largely on those early syllables. The syllable may not be the most appropriate unit to consider for some children.

Basic Units

We have seen from the cross-linguistic comparisons that although all the children have some phonetic tendencies in common (e.g., production of syllables such as [da], [ha], and [hə]), and although certain phonetic tendencies differentially characterize the different language groups (e.g., use of [ko/go] in Japanese or [ti/di] in Swedish), individual differences, even across the children in a single language group (English), are substantial. In fact, it is the individual child who must construct a phonology and a lexicon. Within the constraints of developing neuromotor control and despite the attraction exerted by the phonetic characteristics of the particular adult language, each child follows a unique path from babbling into words. We turn now to a more intensive examination of the longitudinal practiced-syllable profiles for the 10 children learning English. In looking more closely at the syllable inventories developed by these children, we seek clues to the smallest functional unit for the child at this time—syllable, consonant or vowel segment, or articulatory gesture. Three broad types of progress in building a repertoire of practiced syllables can be distinguished for these children.

1. *Stability over time.* Five of the 10 children make use of one or more of the same syllables in all three sessions analyzed. These are all among the most common syllables used: [da], [də], [je], [he], and [hə].
2. *Exploration of novel possibilities.* Two children show continued exploration of new syllables over the three months. Emily begins with [ma], [wa], [ha], and two more [h]-syllables. She adds [da], [de], [do], and [dœ] at 11 months, and shifts to [d]-based syllables more completely at 12 months. Deborah begins with [ba], [da], [ma], plus [de] and [he] at 9 months and shifts to stops or [h] with non-low front vowels only, plus [je], at 11 and 12 months. No one particular syllable, segment, or articulatory gesture can be said to underlie all three sessions for either child, although a variety of consonant and vowel resources appear to be mastered in different combinations in the course of these explorations.
3. *Articulatory gestures.* Three children make use of no one syllable or consonant in all three sessions, but do make consistent use of syllables based on a single articulatory gesture. Alice uses a raised tongue-blade, or palatal articulation, to produce either the glide [j] or a non-low front vowel in every practiced syllable except [na] and [ha] (see Appendix B).

   At 9 months Timmy primarily produces syllables based on a neutral tongue position ([ha], [fə]) and/or raised back of tongue ([fu], [du], [hu]). At 10 months he adds two palatal-gesture-based syllables ([de], [je]), but at 11 months he has consolidated his repertoire and uses only labial and velar consonants and [h] with central vowels (see Appendix B).

   Molly also uses neutral [h] and [ə] as well as a range of raised back-of-tongue or velar articulations ([ga], [gi], [gu], [gə], [go]) at 9 months. At 10 months she adds labials ([ba], [bə]) and at 11 months nasals ([ma], [me], [mə], [nə]).

Appendix B presents a picture of the lexical development of two of these last three children, all of whom are among the more rapidly advancing of the English-speaking subjects (cf. table VI). (The third child, Molly, went on to organize her early lexicon primarily around word-final stops and nasals, which fall outside the scope of the CV syllables we are discussing here [see Vihman and Velleman 1989].) In the case of Alice, the use of the glide [j] (or off-glide [ɪ]) is a prominent feature of the early word productions, as are front vowels and palatalized consonants, even in words that lack such vowels or consonants in the adult model ([œ] in *bottle, mama, ball,* [nj] in *no*). By the time 15 or more words are produced in a half-hour session, Alice has developed her vocal motor scheme, palatal articulation, into a more complete lexical pattern or "word recipe" (Menn 1979) consisting of a disyllable ending in [i], often with a medial palatal consonant (cf. *hi, lady, mommy*). Only a small proportion of Alice's now rapidly increasing lexicon is produced without recourse to the "palatal articulation" set. In the following months we see further elaboration of the palatal motor scheme, with restructuring of *daddy* and *dolly* to [taji] and *(good)night* to [na:ji] at 15 months, for example, and with regression in the production of *clean* as [ti:ni] and *elephant* as [ʔēĩji] or [ʔæĩji] at 16 months.

Turning now to Timmy's lexical profile (Appendix B), we see that at 10 months his lexical output consists entirely of widely ranging phonetic variants of the apparent target-shape <ba> for both *ball* and *block*, while at 11 months he adds <ga(ga)> for *car, girl,* and *Great Gable* (see Vihman and Miller 1988). At 12 and 13 months new "b" and "g" words (and even *Teddy,* produced as <gaga>) are produced with the same motor plans. At 14 months a new Ca syllable appears: <ja> for *eye.* At 15 months, when Timmy's lexicon shows a significant expansion, the basic phonotactic structure remains unaltered, but several consonants are added; just two entirely new forms now appear, both of them onomatopoeia. It is only two months later that we see the first forms with other nuclear vowels, usually [i], and even multisyllabic forms with the shape <CaCi . . . > (*cookie, helicopter*).

Although Timmy's practiced syllables, like Molly's, suggested use of a favored *velar articulation* (as displayed in the use of syllables with [u] in the early months, followed by the addition of syllables with [g]), analysis of his lexical profile shows clearly that the syllables <ba> and <ga>, though variably produced, are the organizing factors over the entire period from 10 to 15 months. Not suprisingly, of the 23 subjects included here, Timmy was the only child whose first four-word session, at 11 months, provided a complete match between word-shapes and previously practiced syllables.

Alice, on the other hand, demonstrates the persistent use of a slightly unusual articulatory pattern—the palatal gesture—not only in her practiced syllables but in the development of a systematic lexical pattern. Every month several of her word tokens are affected by the tendency to produce palatal or palatalized consonants and non-low front vowels, regardless of the shape of the adult target; by 14 months this phonetic tendency appears to have become an organizing pattern for the lexicon, and the pattern continues to shape her words over the next two months of ever-increasing word use.

Recall that only three of Alice's eight words reflected practiced syllables at 11 months (table VI). Although only 2 words—*hello* and *light*—fail to show the influence of the preferred palatal articulation, a word such as *bottle*, with its substitution of front-rounded vowels and a palatal glide for the back-rounded stressed vowel and velarized syllabic [ɬ] of the target, includes none of the practiced syllables. In short, it is the *palatal gesture* that dominates Alice's vocal production, not any particular set of syllables.

DISCUSSION

Cross-linguistic Similarity

We have seen that six top-ranked syllables account for fully half of the practiced syllables in all groups combined; each of these syllables accounts for over 5% of the total syllable use for at least two of the five groups. The only two vowels that occur in the top six syllables, [a/æ] and [ə/ʌ], are both *resting tongue* or *default* vowels. The two highest-use syllables, [da] and [ba], are used by all language groups (the Rutgers sample does not make high use of [ba], but the Stanford sample does). In the four syllables used by two or three of the five groups, French and Japanese make use of syllables with [a], English and Swedish, those with [ə].

What articulatory events must be postulated at a minimum to account for these productions, which are relatively free of specific language influences? The production of [ha] or [hə] involves control of oral breathing and nothing more—a level of control that presumably underlies all intentional vocalization, once the child has begun to produce canonical syllables, but that nevertheless seems to depend on several months of preliminary postnatal anatomical and physiological restructuring (Kent 1981).

The remaining high-use syllables could be taken to require considerable supraglottal control for consonantal production—with different degrees of labial occlusion for [ba] and [wa] and extension of the tongue to achieve apical occlusion for [da] and [də]. However, jaw movement alone has been shown to be sufficient to account for [da/dæ] (Kent this volume). More sweepingly, MacNeilage and Davis (1990) have argued that the rhythmic opening and closing of the vocal tract that characterizes canonical syllables may be "achieved primarily by an alternation between an elevation and a depression of the mandible" (p. 458) (cf. also Netsell 1981). In fact, those authors have suggested that "the common factor underlying the entire initial babbling repertoire may be the induction of what could be called "dummy speech." The child may have developed motor capabilities sufficient to "capture" the fact that speech tends to alternate between louder sounds (the vowels) and sounds that are less loud (the consonants)" (p. 459). Pursuing the idea of "dummy speech," intended to mimic the sound and sight of adults speaking, it is striking that the two supraglottal motor acts that underlie the majority of syllables used, movement of the mandible and movement of the lips, are *visually* as well as *aurally* present to the normally developing child.

Consonant-Vowel Association

But these top-ranked syllables are not the only ones used at this point in the children's development; not all the children restrict themselves to the most basic articulatory movements. The limited evidence of consonant-vowel association in the data seems to have two quite different sources. On the one hand, the association of central (resting tongue) vowels with either [h] or labials for virtually every child seems to reflect continuing reliance on an articulatory "path of least resistance," i.e., a neuromotor "given" that seems to underlie the first (or canonical) syllable production. These particular associations seem best ascribed to the biological factor still partially shaping the children's vocal production in the period of transition from babbling to first words.

The use of high vowels is rare in our data, in conformity with previous findings for vowel production in the first year (Kent and Murray 1982; Lieberman 1980). The association of alveolar with front vowel, which receives no clear support here, may be characteristic of a later stage of lexical acquisition, at least for some children. Davis and Mac-Neilage (1990) emphasize the use of unstressed second-syllable [i] as typical of word use but not babbling for their subject. It is worth noting that the syllable [ti/di] (as well as syllables with the corresponding lax vowel) is highly language-specific in our data (see table II). It occurs in the practiced syllables of three children each in the English- and Swedish-learning groups but is absent from French and Japanese. Japanese actually lacks /ti/ and /di/ in the adult language, in which the syllables /tʃi/ and /dʒi/ fill the structural gap. One Japanese child—Kazuko—reflects this asymmetry in her target language, in her 14-month session only, in the use of [tʃi], which occurs largely in tokens of the words *chun-chun* "cheep-cheep" and *pachin* "snap; clothes-pin." The syllable does not occur elsewhere in our data. Like Davis and MacNeilage's [ti/di], the use of [tʃi] by one child reflects progress toward the ambient adult lexicon and discontinuity with babbling.

In general, the pattern for alveolars, the most frequently produced consonant category, shows great individual variation. Many children restrict themselves to the motorically undemanding syllable [da], which need involve no specific tongue activity or control, while others are mastering certain lingual articulations—the raising and stretching of the tongue for non-low front vowels ([be], [ge], [ɲi]) and palatal ([ja], [jə]) and palatalized consonants ([njæ], [tʃi]) in the case of both Alice and Kazuko, for example. The hypothesized association of alveolars and front vowels is supported only by such lexically related productions as Kazuko's [tʃi], while it is "diluted" or masked by the more common production of [da].

The velar-back vowel association that obtained for three of the four Japanese children seems similarly to reflect not only the facilitating effect of a single back-of-tongue gesture serving for a full syllable but also the influence of an adult language that provides many models with velars. For the Japanese children who make use of [ko/go], the syllable is most characteristic of later sessions, when word use has begun (e.g., for Kazuko, *dakko* "hold me;" for Taro, *koko* "here;" for Kenji, *kore* "this"). The two English-learning children revealing positive velar-back vowel associations are also most likely responding to the relatively frequent occurrence of velars in the adult targets (cf. Boysson-Bardies et al. this volume). However, the children differ in their velar-syllable production patterns, presumably reflecting a difference in the relative contribution of the ambient-language and individual-construction factors: Molly tends to produce back vowels with velars, following the motorically most accessible route. Timmy, on the other hand, develops his own production pattern, combining velars as well as labials with a fixed (neutral, or resting tongue) vowel type, the central vowel (although he did exhibit the ability to make use of back vowels in his early practiced syllables).

Continuity

We found modest evidence of continuity in syllable use from earlier babbling sessions to later sessions when word use had begun. Most of the children included here seem to draw on their pre-established repertoire of practiced syllables in producing early words, although the rate of change in the system is such that prospective analysis yields only weak results. Furthermore, the relation of practiced syllables to word production is clearest for the most vocal and the most rapidly advancing children.

Basic Units

In examining the specific use made of motoric skills acquired earlier in the case of two of the most vocal and lexically advanced children, we found that one—Alice—was not operating with the syllable as a lexical organizing unit, while the other—Timmy—did seem to advance phonologically by very slowly developing a repertoire of different lexical categories based on the syllable-structure [Ca], with <ba> as his prototype. For a child like Alice, there is no evidence of independent (segment-level) planning or control of consonant and vowel production (cf. Studdert-Kennedy and Goodell 1990), but neither is she constrained to follow the most motorically accessible route—the production of front vowels following alveolars. In fact, it is evident that some of the children have already developed the capacity to perform some rather complex maneuvers with the tongue, independently of jaw movements, as they move from prespeech into speech—with definite influence from the available adult target words.

CONCLUSION

What can we conclude from these data, then, with reference to the relative contribution of biological factors, the ambient language, and the individual child? Physiological biases, or ease of motor control, must account for the wide cross-linguistic occurrence of [ha]/[hə]. The fact that [h] is associated with the low/central or resting tongue position in French, which also shows diminishing occurrence of [h] over time, suggests a natural neuromotor source for the syllables involved. The fact that labials are also associated with central vowels for some subjects in every language group lends support to Davis and MacNeilage's hypothesis regarding the change of locus of control. That is, incipient mastery of, or voluntary control over, labial production facilitates no particular lingual movement; as a result, production of a neutral, resting tongue vowel, which dominates vocalizations throughout the prelinguistic period, remains the default choice after a labial for most children.

As the children make the transition from babbling only to the first productions of words, phonetic particularities of the different adult languages begin to exert their influence. Those syllables that are both *salient* in a given language environment, because of their common occurrence in adult models, and *motorically accessible*, because of the facilitating "articulatory neighborhood" effect of consonant-vowel similarity, can serve as entry-points into more sophisticated or motorically complex vocal production. Thus, the biological factor combines here with the ambient language effect to lay down an inviting route for early phonetic development.

When a child is prepared on the basis of word-comprehension and other social and cognitive factors to produce words voluntarily, that child will make use of whatever phonetic resources he or she has been able to develop. Some will base their early lexicon on the simplest "default" phonetic articulations (in our samples, [da], [ba], [ha] in the case of French or Japanese children, [da], [ba], [də], [hə] in the case of American or Swedish children). Others will be ready to go beyond those motorically simplest productions to explore some of the phonetic paths suggested by core words of their ambient language (as in the case of [ko/go] in Japanese, [ti/di] in Swedish). Still others will modulate their babbled repertoire as well as their early words in the direction of some peculiarity of the adult language that departs from the favored phonetics of babble. For example, one English-learning child focussed on final consonants (Vihman and Velleman 1989), while one Japanese child produced an unusually large proportion of many-syllable vocalizations (Vihman 1990).

In effect, we can conclude that the children construct their individual lexical patterns within the limits of broad physiological constraints. However, these constraints are felt less by some, who manage to free themselves from them at an earlier point than others, in relation to the development of the first words. Similarly, the ambient language provides a powerful filter, guiding the child into more advanced phonetic production. Again, however, the power of the filter will depend on individual quirks of attention and organization, and no doubt will be most noticeable in the case of the more vocally precocious children.

REFERENCES

Bickley, C., Lindblom, B., and Roug, L. 1986. Acoustic measures of rhythm in infants' babbling. Proceedings of the 12th International Congress on Acoustics, Toronto.
Boysson-Bardies, B. de, and Vihman, M. M. 1991. Adaptation to language: Evidence from babbling and first words in four languages. Language 67:297–319.
Boysson-Bardies, B. de, Hallé, P., Sagart, L., and Durand, C. 1989. A cross-linguistic investigation of vowel formants in babbling. Journal of Child Language 16:1–18.
Davis, B. L., and MacNeilage, P. F. 1990. Acquisition of correct vowel production: A quantitative case study. Journal of Speech and Hearing Research 33:16–27.
Elbers, L., and Ton, J. 1985. Play pen monologues: The interplay of words and babbles in the first words period. Journal of Child Language 12:551–65.
Fowler, C. A., Rubin, P. E., Remez, R., and Turvey, M. 1978. Implications for speech production of a general theory of action. In Language Production, ed. B. Butterworth. NY: Academic Press.

Fry, D. B. 1966. The development of the phonological system in the normal and the deaf child. In *The Genesis of Language: A Psycholinguistic Approach*, eds. F. Smith and G. Miller. Cambridge, MA: MIT Press.

Goodell, E. W., and Studdert-Kennedy, M. 1990. The child's entry into the lexicon: Evidence for an articulatory model of phonological development. Paper presented at the 5th International Congress for the Study of Child Language, Budapest, July.

Kent, R. D. 1981. Articulatory-acoustic perspectives on speech development. In *Language Behavior in Infancy and Early Childhood*, ed. R. E. Stark. NY: Elsevier/North-Holland.

Kent, R. D. 1984. The psychobiology of speech development: Co-emergence of language and a movement system. *American Journal of Physiology* 246:R888–R894.

Kent, R. D., and Bauer, H. R. 1985. Vocalizations of one-year olds. *Journal of Child Language* 12:491–526.

Kent, R. D., and Murray, A. D. 1982. Acoustic features of infant vocalic utterances at 3, 6, and 9 months. *Journal of the Acoustical Society of America* 72:353–65.

Koopmans-van Beinum, F. J., and Van der Stelt, J. M. 1986. Early stages in the development of speech movements. In *Precursors of Early Speech*, eds. B. Lindblom and R. Zetterstrom. Basingstroke, Hampshire: MacMillan.

Lieberman, P. 1980. On the development of vowel productions in young children. In *Child Phonology*, Vol. 1: *Production*, eds. G. Yeni-Komshian, J. Kavanagh, and C. A. Ferguson. NY: Academic Press.

Locke, J. L. 1983. *Phonological Acquisition and Change*. NY: Academic Press.

McCune, L. 1989. Toward an integrative theory of early language acquisition: Evidence from longitudinal trends in vocal behavior. Paper read at the Biennial Meeting of the Society for Research in Child Development, April, Kansas City, MO.

McCune, L., and Vihman, M. M. 1987. Vocal motor schemes. *Papers and Reports in Child Language Development* 26:72–79.

MacNeilage, P. F. 1980. The control of speech production. In *Child Phonology*, Vol. 1: *Production*, eds. G. Yeni-Komshian, J. Kavanagh, and C. A. Ferguson. NY: Academic Press.

MacNeilage, P. F., and Davis, B. 1990. Acquisition of speech production: Frames, then content. In *Attention and Performance, XIII*, ed. M. Jeannerod. Hillsdale, NJ: Lawrence Erlbaum Associates.

Menn, L. 1979. Towards a psychology of phonology: Child phonology as a first step. In *Proceedings of the 3rd Annual Michigan Conference on Metatheory*, ed. R. Herbert. East Lansing: Michigan State University.

Netsell, R. 1981. The acquisition of speech motor control: A perspective with directions for research. In *Language Behavior in Infancy and Early Childhood*, ed. R. E. Stark. NY: Elsevier/North-Holland.

Oller, D. K. 1980. The emergence of the sounds of speech in infancy. In *Child Phonology*, Vol. 1: *Production*, eds. G. Yeni-Komshian, J. Kavanagh, and C. A. Ferguson. NY: Academic Press.

Oller, D. K., and Eilers, R. E. 1988. The role of audition in infant babbling. *Child Development* 59:441–49.

Oller, D. K., Wieman, L. A., Doyle, W. J., and Ross, C. 1976. Infant babbling and speech. *Journal of Child Language* 3:1–11.

Peters, A. M. 1986. Early syntax. In *Language Acquisition: Studies in First Language Development*, 2nd ed., eds. P. Fletcher and M. Garman. Cambridge: University Press.

Piaget, J. 1952. *The Origins of Intelligence in Children.* Trans. M. Cook. NY: W.W. Norton.

Roug, L., Landberg, I., and Lundberg, L.-J. 1989. Phonetic development in early infancy: A study of four Swedish children during the first eighteen months of life. *Journal of Child Language* 16:19–40.

Stark, R. 1980. Stages of speech development in the first year of life. In *Child Phonology,* Vol. 1: *Production,* eds. G. Yeni-Komshian, J. Kavanagh, and C. A. Ferguson. NY: Academic Press.

Stoel-Gammon, C. 1983. Constraints on consonant-vowel sequences in early words. *Journal of Child Language* 10:455–57.

Stoel-Gammon, C. 1989. Pre-speech and early speech development of two late talkers. *First Language* 9:207–24.

Stoel-Gammon, C., and Cooper, J. A. 1984. Patterns of early lexical and phonological development. *Journal of Child Language* 11:247–71.

Thelen, E. 1981. Rhythmical behavior in infancy: An ethological perspective. *Developmental Psychology* 17:237–57.

Vihman, M. M. 1987. The interaction of production and perception in the transition to speech. Paper read at the Twelfth Annual Boston University Conference on Language Development, October.

Vihman, M. M. 1991. Ontogeny of phonetic gestures: Speech production. In *Modularity and the Motor Theory of Speech Perception,* eds. I. G. Mattingly and M. Studdert-Kennedy. Hillsdale, NJ: Lawrence Erlbaum Associates.

Vihman, M. M., and Miller, R. 1988. Words and babble at the threshold of language acquisition. In *The Emergent Lexicon,* eds. M. D. Smith and J. L. Locke. NY: Academic Press.

Vihman, M. M., and Velleman, S. 1989. Phonological reorganization: A case study. *Language and Speech* 32:149–70.

Vihman, M. M., Ferguson, C. A., and Elbert, M. 1986. Phonological development from babbling to speech: Common tendencies and individual differences. *Applied Psycholinguistics* 7:3–40.

Vihman, M. M., Macken, M. A., Miller, R., Simmons, H., and Miller, J. 1985. From babbling to speech: A reassessment of the continuity issue. *Language* 61:395–443.

Winer, B. 1962. *Statistical Principles in Experimental Design.* (2d ed.) NY: McGraw-Hill.

APPENDIX A.   ANALYSIS OF VARIANCE

Edwin Kay (Lehigh University)

An analysis of variance was carried out on the practiced syllable data. Each syllable consisted of one member of a consonant category: labial (/labiodental), alveolar (/palatal), velar (/uvular), or (glottal) [h] and one member of a vowel category: front, back, or central. The syllables were thus classified in a 4 by 3 design, yielding 12 categories. The number of syllables of each type used by each child was recorded. The data were analyzed with a four factor analysis of variance: Subject (23), Language

Table VIII A.   Results of Analysis of Variance on CV Associations

Source	Sum of Squares	Degrees of Freedom	Mean of Squares	Denominator	F
Language (A)	7877.590	4	1969.40	Subjects (S)	2.76*
Consonant (B)	36244.195	3	12081.40	B × S	8.22**
Vowel (C)	75577.935	2	37788.97	C × S	30.85**
Subjects (S)	12809.333	18	711.63		
A × B	25747.908	12	2145.66	B × S	1.46
A × C	16151.027	8	2018.88	C × S	1.65
B × C	31578.958	6	5263.16	B × C × S	6.73**
A × B × C	21986.336	24	916.09	B × C × S	1.17
B × S	79359.170	54	1469.61		
C × S	44092.600	36	1224.79		
B × C × S	84398.800	100	781.47		

  * = $p < 0.05$
  ** $p < 0.001$

(English: Rutgers sample, English: Stanford sample, French, Japanese, and Swedish), Consonant (Labial, Alveolar, Velar, [h]), and Vowel (Front, Back, Central). Subjects were nested within Language and crossed with Consonant and Vowel. Because the number of subjects per language was unequal (5 each for Rutgers, Stanford, and French and 4 each for Japanese and Swedish), an unweighted means analysis of variance was used (Winer 1962, pp. 600–602). All main effects were significant (see table VIII A, B, and C for the complete analyses of variance as well as the various group means): for Languages, $F(4,18) = 2.76$, $p < .05$, for Consonant, $F(3,54) = 8.22$, $p < .001$, and for Vowel, $F(2,36) = 30.85$, $p < .001$. The Consonant × Vowel interaction was significant, $F(6,108) = 6.73$, $p < .001$. No other interaction was significant at the .05 level.

Table VIII B.   Mean Practiced Syllables (Per Language Group) by Consonant and Vowel Categories

	Labial	Alveolar	Velar	[h]	Mean
Front	11.29	33.95	8.69	11.19	16.28
Back	2.67	7.81	8.41	3.97	5.72
Central	57.99	79.96	18.14	24.33	45.10
Mean	23.98	40.57	11.75	13.16	

Table VIII C.   Mean Practiced Syllables (Per Consonant and Vowel Categories) by Language Group

Rutgers	13.88
Stanford	25.12
French	24.00
Japanese	19.23
Swedish	29.60

APPENDIX B.   PROFILES OF TWO CHILDREN

Alice

I. Practiced syllables

9 mos.		ge			
	na				
	ja			jə	
			wi		
10 mos.		be			
		de			
		ge			
	ja	je			
		le			
	ha				
11 mos.		be	bi		bœ
	na				

II. Early lexicon (spontaneous words only)

10 mos.	baby	[pɛpɛ:], [tɛˡti:], [teˡtɛ]
	mommy	[m:an:ə]
	hiya	[ʔa:jɛ], [haˡje], [ha:ˡ], [ʔa:dʑe]
11 mos.	baby	[be:βI], [bœwœ]
	bottle	[bœjœ], [bœbəp]
	hello	[hʌl:ʌ]
	hi	[ʔaˡ], [jæˡ], [haˡ]
	light	[dæ]
	no	[njæ:næ], [nʌ]
	rubrub	[bɛbɛbɛbɛp], [bʌbʌb]
	yumyum	[jʌm:ʌmjʌm]
12 mos.	ball	[pœ], [pœˡ]
	hi	[haˡ], [ʔaˡ]
	mama	[mœ], [e:m:am:amə]
	whoo	[huˡ]
13 mos.	baby	[pepi]
	dolly	[dal:i]
	elephant	[ʔaˡ], [ʔɛŋi], [ʔe:]

yumyum   [ʔm̩:jʌmjeˡ]

III. 15-word point (14 months)
    A. Palatal articulation ("vocal motor scheme"; "word recipe")

baby	[peˡbi]
bear	[bɛ:]
blanket	[bæŋ:i]
Bonnie	[baŋi]
bottle	[badi]
bye	[baˡ]
clean	[ki:n]
daddy	[tædi]
Ernie	[ʔəŋi]
eye	[ʔaˡ]
hi	[ha:ji]
lady	[jeˡji]
mommy	[ma:ɲi]

    B. Other forms

doll	[da:ə]
hammer	[həv:a]
man	[m:æ]
Oscar	[ʔa]

Timmy

I. Practiced syllables

9 mos.				du
			fə	fu
	ha	he		hu
10 mos.	ba		bə	
		de		
	fa			
		je		
11 mos.	ba		bə	
	ga		gə	
	ha			

II. Early lexicon (spontaneous words only)

10 mos.	ball	[pʰə], [bæ], [bʷæ], [bæp]
	block	[pˤæ:], [ʌv:æ], [ʌpˤæ]
11 mos.	ball	[same range of phonetic variation]
	block	
	car	[[kaə], [ak:aʰ]
	kitty	[kʰə], [kʰḁ], [kaka], [ʔuka], [haəka:ᵏ], [kakaka], etc.
	quack	[kʰə̥], [ka], [kaka], [gaga], [gakaəʰ], [kʰ̥akʰḁ], [kakaga]

12 mos.	\<ba\>	\<ga\>		
	ball	car		
	balloon	girl		
	bell	Great Gable		
	block			
13 mos.	ball	car		
	block	cat		
		Great Gable		
		kitty		
		Teddy		
14 mos.	ball	car	eye	\<ja\>
	block	kitty		
	box	quack		
		Teddy		

III. 15-word point (15 months)

A. Consonant + [a] ("vocal motor scheme;" "word recipe")

\<ba\>	\<ga\>	\<βa\>	\<ɉa\>	\<na\>	\<ja\>
baa	car	Ruth	light	nose	ear
ball	kitty				eye
bird					hair
block					
box					
brush					

B. Other forms (onomatopoeia)

hiss   [s̩]

moo/moon/mushrooms   [mʋ]

Chapter • 14

Early Phonological Acquisition
A Cross-Linguistic Perspective

David Ingram

It is obvious that any research on phonological acquisition must confront directly the question of cross-linguistic similarities and differences. As a consequence, it is not obvious at first glance why this chapter should differ in any important way from the theme of the other chapters in this book. It is well known, however, that discussions of phonological acquisition in the past often focussed almost exclusively on the acquisition of English. I take as my first assumption, therefore, that I am not allowed to do this. Second, theoretical discussions also have, at times, tended to be rather lean on data, either in the sense that only data from one child, or even only isolated examples from a small number of children, were considered. I take my second charge, then, to be to present some data on cross-linguistic acquisition. Last, I have argued in several places in the last few years that children show consistent cross-linguistic differences in their phonological acquisition (c.f. Ingram 1980, 1981/2, 1988, 1989, 1991, in press; Pye, Ingram, and List 1987).

I begin this chapter with a brief discussion of my assumptions about the nature of early phonological acquisition. My position is that children begin the acquisition of their expressive vocabulary with a phonological system that has the formal properties of the adult system. This is followed by a discussion of two aspects of phonological acquisition. The first is the nature of children's phonetic inventories across linguistic communities. Despite individual differences, the data suggest that there are consistent cross-linguistic differences. This finding opposes the view that the nature of the child's first words is solely the consequence of biological factors. The second aspect is how such differences in order of acquisition are phonologically represented. I discuss two hypotheses on how children acquire phonological representations, and demonstrate how they lead to empirically testable claims about the order of acquisition of the phonological features of specific languages.

SOME PRELIMINARY ASSUMPTIONS

The theories of both Jakobson and Stampe are treated by many in recent years to be primarily of historical interest (e.g., Jakobson 1968; Stampe 1969). Jakobson's theory has suffered from its difficulty in accounting for the individual variation of data-oriented studies, and Stampe's has had problems in constraining the extent of variation that it allows. They have been replaced by the versions of the *cognitive theory* of Macken and Ferguson (1983), which has the following properties: (1) emphasis on individual differences; (2) the proposal of developmental stages in the child's phonological units, where progress is roughly from the word to the syllable to the feature; and (3) relatively few general patterns of acquisition across children.

The theory of phonological acquisition I follow, however, differs from this current view. I referred to it elsewhere (Ingram 1988) as a Neo-Jakobsonian theory of acquisition. It is Jakobsonian to the extent that it argues that there are general patterns of acquisition across children, that children begin phonological processing at the time of their first words, and that children begin word acquisition through the acquisition of distinctive features. (A summary of the arguments behind this position is presented in the appendix to this chapter). It is "Neo" in that it attempts to incorporate more recent findings into Jakobson's theory, as well as to elaborate it. For example, it is adjusted to allow for consistent cross-linguistic differences. Also, it adapts the formal apparatus of recent research in nonlinear phonology in general, and feature theory in particular. Last, it incorporates recent methodological advances as initiated in Ferguson and Farwell (1975), and extended in Ingram (1981, 1989).

These beliefs result in part from my interpretation of developmental data, and also from reflections on the logical problem of phonological acquisition. They are not raised here, however, for the purpose of proposing their correctness (although I obviously do not believe they are wrong), nor for the focus of a public debate (although they are worthy issues for such discussion). Rather, I raise these assumptions at the onset because they underlie the line of research discussed in this chapter. Specifically, this research is to examine all of the following questions: (1) the nature of the early phonetic inventories of children acquiring a wide range of phonologically distinct languages; (2) the order of acquisition of the distinctive features of those languages; and (3) the construction of an acquisition theory which, in conjunction with phonological theory, can account for those orders that do occur, and which disallows those that do not.

As is well known, Jakobson (1968) argued that the first consonantal distinction acquired by children is nasal versus oral. Later he suggested (Jakobson and Halle 1956) that features fall into independent groupings, in such a way that the first distinction in one group may be acquired before or after the first feature of another grouping. This enabled him to relax his earlier predictions and allow children to acquire either nasal versus oral or labial versus dental as their first opposition. Current research into feature geometry is exploring the extent to which such groupings exist. Individual differences among children along these lines can be used as one form of evidence for proposals such as these. Such child data can only be useful, however, if we assume that children initiate feature acquisition at the onset of acquisition, rather than some word-based form of representation. Indeed, the extent to which child analyses do or do not support independent phonological evidence on feature geometry can be taken as one form of evidence (among many others) for or against my assumptions above.

PATTERNS OF CROSS-LINGUISTIC PHONETIC INVENTORIES

For some time, I had taken a view that children would fall into categories of individual variation, and that the variation would be consistent cross-linguistically. For example, some children might be naturally disposed to be reduplicators, while others would not. This pattern would then be manifested by these children regardless of the linguistic community into which they were born. This belief led me to look for general patterns of individual differences, as well as general patterns in the form of the use of universal phonological processes.

This belief was altered gradually as I began to look more and more at cross-linguistic data. The first hint of cross-linguistic variation came from my first exposures to the rich diary literature on the acquisition of French (e.g., Roussey 1899–1900). I noted in Ingram (1980) that a process of denasalization, in which a nasal consonant would become nonnasal, was much more common in the French data than in English data.

(1) Some Examples of Denasalization:

> a. English: *room* [wub]; *salmon* [sabud]
> b. French: *mange* 'eat' [ba ʃ]; *menton* 'chin' [ba:to:]

It has been documented in English (e.g., Velten 1943), but only for some children, and only at the earliest stages. I found cases of it for all the French children, however, and often when they were well into their phonological acquisition.

The next piece of data came from a study I did on the phonological system of a bilingual English-Italian girl (Ingram 1981/2). If my view were correct, the girl should show the same phonological system (more or less) for the lexicon of both languages. This was also the interpretation given by Vogel (1975) for her analyses of a bilingual English-Romanian child. I found, however, that the child had a very different phonology for her English words than she did for her Italian ones. For English, she was highly monosyllabic, using either English monosyllabic words, or reducing multisyllabic ones to single syllables. In fact, she did this at a much higher rate than the average English child, based in the analysis of 15 children in Ingram (1981). For Italian, however, she was highly multisyllabic, and rarely reduced words to a single syllable. I concluded that she was acquiring separate phonologies for the two languages, and that the properties of her words were being heavily influenced by the nature of the target language rather than some inherent tendency on her part.

The next and most dramatic set of contradictory data came when I initiated a project with Pye to do phonological analyses on his five K'iche' subjects (Pye 1983). Using the methodological techniques developed in Ingram (1981), we examined their acquisition of initial consonants, imposing a frequency criterion on when we would say that a child had acquired a sound. Roughly, sounds were either marginal, used, or frequent. The general results of this study were reported in Pye, Ingram, and List (1987), and are summarized in table I.

We found that, despite individual differences, the children tended to acquire certain sounds over others. For example, the two most frequent early sounds were [tʃ] and [l]. We then compared this inventory with the one determined for English in Ingram (1981). These two are summarized in (2).

(2)

English	K'iche'
m n	m n
b d g	p t tʃ k ʔ
p t k	x
f s h	
w	w

l

Table I.   The Acquisition of K'iche' Initial Consonants

| | Consonants | | | | | |
	A Tu:n	A Li:n	Al Tiya:n	Al Cha:y	A Carlos	Composite[1]
Nasals						
/m/		m		m	(m)	(m)
/n/	n	n**	n*	n	n	n
Stops						
/p/	(p)	p	p	p*	(p)	p
/t/		t	t*	t	t*	t
/ts/					(ts)	
/tʃ/	tʃ	tʃ*	tʃ	tʃ*	tʃ*	tʃ*
/k/	(k)	k*	k*	k	k	k
/q/		q				
/ʔ/	ʔ**	ʔ**	ʔ***	ʔ*	ʔ*	ʔ*
Ejectives						
/b'/		(b')	(b')		(b')	(b')
/t'/						
/ts'/						
/tʃ'/						
/k'/					k'	
/q'/						
Fricatives						
/s/					s*	
/ʃ/				ʃ*	(ʃ)	
/x/		x*	x*	x*	x*	x*
Liquids						
/l/	l*	l**	l***	l***	l	l*
/r/						
Glides						
/w/	w*	w*	w**	w*	w	w*
/j/		(j)				

(Taken from Pye, Ingram, and List (1987), Table 8.3. Parentheses indicate marginal sounds, and *indicates frequent use of a sound.)

[1]The term *composite* refers to the determination of a single inventory to represent the extent to which the sounds occurred in the speech of all subjects.

There are some similarities in order of acquisition for sounds that occur in both languages. For example, both inventories show early use of the nasals [m] and [n], the stops [p], [t], and [k], and the glide [w]. Differences occurred, however, with several other sounds. The early use of [l] in K'iche' was not matched in English, nor the early use of affricate [tʃ]. Also, the early use of some form of [s] was not matched in K'iche' where the first fricative appeared to be [x]. We concluded that linguistic reasons, rather than some form of articulatory constraint, were at the root of the differences.

I have examined this issue further in two other studies. In Ingram (1988), I selected a sound that is known from numerous studies to be quite late in English, this being the voiced labiodental fricative [v]. I examined three Bulgarian, Estonian, and Swedish diaries which I had previously analyzed and in which I recalled seeing the early use of some form of [v]. These data are summarized in table II. In each case, [v] was one of the first fricatives acquired. (There is a linguistic issue that [v] functions as a glide in these languages. My study, however, was only concerned with the phonetics of the child's articulations and the issue of ease of articulation.)

The other study is one in progress on the acquisition of French vowels. Ignoring nasal vowels and front rounded vowels, French has a five vowel system with some question about the status of the open mid-vowels. The preliminary results have indicated that the first French vowels acquired are [a] and the mid-vowels, not the high vowels of the basic triangle as predicted by Jakobson.

Such results have led me to believe that each language will have its own basic inventory that characterizes the child's first phonemes. Based in part on the kinds of findings discussed in this volume on the perceptual capacities of infants, I believe that children are better pre-pared than we have assumed to acquire a range of speech sounds. Pye, Ingram, and List (1987) suggest that order of acquisition is not solely determined by biological factors, but also by linguistic ones. The lin-guistic factor is something along the lines of what has been referred to in the past as *functional load*. That is, the more words a child acquires that have a particular sound in the adult model, the more likely it is that the sound will be produced. [v] is a late sound in English because chil-dren acquire relatively few words with it. It is because of this problem, for example, that articulation tests have had to rely on words like *valen-tine* and *vacuum cleaner* to test for it. Such is apparently not the case in the languages mentioned above, where the language learner is pre-sented with a number of lexical items with [v].

POSSIBLE FORMS OF EARLY PHONOLOGICAL REPRESENTATIONS

The second aspect of cross-linguistic acquisition concerns the nature of the child's initial phonological representations. I have already stated that I assume that the form of these is consistent with the formalism of adult phonology. Using nonlinear phonology as a frame of reference, we can say that a child stores a CV skeletal tier with each slot associated to phonological features that have been acquired. Acquisition proceeds in a Neo-Jakobsonian manner as features are added, subject to con-straints of the feature geometry, as well as to any marked parameters set in the phonological system being acquired. (More details on the for-mal nature of these representations can be found in Ingram 1988.)

While this account will be capable of capturing current acquisition

Table II. Word Initial Consonantal Inventories of a Swedish Child, Sonia, at 1;9, an Estonian Child, Linda, at 1;7, and a Bulgarian Child, Vlado, at 1;8

Child	Nasals	Stops	Fricatives	Approximants
Sonia	m	p t k	s (h)	r
		b* d* g	v	
Linda	m* n*	p* t* k*	v	l* (j)
Vlado	m* n	p* t k*	(f)	l
		(ts)		
		d g	v	

Source: Based on Ingram (1988).
*Indicates frequent use of a sound.

data, it suffers from the flaws that all new phonological models have shown. Basically, our acquisition models, in conjunction with any phonological theory, always will be capable of describing most acquisition data. The transfer of new proposals in phonological theory, with the exception of Stampean natural phonology, has always had this problem. The significant issue is to constrain our acquisition model in ways that lead to falsifiable predictions.

Let me provide an example of how this occurs for early phonological representations. Suppose we have acquisition data of the form shown in (3), where these are the child's matches and substitutions for word initial consonants.

(3) Adult Phonemes: /p/ /b/ /t/ /d/ /k/ /g/

   Child Sounds: Stage 1   d   d
                  Stage 2   b   b   d   d
                  Stage 3   p   b   d   d
                  Stage 4   p   b   t   d   k   k

In Stage 2 we can suggest that the child acquired the distinction of place. Let's assume that the child acquired the feature [coronal], as shown in (4). (I make this decision with the assumption that the features needed are from /t/, /d/, the first phonemes represented.)

(4) Stage 2   /p b t d /

        cor   − − + +

Next, we observe that the feature [voice] has emerged for /p/ versus /b/ at Stage 3. This is not the case for /t/ and /d/, however, which still show the substitute [d]. How do we represent the child's system at this stage? Various solutions are possible, as given in (5):

(5) Stage 3   /p   b   t   d/

   a.   cor   – – + +
           voice   – + + +

                             /p   b   t   d/

   b.   cor   – – + +
           voice   – + – +
           Production rule t → d

                             /p   b   t   d/

   c.   cor   – – + +
           voice   – +
           Redundancy [voice] → [+ voice]

The first solution, (5)a, represents features in a way that reflects the child's production directly. It also allows the child to represent /t/ as [+ voice], which could be argued for on the grounds of incomplete perception. (This claim, however, would be difficult to justify on the basis of much work on perception [see review in Ingram 1989]). It would also require a restructuring later on the part of the child to change this representation to [– voice]. Because of the autonomy of the child's representation from the adult model, I will call this the *child representation approach*.

The second solution, (5)b, assumes that the child has the adult distinctions underlyingly, and that there are production rules that alter these representations. Such solutions have been around for some time, and have been most argued for in Smith (1973). I will call this the *adult representation approach*. Its problem, which I consider a rather serious one, is that it postulates an ad hoc set of production rules that are not part of the adult phonology.

The third solution, (5)c, follows the basic form of a current view in phonological theory referred to as contrastive specification. It captures phonological representations as consisting of underlying contrasts along with redundancy rules that function somewhat like the rules of natural phonology. For sake of reference, I will refer to this as the *Neo-Jakobsonian approach* (Ingram 1988).

How then, are we to choose between alternatives such as these? I suggest that the basis of such choice be heavily constrained by the restrictiveness of the proposal in question. In this case, only the theory underlying (5)c is restricted in any interesting way. For (5)a, we can always claim the child does not perceive a distinction, or that the child has established an underlying representation distinct from the phonetic input. Because we never have access to the child's representations,

we can never prove such an analysis to be wrong. (5)b is also unfalsifia-
ble, at least in practice, because there is no theory of possible production rules that I am aware of. Even more serious (at least for me) is the
fact that it says nothing very interesting about the acquisition of contrasts, because these are assumed to be adult-like from the time that
words are acquired.

To justify my claim, I need to show the constrained nature of the
position I have advocated. First, it is restricted by assuming a continuity in development between the child and the adult. It also is based
on two crucial hypotheses about phonological acquisition.

(6) Acoustic Representation Hypothesis:

> Children first represent their early vocabulary in the
> form of fully specified phonetic feature matrices.

This hypothesis is based in part on the remarkable findings to date on
how well infants perceive the speech of the linguistic environment. It
suggests that the child has access to the phonetic information he or she
needs for subsequent linguistic analysis. I hedge for the time being
about whether this is in the form of a stored representation, or some
recognitory sensorimotor schema.

The phonetic representations form the basis for the extraction of
distinctive features. This occurs in the following way.

(7) Distinctive Feature Hypothesis:

> Children phonologically analyze and represent their
> first words in distinctive features selected from the
> set of available phonetic features in the fully specified
> phonetic representation.

This hypothesis eliminates any analysis of the form in (5)a where a /t/ is
assigned a feature of [+ voice]. This hypothesis alone restricts greatly
the distance between some early phonological representation and the
adult one. Lastly, a child has available a universal set of redundancy
rules along the lines of Stampe's natural phonology. If a feature is not
represented in a child's underlying representation, it is added through
such rules.

I now show how this set of assumptions captures a set of data from
language acquisition. As before, I present a very simple example to
demonstrate the point. Velten's study (Velten 1943) of his daughter
Joan is probably one of the most detailed reports on vowel acquisition
ever presented. For an extended period, Joan produced just two
vowels, [a] and [u]. Somewhat simplified, [a] was used for all English
low vowels, and [u] was used for mid and high vowels, whether
rounded or unrounded. (8) presents a summary of these facts.

(8) /i,e,o,u/ → [u]   /a, æ, ɔ/ → [a]

What is the feature that Joan has acquired to capture this difference? Three possible candidates present themselves: [round], [high],
and [low]. In (9) and (10) I show how each of the three approaches discussed earlier captures these data depending on whether the feature is
[round] or [low] (I do not include [high], which has analyses comparable in nature to those for [round]).

(9) [round]
   a. *child representation*   / i e o u a æ ɔ /
                        [round]   + + + + − − −
   b. *adult representation*   / i e o u a æ ɔ /
                        [round]   − − + + − − +
                        Production Rules: i,e,o,u → u
                                      a,æ, ɔ → a
   c. *Neo-Jakobsonian*   / i e o u a æ ɔ /
                        *[round]   + + + + − − −

*(not allowed, violates Distinctive Feature Hypothesis)

(10) [low]
   a. *child representation*   / i e o u a æ ɔ /
                        [low]   − − − − + + +
                        [round]   + + + +
   b. *adult representation*   / i e o u a æ ɔ /
                        [low]   − − − − + + +
                        Production Rules: i,e,o,u → u
                                     a,æ,ɔ → a
   c. *Neo-Jakobsonian*   / i e o u a æ ɔ /
                        [low]   − − − − + + +

The first two approaches come up with some way to describe these
data for each of these three features. In (9)a we specify those adult
vowels that surface as [u] as having an underlying [round]. We do not
have to worry that these vowels are not round in English by claiming
that the child misperceives them as such. In (9)b the assignment of
[round] to the adult vowels is accurate, but we then need to postulate
production rules to get the correct output. The first of these, in which
/i,e,o/ go to [u], is unlike any phonological process with which I am
familiar.

    The approach I have described, however, cannot propose either
[round] (or [high]) because both violate the Distinctive Feature Hypothesis. Instead, the approach is forced to choose [low] as the feature

being acquired. The other approaches could be constrained, though I am not aware of anyone trying to do this. The first could be developed by adding a theory of misperceptions, although I am not particularly optimistic about its possibilities. The second needs a constrained theory of possible production rules, although this will not eliminate the problem of separating, as it does, the child's surface distinctions from the underlying ones, as demonstrated in (9)b.

Elsewhere (Ingram in press), I demonstrate other examples of this restrictiveness, including one with the acquisition of vowels in Wikchamni. That example is especially interesting because it demonstrates how the acquisition model can account for the stages a child might go through to reach the adult system proposed in the literature by Archangeli (1985). In work in progress I am pursuing it further, with the attempt to incorporate the language-specific effects discussed in the first part of this paper.

CONCLUSION

I have discussed English, provided less cross-linguistic data than available in my files, and trod beyond description into some issues on children's phonological representations. It is nonetheless true that ultimately cross-linguistic data will be the true test of the extent to which any of these comments are correct characterizations of how children acquire their first phonological representations.

REFERENCES

Archangeli, D. 1985. Yokuts harmony: Evidence for coplanar representations in nonlinear phonology. *Linguistic Inquiry* 16:335–72.

Ferguson, C. A., and Farwell, C. B. 1975. Words and sounds in early language acquisition. *Language* 51:419–39.

Ingram, D. 1980. Cross-linguistic evidence on the extent and limit of individual variation in phonological development. *Proceedings of the Ninth International Congress of Phonetic Sciences*, Vol. 2:150–4.

Ingram, D. 1981. *Procedures for the Phonological Analysis of Children's Language*. Baltimore, MD: University Park Press.

Ingram, D. 1981/2. The emerging phonological system of an Italian-English bilingual child. *Journal of Italian Linguistics* 2:95–113.

Ingram, D. 1988. The acquisition of word initial [v]. *Language and Speech* 31:77–85.

Ingram, D. 1989. *First Language Acquisition: Method, Description and Explanation*. Cambridge: Cambridge University Press.

Ingram, D. 1991. Toward a theory of phonological acquisition. In *Perspectives on Language Disorders*, ed. J. Miller. Austin, TX: Pro-ed.

Ingram, D. In press. Issues in learnability and phonological theory. In *Research on Child Language Disorders*, ed. A. James.

Jakobson, R. 1968. *Child Language, Aphasia, and Phonological Universals.* The Hague: Mouton. (Translation by R. Keiler of original German version published in 1941).

Jakobson, R., and Halle, M. 1956. *Fundamentals of Language.* The Hague: Mouton.

Macken, M. A., and Ferguson, C. A. 1983. Cognitive aspects of phonological development: Model, evidence, and issues. In *Children's Language, Vol. 3*, ed. K. E. Nelson. Hillsdale, NJ: Lawrence Erlbaum Associates.

Pye, C. 1983. Mayan telegraphese: Intonational determinants of inflectional development in Quiche Mayan. *Language* 59:583–604.

Pye, C., Ingram, D., and List, H. 1987. A comparison of initial consonant acquisition in English and Quiche. In *Children's Language, Vol. 6*, eds. K. E. Nelson and A. Van Kleek. Hillsdale, NJ: Lawrence Erlbaum Associates.

Roussey, C. 1899–1900. Notes sur l'apprentissage de la parole chez un enfant. *La Parole* 1:870–80; 2:23–40.

Smith, N. 1973. *The Acquisition of Phonology: A Case Study.* Cambridge: Cambridge University Press.

Stampe, D. 1969. The acquisition of phonemic representation. *Proceedings of the Fifth Regional Meeting of the Chicago Linguistic Society* 433–44.

Velten, H. 1943. The growth of phonemic and lexical patterns in infant speech. *Language* 19:281–92.

Vogel, I. 1975. One system or two: An analysis of a two-year-old Romanian-English bilingual's phonology. *Papers and Reports on Child Language Development* 9:43–62.

APPENDIX

A Summary of Reasons Behind the Claim that Children Use Distinctive Features in their Early Phonological Representations

1. Research on infant speech perception has found that infants are remarkably good at identifying the acoustic characteristics of speech sounds. Their acoustic representations, therefore, should be reasonably complete.

2. When children acquire their 50th word in production around 1;6, they have a much larger receptive vocabulary of around 250 words. The latter vocabulary is sufficiently large to suggest that phonological organization has begun.

3. If children are using holistic representations in their words, then they should not show awareness of segments in their earlier babbling. Research, however, indicates such awareness through babbling sequences such as [bi], [ba], [bu], rather than [bi], [mu], [ta].

4. Developmental theories are unclear as to what is meant by the "word" as an early unit or organization. Does it disappear, or is it retained as further developments take place?

5. What is the mechanism that takes the child from stage to stage?
6. Research on phonological samples using frequency criterion consistently show segmental patterns of acquisition rather than holistic ones. For example, holistic theories predict random substitution patterns rather than the consistent ones that are found.

Research Methods and Assessment Measures

Chapter • 15

Prelinguistic Vocal Development
Measurement and Predictions

Carol Stoel-Gammon

BACKGROUND

The decade of the 1980s witnessed an ever increasing interest in pre-linguistic vocal development and its relationship to subsequent language development. In the past, most studies of phonological development began with scrutiny of the appearance of the first words, later, clinical measures of phoneme mastery (e.g., Templin 1957) often began at three or even four years of age. Today, in contrast, investigators are focusing on increasingly younger aged children with the realization that language acquisition starts well before the first words. Among other findings, we now know that: (1) babies can distinguish their ambient language from other languages shortly after birth (Mehler et al. 1988); (2) at 4 months of age, babies prefer to listen to infant-directed rather than adult-directed speech (Fernald 1985); (3) the infant's perceptual system between 6 and 12 months undergoes changes resulting in a severe reduction of the ability to distinguish between certain phonemic contrasts not found in the maternal tongue (Werker and Tees 1984; Werker and Pegg this volume); (4) prior to the onset of meaning-

Preparation of this article was supported in part by a grant from the National Institutes of Health: NIDCD P01 DC00520. My thanks to Charles Ferguson and Lise Menn for their comments on a draft of this chapter.

ful speech, non-cry vocalizations are used communicatively as indicators of requests, discomfort, and attention-getting devices (Bates 1976); and (5) comprehension of words is evident at 9 months and by 13 months, when most babies begin to produce their first words, their receptive vocabulary is 50 words (Benedict 1979).

Research on infant vocalization in the prelinguistic period has focused primarily on two areas: ages and stages of premeaningful vocalizations and the relationship of babbling to early meaningful speech. In the first category, a number of studies have traced vocal development from the first postnatal utterance types to the establishment of meaningful speech. In spite of differences in methodology, researchers studying a variety of languages are in general agreement regarding the characteristics of the prelinguistic vocalizations. Slight variations in terminology and delineation of stages notwithstanding, investigations of English (e.g., Oller 1978; Stark 1980), Dutch (Koopmans-van Beinum and van der Stelt 1986), and Swedish (Roug, Landberg, and Lundberg 1989) have yielded highly similar timetables for development. The timetables are based on "stages" of development, with onset of a *stage* defined as the appearance of a new type of vocal behavior. The new behavior is not necessarily the most frequent type during the period, and the types of vocal output present in previous stages continue to occur, but the vocalization type was *not* present in the previous stages. The summary below provides a brief description of the major stages that have been documented. The reader is referred to the original sources for more detail.

STAGES OF VOCAL DEVELOPMENT

Stage 1: *Phonation,* ages 0–2 months. The non-cry vocalizations of this stage are described as being mostly "vegetative" and "reflexive" in nature. Phonetically, these utterances consist of vowel-like sounds; grunts and sighs also occur.

Stage 2: *Cooing,* ages 2–4 months. The comfort-state vocalizations of this period are characterized by back vowel-like sounds with some back consonants; all vocalizations have a nasal quality.

Stage 3: *Vocal play,* ages 4–6 months. The new features of this period include the presence of vocalizations exhibiting a wide range of intensity and fundamental frequency differences, resulting in the production of yells, whispers, squeals and growls. Infants may also produce bilabial and uvular trills, sustained vowels, syllabic consonants, and some rudimentary consonant-vowel syllables. These syllables are labeled *rudimentary* or *marginal* because they lack adult-like timing characteristics in overall duration and in consonant-vowel transitions.

Stage 4: *Canonical syllables,* age 6 months and older. The prime feature of this period is the appearance of consonant-vowel (CV) syllables
with adult-like timing. This stage is often divided into two substages:
first, a period of *reduplicated* CV babbles (i.e., strings of identical CV
syllables) and then a period of *variegated* CV babbles (syllable strings
that vary in the C, the V, or both). Recent research, however, casts
doubts upon the view that these two stages are sequential (Mitchell
and Kent 1990; Smith, Brown-Sweeney, and Stoel-Gammon 1989).

The last of these stages seems to be particularly important in terms
of later development because it is at this time that vocalizations first
approximate the timing and phonatory characteristics of adult speech
and, thus, begin to take on the characteristics of words. Some parents
interpret their baby's production of [mama] or [dada] at 7 months as
evidence of the first words. To be sure, it does sound as if the baby is
trying to say "mama" or "daddy;" in most instances, however, there is
no evidence that the infant's productions are semantically linked to any
identifiable referent and, thus, these forms would not be considered
words. Investigations of hearing-impaired infants indicate that it is at
the canonical stage that the vocal development of deaf babies deviates
from the normal timetable (Oller and Eilers 1988; Stoel-Gammon and
Otomo 1986).

THE RELATIONSHIP OF BABBLING TO SPEECH

The second major thrust in investigations of prelinguistic development
has centered around the issue of *continuity,* with a focus on the relationship between prelinguistic (i.e., nonmeaningful) and linguistic (i.e.,
meaningful) vocalizations. Specifically, the researchers seek to determine if the development from one period to the other is a continuous
path or if there is a major break (i.e., a discontinuity) between them. In
his influential monograph on phonological acquisition, Jakobson (1968)
argued strongly that infants' vocalizations prior to the first words were
not related to subsequent phonological development. In his words,
babbling is simply "the purposeless egocentric soliloquy of the child
. . . biologically oriented 'tongue delirium'" (1968, p. 22), and thus
"the appearance of phonemes in a linguistic system has nothing in
common with the ephemeral sound productions of the babbling period" (1968, p. 28). In the babbling period the child is said to produce
"an astonishing quantity and diversity of sound productions . . . consonants of any place of articulation, palatalized and rounded consonants, sibilants, affricates, clicks, complex vowels, diphthongs, etc.
. . . the child then loses nearly all of his ability to produce sounds in
passing over from the pre-language stage to the first acquisition of

words" (1968, p. 21). Although many of Jakobson's predictions regarding phonological acquisition have subsequently been supported, his views on the relationship between babbling and speech have not.

The first major refutation of Jakobson's position was published in 1976 when Oller and colleagues (Oller et al. 1976) provided empirical evidence that the sounds and syllable structures characteristic of the canonical babbling period closely resembled those of early meaningful speech. Since then, this finding has been replicated by a number of different researchers (see Locke 1983, for a summary). Studies show that although infants may produce a wide array of sound types during the prelinguistic period, only a subset of these occurs frequently. Locke's review (1983) of three separate investigations of American infants revealed that 12 consonants: [p,t,k,b,d,g,m,n,w,j,h,s] accounted for 92% to 95% of the consonantal phones produced at 11–12 months. This set of consonants is the same set that predominates in early word productions in English (Stoel-Gammon 1985). Moreover, the CV syllable structure characteristic of the canonical babbling period is also the most frequent in early word productions. Thus, the research shows that babbling and early speech share the same phonetic properties in terms of sound types and syllable shapes.

Further support for continuity between babbling and speech comes from longitudinal investigations of individual children. These investigations provide detailed analyses of data from individual subjects showing that inter-child variability in place and manner of articulation, syllable shape, and vocalization length is present and that differences documented in the prelinguistic period are often "carried forward" to the first words (Stoel-Gammon and Cooper 1984; Vihman et al. 1985; Vihman, Ferguson, and Elbert 1987). This line of research, then, provides another source of support for the continuity view.

The findings of these two lines of research have yielded a substantial body of data on the nature of prelinguistic development and have provided solid documentation of the ages and stages of normal vocal development and detailed descriptions of the course of development followed by individual subjects. Taken as a whole, the research serves as a framework for analyzing vocal productions prior to the onset of meaningful speech. What is missing from this framework, however, is the ability to compare children in order to determine similarities and differences in rate and level of development. If we want to compare *verbal* performance, in contrast, we can calculate the subjects' mean length of utterance (Brown 1973), their percent consonants correct (Shriberg and Kwiatkowski 1982), or their lexicon size, and subsequently rank subjects according to these measures. Currently, our assessments of prelinguistic development are based primarily on broad stages that do not differentiate finely among subjects. If, for example, two children are in Stage 4 (the canonical stage), it would be useful to be able identify one as being more advanced than the other. The question then arises: What measures would allow us to make meaningful interchild comparisons? A related question is: Can prelinguistic measures predict subsequent linguistic development?

MEASURES OF PRELINGUISTIC VOCAL DEVELOPMENT

This section addresses the assessment of prelinguistic vocal development by reviewing available research as it relates to two issues: (1) measures of prelinguistic vocalizations that provide a means for comparing across subjects; and (2) relationships between these measures and subsequent linguistic development. The notion that we might be able to *predict* linguistic development from prelinguistic performance is an appealing one, particularly in the clinical arena where early identification of atypical development could lead to the implementation of early intervention programs. Even in studies of normally developing subjects, it is of interest to determine which features of a child's vocal productions in the first year of life might be linked to phonological and linguistic patterns at later ages.

The following review is not intended to be an exhaustive summary of all studies that have measured prelinguistic development, but rather a representative sampling of the types of studies and their outcomes. The studies are grouped into three main categories: (1) those in which the primary measure was simply *amount* of vocalization; (2) those using measures based on the *stages* of development; and (3) inventory measures based on the frequency and diversity of consonants and CV syllables.

Amount of Vocalization

In the 1970s, Kagan and colleagues and students examined early vocalizations with special attention to the relationships between vocalization rate and other aspects of development. Kagan (1971) reported that the *amount of vocalization* in 4-month-old girls, particularly under "stimulating" conditions (i.e., when they were verbally stimulated by the mother), was related to the subjects' degree of *attentiveness* to a set of paragraphs read to them at 8 months and to their *rate of vocalization* at 13 months. Moreover, the subset of infants who evidenced high rates of vocalization at 4 months (and were from homes with high socioeconomic status) had the highest *vocabulary scores* at 27 months. Interestingly, Kagan did not find the same relationship to obtain for boys.

A few years later, however, Roe's (1975) research on early vocalizations in male infants indicated the presence of such a relationship. Recordings of 14 infants made when the subjects were 3, 5, 7, and 9 months old were analyzed to determine the amount of vocalization at each recording period. Roe found that those infants who scored higher on the Gesell Developmental Quotients (Gesell and Amatruda 1941) at 9 months had an earlier peak in the amount of vocalization (i.e., age at which they produced the most vocalizations) than those with lower Gesell scores. In addition, the subjects with high Gesell scores had vocalized more in response to the mother at 3 months than had the low Gesell babies. Roe (1977) reported the findings of a follow-up study of 12 of the same subjects when they were 5 years old. She found that the amount of vocalization at 3 months, produced when verbally stimulated by the mother, was positively correlated with the *amount of talking* at 3 years, and with *vocabulary size* as measured by the Peabody Picture Vocabulary Test (Dunn 1965) and *performance on a reading task* at 5 years.

Obviously, these findings must be interpreted cautiously due to the relatively small sample sizes and limited measures, but the possibility that amount of vocalization produced by an infant under 4 months of age is related to subsequent measures of linguistic and cognitive development is an intriguing one. The findings are supported by a more recent study by Camp and her colleagues (1987) in which amount of vocalization also was shown to be a valid predictive measure.

Because Roe's findings had not been replicated by other researchers (e.g., Landau 1977; Routh 1969), Camp gathered longitudinal data from a group of 141 infants, aged 6 weeks to 12 months, in order to examine the relationship between early vocalization rate and developmental measures at 12 months. Infants were recorded monthly in a situation in which the mother was asked to stimulate the baby so that he or she would vocalize. The measure was the number of infant vocalizations in a 5-minute period.

Contrary to the findings of Roe, the Camp study found a general pattern of increased amounts of vocalization during the period of study, with the mean number of vocalizations rising from 19.3 at 2 months to 39.6 at 12 months. The most reliable individual differences in vocalization rate appeared at 4 to 6 months, and the average of the observations at 4 and 5 and/or 5 and 6 months showed significant correlations with the subjects' scores at 11 to 15 months on the verbalization factor of the Bayley Scales of Infant Development, based on assessment of vocalization, social contact, and active vocabulary (Bayley 1969). A gross classification of babies into two groups based on performance at 4 to 6 months—a *vocal group* (those who produced at least 20 vocalizations in 5 minutes) and a *silent group* (those producing fewer than 20 vocalizations in two separate observations)—revealed that the vocal babies had quotients above 100 on the verbalization factor of the Bayley Scales.

However, correlations between amount of vocalization and the verbalization scores of the "silent" babies were not found. Noting that rate of vocalization did not show relationships with motor measures or with other cognitive measures of the Bayley Scales, the authors concluded that *amount of vocalization* at 4 to 6 months was specifically related to verbalization at 1 year and not to a more general level of development. Although the critical age for assessing amount of vocalization was somewhat different than that used in the Roe investigations, Camp's study provides evidence of a positive correlation between amount of vocalization under 6 months and subsequent language development.

Stage-Related Measures

Stage-related measures are based roughly on the timetable of vocal development presented in the stages of vocal development section above. The basic measure here is determining the *stage* of the baby and relating it to chronological age, thus allowing one to compare across subjects and to determine if precocity or delay in attainment of a particular stage is correlated with later development.

In one of the first studies of this sort, Stark, Ansel, and Bond (1988) used a seven-level classification system to code nonmeaningful vocalizations from 2 weeks to 18 months. In Stark's system, the onset and expansion of the Canonical Stage were described as follows: *Level 4* (6–8 months): *marginal babbling* characterized by CV syllables with timing slower than that of adult speech; *Level 5* (9–12 months): reduplicated and nonreduplicated CV syllables; *Level 6* (12–16 months): new syllable types, new vowel types; and *Level 7* (16–18 months): jargon babbling, diphthongs, and prewords. The authors used a pass/fail score to determine the infant's highest level of functioning at a particular age, with "highest" level defined as production of at least four vocalizations (out of 40–50 utterances) at that level. The longitudinal findings show that none of the 45 infants evidenced a regression over time; babbling level either remained the same or increased with age. Thus, this measure allows investigators to compare across subjects, to say, for example, that Child A is at Level 6 while Child B, with the same chronological age, is at Level 5 and, therefore, less advanced. Of particular interest in terms of prediction is one of Stark's subjects whose performance was atypical in that he had not yet attained Level 5 (production of reduplicated and nonreduplicated CV syllables) by 12.5 months. According to maternal report, this subject had no words at 18 months. Clinical assessment of his performance showed normal hearing but delayed development in the areas of speech and language. It was also noted that the father had experienced speech problems in school and the mother had reading problems. Subsequent reports showed that the child evidenced a developmental spurt in linguistic development during his second year and appeared to catch up with his peers. In first grade, however, the boy's teacher noted that he was experiencing difficulties in learning to read.

Oller and Eilers (1988) used a stage approach to compare the vocalizations of normally hearing and severely-to-profoundly hearing-impaired (HI) subjects in the first year. The syllables of nonvegetative utterances were classified as being *precanonical* or *canonical*, with a canonical syllable defined as a CV or VC sequence with a supraglottal consonant and adult-like timing. Subjects were considered to be in the *Canonical Stage* when the ratio of canonical syllables to utterances equaled or exceeded 0.2. Thus, to be in the Canonical Stage, a subject had to produce a minimum of 10 canonical syllables in a sample of 50 utterances. Using this criterion, the investigators found that all 21 normally hearing babies in the study entered the Canonical Stage between 6 and 10 months. In contrast, the HI babies were considerably older at attainment of this stage, ranging from 11 to 25 months.

In addition to the late onset of the canonical babbling, Oller and Eilers reported that some of the HI subjects produced a relatively low proportion of canonical syllables after entering the stage. At 11 to 14 months, the babbling ratio (ratio of canonical syllables to utterances) for the normal subjects ranged from 0.5 to 1.8. In contrast, 3 HI subjects in the Canonical Stage evidenced babbling ratios of only 0.1–0.4 six months after onset of the Stage; 3 others evidenced ratios of 0.7–0.9, within the range for the hearing babies. The authors note that during the session in which the babbling ratios were calculated, the latter three HI subjects (those with the higher ratios) showed "emerging speech communications" while the other three showed no meaningful speech. Thus it appears that *age at attainment* of the Canonical Stage and the number of canonical syllables can distinguish among subjects and possibly predict success with speech.

Stoel-Gammon (Olswang et al. 1987; Stoel-Gammon 1989a) developed a measure of prevocalic development based on sound types and the phonetic complexity of syllable structures. We classified nonmeaningful speechlike utterances as Level I, II, or III in accordance with the following criteria. *Level I* utterances are those that consist of a vowel, a syllabic consonant, or a CV or VC syllable in which the consonant is a glottal or a glide, or any combination of these. In terms of stages, *Level I* utterances are all precanonical. *Level II* utterances are vocalizations that contain one or more CV or VC syllables in which the consonant is a *true* consonant (i.e., not a glottal or glide); in multisyllabic utterances with more than one true consonant, the place and manner of the consonant remains constant, although the voicing may change (e.g., [paba] is

Level II; [pada] is not). In terms of stages, these utterances would be described as a single canonical syllable or a sequence of reduplicated canonical syllables. *Level III* utterances are composed of one or more canonical syllables with at least two true consonants that differ in place or manner of articulation. Most Level III utterances conform to the category of variegated babbles. This measure was used to determine a Mean Babbling Level for each of 34 normally developing subjects, ages 9 to 24 months (see Stoel-Gammon 1989a, for details). Mean Babbling Level (MBL) could range from 1.0 for a sample in which all vocalizations were classified as *Level I* to 3.0 if all utterances were *Level III*, and is described as a way of "comparing subjects at a given age and of measuring rate of advance across ages" (1989a, p. 212).

Stoel-Gammon (1989a,b) reported that MBL at 9 months was negatively correlated with age at onset of meaningful speech (as measured by production of at least 10 different adult-based words in a 60-minute recording session); that is, those 9-month-olds with higher MBLs entered the meaningful speech stage earlier than their peers with lower MBLs. Longitudinal analysis showed that the average MBL increased steadily with age, from a mean of 1.33 at 9 months to 1.65 at 18 months for the 32 subjects who entered the meaningful speech stage by 21 months. The remaining two subjects, who were 24 months at attainment of the meaningful speech stage, were labelled as late talkers in accordance with the definitions of Rescorla (1984) and Paul and Shiffer (1987). From 9 to 21 months, the MBL of one of these subjects was substantially lower than that of her peers, ranging from 1.00 (no use of canonical utterances) to 1.26 (24% of the utterances were canonical), a level that was lower than the average of her peer group even at 9 months. At 24 months, when the subject's sample contained 15 identifiable words, her MBL for *nonmeaningful* utterances was 1.93, substantially higher than in any of the previous sessions. Thus, once again, there is an apparent link between paucity of CV syllables in the prelinguistic period and late onset of meaningful speech.

INVENTORY MEASURES

The third major type of measure used in assessing and comparing prelinguistic vocalizations centers around the production of consonants as part of canonical syllables. In reality, these measures form a subset of the stage-based measures described in the previous section because they focus on behaviors that appear after the onset of the Canonical Stage.

Consonantal Types

Stoel-Gammon and Otomo (1986) used a measure of the *size* of the consonantal repertoire (number of different types) to compare the longitudinal development of vocalizations of hearing and hearing-impaired (HI) subjects. Analysis of transcribed samples revealed that the number of consonantal types in the samples of 11 normally hearing babies increased with age, from a mean of 11.3 different consonants at 4 to 6 months to a mean of 29.5 at 16 to 18 months. Prior to 8 months, the repertoire size of the HI subjects differed only slightly from the normals, but thereafter a striking difference appeared between the two groups. Among the normals, the inventories evidenced a steady increase in size until the onset of meaningful speech; among the HI babies, repertoire size remained constant or decreased with age. Thus, this measure revealed that among the hearing subjects, the range of sound types increased, while among the HI babies, no increase was noted.

Consonantal Tokens

The number of consonantal tokens in a sample has been adopted by a number of researchers as a means of inter-subject comparisons. Menyuk and colleagues (Menyuk, Liebergott, and Schultz 1986) carried out a longitudinal study of full-term and premature babies to determine if their prelinguistic vocalizations could serve as a predictor of subsequent linguistic development. They measured the number of *structured vocalizations* (defined as CV syllables) at 12 months and reported two significant correlations: (1) the proportion of CV syllables was negatively correlated with the age at which subjects produced 50 different words; that is, a higher proportion of CV syllables was linked with more rapid lexical acquisition; and (2) the proportion of CV syllables was positively correlated with the accuracy of production of word-final consonants at 29 months.

Vihman and Greenlee (1987) calculated the proportion of vocalizations (both babble and words) containing a *true consonant* (i.e., any consonant except glottals or glides) in each subject at 12 months and found that this percentage was negatively correlated to the subject's *error score* at three years. In other words, those subjects who produced *more* vocalizations with true consonants at one year evidenced *fewer* errors in their word productions two years later. The authors concluded that "high use of vocalizations with true consonants was found to be predictive of phonological advance at age 3" (p. 503).

Most recently, Bauer (1988; Robb and Bauer 1989) proposed an index of phonetic development referred to as the *closant curve,* based on the ratio of consonant-like sounds (*closants*) to vowel-like sounds (*vo-cants*). Among normally developing English-speaking children, this ratio evidences a systematic increase during the first two years as consonants become more frequent. Prior to 9 months of age, the ratio of closants to vocants is less than 0.5 (i.e., vocants are more than twice as frequent as closants); at 13 months, the ratio increases to 0.7. By 18 months, it rises to 1.0, meaning that, on average, consonants and vowels occur with equal frequencies. After 18 months, the ratio continues to increase, reaching 1.6 at 50 months and remaining there into adulthood.

Multiple Measures

In an investigation that followed 20 normal and 9 at risk subjects from birth to six years, a team of Danish researchers (Jensen et al. 1988) used both type and token measures in an attempt to: (1) identify qualitative and quantitative differences in the prelinguistic vocalizations of the two groups; and (2) determine the relationship between prelinguistic vocal development and language skills in the preschool period (in Denmark, preschool extends to 6 years of age). Analysis of premeaningful utterances revealed group differences in two domains: the mean number of different reduplications (diversity) and the mean total number of consonants (quantity) in the samples of the risk group were significantly lower than in the samples of their normal peers. The follow-up at six years revealed that 6 of the 9 subjects in the risk group and 2 of the 20 subjects in the control group failed to achieve "normal" results on a preschool language assessment of receptive and expressive language. In reexamining the prelinguistic data, the authors noted that the number of reduplications from 6 to 14 months and the total number of consonants at 14 months were significantly *lower* for the 8 children with an abnormal language test, whereas the prelinguistic samples from the 3 at risk subjects who tested as normal at 6 years were indistinguishable from the normal controls.

SUMMARY

The findings cited in the previous sections suggest that both the quantity and diversity of vocalizations in the prelinguistic period are linked to subsequent speech and language development. The studies of babies under 6 months of age indicate that *amount* of vocalization, regardless of the phonetic form, is a positive predictor of various aspects of later language development, including verbalization measures at 11 to 15 months, amount of talking at 3 years, and vocabulary scores at 27 months and at 5 years. Given the small numbers of subjects involved, the limited scope of the investigations, and the failure to replicate some of the outcomes, these findings must be viewed as tentative until they are supported in studies with larger subject populations. For the present, however, it appears that amount of vocalization may serve as a useful index for comparing early vocal development in the first 6 months of life and predicting some aspects of language acquisition.

The second finding that emerges from the above review is much more solid, appearing repeatedly in the studies cited. Although the specific measures varied from one study to the next, the key element in all of them was the occurrence of *supraglottal consonants* as part of CV syllables. Consonant use was correlated to long-term as well as short-term outcomes, including onset of speech (Menyuk et al. 1986; Stoel-Gammon 1989a,b), phonological measures at 28 and 36 months (Menyuk, Liebergott, and Schultz 1986; Vihman and Greenlee 1987), and speech, language and academic problems at 5 to 7 years (Jensen et al. 1987; Stark, Ansel, and Bond 1988). In addition, this aspect of infant vocalizations distinguished between hearing and hearing-impaired infants aged 6 to 12 months (Oller and Eilers 1988; Stoel-Gammon and Otomo 1986; see also Stoel-Gammon 1988).

Although the use of supraglottal consonants appears to be a reliable indicator of prelinguistic development, there is considerable variation in the specific measures that have been employed and questions remain regarding the most appropriate overall measure. Stage measures like those of Oller and Eilers (1988) are based on a "yes-no" approach, which specifies the minimum requirement for onset of a particular level of development. In some cases, stages are narrowly defined, as in the study by Stark and colleagues (1988) who identified four distinct stages in what is commonly called the *Canonical Stage*. In contrast, the inventory measures described above are based on a continuum that measures the frequency and/or diversity of consonants or canonical syllables. These measures yield a single number that can be used to distinguish among subjects but questions remain (e.g., Are the measures equally sensitive at all ages? What magnitude of differences actually distinguishes among subjects?).

POSSIBLE EXPLANATIONS

Whether the measure of vocal development is based on the number of consonants in a sample, the ratio of the consonants to vowels, or the number of CV syllables, the general conclusion from the studies reviewed is that "more is better." The baby who produces more canonical syllables generally exhibits more advanced speech and language skills than his peer who babbles less. Why is this the case? There are many possible factors, but two seem to be the most likely candidates: (1) more canonical vocalizations provides more *practice* in producing sounds and syllable types that can serve as the basis for words and (2) more vocalizations provide the opportunity for the establishment of a *feedback loop* that allows babies to determine the relationship between their own oral-motor movements and the sounds that result from these movements.

Practice and Feedback

Speech has a skill component and, as with any skilled activity, practice increases the control and precision with which a movement is performed. Thus, the more often a baby produces the movements that shape the vocal tract to produce particular sounds and sound sequences, the more automatic those movements become and ultimately the easier it is to execute them in producing meaningful speech. Vihman (this volume) was able to identify a set of frequently occurring CV syllables ("practiced" syllables) for each subject and reported that the syllables used in early words were "primarily drawn from the repertoire of practiced syllables." Given this finding, it would seem that babies who have a large stock of practiced CV syllables in babbling will have an advantage in early word acquisition because they will have a larger repertoire of forms to which meaning can be attached. Vihman noted that subjects with slower vocabulary acquisition were those who failed to use their "practiced syllables" in meaningful speech production. This finding is similar to that of Stoel-Gammon (1989a) who reported that one of the two late talkers she studied produced many CV syllables in his nonmeaningful productions but did not use these forms in his attempts at real words.

Practice in the production of speech-like vocalizations is important for another domain—feedback. Infants are exposed to two types of vocal input, the speech of others and their own productions. Both are crucial for the acquisition of adult language and studies of prelinguistic vocalizations of deaf babies demonstrate that the effects of a lack of auditory input can be detected at 7 to 8 months. In addition to improving the skill component of speech production, practice is important because it provides infants the opportunity to hear their own vocalizations.

The nature of feedback loop has been described by Fry (1966, p. 189) in the following way: "As sound producing movements are repeated and repeated, a strong link is forged between tactual and kinesthetic impressions and auditory sensations that the child receives from his own utterances." Awareness of the links between one's own oral-motor movements and the acoustic signal that results is a prerequisite to auditory-vocal matching that underlies word production. It seems logical that the more a child babbles, the greater the opportunity to establish the feedback loops necessary for producing and monitoring its own speech. Moreover, the feedback loop may make infants pay attention to words in the adult language that resemble their own babbled forms. Thus, for example, a baby who frequently produces [ba] or [baba] might be likely to acquire the word "ball" or "bottle" because these words are similar to the baby's forms for which auditory and kinesthetic feedback patterns have been established. (See chapters by Lindblom, Menn and Matthei, and Vihman for additional views on the importance of feedback.)

Practice and feedback are not independent aspects of early vocal development: practice involves the repeated production of sounds; feedback involves hearing and monitoring these practice productions. It is possible to have practice without auditory feedback, but feedback cannot occur in the absence of practice. Hearing-impaired babies, for example, have a normally developing vocal apparatus that would allow them to practice the movements associated with the production of CV syllables; they would have tactile and kinesthetic feedback from oral movements, but their hearing loss prevents them from forming an auditory feedback loop like that of the hearing babies. Interestingly, although they have the capability of producing canonical syllables when other babies do, hearing-impaired babies are significantly delayed in the onset of the Canonical Stage (Oller and Eilers 1988) and in the frequency and diversity of supraglottal consonants in their vocalizations (Stoel-Gammon and Otomo 1986; Stoel-Gammon 1988). Presumably, this failure is linked to the lack of auditory input from others in their environment and from their own output.

Available evidence indicates that lack of practice also affects the timetable of development. Locke and Pearson (1990) examined the linguistic development of a young, cognitively normal girl who was tracheostomized and "generally aphonic" from 5 to 20 months. During this period, she vocalized infrequently, producing utterances that usually consisted of a "single vocalic sound of approximately syllable length" (p. 7). Thus, although exposed to speech from the adults around her, she was unable to produce canonical babbles and had little opportunity to form auditory or tactile feedback loops based on her own vocalizations. Following decannulation (i.e., removal of the tube that prevented normal respiration) just prior to 21 months, the subject evidenced a marked increase in the frequency of vocal output. Of the 909 utterances produced in the weeks following decannulation, however, only 6 met the criteria for canonical syllables. In addition to the lack of well-formed syllables, the girl's speech samples were characterized by a limited repertoire of consonantal types. The authors noted that her speech was similar to that of deaf infants studied by Stoel-Gammon and Otomo (1986) and Oller and Eilers (1988). Thus, the findings of this investigation, though limited to a case study of a single child, suggest that the ability to practice and to hear one's own vocalizations plays a critical role in the normal vocal development.

Social Considerations

McCune (this volume) posits another type of positive interaction between canonical syllables and early word production. She states that the mother of a child who produces speech-like syllables is more likely to attribute meaning to the child's vocalizations and consequently may repeat them as though they were attempts at real words. This type of feedback may in turn cause the child to imitate the adult word and form an association between the vocalization and an object or event in the immediate environment. Thus, the child who uses [ba] in the presence of a ball is likely to evoke the response "ball" from his mother; in contrast, production of the less speech-like form such as [ʔa] is less likely to be viewed as an attempt at a real word and less likely to evoke a modeled form. McCune's view is supported by a study by Murphy et al. (1983) who found that a mother's belief that her child was attempting real words correlated strongly with the child's age at onset of meaningful speech.

Long-Term Effects

While the positive effects of the use of canonical syllables can be explained for short-term phenomena such as age at onset of speech and rate of vocabulary growth, it is more difficult to propose explanations for the long-term relations between babbling and language skills at 3 years and older (Roe 1971; Vihman and Greenlee 1986) and between babbling and language and reading problems in middle childhood (Jensen et al. 1988). If we focus on the linguistic aspects of the relationship, we should consider two opposing views. The first view holds that babies who are "good" babblers (i.e., babies who babble early and produce a high proportion of canonical babbles and a wide range of sound types in those babbles) and who excel in later linguistic skills throughout childhood are endowed with a better language faculty than babies who perform more poorly in both babbling and speech development and later linguistic tasks. According to this view, then, babies are simply born with differing levels of linguistic ability that determine subsequent proficiency with the language. To frame this view in a Chomskyan approach (Chomsky 1965, 1979), one would argue that canonical babbling is part of the innate *language acquisition device* (LAD), and that "good" babblers and "good" talkers and "good" readers are those individuals who have superior language processors. Environmental factors are necessary to trigger the maturation of LAD, but they do not shape particular behaviors.

The other view, in its most basic form, proposes that "good" speech and language skills are directly related to "good" babbling. According to this view, the systematic use of canonical syllables in the prelinguistic period provides a foundation in terms of oral motor practice, auditory-vocal matching, and production of forms to which meaning can be attached. This in turn leads to the early production of words, to rapid lexical development, and to a general advance in all areas of language. On this view, speech and language development progress in an upward spiral wherein each stage springs from the ones that precede it. Thus, a good babbler is a good talker is a good reader; a "slow" babbler is a "late talker" is a "poor" reader. Obviously, this is an oversimplified view because there are often discrepancies between speech, language, and metalinguistic skills associated with reading and other related activities. However, the basic premise merits further consideration.

REFERENCES

Bates, E. 1976. *Language and Context*. New York: Academic Press.

Bauer, H. R. 1988. The ethologic model of phonetic development: I. *Clinical Linguistics and Phonetics* 2:347–80.

Bauer, H. F., and Robb, M. P. 1989. Phonetic development between infancy and toddlerhood: The phonetic product estimator. Paper presented at the Annual Convention of the American Speech-Language-Hearing Association, St. Louis, MO.

Bayley, N. 1969. *Bayley Scales of Infant Development*. New York: Academic Press.

Benedict, H. 1979. Early lexical development: Comprehension and production. *Journal of Child Language* 6:182–200.

Brown, R. 1973. *A First Language*. Cambridge: Harvard University Press.

Camp, B., Burgess, D., Morgan, L., and Zerbe, G. 1987. A longitudinal study of infant vocalizations in the first year. *Journal of Pediatric Psychology* 12:321–31.

Chomsky, N. 1965. *Aspects of a Theory of Syntax*. Cambridge, MA: MIT Press.

Chomsky, N. 1979. Human language and other semiotic systems. *Semiotica* 25:31–44.

Dunn, L. 1965. *Peabody Picture Vocabulary Test*. Minneapolis: American Guidance Service.

Fernald, A. 1985. Four-month-old infants prefer to listen to motherese. *Infant Behavior and Development* 8:181–95.

Fry, D. B. 1966. The development of the phonological system in the normal and deaf child. In *The Genesis of Language*, eds. F. Smith and G. A. Miller. Cambridge, MA: MIT Press.

Gesell, A., and Amatruda, C. S. 1941. *Developmental Diagnosis.* New York: Hoeber.

Jakobson, R. 1968. *Child Language, Aphasia, and Phonological Universals.* A. R. Keiler, Trans. Original work published 1941. The Hague: Mouton.

Jensen, T. S., Boggild-Andersen, B., Schmidt, J., Ankerhus, J., and Hansen, E. 1988. Perinatal risk factors and first year vocalizations: Influence on preschool language and motor performance. *Developmental Medicine and Child Neurology* 30:153–61.

Kagan, J. 1971. *Change and Continuity in Infancy.* New York: Wiley and Sons.

Koopmans-van Beinum, F. J., and van der Stelt, J. M. 1986. Early stages in the development of speech movements. In *Precursors of Early Speech,* B. Lindblom and R. Zetterstrom. New York: Stockton Press.

Landau, R. 1977. Spontaneous and elicited smiles and vocalizations in four Israeli environments. *Developmental Psychology* 14:389–400.

Locke, J. 1983. *Phonological Acquisition and Change.* New York: Academic Press.

Locke, J. L., and Pearson, D. 1990. The linguistic significance of babbling. *Journal of Child Language* 17:1–16.

Mehler, J., Jusczyk, P. W., Lambertz, G., Halsted, N., Bertoncini, J., and Amiel-Tison, C. 1988. A precursor of language acquisition in young infants. *Cognition* 29:143–78.

Menyuk, P., Liebergott, J. and Schultz, M. 1986. Predicting phonological development. In *Precursors of Early Speech,* eds. B. Lindblom and R. Zetterstrom. New York: Stockton Press.

Mitchell, P. R., and Kent, R. D. 1990. Phonetic variation in multisyllabic babbling. *Journal of Child Language* 17:247–66.

Murphy, R., Menyuk, P., Liebergott, J., and Schultz, M. 1983. Predicting rate of lexical development, Paper presented at Biennial Meeting of Society for Research in Child Development, Detroit, Michigan.

Oller, D. K. 1978. Infant vocalization and the development of speech. *Allied Health and Behavioral Sciences* 1:523–49.

Oller, D. K., and Eilers, R. 1988. The role of audition in babbling. *Child Development* 59:441–49.

Oller, D. K., Wieman, L. A., Doyle, W. J., and Ross, C. 1976. Infant babbling and speech. *Journal of Child Language* 3:1–11.

Olswang, L. B., Stoel-Gammon, C., Coggins, T. E., and Carpenter, R. L. 1987. *Assessing Prelinguistic and Early Linguistic Behaviors in Developmentally Young Children.* Seattle: University of Washington Press.

Paul, R., and Shiffer, M. 1987. An examination of communication intentions in speech delayed toddlers. Paper presented at the American Speech-Language-Hearing Convention, New Orleans, LA.

Rescorla, L. 1984. Language delayed at two. Paper presented at the Annual Meeting of the American Academy of Child Psychiatry, Toronto, Canada.

Roe, K. V. 1975. Amount of infant vocalization as a function of age: Some cognitive implications. *Child Development* 46:936–41.

Roe, K. V. 1977. Relationship between infant vocalizations at three months and preschool cognitive functioning. Paper presented at the Annual Meeting of the Washington Psychological Association, Seattle, Washington.

Routh, D. K. 1969. Conditioning of vocal response differentiation in infants. *Developmental Psychology* 1:219–26.

Roug, L., Landberg, I., and Lundberg, L.-J. 1989. Phonetic development in early infancy: A study of four Swedish children during the first eighteen months of life. *Journal of Child Language* 16:19–40.

Shriberg, L., and Kwiatkowski, J. 1982. Phonological disorders III: A procedure for assessing severity of involvement. *Journal of Speech and Hearing Disorders* 47:256–70.

Smith, B. L., Brown-Sweeney, S., and Stoel-Gammon, C. 1989. A quantitative analysis of reduplicated and variegated babbling. *First Language* 9:175–90.

Stark, R. 1980. Stages of speech development in the first year of life. In *Child Phonology, Vol. 1, Production*, eds. G. Yeni-Komshian, J. Kavanagh and C. A. Ferguson. New York: Academic Press.

Stark, R., Ansel, B., and Bond, J. 1988. Are prelinguistic abilities predictive of learning disability? A follow-up study. In *Preschool Prevention of Reading Failure*, eds. R. Masland and M. Masland. Parkton, MD: York Press.

Stoel-Gammon, C. 1985. Phonetic inventories, 15–24 months: A longitudinal study. *Journal of Speech and Hearing Disorders* 53:302–315.

Stoel-Gammon, C. 1988. Prelinguistic vocalizations of hearing-impaired and normally hearing subjects: A comparison of consonantal inventories. *Journal of Speech and Hearing Disorders* 53:302–315.

Stoel-Gammon, C. 1989a. Prespeech and early speech development of two late talkers. *First Language* 9:207–224.

Stoel-Gammon, C. 1989b. From babbling to speech: Some new evidence. Paper presented at the Child Phonology Conference, Northwestern University, Evanston, IL.

Stoel-Gammon, C., and Cooper, J. 1984. Patterns of early lexical and phonological development. *Journal of Child Language* 11:247–71.

Stoel-Gammon, C., and Otomo, K. 1986. Babbling development of hearing-impaired and normally hearing subjects. *Journal of Speech and Hearing Disorders* 51:33–41.

Templin, M. C. 1957. Certain language skills in children: Their development and inter-relationships. *Institute of Child Welfare Monographs, 26*. Minneapolis: University of Minnesota Press.

Vihman, M., and Greenlee, M. 1987. Individual differences in phonological development: Ages one and three year. *Journal of Speech and Hearing Research* 30:503–521.

Vihman, M. M., Ferguson, C. A., and Elbert, M. 1986. Phonological development from babbling to speech: Common tendencies and individual differences. *Applied Psycholinguistics* 7:3–40.

Vihman, M., Macken, M. A., Miller, R., Simmons, H., and Miller, J. 1985. From babbling to speech: A reassessment of the continuity issue. *Language* 61:397–445.

Werker, J. K., and Tees, R. C. 1984. Cross-language speech perception: Evidence for perceptual reorganization during the first year of life. *Infant Behavior and Development* 7:49–63.

Chapter • 16

Assessment of Child Phonology in the Clinical Context

Pamela Grunwell

The assessment of child phonology in the clinical context has a number of particular factors that distinguish it from other investigations of children's phonological development. Notwithstanding, clinical assessment has much in common with other investigations. Clinical phonologists and clinicians need to address the same methodological issues that face all child phonology researchers. Over the past decade these have been identified and discussed by a number of eminent phonologists active in the clinical field (for example, Ingram 1983a, 1989; Schwartz, Messick, and Pollock 1983; Grunwell 1985, 1987a; Elbert and Gierut 1986). These issues are examined in the light of current knowledge and in regard to the particular factors that appertain in the clinical context. The distinction, more apparent than real, between theoretical and clinical requirements is explored in relation to the aims of clinical assessment. Finally, I suggest that in the future it is essential that clinical investigations reflect theories about how children both develop and change their pronunciation patterns.

CLINICAL ASSESSMENT: ISSUES

There are four broad areas in devising and implementing assessment that raise issues that need to be addressed by both researchers and clinicians. These are: (1) data, (2) recording, (3) analysis, and (4) interpretation.

Data

Speech data are assessed in order to arrive at an evaluation of a child's phonology. One question that is raised perennially is what are the most appropriate types of speech data to collect (see especially Ingram 1989, Chapter 4). Another question that is frequently focused on in the clinical context is the optimal size of the data sample (see Grunwell 1987a, Chapter 8). Both of these questions concern the phonetic and phonological configurations of the data. There are also other issues to be addressed. Schwartz, Messick, and Pollock (1983), for example, highlight some nonphonological dimensions that need to be taken into consideration. They discuss syntactic, semantic, and pragmatic factors that, in part, bear on the type of sample to be obtained, but also go beyond this to take account of the influence of children's other language skills on their phonological behavior and vice versa. In addition to productive language skills, information about children's receptive abilities is highly pertinent to the assessment of children's phonology. This has long been a controversial issue in the clinical context, most thoroughly explored by Locke (1980a, 1980b). The problems he raised still remain to be answered (see Elbert and Gierut 1986).

The clinical context places further demands on the assessment process. Because children who are being assessed evidence difficulties in learning to pronounce, phonological and other linguistic assessments must be complemented by information about all the factors that might conceivably impinge upon a child's ability to learn. A multidimensional approach is, therefore, essential; this should include anatomical, physiological, and neurological assessments, evaluation of cognitive abilities, and consideration of socioenvironmental factors (Grunwell 1990).

Recording

The apparently simple issue in recording data for phonological assessment is the same as in any study of pronunciation patterns: what constitutes a reliable and analyzable transcript of speech data obtained for assessment purposes? Furthermore, in clinical context the requirements for recording procedures transcend those routinely required for normative studies. Ideally, for a thorough clinical assessment, full investigations would go beyond auditory-articulatory transcription and include acoustic and articulatory measures in order to investigate for the possible presence of anatomical, physiological, and/or neurological correlates of speech problems (see for example Hardcastle 1989; Gibbon and Hardcastle 1989).

Analysis

The issues concerning analysis of the data address criteria to apply in selecting the type of analytical techniques used. In the study of normal child phonology, the methods of analysis tend to reflect the theoretical frameworks developed in mainstream phonology. This tendency continues despite Menn's insightful and incisive observations at the 1978 conference:

> A theory devised to account economically for an adult behavior cannot generally account for the acquisition of that behavior. The relation between child and adult is among other things the relation between a skilled and an unskilled performer. If the adult produces no unskilled acts the central theory is unlikely to have a way of modelling the production of unskilled acts (Menn 1980, p. 27).

The same tendency can be observed in studies of the speech of children with pronunciation problems (for example, McReynolds and Huston 1971; Compton 1970; Oller 1973; Elbert and Gierut 1986; Ingram 1976; Gandour 1981; Spencer 1984).

The common aim of these studies is to arrive at a characterization of the nature of deviant phonology, and for the most part, the aims of assessment for clinical purposes are a secondary issue. Clinical assessment procedures have, however, been developed from these studies (McReynolds and Engmann 1975; Compton and Hutton 1978; Ingram 1981; Hodson 1980; Shriberg and Kwiatkowski 1980; Weiner 1979; Grunwell 1985). These assessments, perforce, employ modified analytical techniques because of the prerequisites and constraints imposed by the clinical context. In particular, the analysis has to provide a basis for a clinically relevant assessment that will lead to a diagnosis and indications for appropriate remediation strategies. The primarily theoretical issue of selecting an analytical framework, thus, is balanced by practical requirements of clinical context.

Interpretation

By interpretation is meant assessment and evaluation of the findings of the analysis. Different types of interpretation lead to different characterizations of children's speech problems, which in turn may lead to differences in evaluation of the underlying disability and consequently differences in the approach to remediation.

Interpretation is fundamental to construction of a theory that will explain developmental speech disorders. Therefore, the selection of appropriate analytical assessment procedures is crucial to the development of our understanding of these disorders. In addition, information other than that provided by phonological assessment must be taken into account in the clinical evaluation process. This chapter, however, focuses almost exclusively on the phonological assessment.

The Clinical Context

Solutions to these issues are influenced by constraints that are more severe in the clinical context than in other spheres of child phonology research. The clinician works under extreme time pressures and this evidences itself in the approach to assessment and resolution of critical issues. Clinicians routinely point to what they regard as practical drawbacks entailed in using linguistically based analysis and assessment procedures. These drawbacks are:

1. The time required to collect the data
2. The time required to transcribe the data
3. The time required to acquire training and expertise to analyze the data
4. The time required to analyze the data
5. The expertise required to interpret the analysis

As Crystal (1982a) emphasizes, it is the nature of the problem to be solved that requires such time-consuming procedures:

> Phonetic and linguistic handicap is a complex, multi-faceted and variable phenomenon. . . . If one wants understanding, insight and remedial confidence, time must be spent (p. 15).

Essentially the clinician is seeking a rationale and some guidelines for treatment, i.e., answers to the questions: if, when, what, and how to treat? In the clinical context, therefore, there is a constant quest to reconcile time constraints with the need to devise explicitly principled treatment programs.

CLINICAL ASSESSMENT: SOLUTIONS

Given the aims of clinical assessment and the constraints under which it is undertaken it will not be surprising to find that the issues raised above are usually resolved pragmatically. Practical rather than theoretical factors tend to be paramount in arriving at the format and methodology of assessment procedures.

Data

The issue of type of data focuses upon whether the speech sample should be obtained using a specially constructed elicitation procedure or a conversational setting where there would be little or no control over the content of the sample. Each method has advantages and disadvantages. At face value, conversation is more natural and might, therefore, be expected to result in a more typical sample of a child's speech. On the other hand, many children with communication problems are reluctant to engage in conversation. In addition, their spontaneous speech is frequently difficult to understand. Furthermore, the topics of conversation are at least in part in the child's control. This may result in repeated occurrences of a relatively small number of words and a failure to obtain a representative sample of the sounds of the adult language. These seeming disadvantages, on the other hand, can be viewed as advantages. Repeated occurrences of the same words, especially in different phonological and grammatical contexts, provide some indication of the amount of variability in the child's pronunciation patterns. A sample largely determined by the child's lexical selections may provide indications of avoidance strategies.

Notwithstanding, the most common type of elicitation procedure employed in clinical contexts is a picture-naming game, otherwise known as an articulation test (for example Anthony et al. 1971; Goldman and Fristoe 1972).

The advantages of this type of sampling are that:

1. The words to be elicited can be selected to provide a representative sample of the sounds of the adult language
2. The child's responses are, for the most part, glossable
3. An analyzable and representative sample can be obtained in a relatively short time

These advantages are offset by a number of serious shortcomings:

1. The child's pronunciations of the words may not be representative of his or her habitual patterns for a number of reasons:
   A. responses are typically one-word utterances; a child's patterns in continuous speech may be very different (Gibbon and Grunwell 1990);
   B. usually only one token of each target type is obtained; there is no opportunity to investigate variability in the child's pronunciations;
   C. in order to elicit the words required, the clinician may have to provide a model for imitation; this may not be representative of the child's spontaneous speech (see Ingram 1989 for review).
2. The words chosen have to be picturable; this leads to a predominance of nouns in this type of sample (Schwartz, Messick, and Pollock 1983).

A number of other factors have emerged that can influence a child's pronunciation patterns. Ingram et al. (1980) demonstrated that the phonological complexity of a word may affect a child's ability to pronounce a sound. There is a tendency in elicitation samples to include rather complex words in order to maximize the number of sounds elicited through each word, especially with regard to consonant clusters. This may lead to an undervaluation of a child's ability in the more common and shorter words that he or she uses most frequently.

Grammatical, lexical, and prosodic variables have been shown to interact with phonological accuracy (Panagos, Quine, and Klich 1979; Paul and Shriberg 1982; Schwartz et al. 1980; Schmauch, Panagos, and Klich 1978; Panagos and Prelock 1982; Prelock and Panagos 1989; Hughes 1983; Leonard et al. 1982; Grunwell 1981; Campbell and Shriberg 1982; Chiat 1989). If single word naming responses only are obtained, then a child's ability may be overestimated. On the other hand, if the sample is of spontaneous speech, a child's optimum potential may not be discovered, because increased syntactic and morphological complexity tend to lead to a reduction in phonological complexity and/ or accuracy. With regard to prosodic factors, stress placement, especially nuclear stress placement, promotes more accurate pronunciation of the consonants in the stressed syllable.

The ideal solution is to obtain samples of both elicited and spontaneous speech. This ensures a sample representative of both the adult language and the range of the child's habitual speech patterns, including the possibility of obtaining examples of variability. A suitable procedure is to employ elicitation materials designed to obtain a predetermined and representative set of words not confined to single word picture-naming responses. Such a set of elicitation materials is available in PACS Pictures (Grunwell 1987b). Shriberg and Kwiatkowski (1985), in a study of five different conditions to elicit continuous speech samples, found that such directed procedures were successful.

The second issue with regard to the speech data sample is the size of the sample. Most authorities recommend between 80 and 100 words (Crystal 1982b; Ingram 1981; Shriberg and Kwiatkowski 1980; Stoel-Gammon and Dunn 1985). This size of sample is attractive because it usually is obtainable in one clinical session. Nevertheless, Crary (1983) sought to reduce the time even further and suggests that a 50-word sample provides descriptive information similar to samples of 100 words. In contrast, Grunwell (1985; 1987a) suggests 200 to 250 words as the preferred sample size. The discrepancy between these various recommendations is attributable to the conflicting pressures of time and the need for a fully representative sample, allowing for the possible occurrence of variability. Procedures, such as those adopted by Crary, record only the occurrence of types of speech patterns not their frequency, distribution, or variability. Such restricted sampling techniques will fail to provide information about the stability and consistency of children's speech patterns.

There is also concern about the issue of length of time over which the sample is collected. This is rarely given much consideration in clinical context. The assumption appears to be made that data samples will be collected in one, or at the most two, clinical sessions with not much time elapsing between them, usually no more than a week. Ingram (1981) discusses the compilation of a phonological diary, a method also suggested by Grunwell (1985). The advantages of this method are that it provides naturalistic data and the maximum opportunity to record variability and progressive change. There are, however, several major disadvantages. Unless special equipment is used, such as a clip-on radio microphone, there will be no audio recordings. The diary itself almost inevitably will be partial: the diarist is unlikely to be with the child continuously and there is a tendency for diarists not to note all variable forms and to pay more attention to new words and new forms. Notwithstanding, there are clinical settings where a diary-type of method could be employed such as one in which clinicians are in contact with children on a daily basis, for example, in residential schools, assessment centers, special day schools, and language units. In such settings, other informed personnel could be recruited to contribute to the diary. This method of data collection would provide a sample that could yield important information about the processes of change in a child's pronunciation patterns. Indeed, longitudinal recording is to be encouraged in all clinical contexts in order to explore the nature of change in children's speech (see below).

Recording

In routine clinical practice, audio-recording is the most commonly used procedure, though this has increasingly been supplemented by video recordings. Clinicians generally make a simultaneous live transcription to check against the tape recordings, or at least make notes about aspects of a child's speech that might not be clearly detected from the tapes (Anthony et al. 1971; Grunwell 1985; Ingram 1989).

The main issue with regard to recording the data is the reliability of the phonetic transcription. Some authorities consider the problem of ensuring a reliable transcription of certain aspects of speech to be insurmountable and recommend exclusion of analysis of these features from their assessments; for example, Shriberg and Kwiatkowski (1980) exclude voicing. Another factor that impinges upon transcription reliability is listener expectancy. Oller and Eilers (1975) demonstrated that knowledge of the attempted lexical target significantly influences the transcription. This study also found that trained listeners tend to converge, if not exactly agree, in their transcriptions. Most research studies of children's speech, both clinical and nonclinical, employ a number of transcribers and seek to establish a high percentage of inter-transcriber reliability or at best consensus (Shriberg, Kwiatkowski, and Hoffmann 1984; Shriberg, Hinke, and Trost-Steffen 1987). Ingram (1989) recommends that more than one transcriber should be used and that both transcribers should be present at the session(s) when the sample is collected. In everyday clinical practice these recommendations are more often than not unrealistic. Occasionally, if a student clinician is observing, there is an opportunity to compare transcriptions. Alter-natively, the clinician may ask a colleague to listen to parts of the re-cording about which he or she is unsure. The phonetic training of clini-cians must prepare them for the situation of being the sole transcriber and ensure that they are aware of factors that may affect their objec-tivity. It is important also that practicing clinicians seek opportunities to refresh their transcription skills.

Another issue relating to transcribing the data is the amount of phonetic detail recorded. Ideally, the transcriber should attempt to make a narrow phonetic transcription, employing not only the conven-tions of the International Phonetic Alphabet, but those devised to sup-plement these conventions and to record the phonetic phenomena that occur in child and disordered speech (Bush et al. 1973; Grunwell 1983). In practice, busy clinicians use a broad transcription system. Ingram (1981) and Crystal (1982b) suggest that more often than not this will be adequate, provided that it is not just a broad phonemic transcription and that it records the occurrence of "distortions," non-English sound types and phonetic properties that may be contrastive in the child's sound system (see Grunwell 1987).

Analysis

The traditional procedure for the clinical assessment of children's speech is the articulation test. Analysis of the test involves the clinician in sim-ply deciding whether the child has pronounced the test items correctly or not by comparison with the adult target pronunciation. A score is then computed and compared with the standard scores of normal-speaking children within the same age range. Information provided about children's speech patterns and their developmental status is minimal. This lack of information is certainly not a basis upon which to plan a treatment program. Nevertheless, articulation tests remain in the battery of clinical test procedures because they provide a standard score of developmental attainment. Some articulation tests include procedures that go beyond analysis by scoring, for example, Fisher-

Logemann Test of Articulation Competence (Fisher and Logemann 1971); The Edinburgh Articulation Test (Anthony et al. 1971). Neither of these tests, however, addresses the issues of phonological analysis and guidelines for treatment that phonological assessment procedures for the clinical context are specifically designed to do. Using a set of analytical techniques, clinicians identify the systematic patterns in the child's pronunciation and the contrasts that are absent from the child's system by comparing them with the adult system. Usually there are indications, if not an actual procedure, whereby the developmental status of the child's patterns can be gauged. It is not intended here to discuss in detail the criteria for a clinically applicable analysis and assessment procedure. These have been examined comprehensively elsewhere (see Grunwell 1985, 1987a, 1988; for another, somewhat idiosyncratic approach see also Beresford 1987).

Clinical assessment procedures typically include the following analyses:

1. A statement of the child's phonetic inventory of consonant phones/sounds and their phonotactic distribution
2. A contrastive or substitution analysis of the child's realizations of target adult consonants in the various positions in structure; alternatively a similar statement in terms of natural phonological simplifying processes
3. A statement of the child's own phonological system of contrasts, to be compared with the adult system

Most procedures satisfy the first two requirements (e.g., Weiner 1979; Hodson 1980; Shriberg and Kwiatkowski 1980; Crystal 1982b). Only two procedures are designed to address all three requirements: Ingram (1981) and Grunwell (1985). The practical problem with all such procedures is that they are time-consuming. Fortunately, modern technology in the form of automated computer analysis is overcoming this problem (e.g., Shriberg 1986); see also Dyson 1987; Pye and Ingram 1988; Grunwell in preparation). However, computer programs impose constraints of their own. They limit otherwise open-ended procedures such as those described in Ingram (1981) and Grunwell (1985) so that they function in the same way as the other procedures. Indeed the main drawback of most currently available clinical analysis procedures is that their frameworks are limited. In recognition of the time constraints that operate in the clinical context, most procedures provide the clinician with a predetermined framework of analysis. The analysis thus is confined to the discovery of types of phonological patterns already identified as typical of child phonology. Table I lists the patterns or phonological processes included in the five most widely used procedures. By apparently limiting the analysis to identified processes

Table I. Clinical Assessment Procedures Using Phonological Process Analysis

Weiner (1979)	Shriberg & Kwiatkowski (1980)	Hodson (1980)

Syllable structure process
  Deletion of final consonant
  Cluster reductions:
    Initial stop + liquid
    Initial fricative + liquid
    Initial /s/ clusters
    Final /s/ + stop
    Final liquid + stop
    Final nasal + stop
  Weak Syllable Deletion
  Glottal Replacement
 	
Harmony processes
  Labial assimilation
  Alveolar assimilation
  Velar assimilation
  Prevocalic voicing
  Final consonant devoicing
 	
Feature contrast processes
  Stopping
  Gliding of fricatives
  Affrication
  Fronting
  Denasalization
  Gliding of liquids
  Vocalization
	1. Final consonant deletion
	2. Velar fronting:
	    Initial
	    Final
	3. Stopping:
	    Initial
	    Final
	4. Palatal fronting:
	    Initial
	    Final
	5. Liquid simplification:
	    Initial
	    Final
	6. Assimilation:
	    Progressive
	    Regressive
	7. Cluster reduction:
	    Initial
	    Final
	8. Unstressed syllable deletion
		Basic phonological processes
		  Syllable reduction
		  Cluster reduction
		  Prevocalic obstruent singleton omissions
		  Postvocalic obstruent singleton omissions
		  Strident deletion
		  Velar deviations
		
		Miscellaneous phonological processes
		  Prevocalic voicing
		  Postvocalic devoicing
		  Glottal replacement
		  Backing
		  Stopping
		  Affrication
		  Deaffrication
		  Palatalization
		  Depalatalization
		  Coalescence
		  Epenthesis
		  Metathesis
		
		Sonorant deviations
		  Liquid /l/
		  Liquid /rɚ/
		  Nasals
		  Glides
		  Vowels
		
		Assimilations
		  Nasal
		  Velar
		  Labial
		  Alveolar
		
		Articulatory shifts
		  Substitutions of /f v s z/ for /θð/
		  Frontal lisp
		  Dentalization of /t d n l/
		  Lateralization

Table I. *continued*

Ingram (1981)	Grunwell (1985c)	
Deletion of final consonants	Structural simplifications	Gliding:
1. Nasals	Weak syllable deletion:	/r/
2. Voiced stops	Pretonic	/l/
3. Voiceless stops	Posttonic	Fricatives
4. Voiced fricatives	Final consonant deletion:	Context-sensitive voicing:
5. Voiceless fricatives	Nasals	WI and WF
Reduction of consonant clusters	Plosives	Voicing WI
	Fricatives	Voicing WW
6. Liquids	Affricates	Devoicing WF
7. Nasals	Clusters __ 1	Glottal replacement:
8. /s/ clusters	__ 2+	WI
Syllable deletion and reduplication	Vocalization:	WW
	/l/	WF
9. Reduction of disyllables	Other C	Glottal insertion
10. Unstressed syllable deletion	Consonant harmony:	
	Velar	
11. Reduplication	Alveolar	
Fronting	Labial	
12. of palatals	Manner	
13. of velars	Other	
Stopping	S.I. cluster reduction:	
	Plosive + approx.	
14. of initial voiceless fricatives	Fricative + approx.	
15. of initial voiced fricatives	/s/ + plosive	
	/s/ + nasal	
16. of initial affricates	/s/ + approx.	
	/s/ + plosive + approx.	
Simplification of liquids and nasals	Systemic simplifications	
17. Liquid gliding	Fronting:	
18. Vocalization	Palato-alveolars	
19. Denasalization	Stopping:	
Other substitution processes	/f/	
	/v/	
20. Deaffrication	/θ/	
21. Deletion of initial consonant	/ð/	
	/s/	
22. Apicalization	/z/	
23. Labialization	/ʃ/	
	/tʃ/	
	/ʤ/	
	/l/	
	/r/	

(continued)

Table I. *continued*

Ingram (1981)	Grunwell (1985c)
Assimilation processes	
24. Velar assimilation	
25. Labial assimilation	
26. Prevocalic voicing	
27. Devoicing of final consonant	

S.I. = syllable initial
WI = word initial
WF = word final
WW = within word

(Grunwell and Ingram in fact do not; they encourage analysts to search for other patterns), they exclude the flexibility that is demonstrably necessary for the analysis of some clinical data.

There have been numerous case studies published over the last ten years that illustrate this point (for example Grunwell 1981; Fey and Gandour 1982; Ingram 1983b; Leonard and Brown 1984; Leonard 1985; Grunwell and Yavas 1988). As Leonard (1985) demonstrated there are "unusual and subtle" phonological phenomena in the pronunciation patterns of phonologically disordered children that are not amenable to analysis according to the available published procedures. A child I recently studied—MT, aged 3;11—provides a graphic demonstration of this (see table II). Exceptionally he exhibits all the types of unusual behavior that Leonard identifies in his review of previous studies. Personal experience indicates that clinicians constrained to work within predetermined frameworks of phonological analysis are perplexed by a child who shows pronunciation patterns such as these. It is, therefore, essential that clinical phonological assessment procedures build in and prepare clinicians for a flexible approach to analysis.

The "subtle phonological behaviors" that Leonard (1985) describes are those sound differences that are not readily detectable by the adult human ear. A number of studies have revealed that words or consonants that transcribers have recorded as being phonetically identical are in fact phonetically different when subjected to acoustic analysis (Maxwell and Weismer 1982; Weismer, Dinnsen, and Elbert 1981; Smit and Bernthal 1983; Catts and Jensen 1983). These studies suggest that there is a need, in certain cases, to go beyond the customary auditory-articulatory recording and analysis of the data and to carry out acoustic analyses.

Table II. Unusual Phonological Behavior: M.T. 3;11

1. Salient but Unusual Sound Changes with Readily Detectable Systematicity
    —*Early sounds replaced by late sounds*
      /p/ : [k] pencil ['kɛnzəł] teapot ['sikɒʔ]
    —*Additions to adult forms*
    (a) Vocalizations
           clouds ['tɬaʊwi] tights ['taɪʔi] watch ['jɒʔi]
    (b) initial consonant adjunction
           on [lɒ] up [lʌ] umbrella [lu'lɛlg̊]
           icecream [ɔaɪ,n̥ᶠki]
    —*Use of sounds absent from model language*
    (a) [t] clock [tɬɒ] clouds ['tɬaʊwi]
           plate [tɬeɪk] playground ['tɬeɪdaʊ]
    (b) [ɔ] mouse [ɔaʊ] mouth [ɔaʊ]
    —*Use of sounds absent from natural languages*

[n̥ᶠ]				
soft	[n̥ᶠdɒ]	soldier	['n̥ᶠtoʊjə
sand	[n̥ᶠkan; n̥ᶠsdan]		
shoe	[n̥ᶠgu]	sugar	['ŋgʊgə]
shop	[n̥ᶠskɒ]	shaving	['n̥ᶠdeɪji]
spade	[n̥ᶠteɪ]	splash	[n̥ᶠtla]
spoon	[n̥ᶠsku]	spring	[n̥ᶠnɪn]
star	[n̥ᶠsta]	string	[n̥ᶠtɪn]
scarf	[n̥ᶠga]	scribble	['n̥ᶠbɪbł]
square	[n̥ᶠgɛə]		
smoke	[n̥ᶠmoʊk]	snake	[n̥ᶠneɪ]

      [n̥ᶠ]—Voiceless alveolar nasal with audible nasal friction.

2. Salient but Unusual Sound Changes with Less Readily Detectable Systematicity
    —*Assimilations*
    (a) *Reduplications*

birthday	['dɜdeɪ]	chimney	['kɪki]
cupboard	['kʌkə]	ladder	['lala]
drinking	['gɪgi]	rainbow	['weɪwoʊ]
wardrobe	['wɔwoʊ]	window	['nɪnoʊ]

    (b) *Consonant harmony*

flag	[kag]	gate	[geɪg]
ring	[nɪn]		

    —*Metathesis*

bag [ga]	bucket	['gʊʔɪ]	bottle [got]
hedgehog	['jɛgɒ]	motorbike	['noʊgaɪ]
orange	['ɒnɪː]	garden	['ganə]
caravan	['kaŋ,na]		

    —*Syllable structure deletions*
    (a) *Post-tonic weak syllable deletion*

baby	[beɪ]	bottle	[got]
dinosaur	['daɪn̥ᶠθɔ]	caravan	['kaŋ,na]
vinegar	['bɪdə]	finger	[n̥ᶠga]

    (b) *Within-word consonant deletion*

apple	['əu]	laughing	['lɑːi]
sleeping	[tɬiːɪ]	caterpillar	['keɪsɪoʊ]

Interpretation

The assessment and evaluation of children's speech in the clinical context address two questions:

1. Are the child's pronunciation patterns developmentally normal or not?
2. If not, are there identifiable sources of (or causes for) the emergence of the developmentally abnormal patterns?

To answer the first question, a developmental assessment is clearly required that measures both the developmental normality and the chronology of the pronunciation patterns in a child's speech. The use of phonological processes as an analytical technique has greatly facilitated this type of assessment. Using this approach, many studies have demonstrated the normality of apparently disordered child phonologies (for reviews see Ingram 1976, Grunwell 1981; Edwards and Shriberg 1983; Stoel-Gammon and Dunn 1985). With regard to the assessment of the chronology of phonological development, few procedures provide a profile against which to measure developmental attainment. Grunwell (1985) is the exception, and even this profile is incomplete as it does not include phonotactic development. If a child exhibits normal processes at an age long after they have normally disappeared, he or she has delayed phonological development and the severity of the delay can be gauged. A child also may exhibit uneven development with processes from two or more different normal stages of development; this is known as chronological mismatch. The combination of normal processes, chronological mismatch, and some unusual processes makes it difficult if not impossible to match a child's pronunciation patterns with a stage on a normal developmental profile. Experience in using Grunwell's PACS profile has shown that inability to place a child on the normal profile is an indication of a severe developmental phonological disorder.

A developmental assessment leads to easily definable guidelines for therapy. Treatment goals are given priority according to the profile of normal development. This is an attractively simple solution to the primary clinical problem of deciding where to intervene. In consequence, although phonological analyses have provided more informative and appropriate assessments, they have promoted simplistic answers to complex clinical questions. A treatment strategy cannot be based solely on a phonological assessment. A developmental assessment of a child's speech is undoubtedly a crucial element in the clinical context, but the clinician must consider anatomical, physiological, audiological, neurological, psychological, and socioenvironmental factors in deciding on a treatment strategy. This is not to demote the relevance of a decade and a half's study of the phonological characteristics of disordered speech development. Rather it is to promote a balanced multidimensional assessment and evaluation of children's phonological development (e.g., see Grunwell 1988). As the foregoing discussion has demonstrated considerable progress has been made in the clinical assessment of children's phonologies. The importance of phonologically based assessments has been established in clinical practice. Yet fundamental problems still remain. The exigencies of the clinical context demand over-simplified solutions to complex problems. This simplistic approach needs to be modified to take account of theoretical developments in the study of child phonology. Phonological assessment must lead to an evaluation of the child's developmental potential as well as his or her attainment. This would help both in understanding the nature of the child's problem and in selecting an appropriate strategy for intervention.

CLINICAL ASSESSMENT: PROBLEMS

Some of the problems in clinical assessment are engendered by the pragmatism of the clinical context. Evaluation of a child's phonological disorder should aim to explain how the problem has arisen and should, therefore, take into account all dimensions relevant to language learning.

A major factor that contributes to the currently limited perspective is the absence of a strong theoretical dimension to the clinical application of phonological assessment. A number of recent studies have demonstrated how the theoretical implications of assessment might be explored. Stoel-Gammon and Dunn (1985, p. 199) emphasize the chronological aspects of disordered child phonology. They suggest that children with phonological disorders follow "a different time-table for the emergence and mastery of sounds and for the occurrence and suppression of phonological processes." This viewpoint has implications for assessment methods and the interpretation of their results. Firstly, an assessment procedure must provide a method for a detailed evaluation of the developmental status of all aspects of a child's phonology in terms of normality and level. Second, because the routine one-stage assessment method fails to provide information about the introduction of new sounds and the disappearance of phonological processes in a child's speech patterns, assessment should take place over a period of time. During this period, *diagnostic therapy* can be carried out. This will not be targeted at specific phonological patterns but will engage the child in developing and strengthening generally applicable abilities such as listening and metalinguistic skills. Leonard (1985) adds another di-

mension to a possible explanation and thereby introduces further requirements for assessment procedures. He points out that the particular phonological patterns a child uses may result from incomplete
perceptual information, inadequate specification of a word in the memory store, and limitations in a child's ability to organize articulatory sequences and/or to achieve particular articulatory targets. In order to
address these questions in assessment it is necessary to relate a detailed analysis of a speech sample to detailed investigations of a child's
auditory perceptual and memory skills and articulatory sequencing
and production skills.

Ingram (1987) proffers an explanation from a different perspective.
Referring to the normality of many aspects of disordered child phonologies and the range of variation between normal children, he hy-
pothesises that:

> The extent of a child's phonological deviance is the consequence of an in-
> verse relation between his stage of phonological acquisition and the size
> of his vocabulary (see also Ingram 1989 p. 163).

This explanation also has implications for assessment procedures
and practices. It calls for early screening, the measurement of vocabulary as well as phonological development, and regular monitoring of
children who may be at risk of having difficulties learning to pronounce. Problems arise in identifying children at risk and recognizing
the signs of an incipient disorder. Longitudinal research however
would address these problems. From a different point of view, Harris
and Cottam (1985) highlight the relevance of the distinction between
normal and *natural* in the explanation of some types of disordered phonologies. They argue that certain types of phonological behavior, although deemed deviant by comparison with developmental norms,
may be natural when other factors such as anatomy and physiology,
acoustic phonetics, and perceptual psychology, are taken into account.
The focus, thus, is shifted to the question: when should a phonological
assessment be used. Phonological analysis usually is used to assess the
speech development of children with no detectable relevant disability.
Such a restriction is unwarranted. Children with identifiable disabilities are also learning to pronounce. An assessment of their phonological development is, therefore, clinically relevant. Indeed, in such cases,
if one investigates the interaction between developmental processes
and the effects of the identified disabilities that are known to handicap
speech development, one might understand better the nature of phonological learning (Grunwell 1988, 1990; Grunwell and Russell 1988).

If the quality of the assessment and evaluation process were to be
enhanced along these lines, the resultant treatment programs and strat-

egies would be better informed. When time is at a premium, it is well spent at the outset ensuring greater efficiency in the long term.

Current procedures for clinical assessment on the whole fail to address a different set of problems that are related to the results they provide and the data they analyze. First, there is the question of the reliability of the developmental assessment. Grunwell (1981) surveyed the then current state of knowledge about normal phonological development and drew up a developmental profile and a chronology of phonological processes. (See also Grunwell 1985.) This profile has not been tested on a large-scale normal population nor has it been updated. Vihman and Greenlee (1987), however, provide some verification of its accuracy. They found that their 10 three-year-old subjects showed 12 of the 16 processes predicted to be present at that age by Grunwell's chronology of processes. They also found, on the other hand, that there was considerable individual variation between the 10 children, both in the use of processes and in the consistency of process use.

The occurrence of individual variation in the normal population has been recognized as a problem for clinical assessment for some time (Crystal 1982b). Ingram (1987) put forward his hypothesis about the nature of phonological disorders (see above) and the continuity between normal and disordered child phonology in part because there is no clear theory as to what is normal in phonological acquisition. More systematic investigations into phonological patterns in both normal and disordered child phonologies are needed. These will produce measures of developmental normality and level of attainment with which researchers and clinicians can feel confident.

There is another dimension of phonological assessment that requires further investigation especially because it may provide information particularly relevant to treatment planning and delivery. The dimension in question is the occurrence of variability in children's pronunciation patterns. There is a certain irony in emphasizing this point because the direct consequence of the introduction of phonological assessment to the clinical context was the recognition of systematic predictable patterns in disordered child phonology (e.g., Oller 1973). What is now recognized, however, is that alongside these regularities there are instances of irregularities and variability (Grunwell 1981). A number of investigators of normal child speech development consider these phenomena to be important in the process of change in a child's phonology (Hsieh Hsin 1972; Menn 1979; Moskowitz 1980; Local and Brown 1981). It is, therefore, essential that the occurrence of variability is recorded in a phonological assessment and that it is analyzed and evaluated. Traditionally in speech pathology it is consistency of speech production patterns rather than variability that is assessed. Thus a child's pronunciation of a target may be:

consistently correct /k/	[k]	
consistently incorrect /k/	[t]	i.e., never correct
inconsistently correct /k/	[k]	sometimes correct and
	[t]	sometimes incorrect
inconsistently incorrect /k/	[t]	i.e., never correct but
	[d]	several incorrect
	[g]	realizations

These types of statement reveal very little about the nature of the variability in a child's pronunciation patterns. Indeed, apparent inconsistencies (or variability) may in fact be predictable. Different realizations of the same adult target may occur in different word and syllable positions or in different phonetic contexts. This is shown by such processes as context sensitive voicing, consonant harmony, and other types of assimilation patterns. Variable realizations may be associated with other linguistic factors.

Lexical factors are especially important in the occurrence of variability. Moskowitz (1980) points to the occurrence of *progressive and regressive idioms* in children's phonologies. Clinical experience indicates that these warrant attention in phonological assessment. Another lexical factor pertinent to the analysis variability is *lexical diffusion*, which is the gradual spread of a sound change across words involving the same target sound (Hsieh Hsin 1972). Menn (1979) calls this *transitional variation*. Gierut (1986) describes the occurrence of such variation in a phonologically disordered child. It is evident from these studies that destabilization of a child's speech patterns in this way is potentially progressive; it could indicate the beginning of evolution to a changed state and the emergence of a new phonological contrast.

Menn identifies five other kinds of variation all of which she regards as short term. Two of these are potentially progressive: *backgrounding* (or *trade-off*, Garnica and Edwards 1977), where one part of a word is deleted or reduced or reverts to a previous form while the child works on another part; and *imitation effect*, where a child's pronunciation is very different on imitation. Both of these phenomena have been observed in the speech of children receiving speech therapy. They warrant further study because they may shed light on the process of phonological change. Two other types of variation also are familiar in the clinical context: *floundering*, where there is wide fluctuation in the pronunciation of a word, which suggests that the child has no well-formed concept of its phonetic structure; and *lexically controlled variation*, where certain words show considerable phonetic variation, by comparison with other similar words. Neither of these types of variation would appear to be progressive; indeed, in the clinical context, children would need to be assisted to overcome these problems if they persisted. The fifth type of variation, *rule coexistence*, is evidenced when children have two different forms of the same lexical item that are not indicative of transitional variation. The lack of detailed longitudinal records of children with speech disorders renders it difficult to comment on the occurrence of such phenomena.

In disordered phonologies there is another type of variability that needs to be investigated. This is the tendency for there to be multiple matches between adult targets and child realizations. Brenda, Thomas, and Neil exemplify this phenomenon (see tables III, IV, V; figures 1, 2, 3). Most of the patterns or processes in these children's realizations are not unusual, particularly those of Brenda and Thomas. They both have an almost adequate inventory of sound types, but for any one target a number of possible realizations exist. The lack of predictability is less severe in Thomas' speech than in Brenda's. Most of the patterns are normal: stopping, voicing, affrication. Neil, in contrast, has an extremely limited inventory with multiple matches especially for the voiceless targets. Stopping is the major pattern; additionally there is

Table III.   Variability in Clinical Phonology: Brenda

SFWF (Syllable Final Word Final Position)

Multiple realizations of adult targets

[t] /t/		[t] /d/	
		[d]	
[t]		[d]	
[d]/tʃ/		[ts] /dʒ/	
[ts]			
[t]		[t]	
[ts] /s/		[d] /z/	
[z]		[ts]	
		[z]	
[ts]/ʃ/			
[s]			

Multiple loss of phonemic contrasts

	/t/		/d/
	/d/		/tʃ/
[t]	/tʃ/	[d]	/dʒ/
	/s/		/z/
	/z/		
	/tʃ/	[s]	/ʃ/
	/dʒ/		
[ts]	/s/		
	/z/	[z]	/s/
	/ʃ/		/z/

Table IV.   Variability in Clinical Phonology: Thomas

SIWI (Syllable Initial Word Initial position)

Multiple realization of adult targets

[t]	/t/		[d]	/d/
[ʃ]				
[d]	/tʃ/		[ʤ]	/ʤ/
[k]				
[k]	/k/		[g]	/g/
[t]	/s/		[dz]	/z/
[ts]			[k]	
[ʃ]	/ʃ/			
[tʃ]				

Multiple loss of phonemic contrasts

[t]	/t/	[d]	/d/
	/s/		/tʃ/
[ʃ]	/ʃ/	[ʤ]	/ʤ/
	/tʃ/		
	[k]		
[k]	/tʃ/	[g]	/g/
	/z/		
[ts]	/s/	[dz]	/z/
[tʃ]	/ʃ/		

voicing, fronting, and backing. Neil has the most severely disordered pronunciation and a virtually complete lack of predictability. These three examples are, without doubt, instances of *extreme and excessive variability.* It is probable that such variability has extremely deleterious effects on a child's intelligibility. Whether, like other types of variability, they are indicators of the potential for change requires further investigation, but it seems unlikely (see Grunwell 1981 for a preliminary discussion; Grunwell and Russell 1990 for a report on Neil).

In sum, it is apparent that an assessment of variability is an essential component of a phonological assessment that is currently absent from the most commonly used clinical procedures. Its inclusion is necessary because it will provide important guidelines for treatment especially with reference to identifying those aspects of a child's phonology that are most susceptible to progressive change. The different types of variability need to be described and evaluated in regard to both their developmental and communicative implications. There are progressive and nonprogressive variability. Nonprogressive variability occurs when there are multiple matches, none of which is close to the target: for example, Neil's realization of /s/.

Based on the characteristics of normal development, it is sug-

Table V.   Variability in Clinical Phonology: Neil

SIWI (Syllable Initial Word Initial position)

Multiple realization of adult targets

[t] [d] /t/ [g]		[d] /d/ [g]
[k] [d] /k/ [g]		[d] /g/ [g]
[t] [k] /tʃ/ [g]		[d] /dʒ/
[t] [d] /s/ [k] [g]		[d] /z/
[d] /ʃ/ [g]		

Multiple loss of phonemic contrasts

[t]	/t/ /tʃ/ /s/	[d]	/t/ /d/ /k/ /g/ /s/ /z/ /ʃ/ /dʒ/
[k]	/t/ /k/ /tʃ/ /s/	[g]	/t/ /d/ /k/ /g/ /s/ /ʃ/ /tʃ/

gested that the following types of variability are positive indicators of potential for change:

1. Progressive phonological variability.
    a. Potential phonemic contrast (split) at the same position in structure

$$/t/ \rightleftharpoons [t]$$
$$/k/ \rightleftharpoons [k]$$

    b. Potential phonotactic extension (or derestriction):

e.g., context-conditioned "variability," such as in context-sensitive voicing; consonant harmony (assimilation).

2. Progressive phonetic variability.
    a. potential phonetic variability

$$/s/ \rightleftharpoons \begin{matrix} [s] \\ [ts] \end{matrix}$$

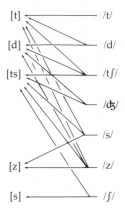

Figure 1.   Variability in clinical phonology: Brenda.

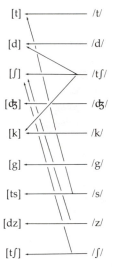

Figure 2.   Variability in clinical phonology: Thomas.

b.   potential phonetic maturation:

e.g., contextually influenced variable phonetic correspondence as in:

| /sp/ | [fp] | /sm/ | [fm] |
| /st/ | [θt] | /sn/ | [θn̩] |

Understanding of the phenomena in child speech that are indicative of ongoing or incipient change needs to be greatly extended. The types of variability and their implications need to be defined and described in more detail. On the basis of this knowledge, the theory and practice of facilitating phonological change in the clinical context will be

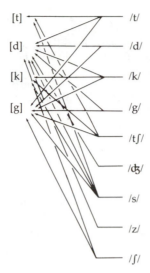

Figure 3.   Variability in clinical phonology: Neil.

founded on more explicit principles. Longitudinal assessments of children experiencing difficulties learning to pronounce are needed in order to investigate the potential for and mechanisms of phonological change in the clinical context. On the basis of such studies, clinicians' ability to identify children at risk and to make prognoses will be enhanced. The results of these studies will also inform treatment planning and intervention strategies. Meanwhile, phonological assessment in the clinical context should be extended to evaluate not only the level and developmental normality of children's phonological attainment, but also children's potential for phonological change.

REFERENCES

Anthony, A., Bogle, D., Ingram, T. T. S., and McIsaac, M. W. 1971. *Edinburgh Articulation Test*. Edinburgh: Churchill Livingstone.

Beresford, R. 1987. What kind of phonological description is clinically most useful? *Clinical Linguistics and Phonetics* 1:35–89.

Bush, C., Edwards, M. L., Luckan, J. M., Stoel, C. M., Macken, M. A., and Peterson, J. D. 1973. On specifying a system for transcribing consonants in child language: A working paper with examples from American English and Mexican Spanish. Unpublished paper, Child Language Project, Stanford University.

Campbell, T. F., and Shriberg, L. D. 1982 Associations among pragmatic functions, linguistic stress & natural phonological processes in speech delayed children. *Journal of Speech and Hearing Research* 25:547–53.

Catts, H. W., and Jensen, P. J. 1983. Speech timing of phonologically disordered children: Voicing contrast of initial and final stop consonants. *Journal of Speech and Hearing Research* 26:501–510.

Chiat, S. 1989. The relation between prosodic structure, syllabification and segmental realization: Evidence from a child with fricative stopping. *Clinical Linguistics and Phonetics* 3:223–42.

Compton, A. J. 1970. Generative studies of children's phonological systems. *Journal of Hearing and Speech Disorders* 35:315–39.

Compton, A. J., and Hutton, J. S. 1978. *Compton-Hutton Phonological Assessment*. San Francisco: Carousel House.

Crary, M. A. 1983. Phonological process analysis from spontaneous speech: The influence of sample size. *Journal of Communication Disorders* 16:133–41.

Crystal, D. 1982a. Terms, time and teeth. *British Journal of Disorders of Communication* 17:3–19.

Crystal, D. 1982b. *Profiling Linguistic Disability*. London: Edward Arnold.

Dyson, A. T. 1987. Review of Pepper (Shriberg 1986). *Child Language Teaching and Therapy* 3:329–35.

Edwards, M. L., and Shriberg, L. D. 1983. *Phonology: Applications in Communication Disorders*. San Diego: College Hill Press.

Elbert, M., and Gierut, J. 1986. *Handbook of Clinical Phonology*. London: Taylor and Francis.

Fey, M. E., and Gandour, J. 1982. Rule discovery in phonological acquisition. *Journal of Child Language* 9:71–81.

Fisher, H. B., and Logemann, J. A. 1971. *The Fisher-Logemann Test of Articulation Competence: Therapists Manual*. Boston: Houghton Mifflin.

Gandour, J. 1981. The non-deviant nature of deviant phonological systems. *Journal of Communication Disorders* 14:11–29.

Garnica, O., and Edwards, M. 1977. Phonological variation in child speech—the trade-off phenomenon. *Ohio State University Working Papers in Linguistics* 22:81–87.

Gibbon, F., and Hardcastle, W. 1989. Deviant articulation in a cleft palate child following the late repair of the hard palate: A description & remediation procedure using electropalatography (EPG). *Clinical Linguistics and Phonetics* 3:93–110.

Gibbon, F., and Grunwell, P. 1990. Specific language learning difficulties. In *Developmental Speech Disorders*, ed P. Grunwell. Edinburgh: Churchill Livingstone.

Gierut, J. 1986. Sound change: A phonemic split in a misarticulating child. *Journal of Applied Psycholinguistics* 7:57–68.

Goldman, R., and Fristoe, M. 1972. *Goldman-Fristoe Test of Articulation*. MN: AGS Inc.

Grunwell, P. 1981. *The Nature of Phonological Disability in Children*. London: Academic Press.

Grunwell, P. (ed.) 1983. *The Phonetic Representation of Disordered Speech (PRDS)*. London: Kings Fund.

Grunwell, P. 1985. *Phonological Assessment of Child Speech (PACS)*. Windson, UK: NFER-Nelson.

Grunwell, P. 1987a. *Clinical Phonology*, 2nd Edition. London: Croom Helm.

Grunwell, P. 1987b. *PACS Pictures*. Windsor, UK: NFER-Nelson.

Grunwell, P. 1988. Phonological assessment, evaluation and explanation of speech disorders in children. *Clinical Linguistics and Phonetics* 2: 221–52.

Grunwell, P. (ed.) 1990. *Developmental Speech Disorders*. Edinburgh: Churchill Livingstone.

Grunwell, P. In preparation. PACS by computer.

Grunwell, P., and Russell, J. 1988. Phonological development in children with cleft lip and palate. *Clinical Linguistics and Phonetics* 2:75–95.

Grunwell, P., and Russell, J. 1990. A case study of a phonological disorder in an English-speaking child. *Clinical Linguistics and Phonetics* 4:29–38.

Grunwell, P., and Yavas, M. 1988. Phonotactic restrictions in disordered child phonology: A case study. *Clinical Linguistics and Phonetics* 1:1–16.

Hardcastle, W. ed. 1989. Clinical applications of electropalatography. *Clinical Linguistics and Phonetics* 3(1).

Harris, J., and Cottam, P. 1985. Phonetic features and phonological features in speech assessment. *British Journal of Disorders of Communication* 20:61–74.

Hodson, B. W. 1980. *The Assessment of Phonological Processes*. Danville, IL: Interstate Inc.

Hsieh Hsin, I. 1972. Lexical diffusion: Evidence from child language acquisition. *Glossa* 6:89–104.

Hughes, R. E. 1983. The internal representation of word final phonemes in phonologically disordered children. *British Journal of Disorders of Communication* 18:78–88.

Ingram, D. 1976. *Phonological Disability in Children*. 1st Edition. London: Edward Arnold.

Ingram, D. 1981. *Procedures for the Phonological Analysis of Children's Language*. Baltimore: University Park Press.

Ingram, D. 1983a. The analysis and treatment of phonological disorders. *Seminars in Speech and Language* 4:375–88.

Ingram, D.(ed.) 1983b. Case studies of phonological disorders. *Topics in Language Disorders* 3(2).

Ingram, D. 1987 Categories of phonological disorders. In *Proceedings of the First International Symposium on Specific Speech and Language Disorders in Children*, eds. P. Fletcher, P. Grunwell, D. Hall, and A. Martin. Surrey: AFASIC.

Ingram, D. 1989. *Phonological Disability in Children*, 2nd Ed. London: Cole and Whurr.

Ingram, D., Christensen, L., Veach, S., and Webster, B. 1980. The acquisition of word-initial fricatives and affricates in English by children between 2 and 6 years. In *Child Phonology, Vol. I, Production*, eds. G. H. Yeni-Komshian, J. F. Kavanagh, and C. A. Ferguson. NY: Academic Press.

Leonard, L. B. 1985. Unusual and subtle phonological behaviour in the speech of phonologically disordered children. *Journal of Speech and Hearing Disorders* 50:4–13.

Leonard, L. B., and Brown, B. L. 1984. Nature and boundaries of phonologic categories: A case study of an unusual phonologic pattern in a language impaired child. *Journal of Hearing and Speech Disorders* 49:419–28.

Leonard, L. B., Schwartz, R. G., Chapman, K., Rowan, L. E., Prelock, P.A., Terrell, B., Weiss, A. L., and Messick, C. 1982. Early lexical acquisition in children with specific language impairment. *Journal of Speech and Hearing Research* 25:554–64.

Local, J., and Brown, K. 1981. Interpreting phonetic variability in children's speech. *Work in Progress* 14:39–45. Dept. of Linguistics, University of Edinburgh.

Locke, J. L. 1980a. The inference of phoneme perception in the phonologically disordered child, Part I: A rationale, some criteria, the conventional test. *Journal of Speech and Hearing Disorders* 45:431–44.

Locke, J. L. 1980b. The inference of phoneme perception in the phonologically disordered child, Part II: Clinically novel procedures, their use, some findings. *Journal of Speech and Hearing Disorders* 45:445–68.

Maxwell, E. M., and Weismer, G. 1982. The contribution of phonological, acoustic and perceptual techniques to the characterisation of a misarticulating child's voice contrast for stops. *Journal of Applied Psycholinguistics* 3:29–43.

Menn, L. 1979. Transition and variation in child phonology: Modeling a developing system. In *Proceedings of the 9th International Congress of Phonetic Sciences*, Vol. II.

Menn, L. 1980. Phonological theory & child phonology. In *Child Phonology, Vol. I, Production*, eds. G. H. Yeni-Komshian, J. F. Kavanagh, and C. A. Ferguson. NY: Academic Press.

McReynolds, L. V., and Engmann, D. 1975. *Distinctive Feature Analysis of Misarticulations*. Baltimore: University Park Press.

McReynolds, L. V., and Huston, K. 1971. A distinctive feature analysis of children's misarticulations. *Journal of Speech and Hearing Disorders* 36:155–66.

Moskowitz, B. A. 1980. Idioms in phonology acquisition and phonological change. *Journal of Phonetics* 8:69–83.

Oller, D. K. 1973. Regularities in abnormal child phonology. *Journal of Speech and Hearing Disorders* 38:35–46.

Oller, D. K., and Eilers, R. 1975. Phonetic expectation and transcription validity. *Phonetica* 31:288–304.

Panagos, J. M., and Prelock, P. 1982. Phonological constraints on the sentence production of language-disordered children. *Journal of Speech and Hearing Research* 25:171–77.

Panagos, S. M., Quine, M. E., and Klich, R. J. 1979. Syntactic and phonological influences on children's articulation. *Journal of Speech and Hearing Research* 22:841–48.

Paul, R., and Shriberg, L. D. 1982. Associations between phonology and syntax in speech delayed children. *Journal of Speech and Hearing Research* 25:536–47.

Prelock, P. A., and Panagos, J. M. 1989. The influence of processing mode on the sentence productions of language-disordered and normal children. *Clinical Linguistics and Phonetics* 3:251–63.

Pye, C., and Ingram, D. 1988. Automating the analysis of child phonology. *Clinical Linguistics and Phonetics* 2:115–37.

Schmauch, V. A., Panagos, J. M., and Klich, R. J. 1978. Syntax influences the accuracy of consonant production in language-disordered children. *Journal of Communication Disorders* 11:315–23.

Schwartz, R. G., Leonard, L. B., Folger, M. K., and Wilcox, M. J. 1980. Early phonological behaviour in normal speaking and language disordered children: Evidence for a synergistic view of language disorders. *Journal of Speech and Hearing Disorders* 45:357–77.

Schwartz, R. G., Messick, D. K., and Pollock, K. E. 1983. Some nonphonological considerations in phonological assessment. *Seminars in Speech and Language* 4:335–49.

Shriberg, L. D. 1986. *Pepper: Programs to Examine Phonetic and Phonologic Evaluation Records*. Madison: Software Development and Distribution Centre.

Shriberg, L. D., and Kwiatkowski, J. 1980. *Natural Process Analysis (NPA)*. NY: John Wiley.

Shriberg, L. D., and Kwiatkowski, J. 1985. Continuous speech sampling for phonologic analyses of speech-delayed children. *Journal of Speech and Hearing Disorders* 50:323–34.

Shriberg, L. D., Kwiatkowski, J., and Hoffmann, K. 1984. A procedure for phonetic transcription by consensus. *Journal of Speech and Hearing Research* 27:456–65.

Shriberg, L. D., Hinke, R., and Trost-Steffen, C. 1987. A procedure to select and train persons for narrow phonetic transcription by consensus. *Clinical Linguistics and Phonetics* 1:171–89.

Smit, A., and Bernthal, J. 1983. Voicing contrasts and their phonological implications in the speech of articulation disordered children. *Journal of Speech and Hearing Research* 26:486–500.

Spencer, A. 1984. A non-linear analysis of phonological disability. *Journal of Communication Disorders* 17:325–48.

Stoel-Gammon, C., and Dunn, C. 1985. *Normal and Disordered Phonology in Children.* Baltimore: University Park Press.

Vihman, M. M., and Greenlee, M. 1987. Individual differences in phonological development: Ages one and three years. *Journal of Speech and Hearing Research* 30:503–21.

Weiner, F. F. 1979. *Phonological Process Analysis (PPA).* Baltimore: University Park Press.

Weismer, G., Dinnsen, D., and Elbert, M. 1981. Analysis of stop consonant production errors in developmentally dysphasic children. *Journal of Speech and Hearing Disorders* 46:320–37.

PART · III

Implications

Overview

Implications of Models and Research

Charles A. Ferguson

        The findings of research on phonological development have had implications for related fields, such as language change, second language acquisition, and the treatment of speech problems in children and adults. Equally significant, although not always sufficiently recognized, have been the implications in the other direction. Insights and findings from these related fields sometimes speak directly to basic issues in phonological development and phonological theory. To take but one example, the phenomenon of *generalization* in learning patterns that occurs in both speech therapy and second language teaching offers important evidence on the validity of phonological units (e.g., features, segments, prosodies) and the representations and rules hypothesized for particular languages or language varieties.

GENERALIZATION

In its simplest form phonological generalization occurs when intervention by therapist or teacher focuses on a particular pronunciation problem of the learner, improvement in the trained pronunciation takes place, and then related improvements are observed in untrained features of pronunciation. If, for example, a particular child has multiple misarticulations including the stopping of fricatives (e.g., pronouncing [p] for adult model /f/, [b] for /v/, [t] for /s ʃ θ/, and [d] for /z ʒ ð/), the clinician may focus on just /f/ and /s/ until the child shows marked improvement. Generalization occurs when the child "spontaneously" improves—although typically to a lesser degree—in the production of other fricatives that the clinician has not addressed. This generalization would provide evidence for the validity of the sound classes or distinctive features of *stop* and *fricative*, the validity of a *process* or *rule* of stopping as part of the child's phonological system, and indeed for the validity of the notion of *phonological system* as such.

Similar instances of *generalization* occur in second language acquisition, as when the teacher drills the learner on a length contrast in one vowel quality and the learner spontaneously improves in the quantity distinction in other vowels.

Although evidence from generalization is striking, it has many problems. It requires careful analysis of the individual L1 or L2 learner's current (and often changing) system, and it is correspondingly difficult to design controlled experiments or even analyses of large number of subjects. Also, the skeptical observer may claim that the "untrained" improvement might have occurred without the "trained" improvement or independently of it. In spite of these and other problems, the evidence from generalization can be valuable, especially if many case studies are recorded and available to professional investigators. The range of atypical, idiosyncratic phonological systems and the possibilities of phonological mismatches across languages are so great that the phenomenon of generalization after intervention is a valuable and underutilized tool of phonological research. Because it is not discussed explicitly in the present volume, reference may be made to Dunn 1983, Elbert, Dinnsen, and Powell 1984, Gierut 1985, *LSHSS* 1988, and Tyler, Edwards, and Saxman 1987 as introductory to the relevant literature.

COMBINED RESEARCH

In several related fields there has been a long tradition of interaction with the findings of research in speech science and linguistics, but until recently with little or no attention paid directly to phonological development in the child. One of these is the area of reading—the process of reading, the acquisition of reading skills, the place of reading in education and life, and the social problems connected with poor literacy skills. Several American structural linguists dealt with reading from their linguistic perspective decades ago (notably Bloomfield 1942, 1955; Fries 1963). In more recent years, linguists, phoneticians, and psychologists, making use of later theoretical tools, have made strenuous efforts to understand the nature of reading (Kavanagh and Mattingly 1972 is an excellent example), but neither the structuralists nor the post-structuralists interested in reading considered the possible contribution of the study of phonological development. Also, the researchers in child phonology for their part did not investigate reading (e.g. Yeni-Komshian, Kavanagh, and Ferguson 1980 does not mention reading).

The two chapters on reading in this volume give some indication of recent trends to combine these lines of research. Barton represents a new approach to reading that assumes there are important similarities between the child's active, "cognitive" role in phonological development and the child's role in learning to read. Bradley represents a vigorous experimental tradition that has demonstrated, by extensive longitudinal studies, the importance of rhyming experience as a precursor to phonological segmentation and learning to read (Bradley and Bryant 1985; Bryant et al. 1989); in doing so the researchers have confirmed hypotheses of contemporary phonologists about onset and rhyme as basic components of the syllable (cf. Halle and Vergnaud 1980). These new lines of research promise to contribute to the understanding of both reading and phonological development.

In these times of great interest in theory construction and model building, it is not surprising that many researchers in the related fields have attempted to sketch out theoretical models that include the phenomena of normal phonological development in children. Thus, in the present volume, Oller and Lynch not only give a convincing account of the differences between the babbling of deaf and normal children that is at odds with the accepted wisdom, but spend most of their chapter elaborating a model of the early stages of phonological development. Leonard's chapter not only discusses the relation between the development of phonologically disordered children and that of normally developing children, but makes use of detailed analyses of two phonologically disordered children to evaluate competing models of phonological development.

Similarly, the chapters by Wode and Flege, which focus on phonology in second language acquisition, attempt to produce models that cover both first and second language acquisition. Wode was a pioneer in his early insistence on the need to include both kinds of phonology acquisition in a unified model (cf., e.g., Wode 1977); Flege, an ingenious and tireless experimenter in L2 phonology, also struggles with the formulation of a theory that will account for the similarities and differences between L1 and L2 phonology and will jibe with his empirical findings. The field of research in L2 phonology, or *interlanguage phonology* as it is often called, has blossomed in the last few years, becoming increasingly sophisticated and more intensively concerned with theories of phonological development and with phonological theory *tout court*. Hammarberg 1988 provides a useful review of this active field.

PHONOLOGICAL THEORY AND LANGUAGE CHANGE

Linguists investigating phonological development in children have naturally turned to phonological theory, i.e., the theory of synchronic,
adult phonological systems, as the nearest body of theory applicable to
their research. Thus, researchers have turned to Jakobsonian structur-
alism (e.g., Leopold 1947), to Stampe's natural phonology (e.g., Edwards 1973), to Firth's prosodic phonology (e.g., Waterson 1987), to the
classical generative phonology of Chomsky and Halle (e.g., Smith
1973), or to Goldsmith's autosegmental phonology (e.g., Spencer 1986).
For many linguists studying child phonology, however, the child's acquisition of phonology or "learning to pronounce" has been an intellectual problem in its own right, not necessarily either an indirect way
of investigating adult phonology or a sphere in which to apply phonological theory. On the one hand, this has meant that they may draw
on bodies of knowledge or theory outside of linguistics, and on the
other hand, it has led some of them to suggest modifications in their
favorite phonological theories.

Mohanan, a phonological theorist rather than a child phonologist,
has contributed in this section a wide-ranging chapter that presents a
full-scale new model for phonological systems in general, drawing in
part on data from child phonology. Although the aim of his chapter is
to change some of the basic assumptions in the generative tradition in
phonology, it is also directly suggestive to researchers in phonological
development, and some comments on it have already been made in
Menn's overview in the section on models.

A connection between phonological development in children and
diachronic change in language has long been assumed, and it could be
expected that a substantial literature on this relationship would be
available. Historical linguists in the nineteenth century, both neogram-
marians and their opponents, tended to assume that one of the chief
factors in sound change was children's imperfect learning of the ambient language, and generative phonologists of the twentieth century,
with their emphasis on the learnability of human language, have often
made that same assumption. It is somewhat surprising, therefore, that
with rare exceptions neither group engaged in systematic study of
phonological development. Studies that compare diachronic sound
change with children's phonological development in a point-by-point
fashion (e.g., Vihman 1980) are relatively rare. One can only hope for
more interaction in these two fields of study, although the assumption
of imperfect learning as a factor in sound change is actually not at all
well supported.

FUTURE IMPLICATIONS

For some of the participants in the Stanford conference that resulted in this book, and probably for many of the readers of the book, the most unexpected and exciting contribution to the whole discussion is the call of the Hauser and Marler chapter to compare the phenomena of children building their phonological systems with various phenomena of animal communication. What is one to make of species of birds that exhibit a kind of babbling behavior before they arrive at their specific song, or of some primates that apparently re-learn a particular vocal signal that they had used for a different function when younger? Although there is no suggestion that such phenomena have any direct evolutionary connection with the phonological development of human children, there is no doubt that both lines of research can benefit from careful comparative study. A conference on phonological development ten years in the future is likely to report significant investigations and speculations growing from this new pairing of previously unconnected fields.

Jenkins, in his comments on the Bethesda conference (Jenkins 1980), referred to research in child phonology as a "vigorous young field" (p. 217) and even as a "very exciting and rapidly maturing field" (p. 227). He acknowledged the interdisciplinary nature of the research and expressed respect for the "staggering burden" (p. 218) of knowledge and skills from various fields that researchers in child phonology needed for their work. Yet nowhere did he recognize the possibility that child phonology research might have implications for other fields. At the Stanford conference ten years later, most of the participants felt that research methodology, research findings, and theoretical models constructed in the course of their research have implications for related fields, and this is evident not only in the chapters of the Implications section but also in other chapters throughout this volume. Research in phonological development will have to continue to draw on related fields, but it is likely also to contribute to other fields, and we may hope that its findings will increasingly be applied to theoretical and practical problems in those fields. The conference ten years from now will have to cast a much wider net and include many more researchers and practitioners whose primary focus is elsewhere but who find an intimate connection with the field of normal phonological development in children.

REFERENCES

Bloomfield, L. 1942. Linguistics and reading. *Elementary English* 18:125–30.
Bloomfield, L. 1955. Linguistics and reading. *Language Learning* 5:94–107.
Bradley, L., and Bryant, P. E. 1985. *Rhyme and Reason in Reading and Spelling.* (I.A.R.L.D. Monograph, 1.) Ann Arbor: University of Michigan Press.
Bryant, P. E., Bradley, L., Maclean, M., and Crossland, J. 1989. Nursery rhymes, phonological skills and reading. *Journal of Child Language* 16:407–428.
Dunn, D. 1983. A framework for generalization in disordered phonology. *Journal of Childhood Communicative Disorders* 7:47–58.
Edwards, M. L. 1973. The acquisition of liquids. *Working Papers in Linguistics* 15:1–54. Columbus, OH: Ohio State University Department of Linguistics.
Elbert, M., Dinnsen, D. A., and Powell, T. W. 1984. On the prediction of phonologic generalization learning patterns. *Journal of Speech and Hearing Disorders* 29:309–317.
Fries, C. C. 1963 *Linguistics and Reading.* New York: Holt, Rinehart and Winston.
Gierut, J. 1985. On the relationship between phonological knowledge and generalization in misarticulating children. Unpub. Ph.D. diss., Indiana University.
Halle, M., and Vergnaud, J. R. 1980. Three dimensional phonology. *Journal of Linguistic Research* 1:83–105.
Hammarberg, B. 1988. Acquisition of phonology. *Annual Review of Applied Linguistics* 9:23–40.
Jenkins, J. 1980. Research in child phonology: Comments, criticism, and advice. In *Child Phonology* Vol. 2. *Perception,* ed. G. H. Yeni-Komshian, J. F. Kavanagh, and C. A. Ferguson. New York: Academic Press.
Kavanagh, J., and Mattingly, I. Eds. 1972. *Language by Ear and by Eye: The Relationships between Speech and Reading.* Cambridge: MIT Press.
Leopold, W. 1947. *Speech Development of a Bilingual Child, A Linguist's Record,* Vol. II. *Sound-learning in the First Two Years.* Evanston: Northwestern University.
LSHSS 1988. Special issue (vol. 19, no. 3) of *Language, Speech, and Hearing Services in the Schools* devoted to generalization.
Smith, N. V. 1973. *The Acquisition of Phonology: A Case Study.* Cambridge: Cambridge University Press.
Spencer, A. 1986. Towards a theory of phonological development. *Lingua* 68:3–38.
Tyler, A. A., Edwards, M. L., and Saxman, J. H. 1987. Clinical application of two phonologically based treatment procedures. *Journal of Speech and Hearing Disorders* 52:393–409.
Vihman, M. M. 1980. Sound change and child language. In *Papers from the 4th International Conference on Historical Linguistics,* ed. E. C. Traugott, R. Labrum, and S. Shepherd. Amsterdam: John Benjamins.
Waterson, N. 1987. *Prosodic Phonology: The Theory and its Application to Language Acquisition and Speech Processing.* Newcastle upon Tyne: Grevatt & Grevatt.
Wode, H. 1977. The L2 acquisition of /r/. *Phonetica* 34:200–217.
Yeni-Komshian, G. H., Kavanagh, J. F., and Ferguson, C. A. Eds. 1980. *Child Phonology.* New York: Academic Press.

Atypical Development

Chapter • 17

Models of Phonological Development and Children with Phonological Disorders

Laurence B. Leonard

This chapter is concerned with a group of children who have significant difficulty acquiring the sound system of their language, yet they exhibit normal hearing, age-appropriate scores on nonverbal tests of intelligence, and show no signs of neurological impairment. The clinical labels *phonologically disordered* and the interchangeable *phonologically disabled* are typically reserved for such children, even though it is recognized that other groups of children, such as those with more general developmental delays, also show limitations in phonology.

Children with phonological disorders often exhibit deficits in other areas of language, most notably, syntax and morphology (see reviews in Bernthal and Bankson 1988; Stoel-Gammon and Dunn 1985). Treatment is effective with these children, but even without treatment these children show gains in phonology through the age of eight years. Changes after that age come much more slowly. School age children whose phonology is still quite limited are at risk for academic difficul-

Thanks go to the participants of the conference on Phonological Development, whose comments on an earlier version of the paper allowed me to clarify certain details. Joseph Stemberger provided especially detailed remarks, for which I am grateful. Any errors of interpretation are mine alone.

ties, although their problems with other aspects of language are no doubt contributing to this.

Given the potential obstacles that phonological deficits represent for children's social and educational development, much research has been aimed at designing more effective assessment and treatment procedures for these children. In the present contribution, the focus is on a different issue: how the study of phonological disorders might inform current models of phonological learning.

SIMILARITIES

In a general way, children with phonological disorders resemble younger, normally developing children. The error patterns most frequently reflected in their speech are well documented in the normal child phonology literature. For English-speaking children, these include final consonant deletion, cluster reduction, gliding, and stopping, among others. These general similarities can be seen when one compares the error patterns of phonologically disordered children and normally developing children who are matched for consonant inventory (or Articulation Score, see Ingram 1981), as well as through comparisons between normal and disordered children who are matched for mean utterance length (see Schwartz et al. 1980). An example of the latter can be seen in table I.

The two groups are also similar in that their errors seem to be influenced by both the phonetic characteristics of the phonemes being acquired as well as the types of sounds in the ambient language that might serve as plausible substitutes. A good example of these two factors at work can be seen in children's acquisition of liquids.

Table I. The Number of Children Studied by Schwartz et al. (1980) for Whom an Error Type Was Noted in At Least Two Words (N = 3 for Each Group)

Error Type	Normally Developing	Phonologically Disordered
Assimilation	3	3
Cluster reduction	3	3
Final consonant deletion	3	3
Fronting	3	3
Voicing	3	3
Reduplication	3	1
Glottal replacement	2	2
Weak syllable deletion	2	2
Backing	1	1
Gliding	1	2
Stopping	1	3

Presented in table II are examples of errors on liquids observed in the speech of both normally developing and phonologically disordered children acquiring two different languages. The examples for English are highly familiar, reflecting the well-documented process of liquid gliding. The examples for Italian (see Bortolini and Leonard 1991) illustrate that each liquid sometimes substitutes for the other, and [n] is occasionally used for both [r] and [l]. The fact that [l] and [r] as well as [n] are dental-alveolar in Italian probably contributes to the substitutions observed. Notice, too, the absence of gliding. Quite probably this is because [j] and [w] occur only after [i] and [u], respectively. (In fact, [j] and [w] are not even represented in the orthography of the language.) With such heavy phonotactic constraints on these glides, they are not very handy substitutes for [l] and [r], at least if the child's substitutions are related at all to the ambient language.

DIFFERENCES

These similarities between the speech of normally developing and phonologically disordered children notwithstanding, there are at least two important differences between the two groups. The most notable, as Ingram (1987) has pointed out, is that phonologically disordered children are usually functioning with a much larger vocabulary than younger, normally developing children who show similar phonological characteristics. That is, although phonologically disordered children are often slow in lexical development, their phonological development typically lags even further behind.

A second difference between normally developing and phonologically disordered children concerns the use of unusual phonological patterns. Error patterns defined as unusual have included the replacement of a presumably earlier-developing sound by a presumably later-developing sound (e.g., [v] for [d] in English), the apparent addition of a sound (e.g., the addition of nasal consonants to the ends of words), and the use of a sound not present in the ambient language (e.g., the use of a bilabial fricative in English) (see Leonard 1985). These are not mutually exclusive subcategories; a single pattern can reflect more than

Table II. Errors on Liquids by Phonologically Disordered as well as Normally Developing Children

English		Italian	
Adult Form	Child Form	Adult Form	Child Form
r	w	r	l, n
l	w, j	l	r, n

one of these characteristics. An example from Leonard and Brown (1984) appears in table III. This phonologically disordered child produced word-final labial consonants as labials; however, all other words were produced with word-final [s]. Consequently, [s] could be described as replacing several early-developing sounds, such as [n] in *airplane*, [d] in *bread*, [g] in *dog*, [t] in *plate*, and [f] in *knife*. However, words whose adult forms end in vowels also contained [s] in final position in the child's productions, which could be described as an addition. Examples included [bus] for *blue*, [gas] for *go*, [tus] for *two*, and so on.

Although unusual patterns are certainly reported for normally developing children, it seems that such patterns are more frequent in the speech of children with phonological disorders (Leonard 1985). This is not simply the impression one gets from the many case studies in the literature on normal and disordered phonology, but seems true as well from the few studies that have involved direct comparisons between normally developing and phonologically disordered children.

Furthermore, there is evidence that unusual patterns are adopted less systematically by phonologically disordered children than by normally developing children. An example from Leonard et al. (1987) can be seen in table IV. In this study, the procedure involved presenting novel object names and their referents to normally developing and phonologically disordered children. These exposures took place over about three weeks, and the children's use of the words was then tested. Three types of words were employed. One type of word contained con-

Table III. Examples of an Unusual Production Pattern Exhibited by a Phonologically Disordered Child Studied by Leonard and Brown (1984)

Word	Production	Word	Production
airplane	[ʌpæs]	Gabe	[gap]
apple	[æpəs]	girl	[gɜs]
bath	[bæs]	go	[gɑs]
blue	[bus]	guy	[gas]
boy	[bɔɪs]	home	[hom]
bread	[bɛs]	juice	[dʒus]
bus	[bʌs]	Kathy	[kadəs]
cook	[kus]	knife	[naɪs]
cow	[kaʊs]	light	[was]
crib	[kɪp]	mom	[mam]
cup	[kʌp]	one	[wʌs]
daddy	[dædəs]	open	[opəs]
dog	[dɔs]	plate	[pes]
door	[dʊs]	snow	[nos]
dress	[dɛs]	stone	[dos]
drive	[daɪs]	sweeper	[sɪpɪs]
eye	[as]	two	[tus]
four	[fɔs]	wood	[wus]

Table IV.   Mean Percentage of Unusual Productions by Normally Developing and Phonologically Disordered Children Studied by Leonard et al. (1987)

Normally Developing			Phonologically Disordered		
In	Attempted	Out	In	Attempted	Out
17.9	20.2	45.0	50.8	47.8	43.8

sonants that the child already used appropriately in the majority of instances ("in phonology" words). A second word type, "attempted" words, contained consonants that the child had apparently attempted a number of times in the past, but never produced accurately. These sounds were subject to more common sound changes such as fronting, stopping, deletion, and the like. Finally, "out of phonology" words contained consonants that the child had neither produced nor attempted in the past.

We found that the normally developing children were more likely to show unusual productions for "out of phonology" words than for the other two word types. Such a finding is not surprising, given that the children did not seem to have an available production solution for these words. Consequently, one was invented. However, the same results did not emerge for the phonologically disordered children. As can be seen from table IV, for these children the percentages of unusual productions were similar for the three word types. There seems to be no clear reason why unusual productions should have been so high for the "in phonology" and "attempted" words, as production solutions existed for these words already (accurate production of "in phonology" words, use of a common, previously employed sound change for "attempted" words).

Summary

Children with phonological disorders are not radically different from younger, normally developing children, but their profiles may differ from younger peers in at least two respects: (1) they show more limited phonological systems than would be expected given the size of their expressive vocabularies; and (2) they make more frequent but less systematic use of unusual patterns.

THE LEARNABILITY PROBLEM

Children with phonological disorders pose an interesting learnability problem. Specifically, one of the empirical conditions that should be met by any satisfactory theory of language learning is the "developmental condition" (see Pinker 1979, 1984), which requires a theory to predict the intermediate stages of development. Recall that phonologically disordered children do not have quite the same profile as normally developing children at any point in time. As just noted, these children's vocabulary development proceeds in the face of a still-limited phonology, and many of the production solutions they adopt in response to this limitation seem to be quite unsystematic. Yet, given that these children eventually acquire the adult system, a theory of phonological learning must also allow for their particular brand of development.

Let us now turn to the question of how the more distinctive characteristics of phonologically disordered children might be handled by different models of phonological learning. For each model, we need first to hypothesize a particular source of disruption. We then assume that the child is an otherwise normal learner who must proceed the best he or she can with the distortions brought on by the disruption. The question, then, is whether the model can predict the correct profile given its currently proposed mechanisms and the assumed source of disruption.

Three different models will be considered. In the interest of space, I present only one in some depth, and then more briefly discuss how the other two will lead to somewhat different predictions.

The Interactive Activation Model

In the interactive activation model of Stemberger (1987, this volume) information is encoded in terms of units that are organized in different levels. Production begins at the semantic level, proceeds to the word and syntactic level, then goes to the syllable level, the phoneme level, then the feature level, before reaching the motor programming system. As processing begins at each new level, partial information is passed down to the next level. Thus, a unit receives activation from sources at various levels. Finally, as the activation of lower-level units increases, the activation is passed back to higher levels and can influence the activity at these higher levels. Probably the clearest example of these feedback effects is seen when the child possesses fewer output patterns than are operative at higher levels. In these instances, the existing output patterns change the higher-level patterns through feedback, so that they are more in line with those at the lower level.

In applying this model to the speech of phonologically disordered children, a plausible source of disruption should be proposed. Let us assume that phonologically disordered children learn in the usual way, but that for these children the activation that is fed back to higher levels is disproportionately high. That is, forms actually produced burn a more lasting imprint on the child's phonology than should occur. The effect is a greater role played by higher levels in the model (e.g., word, syllable levels) than is ordinarily assumed for normally developing children.

Appearing in table V are initial and subsequent words produced by a four-year-old phonologically disordered child. Unfortunately, the child was observed only after her subsequent words had already been acquired. Although the mother's diary information documented which words emerged first, one must take on faith that her productions of the initial words did not change from the point of emergence to the time at which we observed her.

The initial words appear in the first column of the table. The words *mommy, daddy,* and *baby* share several characteristics at the syllable, feature, and even phoneme levels. According to Stemberger's model, this leads to a gang effect in such a way that the shared information is mutually reinforced. The shared information is presented here as a "composite," although in keeping with the model such a composite should be viewed as the product of a dynamic interaction rather than as a static entity. To capture the elements that are statistically favored by the gang effect, the composite is labeled C + V + C + [i].

Three of the words in the next grouping, *broke, duck,* and *coat,* contain word-final stops in the adult form, but were produced with no final consonant. Let us assume, as is allowed in this model, that the child had no available motor programming routine for final stops. The diverted arrows in the table are intended to reflect this. Because these words are produced as open syllables, they are operating functionally like the words *no* and *bee*. That is, the activation that is passed back to higher levels is that of a consonant plus a vowel, hence the composite C + V.

Table V. Productions of a Phonologically Disordered Child

Initial Words	Composite of Gang Effects	Subsequent Words
mommy [mami] daddy [dadi] baby [bebi]	C + V + C + [i]	doggie [gagi]
no [no] bee [bi] broke [bo] duck [dʌ] coat [ko]	C + V	kiss [ki] or [dis]
juice [dus] shoes [dus]	[d] + V + [s]	eyes [das] or [a]
up [ʌ] out [a]	V	

The next two words on the list, *juice* and *shoes* (both produced as [dus]), also share several characteristics. I assume here that no motor programming routine was available for initial fricatives and final voicing, and that the most similar routines available were activated instead. The shared information that was reinforced appears as the composite [d] + V + [s] in the table.

Finally, we have the words *up* and *out*, produced as [ʌ] and [a], respectively. Again we will assume that the absence of a motor programming routine for final stops led to the production of open syllables (note the diverted arrow), and that the activation that was fed back up the system reinforced the shared information, represented here as the composite V.

To summarize thus far, we have some initial words that look fairly typical. *Mommy* is produced as [mami], *no* as [no], *coat* as [ko], *juice* as [dus], and *up* as [ʌ]. There is also some degree of homophony; *juice* and *shoes* are produced in the same way.

Now let us examine some words acquired subsequently by the child. Recall our assumption that the source of disruption for this child is disproportionately high activation that is fed back up the system. The result is that the gang effects will exert a powerful influence on the child's subsequent words. The first example is *doggie*, produced as [gagi]. Surprisingly, this rather common production is not handled especially well by the model. Certainly the gang effects stemming from the child's earlier words make it highly likely that *doggie* would be produced as C + V + C + [i]. However, there is no mechanism that ensures that the two consonants will be the same, although all of the child's earlier multisyllabic words had this characteristic. According to the model, productions such as [dagi] and [dadi] should be just as likely.

The word *kiss* has two different pronunciations, [ki] and [dis]. The first might be described as involving final consonant deletion, the second as fronting of the initial consonant or even alveolar assimilation. However, here the two forms are attributable to the word being subject to two influential gang effects, that labeled C + V, which permits initial velars but no final consonant, and that described as [d] + V + [s], which requires the initial consonant to be [d] but permits final [s].

In the final example, *eyes*, we again have two different pronunciations. The first of these, [das], might be described as involving initial consonant addition, and is representative of the types of productions that have been called unusual. The second, [a], is more typical, involving deletion of the final consonant. As with the preceding example, the presence of two different pronunciations is attributable to the word being subject to two influential gang effects. These are labeled [d] + V + [s], which permits final [s] but requires [d] in initial position, and V, which permits a vowel in initial position but no final consonant.

I have twice used the expression *influential gang effects* to convey our working assumption that the disproportionately high activation back up the system has the effect of forming deeply grooved paths of production for the child. This is not to say that new words subject to a gang effect will not have some distinctive characteristics, for specifications such as C and V permit a variety of possibilities. For example, a new word *cookie* might well be pronounced as [kuki], *TV* might be produced as [titi], *car* as [ka], and so on. In addition, certain new words might be sufficiently different in number of syllables and stress pattern to be free of the influence of all of these gang effects. The word *banana* might be one such example. Here, a production such as [nana] might be highly plausible. Nevertheless, it should be clear that when new words are forced into the grooves of one or another gang effect, the number of segments that are free to vary in the word is restricted. This should have the effect of sharply curtailing the degree of segment analysis that is done, which should in turn slow up the process of phonemic development. Thus, as lexical development proceeds, the child's phonological system might be unable to keep pace.

The second distinctive characteristic of phonologically disordered children's speech centers on unusual production patterns. Such forms are possible when the best-fitting gang effect happens to incorporate a segment that is not found in the adult form. Note that the example in table V illustrates not only an unusual pattern, but a rather unsystematically applied one similar to the type to which I referred earlier. Specifically, the word *eyes* is very similar to the types of words that we classified as "in-phonology" in one of the studies I just summarized (Leonard et al. 1987). That is, this child showed the ability to use word-initial vowels as well as word-final [s]. Therefore, a production such as [as] or [ʌs] would seem likely. But in the present account, this child might sometimes show an unusual pattern in just such instances, as we in fact found for the phonologically disordered children that we studied.

Alternate Models

Although the interactive activation model possesses mechanisms that might be capable of accounting for some of the notable characteristics of phonologically disordered children's speech, it is not clear that this model will prove more satisfactory than alternative models. Let us consider how additional data might allow us to choose among the alternatives. One alternative will be the more traditional model in which it is assumed that the child's underlying representation approximates that of the adult, and rules are applied to derive the child's output form (e.g., Smith 1973). We shall refer to this alternative as the "adult-like representation" model. The other will be the "two-lexicon" model, in which the child has an input lexicon, rules relating it to an output lexicon, and articulatory instructions (e.g., Menn 1983).

Let us assume that we obtain from the child additional productions of all the words noted in table V. (Unfortunately, I have no such data.) Possible outcomes, given additional tokens of some of these words, are provided in table VI. As can be seen from this table, the three models are not identical in their predictions. According to the interactive activation model, one possible outcome of such a larger sample is that additional versions of the words *kiss* and *eyes* could be seen. That is, because the composites shown in table V are actually possible products of gang effects, competition could result in combinations of these forms appearing in production. Thus, in addition to [ki] and [dis] as productions of *kiss*, the child could also produce [kis] and [di]. Similarly, for *eyes* the child might produce [da] and [as] as well as [das] and [a].

Consider now what we should expect given the adult-like representation model. A model of this type would assume that the variability seen in words such as *kiss* and *eyes* was due to optional rules. For *kiss*, final consonant deletion might apply optionally, as might fronting. These two rules might both apply, or neither might apply. Thus, we might expect that all four productions listed for *kiss* in table VI could appear with a large enough sample. However, this might also lead to the expectation that some of the early words, such as *juice*, would be subject to the same optional rules. Such a prediction is quite different from anything predicted by the interactive activation model. Note that the same is true with regard to the word *up*. In this case, the optional initial consonant addition rule assumed for *eyes* might be expected to apply to *up* as well.

In contrast, the two-lexicon model would make the same predictions as the interactive activation model for the child's initial words. However, I believe the predictions would be different for the words *kiss* and *eyes*. In this model, for each of the words the output lexicon se-

Table VI. Predictions of Three Models

Word	Interactive Activation	Adult-Like Representation	Two-Lexicon
juice	[dus]	[dus], [du]	[dus]
up	[ʌ]	[dʌ], [ʌ]	[ʌ]
kiss	[ki], [kis], [di], [dis]	[ki], [kis], [di], [dis]	[ki], [dis]
eyes	[da], [das], [as], [a]	[da], [das], [as], [a]	[das], [a]

lected will consist of a specification of a canonical form plus a specification for each variable parameter. Thus, for *kiss* the canonical form C + V might be specified along with [+ velar] for the consonant, and [+ high] for the vowel. Or, the canonical form [d] + V + [s] might be specified along with [+ high] for the vowel. However, we have no basis for predicting a mixture, for either one canonical form is specified or the other is. A production such as [di] should not occur. Thus, fewer variations should be seen according to this model. The same is true for the word *eyes*.

Even if the child's additional productions of these words were completely in keeping with the predictions of the interactive activation model, one further step might be taken before accepting the proposals discussed here. Specifically, independent evidence of the proposed disruption should be sought. In this case, the assumed disruption is disproportionately high activation that is fed back up the system. One way to test this independently might be to determine if the child is more prone to perseverative productions than are younger normally developing children with comparable phonetic inventories. For example, the child could be asked to imitate, several times in succession, a new word that bears little resemblance to his or her existing words (e.g., *funnel*). Following these imitations, the child could be asked to imitate another new word, bearing some similarity to the first new word, and very little to the child's other words (e.g., *uncle*). We could then determine if the child was more likely than her younger, normally developing peers to carry features of the first word into her productions of the second word (e.g., producing *uncle* with [f] in initial position). A finding of this type could give credence to the view that earlier productions exert a powerful influence on the child's subsequent words.

CONCLUSIONS

Children with phonological disorders are similar to younger, normally developing children in several respects. The substitution and omission patterns of these children resemble those of younger peers, and typically reflect a sensitivity to the phonetic and phonotactic characteristics of the ambient language. However, these children seem to differ from their younger peers in that they are obliged to acquire a relatively large lexicon using a restricted phonology, and they exhibit more frequent but less systematic use of unusual production patterns. Given that these children eventually acquire the adult system, it seems that their learning profiles, too, must be accommodated by any model of child phonology that seeks to explain phonological acquisition.

In this chapter, we started with the more distinctive characteristics of phonologically disordered children's speech and looked at how one possible source of disruption occurring within one particular model might account for these characteristics, and what predictions would be made for additional data. We then saw how these predictions differ from those consistent with other models. If these predictions were to hold, the model would receive considerable support. If they did not hold, the next logical step would be to determine if there is a plausible source of disruption within the model providing the more accurate prediction. In either case, independent evidence for the proposed source of disruption should then be sought.

More generally, the goal of this chapter is to make the case that data from phonologically disordered children might assist us in evaluating our models of phonological learning. After continued work with normally developing children, we may reach a point where the adequacy of two or more viable models can be determined only by seeing how they handle the profiles of these less typical children.

REFERENCES

Bernthal, J., and Bankson, N. 1988. *Articulation and Phonological Disorders*. Englewood Cliffs, NJ: Prentice-Hall.

Bortolini, U., and Leonard, L. 1991. The speech of phonologically disordered children acquiring Italian. *Clinical Linguistics and Phonetics* 5:1–12.

Ingram, D. 1981, *Procedures for the Phonological Analysis of Children's Language*. Baltimore: University Park Press.

Ingram, D. 1987. Phonological impairment in children. Paper presented at the International Symposium on Language Acquisition and Language Impairment, June, 1987, Parma, Italy.

Leonard, L. 1985. Unusual and subtle phonological behavior in the speech of phonologically-disordered children. *Journal of Speech and Hearing Disorders* 50:4–13.

Leonard, L., and Brown, B. 1984. The nature and boundaries of phonologic categories: A case study of an unusal phonologic pattern in a language impaired child. *Journal of Speech and Hearing Disorders* 49:419–28.

Leonard, L., Schwartz, R., Swanson, L., and Loeb, D. 1987. Some conditions that promote unusual phonological behavior in children. *Clinical Linguistics and Phonetics* 1:23–34.

Menn, L. 1983. Development of articulatory, phonetic, and phonological capabilities. In *Language Production, Volume 2: Development, Writing, and Other Language Processes*, ed. B. Butterworth. London: Academic Press.

Pinker, S. 1979. Formal models of language learning. *Cognition* 7:217–83.

Pinker, S. 1984. *Language Learnability and Language Development*. Cambridge, MA: Harvard University Press.

Schwartz, R., Leonard, L., Folger, M., and Wilcox, M. 1980. Evidence for a synergistic view of language disorders: Early phonological behavior in normal and language disordered children. *Journal of Speech and Hearing Disorders* 45:357–77.

Smith, N. 1973. *The Acquisition of Phonology*. Cambridge: Cambridge University Press.

Stemberger, J. 1987. Child phonology: Phonological processing without phonological processes. Unpublished manuscript.
Stoel-Gammon, C., and Dunn, C. 1985. *Normal and Disordered Phonology in Children.* Baltimore: University Park Press.

Chapter • 18

Infant Vocalizations and Innovations in Infraphonology
Toward a Broader Theory of Development and Disorders

D. Kimbrough Oller and Michael P. Lynch

PERSPECTIVES ON THEORY IN THE STUDY OF INFANT VOCAL DEVELOPMENT

There has been considerable progress in the understanding of the emergences of speech capabilities in infancy over the past two decades. However, the recent effort, whatever its accomplishments, clearly needs broadening. The focus of the past has been upon syllables and segments (or "protosyllables" and "protosegments," if one prefers), but it seems likely that infant prespeech development entails much more. Theoretical developments need to be expanded to encompass accounts of higher order rhythmic units, (e.g., the utterance, the phonological phrase). The lack of such descriptive framework in current work may impose a sort of theoretical/empirical blindness on infant vocalization research. If we are not looking for developments in a particular domain, we are unlikely to see them.

The work reported here was supported by a grant from the NIH-NIDCD R01 DC00484 (formerly NINCDS, R01 NS26121) (D. K. Oller, PI), and by NIH-NICHD HD21534 (Rebecca Eilers, PI).

This chapter first reviews the recent progress of description in infant vocal development as a manifestation of an emerging capacity for speech. The work has borne fruit both in terms of a growing consensus about speech-like sound development and in terms of providing a basis for the differentiation of developmental patterns in normal and linguistically disordered infants/children. The second part of the chapter offers a preliminary view of a broadened descriptive framework, designed to provide a basis for a developmental account of suprasyllabic units—utterances and utterance clusters in infant vocal development.

RECENT HISTORY OF INFANT VOCALIZATION RESEARCH

The Problem of Description

Since the middle of the present century, interest in the phonetic characteristics of infant vocalizations has been hampered by uncertainty and controversy regarding proper methods of description. The question was, should one transcribe infant vocalizations utilizing the International Phonetic Alphabet, or should one conduct acoustic analysis and measure properties of the infant vocal output without resorting to auditory evaluation? While Irwin (1947) and his colleagues used the IPA approach, Lynip (1951) attacked the attempt to force infant sounds into the mold of adult speech categories and argued for a strictly acoustic approach.

The inappropriateness of applying the IPA as Irwin did is easy to see, because it is obvious that vocalizations such as gurgles and squeals, so common in early infancy, are not entirely compatible with the critical assumption that sounds being transcribed are phonetically well-formed. In the absence of a clear definition of phonetic well-formedness, there is no solid basis for deciding when transcription should be allowed, and in the case of many infant sounds, there is no basis for describing them at all in a transcriptional framework, beyond pointing out that they are not well-formed.

The problem with using a strictly acoustic approach is, perhaps, not so obvious, but in fact it is equally intractable. When one performs acoustic analysis of infant sounds, a choice must be made about what precise method of analysis is to be used. For example, a bandwidth of analysis must be chosen, assumptions must be made about acceptable and/or appropriate dynamic range of analysis and display, and a time frame must be specified. These and other necessary starting points for the analysis carry with them critical assumptions about what is important (i.e., what is indicative of speech-like quality) in the acoustic signal. Once the acoustic analysis has been performed and a visible recording of the signal is available, the researcher must face a new round of related quandaries. What should be measured? The decision about what data to obtain from the visible recording again requires assumptions about what is important in the signal. In some sense the problem is the same one faced by the researcher who would seek to use an IPA description. What aspect of the signal matters? What is phonetic well-formedness and how can it be assessed?

In the context of the battle over what kind of analysis would be appropriate, infant vocalizations research was in a state of confusion and "descriptive chaos" (van der Stelt and Koopmans-van Beinum 1986). In general, results of studies in infant vocal development were not taken seriously. Perhaps due to the confusion, the preposterous claim (usually attributed to Jakobson 1941) that infant sounds and speech are unrelated, came to be widely accepted. To this day, in many linguistics and psychology circles, it is assumed (while ignoring research in infant babbling) that infants babble all the sounds of all the world's languages randomly, and that young children, when they begin to speak meaningfully, impose a strict hierarchy where certain sounds are highly favored and others are avoided. The descriptive chaos of the mid-century phonetic/acoustic controversy seemed to leave a theoretical vacuum that sucked up a blissfully simple view in which babies were thought capable of producing any speech sound with ease whereas young verbal children were restricted to a small set of favorite sounds.

Similarities of Late Babbling and Early Speech

The Jakobsonian view of babbling has never been in favor among those who have actually devoted research effort to infant vocal sounds. Once one has listened to infants and made an attempt—any attempt—at characterizing those sounds in terms of a relationship with speech, it is hard to miss certain similarities of babbling and early speech. Observers such as Lewis (1936) had pointed out that the most common early words of young children, reflected in nursery terms such as "mama," "dada," and "baba," bear a striking resemblance to favored babbling sequences of infants. A series of studies that began to appear in the 1960s (e.g., Nakazima 1962; Menyuk 1968; Cruttenden 1970; Vanvik 1971; Oller et al. 1976) provided clear indications of the overwhelming similarities of late babbling (in the age range of 8 to 12 months) and early meaningful speech. Both babbling and speech seemed to be characterized by predominant utilization of a small core of syllables that appear to occur nearly universally in languages—[pa, na, ta, ma, wa] and a few others. Conspicuously absent from the list of syllables that occur commonly in infant babbling and speech are nonuniversal syllable types that include consonant clusters, strong final consonants, as-pirated stops, voiced final stops, trills, and so forth. Most people who have spent any time with a baby will recognize the implausibility of babbling with nonuniversal sequences such as [stasta] or [aldald]. Sim-ilarly, such sequences seem improbable candidates for nursery term status.

The relationship of babbling and speech was easy to discern for the post-1960 observers because they took a more phonetically sophis-ticated stance than had Irwin and his colleagues. Instead of transcrib-ing all nonvegetative sounds of infants as Irwin had done, the more recent investigators focused on what we now call *canonical syllables*, the phonetically well-formed utterances of infants. At first the designa-tion of canonical syllables was intuitively directed, but the various in-vestigators seemed persuaded that it was relatively easy to recognize clear cases of canonical babbling. The result was a set of observations of babbled sounds from babies in Europe, Japan, and North America that matched remarkably well and showed a substantial relationship of late babbling and speech. The syllables produced by infants were preferen-tially chosen from a small inventory of more-or-less universal syllable types, in general the same syllables that are favored by young children in early words.

The Emerging Consensus About Precanonical Sounds

The precanonical sounds of earlier infancy present a somewhat more difficult problem for characterization in terms of relationship with speech. The intuitions of observers that led to a distinction between canonical and noncanonical sounds did not offer a clear way of assessing the non-canonical sounds. A variety of investigators in North America and Eu-rope in the 1970s and 1980s described the noncanonical sounds and proposed "stage models" of the development of the vocal capacity from the first month of life through the transition to canonical babbling and later referential speech communication. There is a surprising amount of agreement among the various investigators, though they worked largely independently, about the nature of vocal development in the first year of life. Although not using an IPA style of description, the various investigators characterized infant sounds with a combination of abstract phonetic/acoustic terms and descriptors that are part of the common parlance (gurgles, coos, goos, squeals, shrieks, etc.). In addi-tion, the investigators were drawn to specifying the extent to which infant sounds seemed to approximate well-formed syllables by focus-ing on particular characteristics of precanonical sounds that made them less speech-like than canonical utterances.

The following is a summary of the emerging consensus on stages of vocal development, taking into account research from both sides of the Atlantic (Zlatin 1975; Stark 1980; Oller 1978; Koopmans-van Beinum and van der Stelt 1986; Holmgren et al. 1986; Roug, Landberg, and Lundberg 1989; Vihman, Ferguson, and Elbert 1986; Vihman and Miller 1988; Stoel-Gammon and Cooper 1984; Elbers and Ton 1985). In this synthesis of models, five stages can be seen and ages are allowed to overlap in order to account for individual differences among children (some move much faster through the stages than others) and differences in age specifications of the various investigators. The five stages are: (1) the Phonation Stage (0 to 2 months) is characterized by quasiresonant or quasivocalic sounds (normal phonation with vocal tract at rest, yielding energy concentration at low frequency), sometimes with glottal (stop or fricative) interruptions, and by a variety of reflexive sounds (cries, grunts, hiccoughs, sneezes, etc.). The Primitive Articulation Stage (1 to 4 months), (2), shows appearance of primitive syllables usually with articulation at the back of the vocal tract combined with quasivocalic sounds (these sounds are often called goos, coos, or gurgles). Continuation of quasivocalic sounds with glottal interruptions is seen and laughter begins. The Expansion (or Exploratory) Stage (3 to 8 months), (3), is characterized by many new sounds, including open vowels (called "fully resonant or fully vocalic nuclei"), pitch exploratory sounds such as squeals and growls, amplitude exploratory sounds such as yells and whispers, raspberries, and slowly articulated sequences of vowel-like and consonant-like sounds (marginal babbles). During this period infants are observed to repeat particular sound types systematically in patterns that are referred to commonly as "vocal play." In the Canonical Syllable Stage (5 to 10 months), (4), infants begin to produce well-formed syllables in which both vowel-like and consonant-like elements are combined with quick formant transitions. Reduplicated sequences of such syllables are produced in addition to single syllables. In the Integrative Stage (9 to 18 months), (5), infants begin meaningful speech, mix babbling and speech, and show major individual differences in jargon or gibberish utterances in both amount and kind.

The development of a stage model that encompasses observations of many investigators is useful in providing a schematic of infant vocal trends, but it is most interesting in its implicit indications of increasing phonetic well-formedness of infant utterances and increasing complexity of phonetic skills across the first year and a half of life. During the course of the development of the stage models, investigators have addressed the implicit framework of phonetic well-formedness with mounting interest. The potential for integration of information from a variety of studies within a broad model that includes a straightforward definition of the notion *canonical syllable* raises hopes that infant vocalizations research might progress in heretofore unanticipated ways. The University of Miami group has been heavily involved in the attempt to specify a framework with the capability of integrating phonetic and acoustic information. We have referred to the framework as "metaphonology" (Oller 1986; Oller et al. 1985), and more recently as "infraphonology." We now consider the term infraphonology to be preferable because it more accurately portrays the intent of the model—to provide an explicit characterization of the infrastructure, the underpinnings, of any phonological system, by specifying the nature of phonetically well-formed elements and the relationships that obtain among them.

Infraphonology as an Integrating Approach

The initial focus of infraphonological specification has been the syllable, taken here to be the minimal rhythmic unit of speech. The intuition of observers throughout the modern era of research in vocal development has been that across the first year of life infants progress toward an ability to produce controlled, well-formed syllables. Early in the first year the sounds produced include "primitive syllables" or "protosyllables" (Zlatin 1975), but later the syllables solidify until they seem perfect examples of speech articulation. The Miami group's goal was to specify the nature of that change in sufficient detail and with sufficient insight that a basis could be formed for comparison of infant sounds and speech in general—even more, the goal was to establish a basis for comparison of any kind of sound (human or nonhuman) with well-formed mature speech.

By defining the canonical syllable notion in acoustic terms, we sought to create the comparative reference needed, and we sought to provide some resolution to the conflict between advocates of an acoustic and a transcriptional approach to vocal development descriptions. The canonical syllable is defined as consisting of a sound sequence including a nucleus (a highpoint of energy) and at least one margin (an adjacent lowpoint of energy). The nucleus must be produced with normal phonation and the vocal tract must be postured to yield full-resonance or fully vocalic quality (i.e., a closed tract is disallowed in a canonical nucleus). The margin must be at least 10 dB lower in amplitude than the nucleus and the formant transition between the margin and nucleus must occur within a specifiable time frame (say, 25–140 ms). The whole syllable must also occur within a specifiable time frame (say, 50–500 ms). The pitch and amplitude peaks of canonical syllables in a sequence must fit within a specifiable range. Note that some real syllables in natural languages would not be judged canonical by the stated criteria. Those that would be judged noncanonical (e.g., those including syllabic consonants, wide vocal register shifts, very slow rates of articulation) can be seen either to be nonuniversal, relatively infrequent in languages, or to be representatives of some special case of language use, as in singing. The definitions are intended to specify the class of syllables that are archetypal with respect to the core patterns of speech in normal settings. Other real syllables would be seen as deviations from the canonical standard in specific ways that could be detailed within the context of the definition.

The definitional criteria are a starting point. They will require fleshing out in the future, but even now they offer an indication of the components of the intuition that led observers to judge certain infant sounds as more speech-like than others. Nonvegetative sounds of the Phonation Stage can be seen to represent production of presyllabic sounds with normal phonation, less than full-vocalicness (the vocal tract is closed or nearly closed), and no canonical margins (glottal interruptions produce no formant transitions, and so do not count as canonical). Sounds of the Primitive Articulation Stage show increasing sophistication because the child incorporates margins (usually back articulations) with the sounds of the Phonation Stage. However, the protosyllables of the Primitive Articulation Stage do not abide by all the requirements of canonical syllables because the nuclei are not usually fully vocalic and because the formant transitions between nucleus and margin are too compact (have insufficient slope). During the Expansion Stage, infants explore fully vocalic nuclei and begin articulating marginal syllables, which abide by all the requirements of canonical syllables except those related to timing. Especially formant transitions are too long. In the Canonical Stage, all the requirements of canonical syllables are at last met.

The key accomplishment of the infraphonological model of canonical syllables is the differentiation of speech-like sounds in terms of the extent to which they resemble the archetypal elements of speech. The abstract specification of the archetypes is critical in our view, because it is necessary to provide a standard of comparison that is not biased to a specific language, but rather represents the core toward which we all proceed in the development of a mature speech capacity.

Infraphonology and Disorders of Speech Development

An unexpected benefit of infraphonological modeling has been that it has provided a fruitful basis for comparison of normal and disordered vocal development. Prior to the modern era of vocal development research, it was widely believed that deaf and hearing infants "babbled" alike, although deaf infants were thought to babble less, especially toward the end of the first year of life. This belief seems to have been based on a combination of sheer speculation and transcription-based observation that was blind to the differences between well-formed and ill-formed speech-like vocalization. Without such a differentiation, Mavilya (1969) had transcribed canonical and precanonical sounds of three infants, believed to be deaf, with a broad phonetic alphabet. After comparing her own data with transcriptional data on hearing infants (e.g., from Irwin and Chen 1946), she concluded that deaf and hearing infants babbled similarly.

More modern work on deaf and hearing infants has produced a quite different conclusion. Oller et al. (1985), Kent et al. (1987), and Oller and Eilers (1988) found that the onset of canonical babbling was substantially delayed in deaf infants. While hearing infants begin the Canonical Stage by 10 months of age, deaf infants appear to begin much later. Thus far, comparison of deaf and hearing infants has yielded distributions for the onset of canonical babbling that do not overlap—the slowest normally hearing infants start before the quickest deaf infants. How could the conclusions of this work differ so markedly from those of Mavilya? It seems likely that Mavilya did not notice a difference in canonical syllable production because she was not looking for one. The broad transcriptional framework she adopted offered no encouragement for the distinction of speech-like and nonspeech-like sounds and the investigator appears to have stayed true to the goals implicit in the framework.

In the context of more detailed transcriptional efforts, conducted by investigators sensitized to the need to differentiate speech-like and other sounds, it has been found that deaf and hearing infants differ in additional ways. Stark (1983), Stoel-Gammon and Otomo (1986), and Stoel-Gammon (1988) have shown that the phonetic inventories of deaf infants are more restricted than those of hearing infants and that certain properties of the inventories (e.g., focus on labial sounds) seem predictable based upon the deaf infant's reliance on visual information in vocalization. The fact that Mavilya did not find such differences may be attributable both to differences in the kinds of utterances she was transcribing (presumably less speech-like ones) and to differences in the available repertoire of phonetic units with which to characterize sounds (Mavilya's repertoire being more narrow).

The success of the new descriptive tools in differentiating vocal development in normal infants and one group known to be at serious risk for communication disorders (i.e., the deaf population), has encouraged the search for other communication disordered groups that may show aberrancies in vocalization development. A first attempt (Smith and Oller 1981) showed Down syndrome and normal infants to have similar ages of onset for canonical babbling. Additional work is now underway attempting to provide more detailed characterizations of Down syndrome vocal development in our own laboratories and at

Massachusetts General Hospital (Locke, personal communication). In addition, work on tracheostomized infants (who cannot vocalize until decannulation) at MGH and elsewhere is seeking to demonstrate the role that vocal practice may play in infraphonological development (Locke and Pearson 1990). Stark, Ansel, and Bond (1989) have considered the possibility that late onset of canonical babbling may be an indicator of emerging disorders such as dyslexia or functional language disorders. Other studies in our own laboratories are seeking to characterize vocal development in infants that have been thought to be at risk for communication disorders—premature, low socioeconomic status, and simultaneous bilingual infants. The advent of new methods of description has created a whole new climate for research in infant vocal development. Whereas it used to be thought that infant sounds were unrelated to speech, we now take the relationship to be a given and seek indicators of emerging language/speech disorders by examining the vocal sounds of infants.

PROLEGOMENA TO A BROADER INFRAPHONOLOGY: BEYOND THE MINIMAL RHYTHMIC UNIT

Early Awareness of Multisyllabic Rhythmic Units

While the characterization of the canonical syllable has borne fruit beyond our expectations, it is clear already that additional framework development in infraphonology is required for future progress in describing the emergence of the capacity for speech in infancy. A primary problem seems to us to be the fact that infraphonological studies of infant vocalizations have thus far focused almost entirely on the minimal rhythmic unit of speech, the syllable. Higher order rhythmic units have been ignored.

One reason for interest in developing further information about infant capabilities in the realm of manipulation of multisyllable utterances and clusters of utterances is that there are empirical hints that infants may have substantial awareness of higher order rhythmic units. For example, parents seem to communicate vocally with infants in highly structured prototypical contours that can be superimposed on a wide variety of lexical/segmental messages (Papousek, Papousek, and Haekel 1987; Papousek and Papousek 1988). Rising contours are used to encourage visual contact or vocalization (Stern, Spieker, and MacKain 1982; Ryan 1978), while falling contours at low pitch are used to soothe the distraught infant (Fernald et al. 1989; Papousek, Papousek, and Bornstein 1985). The ritualization of the contour patterns, their apparent universality (a number of cultures and language families have been found to show the same patterns), and the fact that they seem to bear significant pragmatic forces, encourages the belief that humans in general, including infants, are endowed with awareness of the contours and how to identify them. In order to recognize them, the infant would seem to need to be aware of certain broadly applicable principles of chunking of multisyllabic information.

If infants have such awareness, it presumably could be applied to a variety of auditory signals. A recent study of infants' perception of musical phrases has suggested that two-month-olds recognize the phrasal structure of music and prefer to listen to musical passages in which this structure is well-formed (Krumhansl and Jusczyk 1990). In fact, one characteristic that may have been instrumental in the marking of phrase boundaries in the musical stimuli (Mozart minuets) was the regular occurrence of longer notes at the ends of phrases. Lindblom (1978) previously suggested that final lengthening may be important in the demarcation of units such as the phrase in music or the foot in speech. Other possibilities for the indication of temporal unit boundaries in music, such as pitch height, change of melody, change of tempo, and change of register may have analogs in speech units (Clarke and Krumhansl 1990). The universality of acoustic characteristics of speech and music may hint at deep capacities for recognition of units in temporally organized acoustic signals.

In addition to the empirical hints from perception of infants, there are indications in their productions that multisyllabic units may be of major import early in life. By the Integrative Stage of infant vocal development (9 to 18 months), infants commonly produce long sequences of syllables in which there may be identifiable words, but often there is a mixture of words and apparent babble (Vihman, Ferguson, and Elbert 1986; Smith, Brown-Sweeney, and Stoel-Gammon 1989; Elbers and Wijnen this volume). It might seem that in such mixed and variegated utterances, infants are developing broader phonological frames (of multiple syllables and perhaps multiple utterances) within which lexical items can be progressively incorporated as syntactic skills emerge. However, it is unclear how much of the development of such frames takes place earlier, prior to the Integrative Stage, because there has been essentially no research on the multisyllabic structuring of early infant vocalizations. The results discussed below hint at the possibility that such research could yield a bountiful harvest.

On Syllables and Utterances

A key question in the investigation of higher order rhythmic units concerns the definition of such units. For example, it is clear that infants often produce multisyllabic "utterances." But what precisely are *utterances*?

The literature on infant vocalizations has often defined the utterance as a *breath group*. If one could hear a breath (ingress) within a vocalization, an utterance boundary was to be placed there. If no breath could be detected, the breath group was defined as a vocalization separated from other vocalizations by at least one second. This definition was used in all our infant vocalizations research prior to 1988 (see e.g., Smith and Oller 1981; Oller et al. 1985). Others have used similar although not necessarily identical definitions of the utterance (e.g., Stark 1980; Zlatin 1975).

The "breath group/one-second-rule" definition has proved to yield unsatisfactory reliability in recent empirical tests. For years, investigators have been aware that there are important differences between different phonetic judges in how they count the utterances in recorded samples of infant vocalizations. The problem was, however, largely ignored perhaps because the focus of description was on the speech-like quality of syllable-sized units. Our first clear indication of a significant difficulty in utterance counts came from a reliability study conducted with eight observers in training to perform infraphonological categorization at the University of Miami. A half-hour sample of vocalizations from an Expansion Stage infant was presented to the group for utterance counting only. Each observer worked independently, having been instructed that the task was to count all "nonvegetative" utterances (excluding coughs, hiccoughs, sneezes, cries, laughs, and grunts) and to use the one-second rule as a guide (i.e., two utterances with no audible breath between them had to be separated by at least one second, whereas vocal events that were more closely spaced were considered a single utterance). The observers were asked to implement the rule by trying to say the words "one-thousand-one" (a production that presumably takes about one second for a conversational speaking rate) during the silent interval between any two consecutive vocal events that seemed close enough together to be considered a single utterance.

The mean number of utterances counted in the study was 56 but the range across observers was 46 to 74, indicating that the most conservative count represented only a little over 60% of the utterances indicated by the most liberal count. One standard deviation for the distribution of utterance counts was 9.1 or 16% of the mean count. We were surprised at the magnitude of the variance, but subsequent evaluations of criteria utilized by individual judges confirmed that there was ample basis for the discrepancy. A substantial proportion of discrepancies in utterance counts that we evaluated could be attributed to differences in such factors as judgments about whether a particular utterance was a reflexive grunt or a quasivocalic sound. Even though a grunt may indeed possess resonance characteristics resembling the quasivocalic sounds, if the utterance is produced as an artifact of body movement, it is considered vegetative. The observer must make a judgment about the likelihood that the utterance is a grunt based upon other acoustic characteristics (rise time, duration, etc.). In addition, many discrepancies in the obtained utterance counts were attributable to differences in what observers considered audible. Some included very low amplitude utterances and utterances partially obscured by the voices of other people, while others did not. Such discrepancies can be minimized by having observers work together and set common criteria, but a residue of interobserver differences attributable to differing interpretations of the tape-recorded vocalizations has proved to be unavoidable.

The more interesting criterion differences we found among observers concerned whether or not observers perceived a breath between vocal events and how they implemented the one-second rule. In a number of instances, in spite of the instruction to listen for breaths and to count "one-thousand-one" in silent intervals, there were discrepancies among observers on whether or not utterance boundaries were perceived in particular locations. On closer examination we found that some observers felt strong intuitions that the utterance counts resulting from the procedure were often somehow wrong. Boundaries designated on the basis of one second of silence did not always correspond to strong acoustic cues suggesting an intended boundary, and even more commonly, boundaries were often heard in locations where no one-second silence occurred and no breath could be perceived. After additional attempts to correct such discrepancies by enforcing the procedure, we came to the conclusion that the effort was both futile, because agreement was not improving, and unreasonable, because we seemed to be working with an intuitively unsound definition of the utterance.

In order to improve the agreement levels, we found it necessary to adopt a new conception of the notion *utterance,* one that corresponded more to an intuitive "breath group" idea akin to the one utilized to indicate phrasing in music. One does not have to breathe at the boundary of a "breath group" according to the musical definition, and there is no one-second rule implied. At the same time, identification of musical breath groups, even in keyboard music where breathing is irrelevant, is believed by musicians to be relatively straightforward. In Lynch, Oller, and Steffens (1989) we first defined and made use of the new approach. Surprisingly, we found an immediate and substantial improvement in reliability of utterance counts. Essentially we suggested to observers that they listen for breath groups, ignoring whether or not breathing actually occurred, and count as an utterance boundary any silence that did not seem to indicate a consonant, but rather a space within which the speaker could have the option of breathing.

Lynch, Oller, and Steffens found much improved utterance count agreement with the new definition. More recent evaluations of utterance counts with a partially new group of seven infraphonological categorization trainees using the new definition have also yielded encouraging results. The standard deviation of counts across observers has been nearly cut in half (now 9% as opposed to the previous 16% of mean utterance counts), owing to the greater certainty of observers working with the more intuitively satisfying definition.

Results since the new definition show that observers judge utterance boundaries in many instances where the silence between utterances is much less than one second. A spectrographic analysis of an entire taped sample categorized by three of our current team for a canonical stage infant showed that 28 of 68 indicated utterance boundaries occurred at silences less than one second in duration. Many of the boundaries at silences of less than one second did not correspond to audible breaths. It seems reasonable to conclude that the one-second rule, which had been formulated on the assumption that it would correspond to the natural interval duration between breath-groups, was ill-conceived.

To illustrate further the role of silent interval duration in judgments, we have plotted in figure 1 a distribution of utterance boundary durations that were observed in the spectrographically analyzed data on a scale from 0 to 1.5 seconds. For purposes of the display, all values have been rounded to the nearest 50 ms. The figure shows that the modal duration of silences judged as boundaries was about 450 ms, and that the minimum observed silent interval duration of a boundary was 350 ms. It would appear, however, to be unwise to conclude that

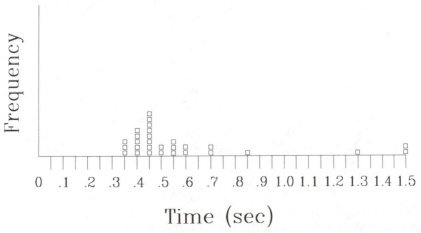

Figure 1.   Distribution of silent interval durations between utterances.

utterance boundaries *cannot* correspond to silences shorter than 350 ms. The infant under consideration did not produce utterance-final consonant-like elements, and consequently our observations apply only to silences that occur after vowel-like elements. Also, it seems probable that at higher rates of speech than are common in infancy, shorter silence durations might be accepted as utterance boundaries.

Figures 2 and 3 provide spectrographic displays to exemplify silence durations that were typically judged to cue utterance boundaries. The vertical grid indicates time in 400 ms units. For figure 2, the silence between the first two utterances (at the point of the # symbol in the transcript) was measured as 2.45 seconds and between the second two, 1.81. These boundaries would, of course, have been unambiguously indicated even according to the old utterance definition. The boundary in figure 3, however, corresponds to an interutterance interval of only about 425 ms, and because there is no audible breath between the indicated utterances, the boundary would not have been designated according to the old definition. It is worth focusing briefly on the burst of energy that occurs between the two utterances in figure 3. The observers resolved to interpret the burst as an extraneous pop on the tape, although it was possible to hear the burst as the release of a stop

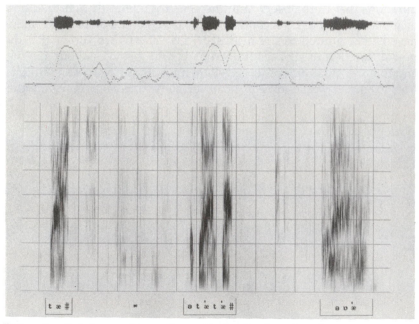

Figure 2. Spectrographic and amplitude display of a three-utterance sequence showing relatively long interutterance intervals. Extraneous adult voice indicated by asterisk (*).

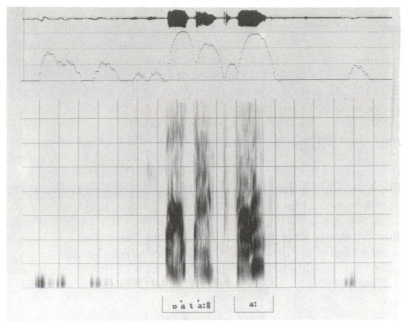

ʋ a t a:#   a:

Figure 3.   Spectrographic display of a two-utterance sequence showing a rela-tively short interutterance interval.

consonant [t]. Interestingly, even under the consonantal interpretation of the burst and with repeated listening, observers maintained the opinion that the utterance boundary was real. If we assume the pop is indeed a consonantal burst, then an appropriate remeasuring of the interutterance interval based on that interpretation would start at the end of the burst, and the new interval duration would be 138 ms. Thus, it appears that the timing criteria that are used by listeners in judging utterance boundaries may vary substantially with specific aspects of the phonetic context.

Given these data, it seems likely that if one were to seek a fixed minimum silence duration as a criterion for utterance boundaries, the value should be, not one second, but less than (perhaps much less than) half a second. It is tempting to speculate that the appropriate value may be tied somehow to common duration of the minimal rhythmic unit of speech, the syllable, or to some subcomponent thereof, perhaps the arresting consonant. If so, the value would seem to be somewhere in the range of 100 to 400 ms. This range is comparable to the pause durations found in samples of spontaneous adult speech by Rochester (1973).

Additional evidence supports the conclusion that while utterances are usually identifiable based primarily on information regarding timing of silences, some utterance boundaries are clearly determined by other factors. In figure 4, we see a sequence of a grunt (which was ignored in the categorizations) and three nonvegetative utterances from the canonical stage infant, the first of which is a whiny, vowel-like syllable with a breathy offset, and the second and third of which are "glottal sequences" of central vowels interrupted by glottal stops. There are clearly five syllables in the two glottal sequence utterances, but the interesting fact is that seven of seven observers who were asked independently to parse this sequence auditorily placed the utterance boundary within the glottal sequences between the third and fourth syllables where duration of silence is shorter (by about 100 ms) than between the second and third syllables. On questioning, the observers insisted that the parsing was correct and unambiguous. The fact that the duration of silence at the boundary point was less than the silence in the previous within-utterance interval was not noticed by the observers, who appeared to think the between-utterance silence was longer; they even tended to imitate the utterance in such a way that the silence between the three syllable and the two syllable glottal sequences was longer

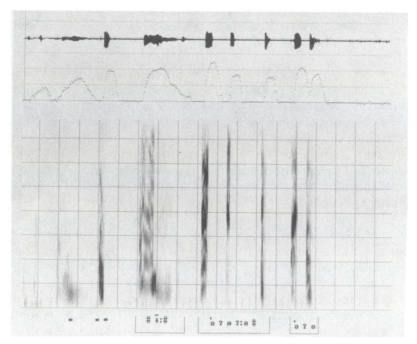

Figure 4. Spectrographic display of a sequence in which duration of silent interval is not the only factor determining utterance boundary location. Extraneous adult voice indicated by asterisk (*). Vegetative grunt produced by child indicated by double asterisk (**).

than any within-utterance silence. Apparently timing was not the only factor that determined the utterance boundary judgments.

Two possibilities regarding the parsing of the utterances in figure 4 are salient. First consider the fact that the two designated glottal utterances end with no glottal stops at their offsets. This can be verified by noting that the amplitude envelopes end abruptly for the nonfinal syllables of each sequence, but that the final syllables end with a gradual offset. Perhaps listeners judging utterance (i.e., breath group) boundaries are aware that the glottal closure implied by a perceived glottal stop precludes breathing, while lack of a glottal stop leaves open the possibility of breathing. Consequently, breath group boundaries would most naturally be assigned to silences that are not glottally stopped. Second, consider the amplitude displays, which show that the two utterances both start with a high amplitude syllable and are followed by lower amplitude syllables. Similarly, though not so clear in the displays, the two utterances begin with a syllable that was a high rising-falling "tone," followed by lower level tones in the noninitial syllables. These pitch and amplitude patterns create a sense of contour and rhythm that seem to encourage the parsing indicated by the observers.

A Definition of Canonical Utterance

A primary goal of our work is to expand infraphonological description into multisyllabic realms. The empirical data we have obtained regarding adult observer judgment of multisyllabic utterances in infant sounds suggest a summary of characteristics of infant utterances that seem to correspond to intuitively satisfying interpretations that we may be able to reconcile at some point with independently motivated characteristics of levels of rhythm in natural languages. In providing the following summary, we attempt to relate units that seem naturally to emerge from observation of infant vocal development to units that can be demonstrated to characterize the infrastructure of human phonology.

1. A canonical utterance consists of at least one minimal rhythmic unit (syllable).
2. Utterances are perceived as coherent units if they show integrity of contours (amplitude and pitch) and occur between breaths (glottal holds are more suggestive of continuation of a canonical utterance than are glottal releases).
3. The silent interval between two utterances exceeds the time frame usually allowed for a syllable margin (approximately 100–400 ms).

This definition summary (especially 2) suggests parallels between our notion of canonical utterance and the traditional notion "breath group." Because there is a wide range of possible durations for canonical utterances, no constraint on acceptable durations has been included. The longest canonical utterances produced by infants, however, are much shorter than a typical adult utterance. Thus, canonical utterances may be precursors to components of adult utterances, such as phonological phrases (see Cruttenden 1986). Constraints 2 and 3 suggest that there may be instances where the timing and other factors are at odds in utterance boundary marking. It will be important to begin to determine how conflicts of constraints are naturally resolved by the perceptual system and to develop a systematic approach to interpreting the infant's intentions with regard to utterance boundaries.

On Utterances and Utterance Clusters

Having once defined the utterance with sufficient intuitive validity that reliable judgments can be made, it quickly becomes clear that additional higher level rhythmic units also are present in infant vocalization samples. Infants even in the first few months of life produce structured sequences, or clusters, of utterances. These sequences may be of fundamental importance in the development of speech capabilities, but they have been essentially ignored in current research.

It is not clear what the optimal definition for the notion "utterance cluster" (UC) would be. However, it is clear that without any special training or instructions on how to group infant utterances, different observers show consistent awareness of groupings of consecutive infant utterances in real samples of vocalizations. In order to assess the ability of listeners to judge utterance clustering, we chose to test the matter with taped samples currently under study. In some samples, utterances are much easier to categorize than in others due to differences in factors such as the presence of obscuring adult voices on the tape, the state of the infant (fussy or angry babies yield utterances difficult to categorize because it proves hard to decide whether many utterances are reflexive/vegetative or not), the developmental level of the infant (older infants tend to be easier to categorize because the distinctiveness of their vegetative and nonvegetative utterances is greater), and so forth. Our approach to studying UC judgments under these circumstances was to choose one taped sample that was relatively difficult to categorize in terms of utterances, and one that was relatively easy.

The difficult-to-categorize tape-recorded sample was subjected to categorization by a designated standard observer who counted 70 nonvegetative utterances of an infant producing primarily precanonical sounds (the canonical babbling ratio [number of canonical syllables divided by number of utterances] was less than 0.1). We subjected the sample to a categorization in which three observers independently judged UCs by simply marking the standard categorization with brackets around utterances that seemed to "go together." No special definitions for the notions, "utterance cluster" or "go together," were given. The observers were required to work within the bounds of the utterance count provided. Note that many of the discrepancies in designation of UCs were potentially due to differences in how the observers would have counted utterances.

The results of the effort showed that the three observers all placed the majority of the 70 utterances in UCs (44, 47, and 59 for the three observers, respectively). The obtained UCs consisted of consecutive utterances. Sixty-eight percent of the utterances that were judged to be in a UC by the most conservative observer (the one who designated 44 as being in UCs) were judged to be grouped with the same consecutive utterances by all three observers. This proportion of agreement is actually quite high. Modelling of randomly placed UC bracketings of the same sizes (2 to 6 utterances) and numbers as those that were actually indicated by the observers yields agreement for three (randomly functioning) observers of only 30 to 40%.

The second tape was chosen to represent an easy-to-categorize sample. The same standard observer indicated 68 utterances from a six-month-old infant who was producing very high proportions of canonical syllables (canonical babbling ratio of 0.91). The three observers again placed the majority of utterances in UCs (53, 57, and 61, respectively). However, the agreement in this case was higher than in the difficult-to-categorize sample. Again, using the most conservative observer (the same individual as in the other case, this time indicating 53 utterances in clusters) as the basis for comparison, 96% of the utterances in the conservatively determined UCs were bracketed the same way by the other two observers. In fact, one of the liberal observers bracketed every one of the conservative judge's utterance clusters in exactly the same way. Clearly, when dealing with babbled utterances that are relatively easy to count, UC determination can be extremely reliable across different judges working with nothing more than their own intuitions about which utterances go together.

The question is, on what basis did observers judge UCs? It is important to consider the possibility that observer intuitions about utterance clustering reflect an underlying awareness of infraphonological constraints on discourse and its structure. By studying the nature of unambiguously clustered utterances we may gain insight into appropriate routes to take in the development of infraphonological models of complex rhythmic groupings. Specification of infraphonological conditions on discourse may foster a deepened study of infant vocal development.

In order to gain a perspective on criteria upon which utterances were judged to be clustered by the three observers in the test, spectrographic displays of the entirety of the easy-to-categorize sample were examined to determine the role of timing of silences in the decisions. Figure 5 shows the distribution of silent intervals between utterances within UCs (squares) and between the last utterance of any UC and the next occurring utterance (o's). In this display, all duration values were rounded to the nearest half second. Within UCs, the durations of silences (at utterance boundaries) ranged from 0.35 to 2.45 sec with a mean of 0.9 sec. The shortest silence between UCs was 1.75 sec and the mean value was nearly 10 sec. Obviously, timing plays an important role in determination of UC boundaries, because there is very little overlap between the distributions of within-UC and between-UC silent interval durations. But, the cases that do overlap are of special interest because they suggest that factors other than timing play a role in how observers judge UC boundaries, just as nontiming factors play a role in single-utterance boundary judgment.

Figure 6 displays the shortest inter-UC interval observed. The 1.75 sec silence between the UCs is shorter than one of the two within-UC interutterance intervals seen in figure 2. The question is, why is the shorter silence sufficient to cue the UC boundary while the longer silence is not? One possibility is that the coherency of acoustic patterns has an effect that can override timing in UC boundary judgments, much the same way it seems to operate in single-utterance boundary judgments. In figure 2, the three utterances, although widely spaced

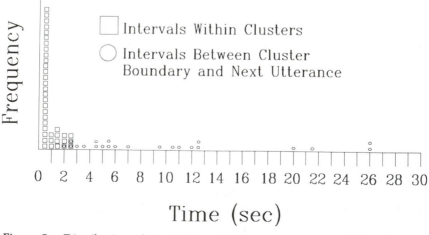

Figure 5.   Distribution of silent intervals between utterances within clusters and between cluster boundaries and the next occurring utterance.

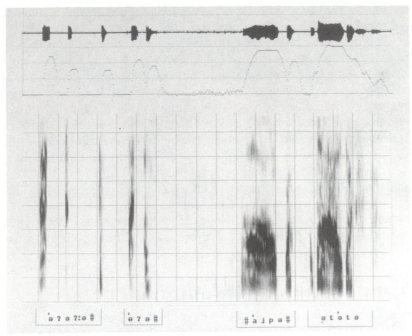

Figure 6. Spectrographic display of the two consecutive clusters with the shortest intercluster interval in the sample.

in time, bear important marks of similarity—all include canonical syllables, with stressed vowels judged to be low and front, and an unstressed central vowel as the initial syllable. In figure 6, on the other hand, the first UC (repeating the second part of figure 5), consists of glottal sequences with central vowels interrupted only by glottal stops, while the second UC shows two utterances with canonical syllables, including "true consonants" (Vihman 1986). The UC boundary seems to be determined by the fact that the child shifts from one coherent utterance pattern (glottal sequences) to another (canonical).

Not surprisingly, given the proximity in time of the two UCs, two of the three observers bracketed the sample in such a way that an utterance supercluster (USC) was indicated in the case of the sequence shown in figure 6. At the first order of utterance clustering, a boundary was indicated between the glottal sequences and the canonical utterances, but at the second order, the two UCs were united.

The other two cases where the durations of intercluster intervals were within the range of durations found for intervals within UCs are also suggestive of a phonetic coherency criterion motivating the UC decisions. In one case, the child shifted from quasivocalic sounds to a canonical syllable sequence, and, in the other, he shifted from a canonical syllable sequence with dental articulations to a canonical syllable sequence with labial articulations.

The durations of the UCs themselves indicate a range from less than two seconds to nearly twelve (mean = 4.6 sec). A closer look, however, at the UCs shows that a number of the longest were heard as having embedded UCs by one or more observers. The existence of consistently identified, embedded UCs suggests a level of structure beyond that of the most commonly identified UCs in the sample. Perhaps there are generally two UC levels in infants. When we break down the USCs that seem to be indicated in the present data into component UCs, the range of UC durations is restricted and falls from that indicated above to 3.2 sec. The longest UC, pictured in figure 7, is 7.7 sec and seems to be indivisible based upon any criteria that have been invoked by the observers—all its five utterances are quickly articulated canonical syllable patterns, and there are no long interutterance intervals.

Preliminary Definition of Canonical UC

In summarizing the observed patterns of clustering of utterances in the study, we again seek to preview the interrelationship of infant vocal patterns and patterns of intonational/metrical structure in mature natural languages. Anticipating the specification of independently motivated infraphonological constraints on vocal unit clustering, we propose the following:

1. A canonical UC is a temporal grouping of 2–6 (or more?) utterances that function as a unit.
2. Canonical UCs range in duration from 1–8 sec, with an optimal duration around three seconds, and are separated from other UCs by intervals in excess of 1.5 sec.
3. Canonical UCs are perceived as coherent by virtue of phonetic and/or suprasegmental resemblance among within-UCs.
4. USCs can be created of UCs by
   a. combining UCs separated at relatively long intervals, more than 1.5 sec and up to around 3 sec;
   b. embedding UCs that are differentiable in terms of phonetic coherency or are separated by relatively longer intervals (up to about 3 sec) than occur between utterances within UCs.

Again, it is tempting to propose that the 3 sec maximum suggested for intervals between UCs embedded within USCs be tied specifically to the optimal UC duration, which appears to be about 3 sec. It seems possible that both are related to the same underlying temporal inclinations of the human perceptual capacity.

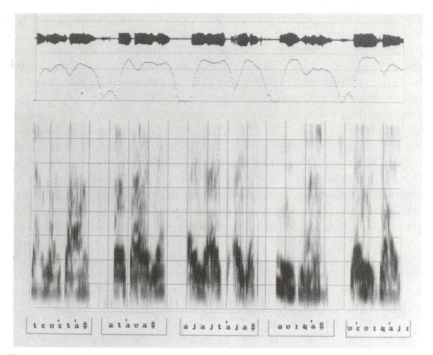

Figure 7.   Spectrographic display of the longest occurring minimal cluster of utterances in the sample.

The duration limits that seem to define utterances within UCs (interval duration > 100–400 ms, interval duration < 1.5 sec) and between UCs (interval > 1.5, < 3 sec) in the study of infant sounds are not far from values found to characterize short, medium, and long pauses in real speech samples as judged by adult listeners (Deese 1980).

Sources of Information on Infraphonological Constraints in Higher Order Rhythmic Units

There is a substantial literature in speech science and linguistics on acoustic means of boundary marking in natural languages. In our work on infant sounds, we have focused primarily on silent intervals, a boundary marker that is considered in depth with regard to adult speech in the field of "pausology" (see Dechert and Raupach 1980). Cruttenden (1986) reviews much of the relevant information on the broad scope of devices that languages use to mark boundaries. Each needs to be accounted for in an infraphonological model of higher order rhythmic units. The means include: (1) pauses, (2) contour unification (both pitch and amplitude play roles here), (3) group final special contours (rising and falling), (4) final syllable lengthening, and

(5) fixed (or nearly fixed) position for stress. The first two and perhaps the third of these methods seem to play roles in adult judgments of infant vocal groupings as indicated in the study reported above. Languages seem to apply principles associated with the first three methods in a relatively universal fashion. The fourth and fifth principles, on the other hand, are applied in language specific ways (some languages lengthen final vowels, others consonants—some languages have final stress, others initial, others do not have fixed stress, etc.). Interestingly, infants do not unambiguously show final lengthening in canonical babbling (Oller and Smith 1979), nor do they consistently show fixed stress positions. They may, however, be auditorily sensitive to final lengthening as a boundary marker (see Krumhansl and Jusczyk 1990). Presumably production of final lengthening and location of fixed stress are patterns that are learned as specific languages are acquired, while the other boundary marking methods are part of a more fundamental, more biologically stable rubric. As study of infraphonological development of higher order rhythmic units proceeds, it will be important to determine in some detail the schedule and manner of development of boundary marking devices.

Levels of rhythmic organization are characterized in a variety of modern theories of phonology. In particular metrical phonology (Liberman 1975; Liberman and Prince 1977; Hayes 1981) offers a perspective on the distinction between syntactic and intonational (or phonological) phrases, and summarizes levels of rhythmic organization and principles of relationship between rhythmic groups and among members of groups. We expect a variety of principles of metrical phonology to play critical roles in the interpretation of infant development of phonological rhythmic structure. An example of a metrical phonological principle that particularly calls out for study in infancy is the "culminative" principle, which suggests that at each level of metrical organization, units tend to have a head member. When and how such a principle may be manifest in infants is unclear, especially because infants commonly seem to produce sequences of reduplicated syllables of equal stress. The metrical distinction between light and heavy syllables (where heavy syllables tend to be closed, have tense full vowels, and tend to be heads) also suggests a potentially important inquiry into the relationship of syllable structure and apparent head members of infant utterances or utterance clusters.

While metrical phonology offers a variety of useful principles for the interpretation of infant sounds, it is our opinion that acoustic characteristics of phonological units at each level need to be specified in terms that cover additional ground. They should relate in a natural way to the levels of analysis of rhythmic units that emerge in studies of two particularly important nonlinguistic or semilinguistic realms—music and poetry—realms in which it appears that the deepest metrical tendencies of humanity are manifest in their most archetypal forms. The theory of musical structure of Lerdahl and Jackendoff (1983) has offered a series of insights that need to be addressed in the study of infant development of rhythmic structures. In particular the distinction between "grouping structure" and "metrical structure" suggests that the human ear may always be capable of differentiating phrasing (or coherency of sequential units) and beat structure of any musical passage. Put another way, one cannot predict where phrase boundaries will be based on where measures begin or end. If Lerdahl and Jackendoff are right, this independence of the two structural domains would appear to apply equally to poetry, and by implication to speech (at least sometimes). It raises the question about whether such an independence of realms can exist in infant vocalizations. Will infant phrasing (as manifest perhaps in our judgments of utterance and cluster boundaries) and infant beat structures be independent from the beginning? Or do they start unified and split at a critical developmental point?

The levels of vocal rhythmic structure that seem reasonable to posit for infants based on our experience clearly need to be related to levels of rhythmic structure that have been the focus of Metrical Phonology, musical theory, and theories of poetic meter. This we take to be a fundamental aspect of the task of infraphonological study of infant vocal rhythmic development. Although it is still very early in the process of study, four levels of structure seem apparent in infants (by the Canonical Stage at the latest): (1) syllables, (2) utterances, (3) minimal clusters, and (4) superclusters. To what levels of speech, music, or poetry do they correspond and how? Clearly a major study needs to be conducted on infants across the first year of life and into a succeeding year or two in order to gain a perspective on relationships of rhythmic groupings in infants and mature systems. At this point, however, certain suspicions are unavoidable.

The infant canonical syllable appears to function in a rhythmically identical manner to the mature syllable of speech or poetry or to the musical note. The infant utterance appears in the vast majority of cases to be composed of a single foot in the terminology of speech or poetry metrics; consequently, the mature speech distinction between foot and intonational or phonological phrase, has not often emerged in our study of infant sounds. Perhaps infants possess a level of organization that must branch at some point in development in order to produce a firm control of the distinction.

The infant minimal cluster seems to correspond to what Chafe (1980) called the "focus of consciousness" in speech groupings. In Turner's (1985) essays on poetic rhythmic organization, he refers to the "fundamental parcel" of human experience, a roughly three-second unit that is the most commonly occurring duration of a poetic line cross-linguistically. It is Turner's thesis that the three-second chunk is an optimal length for information because it is, as he puts it, "the length of the human present moment." One might imagine that if Turner is right, the master rhythm generated within our neural systems should be manifest in the organization of utterances produced in early infancy. Our attention was captured, indeed, by the fact that minimal utterance clusters in the study reported above had durations hovering around three seconds. In music, it seems clear that the infant's minimal clusters correspond to what has been called the musical phrase (see e.g., Lerdahl and Jackendoff 1983).

And the infant supercluster? Perhaps it matches a speech paragraph, or a poetic verse, or a musical passage. As the infraphonological modelling of speech systems expands in the effort to interpret the development of infant vocal capabilities, we are spurred on by the desire to comprehend the roots of language, and poetry, and song.

REFERENCES

Chafe, W. 1980. Some reasons for hesitating. In *Temporal Variables in Speech*, eds. H. Dechert and M. Raupach. The Hague: Mouton.
Clarke, E. F., and Krumhansl, C. L. 1990. Perceiving musical time. *Music Perception* 7:213–52.
Cruttenden, A. 1986. *Intonation*. New York: Cambridge University Press.
Cruttenden, A. 1970. A phonetic study of babbling. *British Journal of Disorders of Communication* 5(2):110–18.
Dechert, H. W., and Raupach, M. 1980. *Temporal Variables in Speech: Studies in Honor of Frieda Goldman-Eisler*. The Hague: Mouton.
Deese, J. 1980. Pauses, prosody and the demands of production in language. In *Temporal Variables in Speech*, eds. H. Dechert and M. Raupach. The Hague: Mouton.
Elbers, L., and Ton, J. 1985. Play pen monologues: The interplay of words and babbles in the first words period. *Journal of Child Language* 12:551–65.
Fernald, A., Taeschner, T., Dunn, J., Papousek, M., de Boysson-Bardies, B., and Fukui, I. 1989. A cross-language study of prosodic modifications in mothers' and fathers' speech to preverbal infants. *Journal of Child Language* 16:477–503.
Hayes, B. 1981. A metrical theory of stress rules. Ph.D. diss., MIT, Cambridge.
Holmgren, K., Lindblom, B., Aurelius, G., Jalling, B., and Zetterstrom, R. 1986. On the phonetics of infant vocalization. In *Precursors of Early Speech*, eds. B. Lindblom and R. Zetterstrom. New York: Stockton Press.
Irwin, O. C. 1947. Infant speech: Consonantal sounds according to place of articulation. *Journal of Speech and Hearing Disorders* 12:397–401.
Irwin, O. C., and Chen, H. P. 1946. Infant speech: Vowel and consonant frequency. *Journal of Speech Disorders* 11:123–25.
Jakobson, R. 1941. *Kindersprache, Aphasie, und allgemeine Lautgesetze*. Uppsala: Almqvist & Wiksell.
Kent, R. D., Osberger, M. J., Netsell, R., and Hustedde, C. G. 1987. Phonetic

development in identical twins who differ in auditory function. *Journal of Speech and Hearing Disorders* 52:64–75.

Koopmans-van Beinum, F. J., and van der Stelt, J. M. 1986. Early stages in the development of speech movements. In *Precursors of Early Speech*, eds. B. Lindblom and R. Zetterstrom. New York: Stockton Press.

Krumhansl, C. L., and Jusczyk, P. 1990. Infants' perception of phrase structure in music. *Psychological Science* 1(1):70–73.

Lerdahl, F., and Jackendoff, R. 1983. *A Generative Theory of Tonal Music.* Cambridge, MA: MIT Press.

Lewis, M. M. 1936. *Infant Speech: A Study of the Beginnings of Language.* New York: Harcourt Brace.

Liberman, M. 1975. The intonational system of English. Ph.D. diss., MIT, Cambridge.

Liberman, M., and Prince, A. 1977. On stress and linguistic rhythm. *Linguistic Inquiry* 8:249–336.

Lindblom, B. E. F. 1978. Final lengthening in speech and music. Paper presented at the Symposium on the Prosody of the Nordic Languages, Lund.

Locke, J. L., and Pearson, D. M. 1990. Linguistic significance of babbling: Evidence from a tracheostomized infant. *Journal of Child Language* 17(1):1–16.

Lynch, M. P., Oller, D. K., and Steffens, M. 1989. Development of speech-like vocalizations in a child with congenital absence of cochleas: The case of total deafness. *Journal of Applied Psycholinguistics* 10:315–33.

Lynip, A. 1951. The use of magnetic devices in the collection and analysis of the preverbal utterances of an infant. *Genetic Psychology Monograph* 44:221–62.

Mavilya, M. 1969. Spontaneous vocalizations and babbling in hearing impaired infants. Ph.D. diss., Columbia University, New York (Univ. Microfilms No. 70-12879).

Menyuk, P. 1968. The role of distinctive features in children's acquisition of phonology. *Journal of Speech and Hearing Research* 11:138–46.

Nakazima, S. A. 1962. A comparative study of the speech developments of Japanese and American English in childhood. *Studia Phonologica* II:27–46.

Oller, D. K. 1978. Infant vocalization and the development of speech. *Allied Health and Behavioral Sciences* 1:523–49.

Oller, D. K. 1986. Metaphonology and infant vocalizations. In *Precursors of Early Speech*, eds. B. Lindblom and R. Zetterstrom. New York: Stockton Press.

Oller, D. K., and Eilers, R. E. 1988. The role of audition in infant babbling. *Child Development* 59:441–49.

Oller, D. K., and Smith, B. L. 1979. Effect of final-syllable position on vowel duration in infant babbling. *Journal of the Acoustical Society of America* 62:994–97.

Oller, D. K., Eilers, R. E., Bull, D. H., and Carney, A. E. 1985. Pre-speech vocalizations of a deaf infant: A comparison with normal metaphonological development. *Journal of Speech and Hearing Research* 28:47–63.

Oller, D. K., Weiman, L. A., Doyle, W. J., and Ross, C. 1976. Infant babbling and speech. *Journal of Child Language* 3:1–11.

Papousek, M., and Papousek, H. 1988. Vocal dialogues between mother and infant. Presented at International and Interdisciplinary Symposium on Origins and Development of Nonverbal Vocal Communication: Evolutionary, Comparative, and Methodological Aspects, July 1988, Munich.

Papousek, M., Papousek, H., and Bornstein, M. 1985. The naturalistic vocal environment of young infants: On the significance of homogeneity and variability in parental speech. In *Social Perception in Infants*, eds. T. Field and N. Fox. Norwood, NJ: Ablex.

Papousek, M., Papousek, H., and Haekel, M. 1987. Didactic adjustments in fathers' and mothers' speech to their three-month-old infants. *Journal of Psycholinguistic Research* 16:491–516.

Rochester, S. R. 1973. The significance of pauses in spontaneous speech. *Journal of Psycholinguistic Research* 2:51–81.

Roug, L., Landberg, I., and Lundberg, L. J. 1989. Phonetic development in early infancy: A study of 4 Swedish children during the first 18 months of life. *Journal of Child Language* 16:19–40.

Ryan, M. L. 1978. Contour in context. In *Recent Advances in the Psychology of Language*, eds. R. N. Campbell and P. T. Smith. New York: Plenum Press.

Smith, B. L., and Oller, D. K. 1981. A comparative study of pre-meaningful vocalizations produced by normally developing and Down's syndrome infants. *Journal of Speech and Hearing Disorders* 46:46–51.

Smith, B. L., Brown-Sweeney, S., and Stoel-Gammon, C. 1989. A quantitative analysis of reduplicated and variegated babbling. *First Language* 9:175–89.

Stark, R. E. 1980. Stages of speech development in the first year of life. In *Child Phonology* Vol. 1, eds. G. Yeni-Komshian, J. Kavanagh, and C. Ferguson. New York: Academic Press.

Stark, R. E. 1983. Phonatory development in young normally hearing and hearing impaired children. In *Speech of the Hearing Impaired: Research, Training, and Personnel Preparation*, eds. I. Hochberg, H. Levitt, and M. J. Osberger. Baltimore: University Park Press.

Stark, R. E., Ansel, B. M., and Bond, J. 1989. Are prelinguistic abilities predictive of learning disability? A follow-up study. In *Preschool Prevention of Reading Failure*, eds. R. L. Masland and M. Masland. Parkton, MD: York Press.

Stern, D., Spieker, S., and MacKain, K. 1982. Intonation contours as signals in maternal speech to prelinguistic infants. *Developmental Psychology* 18:727–35.

Stoel-Gammon, C. 1988. Prelinguistic vocalizations of hearing-impaired and normally hearing subjects: A comparison of consonantal inventories. *Journal of Speech and Hearing Disorders* 53(3):302–15.

Stoel-Gammon, C., and Cooper, J. A. 1984. Patterns of early lexical and phonological development. *Journal of Child Language* 11:247–71.

Stoel-Gammon, C., and Otomo, K. 1986. Babbling development of hearing-impaired and normally hearing subjects. *Journal of Speech and Hearing Disorders* 51:33–41.

Turner, F. 1985. *Natural Classicism: Essays on Literature and Science*. New York: Paragon House.

van der Stelt, J. M., and Koopmans-van Beinum, F. J. 1986. The onset of babbling related to gross motor development. In *Precursors of Early Speech*, eds. B. Lindblom and R. Zetterstrom. New York: Stockton Press.

Vanvik, A. 1971. The phonetic-phonemic development of a Norwegian child. *Norsk Tidsskrift for Sprogvidenskap*, SSIV, Oslo.

Vihman, M. M. 1986. Individual differences in babbling and early speech: Predicting to age three. In *Precursors of Early Speech*, eds. B. Lindblom and R. Zetterstrom. New York: Stockton Press.

Vihman, M. M., and Miller, R. 1988. Words and babble at the threshold of language acquisition. In *The Emergent Lexicon*, eds. M. D. Smith and J. L. Locke. San Diego, CA: Academic Press.

Vihman, M. M., Ferguson, C. A., and Elbert, M. 1986. Phonological development from babbling to speech: Common tendencies and individual differences. *Applied Psycholinguistics* 7:3–40.

Zlatin, M. 1975. Explorative mapping of the vocal tract and primitive syllabification in infancy: The first six months. Paper presented at the American Speech and Hearing Association Convention, Washington, D.C.

Reading

Chapter • 19

The Emergence of Sounds
Parallels between Learning to Read and Learning to Speak

David Barton

INTRODUCTION: TWO SEPARATE ACTIVITIES

In this chapter I document developments in reading research over the past decade so as to demonstrate that two areas that were thought of as quite distinct are in fact closely entwined, and that there are lessons for child phonology to be learned from investigating recent literacy research.

The 1978 Bethesda conference on child phonology is a useful reference point from which to start. The two volumes reporting this conference (Yeni-Komshian, Kavanagh, and Ferguson 1980) can be seen as a comprehensive statement of the state of child phonology at that time. In the twenty-four chapters there is no mention of reading, writing, or spelling. This is not in any way intended as a criticism: it is a comment on the state of the field of language acquisition at that time. The area of literacy was viewed as a quite distinct topic from the acquisition of phonology with no obvious areas of overlap: One is "natural" and "acquired," the other is "imposed" and "taught"—the way of learning associated with each is different and takes place separately at different periods in the child's development. The acquisition of phonology was something that ended at the age of five years. There is no mention of children older than five years except some work on language-delayed children (such as in Menyuk's chapter) and the point that children's speech is not adult-like in phonetic detail (as in Allen and Hawkins' chapter). Although reading was not an explicit topic at that conference, it is still surprising that it was not mentioned in passing.

A similar point can be made about the literature on learning to read. In overviews of learning to read from that period, there is little mention of the acquisition of phonology nor of other areas of language acquisition. For example, if we examine the list of issues in Chall's survey volume (Chall 1983), it is instructive to see what is not covered: how little mention there is of language acquisition or of spoken language. In general, learning to speak and learning to read and write were seen as quite separate activities. Learning to speak finished at age five, while learning to read began at age five. Any signs of literate behavior before five years were marginalized as prereading behaviors.

There were some exceptions to this view of reading. Two people who were making the link between speaking and reading were Carol Chomsky (1972) and Ragnhild Söderbergh (1977), both arguing the similarity of the two forms of learning. These views were not incorporated into reading research at the time and their relevance for child phonology was not apparent. In particular, Söderbergh argued that children could learn both speaking and reading "at the same age and in the same way" (1977, p. 8). It is this position that has become more widespread and that I examine more closely here.

Now it is possible to say more about similarities between speaking and reading and to incorporate both into a coherent approach to language learning. To argue this, I describe one concrete example of reading research that has something to say about the development of sounds, work on *invented spellings.* Then I examine how it can be seen as part of a whole new approach to understanding reading and writing, *emergent literacy.*

THE EXAMPLE OF INVENTED SPELLINGS

Read (1975) and others (e.g., Bissex 1980) have studied invented spellings of children. Read's original work was with preschool children. These children were a small proportion of children who learned to write without formal teaching before going to school, and who, with a basic knowledge of letter names, were willing to guess at and invent their own spellings in the words and messages they wrote. An example would be a notice on a bedroom door:

DO.NAT KM.IN.ANE.MOR.JST.LETL.KES

These messages contain some correct (conventional) spellings, some partly learned spellings and some invented spellings. In this particular message (from Bissex 1980, p. 23), *Do not come in anymore. Just little kids,* we also see information about the segmentation of speech and its analysis into units such as words.

In his original study, Read noticed that where children invented spellings, they invented broadly similar spellings; they seemed to be working on consistent principles. He provides explanations of their spellings in terms of children's knowledge of the sounds of the language. The example above provides instances of most of the principles. Read's data provide examples covering several phenomena of interest to the development of phonology. (They are all examples reflecting American English pronunciation; British English examples are slightly different).

Vowels

The problem in spelling vowel sounds is that English has only five symbols for twenty-odd vowel sounds. Children started with the letter names, letting the letters stand for the sounds of the names, for example:

> *FAS* for *face*
> *LADE* for *lady*
> *TIGR* for *tiger*
> *BOT* for *boat*
> *UNITD* for *united*.

This is relatively straightforward, but what is interesting is how they represented other vowels. One consistent pattern Read observed was the spelling of lax vowels in words like *fish* and *pen*. These had a spelling that is not correct and that is unlikely to have been suggested by adults:

> *PAN* for *pen*
> *LAFFT* for *left*
> *FES* for *fish*
> *SEP* for *ship*.

This solution is unlikely to be suggested by adults in that English spelling makes a different grouping, using an *A* for *FAT* and *FATE*, while using an *I* for both *BIT* and *BITE*. Read's explanation, which seems quite reasonable, is that the children are making a phonetic judgment of identifying the closest sound. In terms of place of articulation the letter name closest to [e] is the letter *A* and the letter name closest to [i] is the letter *E*.

Nasals

Children had no problem with initial nasals or with final nasals, but they tended to omit nasals before other consonants in clusters:

HOM for *home*
NIT for *night*
BOPY for *bumpy*
NUBRS for *numbers*
AD for *and*
AGRE for *angry*
MOSTR for *monster.*

The *-ing* ending was typically spelled *EG:*

SOWEMEG for *swimming*
FEHEG for *fishing.*

There was a greater likelihood of omitting nasals before unvoiced rather than voiced stops (Read 1975, p. 59), but this tendency was not overwhelming. Phonetically, preconsonantal nasals in English are of very short duration and often the nasalization of the vowel is a more important cue to the presence of a nasal. Children's spellings reflect the fleetingness of preconsonantal nasals. There are interesting parallels between children's spellings and their gradual mastery of nasals when learning to speak (Smith 1973, pp. 13, 22) as well as diachronic loss of preconsonantal nasals (Ferguson 1975, pp. 183–184).

Tr-

Children's spellings of *tr-* and *dr-* again reflect consistent phonetic judgments. Phonetically the [t] of *trip* differs from the [t] of the initial singleton stop in *tip;* it is an affricate with a pronunciation between [t] and [ch]. This is reflected in children's spellings:

CHRAY for *tray*
CHRIBLS for *troubles*
CWNCHRE for *country*
JRAGIN for *dragon.*

What is important from all these examples is the consistency and the coherence of children's judgments. When learning to spell, these children are not learning a set of rules of the correct way to act, rather they are trying to work something out on the basis of their knowledge of language. They display knowledge of the sound system of English. They are working on a principle, which is not completely accurate for English, that there is a one-to-one relationship between letters and sounds. Where there is not an appropriate letter they are making co-herent guesses as to which letter fits the best.

This original work was with preschool children who invented their own ways of spelling. Other work has examined children in school, children learning different languages, and adults with spelling prob-lems. More recently, Read (1985) has reviewed children's spellings in different languages and has demonstrated that the deviant spellings that children produce reflect the particular structure of the language they are using. Some of the studies were of invented spellings, while in others they were of the products of dictations given by teachers. To take the example of the spelling of nasals, in Spanish and Dutch there are similar deletions to those described above for English; however, such deletions appear to be much less common in French, which cer-tainly has preconsonantal nasal vowels, in words such as *enfant* and *pinceaux*. Comparing English and French, Read identifies the crucial difference as being that French has a preponderance of open syllables. The preconsonantal nasals which children tend to omit in English usu-ally occur in closed syllables. This brief example suggests that chil-dren's spellings reflect subtleties in the phonological structure of spe-cific languages.

In our own work studying children and adults learning to read, we have observed similar invented spellings and argue that judgments of there being a [t] in *tr-*, for example, come only from experience with the written word (see Barton 1985). Literacy may give adults an additional way of operating on language, but it obscures other knowledge, so that only literate people think that *train* begins with a [t] sound or that the word pronounced [evri] contains three syllables. We can see that by becoming literate, adults have lost some phonetic judgments. As Read puts it "beginning students of phonetics usually have to work to ac-quire (or reacquire) the judgments which the kindergarten children can make" (Read 1978, p. 78). (Parallels can be made with Werker and Pegg's claims, this volume, about very young children losing the ability to make certain judgments.)

EMERGENT LITERACY

Having given a detailed example, I now want to turn to contemporary literacy research and to a framework that provides a way of making sense of the invented spelling research and of incorporating it into a general way of thinking about learning. One of the most significant developments in reading research over the past decade has been the move toward examining in detail the period before children formally learn to read. This is not a search for prerequisites or precursors, with the idea of reading and prereading. Rather, it emphasizes the gradualness of learning to read; this area is united under the term *emergent literacy*.

The approach is captured best in two collections of papers, Goelman, Oberg, and Smith (1984) and Teale and Sulzby (1986), and is summarized in a short book by Hall (1987). In fact, emergent literacy is not yet at a point where there is a set of key ideas that everyone agrees with, and not everyone in the two books of readings necessarily subscribes to one common view. Nevertheless, emergent literacy does represent the beginnings of a new and coherent approach to learning to read and write. It covers topics such as:

—early spoken language and its relation to reading and writing;
—social influences of home and community;
—parent-child interactions around reading;
—children's roles in these activities;
—learning in different cultures.

In the remainder of this chapter I bring together some of the key aspects of emergent literacy, ones that make it distinct from earlier approaches to reading and writing, and see how there are parallels for the acquisition of phonology. I want to make four points, that: *preparations for learning to read begin at an early age*; and that *children participate actively in their learning*; this leads to *questioning the existence of linear skills and of ordered stages*; and results in a view of *learning as a purposeful social activity*.

Early Learning

Part of the interest in what happens in the first five years of life has come from an interest in early readers, children who learn to read before going to school. A significant number of children turn up at school being able to read, the very job to which schools devote so much energy. The idea of early reading has been well documented, discussed, and promoted, and people have addressed the question of how it is that children across a broad range of abilities and social classes can learn to read apparently effortlessly and with no formal teaching. A thorough study of early readers is the work of M. Clark (1976, 1984); she investigated the background of thirty-two children who could read when they entered school. She tried to find what these thirty-two children had in common. She ruled out intelligence or social class and concluded that the main thing the children shared was a desire to read, along with strong oral involvement of the parents. Other researchers, such as Söderbergh, mentioned earlier, and Steinberg and Steinberg (1975) studied children who were learning to read as they learned to speak, in the Steinbergs' case a child who learned to read some letters before beginning to speak.

Early reading is obviously a significant phenomenon, but it is only the tip of the iceberg. Only a few children can actually read unaided before they enter school, but their existence does make us examine more closely the abilities of other children. There are many more children who cannot read when they start school; nevertheless, they bring with them a great deal of knowledge about the task before them. They know a lot about reading and learning to read. This is reflected in the research that has investigated children's awareness of and knowledge of language before formal schooling. One general conclusion from this research is that many children know a lot about reading and writing before reaching school and certainly much more than schools have traditionally taken account of.

In "mainstream" culture, children learn about literacy from an early age. There is more to learn about literacy than the alphabet and phonic rules. Children do not just learn how to read, they learn about literacy: they learn about the role of books and the significance of literacy. They learn, for example, that books are for reading, for talking about, and that pictures are for naming. The whole treatment of books is very different from the treatment of toys, which are played with and acted upon. Snow and Ninio (1986) talk of children learning "the contracts of literacy."

One way in which early learning is important then is that children come across written material at an early age and can understand much about literacy before they can read and write. Another sense in which early learning is significant is that learning to speak is a preparation for learning to read. What children know about spoken language is important and can be drawn upon when approaching reading and writing. This is obvious from research on invented spelling, where children apply their knowledge of sounds to the task of writing. What is important for our discussion is that we cannot separate learning to speak and learning to read: the two activities overlap in time, and children use their knowledge from one in learning the other. Related to this, there is nothing special about the age of five years. There is no reason to wait until age five before teaching children about literacy and, although more ways of learning are available to the child, there is no absolute difference between what children can do before or after this age.

Active Learning

Children are active learners. This is apparent in Read's work which shows that, on their own, children actively work out spellings of words. Part of the meaning of *emergent* is that the child does the work, makes the effort; the child makes sense of the activity and organizes and reorganizes his or her own knowledge.

The division between teaching and learning breaks down. The distinction is often made between the "naturalness" of learning to speak compared with the imposed nature of formal teaching. However, what the child is doing in the two situations is very similar. Children actively work things out. This idea is made explicit in Bissex's notion of the child as teacher (1984), that children teach themselves. Snow (1983) also expands on this point when discussing several of the parallels between reading and general language acquisition. Crucial to active learning is children's developing awareness. As children get older, their growing awareness gives the possibility of more explicit teaching, with explanations. Additional ways of learning are available with reading. To some extent these are socially constructed ways of learning put together before age five.

There have always been anecdotes about children's awareness of language in the child phonology literature. Leopold's classic four volumes contain many examples of his child's observations and questions about the sounds of language, for example the child asking about his grandfather's accent (Leopold 1949). Smith, in his study of his child, makes many comments about the child's awareness, such as when being pressed by his father to pronounce the first sound in *jump*, the child says in exasperation, "Only daddy can say dup" (Smith 1973). These observations have always remained anecdotes, mentioned but not seen as central to the business of learning to speak. Certainly, they were not incorporated into the theories of acquisition that were being proposed and debated. One study where awareness is more central is Weir's study of the presleep monologues of her child (Weir 1962). The child's awareness of sounds and deliberate practicing and learning were the essence of this study, but again these phenomena were not incorporated into theories of the acquisition of phonology. As Elbers put it at the Stanford conference, our theories of child development "don't care whether the child has awareness or not."

It is in studies of reading and in the general psycholinguistic literature that attention has been paid to children's developing awareness. Individual studies of children's awareness of language and its significance for learning to read go back more than two decades with research such as Reid's asking children about the uses and purposes of reading (Reid 1966). Awareness was aired as an important topic at an earlier NICHD conference that resulted in the book *Language by Ear and by Eye* (Kavanagh and Mattingly 1972). In the past decade, there has been a great deal of research into language awareness at all linguistic levels. It has moved from being seen as peripheral to being a common and coherent phenomenon crucial to learning. This interest is part of a general move toward examining the significance of metafunctioning. At the same time it is a complex phenomenon with awareness being studied at many different levels of language. (See, for example, articles in Sinclair, Jarvella, and Levelt 1978; Downing and Valtin 1984). The connections between children's developing awareness of the sound system and learning to read are pursued in Bradley's chapter in this volume.

Deliberate learning and actively being aware become more central in learning as children get older and have greater awareness and control over their learning. Nevertheless, this awareness is a part of the acquisition of phonology from early on. Early awareness is exhibited in the presleep monologues reported by Weir, for example. Of the various approaches to the acquisition of phonology, cognitive theories that stress the active role of the child, the child as active hypothesis-maker (e.g., Macken and Ferguson 1983; Menn 1985), seem most appropriate. In emphasizing the active nature of learning these theories are aligned with recent developments in reading. It now seems possible to have a view of learning that covers both reading and speaking.

I think the points made so far are relatively noncontroversial. The remaining two points are more basic and represent a reconceptualization of what learning to read is.

No Linear Skills or Stages

A decade ago, the best way of conceptualizing learning to read was to regard it as the development of a set of skills, added on one at a time. An example of research in this paradigm was the work on how awareness influences learning to read, whether awareness facilitates reading or whether reading facilitates awareness; whether one is a prerequisite for the other. This approach was one of looking for the skills that contribute to reading, the prerequisites, the precursors. Reading was built from its components. An example of this would be Downing's work on reading readiness, with the idea of children moving from "cognitive confusion" to "cognitive clarity" (Downing 1979.) This approach is now being criticized in the emergent literacy literature. (In fact, if we look back at the invented spelling research, to regard what the children are doing when they invent their own spellings as reflecting "cognitive confusion" would be totally missing the absolute clarity of the child who decides to spell *ticket* as *TIKIT* or *yacht* as *YOT*.)

Reading and speaking are not best thought of as a set of subskills learned separately and later put together, with all children going through the same linear progression. When learning to speak, children are communicating from the beginning, doing the best they can with limited abilities and utilizing all their current knowledge. They engage in purposeful, real-life activities from the beginning. It is accepted that in learning phonology children are engaged in a total activity, and developmental phonology has placed a premium on studying ordinary spontaneous speech. Similarly, with early literacy at home, children get involved in real activities in learning to read or write. We can see this in the three-year-old poring over TV schedules to find the words *Sesame Street*, writing simple messages, and writing names on possessions.

Children engage in whole activities; they try to communicate: they are not trying to use short-term memory, to perceive things, to learn phonic rules. They bring in all their current knowledge to solve everyday problems. In carrying out complex real live activities, children do not all act the same. Different children may solve the same task in different ways. In learning to speak children follow individual coherent paths of development. Children approach the microtasks of learning phonology in different ways. There can be different routes to the same end. Recent emergent literacy research also emphasizes variability. An example is to be seen when adults read to children. Reading to children takes many forms and means many different things. There is not one way of reading to children (Teale 1984).

There is not a linear progression in the acquisition of phonology, there are not precise stages in any detailed way. While there is obviously a biological base, the acquisition of phonology is not some biological unfolding uninfluenced by context. This has been known and accepted in child phonology for some time but, in the 1978 proceedings, the lack of ordered stages seems to have been a fact that did not quite fit with the general way of seeing things. (See, for example, Ingram et al. 1980 and Ferguson 1978 on fricatives.) Rather than regarding this as a hindrance, it can become the cornerstone of a whole way of thinking about learning.

Finally, there is no tidy set of stages through which all children progress. Except in a very general way, there are not obvious orderings or sequences. The orders individual children pursue are built upon what they know already and are strongly influenced by the social context and the interaction. The notion of stage may be useful if we are being very general, such as when referring to the stage of babbling or of early words. However, if we look in detail at any area within these broad stages, such as the acquisition of fricatives, there are no clear stages. (See also Kent's comparison, this volume, of different proposals for stages and the lack of match between them.) We probably need to move away from the notion of stages completely. This is one area where child phonology could reconceptualize its approach.

A Social Activity

I have said that the nature and direction of children's learning is influenced by the social context and by social interaction. The importance of social aspects is being realized as researchers study children learning to speak and learning to read in different cultures. Social context is not just an extra variable that has to be taken into account; rather, social approaches require us to take a fresh look at what is meant by learning. We need to accept that learning is not purely a cognitive activity—it has a social basis. Research on reading moved from a visual or physiological paradigm to a cognitive one more than two decades ago. It is now beginning to move from a cognitive paradigm to a social one. (Explanations of learning to read seem to be in a transition stage at present; social phenomena are studied but cognitive explanations are appealed to. An example of this is to be found in the interesting collection of papers edited by Bertelson [1987] that are interpreted within a cognitive framework; to my mind the argument could be developed [e.g., p. 4] by including some social perspective on learning.)

In the emergent literacy research, it is accepted that there is a social basis to the learning. When speaking or writing, children are trying to achieve other ends; speaking and writing are purposeful social activities—to tell someone something, to ask, to request. Emergent activities are supported by the environment. This is a further part of the meaning of *emergent;* that when they first appear, activities are partly external, they are supported, scaffolded, by the environment. This support is gradually withdrawn as children develop. Even the notion of abilities is called into question if we accept that context is always making a contribution to children's performance; how well a child performs depends on the nature of the environmental support.

There are implications of all this for developmental phonology. The emergent literacy approach reinforces the idea that ways of learning are culturally based. There is now a considerable amount of research emphasizing the extent to which social interaction around learning to speak and learning to read differs qualitatively in different subcultures within the United States (e.g., Fishman 1991; Heath 1983) and in different cultures throughout the world (e.g., Ochs 1983, 1988; Schieffelin 1979; Schieffelin and Ochs 1986). For example, the emphasis in our culture on naming, on labeling, and on identifying individual words as children learn to speak is in many ways a preparation for literacy. These culturally acquired ways of learning probably have as much effect on the acquisition of phonology as they do on learning to read.

The issues that arose in the previous section when we questioned the existence of skills and stages need to be understood within a social framework, not purely a cognitive one. Variability, for instance, has always been recognized in child phonology (e.g., Yeni-Komshian, Kavanagh, and Ferguson 1980); again, it can be seen as central and, most importantly, individual variation is not purely to do with individual cognitive differences between children. Such differences need to be understood within a social framework. It is difficult to think of the development of phonology in these terms, as the social basis of the learning of sounds has been virtually ignored. There has been a little work on parental influences (see Menn 1985, p. 91), but little else. More attention needs to be paid to this.

SUMMARY

In summary, these parallels between reading and speaking bring them much closer together. We now have a much greater understanding of Söderbergh's claim about children learning both speaking and reading "at the same age and in same way." Crucially, similar ways of learning underlie the two.

The point I have tried to keep to in this chapter has been to examine what recent reading research can contribute to our understanding of phonological development. Many of the things I have said about reading reinforce current approaches to phonology. The emergent approach makes phenomena such as individual differences and awareness central. Child phonology has always had a set of phenomena it is slightly ashamed of. They should take center stage and become basic to its theory of learning.

REFERENCES

Barton, D. 1985. Awareness of language units in adults and children. In *Progress in the Psychology of Language*, Vol. I, ed. A. Ellis. Hillsdale, NJ: Lawrence Erlbaum Associates.

Bertelson, P. 1987. *The Onset Of Literacy*. Cambridge, MA: MIT Press.

Bissex, G. 1980, *Gnys at Wrk: A Child Learns To Read and Write*. Cambridge: Harvard University Press.

Bissex, G. 1984. The child as teacher. In *Awakening to Literacy*, eds. H. Goelman, A. Oberg, and F. Smith. London: Heinemann.

Chall, J. 1983. *Learning to Read: The Great Debate*, 2nd edition. New York: McGraw Hill.

Chomsky, C. 1972. Write first, read later. *Childhood Education* 47:296–99.

Clark, M. M. 1976. *Young Fluent Readers*. London: Heinemann.

Clark, M. M. 1984. Literacy at home and at school. In *Awakening to Literacy*, eds. H. Goelman, A. Oberg, and F. Smith. London: Heinemann.

Downing, J. 1979. *Reading and Reasoning*. New York: Springer.

Downing, J., and Valtin, R. (eds.) 1984. *Language Awareness and Learning to Read*. New York: Springer.

Ferguson, C. A. 1975. Universal tendencies and 'normal' nasality. In *Nasálfest*, eds. C. A. Ferguson, L. M. Hyman, and J. J. Ohala. Stanford, CA: Department of Linguistics, Stanford University.

Ferguson, C. A. 1978. Fricatives in child language acquisition. In *Papers on Linguistics and Child Language: Ruth Hirsch Weir Memorial Volume*, eds. V. Honsa and M. J. Hardman-de-Bautista. The Hague: Mouton.

Fishman, A. 1991. Because this is who we are: Writing in the Amish community. In *Writing in the Community*, eds. D. Barton and R. Ivanic. Beverley Hills, CA: Sage.

Goelman, H., Oberg, A., and Smith, F. (eds.) 1984. *Awakening to Literacy*. London: Heinemann.

Hall, N. 1987. *The Emergence of Literacy*. New York: Edward Arnold.

Heath, S. B. 1983. *Ways With Words*. Cambridge: Cambridge University Press.

Ingram, D., Christensen, L., Veach, S., and Webster, B. 1980. The acquisition of word-initial fricatives and affricates in English by children between 2 and 6 years. In *Child Phonology, Vol. 1, Production*, eds. G. H. Yeni-Komshian, J. F. Kavanagh, and C. A. Ferguson. New York: Academic Press.

Kavanagh, J. F., and Mattingly, I. G. (eds.) 1972. *Language by Ear and by Eye*. Cambridge, MA: MIT Press.

Leopold, W. F. 1949. *Speech Development of a Bilingual Child*. 4 vols. Evanston, IL: Northwestern University Press.

Macken, M. A., and Ferguson, C. A. 1983. Cognitive aspects of phonological development: Model, evidence and issues. In *Children's Language*, Vol. 4, ed. K. Nelson. Hillsdale, NJ: Lawrence Erlbaum Associates.

Menn, L. 1985. Phonological development. In *The Development of Language*, ed. J. Berko Gleason. Columbus, OH: Merrill.

Ochs, E. 1983. Cultural dimensions of language acquisition. In *Acquiring Conversational Competence*, eds. E. Ochs and B. B. Schieffelin. London: Routledge & Kegan Paul.

Ochs, E. 1988. *Culture and Language Development*. Cambridge: Cambridge University Press.

Read, C. 1975. *Children's Categorization of Speech Sounds in English*. Urbana, IL: National Council of Teachers of English.

Read, C. 1978. Children's awareness of language, with emphasis on sound systems. In *The Child's Conception of Language*, eds. A. Sinclair, R. J. Jarvella, and W. J. M. Levelt. New York: Springer.

Read, C. 1985. Effects of phonology on beginning spelling: Some cross-linguistic evidence. In *Literacy, Language and Learning*, eds. D. R. Olson, A. Hildyard, and N. Torrance. Cambridge: Cambridge University Press.

Reid, J. F. 1966. Learning to think about reading. *Educational Research* 9:56–62.

Schieffelin, B. B. 1979. Getting it together. In *Developmental Pragmatics*, eds. E. Ochs and B. B. Schieffelin. New York: Academic Press.

Schieffelin, B. B., and Ochs, E. (eds.) 1986. *Language Socialization Across Cultures*. Cambridge: Cambridge University Press.

Sinclair, A., Jarvella, R. J., and Levelt, W. J. M. (eds.) 1978. *The Child's Conception of Language*. New York: Springer.

Smith, N. 1973. *The Acquisition of Phonology*. Cambridge: Cambridge University Press.

Snow, C. 1983. Literacy and language: Relationships during the preschool years. *Harvard Educational Review* 55:165–89.

Snow, C., and Ninio, A. 1986. The contracts of literacy. In *Emergent Literacy: Writing and Reading*, eds. W. H. Teale and E. Sulzby. NJ: Ablex.

Söderbergh, R. 1977. *Reading in Early Childhood*. Washington, DC: Georgetown University Press.

Steinberg, D. T., and Steinberg, M. T. 1975. Reading before speaking. *Visible Language* 9:197–224.

Teale, W. H. 1984. Reading to young children. In *Awakening to Literacy*, eds. H. Goelman, A. Oberg, and F. Smith. London: Heinemann.

Teale, W. H., and Sulzby, E. (eds.) 1986. *Emergent Literacy: Writing and Reading*. NJ: Ablex.

Weir, R. 1962. *Language in the Crib*. The Hague: Mouton.

Yeni-Komshian, G., Kavanagh, J. F., and Ferguson, C. A. (eds.) 1980. *Child Phonology*. Vols. 1 and 2. New York: Academic Press.

Chapter • 20

Rhymes, Rimes, and Learning to Read and Spell

Lynette Bradley

The recent comprehensive report on learning to read by Adams (1990) is the latest of several excellent reviews that have as their central theme the relationship between phonological development and learning to read (Liberman 1985; Stanovich 1987; Wagner and Torgesen 1987; Brady and Shankweiler 1991). Together they detail diverse research reports on different aspects of phonological processing, the reciprocal relationship between phonological awareness and reading, the importance of the orthography, and many issues that still need to be investigated. Yet the papers demonstrate a substantial consensus: phonological development and success in reading are inextricably linked. This chapter explores only one of these strands, not because it is any more important than the others, but because it is possible to trace the origins of this part of the story to the preschool period, where most of the other chapters in this volume are set.

PHONOLOGICAL AWARENESS AND READING

For some time there has been growing evidence that performance on phonological awareness tasks is one of the most potent predictors of early reading acquisition (Share et al. 1984; Stanovich, Cunningham, and Cramer 1984; Tunmer and Nesdale 1985). In their impressive study, Share and his colleagues (1984) looked at a wide variety of factors—39 in all—related to reading achievement in a sample of 543 five-year-old

Australian children starting school for the first time. The phonological task Share used was adapted from Helfgott (1976). The child listened to a word and had to say the initial phoneme and then the remainder of the word with the initial phoneme elided. Then the child was asked to segment the word into initial, medial, and final phonemes. This test, and a test of naming alphabetic letters, proved to be the best predictors of early reading at the end of the first and second years of schooling.

Although Share included the task because other studies had indicated that children need to be explicitly aware that speech consists of phonemic units when learning to read an alphabetic script, the result was surprising to some extent. Earlier, Liberman and her colleagues at Haskins Laboratories (Liberman et al. 1973, 1974) had shown how difficult it was for preschool children to recognize that words and syllables can be divided into phonemes. They found that children could not tap out the number of phonemes in a word consistently until the age of six, and even then 30% of the sample were not successful. At Cambridge, Bruce (1964) asked children to imagine what a word would sound like if a particular sound were taken away from it, for example what the word "stand" would be like without the "t" sound, and concluded that the task was too difficult for children younger than seven. Even illiterate Portuguese adults found equivalent phonological tasks more difficult than did literate adults from a similar background (Morais et al. 1979). The implication that success on such tasks is a consequence of learning to read has been amply supported by the studies of Ehri and colleagues. Her studies have consistently shown that orthographic knowledge affects speech-based processing (Ehri and Wilce 1980; Ehri 1984).

On the other hand the influential work of Clay has clearly demonstrated how much young children learn before they come to school (Clay 1987; Barton this volume), and we know from our own studies how many four- and five-year-old children we have had to exclude from projects because they have already begun to read. So it is quite possible that children in the Share et al. (1984) study could cope with this rather sophisticated phonological task because they had already begun to read. It might not have been a prerequisite of reading at all, because reading was not tested before the study began, but that some of the children had learned to analyze words into their constituent phonemes as a result of their early experience with print. However it would be premature to conclude from this converging evidence that all phonological awareness develops as a consequence of learning to read, as some investigators have suggested. The addition or subtraction of phonemes is just one way of testing phonological awareness, and a rather complex one at that (Yopp 1988). Phonological tasks can be managed by quite young children when they are presented in an appropriate way. Preschool children as young as three years of age were given segmentation tasks by Fox and Routh (1975) with some degree of success. The children were asked to say "just a little bit" of a phrase, a word, or a syllable. The four- and five-year-old children in this study achieved 70% accuracy in segmenting syllables into phonemes. Zhurova (1964) trained three-year-old children to isolate the first sound of their own name, and then was able to train four-year-old children to isolate the initial segment of a word, while Read (1978) used puppets to show that four-year-old children can detect rhymes.

Explanations for these conflicting results from different psychological studies of phonological awareness have been welcomed. Morais and colleagues were among the first to point out that psychologists were testing different levels of phonological awareness, and needed to distinguish between awareness of phonological strings, of phones, and of phonemes (Morais, Alegria, and Content 1987). Some phonological tasks used in these studies do seem to require a more explicit degree of awareness than others, especially those that involve manipulating the phonemes in a word by reversal, or addition, or subtraction. Rebecca Treiman, whose elegant studies have contributed so much to this area of research, suggests that just as reading can refer to the recognition of familiar words, or to the ability to decipher unknown words, so the term *levels of phonological awareness* has at least two possible interpretations. *Levels* can refer to the degree of explicit awareness, or to the linguistic level. So performance on phonological awareness tasks will vary with the cognitive demands of the tasks and the linguistic level that it taps (Treiman and Zukowski 1991). There is good evidence that tasks that involve the detection of single phonemes cause a great deal of difficulty to adults and to older children who have not learned an alphabetic script (Morais et al. 1979; Mann 1986; Morais et al. 1986; Read et al. 1986). The studies mentioned above also suggest that children find the detection of single phonemes difficult, but that they often manage tasks involving syllables. There is now good evidence that young children are aware of and use intrasyllabic units that have been called the *onset* and the *rime*. Because these units are sometimes represented by a single phoneme, they may have an important role to play in developing phonological awareness.

Onsets and Rimes

Speech errors known as spoonerisms were analyzed by MacKay (1972), who noted that people naturally divide monosyllabic words into the consonants that precede the vowel and the rest of the syllable when they combine two words: "don't shell" would be an involuntary combination of "shout" and "yell," rather than "don't shoull." Halle and Vergnaud (1980) argued for the same distinction on the basis of sequential constraints on sequences of phonemes in several different languages, and used the terms *onset* and *rime* to describe the two speech units that they proposed.

Rebecca Treiman has produced evidence from a series of experiments with adults and children in support of onsets and rimes as units of spoken syllables (1983, 1985, 1986, 1988; Treiman and Zukowski 1990). In her example the syllable "trip" contains two subunits, "tr" and "ip." The "tr" unit is called the onset, and the "ip" unit is called the rime. Syllables do not necessarily have an onset—for example "in"— but they must have a rime. The onset and the rime are in turn composed of smaller units. In some cases, onsets and rimes are themselves single phonemes. For example the onset of "bed" is the single phoneme "b" and the rime of "play" is the single phoneme "ay." The boundary between these two units occurs before the vowel. Treiman showed that four-year-old children could isolate and detect some single phonemes with ease. She found that young children isolated the first sound in a word more successfully when the word began with a single phoneme.

Kirtley and colleagues carried this work further with five-, six-, and seven-year-old children at Oxford (Kirtley et al. 1989). The children were given oddity tasks (based on Bradley 1980) and memory control tasks in two separate experiments. In the oddity tasks the experimenter said three or four words to the child and the child had to say which of the words was the odd one out. The onset-rime distinction accounted for the pattern of results in both experiments. In one set of trials the children had to detect which word began (man, mint, peck, mug) or ended (pin, gun, hat, men) with a phoneme different from the other three. In the first of these tasks the odd word has a different onset from the rest, but in the second task all four words have different rimes (as well as different onsets), and so the distinctive feature, being only part of the rime, should be much more difficult to detect. This proved to be the case. Even the prereaders could categorize words on the basis of single phonemes provided that these phonemes coincided with the basic speech unit of the onset. Both the prereaders and children who had begun to read found the onset task much the easier of the two. In the second experiment, a closer relationship was found between final phoneme scores and reading than between initial phoneme scores and reading, which suggests that a major step in learning to read may take place when the child learns to break the rime into smaller units. In the case of the tasks in this experiment, that task entailed detaching the preceding vowel from the final consonant.

RHYMING

The alphabetic system we use to read and to spell in English is infinitely adaptable. New words coined in computer science, or in the exploration of space, can be added and transcribed without difficulty. But for the young child beginning to read and to spell, the number of words he has to learn could seem infinite. The most efficient way to tackle the task is through some form of categorization. Rhyming is a way of categorizing words that we use quite naturally, because rhyming words have more sounds in common than any others, except for identical words. They often differ by only one phoneme, so it is an easy connection to hear. Practice in rhyming seems to begin in the cradle.

Yet rhyming tasks have proved very difficult for older children with reading problems. Bradley and Bryant (1978) showed that ten-year-old backward readers were strikingly insensitive to onset and rime in spoken words when compared with seven-year-old children who were reading normally and at the same level as the backward readers. The tasks they were given were rime and onset oddity tasks. As the children were matched on intellectual level as well as reading level, it seemed likely that the backward readers' difficulty with rhymes was a cause rather than a consequence of their reading problems (Bradley and Bryant use the terms *alliteration* and *rhyme*).

Most children can recognize rhymes at an early age (Knafle 1973, 1974; Lenel and Cantor 1981). Bradley and Bryant (1983, 1985) decided to pursue the causal connection in a longitudinal project with more than 400 young children who were given rhyming and other tests at the age of four and five, before any of them had learned to read. They followed the children in school over the next three years, and gave them tests of reading, spelling, and mathematics when they were eight and nine years old. The children's performance on the onset and rime tasks at age four and five was related to later reading and spelling, but not mathematics, even after differences in intellectual level at the time of the initial and the final tests and differences in memory were controlled.

Although a definite relationship between the child's phonological skill and eventual success at reading had been established, Bradley and Bryant included a training study in their project as a check that any relationship they found was a genuine one, and not due to some other factor they had not taken into account. At the beginning of the project a subsample of the original group were carefully matched for age and intelligence, and on their initially low scores on the onset rime judgment tasks. For one subgroup, the children were taught to categorize words by onset and rime, and then by phonemes. A second group were also taught this information, but in addition were shown how the phonemes in the test words could be represented by letters of the alphabet. A third group, a control group, received instruction in semantic classification of the same set of words, but no attention was given to phonological classification or to spelling. A second control group were given no special training. At the end of the project the two experimental groups had made more progress in reading and in spelling than either of the control groups. The children were tested again when they were 13 years old, and the investigators found that the children in the experimental groups were still ahead on four different tests of reading and spelling, but not in mathematics, although they had not been seen by the team since they were eight years old (Bradley 1988, 1989). Together, these longitudinal and training data offer powerful support for a causal relationship running from phonological awareness to reading and spelling.

Other longitudinal studies have looked at phonological awareness and reading (Mann and Liberman 1984; Stanovich, Cunningham, and Cramer 1984; Fox and Routh 1984; Lundberg, Olofsson, and Wall 1980; Olofsson and Lundberg 1985), but not all of them have included rhyming, or have tested to ensure that the children could not read before the study began. One notable exception are the landmark studies of the Swedish group, particularly their latest one (Lundberg, Frost, and Petersen 1988). These studies are particularly impressive because of the number of different phonological tasks given, and for the variety and ingenuity of the training tasks. Nevertheless I will not review them here for, although rhyming tasks were included, the children were tested at a much later stage, age six or seven, and the rhyming tests were very simple ones, perhaps too easy for children of that age. Consequently the rhyming tasks were not as potent as some of the more complex phonological tests at predicting subsequent reading skill.

NURSERY RHYMES AND READING

It should come as no surprise that onsets and rimes are relevant units to younger children. Linguistic routines such as nursery rhymes and word games play a significant part in the interactions between young children and their carers (Snow, De Blauw, and Van Roosmalen 1979). Mothers recite nursery rhymes to infants as young as three months (Trevarthen 1986, 1987), and in my experience, earlier than this. Trevarthen established that there are striking temporal regularities in the way mothers sing or speak nursery rhymes and lullabies, which may play an important role in helping to develop phonological sensitivity. Children produce rhymes spontaneously in their word play (Vihman 1981; Dowker 1989) to such an extent that Chukovsky (1963) suggested that children get drunk on rhymes. He described rhymes as an inescapable stage of linguistic development, and believed that children who did not indulge in rhyming word play must be abnormal or ill. Rhyming was, in fact, an exercise, and it was difficult to think of a more rational system of practice in phonetics than such frequent repetition of all possible sound variations. Chukovsky gives many examples of children's spontaneous rhyming play, in several different languages, all of which are transcribed alphabetically. Yet in these incidences the orthography can not have influenced such young children.

The Oxford group suggested that these early experiences with rhymes, and particularly nursery rhymes, might play a role in early phonological development. They investigated this in another longitudinal study. This time they followed a smaller group of 64 children from age three years four months until they were almost seven years old. Assessments were made of their knowledge of nursery rhymes and their phonological skills, particularly on the onset rime judgment tasks, at regular intervals. The team found a strong, highly specific relationship between knowledge of nursery rhymes and the development of phonological skills, which remained significant when differences in intellectual level and social background were controlled (Maclean, Bryant, and Bradley 1987). At the end of the study when all the data were analyzed the results suggested that sensitivity to onset-rime units are developmental precursors of phoneme detection, which in turn plays a considerable role in learning to read (Bryant et al. 1989; Bryant et al. 1990). Sensitivity to rhyme also makes a direct contribution to reading, probably by helping children group words with common spelling patterns (see also Bradley 1988).

Most of the chapters in this book are a testament to the early and rapid development of the ability to detect, produce, and categorize different sounds, and the essential role that these impressive skills play in the young child's acquisition of language. We already know that children who are late to speak have problems in learning to read (Rutter, Tizard, and Whitmore 1970). Longitudinal studies that follow infants from birth into school will almost certainly show that this practice in the cradle plays an important role in the development of those phonological skills that are so much a part of beloved childhood linguistic games, and so essential when children come to learn to read.

REFERENCES

Adams, M. J. 1990. *Beginning to Read*. Cambridge, MA: MIT Press.
Bradley, L. 1980. *Assessing Reading Difficulties*. Basingstoke and London: Macmillan Education.

Bradley, L. 1988. Rhyme recognition and reading and spelling in young children. In *Pre-school Prevention of Reading Failure*, eds. R. L. Masland and M. R. Masland. Parkton, MD: York Press.

Bradley, L. 1989. Predicting learning disabilities. In *Learning Disabilities, Vol. 2: Cognitive, Social and Remedial Aspects*, eds. J. J. Dumont and H. Nakken. Amsterdam: Swets Publishing.

Bradley, L., and Bryant, P. E. 1978. Difficulties in auditory organisation as a possible cause of reading backwardness. *Nature* 271:746–47.

Bradley, L., and Bryant, P. E. 1983. Categorizing sounds and learning to read—a causal connection. *Nature* 301:419–21.

Bradley, L., and Bryant, P. E. 1985. *Rhyme and Reason in Reading and Spelling* I.A.R.L.D Monographs No. 1. Ann Arbor: University of Michigan Press.

Brady, S., and Shankweiler, D. (eds.) 1991. *Phonological Processes in Literacy*. Hillsdale, NJ: Lawrence Erlbaum Associates.

Bryant, P. E., Bradley, L., Maclean, M., and Crossland, J. 1989. Nursery rhymes, phonological skills and reading. *Journal of Child Language* 16:407–28.

Bryant, P. E., Maclean, M., Bradley, L. L., and Crossland, J. 1990. Rhyme and alliteration, phoneme detection, and learning to read. *Developmental Psychology* 26:1–10.

Bruce, D. J. 1964. The analysis of word sounds. *British Journal of Educational Psychology* 34:158–70.

Chukovsky, K. 1963. *From Two to Five*. Berkeley: University of California Press.

Clay, M. 1987. *Writing Begins at Home*. Auckland: Heinemann.

Dowker, A. 1989. Rhyme and alliteration in poems elicited from young children. *Journal of Child Language* 16:181–202.

Ehri, L. 1984. How orthography alters spoken language competencies in children learning to read and spell. In *Language Awareness and Learning to Read*, eds. J. Downing and R. Valtin. New York: Springer Verlag.

Ehri, L. C., and Wilce, L. S. 1980. The influence of orthography on readers' conceptualization of the phonemic structure of words. *Applied Psycholinguistics* 1:371–85.

Fox, B., and Routh, D. K. 1975. Analyzing spoken language into words, syllables and phonemes: A developmental study. *Journal of Psycholinguistic Research* 4:331–42.

Fox, B., and Routh, D. K. 1984. Phonemic analysis and synthesis as word attack skills: Revisited. *Journal of Educational Psychology* 76:1059–1064.

Halle, M., and Vergnaud, J. R. 1980. Three dimensional phonology. *Journal of Linguistic Research* 1:83–105.

Helfgott, J. A. 1976. Phonemic segmentation and blending skills of kindergarten children. Implications for beginning reading acquisition. *Contemporary Educational Psychology* 1:157–69.

Kirtley, C., Bryant, P., Maclean, M., and Bradley, L. 1989. Rhyme, rime and the onset of reading. *Journal of Experimental Child Psychology* 48:224–45.

Knafle, J. D. 1973. Auditory perception of rhyming in kindergarten children. *Journal of Speech and Hearing Research* 16:482–87.

Knafle, J. D. 1974. Children's discrimination of rhyme. *Journal of Speech and Hearing Research* 17:367–72.

Lenel, J. C., and Cantor, J. H. 1981. Rhyme recognition and phonemic perception in young children. *Journal of Psycholinguistic Research* 10:57-68.

Liberman, I. Y. 1973. Segmentation of the spoken word and reading acquisition. *Bulletin of The Orton Society* 23:65–77.

Liberman, I. Y. (ed.) 1985. *Phonology and the Problems of Learning to Read and Write*. Special Issue, RASE, 6, 6.

Liberman, I. Y., Shankweiler, D., Fischer, F. W., and Carter, B. 1974. Explicit syllable and phoneme segmentation in the young child. *Journal of Experimental Child Psychology* 18:201–12.

Liberman, I. Y., Shankweiler, D., Liberman, A. M., Fowler, C., and Fischer, F. W. 1978. Phonetic segmentation and recoding in the beginning reader. In *Toward a Psychology of Reading*, eds. A. S. Reber and D. L. Scarborough. NJ: Lawrence Erlbaum Associates.

Lundberg, I., Frost, J., and Petersen, O. 1988. Effects of an extensive program for stimulating phonological awareness in preschool children. *Reading Research Quarterly* 23:263–84.

Lundberg, I., Olofsson, A., and Wall, S. 1980. Reading and spelling skills in the first school years predicted from phonemic awareness skills in kindergarten. *Scandinavian Journal of Psychology* 21:159–73.

Mackay, D. G. 1972. The structure of words and syllables: Evidence from errors in speech. *Cognitive Psychology* 3:210–27.

Maclean, M., Bryant, P. E., and Bradley, L. 1987. Rhymes, nursery rhymes and reading in early childhood. *Merrill-Palmer Quarterly* 33:255–82.

Mann, V. 1986. Phonological awareness: The role of reading experience. *Cognition* 24:65–92.

Mann, V., and Liberman, I. Y. 1984. Phonological awareness and verbal short-term memory: Can they presage early reading problems? *Journal of Learning Disabilities* 17:592–99.

Morais, J., Alegria, J., and Content, A. 1987. The relationship between segmental analysis and alphabetic literacy. *European Bulletin of Cognitive Psychology* 7:2–37.

Morais, J., Bertelson, P., Cary, L., and Alegria, J. 1986. Literacy training and speech segmentation. *Cognition* 24:45–64.

Morais, J., Cary, L., Alegria, J., and Bertelson, P. 1979. Does awareness of speech as a sequence of phones arise spontaneously? *Cognition* 7:323–31.

Olofsson, A., and Lundberg, I. 1985. Evaluation of long term effects of phonemic awareness training in kindergarten. *Scandinavian Journal of Psychology* 26:21-34.

Read, C. 1978. Childrens' awareness of sounds, with emphasis on sound systems. In *The Child's Conception of Language*, eds. A. Sinclair, R. J. Jarvella, and W. J. M. Leveit. Berlin: Springer Verlag.

Read, C., Zhang, Y., Nie, H., and Ding, B. 1986. The ability to manipulate speech sounds depends on knowing alphabetic spelling. *Cognition* 24:31–34.

Rutter, M., Tizard, J., and Whitmore, K. 1970. *Education, Health and Behaviour.* London: Longman.

Share, D., Jorm, A., Maclean, M., and Mathews, R. 1984. Sources of individual differences in reading acquisition. *Journal of Educational Psychology.* 76:1309–1324.

Snow, C., De Blauw, A., and Van Roosmalen, G. 1979. Talking and playing with babies: The role of ideologies of child-rearing. In *Before Speech*, ed. M. Bullowa. Cambridge: Cambridge University Press.

Stanovich, K. (ed.) 1987. Children's reading and the development of phonological awareness. *Invitational Issue of the Merrill-Palmer Quarterly Journal of Developmental Psychology* 33:3.

Stanovich, K. E., Cunningham, A. E., and Cramer, B. 1984. Assessing phonological awareness in kindergarten children: Issues of task comparability. *Journal of Experimental Child Psychology* 38:175–90.

Treiman, R. 1983. The structure of spoken syllables: Evidence from novel word games. *Cognition* 15:49–74.

Treiman, R. 1985. Onsets and rimes as units of spoken syllables: Evidence from children. *Journal of Experimental Child Psychology* 39:161–81.

Treiman, R. 1986. The division between onsets and rimes in English syllables. *Journal of Memory and Language* 25:476–91.

Treiman, R. 1988. The internal structure of the syllable. In *Linguistic Structure in Language Processing,* eds. G. Carlson and M. Tanenhaus. Dordrecht, The Netherlands: Kluwer.

Treiman, R., and Zukowski, A. 1991. Levels of phonological awareness. In *Phonological Processes in Literacy,* eds. S. Brady and D. Shankweiler. Hillsdale, NJ: Lawrence Erlbaum Associates.

Trevarthen, C. 1986. Development of intersubjective motor control in infants. In *Motor Development in Children: Aspects of Coordination and Control,* eds. M. G. Wade and H. T. A. Whiting. Dordrecht: Martinus Nijhoff.

Trevarthen, C. 1987. Sharing makes sense. In *Language Topics—Essays in Honour of Michael Halliday,* eds. R. Steele and T. Treadgold. Amsterdam: John Benjamin Publishing Company.

Tunmer, W. E., and Nesdale, A. R. 1985. Phonemic segmentation skill and beginning reading. *Journal of Educational Psychology* 77:417–27.

Vihman, M. 1981. Phonology and the development of the lexicon: Evidence from children's errors. *Journal of Child Language* 8:239–64.

Wagner, R. K., and Torgesen, J. K. 1987. The nature of phonological processing and its causal role in the acquisition of reading skill. *Psychological Bulletin* 101:192–212.

Yopp, H. K. 1988. The validity and reliability of phonemic awareness tests. *Reading Research Quarterly* 33:159–77.

Zhurova, L. E. 1964. The development of analysis of words into their sounds by preschool children. *Soviet Psychology and Psychiatry* 2:17–27.

Second Language Acquisition

Chapter • 21

Speech Learning in a Second Language

James Emil Flege

Adults and older children learning the sound system of a second language (L2) differ from young children acquiring the sound system of their native language (L1) in two important respects. The L2 learners are better able to control their speech apparatus than the young children acquiring an L1, and they already possess a phonetic system for producing speech. As a result, far more errors in production are likely to arise from the inappropriate use of *previously acquired structures* in L2 learning than in L1 acquisition.[1] It is well known that adult learners are rarely, if ever, completely successful at mastering the sound system of an L2. A widely held view is that when adults encounter an L2 word, they attempt to "decompose" it into the phonemic units of the L1, and then produce the L2 word as if it consisted of phonic elements (allophones, phonemes) from the L1 (Polivanov 1931).

This chapter provides a brief overview of research that has de-

---

[1]We use the term L2 *learning* rather than *acquisition* because of the view that phonetic systems, even those of adults, undergo constant change in the face of new phonetic input. Thus, speech is never fully *acquired*. The term *speech learning* as used here refers to all aspects of learning that affect the production and perception of the sounds making up words. It is used in preference to *phonological learning* because much of our research to date has focused on phonetic-level processes.

The preparation of this chapter was supported by NIH grant DC00257. The author thanks colleagues (O.-S. Bohn, W. Eefting, M. Munro), graduate students (K. Fletcher, S. Jang, C. Wang), and research assistants (L. Cueva, C. Mena, L. Skelton) who have participated in work reported here. Thanks are also extended to O.-S. Bohn, C. Ferguson, and A. Walley for editorial comments.

scribed L2 learners' production and perception of L2 sounds. The view that foreign accent is based on the substitution of the nearest L1 sound for the sounds making up L2 words appears to be inadequate. Such patterns do occur frequently, especially in the earliest stages of L2 learning. Examples of what might be called cross-language "phonetic interference" are presented. However, most adults eventually modify previously established patterns of speech production and perception when attempting to deal with the sound system of an L2. Thus, the differences one might observe between native and non-native speakers often involve more than just the maintenance of old articulatory habits. A recurrent theme of the chapter is that many aspects of L2 production can be understood in terms of how L2 sounds are *categorized*. L2 speech learning is not always just "old wine in new bottles." It seems that, in some instances, even adult L2 learners may be able to learn to savor *new* wine.

PRODUCTION VERSUS PERCEPTION

According to the contrastive analysis (henceforth, CA) approach of the 1950s and 1960s, cross-language differences were the primary source of speech learning difficulty. L2 sounds[2] were expected to be produced authentically (i.e., accurately) by L2 learners if they closely matched L1 sounds, but poorly if they did not. This implied that the authenticity of L2 production would depend on the magnitude of the phonological differences between L2 sounds and the closest sound(s) in the L1. However, a "U" shaped rather than a linear function may describe better the effect of varying differences between L1 and L2 sounds. An L2 sound may be produced authentically if it is identical to a sound in the L1, or if it is *so similar* to an L1 sound that the differences between it and the nearest L1 sound will go unnoticed if the L1 sound is substituted for the L2 sound. We have hypothesized that L2 sounds that differ *substantially* from any sound in the L1 may also be produced authentically, at least once L2 learners have received sufficient phonetic input. The most serious learning difficulty may occur for L2 sounds that are different enough from any L1 sound that L1-for-L2 substitutions could be noticed readily, but not so different as to trigger the formation of new phonetic categories for the L2 sounds.

---

[2]The term *sound* is used here to refer to a class of phones that can be used to contrast meaning. It is used as a terminological convenience to avoid the constant need for drawing a distinction between the phonetic and phonemic levels. For an exposition of this theoretically important distinction, see Flege (1992a).

CA came into disfavor largely because of its failure to predict which particular L2 sounds would, or would not, be difficult. In retrospect, more serious problems existed. First, despite evidence for important differences in phonological and phonetic levels of encoding and decoding (see e.g., Flege 1991 b, c, 1992a), CA did not usually differentiate levels of processing. An attempt was simply made to match the *phonemes* of the L1 and L2. Second, CA never made it clear whether the difficulties encountered by L2 learners had a primarily motoric or perceptual basis.

It has been suggested that L2 production errors arise because the ability to learn new forms of pronunciation diminishes with age (Sapon 1952). Difficulties in L2 pronunciation could arise from an inability to *modify* previously established patterns of segmental production or to develop *new ones.* For example, neither English /r/ nor /l/ is realized with phones that occur on the phonetic surface in Japanese. Not surprisingly, Japanese learners often have difficulty in producing English /r/ and /l/ correctly. They are judged by native speakers of English to make more production errors for word-final singletons than for word-initial singletons, and more errors for word-initial singletons than for word-initial clusters. Such errors probably cannot be attributed solely to inaccurate speech perception. This is because Japanese learners have more difficulty in identifying English /r/ and /l/ tokens that occur in word-initial clusters than in word-initial singletons, and more difficulty for word-initial than for word-final singletons (see Flege 1988a, p. 328 ff).

L2 production difficulties also have been noted for L2 sounds that do have a counterpart in the L1 inventory, but that occur in an unfamiliar phonetic context or position. For example, Spanish learners appear to be less successful in producing English /s/ in word-final than word-initial position, just the reverse of the pattern seen for children acquiring English as an L1 (Turitz 1981, cited by Flege 1988a). This pattern seems to arise because Spanish has few word-final consonants. The word-final fricatives that Spanish *does* have may be weakened or omitted in production, something that might be regarded as a "natural" process. Similarly, Chinese speakers have great difficulty producing an effective contrast between English /p,t,k/ and /b,d,g/ in word-final position, even when their L1 has a voicing contrast much like that of English in the word-initial position. Flege, McCutcheon, and Smith (1987) found that Chinese learners of English did not sustain closure voicing in word-final /b/ to the same extent as native speakers of English. This apparently occurred because the Chinese subjects failed to expand the oral cavity actively during labial closure. And, unlike native speakers, the Chinese learners did not produce /p/ with a more forceful labial closure than /b/ (Flege 1988b).

These differences between native speakers of English and the Chinese subjects probably did not arise from a lack of awareness that /p/ and /b/ contrast phonemically. Chinese subjects in the Flege, McCutcheon, and Smith (1987) study resembled English speakers in producing /p/ with greater peak oral air pressure than /b/. This suggested a difference in laryngeal articulation. The Chinese subjects also made vowels significantly longer before /b/ than /p/, although the magnitude of their voicing effect was considerably smaller than that of the native English subjects' (see also Flege, Munro, and Skelton 1992).

There are many other instances, however, in which a difference in production between native and non-native speakers can probably be traced to an underlying *perceptual* difference. To take an example, Hindi has dental and retroflex stops, but it does not possess stops like English /t/, which are characteristically produced with an alveolar place of constriction (Dixit and Flege 1991). Hindi speakers are reported to use Hindi retroflex rather than dental stops in producing English /t/ (Ohala 1978) even though retroflex stops are considered to be "marked" because of their comparative rarity. This may mean that English /t/ is perceptually more similar to the Hindi retroflex stops and that, in some instances, perceptual similarity is a more important determinant of L1-for-L2 substitution patterns than is articulatory similarity (or difficulty).

A number of studies have demonstrated the existence of differences in phonetic perception between native and nonnative speakers (e.g., Miyawaki et al. 1975). Flege and Hillenbrand (1985) showed that native speakers of Swedish and Finnish differentially labelled the members of a synthetic *peace-peas* (i.e., /s/-/z/) continuum. In this sense, they resembled native speakers of English, but they did not use fricative duration in an English-like fashion. This particular cross-language perceptual difference might be attributed to the absence of final /s/-/z/ contrasts in Swedish and Finnish, but there is also ample evidence of differences for L2 sounds that do have a phonological counterpart in the L1. For example, the phoneme boundaries of native English and Spanish subjects differ for a /da/-to-/ta/ continuum in which VOT (voice onset time) has been varied (Flege and Eefting 1986). This difference reflects how /p/, /t/, and /k/ are produced in English and Spanish. It suggests that phonetic perception is attuned to the acoustic characteristics of L1 stops so as to optimize perception.

Cross-language perception differences may reflect more subtle, multidimensional cues. For example, French learners of English might give greater weight to release burst cues in word-final stops than native speakers of English because French stops, unlike English final stops, are usually produced with an audible release burst (Flege and Hillenbrand 1987). The Chinese subjects mentioned earlier may have failed to produce English /p/ and /b/ authentically because their perceptual representations for these sounds differed from native English speakers'. For example, they may have produced only a small difference in the duration of vowels preceding /b/ and /p/ because their perceptual representations did not encode a large-magnitude difference. Flege (1989b) showed that Chinese speakers of English can accurately identify word-final tokens of /t/ and /d/ when they contain release bursts, but do so more poorly than native speakers when final release bursts and closure voicing cues are removed, even after feedback training (Flege and Wang 1990). This suggests that Chinese learners attempt to apply the representations used to identify Chinese word-initial stops, which are released, to English word-final stops, which are often unreleased. If so, then the relevant level of analysis for describing L2 perception difficulties may be the phonetic rather than the phonemic level (Brière 1966).

Sheldon and Strange (1982) showed that Japanese learners' production of English /r/ and /l/ may be more native-like than their perception of these unfamiliar sounds. Such a finding has not occurred frequently in either the L2 or the L1 literature. It may have arisen from the application of conscious articulation strategies in the context of a formal experiment. It has been hypothesized (e.g., Flege 1981) that accurate phonetic perception is a necessary but not sufficient condition for accurate L2 segmental production. On this view, the Spanish learners mentioned earlier may have omitted word-final fricatives more often than native English speakers because their perceptual representations of word-final fricatives differed from those of native English speakers in terms of how the multiple acoustic dimensions that specify /s/ are integrated. Or, they may have differed from native speakers at a more abstract, phonological level in terms of the hierarchical arrangement of distinctive features (see Weinberger 1990).

The possibility exists, of course, that the Spanish adults' perceptual representations of final /s/ closely resembled those of native English speakers, and that their production difficulty was purely motoric. A speech production difficulty for final /s/ could be localized at a segmental level, or derive from an overall difference in syllable structure between Spanish and English (see Delattre 1951). These are empirical questions. Unfortunately, the L2 literature has seldom resolved such questions because few studies examining both the production *and* perception of L2 sounds have been carried out. Even with the availability of parallel production-perception data sets, it will likely continue to prove difficult to resolve questions concerning the contribution of perceptual and motoric factors to errors in L2 production because of difficulty in finding a common metric for gauging the distance between L1 and L2 sounds in the two domains.

INTERLINGUAL IDENTIFICATION

It is generally assumed that L2 learners identify certain L2 and L1 sounds with one another (Weinreich 1953; Wode 1978, 1981). This process, which is based on judgments of overall phonetic, and perhaps phonological, similarity appears to occur even when the acoustic difference between the L1 and L2 sounds is detectable auditorily. When an L1 sound is identified with a sound in L2, it may be used in place of the L2 sound (Valdman 1976). The use of multiple L1 substitutes for an unfamiliar L2 sound, especially in early stages of learning (Hammarberg 1990), suggests that in some instances an unfamiliar L2 sound may be judged to be perceptually equidistant from two or more L1 sounds.

It has often been claimed that the phonology of L1 causes L2 learners to "filter out" acoustic differences that are not phonemically relevant in the L1 (e.g., Trubetzkoy 1939; Wenk 1985). Flege, Munro, and Fox (1992) examined the perceived dissimilarity of pairs of vowels drawn from Spanish and/or English. Multidimensional scaling (MDS) analyses showed that native Spanish-speaking listeners used fewer dimensions in judging between vowel dissimilarity than native English-speaking listeners. This is analogous to the finding that Spanish *talkers* use a narrower range of tongue positions to produce Spanish /i,a,u/ than English speakers use in producing English /i,ɑ,u/ (Flege 1989a).[3] Listeners whose L1 has a small vowel inventory may use fewer dimensions in identifying English vowels than native speakers of English because there are fewer phonetic contrasts to maintain in the L1.

Flege, Munro, and Fox (1992) found that native Spanish listeners judged certain pairs of phonetically (and phonemically) distinct English vowels to be less dissimilar than native English listeners, apparently because they did not generate two distinct phonetic codes for the vowel pairs. However, pairs that were likely to have been labelled differentially by both English and Spanish listeners often received much the same dissimilarity ratings. For example, both listener groups judged /i/-/a/ pairs to be more dissimilar than /i/-/e/ pairs. Such agreement implies the existence of a universal, auditory-based metric for similarity judgments. Universal "phonetic learning strategies" may also exist. Bohn and Flege (1990a,b; Flege and Bohn 1992) found that inexperienced German and Spanish learners of English relied on duration when asked to identify the members of synthetic vowel continua whose endpoints did not contrast in their L1. Reliance on duration could not

---

[3]This finding agrees with the observation that large-inventory languages will tend to exploit a wider range of articulations than small-inventory languages to ensure a sufficient degree of perceptual contrast (Lindblom 1988).

be attributed to previously learned (i.e., L1) perceptual patterns, at least not for the Spanish subjects. It was, therefore, concluded that L2 learners may exploit temporal cues to a greater extent than spectral cues to identify unfamiliar vowels in a second or foreign language, at least initially.

It is nevertheless true that L1 background may influence importantly the perceived similarity of sounds drawn from two languages (Butcher 1976). Results obtained by Flege and Wang (1990) suggested that learned patterns of attentional allocation may be carried over from the L1 into an L2. Gottfried and Beddor (1988) found that American subjects used duration cues to a greater extent than French subjects in identifying the members of a synthetic French /o/-/ɔ/ continuum. This was attributed to a greater overall use of duration cues in English than French. Munro (1990) found that native speakers of a language with a phonemic length distinction (viz. Arabic) used duration to a greater extent to classify vowels from an unknown foreign language than native speakers of English.

Catford asserted (1968, p. 164) that the only basis for interlingual identification is "substantial . . . rather than formal." It may be difficult to draw a clear distinction between the two, however. For example, the finding by Munro (1990) implies that if native speakers of English and Arabic were asked to judge a pair of vowels differing greatly in duration, the Arabic subjects would rate it as more dissimilar than the English subjects. That is, different judgments of cross-linguistic similarity may be rendered by speakers of different languages because of differences in the prominence given to certain acoustic dimensions, or to the way distinctive features are arranged hierarchically in particular languages (Clements 1985).

There is evidence that speech is processed at auditory, phonetic, and phonemic levels. Listeners' conscious awareness of speech is usually a reflection of phonemic-level processing, but listeners can gain access to the phonetic level under certain circumstances. Flege (1991d) hypothesized that the sound systems of two languages may interface at a phonetic as well as at a phonemic level. This was supported by a study in which Spanish and English subjects estimated degree of rhyme in English words (Flege 1992b). Spanish and English subjects rated pairs of English words with /eⁱ/ and /ɛ/ (e.g., *mate-met*) to rhyme equally, but gave different ratings for other word pairs. This finding suggests that at least one kind of judgment of intervowel distances, viz. rhyming judgments, may be made at a phonetic category level. Had the rhyming judgments been made at a phonemic level, the Spanish subjects should have perceived a greater degree of rhyme than the English subjects, for the Spanish /e/ phoneme is realized with [e] and [ɛ] allophones (see also Flege 1991a).

This finding is not conclusive, however, because of the possibility that the Spanish subjects identified the English /eɪ/ in terms of the /ei/ sequence of Spanish.[4] It seems to agree, however, with results obtained in another recent study using a different technique. Flege, Munro, and Fox (1992) had Spanish and English listeners rate consonant-vowel (CV) pairs containing English /ɛ/ and Spanish /e/ realizations for degree of dissimilarity. If the ratings had been based on phonemic-level representations, the /e/-/ɛ/ pairs should have been judged to be less dissimilar by the Spanish than the English listeners. This is because pairs of vowels that are given the same label are generally rated as more similar than vowel pairs labelled differently. The English and Spanish listeners did not differ, however, suggesting that the comparison was not based on *phonemic* codes. That is, the Spanish listeners appear to have based their judgment on the phonetic quality of the [ɛ] tokens, even though the allophone [ɛ] of Spanish /e/ is not permitted to occur in open syllables. Admittedly, however, the role of phonetic-level processing in interlingual judgments will have to be examined further.

NEW VERSUS SIMILAR SOUNDS

Some sounds in an L2 may be identical to those found in the L1. Most L2 sounds differ from L1 sounds, however, if only in minor details of timing, amplitude, or placement. An important issue is whether interlingual identification persists for all nonidentical L2 sounds after L2 learners have become familiar with the sound system of the L2. We have hypothesized that certain "new" L2 sounds that differ substantially from any vowel in the L1 will cease being identified with a sound(s) in the L1 inventory. "Similar" sounds that more closely resemble a sound in the L1 inventory, on the other hand, will continue to be identified with an L1 sound (i.e., be "equated").

Equivalence Classification

If L2 learners persist in identifying an L2 sound with an auditorily distinct sound in the L1 inventory, it is said to have been "equated" with

---

[4]In Spanish, words like *reina* ([reina] "queen") contrast with words like *reno* ([reno], "reindeer"). English learners of Spanish have difficulty distinguishing Spanish /e/ and /ei/ (Ferguson 1990), apparently because they are accustomed to the absence of an off-glide for English /eɪ/ at fast speaking rates. The /eɪ/ in many English words borrowed by Japanese, a language whose vowel system resembles that of Spanish, has been rendered as a two-vowel /ei/ sequence (Lovins 1975). It is therefore possible that pairs like *mate-met* in the Flege (1992b) study rhymed little for the Spanish subjects because they interpreted the English word *mate* to have the two-vowel sequence /ei/ and *met* to have /e/. Whether or not the extent of formant movement in English /eɪ/ is sufficient to cue the existence of a two-vowel sequence for Spanish speakers is an empirical question that needs to be resolved.

the L1 sound. Equivalence classification is of undoubted importance during L1 development, for it permits the child, and even infants (Kuhl 1980; Hillenbrand 1983), to group disparate phones into functional categories and to perceive constancy in the face of acoustic phonetic variation due to factors such as talker gender, stress, and speaking rate. Flege et al. (1992) provided evidence supporting the effect of equivalence classification in L2 learning. Spanish subjects who were relatively experienced and inexperienced in English gave much the same dissimilarity ratings for vowel pairs consisting of a Spanish /i/ token and an English /i/ token. This finding suggested that the English /i/ did not emerge as a "new" vowel for the experienced Spanish speakers of English, which is hardly surprising because the Spanish /i/ is only slightly lower in an acoustic-phonetic and articulatory space than its English counterpart (Flege 1989a). It was apparent, however, that the Spanish subjects could distinguish the /i/s of Spanish and English auditorily. Both the native Spanish and English subjects rated pairs consisting of a Spanish /a/ token and an English /i/ token as being more dissimilar than pairs consisting of a Spanish /a/ and a Spanish /i/ token.

Defining the New Versus Similar Distinction

Students of bilingualism have long drawn a distinction between what we now call new and similar sounds (Delattre 1964, 1969; Brière 1966). However, at present no standard method exists for determining if an L2 sound will be treated as new or similar. The distinction is based on differences in the perceived phonetic distance between sounds in the L2 and those in the L1 (see Best 1990).[5] Although both new and similar L2 sounds differ acoustically from sounds in the L1, there is thought to be a qualitative as well as a quantitative difference in the degree of phonetic dissimilarity between L1 sounds and sounds in the L2 that are treated as new and similar. Wode (1978), for example, supposed that there is a threshold beyond which an L2 sound will be recognized as distinct from any sound in the L1.

A reliable metric for classifying L2 sounds as new or similar must be developed if predictions concerning these two supposedly different L2 sound types can be tested. Flege (1992a) discussed methods that might be used to operationalize the distinction. An L2 sound may be defined as similar if it is represented by the same IPA symbol as a sound in the L1, provided it can be shown to differ auditorily from the corresponding L1 sound. New sounds, on the other hand, might be defined as L2 sounds that are represented by an IPA symbol that is *not* used to represent a sound in the L1 (and, of course, which differs au-

---

[5]It is uncertain if perceived articulatory similarity enters into cross-language judgments of phonetic similarity.

ditorily from the nearest L1 sound). Problems with this approach do exist, however. This is especially true for the "phonetic symbol" test, for transcriptions may vary according to individual practice and ability (see Flege 1992a).

Alternatively, an L2 sound could be classified as similar if (1) it were shown to be phonetically distinct from L1 sounds using one of several "phonetic distinctness" tests, and (2) it could be shown to differ auditorily from the nearest L1 sound(s). Native speakers of a language having a phonemic writing system, such as Spanish or Finnish, could be asked to be label L2 vowels with the letters used to write vowels in their L1, or to respond "none" if they heard a vowel not found in the L1 (see Flege 1991a). L2 vowels that received the "none" label frequently would be considered phonetically distinct from vowels in the L1 inventory. Other phonetic distinctness criteria might also be used, such as rhyming judgments. So a new L2 vowel might be defined as one that rhymes less with any vowel in the L1 than does any pair of vowels drawn from two adjacent L1 vowel categories.[6] Dissimilarity ratings might also be used as a means for assessing the status of L2 sounds. A new sound might be defined as an L2 sound that is judged to be more dissimilar when paired with realizations of the closest L1 category than pairs of sounds drawn from that L1 category and its closest neighbor.

Vowel Production

The CA approach leads to the view that the rate and eventual extent of learning for various L2 sounds will not differ. However, as predicted by our model of L2 speech learning, evidence is accumulating that certain L2 sounds are learned more readily than others. Pimsleur (1963) found that discrimination training led to an improved pronunciation of new French vowels but not of the "similar" French vowel /o/. Results reported by Henning (1966) suggested that native English subjects who did not speak French were better able to imitate French vowels that partially resemble English vowels than new French vowels. This suggests that, at least initially, the partial resemblance of an L2 sound to a sound in the L1 may prove helpful. However, Mueller and Niedzielski (1963) found just the opposite pattern in a study examining the spontaneous productions of students enrolled in a French class. They were judged by a native French-speaking listener to have produced new French vowels (e.g., /y/) far better than similar vowels (e.g., /e/). These results for French were verified in an instrumental phonetic study (Flege 1987b)

---

[6]A problem with this approach is that different speech communities may have different traditions regarding what constitutes rhyme; and considerable individual differences might be expected (Ferguson 1990).

examining the production of French vowels by native speakers of French, and by native English speakers of French who had resided in Paris for 12 years. Acoustic analysis showed that the native English subjects produced French /y/ authentically. This vowel has no phonological counterpart in English. The native English subjects differed from native French speakers, on the other hand, in producing the similar French vowel /u/, which is not fronted (or made into a diphthong) like its English counterpart.

Several recent studies have provided converging evidence that adult learners are able to master /æ/ if their L1 does not have such a vowel. Perceptual results obtained by Major (1987a, see also Flege 1992a) suggested that as Brazilians' global foreign accent in English improved, the identifiability of their English /æ/s increased. This did not hold true for the production of English /ɛ/, a similar vowel with a counterpart in Portuguese. In an acoustic analysis, Bohn and Flege (1990c, 1992a) found that inexperienced but not experienced German L2 learners differed from native speakers of English in producing the new vowel /æ/.

Flege (1992a) provided perceptual evidence that Dutch learners with a poor pronunciation of English, but not those with a good overall pronunciation of the L2, differed from native English speakers in producing the new English vowel /æ/. L2 learners in both the German and Dutch studies showed small but measurable differences from native speakers for similar English vowels known to differ acoustically from corresponding vowels in the L1. This was predicted from the hypothesis (e.g., Flege 1987b) that L2 learners are unable to establish additional phonetic categories for similar L2 vowels because they are equated with L1 vowels.

L2 Consonant Production

Best, McRoberts, and Sithole (1988) provided perceptual evidence suggesting that Bantu clicks may be sufficiently distinct from any English consonant that they evade equivalence classification by native English speakers during the process of L2 learning. However, no L2 production study to my knowledge has examined the learning of clicks or other so-called "exotic" sounds by native English speakers.[7]

Quite a few studies have examined the production of English /r/

---

[7]In the literature written in English, the term *exotic* usually refers to non-English sounds that occur rarely in human languages. Such sounds are likely to be treated as *new* by native English speakers but, because they are rare, may be articulatorily complex or difficult. To test adequately the hypothesis that adults can master new consonants in an L2, it will therefore be necessary to find L2 consonants that are not known to be difficult articulatorily as shown by, for example, relatively late mastery during L1 acquisition.

and /l/ by L2 learners. These sounds might be treated as new by Japanese speakers, for Japanese has no /l/ phoneme, and the Japanese /r/ is a voiced tip-alveolar flap (Price 1981). MacKain, Best, and Strange (1981) found that Japanese subjects with a great deal of conversational experience in English, but not those without such experience, closely resembled native English subjects in perceiving English /r/ and /l/.

Other studies suggested that the production of English /r/ and /l/ may approach native-like levels. Dissoway-Huff (1981) examined minimally-paired English words spoken by three beginning-level Japanese students. Correct identification rates by native English listeners were 80% (word-initial), 67% (intervocalic), and 67% (word-final). Mochizuki (1981) reported an average 92% correct identification rate for a single Japanese subject reported to have a poor command of English. Sheldon and Strange (1982) examined words spoken by Japanese subjects who had lived in the U.S. for an average of 1.8 years. The correct identification rate for /r/ and /l/ was just 65% for one talker, but it averaged 99% for the other five talkers examined. Although this last finding suggests that English /r/ and /l/ can be mastered, a definite conclusion would be premature. The words examined by Sheldon and Strange (1982) were read from a list, then assessed in a forced-choice identification experiment. There is no guarantee that Japanese learners' /r/ and /l/ attempts will be judged to be fully acceptable (i.e., undistorted) in conversational speech, or even that their production of these English consonants will be as readily *identifiable*. Perhaps more importantly, the data obtained by Sheldon and Strange (1982) for /r/-/l/ production may not generalize to the majority of Japanese learners of English, for their subjects were apparently selected on the basis of pronunciation proficiency. Although English /r/-/l/ learning has been studied often, more work is needed.

Much L2 acoustic research has focused on the voice onset time (VOT) dimension. English /p/, /t/, and /k/ have been examined in several studies. These phonologically voiceless stops are produced with long-lag VOT values. Flege and Hillenbrand (1984; Flege 1987b) hypothesized that even highly experienced French adults would equate realizations of English /p,t,k/ with their counterparts in French, even though the acoustic difference between short-lag and long-lag realization of /p,t,k/ appear to be detectable auditorily (Flege and Hammond 1982; Flege 1984, 1991b). This led to the prediction that French adults would be unable to establish phonetic categories for English /p,t,k/ as the result of equivalence classification, and would, thus, fail to produce English /p,t,k/ authentically.[8]

---

[8]The claim that French and English /p,t,k/ realizations will be equated might at first seem counterintuitive. Many speech perception experiments with synthetic VOT con-

As predicted, the French adults examined by Flege and Hillenbrand (1984) did not produce English /p,t,k/ authentically. Many other L2 production studies with subjects whose L1 has short-lag /p,t,k/ have shown the same thing. Adult L2 learners tend to produce English /p,t,k/ with short-lag VOT values, or with compromise values that are intermediate to the VOT norm for /p,t,k/ in the L1 and L2 (Flege and Port 1981; Port and Mitleb 1980, 1983; Nathan 1987; Flege and Eefting 1987a; Major 1987b; Lowie 1988). Only a few individual exceptions to this general rule have been noted. The fact that experienced L2 learners produce /p,t,k/ with significantly longer VOT values in English than in their L1 demonstrates that they have detected at least some of the phonetic differences between /p,t,k/ in L1 and L2. If late learners did not equate the two kinds of voiceless stops, it would be hard to understand why they so seldom manage to differentiate fully the L1 and L2 versions of /p,t,k/.

Another kind of evidence supporting the hypothesis that long-lag voiceless stops in L2 will be equated with the short-lag voiceless stops in L1 is the existence of L2 effects on L1 stop production. If foreign accent were simply a matter of "interference" one would expect to see effects of the L1 phonetic system on L2 production, but probably not the reverse. However, Flege (1987b) found that Americans who were highly experienced speakers of French produced English /t/ with shorter, and thus slightly more French-like, VOT values than English monolinguals. (The reverse pattern held true for highly experienced French speakers of English; they produced English-like stops in French.) Flege and Hillenbrand (1984) hypothesized that when similar L1 and L2 stops are equated, a learner's L1 voiceless stop category will be restructured so as to accommodate the range of L1 and L2 stops that have been identified as realizations of it.

EARLY VERSUS LATE LEARNERS

In support of this, Major (1990) provided preliminary evidence that the more closely adult learners approximate the L2 VOT norm for voiceless stop consonants, the more their L1 stops will come to resemble L2

---

tinua have shown that subjects whose L1s have short-lag and long-lag versions /p,t,k/ will differ in the location of their voiced-voiceless phoneme boundaries. However, recent work with natural stimuli has shown that VOT is not an overriding cue to stop voicing (Forrest and Rockman 1988). Bohn and Flege (1991b) found that, despite the well-known VOT difference between the /p,t,k/ of Spanish and English, Spanish monolinguals consistently identified long-lag English [tʰ] tokens as /t/. In a surprisingly large number of instances (52%), Spanish [t] tokens were identified by English monolinguals as /t/. Clearly, short-lag Spanish /t/ tokens have a property (or properties) that make them sound like phonologically voiceless stops to native speakers of English.

stops, at least in casual speech (see also Flege 1988a). Major suggested that adult learners may be unable to maintain "two language systems with native-like fluency" because of the mutual effects of L1 and L2. Psycholinguists have claimed, for different reasons, that the two language systems of bilinguals cannot operate completely independently of one another because the L1 and L2 systems are always co-activated to some degree (Obler and Albert 1978; Grosjean 1982, 1985, 1989; Grosjean and Soares 1986).

The seeming upper limit on how authentically English /p,t,k/ can be produced may apply to children and adolescents as well as to adult L2 learners. The strength of global foreign accent in sentences is known to be inversely related to the authenticity of VOT in English /p,t,k/ (Flege and Eefting 1987b; Major 1987a). Sometimes even young children may speak their L2 with an accent (e.g., Asher and Garcia 1969). This leads one to expect that children may not produce the VOT in L2 stops correctly. This inference has, in fact, been supported by studies examining adults who learned English as children or adolescents (Williams 1979, 1980; Suomi 1980; Flege and Eefting 1987b; Schmidt 1988). Caramazza et al. (1973) found that native French speakers who began learning English in Canada by the age of seven years produced English /p,t,k/ with "compromise" VOT values that were intermediate between the values typical for the L1 and L2. Flege and Eefting (1987b) found much the same for native Spanish subjects in Puerto Rico who began learning English by the age of five to six years. (Similar compromise values were observed for early learners who were adults and children at the time of testing.)

These findings raise the issue of whether *anyone* can learn to produce /p,t,k/ authentically in an L2. It appears, however, that English /p,t,k/ can be mastered if L2 learning commences by the age of five to six years. Flege (1991c) examined L1 and L2 stop production by early learners who received native-speaker input when they first began learning English at school in Texas at the age of five to six years. These early learners closely resembled Spanish monolinguals in producing Spanish /t/, and English monolinguals in producing English /t/. That is, they produced a *full phonetic contrast* between /t/ in Spanish and English. Late learners, on the other hand, produced English /t/ with the expected compromise VOT values. It was hypothesized that individuals who begin learning the L2 by about the age of five to six years can accurately produce similar L2 sounds because they are able to establish separate phonetic categories for the corresponding L1 and L2 sounds (see Flege 1988a).

It may be the case that the early learners examined by Flege and Eefting (1987b) and by Caramazza et al. (1973) received accented L2 input. If so, they may have formed phonetic categories that specified the compromise VOT values they had heard as young children. This inference was confirmed by a study of the Puerto Rican subjects examined earlier by Flege and Eefting (1987b). In a study by Flege and Eefting (1988), these subjects imitated the members of a synthetic continuum whose members spanned all three modal VOT categories (i.e., lead, short-lag, long-lag). Spanish monolinguals, English monolinguals, and late L2 learners tended to produce stops with VOT values falling into just two of the three modal VOT categories. Early learners, on the other hand, used *all three* modal categories. This suggested that they had two phonetic categories that might be used to implement /t/: a short-lag category for Spanish /t/ and long-lag category for English /t/.

Realization Rules

It late learners are limited to merely approximating the VOT norm for English /p,t,k/ because they are unable to establish phonetic categories for these similar L2 stops, one might wonder how they manage to produce a VOT difference between the /p,t,k/ of Spanish and English. We hypothesize that they do so by applying different realization rules to a single phonetic category. According to the speech production model sketched in figure 1 (adapted from Keating 1984), phonologically voiced and voiceless stops are implemented by one of three universal phonetic categories corresponding to the traditional distinction between voiced, voiceless unaspirated, and voiceless aspirated. These categories specify broad articulatory (hence acoustic) characteristics of stop consonants. The greater detail needed to account for small but systematic cross-language differences in dimensions like VOT are supplied by language-specific realization rules. This production model might be used to account for bilingual production patterns. By hypothesis, Spanish late learners differentiate Spanish /t/ from English /t/ by applying two different realization rules to a phonetic category originally established to implement just the /t/ phoneme of Spanish. Early learners, on the other hand, produce a more substantial L1 versus L2 difference by implementing /t/ with different phonetic categories in Spanish and English, each motorically output by its own realization rule.

The production model just outlined was evaluated by having Spanish/English bilinguals produce Spanish and English /t/-initial words at the end of alternating Spanish and English sentences and phrases, and in isolation (Flege 1991c).[9] It was predicted that the late

---

[9]In the first condition, the /t/-initial words occurred at the end of English and Spanish sentences "Take another word such as ___" and "Tengo palabras como ___". In the second condition, the same words occurred at the end of English and Spanish phrases ("Take a ___", "Tengo un ___"). The words were spoken in isolation in the third and final condition.

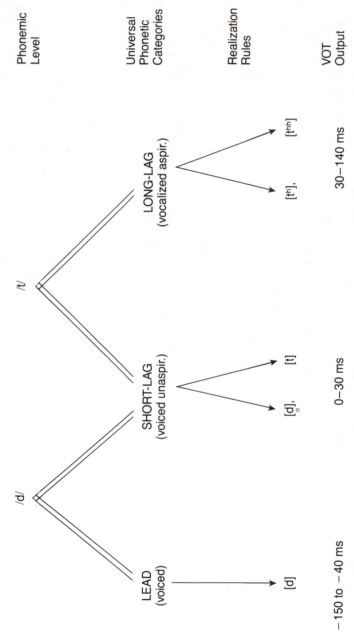

Figure 1. Sketch of a three-level speech production model (see text). Adapted from Keating (1984).

Phonemic Level

Universal Phonetic Categories

Realization Rules

VOT Output

/d/

/t/

LEAD (voiced)

SHORT-LAG (voiced unaspir.)

LONG-LAG (vocalized aspir.)

[d]

[d̥], [t]

[tʰ], [tʰʰ]

−150 to −40 ms

0–30 ms

30–140 ms

learners' small Spanish versus English VOT difference would break down sooner, or to a greater extent, than the early learners' larger L1 versus L2 difference because of the added time needed by the late learners to choose between competing realization rules to output their single /t/ category. The early learners again produced a larger Spanish versus English difference than the late learners (21 versus 60 ms; 22 versus 38 ms), but the magnitude of the difference did not vary significantly across the three conditions for either the late or the early learners.

The results thus failed to confirm the hypothesis concerning how early and late learners distinguish Spanish from English /p,t,k/. However, they did not invalidate the hypothesis either, for it was assumed—incorrectly—that the interval between successive English and Spanish /t/s would be the equal for the early and late learners. The subjects in both groups were told to make the onsets of each successive utterance coincide with the flashes emitted by a timer. Despite this, the "/t/-to-/t/" intervals were significantly longer, by over 300 ms on the average, for the late than the early L2 learners. It is conceivable that this difference arose because the late learners needed additional time to select between competing English and Spanish realization rules. Other interpretations are possible, however, so further experimentation is needed.

Vowel Production

A recent study of English vowel production in our laboratory (Flege and Bohn 1992) also points to important differences between early and late learners. We analyzed five tokens of English words (*beat, bit, bet, bat*) spoken by ten subjects in each of five groups: two English monolingual groups (one from Alabama, one from Texas), two groups of Spanish late learners (one made up of individuals who had lived in the U.S. for 0.4 years on the average, the other 9.0 years), and a group of Spanish early learners. As shown in figure 2, both the early and late learners closely resembled native English speakers in producing temporal contrasts between English vowels. The talkers in each group made /i/ longer than /ɪ/, and /æ/, longer than /ɛ/. Figure 3 and figure 4 show that the native English speakers and the early L2 learners, respectively, produced these four English vowels with little spectral overlap. It is apparent from figure 5, however, that the late learners differed considerably from the native speakers of English. Both late learner groups produced a larger spectral contrast between /ɛ/-/æ/ than the native speakers. Neither the experienced nor the inexperienced late learners managed to produce a significant spectral contrast between /i/ and /ɪ/. These results support the hypothesis (Bohn and Flege 1990a, b)

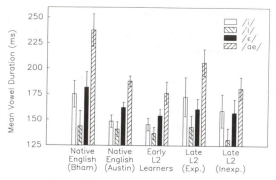

Figure 2.   The mean duration, in msec, of the vowels in *beat, bit, bet,* and *bat* as spoken by native English subjects in two groups, late learners who differed according to English-language experience, and early learners who began learning English as young children. Each mean value is based on 10 subjects × 5 tokens = 50 observations.

that late learners will note temporal differences between a pair of un-familiar L2 vowels more readily than spectral differences.

Flege and Bohn (1992) had three native English listeners identify vowels in the /bVt/ words spoken by the native English and Spanish subjects using one of seven keywords (*beat, bit, bet, bat, bait, but, bot(tle)*). Vowels spoken by the native speakers and the early learners were identified correctly almost without exception, but not vowels spoken by the late learners. The correct identification rates for the ex-perienced late learners were /i/-57%, /ɪ/-61%, /ɛ/-99%, and /æ/-73%; those for the inexperienced late learners were /i/-69%, /ɪ/-51%, /ɛ/-91%, and /æ/-70%. For both groups, /ɪ/ were heard as /i/, and vice versa. Given the traditional description of Spanish /i/ as being somewhat lower than English /i/ (see Flege 1988a), this suggests that the late learn-ers may often have used Spanish /i/ to produce both English /i/ and /ɪ/. The rates for /ɪ/ were slightly higher for the experienced than inex-perienced subjects, some of whose /ɛ/ attempts were heard as /ɪ/. The inexperienced subjects' /æ/ was heard as /ʌ/ in 30% of instances; the experienced subjects' /æ/ was heard as both /ʌ/ (10%) and /ɑ/ (13%).

These results clearly failed to support the hypothesis that the late learners would be able to master two English vowels we had consid-ered new, viz. /ɪ/ and /æ/. With the exception of /ɛ/, the late learners' vowels were identified at far lower rates than vowels spoken by native English speakers. The experienced late learners' /æ/ and /ɪ/ attempts were not more identifiable than the inexperienced late learners' at-tempts. Despite these negative results, it would probably be unwise to reject the hypothesis that late learners are able to master new L2 vow-els. Recall that support for the hypothesis was obtained in earlier stud-

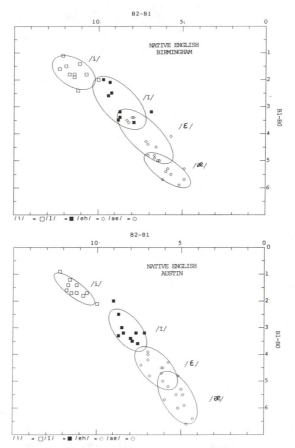

Figure 3.   Mean formant frequencies of the same vowels as in figure 2 for two groups of native English speakers. The y-axis plots the mean difference between F_1 and F_0 (after conversion to barks), which corresponds roughly to the phonological high versus low dimension. The x-axis plots the difference between F_1 and F_2 (in barks), which corresponds roughly to the front-back dimension.

ies (see above). Perhaps an L2 vowel will be treated as "new" only if it is found in a portion of the acoustic phonetic vowel space that is unoccupied by any allophone of an L1 vowel category. Such may be the case for English /æ/ but not English /ɪ/, which is located in a portion of the space occupied by Spanish /i/ (especially the realizations of Spanish /i/ in closed syllables). Interestingly, we noted important differences between the three native English listeners, one of whom identified correctly nearly all of the late learners' /æ/ tokens. We are currently conducting additional listening tests in an attempt to determine why the late learners' /œ/s (and /ɪ/s) were correctly identified by certain listeners but not by others.

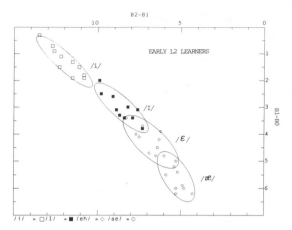

Figure 4.   Mean formant frequencies in English vowels spoken by early L2 learners (see figure 3 legend).

Another reason for not rejecting the "new vowel" hypothesis is the possibility that more native-like performance for /æ/ and /ɪ/ might have been obtained had other words containing these vowels been examined (perhaps words first encountered after category formation had taken place), or had we examined vowels spoken conversationally. Somewhat paradoxically, perhaps, there is evidence that L2 speech may be more authentic when it is produced in a spontaneous conversation than when it is read in a highly formal style, as is typical of phonetics experiments (see, e.g., Oyama 1976; Wenk 1985). Most important, however, is the evidence that some of the L2 learners seemed to have confirmed the prediction that new vowels can be mastered. As shown in figure 6, the correct identification rates for individual subjects varied considerably. Some late learners produced English /æ/, and even /ɪ/, quite well.

To obtain additional insight into the learnability of L2 vowels, we extended the English vowel intelligibility study to native German, Mandarin, and Korean late learners. Each L1 group consisted of 10 experienced and 10 inexperienced subjects.[10] The difference between experienced and inexperienced subjects in the four L1 groups studied was generally quite small and usually nonsignificant. The mean values in figure 7 have therefore been based on all 20 subjects in each L1 group. The late learners' correct identification rates were considerably

---

[10]The experienced and inexperienced German subjects had lived in the U.S. for 7.4 and 0.6 years, respectively; the two Chinese groups for 5.4 and 1.0 years; and the two Korean groups for 7.3 and 0.8 years.

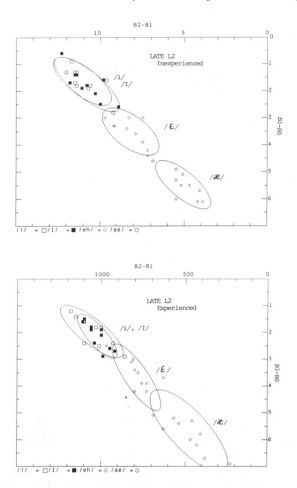

Figure 5. Mean formant frequencies in English vowels spoken by experienced and inexperienced late L2 learners (see figure 3 legend).

lower than the near-perfect rates of the native English speakers in nearly every instance. Exceptions to this general observation are the Germans' /i/ and /ɪ/ productions and the Spanish speakers' /ɛ/ productions. Previous research for German (Bohn and Flege 1989) and Spanish (Dalbor 1980) suggest that these English vowels may have been so similar to vowels in the learners' L1 that, even if the L1 vowel were substituted for the corresponding L2 vowel without any modification, it would probably have gone unnoticed by the native English listeners.

An analysis of vowel confusions revealed differences between the four L1 groups that could be understood in terms of cross-language

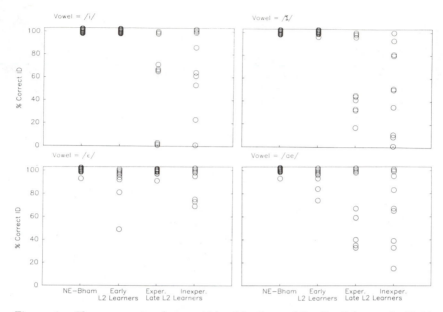

Figure 6.   The mean rate of correct identifications of the English vowels /i/, /ɪ/ (top) and /ɛ/, /æ/ (bottom) as spoken by the native speakers of English from Birmingham, early L2 learners, experienced late L2 learners, and inexperienced late L2 learners (10 subjects per group). Each mean value is based on 75 forced-choice responses (3 listeners × 5 vowels × 5 replicate presentations).

phonetic differences.[11] Our review of the literature suggested that at least one of the four English vowels examined differed sufficiently from vowels in German, Mandarin, Spanish, and Korean to be considered "new." However, even though many of the L2 learners we examined had lived in the U.S. for many years and used English daily, the overall intelligibility rates for the English vowels were usually quite low in the absence of semantic context, some as low as 50%. Based on the acoustic data presented earlier, we thought the German subjects had mastered the /æ/ phoneme, but the intelligibility data suggested otherwise (see Bohn and Flege 1992a, for a discussion). The correct identification rates for the Korean subjects were quite low, especially for /æ/. Korean is not

---

[11]When misidentifications occurred, the native English listeners often heard the German, Chinese, and Korean subjects' /æ/ attempts as /ɛ/. They heard the Spanish subjects' /æ/ attempts as /ʌ/, a vowel that is close acoustically and perceptually to Spanish /a/ (see Flege, Munro, and Fox 1992). It is therefore likely that the Spanish subjects substituted their Spanish /a/ rather than the Spanish [ɛ] allophone of /e/ for English /æ/. Of the four groups, only the Chinese subjects' /ɛ/ attempts were heard as /eʲ/. Their /ɛ/ attempts and those of the Koreans were also heard as /æ/. Some of the experienced Germans' /ɛ/ realizations were heard as /ɪ/, perhaps because the German /ɛ/ overlaps English /ɪ/ (Bohn and Flege 1989a).

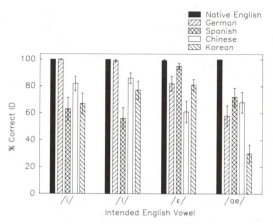

Figure 7. The mean rate of correct identifications of four English vowels spoken by the native speakers of English from Birmingham and by L2 learners who were native speakers of German, Spanish, Mandarin Chinese, and Korean. The means for the native English subjects are based on 3,000 responses (10 talkers × 3 listeners × 4 vowels × 5 tokens × 5 presentations); the means for the nonnative speakers are based on 6,000 responses (10 experienced + 10 inexperienced subjects × 300).

analyzed as having an /æ/, but a perceptual study using a matrix of synthetic vowels (Scholes 1968) indicated that nearly all steady-state, 400-msec vowels identified as /æ/ by native English speakers were consistently identified by Korean listeners in terms of a Korean vowel category rather than being judged as falling outside the Korean vowel inventory (i.e., labelled as not being an L1 vowel). Thus /æ/ might not have been treated as new by Korean learners of English as we originally thought it would be.

As shown in table I, there were usually a few talkers in each L1 group who managed to produce English vowels at rates exceeding 90% correct. For example, nearly half of the Spanish L2 learners were successful in producing English /ɪ/ and /æ/ at this level or better. This last finding shows that cross-language phonetic interference is not inevitable, for some of the late L2 learners were successful in producing an English vowel not found in their L1. There is, of course, no guarantee that this finding would generalize to other speaking styles and situations. It is not known what effect variations in speaking style may have had. As noted earlier, some of the subjects might have produced the English vowels more authentically in casual speech (see, e.g., Oyama 1976). It is also possible, of course, that list-reading tasks yield samples of L2 learners' optimal performance, and thus tend to overestimate their control of the L2 vowel system.

Table I. Number of Subjects in Nine Groups Whose English Vowels were Identified Correctly in More Than 90% of Instances

Group[a]	Vowel			
	/i/	/ɪ/	/ɛ/	/æ/
Native English	10	10	10	10
Native German[b]	10	10	5	4
Native German[c]	10	9	6	2
Native Spanish[b]	3	4	10	5
Native Spanish[c]	4	2	7	4
Native Chinese[b]	7	7	2	5
Native Chinese[c]	5	5	3	3
Native Korean[b]	3	8	5	2
Native Korean[c]	5	5	3	0

The same three native English listeners judged five tokens of each vowel as produced by the subjects in each group (see text).

[a]Five male and five female subjects per group.

[b]Non-natives who were relatively experienced in English.

[c]Non-natives who were relatively inexperienced in English.

Individual Differences

It seems likely, however, that the intersubject differences in table I were real, for we have noted a similar pattern in many of our phonetic studies. In fact, a frequent finding of studies conducted in our laboratory is that the range of individual subject differences is greater than the difference observed between extreme groups of late learners differing in amount of English-language experience. A similar conclusion regarding the relative unimportance of length of residence (LOR) can be drawn from recent experiments examining degree of global foreign accent (or FA, for short). For late learners, added experience in the L2 does not always lead to improvements in L2 pronunciation. Flege (1988c) found that late learners who lived in the U.S. for an average of 5.1 years did not pronounce English measurably better than those who had lived there for only an average of 1.1 years. Flege and Fletcher (1992) found that late learners who had lived in the U.S. for an average of 14.3 years *did* have significantly better accents than those who had lived in the U.S. for just 0.7 years, but the difference was small.

We have compared experienced late learners who lived in the U.S. for more than five years to inexperienced late learners who lived in the U.S. for less than one year in many experiments. The proportion of subjects in the two extreme groups who show production values falling within the native English range is often similar despite what probably amounts to enormous differences in native-speaker input. We suspect that many of the individual subject differences for vowel production seen in table I emerged and stabilized early in the process of L1 learning, perhaps during the first six months. Results obtained in a recent study (Flege 1992) provided preliminary evidence that prosodic errors, such as errors in stress placement or rhythm, may contribute less to FA than do segmental errors. Mueller and Niedzielski (1963) stated that FA derives principally from mismanagement of "allophonic details" in similar sounds. If so, then much of the improvement in FA that does occur in early stages of L2 learning may be due to an improved production of "new" sounds.

We are currently unable to account for the striking individual subject differences in vowel production that have been observed. Several kinds of explanation come to mind. Lambert (1977) provided evidence that some L2 learners ("code users") are more likely to perceive an L2 sound that differs auditorily from any L1 sound in terms of an L1 category whereas others ("code formers") tend to develop new central representations in such instances. Mack (1988) discussed the hypothesis that some L2 learners may make greater use of "bottom-up" processing than do native speakers in attempting to comprehend an L2. L2 learners who show this tendency to the greatest degree may be especially good at L2 segmental production and perception. Extensive use of high-order information might cause L2 learners to overlook the actual *substance* of specific sounds in the L2.

Mochizuki (1981) and Mack, Tierney, and Boyle (1990) provided evidence suggesting that non-natives may remember English words more poorly than native speakers. This may be due in part to a nonoptimal match between incoming English phones and the non-natives' central phonetic representations. Flege, Munro, and Fox (1992) had Spanish and English listeners judge the degree of dissimilarity of pairs of vowels. One finding of this study suggested that L2 learners with good pronunciation of English were better able to perceive sounds at a phonetic than were L2 learners who pronounced English poorly. Another finding was that Spanish subjects who pronounced English well judged pairs of English vowels to be more dissimilar than subjects who pronounced English poorly. This suggested an auditory basis for L2 speech learning ability, perhaps a difference in ability to store and access sensory information for unfamiliar L2 sounds (see also Mayberry and Fischer 1989, for parallels in the learning of ASL).

A CRITICAL PERIOD?

FA is widely believed to be the consequence of a diminished ability to learn speech (Lenneberg 1967). The deficit is usually understood to be the result of faulty speech production, which implies a breakdown in sensorimotor learning ability (Sapon 1952). Scovel (1988) claimed that humans cannot learn to speak an L2 without accent after about the age of 12 years because of lost "plasticity" in "neuropsychological mechanisms" that derive from the completion of cerebral lateralization. Because errors in segmental articulation contribute importantly to the perception of FA (e.g., Flege 1992), the data presented earlier, which showed more authentic production of L2 sounds by early learners than by late learners, could be viewed as supporting the existence of a critical (or sensitive) period for speech learning. It may be unwise to draw this conclusion, however (see Flege 1987a) because a clear relationship between L2 learning ability and lateralization has never been established. Also, chronological (and developmental) age is confounded with so many other factors that it would be difficult, if not impossible, to demonstrate convincingly the existence of a critical period (see below). Even if a critical period were shown to exist, it would provide little insight into *why* adults speak with a FA.

Also, recent experiments have confirmed earlier evidence (e.g., Asher and Garcia 1969) that FAs emerge before the age of 12–14 years, as commonly supposed (Patkowski 1989). Flege (1988c) found that native Chinese adults who began learning English at an average age of 7.6 years spoke English with a slight but detectable accent. A later study using the same stimuli and procedures showed that native Spanish adults who learned English by the age of five to six years did *not* differ significantly from native English speakers (Flege and Fletcher 1992). Although further research is clearly needed, the two studies suggest that FA first becomes evident at some time between the ages of five and seven years.

There are potential explanations for the emergence of an FA other than the passing of a critical period that should be considered. For example, an FA might arise in adults and older children because they do not receive L2 phonetic input that is as rich as the phonetic input received by young children learning an L1 (see Flege 1987a). Adults want and need to communicate in an L2 as soon as possible, so they may begin speaking before they establish accurate perceptual representations for L2 sounds. This could result in incorrect production patterns that are difficult to change later, when more accurate perceptual representations may have been developed (Henning 1966). Alternatively, L2 learners may be less likely than L1 learners to form accurate perceptual representations for L2 sounds. This would probably be the case if the auditory processing of L2 words terminates earlier in adults and older children as the result of more rapid word recognition.[12]

---

[12]More rapid word recognition by adults than young children might come about through the greater, or earlier, use of higher order information in parallel with bottom-up phonetic information.

A classic view of perceptual development is that children become increasingly less reliant on sensory information as they develop cognitively and learn to ignore attributes of sensory stimuli that are irrelevant to classification. Age-related changes in psychosocial or socioaffective factors may account for differences between older and younger L2 learners (e.g., Schumann 1975; Krashen 1985). Others have pointed to cognitive changes that may affect how L2 input is operated upon (Schneiderman and Desmarais 1988). However, a cognitive approach has been applied less often to L2 speech than morphosyntactic learning because of the sensorimotor component of speech production and perception.

CHANGES IN SPEECH LEARNING

The general hypothesis that has motivated our program of speech research over the past decade (e.g., Flege 1981) has been that perceptual and sensorimotor processes that permit children to learn to pronounce their L1 without an accent *remain intact through the lifespan,* that is, do not deteriorate (or become inaccessible) as the result of neurological maturation. We have hypothesized that these processes operate in much the same way in L2 and L1 acquisition, but may yield different results in L2 learning than in L1 acquisition because the phonetic system has often stabilized by the time L2 learning begins. Early learners may learn to pronounce an L2 better than late L2 learners because the late learners are first exposed to the L2 after an important developmental shift in speech processing that has occurred at around the age of five to seven years. Recall that this appears to be the age at which foreign accents first emerge (Flege and Fletcher 1992).

We propose that an important consequence of the hypothesized "phonetic system shift" is that it makes L2 learners more likely to equate L2 sounds with sounds in the L1. This may render late learners less able to establish additional phonetic categories for sounds in the L2 after rather than before the age of five to seven years. If so, it may mean that foreign accents do not arise because speech learning ability has diminished as the result of neurological maturation (Scovel 1988), but because the phonetic system has *developed and stabilized.* Treiman and Zukowski (1990) presented evidence that the smallest portion of a word that might be used in performing explicit perceptual tasks by children between the ages of four and six years changes from a whole syllable, to part of a syllable (i.e., the onset or rime), to a single segment. Walley (1990) suggested that such developmental changes may reflect how words are represented in the lexicon (see also Fowler 1990). Children's first words may be represented holistically whereas words added to the lexicon in later childhood may be stored and retrieved in terms of phonemic segments (Ferguson and Farwell 1975; Ferguson 1986; Jusczyk 1986).

Development of the phonetic system may, itself, be the indirect result of general cognitive changes involving how abstract concepts are formed. The ability to perform tasks that focus on specific formal aspects of a word (e.g., to say the word *pat* without its first sound, or to find the commonality in word pairs such as *player-prayer, cat-cad*) requires explicit, metalinguistic awareness. Cognitive psychologists speak of a "5 to 7 shift" reflecting basic changes in learning strategies and concept formation (e.g., White 1965; Shaffer 1985). The ability to focus attention on specific aspects of stimuli, called *decentering*, epitomizes the stage of concrete operations said to begin between the ages of five and seven years (Piaget and Inhelder 1969). Decentering allows the child to consider alternative hypotheses in attempting to solve a problem. One study showed that five-year-olds who performed poorly on a measure of concrete operations were less successful in reading a year later than children who performed well on the concrete operations measure (Tunmer 1988).

Reading, of course, requires phonemic awareness. Nittrouer and Studdert-Kennedy (1987) found that, in identifying fricatives, children aged three to five years were more influenced by information in the following vowel than seven-year-olds and adults, who tended to base their judgments on spectral properties of the frication noise itself. It was as if the youngest children were unable to focus attention on *just the fricatives*. An increased awareness of segment-sized units in speech processing appears to be motivated by lexical growth. As the number of lexical items increases, so too does the likelihood that "near neighbors" in the lexicon will be confused with one another if the sounds which differentiate them are not represented explicitly (Jusczyk 1989; Charles-Luce and Luce 1990).

The finding that children show increasing perceptual awareness of segment-sized units agrees with the finding that young children may show greater coarticulation than adults in their production of speech as the result of producing words in a somewhat less "segmental" fashion than adults. In a study comparing adults to children aged three to seven years, Nittrouer, Studdert-Kennedy, and McGowan (1989) found an increase with age of the spectral contrast between /s/ and /ʃ/ fricatives. At the same time, they noted a *decrease* with age in the effect of vowel context on the fricative spectra. This suggested that, unlike adults and older children, young children's word production may be organized over a domain "at least the size of the syllable," only later reflecting an organization that is "aligned with perceived segmental components" (Nittrouer, Studdert-Kennedy, and McGowan 1989, p. 120).[13]

There are many such instances of whole-to-part shifts in perceptual development (Aslin and Smith 1988). An increased awareness of segments probably does not occur abruptly; and its timing may differ across sound types. Nor is it likely that increased segmental awareness, in itself, will account for the emergence of foreign accent. We propose that as children's awareness of segments increases during the period from five to seven years, the categories comprising their phonetic system undergo two broad types of change: (1) the core acoustic properties of prototypical exemplars of each phonetic category, and the weighting of those properties, will become better defined; (2) the *range* of phones that are identifiable as a realization of each category will increase. Note that the first hypothesis pertains to category centers, the second to the boundaries between categories.

These two hypotheses concerning phonetic system development are illustrated in figure 8, which shows four hypothetical vowel categories at two times, one prior to the hypothesized phonetic system shift (Time 1), the other after the shift (Time 2). Each box is meant to illustrate a portion of the phonetic vowel space. The two dimensions of the boxes might be thought of as representing acoustic properties such as F1 and F2 frequency but, more realistically, the vowel space should be thought of as an N-dimension psychological space. Four vowel categories, which are represented by circles, change in several respects from Time 1 to Time 2. The categories embrace a wider range of variants (indicated by the increased size of the ellipses); have better defined centers, or prototypes (illustrated by the darkened circles at the approximate center of each category); and have better defined boundaries (indicated by the thickness of the lines). From the standpoint of L2 learning, the most important feature of the change from Time 1 to Time 2 is the reduction of "uncommitted" vowel space not occupied by any L1 vowel category. The hypothesis being advanced here is that unless most realizations of an L2 vowel are found within "uncommitted" space, the L2 vowel will tend to be identified in terms of an L1 category so that new category formation *will not occur*. Thus, an L2 learner

---

[13]It is worth noting that segmentation skills may influence many aspects of speech processing, not just L2 learning. Good readers show better segmentation skills than poor readers. Mann (1984) concluded that good readers use phonetic representations more effectively to process speech than poor readers. Burnham (1986) found that children with good comprehension abilities for their age were more likely to identify sounds in accordance with the phonemic categories of their L1, and to ignore phonetic contrasts that were not phonemically relevant in L1, than children with relatively poor comprehension abilities.

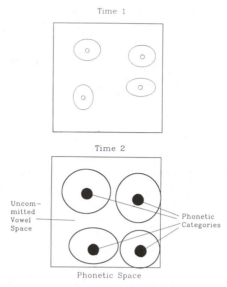

Figure 8.   Illustration of hypotheses concerning how phonetic systems change around the age of five to seven years (see text for explanation).

should be more likely to add new L2 vowel categories at Time 2 in phonetic development than at Time 1.

Based on children's production and perception of vowel duration cues to the contrast between voiced and voiceless stops in word-final position, Krause (1982a, b) concluded that both speech production and perception demonstrate "refinement and stabilization" with increasing age (1982a, p. 25). A better definition of phonetic category prototypes may better enable children to gauge degree of FA as they grow older (Scovel 1988) and to gauge how "clear" or "distorted" the realizations of a particular category may be. The outward expansion of category boundaries should enable children, as they grow older, to correctly identify sounds produced by an ever wider variety of talkers differing in vocal tract size, dialect, and characteristic speaking rate.

Neither of these hypotheses have as yet been tested formally, but they seem to be consistent with previous results. Based on experiments examining the identification of the voicing feature in stops, Simon and Fourcin (1978) concluded that response variability decreases over much of childhood, and a "categorical" mode of response increases up to about the age of five to seven years (depending on the children's L1). This is what one would expect if phonetic category prototypes became better defined. Zlatin and Koenigsknecht (1975, 1976) also examined the identification of stop consonants by children. They found that the slopes of young children's identification functions for voice onset time (VOT) continua were not steep. This meant that a larger number of stimuli from the VOT continua were judged consistently as belonging to either the voiced or voiceless stop category by adults and older children than by young children.

The decrease with age in the number of "ambiguous stimuli" in a forced-choice task implies that the two categories defined by the endpoints of a perceptual continuum embrace a wider range of phones. The hypothesis that the range of phones identifiable in terms of L1 categories expands with age received indirect support from an experiment by Butcher (1976). His experiment assessed the degree of perceived similarity of cardinal vowels by adults and children who spoke English, French, or German. Cross-language comparisons indicated that cardinal vowels were perceived to be closer when they occupied crowded than uncrowded portions of the listeners' L1 vowel space. Perceived dissimilarity ratings (which presumably reflected intervowel distances in a psychological vowel space) tended to be less for adults than children. This suggested that the adult's phonetic space was "filled" to a greater extent than the children's.

LINGUISTIC FACTORS

This chapter has dealt with how sounds in an L2 are produced and perceived. From a linguistic (i.e., phonological) perspective, the research reported here might fall under the general heading of "segmental structure constraints." Although we have focused on segments, many other factors that fall outside the scope of this chapter may influence L2 pronunciation.[14] In particular, properties of language production that encompass more than a single segment are likely to influence segmental production and perception. For example, in agreement with the observation that "segmental phonemes are influenced by the suprasegmentals of language" (Mueller and Niedzielski 1963), Wenk (1985) found that vowel production accuracy may depend on L2 rhythmic accuracy.

Just as L2 segments may or may not be identified with segments in the L1, learners may (or may not) identify strings of segments in the L2 as meeting the structural description for the application of an L1 phonological rule or constraint (Broselow 1983; Rubach 1984; Major 1987c;

---

[14]For treatments of L2 speech learning with a phonological orientation, the interested reader should consult Ioup and Weinberger (1986), James and Leather (1986), James (1988), and Leather and James (1990).

Hammarberg 1990; but see Singh 1990).[15] For example, Hammarberg refers to a beginning German learner of Swedish who pronounced the Swedish word for "bed" ("säng") with an initial /s/ when prompted, but with an initial /z/ (typical for German) once he had learned the word and could produce it spontaneously. The phonological principal of underspecification may be needed to account for which vowel from the L1 inventory is inserted into L2 words in order to make them conform to L1 syllable structure constraints (Weinberger 1990). It might also be needed to account for instances of "differential substitution" (e.g., the use of /s/-for-/θ/ by Japanese learners of English but /t/-for-/θ/ substitutions by Russians, even though both L1s have /s/ and /t/).

It is likely, too, that lexical factors will have an important impact on L2 segmental articulation and learning. Mack, Tierney, and Boyle (1990) found that both native speakers and L2 learners recognized relatively frequent (and presumably familiar) words better than infrequent ones, especially when the words were generated by a computer. Conversely, L2 learners may produce segments more authentically in relatively infrequent than in frequent words. This might be expected if L2 learners tend to mispronounce sounds in the first L2 words they learn because phonetic categories for the L2 sounds have not yet been established, then have difficulty later in correcting these mispronunciations once categories have been established for the L2 sounds.

L2 words that have a cognate in the L1 may be produced differently than words that can not be related to a known L1 word. Wenk (1985) observed more accurate rhythmic properties in L2 words that had a close cognate in the L1 than in those without a cognate. In a recent study, Flege and Munro (1992) found that VOT values in English /t/ tokens were less authentic in an English word with a Spanish cognate (*taco*) than in noncognate words. Differences between cognate and noncognate words may be especially important when L2 learning is mediated by the written word. Hammarberg (1990) found that Germans with no knowledge of Swedish imitated Swedish /ɑː/ (a low, back slightly rounded vowel) with an [o]-quality vowel whereas Germans who knew some Swedish produced it using an German-like [a:]-quality vowel. Orthographic cues may encourage German learners of Swedish to use a "top-down" solution (whereby the Swedish /ɑː/ is identified with German /a:/) rather than a more phonetic "bottom-up"

---

[15]The application of phonological rules may, under certain circumstances, have to await purely articulatory learning. Hammarberg (1990) reported that Germans with no knowledge of Swedish imitated the Swedish retroflex /s/, which is derived by rule from an "underlying" /rs/ sequence (which is evident orthographically) using German /ʃ/. Germans who had just begun learning Swedish produced the underlying sequence (i.e., /rs/). Those with more L2 experience produced the Swedish retroflex /s/ along with German /ʃ/.

solution. The use of L1 vowels was especially apparent in Swedish words that had lexical equivalents in German (e.g., *radio*).

SUMMARY

It seems likely that how well an L2 sound that differs acoustically from any sound in the L1 is produced will depend, to a large extent, on how it is categorized. It is proposed here that the primary difference between early and late L2 learners is that late learners are more likely than early learners to equate L2 sounds perceptually with sounds in the L1, which may prevent late learners from establishing phonetic categories for certain L2 sounds and thus producing them authentically. Another proposal is that the emergence of foreign accent in an L2 at about the age of five to seven years results from the decreasing likelihood that L2 sounds will be judged as falling outside of the existing L1 inventory. This important shift may coincide with an increase in children's segmental awareness, and be linked to changes in the structure and content of their phonetic categories. Paradoxically, the changes in phonetic categories probably result in increased efficiency in perceiving and producing L1 sounds, but they may make it increasingly difficult for children to master sounds not found in the L1 phonetic inventory. If we are correct in thinking that many L2 production errors have a perceptual basis, this may explain why so many skills, including speech motor control (e.g., Smith 1978), seem to increase with age whereas the ability to learn new forms of *pronunciation* seems to decline.

REFERENCES

Aslin, R., and Smith, L. 1988. Perceptual development. *Annual Review of Psychology* 39:435–73.

Asher, J., and Garcia, R. 1969. The optimal age to learn a foreign language. *Modern Language Journal* 53:334–41.

Best, C. T. 1990. The emergence of specific phonemic influences in infant speech perception. In *Development of Speech Perception: The Transition from Recognizing Speech Sounds to Spoken Words*, eds. H. C. Nusbaum and J. Goodman. Cambridge, MA: MIT Press.

Best, C., McRoberts, G., and Sithole, N. 1988. Examination of perceptual reorganization for nonnative speech contrasts: Zulu click discrimination by English-speaking adults and infants. *Journal of Experimental Psychology: Human Perception and Performance* 14:345–60.

Bohn, O.-S., and Flege, J. E. 1989. The establishment of a new phonetic category by German learners of English. *Journal of the Acoustical Society of America* 85:S84(A).

Bohn, O.-S., and Flege, J. E. 1990a. Interlingual identification and the role of foreign language experience in L2 vowel perception. *Applied Psycholinguistics* 11:303–328.

Bohn, O.-S., and Flege, J. E. 1990b. The role of duration differences in the perception of non-native vowel contrasts. Paper read at the Meeting of European Linguistic Society, Bern, Switzerland, September, 1990.

Bohn, O.-S., and Flege, J. E. 1990c. Perception and production of a new vowel category by adult second language learners. In *New Sounds 90, Proceedings of the Symposium of Second-language Speech*, eds. A. James and J. Leather. Dordrecht: Foris.

Bohn, O.-S., and Flege, J. E. 1992a. The production of new and similar English vowels by native speakers of German. *Studies in Second Language Acquisition*, to appear.

Bohn, O.-S., and Flege, J. E. 1992b. Perceptual switching in Spanish/English bilinguals: Evidence for universal factors in stop voicing judgments. *Journal of Phonetics*, under review.

Brière, E. 1966. An investigation of phonological interference. *Language* 42:769–96.

Broselow, E. 1983. Non-obvious transfer: On predicting epenthesis errors. In *Language Transfer in Language Learning*, eds. S. Gass and L. Selinker. Rowley, MA: Newbury House.

Burnham, D. 1986. Developmental loss of speech perception: Exposure to and experience with a first language. *Applied Psycholinguistics* 7:207–240.

Butcher, A. 1976. The influence of the native language on the perception of vowel quality. *Arbeitsberichte, Institut für Phonetik, Universität Kiel* 6.

Caramazza, A., Yeni-Komshian, G., Zurif, E., and Carbone, E. 1973. The acquisition of a new phonological contrast: The case of stop consonants in French-English bilinguals. *Journal of the Acoustical Society of America* 54:421–28.

Catford, J. C. 1968. Contrastive analysis and language teaching. In *Contrastive Linguistics and Its Pedagogical Implications*, ed. J. Alatis. Washington: Georgetown University Press.

Charles-Luce, J., and Luce, P. A. 1990. Similarity neighborhoods of words in young children's lexicons. *Journal of Child Language* 17:205–215.

Clements, G. N. 1985. The geometry of distinctive features. *Phonology Yearbook* 2:223–50.

Dalbor, J. B. 1980. *Spanish Pronunciation*. New York: Holt, Rinehart, and Winston.

Delattre, P. 1951. *Principes de Phonétique Francaise*. Middlebury VT: Middlebury College.

Delattre, P. 1964. Comparing the vocalic features of English, German, Spanish, and French. *International Review of Applied Linguistics* 2:71–97.

Delattre, P. 1969. An acoustic and articulatory study of vowel reduction in four languages. *International Review of Applied Linguistics* 7:295–323.

Dissoway-Huff, P. 1981. Japanese difficulty with English /l/ and /r/: Importance of both perception and production research in second language acquisition. *Research in Phonetics* 2:226–60. (Department of Linguistics, Indiana University.)

Dixit, R. P., and Flege, J. E. 1991. Vowel context, rate and loudness effects on linguopalatal contact patterns in Hindi retroflex /t/. *Journal of Phonetics* 19:213–29.

Ferguson, C. 1986. Discovering sound units and constructing sound systems: It's child play. In *Invariance and Variability in Speech Processes*, ed. by J. Perkell and D. Klatt. Hillsdale, NJ: Lawrence Erlbaum Associates.

Ferguson, C. 1990. Personal communication.

Ferguson, C., and Farwell, C. 1975. Words and sounds in early language acquisition. *Language* 51:418–39.

Flege, J. E. 1981. The phonological basis of foreign accent. *TESOL Quarterly* 15:443–55.

Flege, J. E. 1984. The detection of French accent by American listeners. *Journal of the Acoustical Society of America* 76:692–707.

Flege, J. E. 1987a. A critical period for learning to pronounce foreign languages? *Applied Linguistics* 8:162–77.

Flege, J. E. 1987b. The production of "new" and "similar" phones in a foreign language: Evidence for the effect of equivalence classification. *Journal of Phonetics* 15:47–65.

Flege, J. E. 1988a. The production and perception of speech sounds in a foreign languages. In *Human Communication and Its Disorders, A Review 1988.* ed. H. Winitz. Norwood, NJ: Ablex.

Flege, J. E. 1988b. The development of skill in producing word-final /p/ and /b/: Kinematic parameters. *Journal of the Acoustical Society of America* 84:1639–1652.

Flege, J. E. 1988c. Factors affecting degree of perceived foreign accent in English sentences. *Journal of the Acoustical Society of America* 84:70–79.

Flege, J. E. 1989a. Differences in inventory size affect the location but not the precision of tongue positioning in vowel production. *Language and Speech* 32:123–47.

Flege, J. E. 1989b. Chinese subjects' perception of the word-final English /t/-/d/ contrast: Performance before and after training. *Journal of the Acoustical Society of America* 86:1684–1697.

Flege, J. E. 1991a. Orthographic evidence for the perceptual identification of vowels in Spanish and English. *Quarterly Journal of Experimental Psychology* 43:701–731.

Flege, J. E. 1991b. Perception and production: The relevance of phonetic input to L2 phonological learning. In *Crosscurrents in Second Language Acquisition and Linguistic Theory*, eds. T. Heubner and C. Ferguson. Philadelphia: John Benjamins.

Flege, J. E. 1991c. Age of learning affects the authenticity of voice onset time (VOT) in stop consonants produced in a second language. *Journal of the Acoustical Society of America* 89:395–411.

Flege, J. E. 1992a. The Intelligibility of English vowels spoken by British and Dutch talkers. In *Intelligibility in Speech Disorders: Theory, Measurement, and Management*, ed. R. Kent Philadelphia: John Benjamins.

Flege, J. E. 1992b. The use of rhyming judgments to evaluate the interlingual identification of Spanish and English vowels. MS in preparation.

Flege, J. E. 1992c. The contribution of segmental and prosodic errors to degree of perceived foreign accent: Preliminary evidence. *Studies in Second Language Acquisition.*

Flege, J. E., and Bohn, O.-S. 1989. An instrumental study of vowel reduction and stress placement in Spanish-accented English. *Studies in Second Language Acquisition* 11:35–62.

Flege, J. E., and Bohn, O.-S. 1992. The production and perception of English vowels by native speakers of Spanish.

Flege, J. E., and Eefting, W. 1986. Linguistic and developmental effects on the production and perception of stop consonants. *Phonetica* 43:155–71.

Flege, J. E., and Eefting, W. 1987a. Cross-language switching in stop consonant production and perception by Dutch speakers of English. *Speech Communication* 6:185–202.

Flege, J. E., and Eefting, W. 1987b. The production and perception of English stops by Spanish speakers of English. *Journal of Phonetics* 15:67–83.

Flege, J. E., and Eefting, W. 1988. Imitation of a VOT continuum by native speakers of English and Spanish: Evidence for phonetic category formation. *Journal of the Acoustical Society of America* 83:729–40.

Flege, J. E., and Fletcher, K. 1992. Talker and listener effects on degree of perceived foreign accent. *Journal of the Acoustical Society of America* 91:170–89.

Flege, J. E., and Hammond, R. 1982. Mimicry of non-distinctive phonetic differences between language varieties. *Studies in Second Language Acquisition* 5:1–18.

Flege, J. E., and Hillenbrand, J. 1984. Limits on pronunciation accuracy in adult foreign language speech production. *Journal of the Acoustical Society of America* 76:708–721.

Flege, J. E., and Hillenbrand, J. 1985. Differential use of temporal cues to the [s–z] contrast by native and non-native speakers of English. *Journal of the Acoustical Society of America* 79:508–517.

Flege, J. E., and Hillenbrand, J. 1987. Differential use of closure voicing and release burst as cue to stop voicing by native speakers of French and English. *Journal of Phonetics* 15:203–208.

Flege, J. E., and Munro, M. J. 1992. Acoustic phonetic correlates of language identity: Spanish vs. English *taco*. Ms. in preparation.

Flege, J. E., and Port, R. 1981. Cross-language phonetic interference: Arabic to English. *Language and Speech* 24:125–46.

Flege, J. E., and Wang, C. 1990. Native-language phonotactic constraints affect how well Chinese subjects perceive the word-final English /t/-/d/ contrast. *Journal of Phonetics* 17:299–315.

Flege, J. E., McCutcheon, M., and Smith, S. 1987. The development of skill in producing word–final English stops, *Journal of the Acoustical Society of America* 82:433–47.

Flege, J. E., Munro, M., and Fox, R. 1992. The interlingual identification of Spanish and English vowels. *Journal of the Acoustical Society of America*.

Flege, J. E., Munro, M., and Skelton, L. 1992. Production of the English word-final /t/-/d/ contrast by native speakers of Mandarin and Spanish. *Journal of the Acoustical Society of America*.

Forrest, K., and Rockman, B. 1988. Acoustic and perceptual analysis of word-initial stop consonants in phonologically disordered children. *Journal of Speech and Hearing Research* 31:449–59.

Fowler, A. 1990. How early phonological development might set the stage for phonological awareness. In *Phonological Processes in Literacy*, ed. S. Brady and D. Shankweiler. Hillsdale, NJ: Lawrence Erlbaum Associates.

Gottfried, T., and Beddor, P. 1988. Perception of temporal and spectral information in French vowels. *Language and Speech* 31:57–75.

Grosjean, F. 1982. *Life with Two Languages, An Introduction to Bilingualism*. Cambridge: Cambridge University Press.

Grosjean, F. 1985. The bilingual is a competent but specific speaker-hearer. *Journal of Multilingual and Multicultural Development* 6:467–77.

Grosjean, F. 1989. Neurolinguists, beware! The bilingual is not two monolinguals in one person. *Brain and Language* 36:3–15.

Grosjean, F., and Soares, C. 1986. Processing mixed languages: Some preliminary findings. In *Language Processing in Bilinguals: Psycholinguistic and Neurophysiological Perspectives*, ed. J. Vaid. Hillsdale, NJ: Lawrence Erlbaum Associates.

Hammarberg, B. 1990. Conditions on transfer in phonology. In *New Sounds 90*,

Proceedings of the Symposium of Second-language Speech, eds. A. James and J. Leather. Dordrecht: Foris.

Henning, W. A. 1966. Discrimination training and self-evaluation in the teaching of pronunciation. *International Review of Applied Linguistics* 4:7–17.

Hillenbrand, J. 1983. Perceptual organization of speech sounds by infants. *Journal of Speech and Hearing Research* 26:237–82.

Ioup, G., and Weinberger, S. (eds.). 1986. *Interlanguage Phonology: The Acquisition of a Second Language Sound System.* Rowley, MA: Newbury House.

James, A. R. 1984. Phonic transfer: The structural bases of interlingual assessments. In *Proceedings of the Tenth International Congress of Phonetic Sciences,* eds. M. P. R. van den Broeke and A. Cohen. Dordrecht: Foris.

James, A. R. 1988. *The Acquisition of a Second Language Phonology.* Tübingen: Gunter Narr.

James, A. R., and Leather, J. 1986. *Sound Patterns in Second Language Acquisition.* Dordrecht: Foris.

Jusczyk, P. W. 1986. Toward a model of the development of speech perception. In *Invariance and Variability in Speech Processes,* eds. J. S. Perkell and D. H. Klatt. Hillsdale, NJ: Lawrence Erlbaum Associates.

Jusczyk, P. W. 1990. Infant speech perception and the development of the mental lexicon. In *The Transition from Speech Sounds to Spoken Words: The Development of Speech Perception,* eds. H. C. Nusbaum and J. C. Goodman. Cambridge, MA: MIT Press.

Keating, P. 1984. Phonetic and phonological representation of stop consonant voicing. *Language* 60:286–319.

Krashen, S. 1985. *The Input Hypothesis: Issues and Implications.* London: Longman.

Krause, S. E. 1982a. Developmental uses of vowel duration as a cue to post-vocalic stop voicing. *Journal of Speech and Hearing Research* 25:388–93.

Krause, S. E. 1982b. Vowel duration as a perceptual cue to post-vocalic voicing in young children and adults. *Journal of the Acoustical Society of America* 71:990–95.

Kuhl, P. K. 1980. Perceptual constancy for speech-sound categories in early infancy. In *Child Phonology, Vol. 2, Perception,* eds. G. Yeni-Komshian, J. Kavanagh, and C. Ferguson. New York: Academic.

Lambert, D. 1977. Learning to recognize foreign speech sounds: Strategies of auditory processing. Unpublished Ph.D. diss., University of California, San Diego.

Leather, J., and James, A. R. (eds.) 1990. *New Sounds 90, Proceedings of the Symposium on Second Language Speech Learning.* Dordrecht: Foris.

Lenneberg, E. 1967. *Biological Foundations of Language.* New York: John Wiley & Sons.

Lindblom, B. 1988. Phonetic universals in consonant systems. In *Language, Speech, and Mind, Studies in Honour of Victoria A. Fromkin,* eds. L. Hyman and C. Li. London: Routledge and Kegan Paul.

Lovins, J. 1975. Loanwords and the phonological structure of Japanese. Unpublished Ph.D. dissertation, University of Chicago. (Available from the Indiana University Linguistics Club, Bloomington, IN.)

Lowie, W. 1988. Age and foreign language pronunciation in the classroom. Unpublished M.A. thesis, University of Amsterdam.

Mack, M. 1988. Sentence processing by non-native speakers of English: Evidence from the perception of natural and computer-generated anomalous L2 sentences. *Journal of Neurolinguistics* 3:293–316.

Mack, M., Tierney, J., and Boyle, M. 1990. The intelligibility of natural and

LPC-vocoded words and sentences presented to native and non-native speakers of English. MIT Lincoln Laboratory, Technical Report 869 (32 pps).

MacKain, K., Best, C., and Strange, W. 1981. Categorical perception of English /r/ and /l/ by Japanese bilinguals. *Applied Linguistics* 2:369–90.

Major, R. C. 1987a. Phonological similarity, markedness, and rate of L1 acquisition. *Studies in Second Language Acquisition* 9:63–82.

Major, R. C. 1987b. English voiceless stop production by speakers of Brazilian Portuguese. *Journal of Phonetics* 15:197–202.

Major, R. C. 1987c. The natural phonology of second language acquisition. In *Sound Patterns in Second Language Acquisition*, eds. A. James and J. Leather. Dordrecht: Foris.

Major, R. C. 1990. L2 acquisition, L1 loss, and the critical period hypothesis. In *New Sounds 90, Proceedings of the Symposium on Second Language Speech Learning*, eds. J. Leather and A. R. James. Dordrecht: Foris.

Mann, V. 1984. Reading skill and language skill. *Developmental Review* 4:1–15.

Mayberry, R., and Fischer, S. 1989. Looking through phonological shape to lexical meaning: The bottleneck of non-native sign language processing. *Memory & Cognition* 17:740–754.

Miyawaki, K, Strange, W., Verbrugge, R., Liberman, A., Jenkins, J., and Fujimura, O. 1975. An effect of linguistic experience: The discrimination of /r/ and /l/ by native speakers of Japanese and English. *Perception & Psychophysics* 18:331–40.

Mochizuki, M. 1981. The identification of /r/ and /l/ in natural and synthetic speech. *Journal of Phonetics* 9:283–303.

Mueller, T., and Niedzielski, H. 1963. The influence of discrimination training on pronunciation. *Modern Language Journal* 52:410–16.

Munro, M. 1990. Attention to spectral and temporal cues in vowel perception among native speakers of Arabic and English. *Journal of the Acoustical Society of America* 88:S53(A).

Nathan, G. 1987. On second-language acquisition of voiced stops. *Journal of Phonetics* 15:313–22.

Nittrouer, S., and Studdert-Kennedy, M. 1987. The role of coarticulatory effects in the perception of fricatives by children and adults. *Journal of Speech and Hearing Research* 30:319–29.

Nittrouer, S., Studdert-Kennedy, M., and McGowan, R. 1989. The emergence of phonetic segments: Evidence from the spectral structure of fricative-vowel syllables spoken by children and adults. *Journal of Speech and Hearing Research* 32:120–32.

Obler, L., and Albert, M. 1978. A monitor system for bilingual language processing. In *Aspects of Bilingualism*, ed. M. Paradis. Columbia, SC: Hornbeam.

Ohala, M. 1978. Conflicting expectations for the direction of sound change. *Indian Linguistics* 39:25–28.

Oyama, S. 1976. The sensitive period for the acquisition of a nonnative phonological system. *Journal of Psycholinguistics Research* 5:261–85.

Patkowski, M. 1989. Age and accent in a second language: A reply to James Emil Flege. *Applied Linguistics* 11:73–89.

Piaget, J., and Inhelder, B. 1969. *The Psychology of the Child*. London: Routledge and Kegan Paul.

Pimsleur, P. 1963. Discrimination training in the teaching of French pronunciation. *Modern Language Journal* 47:199–203.

Polivanov, E. 1931. La perception des sons d'une langue étrangère. *Travaux du Cercle Linguistique de Prague* 4:79–96.

Port, R., and Mitleb, F. 1980. Phonetic and phonological manifestations of the voicing contrast in Arabic-accented English. *Research in Phonetics* 1:137–65 (Department of Linguistics, Indiana University).

Port, R., and Mitleb, F. 1983. Segmental features and implementation in acquisition of English by Arabic speakers. *Journal of Phonetics* 11:219–231.

Price, P. J. 1981. A cross-linguistic study of flaps in Japanese and American English. Ph.D. diss., University of Pennsylvania.

Rubach, J. 1984. Rule typology and phonological interference. In *Theoretical Issues in Contrastive Phonology*, ed. S. Eliasson. Heidelburg: Groos.

Sapon, S. 1952. An application of psychological theory to pronunciation problems in second language learning. *Modern Language Journal* 36:111–14.

Schmidt, A. 1988. The acquisition of some American English duration parameters by nonnative speakers of English. Unpublished Ph.D. diss., University of Florida.

Schneiderman, E., and Desmarais, C. 1988. The talented language learner: Some preliminary findings. *Second Language Research* 4:91–109.

Scholes, R. 1968. Phonemic interference as a perceptual phenomena. *Language and Speech* 11:86–103.

Schumann, J. 1975. Affective factors and the problems of age in second language acquisition. *Language Learning* 25:209–235.

Scovel, T. 1988. *A Time to Speak: A Psycholinguistic Inquiry into the Critical Period for Human Speech.* New York: Newbury House.

Shaffer, D. 1985. *Developmental Psychology.* Monterey, CA: Brooks/Cole.

Sheldon, A., and Strange, W. 1982. The acquisition of /r/ and /l/ by Japanese learners of English: Evidence that speech production can precede speech perception. *Applied Psycholinguistics* 3:243–61.

Simon, C., and Fourcin, A. 1978. Cross-language study of speech pattern learning. *Journal of the Acoustical Society of America* 63:925–35.

Singh, R. 1990. The device "phonological rule" and interphonology. In *New Sounds 90, Proceedings of the Symposium on Second Language Speech Learning,* eds. J. Leather and A. R. James. Dordrecht: Foris.

Smith, B. L. 1978. Temporal aspects of English speech production: A developmental perspective. *Journal of Phonetics* 6:37–67.

Suomi, K. 1980. Voicing in English and Finnish stops. Department of English and General Linguistics, Publication 10. Turku University, Finland.

Treiman, R., and Zukowski, A. 1990. Levels of phonological awareness. In *Phonological Processes in Literacy*, ed. S. Brady and D. Shankweiler. Hillsdale, NJ: Lawrence Erlbaum Associates.

Trubetzkoy, N. 1939. *Grundzüge der Phonologie.* Berkeley: University of California Press. English translation by C. Baltaxe, 1969.

Tunmer, W. 1988. Metalinguistic abilities and beginning reading. *Reading Research Quarterly* 23:134–58.

Turitz, N. 1981. The elusive Spanish /s/ and its repercussions in the acquisition of English. Unpublished MS, Department of Linguistics, Georgetown University.

Valdman, A. 1976. *Introduction to French Phonology and Morphology.* Rowley, MA: Newbury House.

Walley, A. C. 1990. Spoken word recognition and vocabulary growth in early childhood. In *Theories in Spoken Language: Perception, Production, and Development*, eds. J. Charles-Luce and J. R. Sawusch. Norwood, NJ: Ablex.

Weinberger, S. 1990. Minimal segments in a second language phonology. In *New Sounds 90, Proceedings of the Symposium on Second Language Speech Learning*, eds. J. Leather and A. R. James. Dordrecht: Foris.

Weinreich, U. 1953. *Languages in Contact, Findings and Problems*. The Hague: Mouton.

Wenk, B. J. 1985. Speech rhythms. *Language and Speech* 28:157–75.

White, S. H. 1965. Evidence for a hierarchical arrangement of learning processes. In *Advances in Child Development and Behavior, Vol. 2*, ed. L. P. Lipsitt and C. C. Spiker. New York: Academic.

Williams, L. 1979. The modification of speech perception and production in second-language learning. *Perception & Psychophysics* 26:95–104.

Williams, L. 1980. Phonetic variation as a function of second-language learning. In *Child Phonology, Vol. 2, Perception*, eds. G. Yeni-Komshian, J. Kavanagh, and C. Ferguson. New York: Academic.

Wode, H. 1978. The beginning of non-school room L2 phonological acquisition. *International Review of Applied Linguistics* 16:109–125.

Wode, H. 1981. *Learning a Second Language*. Tübingen: Gunter Narr.

Zlatin, M., and Koenigsknecht, R. 1975. Development of the voicing contrast: Perception of stop consonants. *Journal of Speech and Hearing Research* 18:541–53.

Zlatin, M., and Koenigsknecht, R. 1976. Development of the voicing contrast: A comparison of voice onset time in stop perception and production. *Journal of Speech and Hearing Research* 19:78–92.

Chapter • 22

Categorical Perception and Segmental Coding in the Ontogeny of Sound Systems
A Universal Approach

Henning Wode

INTRODUCTION

Purpose:
Continuity in Phonological Acquisition

Although there is a sizable amount of research on L1 and L2 phonological acquisition, few if any attempts have so far been made to link the two fields (exceptions are Wode 1977c, 1978, 1981; Macken and Ferguson 1981; or Hecht and Mulford 1982).[1] The difficulties are obvious. If one compares, for example, adult L2 learners with child L1 learners, then one difference is the occurrence of interference, i.e., the incorporation of properties of previously acquired languages into the new target. On the surface of things, such data are hard to relate to each other as long as the comparison is restricted to surface (dis)similarities. Such comparisons can only result in acknowledging the fact that there are many differences between small children and second language

---

[1] I am grateful to Ocke-Schwen Bohn for valuable criticism and suggestions.

learning adults or adolescents. The conclusion can only be to assume a discontinuity with respect to the learning mechanisms involved. This chapter takes a different approach. Instead of looking at surface data, the focus is on the development of the underlying learning abilities. After all, it must be these abilities and their development that determine the nature of the surface data. In this chapter the possibility is explored that at least some language learning abilities develop in a continuous way from early infancy to adulthood, and that continuous changes in the underlying abilities may result in what looks like discontinuous surface data. If the L1 versus L2 surface differences can be accounted for in this way, it would be justified to assume a universal theory of language acquisition (UTA), i.e., one capable of handling not only L1 and L2 acquisition but any acquisitional type.

The Universal Theory of Language Acquisition (UTA)

The central issue for any theory of language acquisition is to determine the nature of the language learning mechanism(s). The ability to learn languages is not restricted to children. The crucial point, therefore, is not to find out how children learn one language, but how people in general learn languages, e.g., in different external settings or at different points during their lifetime. Do humans activate totally different learning mechanisms depending on the learning situation, for example, whether they are tutored or not, or whether it is their L1, L2, or L3? Is there only one single language learning mechanism that is flexible enough to cope with differences in the external settings? The research of the last two decades on L1 and L2 acquisition, foreign language teaching, or on the re-learning of languages, clearly indicates that the first alternative, i.e., to assume a number of totally unrelated learning systems, must be ruled out. Of course, it is not difficult to cite differences between younger and older learners, between L1 or L2 (e.g., Fathman 1975; Clahsen and Muysken 1986; Dulay et al. 1982; Ellis 1985), or when learners are faced with different tasks (e.g., Burmeister, Ufert, and Wode 1979; Wode 1981; Ellis 1985). But none of these differences requires the assumption that they are due to totally independent learning mechanisms, each of them activated for a specific acquisitional type only.

The presently available acquisitional evidence is like this: Some developmental structures have been found with learners of all age groups and acquisitional types. Preverbal negation, as in NP NEG VP, is a case in point. Utterances such as *me no close the window* meaning "I'm not going to shut the window" have been observed with L1 monolingual, L1 bilingual, and L1 trilingual children (e.g., Klima and Bellugi 1966; Lange and Larsson 1973; Wode 1977a; Kadar-Hofman 1983); L2 children (e.g., Wode 1976, 1981; Wong-Fillmore 1976) and adult L2 learners (e.g., Schumann 1978; Clahsen, Meisel, and Pienemann 1983); in L2 re-learning (e.g., Allendorff 1980); and in foreign language teaching (e.g., Felix 1976; Sadownik 1987. Cf. Wode 1981, 1988 for a survey). This wide range of invariant occurrences can hardly be due to different learning mechanisms or to differences in the input situation; they must be due to invariant learning abilities. On the other hand, it will be shown below that the rise of categorical speech perception and segmental coding are clear instances of learning abilities that change as a function of age and experience. These findings are incorporated into UTA by assuming that some language learning abilities change as a function of age and/ or experience, whereas others do not.

Methodological Artifacts: Age

An alternative view to UTA would be to assume separate learning mechanisms to be activated for, say, L1 as against L2 acquisition. One requirement that such an alternative would have to meet is that there be at least one property that categorically differentiates the acquisitional types. Age is probably the most likely candidate to meet this requirement. After all, this is the area where differences between (child) L1 learners and (adult) L2 learners have been reported most reliably, both with respect to differences in the developmental structures (e.g., Clahsen and Muysken 1986; Clahsen 1989) and ultimate level of achievement (e.g., Dulay, Burt, and Krashen 1982; Ellis 1985; Long 1988; Wode 1988). However, even age will not do.

Of course, if one compares adult L2 acquisition to child L1 acquisition, then the age difference is so obvious that age may conveniently be taken as a property that sets these two groups of subjects apart. However, such a procedure involves an artifact. Age is a gradient. The question, therefore, is which age range is to be criterial. This issue cannot be decided arbitrarily, as in McLaughlin (1978) who, arbitrarily, defines L2 acquisition as learning an additional language after the age of three years. What is needed is a functional solution in the sense that the learner's development as reflected in his or her linguistic behavior must provide evidence that a given property occurs only with one age group and not with another.

However, even if age-related differences were found—as indeed, they are reported below—this would not necessarily argue against a universal approach as long as the differences can be shown to develop out of abilities already in existence. Findings of this sort provide the basis for the above claim that some learning abilities change whereas others do not. (For further details on UTA cf. Wode 1981, 1988.)

The methodology needed should be self-evident. The origin and the development of the respective abilities need to be traced starting with very young L1 learners. Their development should be followed through childhood, adolescence, and adulthood.

ONTOGENY AND DEVELOPMENT OF CATEGORICAL SPEECH PERCEPTION

The advent of modern splicing techniques and speech synthesis during the 1960s made it possible for research on categorical speech perception to get under way on a large scale. At first researchers looked at adult, i.e., fully matured, speakers; afterwards the methodology was applied to children and infants as young as four weeks of age. Several techniques are available. All in all, the results are surprisingly compatible across these techniques. For some time the research was directed toward monolingual speakers, both adults and children, (for a general survey cf. Repp 1984; on infants and young children cf. Jusczyk 1981; Aslin, Pisoni, and Jusczyk 1983; Kuhl 1987). Only recently has it been extended to L2 acquisition (for a survey cf. Flege 1988).

The development of categorical speech perception is a complex phenomenon because it does not only imply growth in the sense of increase in perceptual abilities, but also loss or partial loss of originally available ones. Important research questions are: What is the developmental sequence of the target language categories? What is the sequence according to which originally available distinctions are lost because they are not required by the target language? What is the contribution of genetic predisposition and/or external stimulation to these developments? To what extent and in what way can the distinctions not required by the L1, but needed in a language to be acquired subsequently, be developed, either by re-activation of the originally available abilities or by relearning them?

Mature Perception

Speech perception can be said to be categorical if an acoustic continuum is perceived discontinuously. The experimental designs are still much like the ones of the late 1960s and early 1970s (e.g., Liberman et al. 1957; Lisker and Abramson 1964, 1970). At first, researchers were fascinated by the idea that there should be stable category boundaries. These boundaries were found to be language-specific and there was some variation between individual speakers as to the location of their boundaries (e.g., Lisker and Abramson 1964; Williams 1980; Gass 1984). Researchers also came to realize that these category boundaries are more flexible than originally envisaged, even with the same speaker. Howell and Rosen (1984), for example, summarize evidence to show that speed of delivery and other factors can lead to changes in the category boundary values. The term *categorical*, therefore, cannot be taken in an absolute sense but in a slightly looser one, namely, as referring to a high degree of categoriality. This raises the question as to the nature of the mental representation of the speech perceptual categories. Because they are not based on stimuli in which only one single acoustic dimension is varied they can be assumed to be structured like prototypes, as in category formation in the sense of Rosch (1978).

To assume that the perceptual categories in natural speech are structured like prototypes is extremely convenient because their prototypical nature provides for the perceptual basis for phonological/phonetic redundancy, language change, and much of language acquisition. Even if one or a few characteristics of a given prototype change as in diachronic change or synchronic variation, the language, or the particular variety of it, continues to function adequately because the prototype is still recognizable. Furthermore, learners of whatever acquisitional type need not hit the proper target values right away. It suffices for such speakers to get close in order to be able to share verbal interactions as a prerequisite for language learning to get under way (details in Wode 1988). This means that learners can afford to take time to arrive at a match between their own category values and the ones of the target language.

Not long after the first reports on adult categorical speech perception were published, the basic design as well as the theoretical issues were adapted and applied to children, including infants as young as four weeks of age, to check to what extent they were able to discriminate speech sounds in a categorical-like manner. This was an important theoretical development because of the learnability problem associated with categorical speech perception. That is, because the category boundaries cannot be detected in any direct way from the acoustic properties of the speech wave, it was important to determine the origin of these perceptual categorization abilities: Are they due to genetic predisposition, to the impact of external stimulation, or partly to the one and partly to the other?

Development of Perception of Native Contrasts

It now appears that the distinctions utilized for phonological purposes in natural languages are available to infants before they begin to speak. Some of these distinctions have been shown to be available with children as young as four weeks of age; other distinctions become available subsequently before the onset of speech. In the early research infants were reported to fail to discriminate regularly certain contrasts, notably, /θ/ versus /f/ (e.g., Eilers, Wilson, and Moore 1977). However, as more sophisticated experimental techniques were developed even such contrasts were shown to be available to children before the onset of speech. For example, Jusczyk (1981) cites experiments by Jusczyk, Murray, and Bayly (1979) that indicate that children as young as 0;2 can detect place contrasts including such pairs as /θa/ versus /fa/. Moreover, they can do this on the basis of frication and/or formant transitions (Jusczyk 1981). At the present time it seems that there are no distinctions that become available only after children begin to speak.

In terms of the development of abilities required for categorical perception, the presently available evidence is consistent with the following view. Much before children begin to speak, they have available to them the same abilities for categorical speech perception irrespective of the language they happen to be in contact with. For example, the three languages English, Spanish, and Kikuyu, a Bantu language of Kenya, differ as to how voicing is used. English contrasts voiced (unaspirated) stops versus voiceless (aspirated) stops; Spanish has prevoiced versus voiceless (unaspirated) stops; and Kikuyu, according to Streeter (1976), contrasts voiced versus prevoiced stops, except for the labial place of articulation. Kikuyu has only one labial stop and it is prevoiced. Young children, no matter which language they are exposed to, at first distinguish three different VOT ranges, namely, prevoiced, voiced, and voiceless, at VOT values that are the same for all children. This is so, irrespective of the input language. Streeter (1976), for example, found the three categories with Kikuyu children, although, as just noted, Kikuyu has only one labial stop, which is prevoiced. Similarly, English infants are, at first, sensitive to prevoicing although it is not a distinctive feature of the phonological system of English (e.g., Lasky, Syrdal-Lasky, and Klein 1975; Eilers, Gavin, and Wilson 1979; Aslin and Pisoni 1981).

These original abilities subsequently give rise to the category of the input language. The entire process may take many years, in some cases until adulthood, before the full range of target values is established (e.g., Zlatin and Koenigsknecht 1975, 1976; Bailey and Haggard 1980; Flege and Eefting 1985). It is important to note that this development is not only a matter of expanding on the original abilities in a simple additive fashion. There also may be what may look like losses or partial losses in the sense that older children or adults fail to identify or discriminate contrasts that infants regularly perceive. The overall development, therefore, is one of constant reorganization and modification in such a way that the original genetic predisposition interacts with external stimulation via the ambient language(s).

As for methodology, there are two options to trace such developments. One is to investigate monolingual speakers to determine at which age a given category is first available and how the ability for category formation and/or recognition changes over time. The second option is to utilize non-native contrasts. Monolingual speakers of L_i with no prior contact to L_j, are presented with L_j contrasts not used in L_i. The age ranges of such subjects can be varied systematically from pre-speaking to maturity.

Both approaches produce highly comparable results. Invariably, adult monolinguals fare much poorer in perceiving non-native contrasts than either infants for whom the contrasts are native, or infants for whom the contrasts are non-native. What is the nature of these changes? When do they occur? Are adults totally incapable of perceiving non-native contrasts, can they do so but only at a reduced level, or do their abilities vary individually?

Much of the evidence on these points is due to the work by Werker, Tees, and their co-workers on English, Hindi, and Thompson, an Indian language spoken in South-Central British Columbia, Canada. Burnham (1986) has collated several of the Werker and Tees studies into table I.

Among other things, table I documents perceptual changes before the onset of speech. For example, the contrast between the retroflex /ṭ/ versus the dental /t̪/ is phonemic in Hindi but not in English. Until age 0;7 infants from L1 English-speaking environments have the same ability to perceive /ṭ/ versus /t̪/ as infants growing up in a monolingual Hindi environment. Subsequently, this ability diminishes. By age 0;9 only one third of the English-environment subjects were successful up to criterion; by age 0;11 only 2 out 12; and at age 4;0 no child managed to distinguish /ṭ/ versus /t̪/.

The results for the Thompson contrast /k̉/ versus /q̉/ are quite parallel. Thompson is among the few languages with a phonemic contrast between a glottalized velar stop /k̉/ and a glottalized uvular stop /q̉/. This opposition does not exist in English. As with /ṭ/ versus /t̪/ English-environment children appear to begin to fail to discriminate the /k̉/-/q̉/ continuum starting around age 0;7.

Whereas table I provides data on the total disappearance of perceptual abilities, other distinctions may be affected too, but not as radically as /ṭ/ and /t̪/, or /k̉/ and /q̉/. Consider the Hindi contrast /tʰ/ versus /dʰ/. Based on Werker et al. (1981), Werker and Tees (1983), and Tees and Werker (1984), Burnham (1986) points out that children and adults retain some ability to discriminate /tʰ/ and /dʰ/ even without training or exposure. In addition, as little training as 1 to 2 weeks may be so successful that adult students can perform up to criterion in the discrimination of /dʰ/ and /tʰ/. This contrasts with the poor performance of the adults even after training for /ṭ/ and /t̪/, as summarized in table I. Training was successful only with those students who had had some prior exposure to Hindi early in life, which means that these subjects were

Table I. The Perception of Two Place-of-Articulation Contrasts by Infants, Children, and Adults from L1 Monolingual English Environments as well as Native Adult Speakers of Hindi and Thompson. Part (a) Perception; (b) Effect of Training. [Part (a) is based on Werker et al. 1981; Werker and Tees 1983, 1984; (b) on Tees and Werker 1984. Reprinted with permission from Cambridge University Press. D. K. Burnham. Developmental loss of speech perception: Exposure to and experience with a first language. *Applied Psycholinguistics* 7:224.

(a)

	Reached criterion	Infants				Children		Adults		
		0;7	0;9	0;11	4;0	8;0	12;0	Native English	Trained English	Native Hindi/Thompson
/ʈ/ vs. /t̪/	YES	11	8	2	0	0	1	1	0	5
	NO	1	410	12	12	11	9	10	0	
/kʼ/ vs. /q/	YES	8	81	—	—	—	3	—	5	
	NO	2	69	—	—	—	7	—	0	

(b)

	Reached criterion	Untrained English adults	Trained English adults	Native English-speaking adults with 5 years Hindi experience	Students of Hindi with early exposure to Hindi language when tested		Students of Hindi with no early exposure to Hindi language training when tested	
					1–2 wks.	1 year	1–2 wks.	1 year
/ʈ/ vs. /t̪/	YES	1	6	5	9	10	2	3
	NO	14	8	0	1	0	16	15

relearning Hindi rather than being exposed to it for the first time as their L2.

In summary, before children begin to speak, their original perceptual behavior is modified, as a function of the ambient language input. Such modifications continue until, and after, the onset of speech. Adults and children seem to retain some perceptual abilities for contrasts not exploited in their L1s. The degree of retention seems to differ for the various categories.

Perception of Non-Native (L2) Contrasts

Studies on the perception of L2 learners/speakers are indispensable for a proper understanding of both the functioning of the speech perception system and L1 acquisition, because it is through contact with additional languages that the true potential of human beings for speech perception is revealed. How and to what extent can the perceptual abilities of learners be activated for the purpose of learning additional languages? At which state of development are these abilities activated—at the original state at birth; at the state of development at which the learner first has access to L2 input; or at some intermediate state?

Ideally, the data required to answer such questions should be longitudinal and focus on the development of the same individual speaker learning additional languages at different times in his or her life. Obviously, such subjects are not likely to be found. The closest approximation is a cross-sectional study on different people learning additional languages at different ages. Unfortunately, much less research has so far been carried out on L2 than on L1 perception and only a few contrasts have been explored so far, preferably, VOT, e.g., pioneer studies, like Caramazza et al. (1973); Williams (1980); and others in that tradition, such as Albert and Obler (1978); Obler (1983); or Gass (1984).

Others have explored the /r/ versus /l/ contrast, e.g., Mochizuki (1981); MacKain, Best, and Strange (1981); Strange and Dittman (1981); Mann (1986), or vowel distinctions, e.g., Elsendoorn (1981); Flege and Hillenbrand (1984); Bohn and Flege (1989) (cf. Flege 1988 for a survey).

The evidence there is suggests the following overall view: People approach the task of learning an L2 on the basis of the state of development of their perceptual abilities and categories. They form the grid according to which L2 speech is at first processed. As the L2 learner begins to make progress, some category boundaries developed through the prior L1 are modified to serve both languages. As for the acquisition and development of L2 targets, the available evidence suggests that the developmental sequences differ depending on the nature of the specific target item relative to the L2 learner's L1 phonic repertoire. Recent modifications of the notion of perceptual equivalence have proved particularly fruitful in attempts to explain the various observations, notably, age-dependent differences or the fact that in some cases L2 bilinguals may use a compromise VOT boundary for both the L1 and the L2 and which is intermediate between the values of the respective monolingual speakers (e.g., Caramazza et al. 1973; Williams 1979, 1980).

The early pioneer studies on language contact and bilingualism, like Weinreich (1953) or Haugen (1953, 1958), already suggested that phonological transfer in L2 bilinguals was likely to occur only if the phonemes in question were sufficiently similar to each other. Such a claim makes sense only if it is assumed that these phonemes are heard as similar. The insight concerning perceived similarity and/or difference was developed further in the L2 acquisition research during the 1970s (Wode 1977c, 1978, 1981). It was suggested that the way L2 learners acquire the phonological elements of a given L2 depends on equivalence relationships based on the degree of perceived/perceivable similarity between the phonological elements of the target L2 and those of the L1. The central idea is:

> In naturalistic L2 acquisition of phonology learners start from their own L1 phonological capacity. This capacity is the state of development of their L1 phonological system. From their L1 capacity they start towards the L2 targets by substituting L1 elements for those L2 elements that are sufficiently similar to the available L1 targets.

> Those L2 elements that are not sufficiently similar to any L1 elements are acquired differently, very likely in ways parallel to their acquisition in L1. Phonological elements that are sufficiently similar in this sense will be called equivalent to each other; those that are not, are non-equivalent. The process can be likened to a matching procedure. The input is the L2 as spoken by the L2 environment to which the learner is exposed. L2 phonological targets are scanned for equivalencies and for non-equivalences. There seems to be a crucial measure that separates the range of equivalencies from non-equivalencies. L2 elements that fall within this crucial range of equivalence are matched and substituted by their respective L1 equivalents. Those that fall outside this crucial range, undergo other developments (Wode 1981, p. 232).

Flege (1988, in press, this volume), has expanded on this notion of equivalence in two important ways. One is that he distinguishes between three types of phonological elements on the basis of perceptual similarity, namely, identical, similar, and new sounds. Identical elements are perceived by the L2 learner as being the same; consequently, the L2 target is substituted by the L1 equivalent. Similar phones are perceived as different, but not dissimilar enough not to be substituted by the L1 equivalent. New sounds are perceived as different from anything in the learner's L1 repertoire. The perception of the L2 input feeds into the pre-existing system of the L1 categories, i.e., into the L1 prototypes. This has a double effect. The identical and the similar L2 elements are handled via the equivalent L1 prototypes. This allows the L2 learner to make rapid progress on a good number of phonological elements. The new elements, however, require the creation of new categories, which takes time. Consequently, new phones develop later. However, in the long run, the new sounds are likely to be mastered more successfully because there are no pre-existing categories to interfere or that need to be overcome. Because phones in different languages rarely are completely identical, it is flaws in the realization of the similar phonological elements that persist longest, i.e., they take the most time to overcome.

Flege's account of equivalence relationships seems well suited to handle developmental and age-dependent peculiarities observable with L2 learners, including the most difficult cases, namely, similar elements. As for the age issue, Flege's (1988) careful review of the literature confirms that children who learn the L2 before or around age 6 are likely to achieve a native-like competence whereas older learners, in particular adults, rarely do so. Moreover, highly successful L2 learners develop the same category boundaries for both their languages in the same locations as the respective monolingual speakers. Somewhat less successful learners may develop one single compromise boundary intermediate between the L1 and L2 target values to serve both languages in perception and production. This has been found for VOT (e.g., Caramazza et al. 1973; Williams 1979, 1980; Flege and Hillenbrand 1984; Flege 1987). Suppose a given L1 has a VOT boundary between /b/ and /p/ around -4 ms as in the case of Spanish (Williams 1979), and the target L2 has a VOT boundary of $+25$ ms as for English (Lisker and Abrahamson 1964; Williams 1979). In such cases L2 learners may have a VOT boundary that is a compromise between the L1 and the L2 but that matches neither one (e.g., Williams 1979; Flege and Hillenbrand 1984; Flege 1987).

All in all, then, the issue of the availability of perceptual abilities for the acquisition of additional languages, such as L2s or L3s can only be addressed in a relative way. It makes little sense to ask whether certain abilities can be activated. The question has to be whether they can be activated relative to a specific L1 background. For example, can learners of Japanese develop separate categories to distinguish /r/ from /l/ as required by English, although Japanese does not have this distinction? Can speakers of English develop the appropriate sensitivity for the French /u/ that differs from the English equivalent in terms of the location of the second formant? (Flege 1987) Or can Germans learn to perceive and produce the very slight difference between the lax vowel /ɪ/ of English and German? The /r/ versus /l/ distinction may be a new one for the Japanese, hence there is no equivalence for such learners of English. Both, the French /u/ and the German /ɪ/ are cases of (very close) similarity, hence (strong) equivalence, although for most speakers of English and German their respective /ɪ/s are probably mutually identical.

Summary: A Universal Hypothesis on the Ontogeny and Development of Speech Perception

Because of the present state of research, many important issues could not be discussed here. For instance, it is not known whether all L2 learners follow the same developments or whether some of them are able to identify the target L2 category boundaries without being affected at all by their prior L1. There is no research to answer the question of whether all learners retain the ability to separate the category ranges eventually for either all or only some L2 distinctions. And there are no reports on the details of the development of L2 learners who gained a native-like competence. Nonetheless, the following universal hypothesis seems warranted: Speech perception in humans develops out of their auditory system. It constitutes the biological foundation for speech perception.

The auditory system is characterized by areas of heightened sensitivity. These areas constitute the genetically endowed disposition for speech (Eimas et al. 1971) and they form the basis for subsequent development of the characteristics of perceptual categories of the ambient language(s). The areas of heightened sensitivity already respond to sounds of the target language during the prelinguistic period, i.e., while the child does not yet understand the language(s). At this stage, changes in the auditory system are due to the fact that those phonetic properties not exploited for distinctive purposes are either rare in the input or do not occur there at all (Werker and Tees 1984). This way, prelinguistic children lose, discard, and/or become desensitized to those perceptual abilities not needed in the ambient language(s). Consequently, when children begin to talk they have already developed a first approximation between their own abilities and the requirements of the target(s).

As children develop their production capacity after the onset of speech, i.e., around 1;0, the perceptual categories continue to be sharpened toward the target, resulting in the fact that those original abilities not required by the target become increasingly less accessible. This attenuation effect differs depending on the category involved. For some contrasts, the ability, at least with some speakers, gets attenuated to such an extent that it cannot be activated right away if there is contact to an additional language. Recall the difficulty that the adults had in identifying the retroflex versus dental stops of Hindi and the glottalized velar versus glottalized uvular stops of Thompson (table I). The abilities for other contrasts do not seem to attenuate as radically, for example, the relative retention of the ability to identify voiced versus voiceless aspirated stops by speakers of English. The entire development, then, is one of interaction between original biological endowment and experience.

This account fits what is generally known about the rise of cognitive systems in general. Those biological and/or other substrata that are required for the development of specific categories or abilities continue to develop at the expense of others, i.e., attenuation of those substrata not needed. If, subsequently, the need arises to draw on the original abilities, they are not immediately accessible. As far as speech perception is concerned, the details about what happens when such abilities are needed are anything but well understood at the present time. Nonetheless, the impact of experience is not such that its results are completely irreversible. On the contrary, at any given stage of development, i.e., with children as well as with adults, the categories and abilities remain flexible enough to meet new needs, such as imposed by contact with additional languages or the dissemination of language change. The degree to which such new demands can be met differs depending on the categories involved.

The essential point is that this is not a matter of a given category being impossible to learn at a certain age in any absolute sense. Rather, it depends on the relationship between three major factors. One is the state of development of the learner's speech-perceptual system, e.g., his or her system of phonetic prototypes. Another factor is the nature of the phonological elements of the target and their psychoacoustic salience, perhaps in terms of Burnham's distinction between fragile and robust contrasts (Burnham 1986). The third factor is the equivalence relationship between the phones of the learner's L1 repertoire and those of the target. Note that this equivalence relationship is determined by the learner, i.e., as perceived by him or her on the basis of the mutual similarity between the items involved. Taking Flege's three-term distinction of identical versus similar versus new as presenting a cline in similarity rather than three discontinuous categories, the data are consistent with the following generalization: The more similar the distinctions of additional languages, the more they are likely to be perceived in terms of categories already available to a given learner; the less similar a contrast, the less will it be perceived via categories already available. Pre-existing categories tend to block or impede learning and development of those L2 targets that are within the areas already taken up by pre-existing categories. Those targets that fall outside pre-occupied areas are not blocked or impeded. Hence, they may take longer to develop because there are no ready-made categories to fall back on; but they are more likely to get close to the target because there is nothing to block them.

It is difficult at the present state of research to determine how the psychoacoustic salience of perceptual categories relates to the above summary. Burnham (1986) has suggested that perceptual contrasts can be arranged using the two extremes of robust versus fragile. Robust contrasts are quite salient; they occur in many languages; they are learned early in L1 acquisition; and they are easier to activate at later stages in life. Fragile contrasts are less frequent in the languages of the world, they are learned later, and they are probably harder to re-activate if not utilized for L1 acquisition. Burnham's proposal is intuitively quite plausible. However, it is not clear how his distinction interacts with the equivalence relationships and how much room is left for the original psychoacoustic salience/robustness to have an impact.

The above hypothesis allows for a good deal of individual variation. It also allows for categories to change over time. This is reflected in people's ability to adapt to language change and in the fact that some learners do acquire a native-like L2 competence. At the same time the hypothesis suggests a mechanism that explains the basis for differential success. And, above all, the hypothesis is consistent with the fact that, *pace* Lenneberg (1967), there is no principled reason—based on biology or other —human beings should not be able to learn additional languages well.

ONTOGENY AND DEVELOPMENT OF SEGMENTAL CODING

The proposal put forth and explored in this chapter relates to how the phonological components of lexical items are coded. The claim is that at the time a child begins to learn his or her first language(s) this information is not coded in terms of segments as with fully matured speakers, but either in terms of syllables or, more frequently, entire lexical items. Segments become available around 2;0. Afterward, segmental coding is applied to subsequent acquisition of any language.

Learnability of Segments and Lexically Based Coding

On the one hand, no phonetic/phonological theory has so far been proposed that can do without some notion of segment. On the other hand, no instrumental technique is available that allows for the unequivocal identification of the segments of a given utterance. Speech is continuous. This means that on the articulatory and physical level speech cannot be regarded as being structured in terms of individual sounds or segments (e.g., Menzerath and de Lacerda 1933; Zwirner and Zwirner 1966; Truby 1959). What, then, is the nature and the status of segments, phonemes, or the like? How can segments be learned or how can learners learn to identify segments?

The bulk of the literature on child phonology does not deal with the segment issue. For example, Jakobson (1941) simply utilizes phonemes and phonological features as his framework without discussing the issue at all.

In contrast, Moskowitz (1971, 1973) suggested that at the beginning of language acquisition the unit for coding phonological information is not the segment but the syllable. Moskowitz's claim is based on her contention that all children at first reduplicate. This claim is too strong. To be sure, there are such children (e.g., Ferguson, Peizer, and Weeks 1973), but they are rare. Reduplication is much less prevalent in the majority of children. They may have various sorts of reduplication but it is not a property pertaining to all lexical items. It is restricted to the domain of the individual item (cf. survey and discussion in Wode 1988, p. 186). This supports the point repeatedly made by Ferguson and his co-workers that phonological acquisition and the coding of phonological information must initially be based on lexical items rather than on abstract categories (e.g., Ferguson, Peizer, and Weeks 1973; Ferguson and Farwell 1975; Ferguson and Garnica 1975; Macken and Ferguson 1983; Macken 1978, 1979, 1986; Chiat 1979). Lexical items are the only natural starting point for the child.

In addition to reduplication, Ferguson and Farwell (1975) point to the nature of phonological variation in children's first 50 words to support their suggestion concerning lexically based coding. In one word a child may have free variation between three phones A, B, and C; in another word the alternation is between A and B; and in a third word only phone A occurs (table II).

Note that there is no phonetic/phonological reason at all to account for the fact that in one word containing [b –] there is a three-term variation, and in other words also containing [b –], only a two-term variation, and in still other words, no variation at all. The variational pattern is tied to the individual lexical item and does not, yet, apply to the entire lexicon as with fully matured speakers. For the latter to happen, the variation must be statable with respect to individual segments such

Table II. Lexically Based Phonological Variation in Early L1 Speech (Based on Ferguson and Farwell 1975, p. 425)

baby	b-	:	w-	:	p-
bye-bye	b-	:	β-		
bang	b-				

that a segment X has variants A, B, C in every word unless specific constraints of a nonlexical nature, i.e., due to phonetic/phonological peculiarities, intervene. How, then, does segmental coding develop out of lexically based coding?

The Rise of Segments

Two types of data are drawn on for clues as to when segments must become available, namely, the youngest age at which transfer occurs in L2 acquisition and those L1 phonological processes that lead to non-targetlike utterances. (For other types of data cf. Wode 1989). The rationale is the same in either case. For transfer and phonological processes to operate the way they do, it is necessary that the learner/speaker has at his or her disposal a processing device that allows him or her to hit the appropriate spot in a lexical item not by chance but in a systematic and controlled way. This device is the segment.

L2 Transfer in Young Children. The age range at which phonological transfer first occurs with young learners indicates that, at least at that point, segments must have become available.

To date the earliest age reported for transfer to occur is close to 3;0. The data available in the Kiel corpus on L2 German/L1 English include a boy who came to Germany at the age of 2;7 and who was first investigated at 3;4, i.e., 9 months after his first contact with German. At that time the boy's pronunciation was remarkably close to that of his L1 German-speaking monolingual peers. However, there were a number of transfer peculiarities, all of them familiar from English learners of German older than 3;4 (cf. Wode 1978, 1981). Such errors include: the unrounding of rounded front vowels, e.g., [ɛ] in place of lax /œ/ in *Löffel* (spoon); velarization of final /−l/ as [ɫ] in *Löffel*; replacement of front rounded vowels by back vowels, e.g., lax [ʊ] for lax /ʏ/ as in *Brücke* (bridge) or *fünf* (five), [ɔ] for lax /œ/ in *Löffel* (spoon), tense [o] for tense /ø/ as in *schön* (beautiful, nice); or the creation of diphthongs of the German monophthongs /e o/ via [ɛɪ oʊ]. It is not known whether the boy's record at 3;4 illustrates his initial state of affairs or the end of what may have been a much more prevalent characteristic of his L2 phonology. In any event, this type of evidence clearly shows that segments must be available at least around age 3;4. Obviously, much more extensive research needs to be done on the identification of the age range when phonological transfer can first be observed in L2 learners.

L1 Phonological Processes. L1 phonological processes provide a clearer view as to when segments first become available. That L1 children at first do not reproduce the phonetic/phonological features of the target words in exactly the sequence required by the target is one of the most reliably documented findings for early L1 phonology. For example, when English children pronounce *doggie* [gɔgi] instead of /dɔgi/, or when German children render *Decke* (blanket) as [kɛkə] instead of /dɛkə/, the velar feature is displaced, in this case spread to initial position (e.g., Ingram 1976; Smith 1973; Pačesová 1968; Leopold 1939–49). With respect to the segment issue of interest here, note that such phonological processes are highly systematic, and that they are not restricted to exceptional individuals, but that such processes are likely to occur with all children and all languages.

Note further that the displaced features are not moved around lexical items in random ways; they are shifted only to specific segments. In the case of German *Decke*, the velar feature in the child's version [kɛkə] instead of the target /dɛkə/ has been moved to the initial plosive and not to the vowel, which would have resulted in a back vowel. Nor do the displaced features tend to straddle several segments in the target word. All this means that for these early L1 phonological processes to operate the way they do, segments are required either in the mental representation of lexical items or as part of the processing required for the production of such utterances.

To complement the above review on L2 transfer and L1 phonological processes recall Macken's analysis of the early phonology of two Spanish-speaking children (Macken 1978, 1979). Various aspects are pointed out that seem to indicate that, prior to segments, it is words and/or syllables that are of prime importance for coding phonological information. It looks as if Macken focused in on some of the details of how this shift from presegmental to segmental organization may take place. Similar studies with other subjects in other languages, and, in particular, including the onset of speech, are a desideratum.

Phonological Coding in L2 Acquisition

It has been shown in more detail in Wode (1981) that early L2 phonology is conspiciously different from early L1 phonology. Some major differences are: Reduplication does not occur in L2 acquisition, unless the target requires it, as in *bye-bye*. The L2 syllable types are quite different. Such types as CV, VC, CVC that predominate in early L1 acquisition also occur in L2 acquisition, but only if required by the target. That is, consonant clusters may be attempted right away. Such clusters are not necessarily target-like from the outset, but they are certainly not avoided by the L2 learner or simplified via the deletion of one of their members, which is what happens in early L1 acquisition (e.g., Ingram 1976; Wode 1988). The difficulties L2 learners may have with L2 consonantal clusters are primarily due to differences between the target L2 and the L1. L2 learners resolve these difficulties in various ways to make the L2 clusters conform to those of the L1. For example, Spanish speakers learning German as their L2 tend to break up such initial clusters as /ʃtr- ʃpl- ʃn-/, as in *Straße* (street), *Splitter* (splinter), or *schnell* (fast), by preposing [ə] or an [ɛ] -like vowel. This results in two syllables that conform to the syllabification rules of Spanish. German *schnell*, for example, is turned into [ɛsnɛl] (Tropf 1983). In other L2 combinations speakers adopt different solutions to structural clashes between the L1 and the L2, such as the use of different epenthetic vowels, resyllabification, or deletion (e.g., Tarone 1978; Sato 1984; Broselow 1983, 1984; Anderson 1987; Karimi 1987; Hammarberg 1988).

As for phonological processes, the little work that has been done on this topic (e.g., Wode 1978, 1981; Eckman 1977, 1981; Hecht and Mulford 1982; Hyltenstam and Magnusson 1983; Tropf 1983), shows that the L2 processes function on the basis of segments. Processes that displace features from segments and/or spots in the target to other spots in the learner's replica, like L1 [gɔgi] for *doggie*, are rare or nonoccurrent in L2 acquisition. What abounds in L2 acquisition are transfer-based substitution processes. As already mentioned earlier, such L2 processes function on the basis of segments.

Finally, there is no evidence at all to suggest that L2 phonological variation is lexically based as in early L1 phonology. Even transfer works in such a way that variation occurs in all targets containing a given segment.

Creation of Segments

If segmental coding is not available until around age 2;0, how does this ability originate? There are several options to answer this question. One is to argue that children have this ability all along but that they are not mature enough to make use of it at the onset of speech. This line of argument prompts the question, whence does the ability come? Given the learnability problem with segments, the most likely answer is a nativistic one; namely, that the ability to code phonological information on the basis of segments must be part of the biological endowment of human beings for learning natural human languages. This is an easy way out, because it frees the researcher from doing further empirical research.

The rationale adopted here is that nativistic interpretations should be used only as a final escape route, if there is no other alternative to explain a given phenomena. This section is, therefore, intended to explore another possibility; namely, that the ability to code phonological information on the basis of segments is not directly given via biological endowment, but results from a self-organizing system that operates on phonological codings of the presegment stage(s).

The plausibility of the hypothesis crucially depends on the fact

that children have been found to be able to code the phonological information of lexical items in a consistent and stable way right from the
onset of speech. Research currently under way at the English department of Kiel University, Germany, shows that the notorious L1 phonological processes do not necessarily surface in the first words, e.g.,
not in the first 10 words. But, although children may not necessarily
reproduce the phonetic/phonological properties of the target words in
their own first 10 words in exactly the same linear order as required by
the target, their own productions are such that the phonetic/phonolog-
ical properties appear consistently allocated to the same spot(s). This
principle of local allocation applies both to syllables and to strings the
length of a lexical item. Assume that the principle of locally allocated
phonological information is also valid for the structure of the mental
representations of lexical items and not only to—surface—productions. Assume further that these mental representations are activated
for various retrieval purposes as required for decoding and encoding.
Every time a learner identifies a lexical item or wants to produce it, he
or she has to activate his or her mental representation. I take it that it
can be assumed that by going through these operations repeatedly
learners automatically turn these processes into patterns. During the
time these patterns are being established, there need be, at first, nothing that corresponds in any direct way to segments yet. However, the
mere fact that specific phonetic/phonological information is activated
repeatedly in such a way that the same features appear consistently
allocated to the same spot in the lexical item (automatically?) triggers a
process that groups those activities together that need to be coordinated to produce the desired effect. Note that in most cases more than
one phonetic/phonological property appears consistently at a specific
spot in a lexical item, such as voicing plus nasality plus place of articulation in nasal consonants, or unvoicing plus stopping plus labiality at
the beginning of *papa*. It is quite plausible to assume that the repeated
application of whatever it takes to produce these features conjointly,
results in the creation of novel entities reflected in the segments postulated by phoneticians, phonologists, and language acquisition researchers. According to this view, then, the ability to code phonological information on the basis of segments results from, and is based on,
the requirements for the coordination of activities that involve the retrieval of locally allocated phonetic/phonological information.

The argument above does not collapse if it is objected that children
do not really code phonetic/phonological information in the same way
all the time, because there is intrachild variation. This is correct. But
this kind of variation also involves the local allocation of phonetic/pho-
nological information. Recall that these variational patterns are also frequent enough to trigger automation processes with respect to the co-

ordination of controlling processes centering on specific spots and, thus, also lead to segments.

As for the nature and the functioning of the self-organizing system, details are still unclear. The creation of segments cannot be some simple chunking procedure as proposed by Peters (1977, 1983) for the acquisition of syntax or morphology. As indicated earlier, the acoustic nature of speech is not such that the clues needed for the identification of segments unambiguously appear in a linear sequence. More often than not there is co-articulation and co-occurrence of what we think we hear sequentially.

Moreover, the self-organizing system must differ from the model developed by Lindblom and his colleagues via computer simulation (Lindblom, MacNeilage, and Studdert-Kennedy 1984; Lindblom 1989, this volume). In language acquisition there is no external agent to press some button to get the system started. Furthermore, there is no acquisitional evidence to suggest that the starting point and the developmental progression are completely random as in the trial runs in the Lindblom model. To be sure, the developmental sequences in phonological acquisition show much more individual variation than originally envisaged by Jakobson (1941) (recall, notably, Ferguson and Farwell 1975; Leonard, Newhoff, and Mesalam 1980), but in contrast to Ferguson and Farwell (1975) and Lindblom's model, the progression certainly is not random (Wode 1988; Ingram this volume). And, most important perhaps, the stability of the phonological coding in the first 10 words suggests that the self-organizing system does not start with the first word(s). It is, therefore, also doubtful that babbling can be regarded as a precursor to segmental coding.

CONCLUSIONS

UTA should not be viewed as a drastic disruption of previous lines of research but as an attempt to integrate prior work, to fill in gaps, and to overcome undesirable discontinuities, such as the implausible idea that totally different learning abilities should be activated for different acquisitional types. UTA, instead, presents a restatement of the domain of the theory of language acquisition. The basis for UTA is the biological apparatus and certain functional abilities common to all of human kind. UTA attempts to reconstruct and specify them at birth and traces their development as a function of age and/or experience.

Certain areas of the subdomain of phonology were chosen for closer inspection and illustration in this chapter. The biological bases concerned are the perceptual and the vocal systems. Both systems were shown to be capable of producing cognitive abilities/systems indispensable to the learning and functioning of natural human languages. The details in shaping these abilities were shown to be due to the biological substrata interacting with external stimulation.

The reconstruction of the underlying abilities and their development over time has important implications for other theories proposed for language acquisition. First, UTA forces researchers to go beyond surface observations and explain them in terms of the development of underlying abilities. This way the traditional controversy between continuity versus discontinuity in language acquisition, as exemplified in such statements as "do adults have access to . . . " become pointless. The issue is to determine when certain abilities become inaccessible and how such changes come about. On the other hand, it remains to be seen whether and to what extent the approach that works well for certain components of phonological acquisition carries over to other structural areas. This is an empirical issue. To solve it requires that the artifact according to which researchers contrast young L1 children versus adult L2 learners be given up in favor of a cline in terms of the age groups that are investigated.

In addition to providing for explanations, the universal approach, as exemplified by UTA, helps to fill in gaps with respect to previous theories such as structuralist approaches, like Jakobson (1941), the cognitive theory as developed in and around Stanford (e.g., Ferguson and Farwell 1975; Ferguson and Garnica 1975; Macken and Ferguson 1983), or natural phonology (Stampe 1979). For example, one of the major characteristics of the cognitive theory of phonological acquisition emphasizes that it is essentially the learner who determines the course of events by choosing and avoiding items to be learned. This chapter provides for some of the cognitive machinery enabling learners to choose and avoid.

Similarly, UTA provides for a better understanding of some of the central tenets of natural phonology (Stampe 1979). This approach is based on the notion that learners of L1 apply a set of innate natural processes to their representations of adult speech (such as devoicing of final obstruents and stopping of fricatives) and that an important part of acquisition is learning to suppress those processes that conflict with the facts of the ambient language. The L2 learners, in the early stages, transfer from their L1 the patterns both of suppression and lack of suppression acquired in their L1; later their "errors" are more "developmental," including the (re)activation of processes that may have been suppressed in their L1 (Major 1987). The notion of suppression remains vague unless it is made precise in which way and to what extent the natural processes can be suppressed. Recall the development of categorical speech perception and the reactivation of perceptual abilities later in life. The nature of suppression turns out to be much more complex than envisaged by Stampe (1979) or those who use his framework, e.g., Major (1977, 1987).

UTA can help to clarify some of the assumptions of the structural approaches in the tradition of Jakobson (1941) (e.g., Leopold 1939–49; Pačesová 1968). Such notions as feature, segment, or phoneme are not defined at all but are taken for granted. Unless we trace the development of such constructs, it is difficult to understand how such systems ever become functional.

REFERENCES

Albert, M., and Obler, L. 1978. *The Bilingual Brain*. New York: Academic Press.

Allendorff, S. 1980. Wiedererwerb einer Zweitsprache, dargestellt am Beispiel der englischen Negation. Ph.D. diss., Christian-Albrechts-Universität, Kiel.

Anderson, J. I. 1987. The markedness differential hypothesis and syllable structure difficulty. In *Interlanguage Phonology*, eds. G. Ioup and S. H. Weinberger. New York: Newbury House.

Aslin, R. N., and Pisoni, D. B. 1981. Some developmental processes in speech perception. In *Child Phonology Vol. 2, Perception*, eds. G. Yeni-Komshian, J. Kavanagh, and C. Ferguson. New York: Academic Press.

Aslin, R. N., Pisoni, D. B., and Jusczyk, P. W. 1983. Auditory development and speech perception in infancy. In *Handbook of Child Phonology Infancy and Developmental Psychobiology* Vol. 2, eds. M. Haith and J. Campos. New York: Wiley.

Bailey, P., and Haggard, M. 1980. Perception-production relations in the voicing contrast for initial stops in 3-year-olds. *Phonetica* 37:377–96.

Bohn, O.-S., and Flege, J. E. 1989. Interlingual identification and the role of foreign language experience in L2 vowel perception. University of Alabama, Birmingham (submitted for publication).

Broselow, E. 1983. Non-obvious transfer: On predicting epenthesis errors. In *Language Transfer in Language Learning*, eds. S. Gass and L. Selinker. Rowley, MA: Newbury House.

Broselow, E. 1984. An investigation of transfer in second language phonology. *IRAL* 22:261–78.

Burmeister, H., Ufert, D., and Wode, H. 1979. Zur Leistungsfähigkeit experimenteller Datenerhebungsverfahren bei Untersuchungen zum natürlichen Zweitsprachenerwerb. *Linguistische Beiträge* 64: 95–104.

Burnham, D. K. 1986. Developmental loss of speech perception: Exposure to and experience with a first language. *Applied Psycholinguistics* 7:207–40.

Caramazza, A., Yeni-Komshian, G., Zurif, E., and Carbone, E. 1973. The acquisition of a new phonological contrast: The case of stop consonants in French-English bilinguals. *Journal of the Acoustical Society of America* 54:421–28.

Chiat, S. 1979. The role of the word in phonological development. *Linguistics* 17:591–610.

Clahsen, H. 1989. The comparative study of first and second language development. Unpublished manuscript. Universität Düsseldorf.

Clahsen, H., Meisel, J., and Pienemann, M. 1983. *Deutsch als Zweitsprache: Der Spracherwerb ausländischer Arbeiter*. Tübingen: Narr.

Clahsen, H., and Muysken, P. 1986. The accessibility of universal grammar to adult and child learners. A study of the acquisition of German word order. *Second Language Research* 2:94–119.

Dulay, H. C., Burt, M. K., and Krashen, S. D. 1982. *Language Two*. Oxford: Oxford University Press.

Eckman, F. 1977. Markedness and the contrastive analysis hypothesis. *Language Learning* 27: 315–30.

Eckman, F. 1981. On the naturalness of interlanguage phonological rules. *Language Learning* 31: 195–216.

Eilers, R. E., Wilson, W. R., and Moore, J. M. 1977. Developmental changes in speech discrimination in infants. *Journal of Speech and Hearing Research* 20:766–80.

Eilers, R. E., Gavin, W., and Wilson, W. 1979. Linguistic experience and phonemic perception in infancy: A cross-linguistic study. *Child Development* 50:14–18.

Eimas, P. D., Sigueland, E. R., Jusczyk, P., and Vigorito, J. 1971. Speech perception in infants. *Science* 171:303–306.

Ellis, R. 1985. *Understanding Second Language Acquisition*. Oxford: Oxford University Press.

Elsendorn, B. A. G. 1981. The influence of vowel duration in English CVC-words on the word-final perception of the fortis-lenis contrast by Dutch speakers of English, Part 2. *Progress Report Institute of Phonetics Utrecht* 7: Institute of Phonetics, University of Utrecht: 42–57.

Fathman, A. K. 1975. The relationship between age and second language productive ability. *Language Learning* 25:245–53.

Felix, S. W. 1976. Entwicklungsprozesse im gesteuerten Zweitsprachenerwerb. In *Kongreßberichte der 7. Jahrestagung der Gesellschaft für Angewandte Linguistik GAL e.V., Trier*, Vol. IV, eds. K.-R. Bausch and W. Kühlwein. Stuttgart: Hochschulverlag.

Ferguson, C. A., and Farwell, C. B. 1975. Words and sounds in early language acquisition: English initial consonants in the first 50 words. *Language* 51:419–39.

Ferguson, C. A., and Garnica, O. K. 1975. Theories of phonological development. In *Foundations of Language Development (2 Vols)*, eds. E. H. Lenneberg and E. Lenneberg. Paris: UNESCO Press.

Ferguson, C. A., Peizer, D. B., and Weeks, T. E. 1973. Model-and-replica phonological grammar of a child's first few words. *Lingua* 31:35-65.

Flege, J. E. 1987. The production of "new" and "similar" phones in a foreign language: evidence for the effect of equivalence classification. *Journal of Phonetics* 15:47–65.

Flege, J. E. 1988. The production and perception of foreign language speech sounds. In *Human Communication and its Disorders: A Review 1988*, ed. H. Winitz. NJ: Ablex.

Flege, J. E. In press. The intelligibility of English vowels spoken by British and Dutch talkers. To appear in *Intelligibility in Speech Disorders: Theory, Measurement and Management*, ed. R. Kent. Amsterdam: John Benjamins.

Flege, J. E., and Eefting, W. Z. 1985. Linguistic and developmental effects on the production and perception of stop consonants. *Phonetica* 43:155–71.

Flege, J. E., and Hillenbrand, J. 1984. Limits on phonetic accuracy in foreign language speech production. *Journal of the Acoustical Society of America*. 76:708–21.

Gass, S. 1984. Development of speech perception and speech production in adult second language learners. *Applied Psycholinguistics* 5:51–74.

Hammarberg, B. 1988. *Studien zur Phonologie des Zweitsprachenerwerbs*. Stockholm: Almqvist & Wiksell International.

Haugen, E. 1953. *The Norwegian Language in America. A Study in Bilingual Behavior*. Philadelphia, PA: University of Pennsylvania Press.

Haugen, E. 1958. Language contact. In *Proceedings of the 8th International Congress of Linguists*, ed. E. Sivertsen. Oslo: Oslo University Press.

Hecht, B. F., and Mulford, R. 1982. The acquisition of a second language phonology: Interaction of transfer and developmental factors. *Applied Psycholinguistics* 13:313–28.

Howell, P., and Rosen, S. 1984. Natural auditory sensitivities as universal determiners of phonemic contrasts. In *Explanations for Language Universals*, eds. B. Butterworth, B. Comrie, and Ö. Dahl. Amsterdam: Mouton.

Hyltenstam, K., and Magnusson, E. 1983. Typological markedness, contextual variation, and the acquisition of voice contrasts in stops by first and second language learners of Swedish. *Indian Journal of Applied Linguistics* 9:1–18.

Ingram, D. 1976. *Phonological Disability in Children*. London: Edward Arnold.

Jakobson, R. 1941. *Kindersprache, Aphasie und allgemeine Lautgesetze*. Uppsala: Almqvist & Wiksell.

Jusczyk, P. W. 1981. Infant speech perception: A critical appraisal. In *Perspectives on the Study of Speech*, eds. P. D. Eimas and J. L. Miller. Hillsdale, NJ: Lawrence Erlbaum Associates.

Jusczyk, P. W., Murray, J., and Bayly, J. 1979. Perception of place-of-articulation in fricatives and stops by infants. Paper read at the biennial meeting of the Society for Research in Child Development, March 1979, San Francisco.

Kadar-Hofman, G. 1983. Trilingualer Spracherwerb: Der gleichzeitige Erwerb des Deutschen, Französischen und Ungarischen bei einem Kind, dargestellt am Beispiel der Negation. Ph.D. diss., Christian-Albrechts-Universität, Kiel.

Karimi, S. 1987. Farsi speakers and the initial consonant cluster in English. In *Interlanguage Phonology*, eds. G. Ioup and S. H. Weinberger. New York: Newbury House.

Klima, E. S., and Bellugi, U. 1966. Syntactic regularities in the speech of children. In *Psycholinguistics Papers. Proceedings of the 1966 Edinburgh Conference*, eds. J. Lyons and R. Wales. Edinburgh: Edinburgh University Press. Reprinted in *Studies of Child Language Development*, eds. C. A. Ferguson and D. J. Slobin. 1973. New York: Holt, Rinehart and Winston. Revised version in *Child Language. A Book of Readings*, eds. A. Bar-Adon and W. F. Leopold. 1971. Englewood Cliffs, NJ: Prentice Hall.

Kuhl, P. K. 1987. Perception of speech and sound in early infancy. In *Handbook of Infant Perception* Vol. II, eds. P. Salapatek and L. Cohen. New York: Academic Press.

Lange, S., and Larsson, K. 1973. *Syntactical Development of a Swedish Girl Embla, between 20 and 42 Months of Age. Part 1: Age 20-25 Months*. Stockholm: Institutionen för Nordiska Språk.

Lasky, R. E., Syrdal-Lasky, A., and Klein, R. E. 1975. VOT discrimination by four to six and a half year old infants from Spanish environments. *Journal of Experimental Child Psychology* 20:215–25.

Lenneberg, E. 1967. *Biological Foundations of Language*. New York: Wiley.

Leonard, L. B., Newhoff, M., and Mesalam, L. 1980. Individual differences in early childhood phonology. *Applied Psycholinguistics* 1:7–30.

Leopold, W. F. 1939–49. *Speech Development of a Bilingual Child: A Linguist's Record*. (4 vols.) Evanston, IL: Northwestern University Press.

Liberman, A. M., Harris, K. S., Hoffman, H. S., and Griffith, B. C. 1957. The discrimination of speech sounds within and across phoneme boundaries. *Journal of Experimental Psychology* 54:358–68.

Lindblom, B. 1989. Some remarks on the origin of the phonetic code. In *Brain and Language*, eds. C. von Enlew, A. Lundberg, and G. Rennertrand. London: The Macmillan Press Ltd.

Lindblom, B., MacNeilage, P., and Studdert-Kennedy, M. 1984. Self-organizing processes and the explanation of phonological universals. In *Explanations for Language Universals*, eds. B. Butterworth, B. Comrie, and Ö. Dahl. Amsterdam: Mouton.

Lisker, L., and Abramson, A. 1964. A cross-language study of voicing in initial stops: Acoustic measurements. *Word* 20:384–422.

Lisker, L., and Abramson, A. S. 1970. The voicing dimension: Some experiments in comparative phonetics. In *Proceedings of the 6th International Congress of the Phonetic Sciences 1967*, eds. B. Hala, M. Romportl, and P. Janota. München: Hueber.

Long, M. H. 1988. Maturational constraints on language development. *University of Hawaii Working Papers in ESL* 7 (2):1-53.

MacKain, K., Best, C., and Strange, W. 1981. Categorical perception of English /r/ and /l/ by Japanese bilinguals. *Applied Psycholinguistics* 2:369–90.

Macken, M. A. 1978. Permitted complexity in phonological development: One child's acquisition of Spanish consonants. *Lingua* 44:219–53.

Macken, M. A. 1979. The developmental reorganisation of phonology: A hierarchy of basic units of acquisition. *Lingua* 49:11–49.

Macken, M. A. 1986. Phonological development: A crosslinguistic perspective. In *Language Acquisition*, eds. P. Fletcher and M. Garman. Cambridge: Cambridge University Press.

Macken, M. A., and Ferguson, C. A. 1981. Phonological universals in language acquisition. In *Native Language and Foreign Language Acquisition*, ed. H. Winitz. New York: Academy of Sciences.

Macken, M. A., and Ferguson, C. A. 1983. Cognitive aspects of phonological development: Model, evidence, and issues. In *Children's Language*, Vol. IV, ed. K. E. Nelson. New York: Gardner & Hillsdale.

Major, R. 1977. Phonological differentiation of a bilingual child. *Ohio State University Working Papers on Linguistics* 22:88–122.

Major, R. 1987. A model for interlanguage phonology. In *Interlanguage Phonology: The Acquisition of a Second Language Sound System*, eds. G. Ioup and S. H. Weinberger. Cambridge: Newbury House.

McLaughlin, B. 1978. *Second Language Acquisition in Childhood*, Vol. I, *Preschool Children*. Hillsdale, NJ: Lawrence Erlbaum Associates.

Mann, V. A. 1986. Distinguishing universals and language-dependent levels of speech perception: Evidence from Japanese listeners' perception of English /l/ and /r/. *Cognition* 24:169–96.

Menzerath, P., and de Lacerda, A. 1933. Koartikulation, Steuerung und Lautabgrenzung. *Phonetische Studien* 1. Bonn: Dümmlers.

Mochizuki, M. 1981. The identification of /r/ and /l/ in natural and synthesized speech. *Journal of Phonetics* 9:283–303.

Moskowitz, A. J. 1971. Acquisition of phonology. Ph.D. diss., University of California, Berkeley.

Moskowitz, A. J. 1973. The acquisition of phonology and syntax. In *Approaches to Natural Language*, eds. K. K. J. Hintikka, J. M. E. Moravcsik, and P. Suppes. Boston: D. Reidel.

Obler, L. 1983. The parsimonious bilingual. In *Exceptional Language and Linguis-*

tic Theory, eds. L. Obler and L. Menn. New York: Academic: 339–46.

Pačesová, J. 1968. *The Development of Vocabulary in the Child.* Brno: Universität J. E. Purkynè.

Peters, A. M. 1977. Language learning strategies: Does the whole equal the sum of the parts? *Language* 53:560–73.

Peters, A. M. 1983. *The Units of Language Acquisition.* Cambridge: Cambridge University Press.

Repp, B. H. 1984. Categorical perception. Issues, methods, findings. In *Speech and Language: Advances in Basic Research and Practice*, Vol. 10, ed. N. Lass. Academic Press.

Rosch, E. 1978. Principles of categorization. In *Cognition and Categorization*, eds. E. Rosch and B. Lloyd. Hillsdale, NJ: Lawrence Erlbaum Associates.

Sadownik, B. 1987. Implikationen einer psycholinguistisch orientierten Zweit-sprachenerwerbsforschung für die Glottodidaktik. Ph.D. diss., Lublin University.

Sato, C. J. 1984. Phonological processes in second language acquisition: Another look at interlanguage syllable structure. *Language Learning* 34(4): 43–57.

Schumann, J. H. 1978. *The Pidginization Process: A Model for Second Language Acquisition.* Rowley, MA: Newbury House.

Smith, N. V. 1973. *The Acquisition of Phonology.* Cambridge: Cambridge University Press.

Stampe, D. 1979. A dissertation on natural phonology. Ph.D. diss., Indiana University Linguistics Club, Bloomington.

Strange, W., and Dittman, S. 1981. Effects of discrimination training on the perception of /r-l/ by Japanese adults. Paper presented at the 22nd Meeting of the Psychonomic Society.

Streeter, L. A. 1976. Kikuyu labial and apical stop discrimination. *Journal of Phonetics* 4:43–49.

Tarone, E. 1978. The phonology of interlanguage. In *Understanding Second and Foreign Language Learning*, ed. J. Richards. Rowley, MA: Newbury House.

Tees, R. C., and Werker, J. F. 1984. Perceptual flexibility: Maintenance or recovery of the ability to discriminate non-native speech sounds. *Canadian Journal of Psychology* 38(4): 579–90.

Tropf, H. S. 1983. Variation in der Phonologie des gesteuerten Zweit-sprachenerwerbs. Ph.D. diss., Universität Heidelberg.

Truby, H. M. 1959. Acoustico-cineradiographic analysis considerations, with especial reference to certain consonantal complexes. *Acta Radiologica Supplementum* 182, Stockholm.

Weinreich, U. 1953. *Languages in Contact, Findings and Problems.* New York: The Linguistics Club, Reprinted 1964 den Haag: Mouton.

Werker, J., and Tees, R. 1983. Developmental changes across childhood in the perception of non-native speech sounds. *Canadian Journal of Psychology* 37(2): 278–86.

Werker, J., and Tees, R. 1984. Cross-language speech perception: Evidence for perceptual reorganization during the first year of life. *Infant Behaviour and Development* 7:49–63.

Werker, J., Gilbert, J., Humphry, I., and Tees, R. 1981. Developmental aspects of cross-language speech perception. *Child Development* 52:349–55.

Williams, L. 1979. The modification of speech perception and production in second-language learning. *Perception and psychophysics* 26:95–104.

Williams, L. 1980. Phonetic variation as a function of second-language learning. In *Child Phonology, Vol. 2, Perception*, eds. G. Yeni-Komshian, J. Kavanagh, and C. Ferguson. New York: Academic.

Wode, H. 1976. Developmental sequences in naturalistic acquisition: *Working Papers on Bilingualism* 11:1–31.

Wode, H. 1977a. Four early stages in the development of L1 negation. *Journal of Child Language* 4:87–102. Reprinted in: Wode, H. 1983. *Papers on Language Acquisition, Language Learning and Language Teaching*. Heidelberg: Julius Groos Verlag.

Wode, H. 1977b. Developmental principles in naturalistic L2 acquisition. In *Akten der 3. Salzburger Jahrestagung für Psycholinguistik*, ed. G. Drachman. Salzburg: Wolfgang Neugebauer.

Wode, H. 1977c. On the systematicity of L1 transfer in L2 acquisition. In *Proceedings of the Los Angeles Second Language Research Forum*, ed. C. Henning. Los Angeles, CA: University of California at Los Angeles.

Wode, H. 1978. The beginnings of L2-phonological acquisition. *IRAL* 16:109–24.

Wode, H. 1981. *Learning a Second Language: An Integrated View of Language Acquisition*. Tübingen: Narr.

Wode, H. 1988. *Einführung in die Psycholinguistik. Theorien, Methoden, Ergebnisse*. Ismaning: Hueber.

Wode, H. 1989. Maturational changes of language acquisitional abilities. In *Variation in Second Language Acquisition, Vol. II: Psycholinguistic Issues*. eds. S. Gass, C. Madden, D. Preston, and L. Selinker. Clevedon, Philadelphia: Multilingual Matters.

Wong-Fillmore, L. W. 1976. The second time around: Cognitive and social strategies in second language acquisition. Ph.D. diss., Stanford University.

Zlatin, M., and Koenigsknecht, R. 1975. Development of the voicing contrast: Perception of stop consonants. *Journal of Speech and Hearing Research* 18:541–53.

Zlatin, M., and Koenigsknecht, R. 1976. Development of the voicing contrast: A comparison of voice onset time in stop perception and production. *Journal of Speech and Hearing Research* 19:93–111.

Zwirner, E., and Zwirner, K. 1966. *Grundfragen der Phonometrie*. 2. erweiterte u. verbesserte Auflage. Basel, NY: Karger.

Views from Outside

Chapter • 23

Emergence of Complexity in Phonological Development

K. P. Mohanan

The goal of this chapter is to draw attention to an important problem that theories of the organization and the development of phonological systems must jointly address: how does complex order arise in phonological systems? This is not unlike the problem of morphogenesis that other scientists have to wrestle with: how does complex order arise in physical, biological, and social systems (Schrodinger 1935; Prigogine and Stengers 1984)? Current generative linguistics formulates the problem as a "logical" problem of deducing propositional knowledge. I will argue that this formulation is founded on several questionable assumptions. It restricts our field of vision and prevents us from asking questions that could lead to a better understanding of language. I will suggest that, instead, we should view language as a self-organizing dynamical system, and formulate the problem as one of morphogenesis in linguistic systems. This formulation facilitates the use of methods that are analogous to the methods used

This chapter has benefitted greatly from discussions with Lubna Alsagoff, Jen Cole, Cathy Echols, Charles Ferguson, John Goldsmith, Bernado Huberman, David Ingram, Paul Kiparsky, Lise Menn, Tara Mohanan, Douglas Pulleyblank, Richard Schwartz, and Joe Stemberger. I am especially grateful to Joan Bresnan, Eve Clark, Cathy Echols, Charles Ferguson, Lise Menn, and Meg Withgott for detailed comments on a previous draft.

for dealing with the problem of morphogenesis in nonlinguistic systems.

The two conceptions of language development currently available in generative linguistics are hypothesis construction and hypothesis selection. The former conception is adopted in Chomsky and Halle (1968) (henceforth SPE). The latter is the principles-and-parameters program in Chomsky (1981) and subsequent work. Hypothesis construction is data driven in that the child is viewed as constructing principles of the grammar in order to account for the adult input data. Hypothesis selection is universal grammar (UG)-driven in that principles of the grammar are innately available to the child, and what the child does is select the appropriate value for a parametric choice on the basis of the input data. In what follows I argue that neither hypothesis construction nor hypothesis selection is adequate to account for the puzzles of morphogenesis. It would be more enlightening to view language development as structure formation in a dynamical system, and as adaptation to input data.

The conception of language as a dynamical system shares with the principles and parameters model the emphasis on substantive universals in contrast to the emphasis on formal universals in the SPE-inspired formal phonology. It differs from the principles and parameters model in viewing universal principles as being *fields of attraction*. This conception leads to the following consequences. First, it permits infinite variation in a finite *grammar space*. Second, it allows universal principles to have gradient values in their language-particular manifestation. In contrast, parametric choices are generally viewed as discrete. Third, fields of attraction reinforce and conflict with each other, the individual grammar being a result of conflict resolution. Parametric choices do not interact with each other in this manner. Finally, it provides for the possibility that given the same input data, different learners may arrive at different internal linguistic systems. These internal differences may not be noticed in natural situations of linguistic communication, but they become apparent under artificial situations of judgment elicitation or other experimental procedures.

The model of language development advocated in this article is identical in spirit to the "crystal growth" model in Menn (1973), and incorporates the desirable aspects of Natural Phonology (Stampe 1972). I believe that the conception of language structure and development that I have sketched above is not inconsistent with the connectionist models in Smolensky (1986), Goldsmith (forthcoming), and Lakoff (forthcoming), even though actual implementations of connectionism fail to provide for non-unique conflict resolution, and are incapable of structure formation that is not data driven. It is also consistent with the growing body of work on self organization in phonetics (Lindblom, MacNeilage, and Studdert-Kennedy 1983; Lindblom 1988, this volume).

THE PROBLEM OF COMPLEX ORDER IN PHONOLOGICAL SYSTEMS

There are two problems for which current theories of phonological organization have no solutions. First, we do not yet have a mechanism that accounts for recurrent patterns of distribution and alternation in natural languages that nevertheless vary from language to language. Second, we do not have a way of formally expressing the naturalness of these recurrent patterns. These problems have their counterparts in language development and language change. Why is it that children's grammars often exhibit complex patterns that are not present in the adult grammars to which they are exposed? Why do innovations arise in language change? Put together, these four problems constitute the problem of complex order in linguistic systems.

Two Problems for Theories of Phonological Structure

A large number of phonological patterns in natural languages are variable manifestations of a small number of archetypal or core patterns. To take an example, almost all languages require adjacent obstruents in some domain to agree in voicing, even though the details are not quite the same in different languages. This regularity holds syllable internally in English, but in most varieties of English it does not hold across syllables: onsets like *[sg], *[zk], *[sd], and *[zt], and codas like *[fd], *[vt], *[kd], *[gt], *[zp], and *[sb] are ill formed, even though words like *a[bs]olute* and *a[sb]estos* show that these sequences are permitted across syllables.[1] In South Asian languages like Malayalam and Hindi, such sequences are prohibited morpheme internally, whether or not they are tautosyllabic. In languages like Russian, the effects of this prohibition hold across words as well. Languages also vary in the way in which the pattern is manifested in alternations. In English, the voiced consonant assimilates to the voiceless (regressive in *five* versus *fifth*, progressive in *John'[z] here* versus *Jack'[s] here*) whereas in Spanish and Russian, the first consonant assimilates to the second, irrespective of which one is voiced.

Another pattern that is recurrent in natural languages is that of

---

[1]It appears that in some varieties, the regularity holds across syllables as well. Thus, *absolute* is pronounced with [ps] and *asbestos* with [sp] (Ferguson personal communication). In yet other varieties, assimilation occurs only within a foot (Menn personal communication).

place agreement of oral or nasal stops with the following consonant. For example, English does not allow nonhomorganic codas like *[mk], *[mc], *[nk], *[np], and *[nf], even though it allows the nonhomorganic coda [mt] (e.g., *pre-empt*). The generalization is that the nasal must be homorganic with the following consonant if the latter is a noncoronal. Across syllables, this restriction does not hold, as shown by heterosyllabic sequences like [nk] (e.g., *concave* [kɔnkeyv]).[2] Like English, Malayalam exhibits homorganic nasal assimilation. However, nasals in Malayalam must agree in place with the following plosive word internally, even if the plosive is coronal, unlike in English. Another difference between English and Malayalam is that in English, place assimilation is triggered by both fricatives and plosives: thus, tautosyllabic *[nf] is disallowed in English, and /n/ assimilates optionally to /f/ across words (e.g., *te[m]fingers*). In contrast, place assimilation is triggered only by plosives in Malayalam: even though word internal [mt], [mc], etc. are forbidden, [ms], [nš], [ml], [mn], [nm], etc. are not. Yet another pattern of place assimilation is found in Korean, in which the alveolar consonants assimilate to the palatal, labial, and velar triggers, while palatal and labial consonants assimilate only to velar triggers, and the velar does not undergo assimilation at all.[3]

Clearly, both voicing assimilation and place assimilation are universal in the sense that they are repeatedly found in natural languages. Yet current phonological theory has no mechanism to express the universality of these phenomena, because the details of their actual manifestation vary from language to language. As a result, current practice in phonological theory is to state them formally as language particular rules in each individual grammar, thereby missing important universal generalizations.

Another problem that current phonological theory faces is the mismatch between naturalness and formal simplicity. An assumption that has either implicitly or explicitly been incorporated in all phonological theories since SPE is that formal simplicity is a measure of naturalness: given two rules or two grammars, the one that carries fewer specifications (or counts as "simpler" on the basis of some other evaluation metric) is more natural. This assumption, however, runs counter to actual observations under existing theories of phonology. For example, under existing theories, a grammar that contains a rule that changes /nk/ to [ŋk] is formally more complex than one that does not contain such a

---

[2]For most speakers, assimilation to the velar occurs in fast speech in words like *concave*. The point is that [ŋ] before [k] is not obligatory in *concave* for all speakers of English, unlike a tautosyllabic [ŋ] before [k], as in *sink*.

[3]For a detailed discussion of the data on obstruent voicing agreement and place assimilation, the reader is referred to Mohanan (forthcoming) and the references cited therein.

rule, thereby leaving word final /nk/ to be realized as unassimilated [nk] (e.g., [sink]). Yet, the former grammar is more natural than the latter one. Similarly, existing dialects of English that contain the rule of voicing assimilation are more complex than a hypothetical dialect that does not have such a rule, allowing *dogs* [dɔgz], *cats* [kætz], etc. Again, the former is more natural. In both cases, there is a mismatch between naturalness and formal simplicity of grammars: the more complex is in fact the more natural. How do we resolve this conflict?[4]

These two problems are not limited to assimilatory phenomena. They are far more general, and reappear in other phenomena, like consonant lenition, vowel reduction, neutralization, deletion, and so on (Mohanan forthcoming).

Phonological Development and Phonological Change

The problems of phonological structure raised above have their counterparts in phonological development and phonological change. Generative theories conceive of phonological development as a process whereby the learner constructs the simplest grammar that is compatible with the input data and universal grammar. This view, explicitly articulated in SPE, holds that children construct grammars to account for the data they are exposed to within the constraints imposed by the formalism, and an evaluation metric selects the simplest possible grammar for the given data (Chomsky and Halle 1968, p. 331).[5] The idea that acquisition of phonology is determined by the evaluation metric has been implicitly or explicitly accepted in post-SPE theories of generative phonology as well, in spite of the obvious problems of implementing this proposal.[6] Under this conception of phonological development, children's grammars should not contain any complexity not warranted by adult data. In other words, we must expect that developing grammars do not have all the rules or constraints that adult grammars have, but the prediction is that the reverse situation is not

---

[4]The simplicity addressed here is that of formal simplicity, not functional simplicity. No doubt [ŋk] and [ts] are articulatorily simpler than [nk] and [tz], but this "phonetic motivation" is not reflected in the formal description. The only simplicity that the formal paradigm recognizes is that of formal simplicity. The problem I am raising here is that the articulatory simplicity does not correlate with formal simplicity.

[5]As pointed out in Chomsky (1965), this notion of "simplicity" is crucially defined by the linguistic theory. Because the choice of different formalisms has different consequences for what counts as simple, the choice of formalism constitutes an empirical hypothesis about the nature of the human language faculty and language acquisition.

[6]For example, proposing a revised evaluation metric, McCarthy (1981) says: "This metric, like its counterpart in Chomsky and Halle (1968), must evaluate entire grammars on the basis of specific criteria of formal simplicity in the domains of phonological processes, readjustment rules, and the lexicon" (p. 246).

possible. Actual data on phonological development falsify the claim, as there are a number of instances of greater complexity in children's phonological systems, not warranted either by the adult data or by the difficulties of articulation. Classic examples are those of consonant harmony, documented in Menn (1973), Vihman (1978), and Barton (this volume) among others, which cannot be attributed to articulatory difficulties.[7] Ingram (1984) and Stemberger (1988) report other patterns in children's speech not attributable to the adult grammars to which the children are exposed. Regularities of this kind are documented in the speech of phonologically disordered children as well (e.g., Schwartz et al. 1980; Leonard and Brown 1984). If a child's business is to construct, within the boundaries of UG, the simplest account of the input data, why does the child impose additional complexity on the grammar, the effect of which is to make the output deviate from the "target" adult input? It was the intuitive recognition of this problem that led to the proposal for the "crystal growth" model of language development in Menn (1973).

It must be pointed out that this problem of novel complexity is not the same as the problem of novel forms discussed in Macken and Ferguson (1983). As evidence for "creativity" in language acquisition, they observe that children often create forms that are not found in adult language. Thus, Adam, one of the children studied in Brown and Hanlon (1970), produced the novel tag question *I am magic, amn't I?* and Leslie, studied in Ferguson, Peizer, and Weeks (1973), produced a word initial velar nasal when she was acquiring English. These novel forms are actually the result of grammars that are simpler than the adult grammars, and therefore do not pose any challenge to the traditional views of language acquisition in generative linguistics. They are not significantly different from well known examples like *goed* instead of *went*, cited as evidence for the generative view of language acquisition. In contrast, the novel patterns of consonant harmony (e.g., [gʌk] for *duck*) are indicative of grammars that are in fact more complex than adult grammars.[8] It is the latter type of creativity that I am concerned with.[9]

The problem of complexity in language development has its corol-

---

[7]In children's consonant harmony, constraints on place or manner features hold between consonants across vowels. Thus, Daniel pronounced *bug, duck,* and *seat* as [gʌg], [gʌk] and [dit] (Menn 1973). As Menn clearly shows, though articulatorily motivated, these assimilatory patterns are phonological. They cannot be attributed to articulatory difficulties. Daniel was perfectly capable of mimicking his mother to say [dʌk], but chose to say [gʌk] in his own speech (Menn and Matthei this volume).

[8]Once again, it must be borne in mind that the issue under discussion is formal simplicity.

[9]Among the examples cited in Macken and Ferguson (1983), the only instance of children's grammars exhibiting added complexity is that of the word patterns in Si's language, where the first consonant had to be labial and the second one dental.

lary in language change. Language change generally is viewed in generative linguistics as the result of the chain of transmission of language from one generation to the next. Under perfect conditions of input data, the grammar that children construct in order to account for the adult data would be identical to the adult grammar, exhibiting the same amount of complexity. Under less ideal conditions, however, where the data are incomplete, in addition to being riddled with random errors and noise, one would expect that the new phonological system would be less complex than the previous one. Under repeated cycles of such simplification, one would further expect a stage completely devoid of all complexity, that is, a phonological system without rules or constraints. However, we never find such complete loss of complexity in language change. When some regularities are lost, new ones emerge. Unless linguistic theory provides for a mechanism for the emergence of novel complexity, innovations in language change would be a puzzle, whether these innovations are to be traced to early stages of language development, or later stages.[10]

All four problems raised above, in phonological structure, development, and change, can be summed up as: what are the reasons for the emergence of complex organization in phonological systems? This question is unanswerable within the conception of language and language development implicit in current generative research. In the following section, I examine the deep-rooted biases in the current paradigm that have prevented us from perceiving the problem of complexity, and from seeking an explanation.

THE LOGICAL PROBLEM OF LANGUAGE ACQUISITION

The central problem of language development is viewed in generative linguistics as "Plato's problem" (Chomsky 1986), or the "logical problem" of language acquisition (Baker and McCarthy 1981). The question asked is: how does the learner deduce the grammar from the data to which he or she is exposed? Underlying this formulation of the problem and the proposed solutions are the following assumptions:

1a. Different learners in a given community arrive at the same grammar.
1b. The formation of grammar in a human individual is an operation of induction and deduction: children deduce the grammar from the combination of the propositions in universal grammar, and

[10]I am assuming that language development is a process that begins soon after birth, and goes on until the death of the individual.

the propositions that can be inductively arrived at from the data that they are exposed to.

1c. Learnable grammars are those for which there exists an algorithm such that when provided the data as the input, it yields the adult grammar as the output. A grammar for which such an algorithm does not exist is unlearnable.

The assumptions in (1a–c) are reflected in statements such as the following:

> A non-decidable language is unlearnable, even if the learner benefits from an informant. In short this means that there is no algorithm by which an (observationally) adequate grammar can be derived from a sequence of strings marked "grammatical" and "ungrammatical." *If there is no learnability in terms of an algorithm, there is certainly no learnability in terms of human cognitive capacities, given the finite character of the latter* (Levelt 1974, quoted in Lasnik 1981, italics mine).

> . . . one goal of linguistic theory has been to provide a sufficiently rich account of universal grammar to explain a child's acquisition of language. A linguistic explanation is achieved if, given exposure to a representative set of sentences, a child equipped with universal grammar can induce *the particular grammar of his community.* . . . This essay has two goals. The primary goal is to provide a demonstration of the claim that universal grammar can be enriched to the point where an explicit *deductive acquisition procedure* can be provided for an important domain of grammar . . . " (Roeper 1981, italics mine).

> The task is to *predict* what grammar a learner will internalize as a function of the data available (Grimshaw 1981, italics mine).

> The child cannot learn just any useful communicative system; nor can he or she learn just any natural language. He or she is stuck with having to learn the particular kind of language the species eventually converged upon and *the particular variety the community has chosen* (Pinker and Bloom 1990, italics mine).

Take assumption (1a). What is the evidence for the assumption that children exposed to a single speech community arrive at the same internal grammar? Practicing linguists have always recognized that speakers of the same "language" or "dialect" need not have identical linguistic systems. Yet, most linguists also believe that for practical purposes of grammar construction, the idiolectal differences between individual speakers in a speech community can be ignored. In particular, the unstated assumption in generative linguistics has been that variability does not exist in those domains that linguistic *theories* are based on. Examples such as the following show that this naive belief is in fact incorrect:

2a. The boys told Mary that Sally liked each other's pictures.
2b. The boys told Mary that each other's pictures would be on sale.

2c.   Mary told the boys that each other's pictures would be on sale.
2d.   The boys told Mary that each other's girl friends were pretty.

Sentences like (2a,b) have been used as crucial evidence for universal grammar in syntactic theories. The conventional position on the data has been that speakers of English find (2a) to be ungrammatical and (2b–d) to be grammatical. And yet, in actual practice, speakers of English exhibit a great deal of variability in their judgments, ranging from the total acceptance of all the sentences in (2) to the total rejection of all of them. Among the speakers who accept (2b) and reject (2a) are those who accept (2b,c) but not (2d), requiring *picture* noun phrases for nonclause-bounded reciprocals. There are also those who accept (2b) but not (2c), requiring subject antecedents for nonclause-bounded reciprocals. Though the unquestioned acceptance of the dogma in (1a) has prevented researchers from reporting situations of this kind, it is not difficult to find variability of core grammar in the same community.[11]

Interestingly enough, the assumption in (1a) is explicitly rejected by Chomsky himself.

> . . . I am using the term "language" to refer to an *individual* phenomenon, a system represented in the mind/brain of a particular individual. If we could investigate in detail, we would find that no two individuals share exactly the same language in this sense, even identical twins who grow up in the same social environment. Two individuals can communicate to the extent that their languages are sufficiently similar.

> In the ordinary usage, in contrast, when we speak of a language, we have in mind some kind of *social* phenomenon, a shared property of a community. . . . The term "language" as used in ordinary discourse involves obscure sociopolitical and normative factors (Chomsky 1988; p. 36–37).

Saussure's conception of LANGUE as a set of conventions common to the community crucially presupposes language as a social entity. In contrast, Chomsky's notion of COMPETENCE (Chomsky 1965), or I-LANGUAGE in his subsequent work (Chomsky 1986, 1988) focuses on language as a psychological entity, as part of an individual's mental system. *Langue* is the system of the community, whereas *competence* is the system of the individual. The members of a language community share a langue, but no two speakers of a language have the same competence. Labels like "the French language" and "the English language" refer to collections of diverse grammars bound together by a sociolinguistic bond. There-

---

[11]It is true that the individuals belonging to the same community share a great deal of properties in their grammars: otherwise communication would be impossible. However, that they share a number of properties does not entail that they have identical grammars.

fore, investigation of the nature of such entities belongs to the domain of sociolinguistics, not generative linguistics in Chomsky's sense.

Now, if no two individuals develop the same internal linguistic system even when exposed to the same input data from a community, it could not be the case that the internal linguistic system is arrived at through a process of logical *deduction*.[12] In other words, the Chomsky-inspired learnability theories of language acquisition are predicated on assumption (1a), which Chomsky himself denies. Once we reject assumption (1a), the remaining assumptions in (1b,c) have no place in the theory. If, as Chomsky implies, LANGUE is not the right notion for language acquisition, and the object of inquiry in generative grammar is the COMPETENCE that differs from individual to individual in a language community, the "logical problem" of language acquisition turns out to be a red herring that arises out of the profound confusion between *langue* and *competence*. If Chomsky is right, there is no "target" grammar that learners attempt to arrive at through inductive and deductive means.

THE MISLEADING METAPHORS IN GENERATIVE LINGUISTICS

Why is it that the obvious contradiction between Chomsky and the Chomsky-inspired approaches to language acquisition has not attracted very much attention? One of the reasons, as I suggested above, is that many generative linguists believe at heart that entities denoted by labels such as "the English language" and "the French language" are the objects of inquiry in generative grammar. In other words, they consider LANGUE, not COMPETENCE, to be the object of inquiry. A more fundamental reason, I will suggest, is the "entropic conception" of the language faculty: that is, the belief that the complexity in an adult

---

[12]One may argue that the differences between individual grammars arise out of being exposed to different input data albeit from the same community. Granted this possibility, it would nevertheless be hard to relate individual differences in examples like (2) to differences in input. Furthermore, the claim implicit in the research on the logical problem of language acquisition is that differences in the input data for different individuals growing up in the same speech community do not affect the output grammars. Once we admit that input differences from the same community can cause significant differences in the grammar, then the only way of studying acquisition would be by pairing the input data and the grammar for each individual. Such a commitment, however, has been absent in most research in this paradigm.

Given two learners with identical neural systems, and given identical input data in identical sequence in identical environment, one might speculate that the learners will develop identical grammars (cf. Leonard, Newhoff, and Mesalem 1972). The question is, are the individual differences marginal enough to justify an idealization to this hypothetical situation? If, as I suggest below, the language faculty is a chaotic system that exhibits sensitivity to initial conditions, then such idealization is totally misleading.

grammar cannot exceed the sum total of the complexity of the input data and the initial state of UG.

In order to come to grips with the nature of the entropic view of language, it is necessary to examine the metaphors of language acquisition that have been the driving force behind generative theories of language acquisition for the past three decades, namely: (1) the learner is a scientist, (2) the learner is a data processing serial digital computer, and (3) grammar is knowledge. Tied up with these metaphors is the notion of evaluation procedure in generative linguistics. In what follows, I turn to a discussion of these issues.

The Language Learner as a Scientist

Chomsky (1956) says:

> . . . linguistic theory characterizes a system of levels, a class of potential grammars, and an EVALUATION PROCEDURE with the following property: given data from language L, and several grammars with the properties required by linguistic theory, the procedure of evaluation selects the highest-valued of these. It is suggested that the language learner (*analogously, the linguist*) approaches the problem of language acquisition (grammar construction) with a schematism that determines in advance the general properties of human language and the general properties of the grammars that may be constructed to *account for linguistic phenomena*. His task is to select the highest-valued grammar of the appropriate form compatible with available data (p. 12, italics mine).

As far as phonology is concerned, the notion of "most highly valued" has two dimensions of meaning. In terms of language acquisition, it refers to the grammar picked out by the learner from the set of grammars provided by the formalism. In terms of cross-linguistic distribution, it refers to the most recurrent. The claim implicit in many discussions is that the two notions converge (see McCarthy 1981).

The metaphor of the learner as a linguist/scientist has led to the program of the formal algebra of grammars, incorporated into phonological theory in Chomsky and Halle (1968). In this approach, it is assumed that the learner constructs an *account for the data* he or she is exposed to, using the hypothetico-deductive method, exactly as a linguist would. The formalism of linguistic theory allows a large (if not infinite) number of grammars for the same data. Just as a scientist chooses the simplest theory that accounts for the data, "a learner adopts the most highly valued rules (i.e., rules requiring fewest features) consistent with and sometimes overriding the available data" (Dresher 1981, p. 192).

The fundamental claim in the SPE approach to phonological theory is that it is possible to devise a formal system such that the "highest-valued" corresponds to the "simplest" in terms of the formalism. The test for the adequacy of a formal system since SPE has been the ability of the formalism to express "highly-valued" as "formally simple." A majority of arguments in phonological theory have been made on the basis of the assumption that the formalism provided by phonological theory must facilitate selection of the most highly-valued grammar from a set of alternatives. Thus, the demand on a linguistic theory is that the formalism it employs must provide an explanation for language acquisition.

The goal of linguistic theory, therefore, is viewed to be the construction of a formal algebra for the statement of grammars such that the following conditions are met:

3a.   The space for hypothesis is *severely constrained* by the formal algebra of UG.
3b.   States of affairs not attested in human languages are those that cannot be described in terms of the formal algebra.
3c.   Natural states of affairs in human languages are those that lend themselves to a *simpler* description in terms of the formal algebra.

Thus, the evaluation procedure for the scientist and the language learner is the choice of grammar that has the maximum formal simplicity. This approach claims to solve the problems of language acquisition, and thereby satisfy the criterion of explanatory adequacy, by constraining the power of the formal system used for the construction of grammars. The class of possible human grammars, which are claimed to be the only learnable grammars, are those that are expressible in terms of the formal system (3b). Natural grammars, which are those that children select from the class of possible grammars, are the simplest ones compatible with the data (3c). It follows, therefore, that the goal of linguistic theory is to construct a formal system (3a) so as to meet the requirements in (3b,c).[13]

The Language Learner as a Data Processing Computer

In the late fifties and sixties, the approach in (3) generated heated discussions on various types of automata and formal grammars, currently carried on in the GPSG (generalized phrase structure grammar)-

---

[13]It must be noted that the model of acquisition proposed in Macken and Ferguson (1983) is a variant of the SPE model, in that both assume that the child constructs hypotheses in order to account for the data. According to SPE, grammars meeting the conditions of the formal system of UG are "entertained as hypotheses" by the child who acquires the language (Chomsky and Halle 1968, p. 331). This position is not different from the view that the child is "an active seeker and user of information—an active hypothesis-generator" (Macken and Ferguson 1983, p. 257). Irrespective of the assumptions about the nature of innate specifications, both models are essentially "data driven" in that both assume that the child constructs hypotheses *in order to account for* the input.

inspired approaches to syntax (Gazdar et al. 1985). Within GB (government and binding)-inspired syntax, however, it soon became obvious that the program of choosing a formal algebra and the evaluation procedure based on formal simplicity was insufficient. The essential problem was the discovery of universals that have exceptions and that exhibited variability across languages. The program in (3) by itself could not cope with this problem. As a result, the focus shifted from formal universals to substantive universals, one version of which is the program of principles and parameters. The fundamental claim of this program is that there is only a finite number of core grammars that UG allows, and children select the simplest grammar that is compatible with the data (Chomsky 1981). The guiding metaphor behind this program is that of the language learner as a data processing computer, rather than as a scientist who employs the hypothetico-deductive method to discover the grammar. The central assumptions of the program are given in (4):

4a. There are only a finite number of core grammars provided by UG.
4b. States of affairs not attested in human languages are those that are not compatible with any of the options provided by UG.
4c. Natural states of affairs in human languages are those that result from choosing the default options in UG.

The program of principles and parameters views the learner as a machine whose switches are set when the input data is provided (Chomsky 1981 and subsequent work). The program in (3) requires the learner to search through a space of infinite possibilities. The program in (4) has the advantage of providing a finite number of prefabricated grammars, so that the problem of selection is trivial: the learner selects the grammar the output of which matches the observed data. This task is achieved essentially by focussing on the CORE grammar (i.e., that part of the grammar that cannot be arrived at from the data through inductive means). Unlike (3), the program in (4) does not require an evaluation procedure based purely on formal simplicity, because the substantive statements in UG specify the default choices that the learner will make.

While the program in (3) continues to be employed for phenomena that typically have been dealt with in terms of "rules" (such as in phonological alternations), the program in (4) is employed for the phenomena that typically have been dealt with in terms of "constraints" (such as the binding conditions in syntax). The general feeling is that (4) is appropriate for the "core grammar" where the variability across grammars is expected to be limited, while (3) is appropriate for the periphery that allows greater variability. To some extent, research in phonology has been influenced by the principles and parameters pro-

gram in syntax, particularly in theories of stress and underspecification. However, the idea that even "rules" can have their origin in UG
and, hence, can be "innate" in a sense, is somewhat alien to the intellectual climate in phonology. Earlier we argued precisely for this position. We must therefore re-examine the use of the two programs in
phonology.

Whether the language learner is viewed as a scientist or as a data
processing serial computer, the central assumption in the generative
paradigm of research has been that grammar is a form of knowledge.
Furthermore, both programs crucially demand an evaluation procedure to choose the "correct" grammar for a given body of data, implicitly assuming that given the same data, all children converge on a
single grammar (1a). It is this assumption that has led to the search for
an evaluation metric. If there is no unique grammar that a given body
of data triggers in a child, then what we need in a theory of language
development is not an evaluation procedure that selects *the* "correct"
grammar, but a way of (1) constraining the space in which grammars
develop, and (2) identifying the most likely locations in the space.

Grammar as Knowledge of Language

The generative paradigm of research on language conceives of grammar as knowledge of language. This metaphor has given rise to a mode
of research that has focussed on Plato's problem or the problem of
"knowledge not grounded on experience." The way the problem is formulated has led to hasty assumptions about the genetic specifications
of human beings.

Consider the mode of argument for innately specified universals
in generative grammar, which can be illustrated with the sentences
in (5):

5a. Who married John?
5b. Who did Mary marry?
5c. Who married who?
5d. *Who did who marry?[14]

The argument runs as follows:

6a. An adult speaker of English accepts (5a–c), but rejects (5d).
6b. The contrast between (5a–c) on the one hand and (5d) on the
     other can be accounted for by assuming that the speaker knows
     some principle, *P*.

---

[14]Needless to say, (5d) is perfectly acceptable as an echo question. The point here is
that the response to (5c) can be "Mary married John, Suzan married Bill, Amelia married
Gus. . . . " Such a response is not available for (5d).

6c.   Principle *P* could not have been inductively arrived at from expe-
      rience, i.e., from the kinds of data that language learners are nor-
      mally exposed to.
6d.   Therefore, principle *P* is innately specified as part of UG.

The idea of "knowledge that is not grounded on experience" has been
the driving force behind generative linguistics for more than two decades. The metaphor of knowledge of language is an extremely misleading one, because it leads to the illusion that the knowledge that different individuals have of the same language is identical (1a). This
assumption, as pointed out earlier, conflicts with the facts. It also conflicts with Chomsky's own position on the nature of the mental linguistic system of human individuals. If the "language" in "knowledge of
language" refers to the input data for children, clearly, each child
is exposed to a unique grammar. On the other hand, if "language"
means entities such as English and French, it is inconsistent with
Chomsky's position that this notion of language is irrelevant for generative linguistics. In spite of this clear contradiction, the "knowledge-of-
language" metaphor has led researchers to conduct their research as if
there exist clearly defined entities such as English and French, and
learners acquire knowledge of the structure of these languages.

Language as an Entropic System

A more serious objection to the mode of argument in (6) is its implicit
assumption that the language faculty is entropic. In an entropic system, the total order or energy at the final state cannot exceed the sum of
the order or energy at the initial state and the input. That is to say, disorder can only increase in an entropic system. Central to the formulation of the problem of language acquisition as the acquisition of
KNOWLEDGE OF LANGUAGE in generative grammar is the assumption
that complexity of the final state (grammar) cannot exceed the complexity of the combination of the initial state (universal grammar) and
the input (data to which learners are exposed). In order to see the hidden assumptions behind the argument in (6), consider the model of
the Language Acquisition Device (LAD) that has appeared in several
discussions of explanatory adequacy and language acquisition (figure 1).
      The argument in (6) has the following form: the output of LAD
contains principle *P*. Principle *P* could not have been inductively arrived at from the input. Therefore, it must have been innately specified
as part of LAD. For this conclusion to be valid, we need to appeal to the
hidden assumption that every organizational principle found in the
output must be present either in the initial state (LAD) or in the input
(data). That is to say, LAD is essentially entropic: the complexity of the

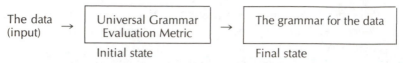

Figure 1. Language Acquisition Device (LAD) model.

output cannot exceed the sum total of the complexity of the input and the initial state.

Why should we make this assumption? Why couldn't it be the case that the complexity of organization in the final state is the result of the *formation* of novel regularities in LAD, triggered by the impetus from the input data? Suppose the black box contains a concentrated solution of some sort. If we produce a disturbance in the solution, say by cooling, the final state will be a set of highly structured crystals. When extended to crystal formation, the logic of the argument for innately prespecified principles in LAD would force us to conclude that the black box originally contained crystals (not just the solution) because crystals are part of the final state but not the input. This analogy brings out the dubiousness of the conclusions about the nature of innate specification. It is more reasonable to hold that what is innately specified is not the set of "macro" prefabricated principles of core grammars, but only the "micro" atomic entities that go into the formation of principles. These atomic entities organize themselves into complex order at a macro level of organization that we call grammar. I will provide examples of such atomic entities in the section on Fields of Attraction.

In sum, the metaphor of grammar as knowledge creates the illusion of a unique grammar shared by a linguistic community. This illusion has led to the formulation of the problem of language development as a "logical problem," and has given birth to the demand for an evaluation procedure that selects the "correct" grammar for the given data. Underlying the entire program is the entropic conception of the language faculty.

EMERGENCE OF COMPLEX ORDER IN NATURAL SYSTEMS

While it is true that closed systems in the universe do exhibit entropy, it has become increasingly clear to physicists and biologists that there exist large classes of open systems in nature that have the property of increasing the complexity of organization by absorbing energy from the environment. According to current cosmology, there was little order in the universe at the point of the big bang, when the universe came into existence. How did this original random state gradually evolve into the complex organization of atoms, molecules, crystals, living cells, animals, and the human mind? How does the exquisite order of snowflakes continue to arise out of the disordered collection of water molecules, with a unique pattern of organization for each snowflake? These questions have been raised during the recent years by many scientists. Schrodinger (1935), one of the earliest who was interested in this question, distinguishes between three types of processes in nature. First, there is the domain of Newtonian mechanics in which ordered states are changed into other ordered states. Second, there is the domain of equilibrium thermodynamics in which ordered states give way to disordered states. Finally, there is the newly discovered domain in which disorder gives way to order. This third domain belongs to the "science of complexity" that raises the question of how order arises in nature (Prigogine and Stengers 1984). Variously referred to as "chaos," "self organization," and "non-linearity," this domain has turned out to be the most exciting since quantum mechanics and relativity in physics, and has proved to be central to many problems in biological and social systems as well.

In what follows, I briefly sketch some of the ideas that I think will prove to be valuable in theories of phonological structure and development, leaving the reader to other sources for the details of the types of phenomena and solutions that come under chaos and self organizations (Hofstadter 1981; Prigogine and Stengers 1984; Crutchfield, Farmer, and Light 1986; Davis 1988; Stewart 1989).

A fundamental notion in these theories is that of ATTRACTORS. An attractor is a point or region that an evolving system settles down to. In a FIXED POINT ATTRACTOR the system comes down to rest at a fixed location, as in the case of a simple pendulum subject to friction. In a PERIODIC ATTRACTOR, the system repeats itself indefinitely, as in the case of the human heart, a planet going around a star, or a simple pendulum without friction. In a STRANGE ATTRACTOR (or chaotic attractor), the system never repeats itself, but describes an infinite set of possibilities in a finite space. An example of such a situation would be a planet orbiting around two stars, or a pendulum caught in the magnetic field of three magnets.[15]

In the case of both fixed point attractor and periodic attractor, it is possible to predict the future state of the system on the basis of the state of the system at any previous point of time. In contrast, this prediction is impossible in a strange attractor. Even though the behavior of a system, with a strange attractor is governed by *deterministic* laws, its

---

[15]*Attractor* is a descriptive term that refers to a set of states in a dynamical system, not to the causes that give rise to the behavior. Thus, the cause that governs periodic oscillation in a simple pendulum is the earth's gravitational field, but the attractor is its history of pairs of velocity and position.

behavior in the long run is *unpredictable*. We can tell where the system cannot be, and we can identify the states that the system is most likely to be, but we cannot tell exactly where the system will be. In other words, a chaotic attractor exhibits the property of *constrained randomness*. An international conference on chaos held by the Royal Society in London defines the property as "stochastic behaviour occurring in a deterministic system" (Stewart 1989, p. 17).

A strange attractor is often the result of the interaction of two or more interacting atomic "fields of attraction" which, in isolation, would have given rise to fixed point or periodic attractors. Thus, even though a planet going around a star yields a periodic attractor whose motion is entirely predictable in terms of Newtonian mechanics, the motion of a planet in the field of two stars can be totally unpredictable. The same forces of nature that yield predictable motion also yield unpredictable motion in a different combination or different strength.

The reason for the constrained randomness of chaotic systems lies in their *sensitivity to initial conditions*. That is to say, immeasurably small differences in the initial input or initial state can cause extremely large differences in the final state. Therefore, their state at time t_j can be predicted only if we know the nature of their state at t_0, as well as the input with total precision. Their state at t_j cannot be predicted on the basis of some non-initial state at t_i or a less precise measurement of t_0.

There are several reasons we must explore the possibility that the language faculty is a self-organizing system with the properties of a strange attractor. First, computer implementations show that distributed systems with built-in attractors exhibit the properties of adaptability, goal orientedness, self-repair, and efficient learning and recognition under noisy conditions (Hogg and Huberman 1984; Huberman and Hogg 1986). These properties are characteristic of linguistic systems, like other cognitive and biological systems. Second, if, as Chomsky recognizes, no two individuals have the same grammar, the property of constrained randomness in dynamical systems makes them ideal for modeling language development. Third, these systems can be nonentropic: that is, they have the property of creating order where none existed before. The last property makes them the right candidates for answering the question of how novel order arises in linguistic systems.

LANGUAGE AS A SELF-ORGANIZING DYNAMICAL SYSTEM

Suppose we abandoned the metaphor of the language learner as a scientist or a data processing serial computer, and viewed language development as being analogous to the growth of form in a growing plant or the formation of a snowflake. This shift of metaphor has far-reaching consequences for the way we formulate the problems of language structure and development. Take the problems of symmetry in snow-flakes. It is well known that snowflakes have six branches, and that there are infinite ways of structuring each branch (figure 2). Yet, they obey a symmetry condition: within each snowflake, the patterning of all the six branches must be identical.

One problem that physicists have been seeking an answer to is: what is the mechanism that guarantees the symmetry constraint on snowflakes in spite of their infinite variability? Observe that this is a problem that is similar to the problem of variability of human gram-mars: no two grammars are identical, even when the input data are the same, and yet the variability across grammars is severely constrained. If we were to adopt the formulation of the "logical" problem of lan-guage acquisition, we should ask: how do the water molecules in a branch "deduce" the organization in the other branches? Clearly, this is a meaningless question. If the growth of form in language formation is analogous to that in snowflake formation, we must formulate it as a problem of morphogenesis: how does a grammar arise and develop in an individual through interaction with the linguistic environment? In-stead of thinking of grammar as knowledge of language, we must think of it as an individual's internal linguistic system. This system governs the external behavior of the individual in the production and processing of language, in making acceptability judgments, and so on. As a result, it creates the illusion of containing propositional knowledge.

Suppose we free ourselves from the idea that language develop-ment is the deduction of the adult grammar from the input data, and

Figure 2.   Possible structures for snowflakes with six branches.

think of it as the formation of patterns triggered by the data. The patterns that arise in this fashion can vary from individual to individual, even when triggered by the same data. Furthermore, the data from the adult systems need not trigger the same patterns as the adult systems.

Given this scenario, the question is how the different grammars that are formed in the same community happen to share sufficient common properties so as to allow linguistic communication. The answer is that the grammars in a community adapt to each other. Some of the patterns that appear in the growing individual are "overt" in ordinary communication, whereas others are "covert" in the sense that they do not affect ordinary communication. Thus, allowing the determiner to precede or follow the noun is an overt pattern because it is directly relevant for communication, whereas allowing the reciprocal to take object antecedents in the nonclause-bounded domain is hardly a candidate for causing misunderstanding in ordinary communication in English. After all, how many times does one come across sentences like (2c) in actual speech? The overt patterns of the individuals of a community must be the same, while they are free to vary within some limits as far as covert patterns are concerned.[16] In the course of language development, the overt patterns that are "unfit" to survive because of conflict with the input data disappear, while the covert patterns are retained by the individuals.[17]

The basic premises that define this conception of phonological structure and development can be stated as follows:

1. The emergence of order/complex organization in linguistic systems is analogous to the emergence of order/complex organization in nonlinguistic systems. The formation of grammar in an individual does not involve a logical problem of deducing propositional knowledge, but involves growth of form in a system that governs the external behavior of the system.

2. Linguistic systems are dynamical systems. If so, it is reasonable to expect them to exhibit properties of dynamical systems, namely, (A) sensitivity to initial conditions characteristic of strange attrac-

---

[16]Needless to say, this does not rule out the possibility of total convergence in some domains even in covert patterns.

[17]Pronunciation, word order, and word meanings are part of the overt patterns that enter into normal language interaction. In contrast, the principles responsible for acceptability judgments on (2) or the representation of *president* as [[preside]ent] (bimorphemic) or as [president] (monomorphemic)], hardly affect the kinds of communicative interaction that human beings indulge in. Given everything else the same, we would expect greater variability in the unstable covert parts which do not interact frequently with environment. Thus, the use of overt pronouns is extremely rare in "pro drop" languages like Malayalam and Japanese, and hence the pronominal anaphora of these languages exhibit a great deal of variability across speakers. When the occurrence of overt pronouns is infrequent in actual language use, the differences in the internal grammars go undetected.

tors; (B) self-organization: random behavior at the micro level leading to stable order at the macro level (Prigogine and Stengers 1984);
(C) goal orientedness: alternative paths lead to the same target;
and (D) self-repair, adaptability, and efficient learning and recognition under noisy conditions.

3. Linguistic patterns appear spontaneously in the language faculty,
    when triggered by the environment, like the patterns in snow-
    flakes. Unlike snowflakes, however, linguistic systems exhibit
    adaptability. Their internal changes are governed by the pressure to
    conform in their overt behavior to those of the other members of
    the community. The overt patterns of a system are those that affect
    the normal linguistic interaction; the covert patterns do not enter
    into the normal linguistic interaction and are open only to the lin-
    guist's experimental techniques that probe into the system.

4. Small differences in the input can cause large differences in the
    covert patterns, as in other dynamical systems. Therefore one can-
    not predict the grammar of the learner from the combination of UG
    and input data. There can be no algorithm to deduce the grammar
    from the data.

5. Growth of form in linguistic systems is governed by (A) universal
    fields of attraction, (B) relative strengths of these fields, and (C)
    reinforcement and conflict between different fields of attraction.
    The same principles may yield discrete/robust/predictable results
    when close to an attractor, and gradient/variable/random results at
    the boundary between two attractors.

In the following section, I summarize some of the ideas and analyses in Mohanan (forthcoming) in order to provide a brief example of
how the conception of language as a dynamical system can be implemented in a theory of phonological structure, and to show how we can
seek answers to the problems of morphogenesis posed earlier. Because
I am not a developmental phonologist, I am in no position to substanti-
ate this program in terms of data from phonological development per
se. Due to limitations of space, even the "internal" motivation will be
very sketchy. My intention is to outline a promising possibility, rather
than provide a detailed defense.

FIELDS OF ATTRACTION IN PHONOLOGY

In order to understand the nature of the internal phonological system
of human individuals, most phonological theories have focussed their
attention on two types of phenomena, namely, patterns of distribution
and alternation. A regularity in distribution is the systematic correla-

tion between an entity and its environment, whereas a regularity of alternation is the systematic covariance between two corresponding entities in related environments.[18] The two staple tools in phonological theories used for the formal statement of the patterns of distribution and alternation are RULES and CONSTRAINTS. A rule is a statement that takes a representation as its input and yields another representation, whereas a constraint is a statement that holds on either entities internal to a representation, or on entities in two different levels of representation, without implying an input-output relation. Either distribution or alternation can be described in terms of either rule or constraint.

Instead of thinking about phonological regularities in terms of the formalism of rules and constraints, let us think of them as FIELDS OF ATTRACTION in a dynamical system. The gravitational field is neither a rule nor a constraint, but it has the observed effects that phonologists might be able to describe in terms of rules or constraints.[19] Examples of centers of attraction in phonological systems ("states" or "locations" that attract phonological systems) are given in (7) and (8). These statements define the most natural or "unmarked" states for phonological systems to be. (7a–c) define cross-segmental naturalness, while (8a–d) define segment-internal naturalness.

7a.   If a [+ stop] consonant is followed by another consonant, the former must share its place of articulation with the latter.[20]
7b.   Adjacent obstruents must agree in voice.
7c.   A segment adjacent to a [+ nasal] segment is [+ nasal].

8a.   If a segment is [+ nasal], it is [+ sonorant].
8b.   If a segment is [+ nasal], it is [+ stop].
8c.   If a segment is [+ sonorant], it is [+ voiced].
8d.   If a segment is [+ consonantal], it is [+ coronal].

These fields of attraction differ in the strength of attraction they exert on the system. For example, the field of attraction in (8a) is extremely strong: natural languages do not allow nasal obstruents. The fields of (8b) and (8c) are relatively weak, as some languages do allow non-stop nasals (e.g., nasal vowels) and voiceless sonorants. The field of attrac-

---

[18]Examples of distributional regularity would be: in English, [u] does not occur at the beginning of a word, and [h] does not occur at the end of a syllable. An example of a regularity of alternation would be: in English, [m] systematically alternates with [mn] as illustrated in *damn-damnation*.

[19]This conception of phonological patterns has the immediate advantage of eliminating the illusory dichotomy between rules and constraints, thereby eliminating the freedom to use either the rule formalism or the constraint formalism to suit the contingencies of description (see Mohanan forthcoming).

[20]A sound is [+ stop] if there is no oral air flow in its production. Plosives and nasal stops are [+ stop], while fricatives, laterals, and vowels are [− stop].

tion of (8d) is the weakest, because almost all languages allow noncoronal consonants.

An advantage of the conception of fields in phonological systems is that it allows interactions involving REINFORCEMENT and CONFLICT RESOLUTION. An example of reinforcement is (8b) and (8c). Even though both (8b) and (8c) can be individually violated in human languages, the force they exert when they are in combination cannot be overcome: no language has voiceless nasal vowels or voiceless nasal laterals. (7c) and (8b) constitute an example of conflict resolution. When a vowel precedes a nasal consonant, (7c) has the effect of making the vowel [+nasal]. However, (8b) opposes this force, retaining the vowel as [−nasal]. The outcome of this conflict cannot be predicted on universal grounds: in some languages, (7c) effects phonological nasalization, whereas in others it does not. The interaction of these atomic attractors yields the strange attractor that we call UG. If so, the atomic fields of attraction and the theory of their interaction can give us an explanation for why UG is the way it is.

The assumption that statements such as (7) and (8) constitute universal fields of attraction provides an answer to one of the questions that we raised in the first section of this chapter. Why is it that homorganic nasal assimilation and obstruent voicing assimilation are found in language after language? If the idea of fields of attraction is accepted, we can view the recurrent but infinitely variable patterns as being caused by universal fields of attraction. It also solves the problem of the mismatch between naturalness and formal simplicity. Natural states of affairs are those that are closer to universal attractors. A grammar that violates (7a) and (7b) is less natural than one that does not. The presence of homorganic nasal assimilation and obstruent voicing assimilation in a language is not a complexity that is language particular: it stems from universal grammar.

An advantage of thinking about the statements in (7) and (8) as fields of attraction is that we will not expect them to be exceptionless; nor will we expect them to be invariant across languages. (7a) and (7b) characterize a region near which most languages can be found, they do not specify the precise details of the patterns of distribution and alternation in a given language. In order to relate the "archetypes" to their actual manifestation in a given language, further details have to be added.

This approach provides for a way of capturing the variability and invariance of the recurrent patterns of distribution and alternation. In English, for example, we have to add the following specifications to (7a): in the syllable internal domain, (7a) holds only if the following consonant (the trigger) is [−coronal]; across syllables, it holds only if the undergoer of assimilation is [+coronal]. In Malayalam, on the other hand, the specifications would be that the undergoer is [+nasal], and the trigger is a plosive. These additional specifications themselves are governed by universal principles of attraction interaction, such as those in (9):

9a. The strength of assimilatory attraction is greater in smaller domains.
9b. The strength of assimilatory attraction increases with more dominant triggers.[21]
9c. Resistance to change is greater in more dominant segments.
9d. The values [−son], [+stop], [−cor], [−ant] and [+back] are dominant in place assimilation.

These principles yield a large number of cross-linguistic predictions, most of which are unavailable in existing phonological theories. For example, the specification that [−son] is the dominant value of [son] has the effect of making plosives ([−son, +stop]) more dominant than nasals ([+son, +stop]). The effect of (9c) is to make dominant segments resist assimilatory change more than nondominant segments. When (9c) is combined with (9d), we get the result that nasals are more likely to undergo assimilation than plosives. Thus, (9c) and (9d) together allow languages such as English in which both nasals and plosives undergo place assimilation, and languages like Malayalam in which only nasals undergo place assimilation. They also predict that there will be no language in which plosives undergo place assimilation, but not nasals. The effect of (9b) is to make dominant segments stronger triggers of assimilation than nondominant ones. The specification of [+stop] as the dominant value of [stop] (9d), in conjunction with (9b), predicts that in a language in which fricatives ([−stop, −son]) trigger place assimilation, plosive ([+stop, −son]) will also trigger assimilation. The stipulation of [−cor], [−ant], and [+back] as dominant (9d) correctly predicts the possibility of labials ([+ant, −cor, −back]) assimilating to velars ([−ant, −cor, +back]) but not alveolars ([+ant, +cor, −back]), as in English and Korean (9b). It also predicts that in the environment in which labials undergo assimilation, coronals also will (9c). When we combine this result with (9a), we understand why labials in English obligatorily undergo assimilation to velars within syllables, but not across syllables: the assimilatory force is greater in the syllable domain than in a larger domain, and, hence, it overcomes the greater resistance of labials to undergo assimilation in this domain.[22] These predictions crucially depend upon the use of gra-

---

[21]Dominance is a property which allows entities to survive in a conflict. Dominant entities typically trigger assimilation, but fail to undergo it. They also typically fail to undergo deletion and neutralization.

[22]For the details of other predictions and the data and analyses that support them, the reader is referred to Mohanan (forthcoming).

dient strength, reinforcement, and conflict resolution in multiple fields of attraction. These ideas are unavailable in the traditional models that employ either evaluation procedures (3) or parameter setting (4).

What is interesting is that principles such as (9a–d) that are motivated by cross-linguistic generalizations also are supported independently by phonological development. To take an example, the dominance values in (9d) derive the dominance hierarchy of alveolar < labial < velar, the less dominant assimilating to the more dominant. This hierarchy, which accounts for the facts of assimilation in Korean adult speech, also accounts for the speech of English-speaking children. For Daniel's speech, Menn (1973) argues for a strength hierarchy of "velar, labial, dental, in descending order of strength (p. 381)."

In addition to accounting for the invariance and variability of archetypal patterns across languages, the approach sketched above also provides an account of the variability across speakers within a language, as well as within the grammar of a single individual. Thus, most speakers of English allow place assimilation across words in both *hot cakes* and *ten kings*, while some allow only the nasal to undergo assimilation. As predicted by the specification that [−son] is dominant (9d), there are no speakers who allow only the plosive to assimilate.

We now have a solution to the problem of emergence of complexity in phonological development. Why do children's grammars exhibit complex patterns that cannot be "logically" deduced from the adult speech to which children are exposed? The answer provided by the dynamical systems model is that universal attractors of the kind illustrated in (7) and (8) create complex patterns of phonological organization in a developing individual even when not required by the input data. When these patterns are external and are in conflict with the observed patterns of the rest of the community, some of them tend to get modified or eliminated altogether in the course of adaptation. Occasionally, the individual wins, retaining the pattern and letting it spread to the rest of the community, resulting in innovations in language change. Phonological development, in other words, is pattern formation and adaptation, not knowledge discovery and deduction.

Neither the formal algebra program nor the principles and parameters program has a satisfactory answer to the emergence of complexity in a domain that exhibits constrained but random variability. Extending the principles and parameters program to solve the kinds of problems raised above will involve three modifications crucially. First, the values of parameters will have to be gradient, ranging from 0 to 1, rather than discrete. Second, we will have to allow the parametric choices to reinforce each other and resolve conflicts with each other. Third, some degree of randomness must be allowed in the parameter setting, so that given the same input, different individuals may choose different settings. If these modifications are made, the principles and parameters model will have the properties of a dynamical systems model.

I believe that a large number of phonological fields of attraction can be ultimately traced to the properties of the production and perception of speech, although phonology cannot be "reduced" to phonetics. Thus, the physiological basis of assimilation, consonant lenition, and vowel reduction phenomena is the interaction between two opposing fields: the inertia of the production system that tends to reduce articulatory cost (Lindblom this volume) and the need of the perceptual system to maintain phonological contrasts.[23]

CONCLUDING REMARKS

In this chapter we examined the problem of the emergence of complex order in phonological systems. Children's grammars frequently show novel complex patterns of organization that are not present in the adult grammars that surround them. In order to offer a solution to this problem, we suggested that the language faculty is a self-organizing dynamical system that has the property of creating complex patterns when interacting with the linguistic environment. In particular, we suggested that it would be enlightening to view the phonological module of the language faculty as containing a number of atomic fields of attraction. These fields interact with each other, as well as with the articulatory and auditory systems, to create patterns that are not necessarily present in the input data. If they enter into linguistic interaction, these patterns are subject to the requirements of adaptation in a language community to serve the purposes of communication.

In the course of arriving at this proposal, we rejected the formulation of the problem of language development as the "logical problem of language acquisition," and suggested that it should be viewed as the problem of morphogenesis. In doing so, we also rejected the assumptions that language development involves a discovery of the grammar of the community, and that it is governed by inductive and deductive operations. Instead, we suggested that what language development involves is a creation of grammar that adapts itself to the overt patterns of the grammars of the other individuals of the community. The formation of grammars is governed by nonlinear dynamics.

---

[23]For a discussion on the basis of phonological fields of attraction, see Mohanan (forthcoming).

REFERENCES

Baker, C. L., and McCarthy, J. J. 1981. *The Logical Problem of Language Acquisition*. Massachusetts: MIT Press.

Brown, R., and Hanlon, C. 1970. Derivational complexity and order of acquisition. In *Cognition and the Development of Language*, ed. J. R. Hayes. New York: Wiley.

Chomsky, N. 1956. *The Logical Structure of Linguistic Theory*. Chicago: The University of Chicago Press.

Chomsky, N. 1965. *Aspects of the Theory of Syntax*. Massachusetts: MIT Press.

Chomsky, N. 1981. *Lectures on Government and Binding*. New York: Foris Publications.

Chomsky, N. 1986. *Knowledge of Language*. New York: Praeger.

Chomsky, N. 1988. *Language and Problems of Knowledge: Managua Lectures*. Massachusetts: MIT Press.

Chomsky, N., and Halle, M. 1968. *The Sound Pattern of English*. New York: Harper and Row.

Crutchfield, J. P., Farmer, J. J., and Light, D. 1986. Chaos. *Scientific American* 12.

Davies, P. 1988. *The Cosmic Blueprint*. New York: Simon and Schuster.

Dresher, B. E. 1981. On the learnability of abstract phonology. In *The Logical Problem of Language Acquisition*, eds. C. L. Baker and J. J. McCarthy. Massachusetts: MIT Press.

Ferguson, C. A. Personal communication.

Ferguson, C. A., Peizer, D. B., and Weeks, T. E. 1973. Model-and-replica phonological grammar of a child's first words. *Linqua* 31:35–65.

Gazdar, G., Klein, E., Pullum, G. K., and Sag, I. 1985. *Generalized Phrase Structure Grammar*. Oxford: Basil Blackwell.

Goldsmith, J. Forthcoming. Harmonic phonology. In *Rules and Constraints*, ed. J. Goldsmith. Chicago: The University of Chicago Press.

Grimshaw, J. 1981. Form, function, and the language acquisition device. In *The Logical Problem of Language Acquisition*, eds. C. L. Baker and J. J. McCarthy. Massachusetts: MIT Press.

Hofstadter, D. 1981. Strange attractors: Mathematical patterns delicately poised between order and chaos. *Scientific American* 5.

Hogg, T., and Huberman, B. 1984. Understanding biological computation: Reliable learning and recognition. In *Proceedings of the National Academy of Sciences, USA, Vol 81*. November.

Huberman, B., and Hogg, T. 1986. Complexity and adaptation. *Physica* 22 D:376–84.

Ingram, D. 1974. Phonological rules in young children. *Journal of Child Language* 1:49–64.

Lakoff, G. Forthcoming. Cognitive phonology. In *Rules and Constraints*, ed. J. Goldsmith. Chicago: The University of Chicago Press.

Lasnik, H. 1981. Learnability, restrictiveness, and the evaluation metric. In *The Logical Problem of Language Acquisition*, eds. C. L. Baker and J. J. McCarthy. Massachusetts: MIT Press.

Leonard, L. B., and Brown, B. L. 1984. Nature and boundaries of phonologic categories: A case study of an unusual pattern in a language impaired child. *Journal of Hearing and Speech Disorders* 49:419–28.

Leonard, L. B., Newhoff, M., and Mesalam, L. 1972. Individual differences in early child phonology. *Applied Psycholinguistics* 1:7–30.

Levelt, W. J. M. 1974. *Formal Grammars in Linguistics and Psycholinguistics*. The Hague: Mouton.

Lindblom, B. 1988. Some remarks on the origin of the phonetic code. Paper presented at the Symposium on Developmental Dyslexia at the Wenner-Gren Center, Stockholm, Sweden.

Lindblom, B., MacNeilage, P. F., and Studdert-Kennedy, M. G. 1983. Self-organizing processes and explanation of phonological universals. In *Explanations of Linguistic Universals*, eds. B. Butterworth, B Comrie, and O. Dahl. The Hague: Mouton.

McCarthy, J. J. 1981. The role of the evaluation metric in the acquisition of phonology. In *The Logical Problem of Language Acquisition*, eds. C. L. Baker and J. J. McCarthy. Massachusetts: MIT Press.

Macken, M., and Ferguson, C. 1983. Cognitive aspects of phonological development: Model, evidence, and issues. In *Children's Language*, ed. K. Nelson. Hillsdale, NJ: Lawrence Erlbaum Associates.

Menn, L. 1973. On the origin and growth of phonological and syntactic rules. *Chicago Linguistic Society* 9.

Menn, L. Personal communication.

Mohanan, K. P. Forthcoming. Universal attractors in phonology. In *Rules and Constraints*, ed. J. Goldsmith. Chicago: The University of Chicago Press.

Pinker, S., and Bloom, P. 1990. Natural language and natural selection. *Behavioral and Brain Sciences*.

Prigogine, I., and Stengers, I. 1984. *Order Out of Chaos*. New York: Fontana.

Roeper, T. 1983. On the deductive model and the acquisition of productive morphology. In *The Logical Problem of Language Acquisition*, eds. C. L. Baker and J. J. McCarthy. Massachusetts: MIT Press.

Schrodinger, E. 1935. *What Is Life? and Mind and Matter*. Cambridge: Cambridge University Press.

Schwartz, R. G., Leonard, L. B., Folger, M. K., and Wilcox, M. J. 1980. Early phonological behaviour in normal speaking and language disordered children: Evidence for a synergistic view of language disorders. *Journal of Speech and Hearing Disorders* 45:357–77.

Smolensky, P. 1986. Information processing in dynamical systems: The foundations of harmony theory. In *Parallel Distributed Processing, Vol. I.*, eds. D. Rumelhart et al. Massachusetts: MIT Press.

Stampe, D. 1972. How I spent my summer vacation. Doctoral dissertation, University of Chicago.

Stemberger, J. P. 1988. Between word processes in child phonology. *Journal of Child Language* 15:39–61.

Stewart, I. 1989. *Does God Play Dice? The Mathematics of Chaos*. Oxford: Basil Blackwell.

Vihman, M. 1978. Consonant harmony: Its scope and function in child language. In *Universals of Language, Vol. 2: Phonology*, eds. J. P. Greenberg, C. A. Ferguson, and E. A. Moravcsik. Stanford: Stanford University Press.

Chapter • 24

How Do and Should Studies of Animal Communication Affect Interpretations of Child Phonological Development?

Marc D. Hauser and Peter Marler

Observations of nonhuman animal behavior have played three different roles in the study of human behavior generally, and of human vocal communication or language more explicitly. First, it has been clear since Darwin (1872) that data on nonhuman animals (hereafter, animals) are important because they provide an understanding of continuity or discontinuity between our own and other species. Second, animals have frequently been used as models for testing particular hypotheses about human behavior (reviews in: Lieberman 1984; Petersen and Jusczyk 1984; Kuhl 1989). In a number of cases, having an animal model has been critical to our understanding of a particular theoretical issue because the decisive experimental tests could not be conducted with human subjects. Third, there has been

We thank Charles Ferguson for inviting outsiders to contribute to this volume and for making this an exciting event. For comments on earlier versions of this chapter, we thank Chris Evans, Lisa Hauser, and especially, John Locke and Michael Studdert-Kennedy. For access to the facilities and permission to work on Cayo Santiago and in Sabana Seca, we thank the Caribbean Primate Research Center, Matthew Kessler, and John Berard. Funding was provided by the National Institute of Child Health and Human Development and a National Geographic Society Grant to the authors.

a long history of attempts to identify features of human behavior (typically, features related to the mind) that are not found in animals and from such observations, to argue for the uniqueness of humans (Chomsky 1980; Lieberman 1984; Premack 1986).

In this chapter, we begin by discussing how observations of animal behavior have been used, how we think they might be more appropriately used, and how, with regard to our understanding of child phonology, they must be used. We then discuss recent research on referential signalling and the mechanisms underlying phonation in nonhuman primates, and argue that such data are critical to our understanding of both evolutionary and developmental precursors to speech. Throughout, we focus on similarities and differences between humans and animals with regard to vocal production rather than perception. We emphasize production not because of lack of research on perception (see below), but because a number of interesting problems and data have recently emerged that challenge the proclaimed uniqueness of human speech and the mechanisms underlying its production. We do, however, refer to reviews of research on nonhuman animal vocal perception wherever it is relevant.

NONHUMAN ANIMALS AS MODELS FOR THE STUDY OF HUMAN SPEECH

Ethologists studying vocal communication in animals commonly refer to studies of human speech in order to argue for evolutionary precursors. Similarly, linguists frequently draw upon studies of vocal communication in animals to give credence to the idea that there is a biological basis to the observation or phenomenon at hand. There is no question that such cross-species comparisons are necessary and can provide important insights regarding both phylogeny and functional organization. However, when making such comparisons, we must be cautious in distinguishing similarities that are homologous, as may be anticipated when comparing our own species with other primates, and those that are analogous, as when making more remote phylogenetic comparisons between humans and birds that engage in vocal learning. To illustrate this point, let us consider first research on nonhuman primate vocal development and second, observations of song learning in birds.

Vocal Development in Nonhuman Primates

The most comprehensive research on vocal development in nonhuman primates has been conducted with squirrel monkeys (for a review, see Newman and Symmes 1982). Results show that young squirrel monkeys raised in isolation produce all of the calls in the adult repertoire. Acoustic isolation experiments suggest that auditory experience has little affect on subsequent modification of call structure. This conclusion is based primarily on a careful study of vocal development in four infants raised by muted mothers living in isolated mother-infant pairs (Winter et al. 1973). One of the four was separated from the mother and raised in isolation after two weeks of age. Two others were separated from their hearing mothers and raised in isolation, one from 2 days and the other from 19 days. Finally, one infant was deafened by bilateral cochleaectomy at four days of age. Six other infants served as controls.

No differences were reported in the vocal development of the deaf infant, the isolates with intact hearing, and the controls. All of the major vocal categories were recorded from all subjects within the first week, except for *twitter/trills*. *Twitter/trills* developed out of another category, in both experimentals and controls, at about three months of age. Ontogenetic changes also were recorded in other vocal features, such as the duration of the isolation peep. Both experimentals and controls reached adult values of isolation peep duration at about nine months of age. The only major abnormality noted was the low rate of vocal production in the deaf infant and in some isolates; rates of vocal production changed when they were allowed to interact with other age-mates. We can conclude then, that in the squirrel monkey, normal development of all major vocal categories occurs in auditory isolation and without the need for auditory feedback. The question of within-category variations, however, and the possibility that their use might be susceptible to influence by the auditory environment was not addressed in these studies.

Another study confirmed that, although deafening of two adult female squirrel monkeys drastically modified rates of production and loudness of certain call types, as well as the sequential ordering of call categories, the acoustic morphology of all classes of calls studied remained unchanged (Talmage-Riggs et al. 1972). Finally, there is evidence that subspecific differences in vocal morphology develop irrespective of the acoustic environment in which squirrel monkeys are raised (reviewed in Newman and Symmes 1982).

Should we then conclude that learning plays no role at all in the development of fully normal vocal communication in squirrel monkeys? Herzog and Hopf (1984) found no abnormalities in responses of isolates to playbacks of alarm calls, but the number of response assays available to them in the laboratory was limited. Experience, however, almost certainly plays some role in nature in shaping the contexts in which call types are produced, and in the responses that vocal signals elicit in others. Until these aspects of the vocal communication system have been investigated more exhaustively, it is appropriate to reserve judgment about the role of learning in the ontogeny of vocal communication in the squirrel monkey. It seems unlikely, however, that further research will change the conclusion reached by Winter et al. (1973), that auditory experience has little bearing on the course of development of normal vocal morphology in this species, unless vocal stimulation proves to influence the frequency of use of certain within-category variants (Newman and Symmes 1982).

A further question arises about the degree to which one can generalize from the squirrel monkey to other nonhuman species. First, squirrel monkeys, like other New World monkeys (e.g., tamarins and marmosets) are precocial. In contrast, the Old World monkeys (e.g., macaques and baboons) and the Great Apes (e.g., chimpanzees and gorillas) are altricial species and, thus, are unlikely to show the same patterns of vocal development. Second, if one looks at vocal development as a multidimensional process that includes production, contextual usage, and comprehension, then lack of support for the role of learning in call production should not be taken as evidence against the role of learning in other prerequisites of a communicative system such as comprehension of call meaning.

Other lines of recent research (Snowdon 1982; Snowdon, French, and Cleveland 1986; Seyfarth and Cheney 1986; see thorough review in Snowdon 1987) also suggest that closer investigation of the developmental patterns exhibited by squirrel monkeys would repay further investigation, and may reveal more evidence of developmental plasticity than previously thought. For example, Hauser (1989) has described the development of a trill-like vocalization (the *wrr*) produced by vervet monkeys living in Kenya. The aims of that study were to provide data on the developmental changes in (1) acoustic morphology, (2) contextual usage and, (3) comprehension. Young vervet infants (birth to three months) produce a *wrr*-like call when they are in distress (e.g., separated from their mothers). Although this call is no longer produced after the age of three months, the context that elicits it persists for several more months. At the age of ten months, the *wrr* re-enters the repertoire, but in a different context . . . i.e., when one group of vervets sees another group near their territorial boundary.

There are four aspects of the development of the *wrr* that display significant change. First, the acoustic morphology of the *wrr* given by individuals over the age of ten months and less than 3.5 years is different from that of adults. The difference in morphology seems to be due to the difficulty that young individuals have in producing distinct pulses of energy separated by silence, the most characteristic features of the *wrr*. Second, production of the *wrr* in an appropriate social context, as well as comprehension of call meaning, develop gradually over time, with comprehension preceding production. Both social and auditory experience affect the age at which infants first begin to produce and comprehend the meaning of *wrr*s. Last, and perhaps most intriguingly, the acoustic morphology of the *wrr* given by infants from birth to three months is more adult-like than that of older infants and juveniles.

In discussing the four points above, the following statements were made (Hauser 1989). Vervets appear to be born with the ability to produce an adult-like *trill*, as evidenced by the acoustic morphology of young infants' *wrr*s. When these early *wrr*s drop out of the repertoire at three months, a number of other adult-like vocalizations enter the repertoire. However, these new vocalizations are associated with different articulatory gestures. When the *wrr* re-enters the repertoire at ten months, its acoustic morphology suggests that the infant has, in some sense, lost articulatory control. It was inferred that this loss was due to interference from other calls with different articulatory routines and that this developmental pattern was comparable to the phenomenon of phonemic regression in human vocal development (Moskowitz 1970; see also, Macken this volume). After further reflection, we would now claim that some of the references to human vocal development were premature given our lack of knowledge of nonhuman primate phonation and cognitive abilities. Specifically, we do not know how nonhuman primates produce the sounds in their repertoire and what is known suggests that the vocal tract of a nonhuman primate differs in significant ways from that of a two-year-old child (Negus 1962; Crelin 1987), the approximate age for which phonemic regression has been described. If the mechanisms underlying phonation in nonhuman primates differ from those in human children and adults, then our analogies reflect ontogenetic parallelisms and do not tell us about possible evolutionary precursors.

Given current knowledge, three points are warranted with regard to the comparison between human and nonhuman primate vocal development. First, there is little evidence that learning contributes significantly to the ontogeny of an acoustically appropriate call repertoire. Most observations suggest that maturational changes in the vocal tract carry the primary burden for shaping developmental changes in call morphology (e.g., Seyfarth and Cheney 1986; Hauser 1989). However, we should exercise some restraint in drawing the conclusion that auditory feedback plays no role in vocal production given the results presented by Sinnott, Stebbins, and Moody (1975) that adult macaques subject to an environment with white noise will raise the amplitude of their own vocalizations (i.e., the Lombard effect). Second, learning may play a more important role than maturational factors in guiding developmental changes in the contextual usage of calls and their com-

prehension. And third, we believe that evidence of a hiatus in call production need not imply evidence of developmental discontinuities, as
has often been suggested for the transition period between babbling
and early speech. For example, we interpret the observation that vervet
infants stop producing the *wrr* for a seven month period (during which
other calls enter the repertoire) as evidence for reorganization of the
vocal developmental pathway, rather than as evidence of a "break" in
the ontogenetic sequence leading to adult renditions of the call.

Vocal Development in Birds

The phylogenetic distance between birds and humans is much greater
than that between us and nonhuman primates. There are, of course,
many homologies between birds and our own species at the level of
organ systems, cellular and subcellular physiology, and biochemistry.
At the behavioral level, however, we are more likely to ascribe similarities to convergent evolution. This does not mean that such comparisons lack scientific value. On the contrary, interpreted with care,
examining the process of convergent evolution has led to many fundamental insights into the historical forces that have shaped the phylogeny of organisms, whether the subject matter be anatomical or
behavioral. Such is the case, we believe, with comparisons of vocal
learning in songbirds and humans.

The list of similarities is now impressively long. This is not the
place for a comprehensive catalog. Such a list would encompass such
characteristics as the temporal separation of acquisition and production, the existence of sensitive periods for acquisition of new patterns
of vocal morphology (for reviews, see Marler 1987; Flege this volume),
the emergence in infancy of sensory predispositions that sensitize but
do not restrict responsiveness to certain patterns of vocal sound (e.g.,
Marler and Peters 1989; Jusczyk this volume), and the occurrence of
distinctive programs of motor ontogeny, variable in some degree according to circumstances, and yet displaying modal tendencies characteristic of a species as a whole. There is also evidence of categorical processing of adult vocal stimuli in both cases (Nelson and Marler 1989;
Harnad 1987).

As one example of an intriguing parallel, consider the phenomenon of subsong (an acoustically variable vocal utterance produced by
birds prior to reaching the state known as crystallized song), which is
so obviously reminiscent of the babbling stage of speech development.
Are the parallels meaningful, and if so, what do they tell us about the
vocal learning process? Most birds, such as flycatchers, have songs that
are innate rather than learned. When a bird with an innate song starts
to sing, the first efforts are clearly identifiable as immature versions of

normal crystallized song. These early efforts may be noisy and fragmented, but the maturational progression is clear, predictable, and linear, from the earliest efforts to the latest efforts.

In birds that can learn their songs, the developmental sequence is quite different. There is a virtual metamorphosis between subsong and the subsequent stages of plastic and crystallized song. Once again there is a certain range of individual variation in the timing of these various stages, but a modal pattern can always be discerned that varies in detail from species to species. As far as we can tell, in every species for which we have observed the subsong phase, vocal learning has been critically involved in the development of normal song.

Irrespective of whether or not a bird has been tutored with song, subsong reveals little or no impact of that experience. It is only with the onset of plastic song, which may begin weeks or months after the last experience of song tutoring, that a bird begins to show signs of retrieving learned songs from memory and attempting to reproduce some of their characteristics. We still do not know for certain what the functions of subsong are. It is believed, however, that subsong provides the opportunity to practice the skills of singing, and to fine tune the ability to guide the voice by ear (Nottebohm 1972). Such guidance is a prerequisite for vocal imitation, but is irrelevant for species in which the song is innate.

It has been shown recently that even the earliest stages of subsong are monitored by auditory feedback. There are species differences in song note duration in certain species of sparrows, and it turns out that these differences are present even in the earliest renditions of subsong. We have found that this contrast is lacking in the early subsong of sparrows that have been deafened in infancy (unpublished data). We believe that subsong is concerned with preparing the articulatory and perceptual substrates for the generation of vocal imitations, rather than with the imitation process per se, which begins later. It seems conceivable that babbling plays a similar role, by establishing an extensive repertoire of sensory-motor routines that form a basic substrate, out of which a subset is subsequently selected, appropriate to sustain the more refined skills needed for production of the speech sounds of a particular language.

Assuming that there is some validity to this comparison, no one would, of course, claim homology between subsong and babbling. Rather, similarities would be viewed as convergences, illustrating a basic set of strategies that any species is likely to employ if it embarks on the development of a system of communication based on learned signals. It is at this level that comparisons between speech development, and vocal learning in birds, are potentially illuminating. Why, then, are there no examples of subsong/babbling in other organisms, especially nonhuman primates? Snowdon (1982, 1987, 1988) has claimed to have found evidence of babbling in marmosets, a small New World monkey. However, no quantitative data have yet been presented to buttress this argument and the results that have been discussed show that young animals are actually producing a juxtaposed jumble of imperfectly rendered adult calls (Snowdon personal communication). Such utterances stand in contrast to true babbling/subsong where the difference between infantile and adult vocalizations is more radical. At this stage, it therefore seems that the avian-human comparison is more compelling. Nonetheless, we would argue that organisms other than oscine songbirds believed to engage in vocal learning (e.g., parrots, hummingbirds, kittens, and dolphins) are all worthy of study. More specifically, there is an urgent need for detailed studies of vocal ontogeny in a diversity of nonhuman primate species, to establish once and for all whether the transition in vocal ontogenetic strategies from monkeys and apes to man is indeed as radical as it seems to be.

In summarizing our stance, we would urge that birds and nonhuman primates can most profitably be used as models for early speech development if they are employed together, rather than as competing models. Close attention should be given to the possibility that vocal stimulation can affect the frequency of usage of call subtypes within the major vocal categories. Otherwise, it seems that studies of the behavioral correlates and physiological underpinnings of vocal imitation are best conducted on birds, and observations on the development of the comprehension and contextual usage of vocal signals are best approached in nonhuman primates.

WHY IS THE STUDY OF NONHUMAN ANIMAL COMMUNICATION CRITICAL TO OUR UNDERSTANDING OF HUMAN SPEECH?

Recent research in child phonology has embarked on a quantitative and objective assessment of what constitutes speech (see Oller this volume). This new framework is important for at least two reasons. First, it integrates objective and easily measurable acoustic variables with measures of relevant linguistic features. Second, it permits researchers working with individuals in different linguistic environments to compare observations readily. As Oller points out (this volume), without an integration of acoustic and linguistic measures, one is left with a suite of acoustic parameters that have no functional relationship to the language environment. Although Oller's synthesis represents a significant advance in the area of child phonology, as ethologists we see three problems with the current structure. First, although there are some objective criteria for distinguishing between sounds that are precursors to speech and those that are not (e.g., Oller's measure of mouth opening rates for syllables), there is still an overall lack of consideration for the mechanisms underlying phonation and, thus, for the mechanisms underlying the great variety of sound patterns generated by young children. Acoustic analyses of the young child's utterances cannot substitute completely for analyses of the articulatory gestures used in the production of such utterances (see Kent this volume).

Because the vocal tract undergoes substantial developmental modifications, it is unlikely that vocalizations produced by the young child, which may sound like those produced later on in life, will be based on the same articulatory routines. This in itself is of interest, because it suggests an early form of "functional equivalence." Second, discussions of speech precursors have generally failed to make the distinction between evolutionary and developmental precursors. And third, there is much to gain if those studying humans and those studying nonhuman primates share methods and conceptual frameworks: after all, the subjects are in both cases primates. Failure to use comparable techniques may hinder us from the discovery of true homologies in the patterns of processes of vocal development that are shared between human and nonhuman primates.

We propose a conceptual framework that might allow us to determine when and how animal communication differs from human speech. First, we suggest that a distinction be made between evolutionary and developmental precursors; the first refers to phylogeny and function and the second to chronological time in an individual's lifetime. This breakdown allows us to talk about the abilities or faculties that a child is born with or must learn about, and whether such faculties are derived from an ancestral stock. Both evolutionarily and developmentally, three different faculties must be distinguished in order to properly evaluate what kind(s) of precursor(s) to speech an individual has: (A) mechanistic, (B) acoustic and, (C) linguistic.

A mechanistic precursor refers to the anatomical components of the vocal tract and its associated neuromuscular equipment and the range of articulatory gestures that it is capable of producing. Based on comparative anatomical studies by Negus (1949) and more recent work by Lieberman (1984) and Crelin (1987), it is clear that the human adult vocal tract configuration is unique among animals and different from that of the human child. In particular, no other animal has more than a relatively simple one-tube vocal tract with the possible exception of nonhuman primates, such as howler monkeys and chimpanzees, who have air sacs opening into the ventricle of the larynx. Also, due to the relative size and placement of the tongue in relation to the oral cavity, there appears to be little opportunity for changing cross-sectional areas. As a result, the nonhuman animal vocal tract is more limited than the human vocal tract with regard to speech producing capabilities. Nonetheless, species with anatomically different vocal tracts (e.g., parrots, starlings) and humans born with vocal tract abnormalities (e.g., no tongue, cleft palate) are able to produce fairly comprehensible speech. Thus, some articulatory features may be more important than others with regard to the acquisition of a spoken language. Given our current lack of knowledge about mechanisms of a vocal production and vocal tract anatomy in nonhuman primates, it may be premature to speculate about which features are necessary and which sufficient for the production of the sounds of speech (but see below). Moreover, because nonhuman primates are capable of perceiving a number of subtle distinctions within human speech (e.g., categorical perception of the ba-da continuum; see review in Kuhl 1989), it is important to consider how perception might guide and constrain articulation of speech-like sounds.

Some nonhuman species produce sounds that are present in the natural languages of the world (e.g., parrots "speaking" English) and yet these would not be considered as mechanistic precursors to speech. Rather, the parrots' utterances represent acoustic similarity. This argument raises two points concerning the distinction between mechanistic and acoustic precursors. First, by looking at the mechanisms for generating sounds, we can better understand the range of sounds that could be produced. Thus, although parrots may be able to produce some English utterances, we know less about the entire range of English sounds parrots could produce (although see Klatt and Stefanski 1974 for data on mynah bird productions of human speech). Perhaps more to the point, we know that any human child can develop into a competent speaker of Chinese, French, or English, but can a well-trained parrot produce all of the relevant sound contrasts in these different languages? Second, by looking at mechanistic and acoustic precursors, we allow for the possibility that acoustic precursors could exist even with a vocal tract that differs from the typical human adult.

Linguistic precursors describe the formation of sound-meaning associations as well as the rules by which such associations are combined into a potentially infinite set of meaningful utterances. We, like others in linguistics, leave the reference/semantics definition and distinction in somewhat woolly form. However, we do so intentionally in order to allow for the possibility that semantic or referential properties can be ascribed to sounds that do not appear in a natural language. Thus far, although there is accumulating evidence of a semantic and rudimentarily referential system of vocal communication in nonhuman animals (see review in Gouzoules, Gouzoules, and Marler 1985; Pepperberg 1988), there is minimal evidence of lexical syntax (*sensu stricto* of Marler 1977). On the other hand, the observation that some nonhuman primates combine discrete calls into new utterances (e.g.,

Robinson 1979, 1984; Mitani and Marler 1989) hints at primitive forms of both phonological and lexical syntax, thereby qualifying as possible evolutionary, linguistic precursors. The crucial question, still not satisfactorily answered, is whether any animal can rearrange inherently meaningful vocalizations into new combinations whose meanings derive from those of its components.

To clarify the distinctions between types of precursors, let us examine one example in some detail. Consider, a ten-month-old child who is sitting alone in a room, repetitively babbling the sound *hak*, but not looking or pointing to any object or event in the room. Based on a number of presentations at the conference on which this book is based, it seems that *hak* would be considered a precursor to speech. However, the red-tailed monkey also utters a sound which, to the human ear, sounds like and would be transcribed as *hak* (Marler 1973). Given the similarity between the two sounds, in what sense would one want to label *hak* as a precursor to human speech? We claim that *hak* should be classified, evolutionarily and developmentally, as a mechanistic and acoustic precursor to speech. Evolutionarily, both the red-tailed monkey and the human infant show evidence of some homology in their sound producing capabilities (e.g., see Crelin 1987, for vocal tract anatomy of young children and nonhuman primates). In addition, *hak* is a sound that is represented in a spoken natural language.

Developmentally, the child's utterance can be seen as both a mechanistic and acoustic precursor. If, however, the child and red-tailed monkey were to use *hak* in a fairly restricted range of contexts (e.g., whenever the child sees a hat or cap and whenever the red-tailed monkey sees a threatening conspecific), then we would describe *hak* as a linguistic precursor as well; in other words, *hak* has now acquired some referential specificity.

It is our contention that the most radical evolutionary break between human and animal precursors to speech occurs when the child begins to string referential vocalizations into rudimentary sequences or compounds. For example, the child who had been producing *hak* in the context of hats and caps, now utters *give hak* and places its hand on its head. This utterance represents a combination of mechanistic and linguistic precursors that, so far as we know, no animal has produced in the course of normal communication. Moreover, and as argued by a number of linguists and philosophers of language, even such one- and two-word utterances represent a rudimentary transformation of the deep structure that involves syntax.

One of the primary benefits of the position we have sketched above is that it will alleviate the common tendency of seeing in development the end in the beginning. As Studdert-Kennedy (1986) and others have pointed out, we must avoid the idea that because a child will one day possess a natural language, sounds produced early in life are all or primarily precursors to adult forms. Describing the sounds produced by a young child as mechanistic, acoustic, or linguistic precursors allows one to evaluate the *potential* of a given utterance to develop into a word in the natural language environment. A corollary to this general argument is that for humans with neurological disorders (e.g., Down syndrome), where an adult-like vocabulary is unlikely to emerge, we are liberated from any necessity to describe their sounds as precursors to speech or what we would call rudimentary words. An utterance produced by the child with Down syndrome would, under the above scenario, be examined for what it is (e.g., a bilabial or an utterance with a fundamental frequency of 180 Hz that is typically associated with the presence of food) rather than what, under normal circumstances (i.e., lack of a neurological impairment), it would eventually be (e.g., a linguistic utterance).

In sum, the distinction between speech and nonspeech can be seen as representing a continuum of possibilities. Along this continuum, some nonhuman species will have sounds that are represented in the different languages of the world. As a result, the vocal repertoires of young infants may share some features with those of a given nonhuman animal. At some point, however, there will be sufficient divergence to allow one to conclude that the human child has produced a set of sounds that, from both mechanistic, acoustic, and linguistic viewpoints, no nonhuman animal has produced. It is at this point that one could convincingly talk about the child having rudimentary speech. Put somewhat differently, when the human child produces an utterance with linguistic potential that no nonhuman animal can or could match, then we should, in theory, be able to isolate the necessary and sufficient components for its production.

MECHANISMS OF VOCAL PRODUCTION
IN NONHUMAN PRIMATES: A GLIMPSE AT SOME NEW DATA

Quantification of the differences between animal communication and human speech relies, among other things, upon a thorough description of how animals produce their vocalizations. As previously argued, if the mechanisms underlying vocal production in animals are different from those in humans, then observations of acoustic similarity are functionally interesting but phylogenetically irrelevant.

Knowledge of the mechanisms underlying phonation in our closest relatives, the nonhuman primates, is sadly deficient. To meet this deficiency and to allow us to address the issue of precursors to speech

more properly, we have conducted research on the articulatory gestures used by rhesus macaques (*Macaca mulatta*) to produce the sounds
in their repertoire, designed to answer three questions. Only a small
subset of the data will be presented.

First, what are the roles of lip configuration and tongue movement
in sound production? Second, given the role of various articulatory
routines in sound production, how is a given call's morphology affected by (1) the rapidity with which other calls precede or follow, and
(2) the type of call that precedes or follows? For example, if call *Y*
follows call *X* within a relatively short time, and thereby physically
hinders the individual from resetting the vocal tract to some baseline
position, is the acoustic morphology of *Y* different from the *Y* produced when no call immediately precedes or follows it? In essence, is
there a coarticulatory effect in nonhuman primate vocalizations? And
third, given the striking cases of compensation in human speech (e.g.,
MacNeilage 1970; Lindblom, Lubker, and Gay 1979), can a rhesus monkey whose vocal tract has been perturbed, compensate by producing
perceptually meaningful vocalizations? Evidence of vocal compensation would show that like humans, nonhuman primates are also "searching" for acoustic targets when they vocalize and there is more than one
articulatory routine associated with the production of a given call.

Bauer (1987), based on initial work presented by Marler and Tenaza (1977), examined the relationship between mouth opening and
fundamental frequency in a graded series of calls produced by a male
chimpanzee. He found that when the mouth was wide open, fundamental frequency was high and when there was a narrow mouth opening, fundamental frequency was low. In addition, the lips tended to be
in a retracted position when the mouth was wide open but were pro-
truded when there was a narrow mouth opening.

Bauer's results do not show how gradual changes in mouth opening might influence call morphology from moment to moment. However, based on similar work conducted with human speech (Ohala
1983, 1984; see Kent and Lindblom this volume), it has been shown that
data on changes in lip configuration over relatively short time intervals
allows one to determine (1) how an individual sets up for a call, and (2)
where, precisely, call onset and offset occur in relation to lip configuration. The latter provides the necessary data for examining the correlation between lip configuration and acoustic morphology.

We have looked at the relationship between lip configuration and
call morphology in two types of calls: noisy, atonal calls and clear, tonal
calls, which are vowel-like. Analyses were made using freeze-frame
video images and a computer software package that enabled us to
readily calculate distances between different articulators. Lip config-

uration is a poor predictor of call morphology for the first class of noisy calls (i.e., alarm barks), but a better predictor for the second class of clear tonal calls (i.e., coos). Figure 1a shows a wide band (300 Hz) spectrogram of a coo produced by an adult female rhesus macaque in anticipation of food. Figure 1b presents data on the mean changes in lip height as a function of time for one female and ten exemplars of the coo. There are two points to note about these data. First, lip configuration changes gradually over time and, as shown in figure 1c, seems to be closely related to changes in the dominant frequency. Second, the pattern of change in lip height for this particular call tends to show little variation across individuals.

We have also looked at the changes in tongue position (distance between tongue tip and lower dental arcade) during the production of an alarm bark. Contrary to early speculations that nonhuman primates do not use their tongues in sound production (Lieberman, Klatt, and Wilson 1969; Lieberman 1984), our data show that during the production of an alarm bark, the tongue is maximally retracted from the lower dental arcade at call onset and is then moved forward, with the tongue tip reaching the base of the dental arcade by the termination of the call. Moreover, our video records indicate that as the tongue is retracted, it also becomes more concave in shape. Preliminary analyses suggest that these tongue movements are associated with changes in the bark's acoustic structure.

Future analyses will concentrate on showing whether lip configuration is a strong predictor of more subtle features of call morphology and the extent to which perturbations of lip configuration affect sound structure. Preliminary results suggest that rhesus monkeys whose lips have been temporarily anesthetized with lidocaine or, who have been fitted with a dental prosthesis, which decreases the volume of the oral cavity by 50%, can compensate for some calls but not others. Although it is unclear, in the case of the lidocaine treatment, whether such manipulations cause a sensory or motor deficit (Borden 1980), these results have at least two implications for the study of human speech and its origins. First, suppose that the pattern of lip configuration change in a nonhuman primate and a human were comparable even though two fundamentally different vocalizations were produced. If this were the case, then we would be forced to challenge the role of lip configuration as a diagnostic predictor of acoustic morphology. Second, if nonhuman primates can compensate for perturbations of the vocal tract, then we should no longer view them as severely restricted by the range of articulatory routines accessible for sound production, and we must seriously entertain the possibility that they are capable of controlling the structure of their calls in precise, dynamic fashion, which must be critical to their meaning.

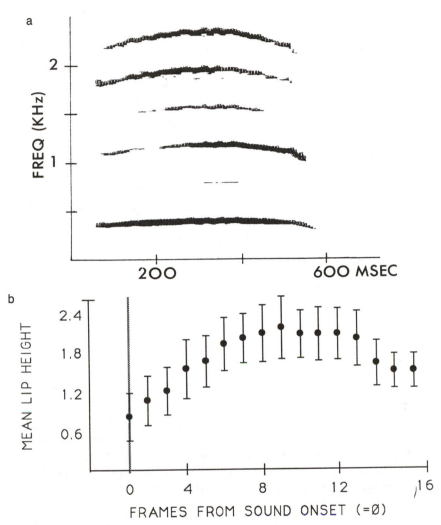

Figure 1.   A. Spectrogram of an adult female rhesus monkey's coo given in the context of waiting for food. B. Mean changes (with standard error bars shown) in lip height (*n* = ten call exemplars) for one female during the production of coos. C. The relationship between mean lip height and mean dominant frequency for coos. Values for figure 1b were obtained from freeze-frame analysis and a computer program that enabled us to measure accurately the distance between lips. All values were standardized to a reference point to control for head movement; values for lip height were measured in pixels.

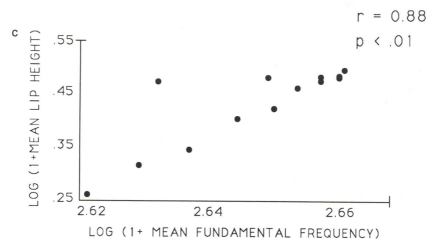

Figure 1. continued

CONCLUDING REMARKS

In conclusion, the authors in this volume show that our understanding of child phonology has exploded over the past two years. This explosion is due to a greater sensitivity to methodological issues and an increasing awareness of the importance of establishing how different sensory modalities interact to shape the pattern of vocal development in human children. What we have argued is that child phonologists might begin to consider how the Zeitgeist could include studies of animal communication, which may prove essential to our discovery of the ultimate significance of the precursors to speech, not only in animals, but perhaps in prespeech human infants as well.

REFERENCES

Bauer, H. 1987. Frequency code: Orofacial correlates of fundamental frequency. *Phonetica* 44:173–91.

Borden, G. 1980. Use of feedback in established and developing speech. In *Speech and Language: Advances in Basic Research and Practice. Vol. 3*, ed. N. Lass. New York: Academic Press.

Chomsky, N. 1980. Rules and representations. *Behavioral and Brain Sciences* 3:1–61.

Crelin, E. 1987. *The Human Vocal Tract.* New York: Vantage Press.

Darwin, D. 1872. *The Expression of the Emotions in Man and Animals.* New York: D. Appleton & Co.

Gouzoules, H., Gouzoules, S., and Marler, P. 1985. External reference and affective signalling in mammalian vocal communication. In *The Development of*

Expressive Behavior: Biology-Environment Interactions, ed. G. Zivin. New York: Academic Press.

Harnad, S. 1987. *Categorical Perception*. Cambridge: Cambridge University Press.

Hauser, M. D. 1989. Ontogenetic changes in the comprehension and production of vervet monkey (*Cercopithecus aethiops*) vocalizations. *Journal of Comparative Psychology* 103:149–58.

Herzog, M., and Hopf, S. 1983. Effects of species-specific vocalizations on the behavior of surrogate-reared squirrel monkeys. *Behaviour* 86:197–214.

Klatt, D. H., and Stefanski, R. A. 1974. How does a mynah bird imitate human speech? *Journal of the Acoustical Society of America* 55:822–32.

Kuhl, P. 1989. On babies, birds, modules, and mechanisms: A comparative approach to the acquisition of vocal communication. In *The Comparative Psychology of Audition*, ed. R. J. Dooling and S. H. Hulse. Hillsdale, NJ: Lawrence Erlbaum Associates.

Lieberman, P. 1984. *The Biology and Evolution of Language*. Cambridge, MA: Harvard University Press.

Lieberman, P., Klatt, D. H., and Wilson, W. H. 1969. Vocal tract limitations on the vowel repertoires of rhesus monkeys and other nonhuman primates. *Science* 164:1185–1187.

Lindblom, B. E. F., Lubker, J., and Gay, T. 1979. Formant frequencies of some fixed-mandible vowels and a model of speech motor programming by predictive simulation. *Journal of Phonetics* 7: 147–61.

MacNeilage, P. F. 1970. Motor control of serial ordering of speech. *Psychological Review* 77:182–96.

Marler, P. 1973. A comparison of vocalizations of red-tailed monkeys and blue monkeys, *Cercopithecus ascanius* and *C. mitis*, in Uganda. *Zeitschrift fur Tierpsychologie* 33:223–47.

Marler, P. 1977. The structure of animal communication sounds. In *Recognition of Complex Acoustic Signals*, ed. T. H. Bullock. Berlin: Springer-Verlag.

Marler, P. 1987. Sensitive periods and the roles of specific and general sensory stimulation in birdsong learning. In *Imprinting and Cortical Plasticity*, eds. J. P. Rauschecker and P. Marler. New York: J. P. Wiley & Sons.

Marler, P., and Peters, S. 1989. Species differences in auditory responsiveness in early vocal learning. In *The Comparative Psychology of Audition: Perceiving Complex Sounds*, eds. R. J. Dooling and S. H. Hulse. Hillsdale, NJ: Lawrence Erlbaum Associates.

Marler, P., and Tenaza, R. 1977. Signalling behaviour of apes with special reference to vocalizations. In *How Animals Communicate*, ed. T. A. Sebeok. Bloomington: Indiana University Press.

Mitani, J. C., and Marler, P. 1989. A phonological analysis of male gibbon singing behavior. *Behaviour* 109:20–45.

Moskowitz, A. I. 1970. The two-year old stage in the acquisition of English phonology. *Language* 46:426–41.

Negus, V. 1962. *The Comparative Anatomy and Physiology of the Larynx*. New York: Hafner.

Nelson, D., and Marler, P. 1989. Categorical perception of a natural stimulus continuum: Birdsong. *Science* 244:976–78.

Newman, J. D., and Symmes, D. 1982. Inheritance and experience in the acquisition of primate acoustic behavior. In *Primate Communication*, eds. C. T. Snowdon, C. H. Brown, and M. R. Petersen. Cambridge: Cambridge University Press.

Nottebohm, F. 1972. Neural lateralization of vocal control in a passerine bird. II.

Subsong, calls, and a theory of vocal learning. *Journal of Experimental Zoology* 79:35–49.

Ohala, J. J. 1983. Cross-language use of pitch: An ethological view. *Phonetica* 40:1–18.

Ohala, J. J. 1984. An ethological perspective on common cross-language utilization of Fo of voice. *Phonetica* 41:1–16.

Pepperberg, I. M. 1988. Second language acquisition: A framework for studying the importance of input and social interaction in exceptional song acquisition. *Ethology* 77:150–68.

Petersen, M. R., and Jusczyk, P. 1984. On perceptual predispositions for human speech and monkey vocalizations. In *The Biology of Learning*, eds. P. Marler and H. S. Terrace. Berlin: Springer-Verlag.

Premack, D. 1986. *Gavagai*. Cambridge: MIT Press.

Robinson, J. G. 1984. Syntactic structures in the vocalizations of wedge-capped capuchin monkeys, *Cebus olivaceus*. *Behaviour* 90:46–79.

Robinson, J. G. 1979. An analysis of the organization of vocal communication in the titi monkey, *Callicebus moloch*. *Zeitschrift fur Tierpsychologie* 49:381–405.

Seyfarth, R. M., and Cheney, D. L. 1986. Vocal development in vervet monkeys. *Animal Behaviour* 34:1640–1658.

Sinnott, J. M., Stebbins, W. C., and Moody, D. B. 1975. Regulation of voice amplitude by the monkey. *Journal of the Acoustical Society of America* 58:412–14.

Snowdon, C. T. 1982. Linguistic and nonlinguistic approaches to nonhuman primate communication. In *Primate Communication*, eds. C. T. Snowdon, C. H. Brown, and M. R. Petersen. New York: Van Nostrand Reinhold.

Snowdon, C. T. 1987. A comparative approach to vocal communication. In *Nebraska Symposium on Motivation, Vol. 35. Comparative Approaches in Modern Psychology*, ed. D. W. Leger. Nebraska: University of Nebraska Press.

Snowdon, C. T. 1988. Communication as social interaction: Its importance in ontogeny and adult behavior. In *Primate Vocal Communication*, eds. D. Todt, P. Goedeking, and D. Symmes. Berlin: Springer-Verlag.

Snowdon, C. T. Personal communication.

Snowdon, C. T., French, J. A. and Cleveland, J. 1986. Ontogeny of primate vocalizations: models from birdsong and human speech. In *Current Perspectives in Primate Social Behavior*, eds. D. Taub and F. King. New York: Academic Press.

Studdert-Kennedy, M. 1986. Sources of variability in early speech development. In *Invariance and Variability in Speech Processes*, eds. J. S. Perkell and D. H. Klatt, Hillsdale, NJ: Lawrence Erlbaum Association.

Talmage-Riggs, G., Winter, P., Ploog, D., and Mayer, W. 1972. Effect of deafening on the vocal behavior of squirrel monkeys (*Saimiri sciureus*). *Folia primatologica* 17:404–20.

Winter, P., Handley, P., Ploog, D., and Schott, D. 1973. Ontogeny of squirrel monkey calls under normal conditions and under acoustic isolation. *Behaviour* 47:230–39.

Index

(Page numbers in italics indicate material in tables or figures.)